Policy Success in Canada:
Cases, Lessons, Challenges

Policy Success in Canada

Cases, Lessons, Challenges

Edited by

EVERT A. LINDQUIST
MICHAEL HOWLETT
GRACE SKOGSTAD
GENEVIÈVE TELLIER
PAUL 'T HART

OXFORD
UNIVERSITY PRESS

Great Clarendon Street, Oxford, OX2 6DP,
United Kingdom

Oxford University Press is a department of the University of Oxford.
It furthers the University's objective of excellence in research, scholarship,
and education by publishing worldwide. Oxford is a registered trade mark of
Oxford University Press in the UK and in certain other countries

© the several contributors 2022

The moral rights of the authors have been asserted

Impression: 1

Some rights reserved. No part of this publication may be reproduced, stored in
a retrieval system, or transmitted, in any form or by any means, for commercial purposes,
without the prior permission in writing of Oxford University Press, or as expressly
permitted by law, by licence or under terms agreed with the appropriate
reprographics rights organization.

This is an open access publication, available online and distributed under the terms of a
Creative Commons Attribution – Non Commercial – No Derivatives 4.0
International licence (CC BY-NC-ND 4.0), a copy of which is available at
http://creativecommons.org/licenses/by-nc-nd/4.0/.

Enquiries concerning reproduction outside the scope of this licence
should be sent to the Rights Department, Oxford University Press, at the address above

Published in the United States of America by Oxford University Press
198 Madison Avenue, New York, NY 10016, United States of America

British Library Cataloguing in Publication Data

Data available

Library of Congress Control Number: 2022931243

ISBN 978–0–19–289704–6

DOI: 10.1093/oso/ 9780192897046.001.0001

Printed and bound by
CPI Group (UK) Ltd, Croydon, CR0 4YY

Links to third party websites are provided by Oxford in good faith and
for information only. Oxford disclaims any responsibility for the materials
contained in any third party website referenced in this work.

Acknowledgements

This edited collection represents the collaborative efforts of many people and we are delighted to be able to acknowledge them here. This book would not exist if not for Alan Fenna, our Canadian-born colleague at Curtin University in Western Australia, who was a participant in a prior Australia and New Zealand-focused collection of policy success cases, and who suggested that something similar should and could be done about Canada. Alan, we hope you like what has come of it, and thanks for planting the seed.

We thank Dominic Byatt, our editor, for his enthusiastic support for this collection from the outset. We are grateful to our authors for their willingness to fit this project in amongst their other writing commitments, their discipline in meeting our deadlines, their responsiveness to our feedback on their draft chapters, and, above all, for producing such high-quality chapters. We are also grateful to Professor Michael Mintrom of Monash University for providing formal comments on the entire collection at an editors' panel as part of the CPSA-CAPPA Section of the Annual Conference of the Canadian Political Science Association (9 June 2021).

We thank Busra Hacioglu, PhD candidate in the Department of Political Science at the University of Toronto, for her meticulous proof-reading of all chapters. No missing reference or verb failed to catch Busra's eye. We are also very appreciative of OUP's anonymous reader: those constructive comments were extremely valuable in helping us to pull together the chapters' findings and broader lessons in the Conclusion to the collection. We would like to thank Alexander Howlett for his thorough work in preparing the index for this collection. We would like to thank Alexander Howlett for his thorough work in preparing the index for this collection.

Last but not least, we are grateful to the European Research Council (ERC) for funding the book's publication under the European Union's Horizon 2020 research and innovation programme (grant agreement n° 694266). Without this financial support, we would have been unable to publish this collection as an open access book.

Evert A. Lindquist
(*University of Victoria*)
Michael Howlett
(*Simon Fraser University*)
Grace Skogstad
(*University of Toronto*)
Geneviève Tellier
(*University of Ottawa*)
Paul 't Hart
(*Utrecht University*)

Contents

List of Figures	x
List of Tables	xi
List of Contributors	xii

1. Introduction: Exploring Canadian Experiences with Policy
   Success
   *Evert A. Lindquist, Michael Howlett, Grace Skogstad,
   Geneviève Tellier and Paul 't Hart* — 1

PART I. HEALTH POLICY SUCCESSES

2. Canadian Medicare as a Policy Success — 17
   Gregory Marchildon

3. Canada's Long March against Tobacco — 36
   Cynthia Callard

4. Insite in Vancouver: North America's First Supervised Injection
   Site — 56
   Carey Doberstein

PART II. EDUCATION POLICY SUCCESSES

5. Schooling Successfully: The Elementary and Secondary
   Education Sectors in Canada — 77
   Jennifer Wallner

6. Québec's Subsidized Childcare Network — 98
   Nathalie Burlone

7. Early Years Policy Innovations across Canada: A Policy Success? — 117
   Adrienne Davidson and Linda A. White

8. Modernizing Canada's Research Universities — 139
   Allan Tupper

PART III. SOCIAL POLICY SUCCESSES

9. Good and Lucky: Explaining Canada's Successful Immigration Policies 161
   Triadafilos Triadafilopoulos

10. Multiculturalism Policy in Canada: Conflicted and Resilient 183
    Keith Banting

11. The Magic Is in the Mix: How the Guaranteed Income Supplement and Old Age Security Interact in Canada's Pension System to Tackle Successfully Poverty in Old Age 206
    Daniel Béland and Patrik Marier

12. The Federal Equalization Program as a Controversial and Contested Policy Success 225
    Daniel Béland, André Lecours, and Trevor Tombe

PART IV. ECONOMIC AND INDUSTRIAL POLICY SUCCESSES

13. Regulating Canada's Banking System: Tackling the 'Big Shall Not Buy Big' Problem 247
    Russell Alan Williams

14. Supply Management in Canada's Dairy and Poultry Sectors 267
    Grace Skogstad

15. From R&D to Export: Canola Development as a 'Resilient Success' 286
    Matt Wilder

16. Developing the Canadian Wine Industry: A Contested Success 307
    Andrea Riccardo Migone

PART V. ENVIRONMENTAL POLICY SUCCESSES

17. Managing Canada's National Parks: Integrating Sustainability, Protection, and Enjoyment 327
    Robert P. Shepherd, Diane Simsovic and Alan Latourelle

18. The Great Lakes: Embracing the Complexity of Policy Success 348
    Carolyn M. Johns

19. Phasing Out Coal-Fired Electricity in Ontario 372
    Mark S. Winfield and Abdeali Saherwala

CONTENTS ix

PART VI. GOVERNANCE POLICY SUCCESSES

20. How Indigenous Nations Have Been Transforming Public Policy through the Courts 395
Satsan (Herb George), Kent McNeil and Frances Abele

21. The Canadian Federal 1994–1996 Program Review: Appraising a Success 25 Years Later 416
Geneviève Tellier

22. Canadian Airport Authorities: A Success Story 438
David J. Langlois

23. Canada's Response to the Global Financial Crisis: Pivoting to the Economic Action Plan 457
Evert A. Lindquist

24. Conclusion—Public Policy Success: Lessons from the Canadian Experience 478
Grace Skogstad, Geneviève Tellier, Paul 't Hart, Michael Howlett, Evert A. Lindquist

Index 492

List of Figures

10.1.	How Important is Multiculturalism to Canadian Identity?	196
12.1.	Actual vs. 'Full' Equalization Payments in Canada	239
16.1.	Major Wine and Grape Associations in Canada	311
17.1.	The Mission Mystique Framework	329
18.1.	Map of Great Lakes Basin and Areas of Concern	353
19.1.	Total Annual Ontario Electricity Demand (in TWh) 1997–2018	382
19.2.	Average Global Adjustment vs. Average Market Electricity Price (2009–2019)	385
21.1.	Canadian Federal Budget Balance, 1970–2008	419
21.2.	Canadian Federal Revenues and Expenditures, 1970–2008	419
21.3.	Canadian Federal Interest Payments, 1970–2008	420
21.4.	Canadian Federal Net Debt, 1970–2008	421
21.5.	Public Opinion about the Size of the Federal Deficit, 1988–1997	430
22.1.	The National Airports System—Transfer Dates	439

List of Tables

1.1. Dimensions of Policy Success: A Map for Case Assessment 6

2.1. Competing Design Differences of Saskatchewan and Alberta Hospital Plans 20

3.1. Key Events in Canadian Tobacco Policy 37

3.2. Obligations under the Framework Convention on Tobacco Control 47

7.1. Metrics of Success 120

10.1. Multiculturalism Policy Index, 1980–2020 186

10.2. Public Attitudes towards Multiculturalism Policies: Recognition 197

10.3. Public Attitudes towards Multiculturalism Policies: Accommodation 197

11.1. GIS, by Family Types, 2020 217

11.2. Seniors Income Plan (Saskatchewan), by Family Types and Living Situations, 2020 218

13.1. Evaluating Policy Success—Preparing the Canadian Financial Services Industry for Globalization 250

18.1. State of the Great Lakes Ecosystem Indicators, 2019 359

18.2. Assessing Policy Success 361

19.1. Electricity-Sector Emissions Reductions in Ontario 373

19.2. Ontario's Coal-Fired Electricity Plants 374

19.3. Ontario Power Generation's Coal Plants: Electricity Generation and Emissions 1995–2001 376

19.4. Assessing the Ontario Coal Phase-Out 389

21.1. 1995–1996 Program Review Department Spending Reductions 428

21.2. Federal Fiscal Transactions, $ million 431

24.1. Summary of Case Assessments on the Success Spectrum 480

List of Contributors

Frances Abele is Chancellor's professor of public policy and administration in Ottawa, and research fellow at both the Carleton Centre for Community Innovation and the Institute for Research on Public Policy.

Keith Banting is the Stauffer Dunning fellow in the School of Policy Studies and professor emeritus in the Department of Political Studies at Queen's University, and a member of the Order of Canada and a fellow of the Royal Society of Canada.

Daniel Béland is director of the McGill Institute for the Study of Canada and James McGill professor in the Department of Political Science at McGill University.

Nathalie Burlone is a professor at the School of Political Studies at the University of Ottawa. https://uniweb.uottawa.ca/members/963

Cynthia Callard has assisted the development of federal and provincial policies on tobacco since the mid-1980s, when working in Parliament on the first successful reforms. Since the mid-1990s she has worked for the health charity, Physicians for a Smoke-Free Canada.

Adrienne Davidson is assistant professor in the Department of Political Science at McMaster University.

Carey Doberstein is associate professor of political science at the University of British Columbia in Vancouver, and associate editor of *Canadian Public Administration*, with books on *Building a Collaborative Advantage* and *Distributed Democracy*.

Satsan (Herb George) is a Wet'suwet'en hereditary chief of the Frog Clan and a long-time speaker for the Wet'suwet'en Nation and, for over 40 years, has worked towards securing recognition and respect for the inherent right of Indigenous self-government in the courts, classrooms, and communities.

Paul 't Hart is professor of public administration at Utrecht University, the Netherlands, and co-editor of similar open access case study collections on policy successes globally (OUP, 2019), in Australia and New Zealand (ANU Press, 2019) and in the Nordic Countries (OUP, 2022).

Michael Howlett is Burnaby Mountain Professor and Canada Research Chair (Tier 1), Department of Political Science, Simon Fraser University, and a Fellow of the Royal Society of Canada.

Carolyn M. Johns is professor in the Department of Politics and Public Administration at Ryerson University, chair of the Geoffrey Bruce Fellowship in Canadian Freshwater Policy, and a member of the International Joint Commission's Great Lakes Water Quality Board.

LIST OF CONTRIBUTORS xiii

David J. Langlois has worked for the private sector as an aerospace engineer, computer programmer, systems analyst, and manager. Since 2002 he has conducted over 45 performance reviews of 17 Canadian Airport Authorities, with more in progress.

Alan Latourelle is a former chief executive officer at Parks Canada, and recipient of the Order of Canada.

André Lecours is professor in the School of Political Studies at the University of Ottawa and has published widely on Canadian, Québec, and European politics, nationalist movements, and federalism.

Evert A. Lindquist is professor of public administration in the School of Public Administration, University of Victoria, BC, and editor of *Canadian Public Administration*, the scholarly journal of the Institute of Public Administration of Canada.

Gregory P. Marchildon is professor and Ontario research chair in health policy and system design at the Institute of Health Policy, Management and Evaluation's Dalla Lana School of Public Health and Munk School of Global Affairs and Public Policy, University of Toronto.

Patrik Marier is professor, Department of Political Science, Concordia University in Montréal and principal researcher l'Équipe VIES, and directeur scientifique, Centre de recherche et d'expertise en gérontologie sociale (CREGÉS).

Kent McNeil is a distinguished research professor (emeritus) at York University's Osgoode Hall Law School. His research focuses on the rights of Indigenous peoples in Canada, the United States, Australia, and New Zealand.

Andrea Migone is assistant professor at Ryerson University in Toronto and has published widely on public policy, public administration, government innovation, and advisory systems.

Abdeali Saherwala is a clean energy policy and finance analyst at National Renewable Energy Laboratory and completing an MA at the Yale School of the Environment in New Haven, CT.

Robert P. Shepherd is associate professor in the School of Public Policy and Administration at Carleton University, Ottawa, Ontario, Canada.

Diane Simsovic is lecturer and PhD candidate in the School of Public Policy and Administration at Carleton University, Ottawa, Ontario, Canada.

Grace Skogstad is professor of political science at the University of Toronto and University of Toronto Scarborough, a past president of the Canadian Political Science Association, and president of the International Public Policy Association.

Geneviève Tellier is professor of public administration at the University of Ottawa's School of Political Studies and editor of the Politics and Public Policy series for the University of Ottawa Press.

Trevor Tombe is professor of economics in the Department of Economics and Research Fellow at the School of Public Policy at the University of Calgary.

xiv LIST OF CONTRIBUTORS

Triadafilos (Phil) Triadafilopoulos is associate professor of political science at the University of Toronto Scarborough and the Munk School of Global Affairs and Public Policy.

Allan Tupper is professor and former head of the Department of Political Science at the University of British Columbia, who has published widely on Canadian politics and government, public management, public policy higher education, and government ethics.

Jennifer Wallner is associate professor with the School of Political Studies at the University of Ottawa and the Jean Luc Pepin Research Chair in Canadian Politics.

Linda A. White is RBC Chair in Economic and Public Policy and professor in the University of Toronto's Department of Political Science and Munk School of Global Affairs and Public Policy.

Matt Wilder is a political economist and public policy specialist whose research and publications have focused on innovation, industrial policy, public finance, and methodology. Matt is currently a visiting fellow in the Department of Government at Harvard University.

Russell Alan Williams is associate professor of political science at Memorial University. He researches the impact of globalization on Canadian public policy trade and labour market policy, financial services regulation, and global climate change governance.

Mark S. Winfield is professor of environmental studies in the Faculty of Environmental and Urban Change (EUC) at York University, and co-chair of the Faculty's Sustainable Energy Initiative.

1

Introduction

Exploring Canadian Experiences with Policy Success

*Evert A. Lindquist, Michael Howlett, Grace Skogstad,
Geneviève Tellier, and Paul 't Hart*

Overcoming the Dominance of Policy Failure
in Public Policy Studies

Through their public policies, governments have enormous potential to shape the lives of their citizens. Much is at stake when new public policies are forged or when established ones are reformed and it behooves governments to learn from past experiences and both avoid earlier errors as well as emulate past successes. Actions taken at any given time can affect both present conditions and future trajectories, and whether or not those actions successfully accomplish government and public goals and aims in an enduring fashion is a critical aspect of policy-making and political life.

In the 1970s scholars produced classic accounts of public policy-making and outcomes, now ensconced in the canon of academic research worldwide and academic curricula in universities everywhere. In part in order to avoid the somewhat Panglossian accounts of a first generation of policy scholars who sometimes over-promised the positive impact of applying cost-benefit calculus and other economics-derived tools to previously highly partisan and political processes of decision-making (Tribe, 1972; Banfield, 1977), these studies often tended to focus on 'negative exemplars' rather than 'positive' ones. That is, they emphasized the lessons that could be derived from avoiding policy failures rather than those which might be gained from efforts to emulate success.

Two well-known foundational works of policy studies in the US, for example, set the tone for the next several decades of research into policy success and failure. Pressman and Wildavsky's (1984) *Implementation* and Peter Hall's (1982) *Great Planning Disasters* showcased and explored high profile public policy failures. They showed that although having seized a much more prominent role in public life following their successful prosecution of World War II, Western governments continued to suffer from internal complexities which, combined with the vagaries

---

Evert A. Lindquist et al., *Introduction*. In: *Policy Success in Canada*.
Edited by Evert A. Lindquist et al., Oxford University Press. © Evert A. Lindquist et al. (2022).
DOI: 10.1093/oso/9780192897046.003.0001

2 INTRODUCTION

of democratic political decision-making, often operated to thwart their ambitions, despite their best intentions and efforts.

Somewhat unintentionally, subsequent generations of public policy and public administration students became steeped in pessimistic diagnoses of government action and many similar studies followed. They included Butler et al.'s (1994) *Failure in British Government*, 't Hart and Bovens' (1996) *Understanding Policy Fiascos*, and Gray and 't Hart's (1998) *Public Policy Disasters in Europe*. More recent works in the same vein are Allern and Pollack's (2012) *Scandalous!*, Crewe and King's (2013) *The Blunders of Our Governments*, Light's (2014) *A Cascade of Failures*, Schuck's (2014) *Why Government Fails So Often,* and Opperman and Spencer's (2016) *Telling Stories of Failure.*

These readings and research provide a firm analytical grounding of the institutional, behavioural, political, and media problems and dynamics contributing to the occurrence, framing, and escalation of public policy failure. But they also provided a distorted view of policy-making and policy outcomes as they largely ignored or downplayed the study of the other side of the success/failure coin, namely, policy success, its causes and consequences.

The Need to Study (and Learn from) Experiences with Policy Success

The 'policy failure' discourse has been very influential. Day in, day out, media reports and social media discussions about alleged government failures perpetuate a negative frame on government activity, and much public and electoral discourse and partisan activity is obsessed with the naming, shaming, and blaming activities linked to rooting out and highlighting policy failures big and small. This practice, seen in many countries, was especially prominent in the United States from the Reagan to Trump era. It had significant implications for public perceptions and the lack of or under appreciation of government institutions which accompanied it. Although the success of public-led health efforts to control and stop the Covid-19 coronavirus has shifted some public views of government institutions in some countries, government failure and blame for errors in handling the pandemic has also been a prominent feature of political discourse in many others (Greer et al., 2020; Capano et al., 2020).

Under the spell of high-profile scandals and other forms of ambulance-chasing, many public and media accounts of public policy still have little to say about instances where governmental steering efforts have been effective, generate benefits for all, remain popular and have stood the test of time, including in areas of activity such as healthcare, pensions, banking regulation, or infrastructure development. But as recent events around the coronavirus response serve to emphasize, such stories of endemic government failure ignore or neglect just as many, if not many more, cases from day-to-day to long-term policy-making where governments succeed in creating and maintaining projects, programs, and services. In areas such as health, education, and social policy, for example, policies and programs in many countries have performed well, sometimes exceptionally well, often for decades or more, making their study and analysis of the factors driving or leading to success equally if not more important than deriving the negative lessons of occasional failure (see Bovens, 't Hart and Peters, 2001; McConnell, 2010a and 2010b; Moore, 2013; Goderis, 2015; Roberts, 2018).

The 'negativity' bias towards government (Hood, 2010) and related public discourses have continuously focused attention on the politics of blame, engendering and contributing to widespread and undeserved cynicism about the possibility of effective governments and governance. The net impact of the concentration on the downside of government failure and neglect of the 'upside' of government performance is that many observers and members of the public cannot properly 'see' and recall, let alone recognize and explain successful public policies and programs. In some cases these views have helped undermine the legitimacy of representative democratic institutions and contributed to the rise of anti-expert and anti-knowledge 'populist' politics, discourses, and actions (Stoker, 2018; Facchini and Milki, 2019; Moynihan and Roberts, 2021).

What is needed is a more balanced focus on both the 'light' and the 'dark' sides of the performance of our political and public sector institutions. This book is designed to help turn that tide and re-balance these efforts. It accompanies more recent studies of public policy successes such as McConnell's (2010) *Understanding Policy Success*, Compton and 't Hart's (2019) *Great Policy Successes*, and Luetjens, Mintrom and 't Hart's (2019) *Successful Public Policy* which all aim to help reset agendas for teaching, research, and dialogue on public policy performance.

Like those works, the present study systematically examines outstanding cases of policy success, providing a foil to those who neglect these cases and focus overly on errors and mistakes. It offers a series of close-up, in-depth case study accounts of the genesis and evolution of significant public policy achievements, across a range of sectors, jurisdictions, and time periods in Canada: a country generally regarded as having an effective and efficient government which has delivered high quality services to its citizens for over 150 years. By constructing detailed case narratives and overviews while systematically engaging with the conceptual, methodological, and analytical challenges of researching and debating success and failure in Canadian public policy, we hope the chapters in this collection will inspire a generation of teachers and researchers in policy analysis, and the public, to take policy success more seriously.

The Canadian Case

Since its nineteenth century development as an outpost of the British Empire, successive national and provincial governments in Canada have progressively

4   INTRODUCTION

carved out independent identities and policies for the populations within their jurisdictions. In so doing they have attained a high level of social and economic development operating within a set of governing institutions and practices envied by many (Lower, 1977; Hodgetts, 1955 and 1973).

Canada has long been regarded as among the world's most stable and progressive countries. Although not seen as a 'radical innovator', it often has been rated as one of the best places to live in the world, with strong governance traditions and public service institutions and a commitment to steady progress in public service delivery and social and economic development (Quirk, 2019; Goderis, 2015). Canadian political leaders and public service institutions are regularly consulted and asked to share insights with governments in the developing world and elsewhere due to the country's rich experience in public policy development and implementation (Dewitt and Kirton, 1983).

Although Canada lacks the strong anti-government sentiments found in neighbouring countries like the United States, as in many other countries, this record or success is often obscured by a focus on scandal and failure. This is especially true of the media and public sentiments which both have focused on scandals and failures, while the Canadian academic policy literature has not grappled directly with the issue of policy success, per se. High profile fiascos and scandals have all been widely covered in the media, been studied, and have entered the Canadian political and policy lexicon (Campbell et al., 2004; Allen and Doern, 2006; Free and Radcliffe, 2009; Trottier, 2018). In the recent past they include the cost overruns of the 1976 Montréal Olympic Games (Roult and Lefebvre, 2010; Todd, 2016); the tragedy of the Westray mine explosion in Nova Scotia (McCormick, 1998); the Mirabel Airport construction (Edwards, 2016); the Sponsorship Affair and 2004–06 Gomery Commission into political corruption in the federal Liberal Party and Prime Minister Jean Chrétien (Ruderman and Nevitte, 2015); the contaminated blood tragedy (Paquet and Perrault, 2016); the appalling treatment of Indigenous children in residential school care and their removal in the 1960s from their families and adoption into predominantly non-Indigenous families (Milloy, 2017); deep scandals in Canadian peacekeeping in Somalia (Dawson, 2007); persistent gender discrimination in the Royal Canadian Mountain Police (Bastarache, 2020); the implementation of the Government of Canada's Phoenix payroll system (Office of the Auditor General, 2018); and the province of Newfoundland and Labrador's investment in the troubled Muskrat Falls dam to name only the latest in a history of problematic resource mega-projects (Mathias, 1971).

Not surprisingly, as in other countries, such examples have contributed to the idea that governments are chronically incompetent, overly politicized, lacking capacity to deliver, and tending towards avoiding accountability (e.g. Scott, 1998; Schuck, 2014; and for Canada, Savoie, 2015). Although Canadians may have a less negative view of government and the public sector than found in some other countries, Canada nevertheless does have a history of neglecting or failing to pay sufficient attention to many of the successful public policies enacted by its three levels of government.

Notwithstanding the high-profile negative examples cited above, most public projects, programs, and services in Canada perform well, and many are very successful and endure for decades with wide popular support. But these policy success cases are consistently underexposed in public discourses and understudied in the policy literature (see Little, 2008, for an exception).

This volume provides an opportunity to rectify this neglect and analyse what is similar and distinctive about introducing and implementing successful public policies in one of the world's wealthiest economies, one of its most politically decentralized and regionally diverse federations, and one of its oldest continuous democracies.

Theoretical Framework: What Is Policy Success?

In this volume, we adopt as our working definition the description of a successful public policy used by 't Hart and his colleagues in their 2019 volumes (Compton and 't Hart, 2019; Luetjens et al., 2019). They situate policy success on a continuum between failure and total success. A policy at the success end of the continuum (a) demonstrably achieves highly valued social outcomes and has a broad base of public and political support for these achievements and the associated processes and costs; and (b) manages to sustain this performance for a considerable period of time even in the face of changing circumstances. A policy at the policy failure end of the continuum achieves neither (a) nor (b).

The conceptualization of policy success/failure as a continuum acknowledges that policy success (like policy failure) is not an either/or binary. As McConnell (2010b) notes, there are many 'grey areas' between total failure and complete success in which success is partial or contested and not endorsed or viewed as such by all participants. Compton and 't Hart (2019) and Luetjens et al. (2019) helpfully disaggregate policy success into four dimensions of programmatic, process, political, and temporal success. Their definition of policy success recognizes that many policies, including those which have endured for some time, may accomplish one or more, but not all four of these criteria of success (see Table 1.1). Some policies, for example, may achieve their identified programmatic goals but never achieve popular acclaim. Similarly, many may be quite popular but fail to be regarded by experts as effective or optimally efficient.

This situation is made more complex, of course, when public or expert opinion is divided on the criteria for judging policy success. Labelling a policy or a programme as successful depends upon the perceptions of the stakeholders involved, the positions they take, and the political environment. Public perceptions, political support, program legitimacy, and institutional reputations all come into play

6 INTRODUCTION

Table 1.1 Dimensions of Policy Success: A Map for Case Assessment

Programmatic success: Purposeful and valued action	Process success: Thoughtful and effective policy-making practices	Political success: Many winners, firm support and reputational benefits
• A well-developed *public value proposition* and *theory of change* underpin the policy • *Achievement* of (or, considerable momentum towards) the policy's intended and/or of other *beneficial social outcomes* • The pleasure and pain resulting from the policy are *distributed fairly* across the field of institutional and community stakeholders	• The design process ensures carefully considered *choice of policy instruments appropriate to context* and in a manner perceived to be correct and fair • The policy-making process offers reasonable opportunities for *different stakeholders to exercise influence* and *different forms of expertise* to be heard, as well as for *innovative practices and solutions* to be attempted before key policy choices are made • The policy-making process results in *adequate levels of funding, realistic timelines, and administrative capacity* • The delivery process effectively and adaptively deploys (a mix of) policy instrument(s) to *achieve intended outcomes with acceptable costs*, and with limited unintended negative consequences	• A *wide array of stakeholders* feel they could advance their interests through the *process and/or outcomes* of the policy • The policy enjoys relatively high levels of *social, political, and administrative support* • Being associated with the policy *enhances the reputations* of the actors driving it (both inside and outside government).

Success over time:
Consolidation and endurance

- *High levels of programmatic, process, and political efficacy are maintained* over time
- Stable or growing *strength of social, political, and administrative coalitions favouring continuation* of the policy over time
- Emerging narratives about the policy's success *confer legitimacy on the broader political system*

in shaping whether a government policy, programme, or governance initiative is judged successful or not.

In short, 'success', like 'failure', is usually not a matter of indisputable fact. We can try to monetize or otherwise standardize costs and benefits of policy processes and outcomes, and we can set time frames and construct comparators across time and space to document our assessments. But there are also the lived realities and situated perceptions which mean that 'where you stand depends on where you sit', in the sense that different actors and stakeholders have different needs, desires, goals, and expectations and may disagree fundamentally—or marginally—about what a policy has achieved or failed to achieve. Moreover, the perspectives of actors on a policy may also vary greatly from a more macro 'helicopter' (e.g. 'net benefits to society') perspective to the more granular ('inequitable distribution of costs and benefits to different groups in society') vantage point. Such differences, of course, may also lead to stark differences in assessments and interpretations of policies and program outcomes (McConnell, 2010a and 2010b).

Thus, as McConnell, Grealy and Lea (2020) remind us, case studies of policy outcomes should go beyond ascertaining whether a particular program is viewed as successful from the point of view of the government that undertook it, to include the extent to which key actors within and outside government have been successful in shaping the program and reaping its benefits. In that sense, all policies and programs harbour particular configurations of success and failure depending on which and whose vantage points one uses in assessment.

In each case examined in this collection, then, many questions abound about policy processes, actors, and outputs. Successful in what regard, for whom, at which point in time, and relative to what benchmark? Successful in actually 'doing better' to achieve public purposes, or primarily in making the public 'feel better' through more effective framing? How do luck (context, zeitgeist, chance events, crises) or skill (political and public service craftsmanship in design, timing, political management, public relations) each play their part, and how do they affect one another?

Within Canada Case Selection and Volume Outline

The aim of the book is to see, describe, acknowledge, and promote learning from past and present instances of highly effective and highly valued public policy-making, drawing on examples from Canadian experiences. Through detailed examination of 22 case studies of policy success that span different eras, governments, and policy domains in Canada, we hope to contribute to the broader literature on the conceptualization of policy success and to draw attention to how endogenous country-specific factors affect the prospects of policy success.

8 INTRODUCTION

The case studies of highly successful public policy-making in Canada were chosen after canvassing dozens of public policy experts and former officials across the country, who were asked to identify cases they considered exemplary examples of successful Canadian public policies. These policy experts were provided with the definition of what constituted a successful policy and shown the lists of cases covered in Compton and 't Hart (2019) and Luetjens, Mintrom and 't Hart (2019) in order to promote possible comparative case selections where possible.

Following this process, the editorial team compiled a long list of well over a hundred suggestions for cases. This list was reduced by virtue of the requirement for policy successes to meet the consolidation and endurance dimension; public policy cases that were 'too recent' to be certain of their trajectory and fate were eliminated. The list of policy success cases was then further refined in order to attain variation between degrees of success: with some high-profile cases included where public policies persisted seemingly effortlessly over long periods, while other policies were included which were considered successes overall but nevertheless were contested, frayed, and required significant adjustments over time. We also decided to focus predominantly on national cases although many of these have a very strong provincial or regional dimension. However, given Canada's decentralized federal system of government, wherein provinces enjoy extensive autonomy and independence in many major areas of social and economic life, we also included examples of solely provincial, and in one case, municipal, policy success. More inevitably and pragmatically, the cases included in this collection were ones where Canadian policy experts were willing to author a chapter.

In each case study included in the book, the authors provide narratives and analyses using the same framework adapted by Compton and 't Hart (2019) and Luetjens et al. (2019) in their studies of Australia and New Zealand and other countries. This requires them to consider several factors and employ certain analytical perspectives in designing and reporting their findings.

Despite their differences in subject matter, approach, and coverage, two assumptions underpin each case study. First, building on Bovens and 't Hart (1996) and McConnell (2010), each author presupposes that balanced evaluation of policy success requires a multi-dimensional, multi-perspectivist, and multi-criteria approach to assessment. Second, following other longitudinal research in the policy sciences (Sabatier, 1988) each presumes that the success or failure of a public policy program or project cannot be properly assessed unless one looks at its evolution and impact over a period of at least a decade since it came into being.

The 22 cases found in the book can be grouped into six sectoral or thematic areas based on their central policy focus or topic. Three cases deal with *health policy successes*—from the nation's premiere flagship success in national health insurance or Medicare, to successful efforts to reduce tobacco use and municipal initiatives to deal with drug use in Canada's cities through supervised injection sites for hard drug users.

Four cases deal with *education policy successes* ranging from the development of the now standard system of Kindergarten to Grade 12 public schools to province-wide subsidized daycare and early childhood education, to the country's well-known and much admired post-secondary education system of Universities and Colleges.

Four other cases deal with *social policy successes*. These include the linked system of immigration and multiculturalism for which the country is often celebrated, as well as older programmes establishing effective pensions and schemes and the financial wherewithal to fund them through equalization payments and federal-provincial sharing of their costs.

Another four cases deal with successes in the *economic and industrial realm*. These include studies of the country's well-known highly stable and well-organized banking system and its lesser known but sometimes contentious system of agricultural marketing boards in key areas such as poultry and dairy products. It also includes two cases of successful government-initiated or supported product innovation in its world leading canola crop and similar, if smaller scale, efforts currently underway in the wine industry.

Three case studies examine *environmental policy successes*. They examine one of the oldest enduring and popular successes in the country's unparalleled system of national and provincial parks and its pioneering efforts, with the United States, to preserve and protect the water quality of the Great Lakes, and the more recent climate change mitigation measure of phasing out of coal-fired electricity generators in Ontario.

Each of these areas and subjects is more or less amenable to standard treatment applying the PPPE framework to a government policy effort within a given policy sector. However Canada, like some other countries, also has featured a series of successes within its *constitutional and administrative system of governance*, an area which has largely escaped detailed analysis in previous studies of policy success. These kinds of constitutional and governance-related policy successes include efforts with respect to claims of Indigenous Nations to lands and resources which predate the country. They also include federal government systemic efforts to reduce deficits and streamline the public sector ('programme review') including the 'privatization' of the country's main airports (and harbours). In the past decade, as well, Canadian administrative policy success was tested by the government of Canada's response to the economic and social fallout of the Global Financial Crisis (GFC), and more recently, by ongoing efforts to deal with the Covid-19 pandemic.

In each case study the authors set out what the case is about and why the topic—whether a policy or program or project—should be included in the volume. In other words, they explore was its fundamental 'claim to success' in terms of the definition and the four assessment dimensions of Table 1 set out above.

10   INTRODUCTION

Following the PPPE framework, the authors then examine the *programmatic* component of success by setting out what social, political, and institutional contexts are relevant to understand the framing, design, and execution of the policy. In providing a chronology of how the policy developed, they examine the history, fault lines, alliances, and opportunities that played into its origins and evolution. Authors also address what specific challenges the policy was seeking to tackle and what, if any, specific aims it sought to achieve.

Authors also address the 'who' of the programme, or its *political* dimension. Which actors were principally involved in the policy process, and which were most affected by its enactment and implementation? Who were the policy's main advocates, entrepreneurs, and stewards? What drove them to take up these roles? How did they raise and maintain support for the policy? And which actors were opposed to it, skeptical about it, or trying to get it amended or terminated? What tactics did these actors/coalitions use? What if any 'counternarratives' to the success assessment have been offered?

The authors also look at the *process* dimension of success. How did the policy design process—the progression from ambitions and ideas to plans and instruments—unfold? What role did evidence/analyses play in this process? What, if any, innovative practices were employed and to what effect? How did the political decision-making process leading up to its adoption—the progression from proposals to policy decisions to budgets—unfold? And, in this constellation of actors, interests, design practices, political moves, and countermoves, when and how did a supporting coalition that helped carry the policy forward come into being?

Finally, each author also examines the *endurance* dimension of success by examining how the implementation process unfolded, and how it shaped the eventual reception and impact of the policy. Did the policy's key components (goals, objectives, instruments, delivery mechanisms) remain intact over time? If not, what level of change (or abandonment) ensued, and how did it come about? How did the political and public support for the policy evolve over time? And, to what extent did the original coalition driving its adoption remain intact (or expand, or contract) and how did this affect its continuing success?

In their examination of the multiple dimensions of policy success, the chapters in the book comprise a salient mix of examples of successful public policy in Canada covering at least a decade or more. Each case study in its own right offers a powerful story about when governments get things right in important areas, and how this often happens. As such, each case study presents an instance of actors, institutions, and processes of public policy-making coalescing to positive effect. In our concluding chapter, we draw together the broader lessons that can be learned from the 22 case studies and which can help to offset the neglect of policy success and the over-emphasis of scandal and failure discussed at the outset of this chapter.

References

Allen, B., and G. B. Doern. "How Ottawa Buys: Procurement Policy and Politics Beyond Gomery." In *How Ottawa Spends: 2006–2007: In From the Cold: The Tory Rise and the Liberal Demise*, edited by G.B. Doern, pp. 95–115. Montreal: McGill Queen's University Press, 2006.

Allern, S. and E. Pollack. 2012. *Scandalous! The Mediated Construction of Political Scandals in Four Nordic Countries*, Gothenburg, SE.

Bakvis, H. and G. Skogstad. 2020. *Canadian Federalism: Performance, Effectiveness and Legitimacy*. Toronto: University of Toronto Press.

Banfield, E. C. 1977. "Policy Science as Metaphysical Madness." In *Statesmanship and Bureaucracy*, edited by Robert A. Goldwin, pp. 1–35. Washington, DC: American Enterprise Institute for Public Policy.

Bastarache, M. 2020. *Broken Dreams, Broken Lives: The Devastating Effects of Sexual Harassment on Women in the RCMP. Final Report on the Implementation of the Merlo Davidson Settlement Agreement*, Royal Canadian Mounted Police. Ottawa: Government of Canada.

Béland, D., A. Lecours, G. P. Marchildon, Haizhen Mou, and G. P. Rose Olfert. 2017. *Fiscal Federalism and Equalization Policy in Canada: Political and Economic Dimensions*, Toronto: University of Toronto Press.

Bovens, M., P. 't Hart, and B. G. Peters (eds). 2001. *Success and Failure in Public Governance: A Comparative Analysis*, Cheltenham: Edward Elgar.

Bovens, M and P. 't Hart 1996. *Understanding Policy Fiascos*. New Brunswick, NJ: Transaction Books.

Boyd, B. and A. Olive. 2021. *Provincial Policy Laboratories: Policy Diffusion and Transfer in Canada's Federal System*. Toronto: University of Toronto Press.

Doern, G. B. and G. B. Toner. 2019. *The Politics of Energy: The Development and Implementation of the NEP*. 2nd edn. (1985). Abingdon, Oxon: Routledge.

Butler, D., A. Adonis, and T. Travers. 1994. *Failure in British Government: Politics of the Poll Tax*. Oxford: Oxford University Press.

Campbell, R. M., L. A. Pal, and M. Howlett. 2004. *The Real Worlds of Canadian Politics: Policy and Process in Canadian Political Life*. 4th edn. Peterborough, ON: Broadview Press.

Capano, G. 2012. "Policy Dynamics and Change: The Never-Ending Puzzle." In *Routledge Handbook of Public Policy*, edited by E. Araral, S. Fritzen, M. Howlett, M. Ramesh, and X. Wu, pp. 451–472. New York: Routledge,.

Capano, G., M. Howlett, D. S. L. Jarvis, M. Ramesh, and N. Goyal. 2020. "Mobilizing Policy (In)Capacity to Fight COVID-19: Understanding Variations in State Responses." *Policy and Society* 39 (3): pp. 1–24.

Compton, M. and P. 't Hart (eds). 2019. *Great Policy Successes*, Oxford: Oxford University Press.

Crewe, I. and A. King. 2013. *The Blunders of our Governments*, London: Oneworld.

Dawson, G. 2007. *"Here Is Hell": Canada's Engagement in Somalia*. Vancouver: UBC Press.

Dewitt, D. B., and J. J. Kirton. 1983. *Canada as a Principal Power: A Study in Foreign Policy and International Relations*. Toronto and New York: John Wiley & Sons Inc Canada Ltd.

Dunlop, C. A. and C. M. Radaelli. 2018a. "The Lessons of Policy Learning: Types, Triggers, Hindrances and Pathologies." *Policy and Politics* 46 (2): pp. 255–272.

12 INTRODUCTION

Dunlop, C. A. and C. M. Radaelli (eds). 2018b. *Learning in Public Policy: Analysis, Modes and Outcomes.* Basingstoke: Palgrave Macmillan.

Edwards, B. 2016. "Breaking New Ground: Montreal-Mirabel International Airport, Mass Aeromobility, and Megaproject Development in 1960s and 1970s Canada." *Journal of Canadian Studies,* 50 (1): p. 5–35.

Facchini, F. and M. Melki. 2019. "The Democratic Crisis and the Knowledge Problem." *Politics and Policy* 47 (6): pp. 1022–1038.

Free, C. and V.Radcliffe. 2009. "Accountability in Crisis: The Sponsorship Scandal and the Office of the Comptroller General in Canada." *Journal of Business Ethics* 84 (2): pp. 189–208.

Goderis, B. 2015. *Public Sector Achievement in 36 Countries.* Sociaal en Cultureel Planbureau: The Netherlands Institute for Social Research.

Gray, P. and P. 't Hart (eds). 1998. *Public Policy Disasters in Europe.* London: Routledge.

Greer, S. L., E. J. King, E. M. da Fonseca, and M. Peralta-Santos. 2020 "The Comparative Politics of COVID-19: The Need to Understand Government Responses." *Global Public Health* 15 (9): pp. 1413–1416.

Hall, P. 1982. *Great Planning Disasters.* Berkeley: University of California Press.

Hodgetts, J. E. 1955. *Pioneer Public Service: An Administrative History of the United Canadas, 1841–1867.* Toronto: University of Toronto Press.

Hodgetts, J. E. 1973. *The Canadian Public Service: A Physiology of Government 1867–1970.* Toronto: University of Toronto Press.

Hood, C. 2010. *The Blame Game: Spin, Bureaucracy, and Self-Preservation in Government.* Princeton, NJ: Princeton University Press.

Howlett, M. and B. Cashore. 2009. "The Dependent Variable Problem in the Study of Policy Change: Understanding Policy Change as a Methodological Problem." *Journal of Comparative Policy Analysis: Research and Practice* 11 (1): pp. 33–46.

Kingdon, J. W. 1984. *Agendas, Alternatives, and Public Policies.* Boston: Little, Brown.

Light, P. 2014. *A Cascade of Failures: Why Government Fails, and How to Stop It.* Washington, DC: Brookings Institution, Centre for Effective Public Management.

Little, B. 2008. *Fixing the Future: How Canada's Usually Fractious Governments Worked Together to Rescue the Canadian Pension Plan.* Toronto: University of Toronto Press.

Lower, A. R. M. 1977. *Colony to Nation: A History of Canada.* Toronto: Methuen.

Luetjens, J., M. Mintrom, and P. 't Hart (eds). 2019. *Successful Public Policy: Lessons from Australia and New Zealand.* Canberra, Australia: ANU Press and Australian and New Zealand School of Government (ANZSOG).

Lutz, J. M. 1989. "Emulation and Policy Adoptions in the Canadian Provinces." *Canadian Journal of Political Science* 22: pp. 147–154.

Macfarlane, E. (ed.) 2018. *Policy Change, Courts, and the Canadian Constitution.* Toronto: University of Toronto Press.

Mathias, P. 1971. *Forced Growth: Five Studies of Government Involvement in the Development of Canada.* Toronto: James Lewis.

McConnell, A. 2010a. *Understanding Policy Success: Rethinking Public Policy.* Basingstoke: Palgrave Macmillan.

McConnell, A. 2010b. "Policy Success, Policy Failure and Grey Areas In-Between." *Journal of Public Policy* 30 (20): pp. 345–362.

McConnell, A. 2017. "Policy Success and Failure." In *Oxford Research Encyclopedia of Politics,* edited by W. R. Thompson. Oxford: Oxford University Press.

McConnell, A., L. Grealy, and T. Lea. 2020. "Policy Analysis for Whom? A Framework for Analysis." *Policy Sciences* 53 (4): pp. 589–608.

McCormick, C. R. 1998. *The Westray Chronicles: A Case Study in Corporate Crime.* Halifax: Fernwood.

Milloy, J. 2017. *A National Crime: The Canadian Government and the Residential School System, 1879 to 1986,* 2nd edn. Winnipeg: University of Manitoba Press.

Moore, M. 2013. *Recognizing Public Value.* Cambridge, MA: Harvard University Press.

Moynihan, D. and A. Roberts. 2021. "Dysfunction by Design: Trumpism as Administrative Doctrine." *Public Administration Review* 81 (1): pp. 152–156.

Office of the Auditor General. 2018. *Building and Implementing the Phoenix Pay System: Independent Auditor's Report.* Ottawa: Parliament of Canada.

Oppermann, K. and A. Spencer. 2016. "Telling Stories of Failure: Narrative Constructions of Foreign Policy Fiascos." *Journal of European Public Policy* 23 (5): pp. 685–701.

Paquet, G. and R. A. Perrault. 2016. *The Tainted-Blood Tragedy in Canada: A Cascade of Governance Failures.* Ottawa: Invenire.

Poel, D. H. 1976. "The Diffusion of Legislation among the Canadian Provinces: A Statistical Analysis." *Canadian Journal of Political Science* 9: pp. 605–626.

Pressman, J. L. and A. Wildavsky. 1984. *Implementation*, 3rd edn. Berkeley: University of California Press.

Quirk, P. J. (ed.) 2019. *The United States and Canada: How Two Democracies Differ and Why It Matters.* 1st edn. New York: Oxford University Press.

Roberts, A. 2018. *Can Government Do Anything Right?* Oxford: Polity Press.

Rose, R. 1993. *Lesson-Drawing in Public Policy: A Guide to Learning across Time and Space.* Chatham: Chatham House Publishing.

Roult, R. and S. Lefebvre. 2010. 'Planning and Reconversion of Olympic Heritages: The Montreal Olympic Stadium', *International Journal of the History of Sport* 27 (16–18): pp. 2731–2747.

Ruderman, N. and N. Nevitte. 2015. "Assessing the Impact of Political Scandals on Attitudes toward Democracy: Evidence from Canada's Sponsorship Scandal." *Canadian Journal of Political Science* 48 (4): pp. 885–904.

Sabatier, P. 1988. "An Advocacy Coalition Framework of Policy Change and the Role of Policy-Oriented Learning Therein." *Policy Sciences* 21: pp. 129–168.

Savoie, D. 2015. *What Government Is Good At: A Canadian Perspective.* Montreal: McGill-Queens University Press.

Scharpf, F. W. 1997. "Introduction: The Problem-Solving Capacity of Multi-Level Governance." *Journal of European Public Policy* 4 (4): pp. 520–538.

Schuck, P. 2014. *Why Government Fails So Often and How It Can Do Better.* Princeton, NJ: Princeton University Press.

Scott, J. C. 1998. *Seeing Like a State: How Certain Schemes to Improve the Human Condition Have Failed.* New Haven, CT: Yale University Press.

Stimson, J. A. 1991. *Public Opinion in America: Moods, Cycles and Swings.* Boulder, CO: Westview Press.

Stoker, G. 2019. "Can the Governance Paradigm Survive the Rise of Populism?" *Policy and Politics* 47, 1: 3–18.

Todd, J. 2016. "The 40-Year Hangover: How the 1976 Olympics Nearly Broke Montreal." *The Guardian*, 7 July.

14   INTRODUCTION

Tribe, L. H. 1972. "Policy Science: Analysis or Ideology?" *Philosophy and Public Affairs* 2 (1): pp. 66–110.

Trottier, D. 2018. "Scandal Mining: Political Nobodies and Remediated Visibility." *Media, Culture, and Society* 40 (6): pp. 893–908.

Wu, X., M. Ramesh, and M. Howlett. 2015. "Policy Capacity: A Conceptual Framework for Understanding Policy Competences and Capabilities." *Policy and Society* 34, 3–4: pp. 165-171.3/4

PART I
HEALTH POLICY SUCCESSES

2

Canadian Medicare as a Policy Success

Gregory Marchildon

Introduction

In Canada, Medicare refers to universal health coverage (UHC) programs administered by provincial and territorial governments under broad national standards legislated and enforced by the federal government. Established in successive steps over a quarter of a century, Medicare is the financed by the Government of Canada and the 13 provincial and territorial (PT) programs to provide full coverage for hospital, diagnostic, and medical care services. Since its inception, Medicare as an ideal has become an important dimension of the Canadian identity as well.

Medicare has been a *programmatic* policy success based on the policy's original objectives as conceived by successive federal governments and the originating provincial governments. Medicare has also been successful in establishing and maintaining a single-tier of hospital and medical care services, even though there have been numerous attempts to introduce a second private tier of services reserved for a minority of wealthier Canadians. *Politically*, it has been able to attract broad and steadfast support among the public. Over its life course, Medicare should be seen as a success in terms of *endurance*, too: it has preserved universal access to necessary physician, hospital, and diagnostic services for no cost at the point of service for all Canadians. Moreover, it has done so through a decentralized system in which provincial and territorial governments pay the bills while preserving the portability of coverage for Canadians within the country.

This chapter begins with a summary of the evolution of Medicare with a focus on the contingency of historical events during the discrete stages of Medicare's evolution, initially an against-the-odds accomplishment but one that eventually became a path-dependent policy norm in Canada. This historical section is followed by an analysis of the various components of Medicare's enduring accomplishments as a program, as a policy process with public support, and as a contested political success. The chapter ends with a reflection on the policy lessons that can be drawn from Medicare's success.

Gregory Marchildon, *Canadian Medicare as a Policy Success*. In: *Policy Success in Canada*.
Edited by Evert A. Lindquist et al., Oxford University Press. © Gregory Marchildon (2022).
DOI: 10.1093/oso/9780192897046.003.0002

18 CANADIAN MEDICARE AS A POLICY SUCCESS

Against the odds: Tommy Douglas and the Birth of Medicare, 1944–47

Medicare, as we now know it in Canada, began with Tommy Douglas and a new social democratic party that emerged in the depths of the Great Depression. Originally a Baptist preacher and social activist, Douglas was drawn to reformist socialism espoused by the newly forming Co-operative Commonwealth Federation (CCF). Although his first electoral effort failed provincially in 1934, he was elected to the House of Commons the following year as a CCF member of parliament (MP). However, as a member of a marginal party, Douglas could only have the most limited influence in pushing the federal government to introduce the social welfare measures needed to offset the impact of the depression. Douglas's support for social welfare measures was influenced by almost losing his leg as a child due to inadequate access to medical care, and, later, observing the medical needs of relief recipients in Saskatchewan in the early 1930s when he provided charitable relief through his church. When the opportunity arose during World War II, he took over the leadership of the provincial CCF in Saskatchewan. In the election platform, issued as a 20-page document in late 1943, Douglas and his party promised 'a complete system of socialized health services' (Marchildon, 2021, 21).

With the landslide victory of the CCF in June 1944, the policy of universal health coverage was placed at the top of the government's agenda. In John Kingdon's metaphor, the problem, policy, and political streams converged. Douglas appointed himself as minister of public health in his cabinet in order to ensure rapid policy design and program implementation. While federal and provincial Liberal governments in Canada had considered the idea of public coverage, Douglas actually intended to follow through on this promise during his first term in office. The only question was: how? There were two options. The first option was to work with the federal government from the beginning to devise a program that would have national standards and contributory financing—an option that had been put on the table by the federal Advisory Committee on Health Insurance (1943). The second option was for the province to go it alone: a less attractive approach given Saskatchewan's precarious fiscal position in the wake of the Great Depression (Johnson, 2004).

In August 1945, Douglas attended the Dominion-Provincial Conference on Reconstruction in order to lobby strenuously in favour of a national system of health insurance, in which the province administered health insurance under national standards and 60 per cent federal cost sharing. This proposal was almost identical to the position in the federal government's Green Book proposal on health insurance. However, given that the federal proposal was tied to the continuation of the wartime tax rental agreement by the federal government, Douglas's enthusiasm was met with opposition to the plan by the most populous and powerful provinces in the country (Finkel, 1993). Although the conference was adjourned to April 1946, no compromise emerged in the meantime, and Douglas moved to Plan B, which was to go it alone (Canada, 1946; Taylor, 1987).

The Douglas government had been working on a bill for universal hospital coverage throughout 1945 in preparation for either Plan A or Plan B. First introduced in the provincial Legislature in March 1946, the new hospital bill was rapidly passed by the massive CCF majority in the Legislature. The bill had two characteristics that would persist as design features of Medicare, despite periodic challenges to both over the next 75 years. The first was a centralized *single-payer* financing mechanism, in which all hospitals and diagnostic services would be paid by the government through public sources. The second feature was *single-tier* access to one set of hospitals and related services in the province, even though the hospitals would not be owned and managed by the provincial government. This second feature bore a key difference with the National Health Service (NHS) in the United Kingdom, which achieved single-tier delivery through the government's nationalization of all hospitals by placing them under NHS ownership and control when the policy was implemented in July 1948 (Carrier and Kendall, 2016). The Saskatchewan, and ultimately Canadian, approach was to achieve single-tier delivery by having governments pay patient bills in all hospitals, whatever their ownership structure (Tuohy, 2009).

In his design of hospital coverage, Douglas implicitly rejected a publicly owned and managed hospital system that had been recommended by Henry Sigerist of Johns Hopkins University in his report to the provincial government—an approach borrowed from the Soviet medical model and supported by some CCF activists, as well as Dr. Mindel Sheps, the first secretary to the provincial Health Services Survey Commission (Sigerist, 1944; Duffin and Falk, 1996; Jones, 2019). Douglas also rejected outright the Sigerist Commission's recommendation to place doctors on salary (Sigerist, 1944). Although these were difficult decisions that brought Douglas and his government in conflict with the more ardent leftists in his own party, his first priority was to get the universal hospital coverage implemented with as little opposition as possible from the hospital sector—then led by the powerful Saskatchewan Hospital Association—and from the province's doctors (Jones, 2019; Lawson, 2009).

The province's limited fiscal resources meant that Douglas had to restrict the basket of coverage to hospital coverage to include the few doctors, such as radiologists, that worked on salary for the hospitals, and to the diagnostic services, such as x-rays, blood specimen and associated laboratory services, and the drugs, including chemotherapy administered within hospitals. He wanted to include other services, such as outpatient prescription drugs, as well as the services of general practitioners and non-salaried specialists, but until his province received federal cost-sharing, he could not expand universal health coverage (UHC) in Saskatchewan (Dyck and Marchildon, 2018).

20 CANADIAN MEDICARE AS A POLICY SUCCESS

Single-Payer and Single-Tier National Hospital Coverage, 1947–61

Tommy Douglas hoped that the success of his hospital plan would eventually entice the federal government into cost-sharing arrangements with other provincial programs in the rest of Canada. In fact, the Saskatchewan hospital plan quickly proved itself in terms of its effectiveness and efficiency, regularly attracting delegations from other provincial governments (Taylor, 1987). In 1948, the Liberal coalition government in British Columbia actually implemented universal hospital coverage using the Saskatchewan single-payer design (Marchildon and O'Byrne, 2009).

At the same time, a powerful coalition of health care professionals, businesses, and political interests had been spurred into offering a policy alternative to the Saskatchewan hospital design. A conservative Social Credit government in Alberta, under Premier Ernest Manning, implemented a multi-payer and multi-tier hospital insurance plan in 1950. Like Douglas, Manning wanted influence beyond Alberta, and hoped that his insurance scheme would eclipse its Saskatchewan rival as the preferred template for the rest of the country (Marchildon, 2016). Although Premier Manning's program was heavily supported by organized medicine and the insurance industry, it was not as well received by Paul Martin Sr., the federal minister of health and welfare in Canada between 1946 and 1957.

Martin preferred the Saskatchewan plan on the pragmatic ground that it was designed to cover all provincial residents, while the hospital plan in Alberta, voluntary for both individuals and municipalities, covered only part of the population (see Table 2.1). From his perspective, any sizeable federal investment would only

Table 2.1 Competing Design Differences of Saskatchewan and Alberta Hospital Plans

Competing design features	Saskatchewan plan, 1947–present	Alberta plan, 1950–58
Universal coverage vs. partial or targeted coverage	Compulsory enrolment based on status as provincial resident	Voluntary enrolment with public subsidies for low-income individuals
Public vs. private governance	Government responsible for payment of all covered services	Private insurance carriers responsible for payment of covered services for those with plans
Breadth of coverage	Access to single coverage package based on uniform terms and conditions	Access to multiple coverage packages (choice)
Financial coverage at point of access to services	No user charges for any covered service	User fees for hospital stays based on number of days (with maximum)

be worthwhile if UHC could be achieved quickly through covering the entire population. Unfortunately for Martin, many of his cabinet colleagues, as well as Prime Minister Louis St-Laurent, were lukewarm to the idea of federal cost-sharing to support universal health coverage. It was not until the First Ministers' Conference of 1955, when Martin and Douglas were joined by the premiers of Ontario and British Columbia—wealthier and more populous, and therefore, more politically powerful provinces—that universal hospital coverage was even placed on the federal-provincial agenda (Marchildon, 2020a). Although there was no unanimity among the provincial premiers as to the merits of hospital coverage, much less a consensus on design, Martin used his position as federal minister of health to tip the balance in favour of the Saskatchewan design. While St-Laurent and organized medicine throughout the country preferred a multi-payer model based on subsidizing private insurance carriers, the Canadian public and organized labour supported the public, single-payer approach of the Saskatchewan government (Maioni, 1997). Their support reinforced Martin's position in cabinet, and the end result was the Hospital Insurance and Diagnostic Services Act (HIDSA), a national law that required provincial hospital insurance programs to be based on 'uniform terms and conditions', which fostered a model of single-tier health insurance and discouraged two-tier service delivery. The law's requirement for public administration, and therefore public accountability to the provincial legislature, knocked out the possibility of private insurance companies running the system on behalf of government (Marchildon, 2016; 2019).

However, HIDSA also had a double majority rule: it would not be implemented, and no provincial government could receive federal cost-sharing until a majority of provinces, representing a majority of the Canadian population, had eligible hospital insurance programs. As premier of a province whose program had met the eligibility requirements for a decade, Tommy Douglas was infuriated by the double majority rule and perceived it as a political ploy by Prime Minister St-Laurent to delay, perhaps indefinitely, the implementation of national hospital coverage. St-Laurent called a federal election shortly after HIDSA was passed in Parliament and the Liberal Party used the promise of national hospitalization as a major plank in its platform. However, to almost everyone's surprise, the Liberals lost the election to the Progressive Conservatives, led by John G. Diefenbaker (Marchildon, 2020a).

Douglas took advantage of this electoral change to lobby Diefenbaker to eliminate the double majority clause in the legislation. Heavily impressed by his mother's hospital care through the Saskatchewan hospital plan, Diefenbaker amended the law, which allowed provinces to become part of the national plan as soon (or as late) as they met the HIDSA's conditions. On 1 July 1958, HIDSA's initial implementation date, Saskatchewan began to receive 50 per cent federal cost-sharing for its program of universal hospital coverage. It was joined by British Columbia, which also had implemented a hospital plan without federal assistance for years; by Manitoba, which had just established a program that met the eligibility

22   CANADIAN MEDICARE AS A POLICY SUCCESS

requirements; and by Alberta, which reconfigured its multi-payer program into a single-payer government-run program in order to receive federal cost-sharing. Between 1959 and 1961, the remaining six provinces would also establish eligible programs, thereby ensuring that Canadians from coast to coast had access to universal hospital coverage (Taylor, 1987).

Organized Medicine's Opposition to Universal Single-Tier Medical Care Coverage

In this next phase, UHC was extended to inpatient medical care in the 1960s and early 1970s in a similar manner although, this time, federal and provincial governments faced significant opposition from organized medicine and an anti-Medicare coalition of insurance companies, health professionals, and business organizations. In addition, the federal government faced the opposition of a number of provincial governments. While the national standards set by the federal government had very similar design features to those embedded in universal hospital coverage, thereby reflecting a degree of path dependence, there was no political inevitability to the establishment of national medical care coverage.

At the heart of this opposition was organized medicine's rejection of single-payer and single-tier Medicare as originally designed by a social democratic Saskatchewan government and accepted, and then fortified, by the Government of Canada. By the early 1960s, the doctors in charge of provincial medical associations, as well as the Canadian Medical Association (CMA), had become much more extreme in their opposition to any form of single-payer and single-tier Medicare. Radicalized by immigrant doctors, who had left the United Kingdom because of their discontent with the National Health Service, organized medicine in Canada became unyielding in its opposition to extending universal coverage from hospitals to doctors (Naylor, 1986; Wright et al., 2010).

Saskatchewan quickly became the front line in the battle between physicians and the state. The Douglas government took the opportunity offered by federal cost-shared financing of hospital care to extend universal coverage to physician billing. The 1960 provincial election became a referendum on the issue, with Saskatchewan doctors, assisted by the CMA and the Ontario Medical Association, spending more money on ads during the campaign than the two major political parties combined. Although the Douglas government emerged victorious, the provincial medical association continued to obstruct the program's implementation. At the high point of the conflict, Saskatchewan doctors staged a 23-day strike that only ended after both sides made significant concessions. The doctors grudgingly accepted that the government would henceforth finance the payment of medical care, and the government guaranteed the right of doctors to continue to operate as independent businesses on a fee-for-service basis (Marchildon and Schrijvers, 2011).

Rejecting the Saskatchewan single-payer design, three provincial governments set up their own multi-payer plans, hoping to set the national pattern. In 1963, one year after the Saskatchewan plan had been implemented, the Alberta government under Premier Ernest Manning established a plan that subsidized the voluntary purchase of private health coverage for low-income residents—a program dubbed 'Manningcare' by the media (Marchildon, 2016). Two years later, BC Premier W.A.C. Bennett's government implemented 'Bennettcare', a multi-payer plan that differed from Manningcare in its restriction to non-profit insurance carriers (Marchildon and O'Byrne, 2009). In 1966, Premier John Robarts' Ontario government established 'Robartscare', a program that closely resembled Manningcare (Marchildon, 2020b).

The federal cabinet under Liberal Prime Minister Lester B. Pearson itself was divided on the issue (Bryden, 1997). The left-wing members of the party supported the 1964 recommendation of the Royal Commission on Health Services (the Hall Commission), which suggested that the federal government cost-share the medical care programs of the provinces on a single-payer and single-tier design. The fiscally conservative members of the Liberal cabinet felt that the government should consider the less expensive option of cost-sharing multi-payer plans, which would subsidize the purchase of insurance by Canadians below a low-income threshold. Pearson eventually sided with the left-wing members of the party, and the Medical Care Act (1966) required that provincial governments adopt a strong form of single-tier universality.

Between 1968 and 1971, all provincial governments established eligible programs despite challenges like the continued opposition by physicians, a doctors' strike in Québec, and provincial demands for more money from Ottawa by individuals such as the Liberal premier of New Brunswick (Taylor, 1987; Marchildon and O'Byrne, 2013). The governments of Alberta, BC, and Ontario grudgingly replaced their existing programs with those that met federal eligibility requirements. The attraction of cost-shared financing, as well as public pressure within their provinces for Medicare, overpowered their respective convictions concerning the superiority and affordability of a multi-payer design.

In less than 15 years, the federal government spearheaded two significant changes to this institutional arrangement. The first was the replacement of cost-shared financing with a combination of a permanent tax transfer with a block cash transfer, known as Established Programs Financing (EPF), introduced in 1977. Offering greater flexibility to the provinces and less federal oversight, the provinces readily agreed to the new federal transfer (Lecours et al., 2020). However, the mechanics of the new transfer exacerbated an emerging problem. In some provinces, governments were turning a blind eye to the practice of physician extra-billing and user fee charges imposed by hospitals. Although not prohibited in federal legislation, the implicit agreement between Ottawa and the provincial governments was that such practices would be discouraged and marginalized by provincial governments (Taylor, 1987).

This change in the funding arrangements for Medicare had little impact on the general public. The complicated mechanisms used by the federal government to transfer money to the provinces for specific purposes, such as health, or for general purposes, such as equalization, were difficult to understand even for the public servants and politicians responsible for Medicare's stewardship, much less for members of the public and the media. However, the introduction of EPF was accompanied by user fees in some provinces. Although discouraged, some very limited hospital user charges and physician extra billing had been tolerated by certain provincial governments and the federal government. However, this practice became prevalent—even common in some parts of Canada—after EPF, leading several experts to begin to point the finger at EPF as the possible culprit (Bégin, 2019).

By the early 1980s, a groundswell of discontent with such user fees prompted Monique Bégin, the federal minister of health and welfare, to replace the Hospital Insurance and Diagnostic Services Act (1957) and the Medical Care Act (1966) with a new single law that would discourage provincial governments from allowing the practice to continue. The Canada Health Act (1984) did this by legislating a dollar-for-dollar reduction in transfers for any provincial government that permitted extra-billing or user charges (Bégin, 2019; Taylor, 1987).

Although the provincial governments that were most permissive in terms of extra-billing and user charges were most opposed to the legislation, they nonetheless took legislative action to prohibit doctors from extra-billing and hospitals from imposing user charges. They did so because they were eligible for a federal reimbursement of all health transfer withholdings between 1984 and 1987 if they could demonstrate that they had eliminated these practices by 1987. A major confrontation occurred when the Ontario government proposed a ban on extra-billing to comply with the provisions of the Canada Health Act. Ontario specialists were responsible for roughly 70 per cent of all extra-billing in Canada by the mid-1980s, and the Ontario Medical Association led a 25-day strike to pressure the provincial government to withdraw its proposed ban. However, the government held firm, the strike collapsed, and extra-billing was banned in the province (Heiber and Deber, 1987; Tuohy, 1988; Butt and Duffin, 2018; Stevenson et al., 1988).

The passage of the Canada Health Act marks the final stage in the evolution of Medicare as Canadians understand and experience it today. Although there have been some political challenges to Medicare in the 1990s and legal challenges since the 2000s, the original policy objectives remain intact. The institutional structures and processes, albeit with the addition of some supporting pan-Canadian organizations and some tinkering with the federal health transfer, remain largely the same. This history sets the stage for a more contemporary assessment of Medicare's success in 21st century Canada.

Medicare's Success in Twenty-First-Century Canada

Adopting the programmatic, policy and political assessment framework used in this volume, Medicare can be judged to be a complete success if: 1) Medicare has achieved its original policy objectives (program success); 2) support for Medicare's value proposition, architecture, and processes remains consistently high among citizens (enduring process and political success); and 3) the politics of Medicare continue to confer benefits to the governments responsible for its stewardship (enduring political success). As will be seen below, Medicare in contemporary Canada meets most, if not all, of these criteria.

Programmatic Success: Universal Access to Health Services

Medicare has been a success, as measured by its main objective—making essential health services accessible by removing the financial barrier to them. Historically, the prime objective of Medicare was to ensure that Canadians could obtain all necessary hospital, diagnostic, and medical care on the basis of need, rather than ability to pay. Without question, Medicare has been a programmatic success, as evidenced by the financial protection it provides Canadians from catastrophic medical costs. Although it is narrowly focused on hospital and medical care, as well as diagnostics and inpatient drugs, these are generally the most expensive areas of health care. These areas are also least predictable in terms of need and, therefore, result in large unanticipated and unplanned costs for patients.

The Canada Health Act has helped ensure that all Medicare services are freely available at the point of service in all provinces and territories. Moreover, the portability condition in the Canada Health Act guarantees Canadians financial protection across all provinces and territories, as well as some protection outside of Canada.

An additional but often overlooked advantage of Medicare is that it relieves Canadian businesses of the cost of insuring Canadians for the most expensive forms of medical treatment. As a consequence, it has given a cost advantage to companies based in Canada, relative to those in the United States, and has influenced the investment decisions of businesses (Monk, 2008). Simply put, US firms with unionized workforces have to spend more than Canadian companies on their health insurance coverage for their employees.

Single-payer Medicare is also an unquestioned success in terms of the low cost of administration relative to multi-payer systems. In general, because they eliminate the considerable administrative overhead involved in having multiple insurers and payers, single-payer systems are less expensive than multi-payer private and public health insurance systems (Bichay, 2020). This difference is very large when comparing Canada to the United States. Based on a 2017 estimate, Canadians paid roughly 80 per cent less per capita on overall administrative overhead than Americans (Himmelstein et al., 2020).

As pointed out by Dave (2017), there is also a feedback effect of health insurance policies on the behaviour of citizens and, hence, to society as a whole. Systems that tolerate non-insurance and underinsurance, such as the US system, also encourage delayed care and preventable hospitalizations, resulting in higher societal costs overall. By contrast, Canadian Medicare, which insures everyone and removes all financial barriers to hospital, diagnostic, and medical care, encourages Canadians to seek more primary and preventative care. As a result, Canadian Medicare reduces the need for, and cost of, avoidable downstream treatment, which in turn helps reduce the burden of disease and improves public health outcomes.

The health outcomes for Canadians confirm the validity of this value proposition: in international comparisons, Canada consistently has rates of life expectancy at birth and low rates of maternal mortality, avoidable hospitalization rates, and amenable mortality roughly comparable to high-income countries such as the United Kingdom, Sweden, the Netherlands, Germany, France, and Australia, and considerably better outcomes in almost all cases than the United States (Marchildon et al., 2020, 11, 154, 158).

However, since the budget cuts by provincial governments in the early to mid-1990s, exacerbated by major reductions in the cash value of health transfers from the federal government to provincial governments beginning in 1995, there has been a deterioration in access to, and the quality of, some Medicare services (Tuohy, 2002). In particular, longer-than-usual wait times for non-urgent surgeries (e.g. hip and knee replacements), as well as some specialized physicians services (e.g. psychiatry), have been a persistent feature of provincial health systems (Commonwealth Fund, 2016; Marchildon et al., 2020).

The inability of provincial governments to reduce such wait times over the last two decades poses a challenge, not only to the political success of Medicare as discussed below, but also to the success of Medicare as a program (Martin et al., 2018). As a public program financed and managed by provincial governments in Canada, Canadian residents expect their respective governments to ensure that these services are provided in a timely manner. Despite major efforts by a number of provincial governments and some successes in the short-term, progress on wait times for a number of elective surgeries has again stalled in recent years, reducing the confidence of Canadians in the public management of Medicare (Marchildon et al., 2020).

This shortcoming in the delivery of some Medicare services, particularly elective surgical services, has provided considerable ammunition for anti-Medicare advocates to call for a two-tier system of Medicare. These individuals and interest groups argue that this parallel private tier would compete with the public tier, forcing public sector managers and political stewards to improve services. If policy-makers thought that this solution was likely to succeed, it is likely that some market-friendly provincial governments would have considered making the change. However, these same governments are well aware that this argument is both misleading and irrelevant, as physicians have been permitted to opt out of Medicare to provide services for patients who agree to pay privately since the inception of the program.

In recent years, the most vocal proponents of this change have been orthopaedic surgeons, who own and manage private clinics. They have opted out of Medicare in order to provide services to patients who are willing to pay out-of-pocket for their treatments. What these physicians really want is for provincial governments to eliminate the rules that require a separation between public and private practice in order to allow them to bill Medicare at the same time they are billing private patients—what is known as dual practice. The restriction was originally put in place (and remains in place) by provincial governments to prevent the public cross-subsidy of non-Medicare practices and to prevent a situation in which dual-practice physicians would always have an incentive to give priority to patients paying privately (Garcia-Pardo and Gonzalez, 2011; Thomas, 2020)

Process Success: A Pillar of Canadian Identity

Medicare has also been successful in terms of the general public's support of its single-payer design and the strong form of single-tier universality, which has held steady in the last fifty years (Mendelsohn, 2002; Marchildon, 2014). The high point of this satisfaction was likely in 1990, just before provincial government budget constraints on Medicare were imposed. A ten-nation survey comparing high-income countries revealed that Canadians had (by far) the most positive view of their health care system that year, and this view still remained evident when the Royal Commission on the Future of Health Care in Canada commissioned a major public opinion survey in 2001 (Blendon et al., 1990; Romanow, 2002).

This attachment to Canadian Medicare extends well beyond Canadians' individual interests and represents a broader loyalty to fellow Canadians and their right to access necessary health care based solely on need (Cohn, 2005). Finally, over the past 60 years, Medicare has emerged as a defining aspect and symbol of Canadian citizenship, and thus, identity (Béland et al., 2020). Historically, the contrast between Canadian Medicare and the lack of universal health coverage in the United States has been key in defining this identity; however, the strong form of single-tier universality in Canada—as one that bears more resemblance to Nordic countries than to the United Kingdom and the social health insurance countries of Western Europe—should also be recognized (Marchildon, 2019).

The process by which Canadian governments manage the tax-based system of financing Medicare also has broad legitimacy. Provincial governments use general taxation funds to finance Medicare services and then allocate these funds among hospitals and providers. While a few interest groups and individual commentators have argued that provincial government restrictions on private health insurance for Medicare services should be removed, most provincial governments, supported by pro-Medicare interest groups and public opinion, have opposed this position (Marchildon, 2020b). Moreover, a concerted effort to overturn the provincial ban on private health insurance for Medicare services as contrary to the Canadian Charter of Rights and Freedoms was rejected in the BC Supreme Court in the Cambie Surgeries case (British Columbia, 2020). However, this hardly ends the argument, as the case will likely be appealed, and eventually reviewed, by the Supreme Court of Canada.

Political Success: Increasingly Contested Yet Resilient

After surviving numerous challenges in its early years, Medicare was generally perceived as a political success by the 1980s. Indeed, the ease with which the Government of Ontario was able to defeat the Ontario Medical Association's challenge to the provincial ban on extra-billing in 1986 reflected public support for Medicare at the time and the desire of the governing Progressive Conservatives to keep public support (Heiber and Deber, 1987; Tuohy, 1988). Although anti-Medicare sentiment among special interest groups, including physicians and business organizations, has continued, and perhaps even grown in the last two decades, public support for the general principles of Medicare and its single-payer and single-tier design remain strong.

At the same time, the CMA and provincial medical associations have chosen not to challenge Medicare openly. Indeed, the frustration of anti-Medicare physicians with their own associations has led them to change venues and use litigation through the courts to achieve policy change. Dr. Jacques Chaoulli, for example, launched a court challenge to Medicare in the Québec courts which was successfully upheld, in part, by the Supreme Court of Canada in 2005. As a result, the Québec government permitted elective hip, knee, and cataract surgeries to be covered by private health insurance and performed in private clinics by doctors who have opted out of Medicare. However, given that demand for this type of insurance is largely limited to those individuals with pre-existing hip or knee problems, the cost of offering such insurance is prohibitive. As a consequence, no private market has emerged in Québec (Quesnel-Vallée et al., 2020). At the same time, the media coverage of the case and the victory of Dr. Chaoulli, however symbolic, provided political support for anti-Medicare advocates in Canada, like the orthopaedic surgeon, Dr. Brian Day (Jackman, 2020).

In 1995, Day established the Cambie Surgery Centre, a for-profit orthopaedic surgical clinic in Vancouver, that catered to patients willing to pay out-of-pocket for surgeries in order to avoid public wait times. In 2006, Dr. Day was elected president of the CMA. Day used his presidency to advocate the replacement of single-tier Medicare with a two-tier system, but could not obtain majority within the CMA's membership to lobby both levels of government for major change. In 2009, Day filed a legal claim on behalf of his clinic and some of his patients, challenging the BC government's ban on private health insurance for Medicare services. The case went on for years and eventually resulted in a trial that saw dozens of health experts being examined and cross-examined on the merits and demerits of a single-payer and single-tier model of health care. In 2020, the trial judge delivered an 880-page decision refusing the argument that wait lists for elective surgical procedures deprived the life or liberty of Day's patients and, therefore, rejected the premise that BC's Medicare laws and regulations infringed the Charter of Rights and Freedoms (British Columbia, 2020).

There are two ways to view such legal challenges to Medicare. The first is that litigation offers an alternative and viable venue for anti-Medicare advocates frustrated with their failed attempts to convince the federal and, in particular, provincial governments, to alter the rules of the policy game. The second is that, irrespective of the political success of Medicare—and the general support of all governments and the majority of their residents for the current system—the single-payer and single-tier health care model could one day be altered through a court decision based on a lawsuit brought on by individuals supported by interest groups with deep pockets. Such a reversal, if it were ever to come, would likely have to be triggered through a court decision, as no government of any ideological or partisan persuasion in the last half century has shown the desire to either reduce coverage under Medicare or change any of its fundamental design principles.

As noted in the history above, Medicare is very much an intergovernmental policy. The establishment of numerous pan-Canadian agencies to support various dimensions of Medicare, including the Canadian Institute for Health Information, the Canadian Blood Agency, and the Canadian Agency for Drugs and Technologies in Health, reflects innovative ways that federal, provincial, and territorial governments provide a common infrastructure to support health care in Canada. The one area that has proven conflict-ridden in the political arena involves the intergovernmental financing of Medicare. Since the early 1980s, the federal health transfer has proven to be a bone of contention between the federal and provincial orders of government. The federal government has made periodic changes to the health transfer, including the inflationary rate of increase, and this has sometimes precipitated major conflicts with the provinces. However, contrary to what some provincial governments have argued, the federal government's contribution now actually exceeds its historic contribution to Medicare services (Marchildon et al., 2020).

At the same time, Medicare has been difficult to change even by pro-Medicare advocates who want to see it expanded to other services. Instead, it seems frozen in

30   CANADIAN MEDICARE AS A POLICY SUCCESS

time in terms of the services covered, even though the original intention behind the policy was that UHC would grow with changing needs (Marchildon, 2007). Although part of most UHC policies in Western Europe and Australasia, outpatient prescription drugs remain outside of Medicare and a number of past efforts to introduce universal Pharmacare (or add prescription drugs to Medicare) have failed. The core of the coalition that opposes the expansion of Medicare remains largely the same but we can now add some of Canada's largest law firms representing private clients, who see a major market opportunity for themselves if the rules around health insurance and dual practice, for example, can be forcibly changed through the courts.

The long wait times for elective surgery, poor coordination of health services across the continuum of care, poor patient responsiveness by physicians and some healthcare organizations, and the treatment of chronic conditions constitute the main fault lines threatening the policy. At the same time, there has been little or no public disappointment with the provincial and territorial single-payer financing mechanism, the single-tier set of services, and the five principles of the Canada Health Act, including portability. However, the old mechanisms of federalism (federal direction through shared-cost financing and standard-setting) cannot work as they did half a century ago due to the increase in provincial power, capacity, and expectations. New approaches that are better suited to the structures and norms of Canadian federalism in the twenty-first century are required to expand and refine Medicare.

What Might Be Learned from the Medicare Experience?

In the early postwar years, particularly after the failure of the federal government's reconstruction proposals in 1946, UHC in Canada seemed unlikely. However, the tenacity of one provincial government put the option on the table and, by 1961, universal hospital coverage had been introduced by every provincial government in Canada. A second round followed, allowing for the extension of UHC to medical care services in the 1960s and early 1970s. The Canada Health Act of 1984 covered off the loose ends by discouraging user fees to ensure that Canadians would not face any financial barriers in accessing Medicare services.

Overall, Medicare must be judged a success based on the evaluative dimensions of process and politics. Medicare's success from a federal program perspective has been more limited. Although national standards in terms of extra-billing and user charges have been upheld consistently, there has been a limited departure from two of the five national criteria in the Canada Health Act.

Each of the 10 provincial and three territorial governments is responsible for the governance and management of its single-payer Medicare programs. Provincial governments must also raise most of the revenue needed for UHC expenditures, although they receive an average of roughly 30–35 per cent of their required Medicare revenues (and some 20 per cent of their total health expenditures) through the Canada Health Transfer in return for adhering to the requirements of the Canada Health Act. In addition, lower-income provinces receive equalization payments from Ottawa, which allow them to provide Medicare services of roughly comparable quality to high-income provinces.

On the whole, Medicare has been implemented and managed consistently with the original objectives of governments. As a statement of principle and general policy, Medicare remains supported by a majority of Canadians and sustained by an enduring coalition of civil society advocacy groups, trade unions, and non-physician provider groups. In recent years, it has lost some program support due to the long wait times for elective surgery and the inability to expand UHC beyond inpatient and outpatient medical care. One noticeable trend is the use of court challenges by anti-Medicare interest groups in recent years.

Despite these challenges, the majority of Canadians remain loyal to the original objectives of the policy and have continually worked to replenish their support for Medicare through citizen-based organizations, such as the Canadian Health Coalition, or by establishing pro-Medicare voices within historically anti-Medicare organizations, such as Canadian Doctors for Medicare. This activity has prevented the gradual unwinding of 'general interest reforms' as described by Eric Patashnik (2008) and has contributed to the long-term political sustainability of Medicare. In response to the popularity of Medicare, members of anti-Medicare coalitions in Canada have avoided challenging the redistributive ethos of Medicare and have tended to posit their policy recommendations as improving, rather than replacing, Medicare. Finally, no provincial government has redesigned its policy to replace single-payer and single-tier Medicare with multi-payer or two-tier alternatives, despite threatening at times to do so.

The first lesson that can be drawn from this case study of Canadian Medicare is that a policy originating from fragile and highly contingent beginnings can become dominant and difficult to change with time. At first, nothing was certain. The Saskatchewan experiment could have failed or been ignored in favour of an alternative approach. However, once it was established on a national basis through the federal spending power, and national standards entrenched the single-payer and single-tier design for universal hospital coverage, it became the easier path to take by the Saskatchewan and federal government when universal medical care coverage was subsequently introduced.

The second lesson is that the resilience of the policy can cut both ways. For anti-Medicare advocates, it has been extremely difficult for special interests to challenge the status quo in large part because of the easily identifiable benefits flowing to members of the general public (Scott and Mendez, 2015). But, paradoxically, pro-Medicare advocates have found it equally difficult to reform basic delivery mechanisms and to add new services to the existing basket. A classic case of 'lock-in' (Hacker, 2002), the system seems highly resistant to reforms of any type whether they threaten the basic design features of Canadian Medicare or are intended to strengthen and expand it. This situation has been referred to as paradigm freeze in Canadian healthcare (Lazar, 2013). As a consequence, problems that have existed since Medicare was introduced, including physician accountability and payment systems, have been difficult to root out and repair (Marchildon and Sherar, 2018).

The third lesson is that federalism brings with it great opportunities in terms of policy experimentation. When the federal government failed in its efforts to initiate a pan-Canadian UHC scheme immediately following World War II, provincial governments had the constitutional and legal capacity to go it alone. As a result, three provincial governments implemented their own hospital insurance plans: Saskatchewan in 1947, BC in 1948, and Alberta in 1950. Moreover, their innovations allowed the federal government to evaluate the results of these program experiments, make its own decisions as to which design to support through federal transfers, and to enable the adoption of UHC in all provinces and territories under some common national standards, including mechanisms which facilitate the almost seamless portability of coverage across jurisdictions in Canada. This advantage of federalism, however, has not been as obvious in recent decades due to the less bold health system experiments and innovations undertaken by provincial and territorial governments.

References

Advisory Committee on Health Insurance. 1943. *Health Insurance: Report of the Advisory Committee on Health Insurance*. Ottawa: House of Commons Special Committee on Social Security, presented by Hon. Ian Mackenzie on 16 March.

Bégin, M. 2019. *Ladies, Upstairs! My Life in Politics and After*. Montreal and Kingston: McGill-Queen's University Press.

Béland, D., G. P. Marchildon, M. J. Prince. 2020. "Understanding Universality within a Liberal Welfare Regime: The Case of Universal Social Programs in Canada." *Social Inclusion* 8 (1): pp. 124–132. http://dx.doi.org/10.17645/si.v8i1.2445

Bichay, N. 2020. "Health Insurance as a State Institution: The Effect of Single-Payer Insurance on Expenditures in OECD Countries." *Social Science & Medicine* 265 (11): 113454. https://doi.org/10.1016/j.socscimed.2020.113454

Blendon, R. J., R. Leitman, I. Morrison, and K. Donelan. 1990. "Data Watch: Satisfaction with Health Systems in Ten Nations." *Health Affairs* 9 (2): pp. 185–192.

Bryden, P. E. 1997. *Planners and Politicians: Liberal Politics and Social Policy, 1957–1968*. Montreal and Kingston: McGill-Queen's University Press.

Butt, H. and J. Duffin. 2018. "Educating Future Physicians for Ontario and the Physicians' Strike of 1986: The Roots of Canadian Competency-Based Medical Education." *Canadian Medical Association Journal* 190 (7): E196–E198.

Canada. 1946. *Dominion-Provincial Conference on Reconstruction: Dominion and Provincial Submissions and Plenary Conference Discussions.* Ottawa: King's Printer, Government of Canada.

Carrier, J. and I. Kendall. 2016. *Health and the National Health Service.* Abingdon and New York: Routledge.

Cohn, D. 2005. "Canadian Medicare: Is There a Potential for Loyalty? Evidence from Alberta." *Canadian Journal of Political Science* 38 (2): pp. 415–433.

British Columbia. 2020. Hon. Justice Steeves Reasons for Judgment, Supreme Court of British Columbia in the *Cambie Surgeries Corporation v British Columbia (Attorney General)*, 10 Sepember 2020.

Commonwealth Fund. 2016. *2016 Commonwealth Fund International Health Policy Survey of Adults.* New York: Commonwealth Fund. https://www.commonwealthfund.org/publications/surveys/2016/nov/2016-commonwealth-fund-international-health-policysurvey-adults.

Dave, D. 2017. "Health Care: Multi-Payer or Single-Payer?" *Eastern Economic Journal* 43 (1): pp. 180–182.

Duffin, J. and L. Falk. 1996. "Sigerist in Saskatchewan: The Quest for Balance in Social and Technical Medicine." *Bulletin of the History of Medicine* 70 (4): pp. 658–683.

Dyck, E. and G. P. Marchildon. 2018. "Medicare and Social Democracy in Canada." In *Party of Conscience: The CCF, the NDP, and Social Democracy in Canada,* edited by R. Lexier, S. Bangarth, and J. Weier, pp. 174–182. Toronto: Between the Lines Press.

Finkel, A. 1993. "Paradise Postponed: A Re-examination of the Green Book Proposals of 1945." *Journal of the Canadian Historical Association* 4 (1): pp. 120–142.

Garcia-Pardo, A. and P. Gonzales. 2011. "Whom Do Physicians Work For? An Analysis of Dual Practice in the Health Sector." *Journal of Health Politics, Policy and Law* 36 (2): pp. 265–294.

Greer, S. L. and C. A. Méndez. 2015. "Universal Health Coverage: A Political Struggle and Governance Challenge." *American Journal of Public Health* 105 (55): S631–S632.

Hacker, J. S. 2002. *The Divided Welfare State: The Battle over Public and Private Social Benefits in the United States.* New York: Cambridge University Press.

Heiber, S. and R. Deber. 1987. "Banning Extra-Billing in Canada: Just What the Doctor Didn't Order." *Canadian Public Policy* 13 (1): pp. 62–74.

Himmelstein, D. U., T. Campbell, and S. Woolhandler. 2020. "Health Care Administrative Costs in the United States and Canada, 2017." *Annals of Internal Medicine* 172 (2): pp. 134–142.

Jackman, M. 2020. "Chaoulli to Cambie: Charter Challenges to the Regulation of Private Care." In *Is Two-Tier Health Care the Future?* edited by C. M. Flood and B. Thomas, pp. 39–68. Ottawa: University of Ottawa Press.

Johnson, A. W. 2004. *Dream No Little Dreams: A Biography of the Douglas Government of Saskatchewan, 1944–1961.* Toronto: University of Toronto Press.

Jones, E. W. 2019. *Radical Medicine: The International Origins of Socialized Health Care in Canada.* Winnipeg: ARP Books.

Kent, T. 1962. *Social Policy for Canada: Towards a Philosophy of Social Security.* Ottawa: Policy Press.

Lawson, D. 2009. "The Road Not Taken: The 1945 Health Services Planning Commission Proposals and Physician Remuneration in Saskatchewan." *Canadian Bulletin of Medical History* 26 (2): pp. 295–293.

Lazar, H. 2013. "Why Is It So Hard to Reform Health-Care Policy in Canada?" In *Paradigm Freeze: Why it is so Hard to Reform Health-Care Policy in Canada,* edited by

H. Lazar, J. N. Lavid, P.-G. Forest, and J. Church, pp. 1–20. Montreal and Kingston: McGill-Queen's University Press for the Institute of Intergovernmental Relations, Queen's University.

Lecours, A., D. Béland, and G. P. Marchildon. 2020. "Fiscal Federalism: Pierre Trudeau as an Agent of Decentralization." *Supreme Court Law Review* 99: pp. 77–99.

MacDougall, H. 2009. "Into Thin Air: Making National Health Policy, 1939–1945." *Canadian Bulletin of Medical History* 26 (2): pp. 283–313.

Maioni, A. 1997. "Parting at the Crossroads: The Development of Health Insurance in Canada and the United States, 1940–1965." *Comparative Politics* 29 (4): pp. 411–431.

Marchildon, G. P. 2007. "The Douglas Legacy and the Future of Medicare." In *Medicare: Facts, Myths, Problems and Promise*, edited by B. Campbell and G. P. Marchildon, pp. 36–41. Toronto: Lorimer.

Marchildon, G. P. 2014. "The Three Dimensions of Universal Medicare in Canada." Canadian Public Administration 57(3): 362–382.

Marchildon, G. P. 2016. "Douglas versus Manning: The Ideological Battle over Medicare in Postwar Canada." *Journal of Canadian Studies* 50 (1): pp. 129–149.

Marchildon, G. P. 2019. "The Single-Tier Universality of Canadian Medicare." In *Universality and Social Policy in Canada*, edited by D. Béland, G. P. Marchildon, and M. J. Prince, pp. 49–62. Toronto: University of Toronto Press.

Marchildon, G. P. 2020a. "The Cautious Liberal: St-Laurent and National Hospitalization." In *The Unexpected Louis St-Laurent: Politics and Policies for a Modern Canada*, edited by P. Dutil, pp. 281–291. Toronto: University of British Columbia Press.

Marchildon, G. P. 2020b. "Private Finance and Canadian Medicare: Learning from History." In *Is Two-Tier Health Care the Future?* edited by C. M. Flood and B. Thomas, pp. 15–35. Ottawa: University of Ottawa Press.

Marchildon, G. P. 2021. "Thomas Clement Douglas." In *Dictionary of Canadian Biography* 21, available online at: http://www.biographi.ca/en/bio/douglas_thomas_clement_21E.html.

Marchildon, G. P., S. Allin, and S. Merkur. 2020. "Canada: Health System Review." *Health Systems in Transition* 22 (3): pp. i–194.

Marchildon, G. P. and N. C. O'Bryne. 2009. "From Bennettcare to Medicare: The Morphing of Medical Care Insurance in British Columbia." *Canadian Bulletin of Medical History* 26 (2): pp. 453–475.

Marchildon, G. P. and N. C. O'Byrne. 2013. "Last Province Aboard: New Brunswick and National Medicare." *Acadiensis* 42 (1): pp. 150–167.

Marchildon, G. P., and K. Schrijvers. 2011. "Physician Resistance and the Forging of Public Healthcare: A Comparative Analysis of the Doctors' Strikes in Canada and Belgium in the 1960s." *Medical History* 55 (2): pp. 203–222.

Marchildon, G. P. and M. Sherar. 2018. "Doctors and Canadian Medicare: Improving Accountability and Performance." *Healthcare Papers* 17 (4): pp. 14–26.

Marier, P. 2013. "A Swedish Welfare State in North America? The Creation and Expansion of the Saskatchewan Welfare State, 1944–1982." *Journal of Policy History* 25 (4): pp. 614–637.

Martin, D., A. P. Miller, A. Quesnel-Vallée, N. R. Caron, B. Vissandjée, and G. P. Marchildon. 2018. "Canada's Universal Health-Care System: Achieving its Potential." *The Lancet* 391 (10131): pp. 1718–1735.

McConnell, A. 2010. "Policy Success, Policy Failure and Grey Areas In-Between." *Journal of Public Policy* 30 (3): pp. 345–362.

McConnell, A. 2017. "Policy Success and Failure." In Oxford Research Encyclopedia, Politics. Available online: https://doi.org/10.1093/acrefore/9780190228637.013.137

Mendelsohn, M. 2002. *Canadians' Thoughts on their Health Care System: Preserving the Canadian Model through Innovation*. Saskatoon: Commission on the Future of Health Care in Canada.

Monk, A. H. B. 2008. "The Interplay between Social Welfare and Competitiveness: The Case of Canadian Medicare." *Geoforum* 39 (6): pp. 2009–2018.

Naylor, C. D. 1986. *Private Practice: Public Payment: Canadian Medicine and the Politics of Health Insurance, 1911–1966*. Montreal and Kingston: McGill-Queen's University Press.

Patashnik, E. M. 2008. *Reforms at Risk: What Happens after Major Policy Changes Are Enacted*. Princeton, NJ: Princeton University Press.

Quesnel-Vallée, A., R. McKay, and N. Farmanara. 2020. "*Chaoulli v Quebec*: Cause or Symptom of Quebec Health System Privatization." In *Is Two-Tier Health Care the Future?* edited by C. M. Flood and B. Thomas, pp. 93–121. Ottawa: University of Ottawa Press.

Romanow, R. J. 2002. *Building on Values: The Future of Health Care in Canada*. Saskatoon: Commission on the Future of Health Care in Canada.

Sigerist, H. 1944. *Saskatchewan Health Services Survey Commission: Report of the Commissioner Henry E. Sigerist*. Regina: King's Printer.

Stevenson, H. M., A. P. Williams, and E. Vayda. 1988. "Medical Politics and Canadian Medicare: Professional Response to the Canada Health Act." *Milbank Quarterly* 66 (1): pp. 65–104.

Taylor, M. G. 1987. *Health Insurance and Canadian Public Policy: The Seven Decisions That Created the Canadian Health Insurance System*. Montreal and Kingston: McGill-Queen's University Press.

Thomas, B. 2020. "Contracting our Way around Two-Tier Care? The Use of Physician Contracts to Limit Dual Practice." In *Is Two-Tier Health Care the Future?* edited by C. M. Flood and B. Thomas, pp. 315–333. Ottawa: University of Ottawa Press.

Tuohy, C. H. 1988. "Medicine and the State in Canada: The Extra-Billing Issue in Perspective." *Canadian Journal of Political Science* 21 (2): pp. 267–296.

Tuohy, C. H. 2002. "The Costs of Constraint and Prospects for Health Care Reform in Canada." *Health Affairs* 21 (3): pp. 32–46.

Tuohy, C. H. 2009. "Single Payers, Multiple Systems: The Scope and Limits of Subnational Variation under a Federal Health Policy Framework." *Journal of Health Politics, Policy and Law* 34 (4): pp. 453–496.

Wright, D., S. Mullally, and M. C. Cordukes. 2010. "'Worse Than Being Married': The Exodus of British Doctors from the National Health Service in Canada, c.1955–1975." *Journal of the History of Medicine and Allied Sciences* 65 (4): pp. 546–575.

3

Canada's Long March against Tobacco

Cynthia Callard

Introduction

For Canadian children entering high school in the late 1960s, the cigarette was part of everyday life. Most likely they had parents, family, and friends who smoked, watched television programs sponsored by cigarette brands, spent their allowance at stores where they could buy cigarettes without anyone questioning their age, and spent their days in schools with smoke-filled bathrooms and teachers' lounges. Governments acknowledged that cigarettes caused cancer, but they seemed unwilling to do very much about it. More than half of this generation were smokers by the time they left school (and one-quarter of those are still smoking).

For the children (and grandchildren) of these baby-boomers, this tobacco-friendly backdrop has largely disappeared. Canadian children entering high school in 2020 were more likely than not to have been raised in a smoke-free home. It is also likely that they have not seen a billboard or television ad for cigarettes, have never seen a package of cigarettes without an illustrated warning about the dangers of smoking, and have only eaten at restaurants where smoking was not permitted.

In the late 1960s, government restrictions on cigarette marketing and smoking were considered unimaginable. Today, removing those restrictions would be considered unthinkable. This change results from decades of sustained activism, health research, and multiple policy changes by all levels of government. This chapter tells the story of those changes, and evaluates the extent to which they can be considered a policy success. This abridged version draws on the detailed accounts of others (Collishaw, 2009; Cook, 2012; Cunningham, 1996; Robinson, 2021; Rudy, 2005; and Tait, 1968, and elaborates on a chronology of events shown in Table 3.1). This story of policy change has two false starts: the failed attempt to prevent the cigarette epidemic in the early 20th century, and the failed attempt to impose regulatory constraints on its trade in the early 1970s. In the two decades following the mid 1980s, all levels of government made progressive policy changes with respect to tobacco, which was supporting and supported by a changed social consensus about how this product should be managed.

Cynthia Callard, *Canada's Long March against Tobacco*. In: *Policy Success in Canada*.
Edited by Evert A. Lindquist et al., Oxford University Press. © Cynthia Callard (2022).
DOI: 10.1093/oso/9780192897046.003.0003

Table 3.1 Key Events in Canadian Tobacco Policy

Decade	Policy Events	Annual Number of Cigarettes sold in Canada	Percentage of Canadians who smoke
		Mid-decade	
1950s	Scientists firmly establish link between smoking and lung cancer Industry promotes filter cigarettes	33 billion	Both sexes: 58% Men: 68% men Women: 47%
1960s	Governments acknowledge that smoking causes cancer Canada's Smoking and Health Program launched Parliamentary committee holds hearings into the 'cigarette issue'	51 billion	Both sexes: 50% Men: 61% Women: 38%
1970s	Federal legislation is introduced and abandoned Industry voluntary code is implemented Broadcast advertising disappears Health warning labels appear on cigarette package sides Federal government asks for tar levels in cigarettes to be reduced and Industry promotes 'light' cigarettes Tobacco control advocacy groups are formed First 'no-smoking' bylaws in hospitals and other areas	64 billion	Both sexes: 45% Men: 51% Women: 38%
1980s	National Strategy to Reduce Tobacco Use is adopted Federal legislation is adopted Tobacco taxes significantly increased Advertising is banned, but sponsorship ads are tolerated First 'smoke-free' workplaces and public places Front-of-pack health warning messages are mandated	66 billion	Both sexes: 34% Men: 36% Women: 32%

1990s	Taxes are rolled back in 5 provinces Scientists establish that second-hand smoke causes lung cancer Supreme Court strikes down federal *Tobacco Products Control Act*, which is replaced with *Tobacco Act*. Most tobacco advertising is phased out Provincial tobacco control laws are implemented Health warnings become larger and more visible Minimum age is raised to 18 or 19 in most provinces	51 billion	Both sexes: 26% Men: 29% Women 26%
2000s	Canada pioneers graphic health warning messages Taxes are re-established in most provinces Sponsorship promotions are phased out National Strategy to Reduce Tobacco Use replaced with separate federal and provincial strategies Provinces sue tobacco companies to recovery health care costs Framework Convention on Tobacco Control comes into force Provinces across Canada ban smoking in bars, restaurants and other indoor public settings across Canada, as well as private vehicles when children are present Provincial governments ban retail displays of cigarettes Tobacco advertising in publications is banned	36 billion	Both sexes: 22% Men: 24% Women: 20%
2010s	Québec courts hold tobacco companies liable for wrongdoing and harming smokers Flavourings and menthol in tobacco products are banned Federal government legalizes vaping products	29 billion	Both sexes: 17% Men: 20% Women: 15%
2020s	Plain packaging is required for tobacco products Minimum age is raised to 21 in Prince Edward Island Restrictions on e-cigarettes are tightened, including some bans on flavours and nicotine levels		

Sources: Consumption: 1955–2005 (Barbara Forey, 2012); *2015* (Health Canada, 2017) Prevalence: *1955* (Robinson, 2021), *1965–1995:* (University of Waterloo School of Public Health and Health Systems, 2019), *2005–2019* (Statistics Canada, 2020)

The market has continued to adapt to these changes, presenting new problems and new challenges for policy-makers.

The Invention of the Cigarette

When Canada became a nation in 1867, tobacco use was well-established in both settler and indigenous communities, as it was in many parts of the world. In the 19th century, unlike today, few people smoked cigarettes, instead smoking pipes or cigars, or chewing 'plugs'. Unlike today, cultural traditions and social pressures restricted tobacco use primarily to men; smoking was considered unhealthy for children or women, but not especially risky for men. Unlike today, ethnicity and class largely prescribed a range of tobacco use patterns—with various types of pipes, cigars, and blends of tobacco used in different communities. These social controls (and the luxury taxes that made tobacco expensive) were not formally adopted as a way to protect communities from disease, although they would have had some effect in doing so.

The invention of the cigarette machine in the 1880s and the subsequent development of cigarette marketing that soon followed changed everything about how this product was consumed. The introduction of the Bonsack machine to Canada in 1888 (by the company now part of the British American Tobacco chain), initiated a transformation. It was a disruptive technology which introduced mass production and displaced hand-rolling of cigarettes.

Suddenly cigarettes were affordable and—courtesy of the also newly-invented safety match and lighters—they were convenient, too. This new form of tobacco use was an inexpensive, discrete, and efficient way to use nicotine and was not weighed down by social and class taboos. Mass production, lower prices, and extensive advertising democratized tobacco use—removing social, gender-based, and other barriers that had previously kept consumption low.

Not all Canadians were happy with this turn of events. From the 1890s, social gospel activists and temperance societies like the Women's Christian Temperance Union (WCTU) expressed their blended concern for the moral and public health consequences of cigarette smoking by calling on the government to restrict or ban cigarettes. Women were not allowed to vote or hold office, but they could lobby. In 1904, the WCTU persuaded a majority of members of parliament to support a law to ban the sale of cigarettes (the preferred tobacco product for younger men), while allowing pipes and cigars (then the smoke of choice of adult men). At the time, the number of cigarettes made in Canada was only about 22 cigarettes per adult per year (Alston et al., 2002).

Tobacco companies then, as later, fought to block legislation that would affect their business. Mortimer Davis, head of the largest tobacco company operating in Canada and the major producer of manufactured cigarettes, threatened the Canadian government by indicating that a ban on cigarettes would result in political retaliation from the 36,000 merchants who sold tobacco. Others also opposed the law, including the Anglican and Roman Catholic Churches, who saw such a law as a state intrusion into the jurisdiction of parents.

The proposed cigarette ban had the support of back benchers in the House of Commons, but not the support of the Cabinet, which controlled the legislature's time. Alongside other uncompleted business, the bill expired when the House of Commons recessed that summer. Subsequent attempts to limit tobacco use by law were made and failed. The pressure of these efforts resulted in the government adopting a lesser measure, the Tobacco Restraint Act in 1908. This law, which was in force but rarely enforced for the following eight decades, prohibited the sale or use of cigarettes to children under 16.

Those leading the campaign for cigarette prohibition did not support this compromise, seeing it as a hollow measure. The WCTU and other supporters continued to press for controls on cigarettes. In 1914, a House of Commons Select Committee on Cigarette Evils was given the mandate to examine whether a prohibition on cigarettes should be put in place or whether there were other measures available for 'remedying or preventing any evils arising from the use of cigarettes'. Medical researchers identified the toxic properties of nicotine, and the deeper inhalation that resulted from cigarettes in comparison with pipes (McQuarrie, 2016). Children's advocates promoted policies that were adopted some decades later (including taxes, package labelling, licence fees, and advertising restrictions). The committee, however, never came to any conclusions and its review was interrupted by a summer recess that also saw the beginning of World War I.

These early failed attempts to restrain the trade of tobacco were reflected in Canadian government approaches to smoking for the following century. Arguments based on morality were rejected, the right of an individual to smoke tobacco was not challenged, and the free exchange of this market commodity was left unchecked.

The Growth of Smoking

World War I halted policy concerns about cigarettes and accelerated their use. Worries about the longer-term health effects of tobacco were swept aside by the very immediate concerns for young men sent into battle. Cigarettes ceased being a degenerative object of prohibitionist ambition and became an icon of soldierly masculinity. Buying cigarettes for soldiers became an expression of patriotic support, mobilizing service clubs, school groups, and other members of the public to purchase tobacco products for soldiers. Most of the soldiers who survived the Great War returned as regular smokers (Chandler, 2018).

After the war, an increasing number of men (and then women) took up cigarette smoking. They were encouraged to do so through new advertising techniques, like collector-cards, loyalty programs, and the glamorous role-modelling of movie stars. Concerns about 'coffin nails' and 'little white slavers' were largely swept aside by a new pro-smoking social norm.

The main policy concern of government in the first half of the twentieth century was about how some companies treated retailers, farmers, and workers engaged in the tobacco industry. In 1935, the Conservative government set up a Royal Commission on Price Spread, which, in its review of monopolistic business practices, targeted tobacco companies. The companies used advertising and public relations campaigns to build public support during this review. That same year, the Liberal Party was returned to power under Prime Minister Mackenzie King, and the companies could rely on their close Montréal ties and common interests with the party—'a near monopoly industry had for its political bedfellow a quasi one-party state' (Robinson, 2021).

With the Second World War underway, the social acceptability of women smoking was well established. Mirroring their association with fighting men, cigarettes became an emblem for women serving on the home front in munitions factories or other roles that supported the war effort. Federal policy favoured cigarettes: the government increasingly relied on cigarette tax revenues to help fund its tight wartime budgets, and exempted tobacco from the rationing and controls imposed on other non-essential consumer goods.

After the war, Canadians were among the world's heaviest smokers. More than half the men born in the first decades of the twentieth century—and more than 70 per cent of those born between 1920 and 1940—were cigarette smokers. A parallel increase in women's smoking came a couple of decades later—rising to more than half the women born between 1930 and 1960 (Ferrence, 1988).

'Smoking Kills': The Proof of Causation

In the post war years, the case for a public health response to smoking steadily grew. Lung cancer takes many years to manifest but, once established, it is dramatic and severe. By the 1950s, the rise in lung cancer cases that resulted from increased smoking earlier in the century could no longer be ignored. Medical research and epidemiological methods were improving, and thus, it was easier to connect current diseases with past events. Many studies had been published linking smoking to ill health before 1950, but it was the studies published by British and American researchers like Richard Doll, Ernest Wynder, and their colleagues that firmly and publicly implicated cigarette smoking as a cause of cancer (Robinson, 2021).

The scientific consensus behind this conclusion of these studies set a new path for policies to reduce smoking. Early in the century, it had been easier to scoff at the views of temperance women. By the 1960s, it was much harder to dismiss the conclusions of scientific men.

Nonetheless, tobacco companies in Canada and elsewhere worked hard to prevent the public from learning about the harms of smoking and to delay the government from adopting protective measures (Létourneau c. JTI-MacDonald Corp., 2015). Beginning in the 1950s, Imperial Tobacco regularly polled the public on their smoking habits to gain insight into the impact of these scientific reports. It also launched extensive advertising and public relations campaigns to address prevalent concerns.

With one notable exception, throughout the twentieth century, none of the companies publicly acknowledged that their products caused lung cancer or other diseases. The exception was in early 1958, shortly after Rothmans (the South African tobacco company) began selling cigarettes in Canada. In an effort to make a big splash and rapidly gain market share, the company placed full-page newspaper ads in which it acknowledged 'the statistical evidence linking lung cancer with heavy smoking' and encouraged smokers to reduce their tar intake by switching to the new Rothmans King Size filter cigarette. The response of other tobacco companies was fast and furious. Rothmans soon re-aligned its position with its competitors, denying that the link between smoking and cancer had been proven. Many years later their conspiracy to 'impede the public from learning of the inherent dangers of smoking' and to 'delay and water down' government action would be reviewed and denounced by Québec courts, leading to a $13 billion award against them (Létourneau c. JTI-MacDonald Corp., 2015).

Reluctant Regulation: The Beginning of Government Involvement

By the early 1960s, leading health organizations, like the Canadian Cancer Society and the Canadian Medical Association, had formally accepted that smoking caused cancer. Pressure was on the federal government to follow suit. In the spring of 1963, the newly appointed minister of national health and welfare, Judy LaMarsh, sought permission from her cabinet colleagues to do so. That June, she informed the House of Commons that she accepted the scientific evidence that cigarette smoking contributed to lung cancer and could be associated with chronic bronchitis and coronary heart disease. She also announced that she would be hosting a conference to address the issue.

Within a few months, delegates from provincial and municipal governments, civil society, tobacco farmers, and manufacturers were assembled to discuss a national plan of action to reduce the prevalence of lung cancer and other diseases caused by smoking. This conference birthed the first Canadian Smoking and Health Program, a policy approach with no intention to impose restrictions on tobacco companies or the products they sold. Instead, it would focus on health education and research with the objective of informing the public about the risks, encouraging smokers to quit, and discouraging non-smokers from picking up the habit. Furthermore, the government began to measure how many Canadians were smoking. The resources to accomplish these tasks, however, were modest: the annual budget would be worth about $1 million today (LaMarsh, 1963). This poorly-funded, multi-stakeholder, consensus-seeking, demand-sided, and regulation-shy approach was the starting point of a multi-generational Canadian effort to reduce smoking.

The efforts of governments and communities to discourage smoking through 'health education' were dwarfed by the promotional activities of tobacco companies. It soon became clear to some that this was a losing battle and, in order to be successful, tobacco promotions needed to be curbed. Throughout the 1960s, the government was peppered with proposals for doing this. Parliamentary backbenchers repeatedly introduced private members' bills that aimed to ban cigarette advertising and intended to introduce health warnings on tobacco product packages. Departmental officials repeatedly wrote memos calling for such regulations, along with others that would require the manufacturing of 'safer' cigarettes with lower tar levels and which would oblige tobacco manufacturers to publish information on tar and nicotine levels. There was no great appetite to regulate the industry, however, not even by the health minister. For Allan MacEachen, who had replaced Judy LaMarsh at the end of 1965, regulating the tobacco trade was 'a quixotic effort to stuff a statute book in a vacuum that can only be filled by the exercise of personal responsibility'. Although the idea of legislation on advertising and packaging was toyed with as early as 1967, the deputy minister squashed this plan, calling it 'unrealistic' and 'silly' (Robinson, 2021).

A new policy window opened in the summer of 1968 when John Munro was appointed health minister, and a new deputy minister was put in charge of the department. Munro, himself a smoker, nevertheless took a more forceful approach, surprising the tobacco companies by forcing them to publicize the tar and nicotine levels of their individual brands (Stewart, 1968). By the end of the year, he had arranged for the House of Commons Standing Committee on Health, Welfare and Social Affairs, chaired by Dr. Gaston Isabelle, to open hearings into the cigarette smoking issue. Munro was the first (and one of the few) federal health ministers willing to openly lead on this file. He opened the committee hearings with a forceful and personal statement, where he acknowledged that health education was not enough: the time had come to move from 'cooperation and voluntary action' to 'legislation and regulation'. Prohibition, however, was firmly off the table, in his view, as this could increase the unregulated illicit trade of cigarettes and prevent the use of product regulation to make cigarettes less hazardous (Munro, 1968).

The committee presented its report a year later, calling for new policy objectives. Among these were bans on advertising, increased educational efforts, promotion of less hazardous smoking, assistance to farmers, and standards to reduce

44 CANADA'S LONG MARCH AGAINST TOBACCO

fires caused by cigarettes. Their detailed recommendations anticipated the core tobacco-control measures in place today: warning labels, smoke-free areas, preventing purchases by children, and providing support to smokers who want to quit. The committee understood that 'young people can hardly be expected to believe that governments really consider cigarette smoking to be hazardous if they allow unlimited cigarette promotion' (House of Commons, 1969).

Over the following year, Munro signalled his desire for legislation to curb industry activities and, in spring of 1971, a draft law was submitted to cabinet for approval. However, by the time the legislation was drafted, his cabinet colleagues and other senior public servants had been persuaded by tobacco companies to close the policy window. Even before the health minister had made his case to cabinet, other ministers had negotiated a voluntary agreement with tobacco companies that would substitute for legislation (Paré, 1971) and senior public servants were mobilizing to block the law. Munro introduced Bill C-248, 'An Act respecting the promotion and sale of cigarettes' but no further legislative review was authorized. The bill was effectively dead in the water when presented to the House of Commons just before the summer break in 1971. The government de facto accepted the industry's alternative approach of a voluntary code, which came into effect at the start of 1972. The agreement covered some of the objectives of C-248, such as warning labels on packaging, an end to cigarette advertising on television, and measures to persuade smokers to switch to lower tar cigarettes.

For the next seventeen years, the voluntary code drafted and enforced by the industry would form the core federal policy instrument to reduce smoking. British Columbia was the only provincial government to take steps to restrict tobacco marketing, implementing partial measures in 1971. The notion of a federal law restricting commercial activities in tobacco had run against a federal government preference for non-intervention. Instead of a parliamentary debate and decision, the issue was settled through elite accommodation. The policy direction was decided behind closed doors, through a discussion between government and an industry that was a political ally, a powerful employer, and tax provider—not by the legislature. It would be almost two decades before tobacco policy emerged from this back-room process.

Forging a Consensus for Regulation

For the following decade, the tobacco industry's voluntary code set the rules for how cigarettes and other tobacco products could be advertised and packaged. The federal health department continued to run educational programs aimed at reducing smoking, but on a diminishing budget. Officials remained keen on making cigarettes 'less hazardous' and looked into new varieties of tobacco that might accomplish this. They monitored the tobacco companies' activities and measured their practices against their voluntary undertakings. At times, they pressured non-compliant companies, through increasingly stern and sometimes testy letters, to reduce the amount of tar and nicotine in their cigarettes and to make warning messages more visible. At the same time, the department prepared to make a case for legislative controls on tobacco.

Civil society organizations began to organize in favour of public policy that restricted tobacco usage. Major health charities—like the Canadian Cancer Society, the Heart and Stroke Foundation and the Canadian Lung Association—decided to expand their efforts beyond public education, and started advocating for policy change. In 1974, they collectively set up the Canadian Council on Smoking and Health, and in the same year, the Non-Smokers Rights Association was also founded. Health charities became more comfortable with advocating for policy change and the Canadian Cancer Society soon opened up offices in Ottawa for that purpose. From the early 1980s, advocates for health strategized to counter the lobbying efforts of the tobacco industry.

New policy measures were piloted, including smoking bans and higher taxes. Beginning in the 1970s, municipalities began to pass smoke-free bylaws, revising them repeatedly over the next decades to expand their application. In the 1980s, public servants began to demand smoke-free workplaces, and Air Canada began to ban smoking on some short-haul domestic flights.

Health officials in provincial and federal governments began to prepare for co-ordinated policy change. In 1983, federal and provincial deputy ministers of health agreed to a 10-point plan to reduce smoking, and then invited civil society partners to join them on what would become the Steering Committee for the National Strategy to Reduce Tobacco Use (NSTRTU) (Health and Welfare Canada, 1988). The 1987 NSTRTU directional paper, agreed to by this multi-sectoral group, put 'legislation' at the top of its list of seven strategic directions to achieve its pillar goals of 'prevention', 'protection', and 'cessation' (Health and Welfare Canada, 1987). The federal government provided financial support to NSTRTU and some non-governmental partners.

The opportunity for legislation improved after the 1984 election. The new Conservative government had fewer close ties with tobacco companies and had also made an election commitment to increase the power of members of parliament to introduce legislation. One of the first parliamentary initiatives to succeed through this new process was a bill introduced by a New Democratic Party (NDP) backbencher, who proposed to ban tobacco advertising and to make federally-regulated workplaces (federal workers, banks, transportation, broadcasters, etc.) smoke-free. The bill was chosen by an all-party committee as one of the first 'votable' items under the new parliamentary reforms, and support for the bill was evident on all sides of the House. This show of support (and risk of being scooped by another party) nudged the new health minister, Jake Epp, to obtain cabinet backing for government proposals that would accomplish similar goals.

46 CANADA'S LONG MARCH AGAINST TOBACCO

As they had done in the past, tobacco companies tried to forestall the legislation, offering to mend their ways and suggesting a stronger voluntary code in lieu of a new law. This time their offers were refused. A new government was in power, a new style of decision-making was in place, and aggressive lobbying by health charities was underway. In 1988 parliament approved not one, but two bills to control tobacco: the government's Tobacco Products Control Act and the private member's Non-Smokers' Health Act. With these first legislative successes, the foundations of modern tobacco control appeared firmly in place: tobacco ads were banned, more powerful warning labels were required, federal workplaces were smoke-free, cigarettes were more expensive, and a community was working together to provide education and support.

This foundation, however, was far from stable. The companies adapted their approach to changing circumstances, moving from quiet recalcitrance to open defiance. They challenged the advertising ban in court. They ran a campaign to stoke smokers' anger about cigarette taxes and then flooded the illicit market with their brands. They shifted their promotional dollars away from traditional advertising to sponsorship advertising, exploiting a legal loophole that allowed ads by corporate identities like 'du Maurier Jazz Inc.' Before long, key elements of the comprehensive federal policy approach to control tobacco were in tatters, and measures were being rolled back. In early 1994, provincial and federal governments addressed run-away illicit sales by cutting tobacco taxes in half. In 1995, the Supreme Court found that the Tobacco Products Control Act was inconsistent with the newly created constitutional rights of companies to commercial free speech.

These major setbacks did not cause the overall approach to collapse. The federal government re-legislated, introducing a new Tobacco Act in 1997. This amended approach addressed the concerns of the Supreme Court, but also closed loopholes in the previous law and effectively phased out most traditional and sponsorship tobacco ads by 2003. In the early 1990s, health organizations established provincial coalitions, like the Ontario Campaign for Action on Tobacco and the Québec Coalition for Tobacco Control. Soon provincial governments entered the field in significant ways.

Over the following decade, the comprehensive tobacco control approach adopted by the NSTRTU expanded across Canada. At the federal level, Health Canada pioneered new regulatory controls for tobacco companies. These included mandatory graphic health warning messages on cigarette packages, new reporting requirements, and setting new standards for how toxic emissions from cigarettes were measured. Canadian provinces were also at the global forefront, pioneering key regulations like bans on retail displays of tobacco products, second-hand smoke protections for bar and casino workers and customers, prohibitions on smoking in cars when children were present, and sanctions on selling menthol or flavoured cigarettes. Some provinces significantly beefed up their support to smokers trying to quit, and some used taxes to deter young people from smoking by making the practice less affordable. Hundreds of municipalities adopted by-laws that restricted smoking in certain workplaces and public places, and also set licence fees for tobacco retailers (Canadian Cancer Society, 2017).

Canada moved to expand this approach globally, as well. The emergence of globalization in the late 1980s, along with the collapse of the iron curtain, had allowed multinational tobacco companies to expand into previously closed markets. The World Bank was strongly encouraging the formerly centralized economies of Asia and Eastern Europe to privatize their state tobacco monopolies, and multinationals like Philip Morris and British American Tobacco were eager to purchase them (Holden, 2009). Soon, outside a few countries like China and Vietnam, the global tobacco market was controlled by a small handful of multinational companies.

The global tobacco control community noted these developments with concern and identified the need for a globalized response to this increasingly international problem. The Canadian government supported this aim and encouraged the World Health Organization to negotiate a global treaty on tobacco. The

Table 3.2 Obligations under the Framework Convention on Tobacco Control (World Health Organization, 2003)

OTHER MEASURES	DEMAND REDUCTION MEASURES	SUPPLY REDUCTION MEASURES
Article 5 General obligations to implement multisectoral national tobacco control strategies and policies and to protect these strategies and policies from commercial and other vested interests of the tobacco industry **Article 19** Questions related to liability **Articles 20, 21, 22** Scientific and technical cooperation and communication of information	**Article 6** Price and tax measures to reduce the demand for tobacco **Article 8** Protection from exposure to tobacco smoke **Articles 9 and 10** Regulation of the contents of tobacco products and their disclosure **Article 11** Packaging and labelling of tobacco products **Article 12** Education, communication, training, and public awareness **Article 13** Bans on tobacco advertising, promotion, and sponsorship **Article 14** Providing support for smokers to quit	**Article 15** Controls on illicit trade in tobacco products **Article 16** Ban on sales to and by minors **Article 17** Provision of support for economically viable alternative activities (for farmers) **Article 18** Protection of the environment and the health of persons

48　CANADA'S LONG MARCH AGAINST TOBACCO

Framework Convention on Tobacco Control, which came into force in February 2005 (see Table 3.2), established an international standard for tobacco control policy, obliging parties to adopt a comprehensive approach similar to what had been implemented in Canada (Roemer, 2005).

Loss of Cohesion

By the early part of the twenty-first century, the policy recommendations of the 1969 parliamentary committee and the 1987 national strategy were largely and securely in place. The united approach of the pan-Canadian multi-sectoral steering committee, however, could not be sustained. Its last formal action was the adoption of a renewed plan of action that added 'denormalization' to the three pillar goals ('prevention', 'cessation', 'protection') (Health Canada, 1999). Some US states had publicized the actions of the tobacco industry to further erode the social acceptability of smoking (Malone, 2012) and every state sought compensation from the companies for the deterioration of public health, resulting from the industry's wrongful actions. The majority of members of the NSTRTU Steering Committee thought that mass media messages about tobacco industry behaviour, and other forms of tobacco industry accountability, should be included in the next phase of Canadian public health measures on tobacco. The federal Liberal government led by Jean Chrétien, however, did not agree with this approach and announced a different fourth goal (exploring ways to make tobacco products less harmful) when it adopted its revised Federal Tobacco Control Strategy in 2001.

The NSTRTU was quietly shelved soon after, with federal funding for non-governmental organizations ending in 2012 under the Harper government. Over the coming years, several tobacco-specific agencies—including the Canadian Council on Smoking and Health (which had been renamed as the Canadian Council on Tobacco Control), the Non-Smokers' Rights Association, and the Ontario Campaign for Action on Tobacco—closed their doors. The era of multi-stakeholder strategies was over: the forged consensus among diverse governments and civil society had come to an end.

Provincial governments sued tobacco manufacturers to hold them accountable for their practices and to recover healthcare costs associated with wrongful actions of tobacco companies. The first lawsuit was filed by British Columbia in 1999 (and refiled in 2001). Currently, in the winter of 2021, the provinces are in mediated negotiations with the industry to resolve these actions (Physicians for a Smoke-Free Canada, 2020). To date, none of the provinces has indicated whether these lawsuits are intended to reduce tobacco use.

Around 2008, electronic nicotine products began appearing on the Canadian market. The sale of these nicotine products was illegal under the federal Food and

Drugs Act. Initially the federal government indicated that it would shut down this trade, cautioning Canadians that these products had 'not been fully evaluated for safety, quality and efficacy' (Canadian Broadcasting Corporation, 2009). Few enforcement actions were taken, though, and soon vape stores were commonplace across Canada. Not all businesses were willing to sell these products since they were illegal, and convenience stores and tobacco manufacturers largely refrained from participating in this illegal-but-tolerated business. In September 2014 the then minister of health, Rona Ambrose, asked the Commons Health Committee to review the benefits and drawbacks of legalizing e-cigarettes and to make recommendations on whether or how this should be done. The following spring, the committee recommended that the government develop new legislation to cover these products but was vague on the measures that should be included (House of Commons, 2015).

By this time, it was clear that there was no consensus in the medical and health community about whether to use e-cigarettes as a harm reduction approach or whether, like the filters and low-tar cigarettes of the past, they would serve to encourage would-be quitters to continue and recruit new users. Health Canada revealed its approach to the topic only when it introduced legislation in November 2016 (Senate of Canada, 2016). The bill would legalize e-cigarette sales and not require them to be evaluated for safety, quality, or efficacy. Health Canada opted for more relaxed conditions on the marketing of e-cigarettes than they did for tobacco.

The passage of the Tobacco and Vaping Products Act exposed the breakdown in the consensus that had driven tobacco control policy for decades. The federal approach to the marketing of vapes was generally supported by tobacco companies and by many academic researchers, but not by all health charities (Senate of Canada, 2017). In the same week that the new law came into force, Health Canada publicly released Canada's Tobacco Strategy (Health Canada, 2018). This was the third time that the federal government's tobacco control policy formally included a harm reduction approach, but the first time it was controversial within the community.

Across Canada, governments initially took different approaches to the new challenge. None of the provincial governments formally adopted a harm reduction approach, and some took the precaution of imposing stronger marketing controls than those proposed by the federal government (Canadian Cancer Society, 2017). Within a year of the new federal law coming into place, however, Health Canada acknowledged that stronger measures were needed as 'a marked increase in youth experimentation and uptake of vaping [were] threatening Canada's hard-earned gains in tobacco control' (Health Canada, 2019). The pan-Canadian committee of chief medical officers of health stepped in, offering a consensus on additional tobacco control policies that should be adopted (Council of Chief Medical Officers of Health, 2020).

Assessing Canada's Tobacco Control Regime

For half a century, the tobacco control community has worked collaboratively to implement policies and programs that reduced tobacco use. These policies reflected the broad consensus of Canadians working in government, research institutions, clinical settings, civil society organizations, funding bodies, and the community. By 2000, this community had largely achieved the goals it had been pursuing since the 1960s. Their achievements were not only sustained and expanded; they became culturally adopted and legally entrenched locally and globally. Through a series of near-term goals, these Canadians have nudged their communities pragmatically and incrementally, and have dramatically reduced tobacco use among the Canadian population.

This progress can be attributed to the consistent approach of the tobacco-control community over several decades, which is comprised of several features that McConnell (2010) would view as the 'process' dimension when appraising policy success. These process features were:

- *Science-based.* The set of policies remained grounded in health sciences and were supported by evidence. Measures were not advocated or adopted without evidence of their effectiveness.
- *Incremental.* There were some significant shifts in policy (e.g. adoption of legislation), but most of the measures were implemented one at a time, ensuring that each measure was firmly in place before reaching for the next step.
- *Pan-partisan.* Tobacco control was not aligned with any political philosophy and its advocates worked to secure support for these policies from all political parties. This reduced the likelihood of policy change or roll-backs when governments changed.
- *Popular.* Public support was established before policy changes were implemented.
- *Expert driven.* Tobacco control measures were presented and validated by experts, helping frame public discussion as questions of fact, not opinions.
- *Dispersed leadership.* There were many governments and many entities which led the advocacy for, and implementation of, tobacco control policies. Provinces have leap-frogged their implementation of innovative measures, like flavour-bans, smoke-free spaces, and retail restrictions.
- *Collaboration.* The advocacy groups that supported these changes largely worked as an unbranded, consensus-driven 'anti-smoking movement'.

In short, the ultimate success of this movement can largely be traced to pragmatic decision-making, whereby incremental innovations helped to realize long-standing policy objectives.

This method came at the cost of not trying alternative process approaches. Ensuring that every measure was well-supported by scientific evidence, for example, meant that the advantages of using the precautionary principle were not explored, and the strengths of values-based decisions or human rights processes were not evaluated. Avoiding direct challenges to economic liberalism allowed tobacco manufacturers and retailers to continue their trade essentially unchanged. By engaging experts and advocates, the potential for organizing a popular movement was not pursued. The focus on demand-reduction policy measures meant that supply-side approaches were not deeply explored. Their alignment with the Framework Convention on Tobacco Control or other best practices has not encouraged innovation or experimentation. It is difficult to measure the opportunity cost of these decisions because few other jurisdictions took a materially different policy approach.

Nevertheless, from a 'program' perspective (McConnell, 2010), Canadians and a succession of federal, provincial, and municipal governments succeeded in substantially reducing tobacco use. About 60 per cent of men (and 40 per cent of women) born between 1920 and 1960 smoked cigarettes, compared with about 20 per cent of those born in the 1990s (Manuel, 2020). Since the first government smoking survey in 1965, overall smoking rates have fallen from 50 per cent to 15 per cent (Reid, 2019). Policy investments have continued to pay dividends: smoking rates in Canada have fallen steadily, stalling only when the policy measures faced temporary setbacks (e.g. the mid 1990s) and dropping more steeply following the introduction of new measures (e.g. the early 2000s). On the other hand, these policies were not strong enough to prevent the recruitment of new smokers to replace those who have died. Government surveys estimated that in 1965 there were 5.6 million Canadian smokers (Thompson, 1970), a number that had fallen to only 5 million in 2019. One-fifth of those smoking today were born after 1990 and started smoking after these measures were largely in place (Statistics Canada, 2020). Canada's tobacco control policies have flattened the curve of the smoking epidemic but have not yet ended it.

High measures of success along the 'political' dimension (McConnell, 2010) can also be seen in the sustainability, political benefits, and outcomes of these policy changes. The strategy of incremental discouragement of smoking secured the support of many governments and many courts over the years. While governments rarely adopted 'bold' interventions, which might have risked push-back from many voters and the tobacco companies, the multi-party consensus, which was steadily cultivated, meant there was far less political risk involved. On only rare occasions were elements of this comprehensive approach rolled-back, or were handed permanent legal or political defeats. Tobacco control has enhanced the broad standing of the public-health system, which worked collaboratively and collectively to put such policies in place. This has accorded the public-health system a political and reputational benefit, which has strengthened its influence in other health challenges.

52 CANADA'S LONG MARCH AGAINST TOBACCO

One can also consider another political dimension of this case: that of 'bureaucratic politics' (Allison, 1971). Public health authorities have been less successful in being able to shape and steer the direction of policy development. No Canadian government has yet developed the 'whole-of-government' approach to reducing tobacco use that would, for example, engage the support of finance ministries on taxation and funding. The limited influence that health ministries have on senior and central branches of government further restricts their ability to achieve the highest levels of tobacco control implementation in Canada (World Health Organization, 2019). Lacking the support of their cabinet colleagues, Canadian provincial and federal health ministers have repeatedly been forced to delay, weaken, or abandon measures, which were later shown to be effective. Plain packaging was first recommended by a parliamentary committee in 1994, but two decades would pass before a health minister was given the green light to require them.

A discussion of tobacco control policy is not complete without an acknowledgement of the role of the tobacco industry. This industry has also acted collectively to resist and to overcome the measures designed to reduce the harms caused by tobacco use. This group has often succeeded in framing the responses of governments and sought to shape public attitudes. By doing so, the tobacco industry limited policy options and succeeded in delaying, defeating, and diminishing measures that would have reduced harm to Canadians (Robinson, 2021; Létourneau, 2015). The corporate and commercial rights of the companies and their ability to maintain a customer base have been sustained by government, thereby maintaining the legitimacy and legality of tobacco trade by the industry and externalizing the economic burden of its commercial activities. In 2015, the companies were estimated to extract about $1 billion in earnings from Canada, while burdening our economy with $12 billion in healthcare and other economic costs (Canadian Centre on Substance Use and Addiction, 2020). They, too, have reason to claim success as they look back at Canada's long march against tobacco.

References

Allison, G. T. 1971. *The Essence of Decision: Explaining the Cuban Missile Crisis*. New York: Harper Collins

Alston, L., R. Dupré, and T. Nonnenmacher. 2002. "Social Reformers and Regulation: The Prohibition of Cigarettes in the United States and Canada." *Explorations in Economic History* 39 (1): pp. 425–445.

Canada Revenue Agency. 2016. "Comprehensive Settlement Agreements with Tobacco Companies." CRA. 15 February. https://www.canada.ca/en/revenue-agency/news/about-canada-revenue-agency-cra/comprehensive-settlement-agreements-tobacco-companies.html. Accessed 15 January 2021.

Canadian Broadcasting Corporation. 2009. "Health Canada Puts Foot down on Electronic Cigarettes." CBC News. 27 March. https://www.cbc.ca/news/health-canada-puts-foot-down-on-electronic-cigarettes-1.798958. Accessed 15 January 2020.

Canadian Cancer Society. 2017. "Overview Summary of Federal/Provincial/Territorial Tobacco Control Legislation in Canada." Canadian Cancer Society. October. http://support.cancer.ca/documents/Legislative_Overview-Tobacco_Control-F-P-T-2017-final.pdf. Accessed 15 January 2021.

Canadian Centre on Substance Use and Addiction and the Canadian Institute for Substance Use Research, 2020. *Canadian Substance Use Costs and Harms 2015–2017*. Ottawa. Available at: https://www.ccsa.ca/sites/default/files/2020-06/CSUCH-Canadian-Substance-Use-Costs-Harms-Report-2020-en.pdf

Chandler, G. 2018. "The Smoke of War." *Legion*. 23 February. https://legionmagazine.com/en/2018/02/the-smoke-of-war/. Accessed 15 March 2021.

Collishaw, N. E. 2009. *History of Tobacco Control in Canada*. Ottawa: Physicians for a Smoke-Free Canada. Available at: http://www.smoke-free.ca/pdf_1/2009/History%20of%20tobacco%20control%20in%20Canada.pdf. Accessed 15 March 2021.

Cook, S.A. 2012. *Sex, Lies, and Cigarettes: Canadian Women, Smoking, and Visual Culture, 1880–2000*. Montreal: McGill-Queen's University Press.

Council of Chief Medical Officers of Health. 2020. *Statement on Nicotine Vaping in Canada*. Government of Canada. 22 January. https://www.canada.ca/en/public-health/news/2020/01/statement-from-the-council-of-chief-medical-officers-of-health-on-nicotine-vaping-in-canada.html. Accessed 15 March 2021.

Cunningham, R. 1996. *Smoke and Mirrors: The Canadian Tobacco War*. Ottawa: IDRC.

Ferrence, R. 1988. "Expert Opinion. Trends in Tobacco Consumption in Canadas: 1900–1987." Trial Record *RJR Macdonald v AG Canada*.

Forey, B., J. Hamling, A. Thornton, and P. Lee. 2012. *International Smoking Statistics*. Sutton, UK: P N Lee Statistics & Computing Ltd.

GBD Collaborators. 2019. "Global Burden of 87 Risk Factors in 204 Countries and Territories, 1990–2019: A Systematic Analysis for the Global Burden of Disease Study 2019." *The Lancet* 396 (10258): pp. 1233–1249.

Health and Welfare Canada. 1987. *Directional Paper of the National Program to Reduce Tobacco Use in Canada*. Ottawa: Health and Welfare Canada.

Health and Welfare Canada. 1988. *National Program to Reduce Tobacco Use: Orientation Manuals and Historical Perspective*. Ottawa: Health and Welfare Canada. https://www.industrydocuments.ucsf.edu/tobacco/docs/#id=rthx0149. Accessed 15 March 2021.

Health Canada. 2017. *National and Provincial/Territorial Tobacco Sales Data*. Ottawa: Health Canada. www.canada.ca/en/health-canada/services/publications/healthy-living/federal-provincial-territorial-tobacco-sales-data. Accessed 15 March 2021.

Health Canada. 2019. *Notice of Intent—-Potential Measures to Reduce the Impact of Vaping Product Advertising on Youth and Non-Users of Tobacco Products*. Ottawa: Government of Canada. Available at: https://www.canada.ca/content/dam/hc-sc/documents/programs/consultation-measures-reduce-impact-vaping-products-advertising-youth-non-users-tobacco-products/notice-document/summary/consultation-summary-vaping.pdf

Health Canada. 1999. *New Directions for Tobacco Control in Canada: A National Strategy*. Ottawa: Health Canada. https://www.industrydocuments.ucsf.edu/tobacco/docs/#id=nnxx0149. Accessed 15 March 2021.

Health Canada. 2018. *Overview of Canada's Tobacco Strategy*. Ottawa: Health Canada. www.canada.ca/en/health-canada/services/publications/healthy-living/canada-tobacco-strategy/overview-canada-tobacco-strategy. Accessed 15 March 2021.

54 CANADA'S LONG MARCH AGAINST TOBACCO

Holden, C. and K. Lee. 2009. "Corporate Power and Social Policy: The Political Economy of the Transnational Tobacco Companies." *Global Social Policy* 9 (3): pp. 328–354.

House of Commons Standing Committee of Health, Welfare and Social Affairs. 1969. *Report of the Standing Committee of Health Welfare and Social Affairs on Tobacco and Cigarette Smoking.* Ottawa: House of Commons.

House of Commons Standing Committee on Health. 2015. *Vaping: Towards a Regulatory Framework for E-Cigarettes. Report of the Standing Committee on Health.* Ottawa: House of Commons.

LaMarsh, J. V. 1963. *Memorandum to Cabinet: The Effects of Smoking on Health.* Ottawa: Government of Canada. https://www.industrydocuments.ucsf.edu/tobacco/docs/#id=jqnw0223. Accessed 15 March 2021.

Létourneau c. JTI-MacDonald Corp. 2015. QCCS 2382

Malone, R. E., Q. Grundy, and L. A. Bero. 2012. "Tobacco Industry Denormalisation as a Tobacco Control Intervention: A Review." *Tobacco Control* 21 (2): pp. 162–167.

Manuel, D. G., A. S. Wilton, C. Bennett, A. Rohit Dass, A. Laporte, and T. R. Holford. 2020. *Smoking Patterns Based on Birth-Cohort-Specific Histories from 1965 to 2013 with Projections to 2041.* Ottawa: Statistics Canada.

McConnell, A. 2010. "Policy Success, Policy Failure and Grey Areas In-Between." *Journal of Public Policy* 30 (3): pp. 345–362.

McConnell, A. and L. Grealy. 2020. "Policy Success for Whom? A Framework for Analysis." *Policy Sciences* 53 (4): pp. 589–608.

McQuarrie, J. R. 2016. *From Farm to Firm: Canadian Tobacco c.1860–1950.* Doctoral dissertation, University of Toronto.

Munro, J. 1968. *Report on Cigarette Smoking and Health: Presentation to the Health, Welfare and Social Affairs Committee of the House of Commons.* Ottawa: House of Commons. https://www.industrydocuments.ucsf.edu/tobacco/docs/#id=zqnw0223. Accessed 15 March 2021.

Paré, P. 1971. Letter to the Hon. C.M. Drury, President, Treasury Board on behalf of the Canadian Tobacco Manufacturers' Council. https://www.industrydocuments.ucsf.edu/docs/qynv0223

Physicians for a Smoke-Free Canada. 2020. *Tobacco Companies and their Use of Insolvency Protection.* Ottawa: PSC. www.smoke-free.ca/SUAP/2020/Litigation%20update.pdf. Accessed 15 March 2021.

Reid J. L, D. Hammond, U. Tariq, R. Burkhalter, V. L. Rynard, and O. Douglas. 2019. *Tobacco Use in Canada: Patterns and Trends, 2019 Edition.* Waterloo: Propel Centre for Population Health Impact, University of Waterloo.

Robinson, D. J. 2021. *Cigarette Nation: Business, Health and Canadian Smokers, 1930–1957.* Montreal: McGill-Queen's University Press.

Roemer, R., A. Taylor, and J. Lariviere. 2005. "Origins of the WHO Framework Convention on Tobacco Control." *American Journal of Public Health* 95 (6): pp. 936–938.

Rudy, J. 2005. *The Freedom to Smoke: Tobacco Consumption and Identity.* Montreal: McGill-Queen's University Press.

Senate of Canada. 2016. *Bill S-5, An Act to Amend the Tobacco Act and the Non-Smokers' Health Act and to Make Consequential Amendments to Other Acts.* House of Commons. 22 November. Available at: https://www.parl.ca/DocumentViewer/en/42-1/bill/s-5/first-reading.

Senate of Canada Standing Committee on Social Affairs, Science and Technology. 2017. *Bill S-5, An Act to amend the Tobacco Act and the Non-smokers' Health Act and to make consequential amendments to other Acts. Briefs and other documents.* Senate of Canada. Available at: https://sencanada.ca/en/committees/SOCI/Briefs/ 42-1?oor_id=445224. Accessed 15 March 2021.

Statistics Canada. 2020. *Health Characteristics, Annual Estimates.* Statistics Canada. www150.statcan.gc.ca/t1/tbl1/en/tv.action?pid=1310009601. Accessed 15 March 2021.

Stewart, D. 1968. *Letter to Minister Munro.* Canadian Tobacco Industry Collection. www.industrydocuments.ucsf.edu/tobacco/docs/#id=xpnv0223/ Accessed 15 March 2021.

Tait, L. 1968. *Tobacco in Canada.* Toronto: T.H. Best Printing Company.

Thompson, M. W. 1970. *Statistics on Smoking in Canada.* Ottawa: Health Canada. www. industrydocuments.ucsf.edu/tobacco/docs/#id=tfjl0200. Accessed 15 March 2021.

World Health Organization. 2003. *Framework Convention on Tobacco Control.* Geneva: World Health Organization.

World Health Organization. 2019. *WHO Report on the Global Tobacco Epidemic 2019: Offer Help to Quit Tobacco Use.* Geneva: World Health Organization

4

Insite in Vancouver

North America's First Supervised Injection Site

Carey Doberstein

Introduction

In 2003, the first legal supervised safe injection site in North America ('Insite') opened in Vancouver—the epicenter of the injection drug epidemic in Canada. The creation of Insite was the culmination of an extraordinary political struggle initiated by an activist movement of drug users, pioneering local elected leadership, and a delicate multi-level governance negotiation with legal, health, and public safety dimensions. Insite has been an unqualified success in its core objective: saving lives through a harm reduction model by treating drug use as a health, rather than criminal, issue. There are broader issues that intersect with drug addiction in Vancouver—such as poverty, homelessness, and mental health—that fall well outside the scope of a safe injection site to solve, and thus remain a significant policy problem. But on the specific task for which Insite was designed, it is a clear success. Insite, and the subsequent additional sites created in Vancouver, enjoy enormously high public support in the city, the province and most parts of the country, representing a robust policy success that has survived several government turnovers at all three levels of government. This firmly institutionalized policy model has also since diffused to other cities in Canada, further demonstrating its popularity among policy-makers.

A Policy Success

This chapter describes how a diverse group of people in Vancouver—activists, service providers, health professionals, policy advisors, and local elected officials—mobilized a challenge to the prevailing paradigm that viewed drug addiction as a criminal activity and offered an alternative response to the health crisis drug addiction produced. It describes how, in various public venues and behind the scenes,

Carey Doberstein, *Insite in Vancouver*. In: *Policy Success in Canada*.
Edited by Evert A. Lindquist et al., Oxford University Press. © Carey Doberstein (2022).
DOI: 10.1093/oso/9780192897046.003.0004

this coalition was able to persuade policy-makers that a harm reduction strategy would be effective in treating drug addiction.[1] The chapter also appraises the extent to which the harm reduction coalition remains influential as new problems emerge.

The success of Insite is assessed by deploying the PPPE frameworks of McConnell (2010) as well as Compton and 't Hart (2019), which include programmatic, process, and political dimensions. In other words, an unambiguous policy success will generate measurable social value (programmatic dimension), from a set of policy-making practices that are appropriately inclusive and effective (process dimension) and enjoy broad and sustainable political support (political dimension). The PPPE framework is not binary with respect to success-failure, but rather conceptualizes tiers of success in relation to these dimensions to help understand the 'bundles of complex outcomes' and identify patterns in this realm. Insite is best described as a 'durable success' (McConnell, 2010), in that it generally achieves what it was set to do (though perhaps not perfectly), remains resilient to challenge from opponents, and any controversy around it is manageable by policy-makers. It has a demonstrated record of saving thousands of lives among vulnerable populations, for whom political attention and public empathy have traditionally been scarce. Insite was both the *product* of a concerted challenge to the dominant paradigm of drug policy in Vancouver, as well as the *cause* of a larger revolution in drug policy and treatment in Canada that now enjoys broad scientific and political legitimacy.

Marginalization and Risk in Vancouver's Downtown Eastside

North America's first safe injection site in Vancouver emerged out of a particular social, political, and institutional context characterized by urgency, activism, and collaboration. The Downtown Eastside (DTES) in Vancouver became what it is today through a series of economic, social, city planning, and societal changes that channelled marginalized folks into the neighbourhood. Once one of many areas in the city in which low-income residents could find affordable housing, aggressive gentrification elsewhere in Vancouver made the DTES virtually the only remaining central area not transformed to middle class aesthetic and behavioural norms. Low-income and other support services to assist marginalized populations were then disproportionately located in the DTES in response to this trend.

---

[1] The development and institutionalization of safe injection sites in Canada can be understood through the Advocacy Coalition Framework (ACF), a leading policy-process theory, which holds that various people and groups with shared core beliefs in a policy subsystem coordinate with each other to translate their beliefs into action (Sabatier and Jenkins-Smith, 1993; Weible and Ingold, 2018). ACF suggests we generally see paradigmatic policy change, like that associated with the shift from criminalization of drug use to harm reduction policies, when the dominant coalition is displaced by a challenger coalition, often due to policy failure or an external shock, like a crisis.

58 INSITE IN VANCOUVER

Insufficient community support associated with the mental health deinstitution-alization movement resulted in the migration of people who were not welcome elsewhere and vulnerable to self-medication with illicit drugs.

The economic and social anxieties in the area in the late 1980s, combined with the newly inexpensive but highly addictive heroin being trafficked into the city, contributed to a neighbourhood consumed by drug use (Campbell et al., 2009). In 2012, Andresen and Jozaghi (2012) estimated about 5,000 persons who inject drugs (PWID) in the DTES, but the figure could be as high as 9,000. Widespread injection drug use and needle sharing among marginalized persons contributed to a rapid rise of HIV and Hepatitis C infections, which became among the highest in the Western world. In 1997, health researchers in Vancouver estimated that 25 per cent of PWID acquired HIV and nearly 90 per cent were infected with Hepatitis C (Campbell et al., 2009). Increasing drug potency and mixing contributed to a new problem of 'multiple drug toxicity' that resulted in an explosion of fatal overdoses among PWID in the mid 1990s (Boyd, 2013).

The problems associated with needle sharing and drug overdoses were the key issues that a safe injection site, as part of a harm reduction policy, was seeking to tackle. The goal was to save lives of PWID, who, until the 1990s, were generally a group that earned limited sympathy from most citizens. However, since then, the profile of drug users had evolved, and the problem had begun to touch families of diverse socioeconomics and histories. To recognize the *programmatic* success of Insite, it is important to understand how a safe injection site typically works. They are facilities staffed by medical professionals, usually nurses, who provide clean materials and space for drug users—who bring their own supply—to inject under supervision. Clean materials are a critical intervention to reduce the spread of HIV and Hepatitis C, and supervision by medical professionals is critical to reverse overdoses.

Insite and the broader drug use patterns in and around Vancouver's DTES have been subject to considerable academic study, and the results of the intervention are unambiguous: HIV and Hepatitis C acquisition rates have declined (Andresen and Boyd, 2010), needle sharing has dropped among users outside of the facility (Boyd, 2013), Insite clients are more likely to initiate and maintain addiction treatment (DeBeck et al., 2011), not a single supervised overdose has resulted in death at the facility (Vancouver Coastal Health n.d.), and, prior to the arrival of fentanyl, the fatal overdose rate in the region had significantly declined (Marshall et al., 2011). Other studies have found additional benefits, such as lower public injection drug use (Boyd, 2013), positive benefit-cost ratios ranging from $3–25 million annually[2] (Bayoumi and Zaric, 2008; Des Jarlais et al., 2008; Andresen and Boyd, 2010), and no evidence that this intervention 'encourages' drug use, (Andresen and Jozaghi, 2012) increases drug trafficking or crime (Wood et al., 2006).

[2] These estimates are dependent on assumptions of averted HIV infections.

The data from Insite are clear: it works for what it is designed to address. The fact that drug use, crime, and poverty are still prevalent in the DTES is not a failure of Insite. Safe injection sites (SIS) are not a solution to poverty, homelessness, and mental health crises. These are all critical issues that intersect with drug addiction, yet they are clearly broad and daunting policy challenges beyond the mandate of SIS. As such, Insite sought to address one element: reducing the harm associated with drug use.

How Safe Injection Sites Emerged

Activists and advocates in the DTES were drawing attention to this crisis throughout the 1980s, and directly challenging the dominant paradigm through which policy-makers viewed drug use. The so-called War on Drugs paradigm held that drug use in society could be curbed by the enforcement and incarceration of suppliers and users of drugs. However, there is limited evidence of its success in discouraging drug use, and considerable evidence of its unfairness and stigmatizing effects (Baum, 1996). Activists rallying against the War on Drugs paradigm had both allies and opponents among health professions and public authorities, but they sought out collaborative opportunities to marshal evidence of the emerging crisis, which they used to advance new approaches to deal with the presence of drugs in society (Lupick, 2019). Such 'epistemic communities' are found in all policy domains, and they mobilize knowledge to define problems and craft solutions (Muhkerjee and Howlett, 2015). The harm reduction paradigm accepts drug use as part of our world, and suggests that policy-makers should prioritize policies that reduce its harms through non-judgmental and non-coercive support services (Marlatt, 1996).

The origins of Insite in Vancouver can be unambiguously traced to community activists and advocates who, along with health professionals, continually pushed controversial initiatives and ideas into the policy debate, slowly chipping away at their opposition. Activists and advocates had been addressing the drug crisis developing in the DTES for many years before any government took notice, let alone action. In the late 1980s, recognizing the increasing transmission of HIV and Hepatitis C among injection drug users who shared needles, activists created mobile needle exchange services through private donations. This generated a sufficient demonstration of the efficacy of needle exchanges to municipal and provincial leaders, prompting them to begin funding such initiatives in 1989 (Lupick, 2019). Needle exchanges helped cut the transmission of HIV and Hepatitis C in half by 2002, but the problem was evolving. When toxicity and mixing of recreational drugs became a problem in the mid 1990s, activists once again pushed the legal boundaries by creating unsanctioned safe injection sites in back alleys or in community residences, with unofficial cooperation from street nurses who supplied

60   INSITE IN VANCOUVER

syringes and other materials. From 1995 to 2003 several unauthorized SIS were opened in the DTES, some of which later closed due to community complaints or organizational funding cuts. It was clear to health professionals that they were saving lives, even while the harm reduction debate simmered in the medical and policy communities.

DTES activists worked within the system (e.g. sitting as community representatives on health boards to push for reforms), while continually applying pressure with direct action protests (e.g. mock gravesites in a prominent DTES park). They were willing to push legal boundaries with their services to the community when change was not moving fast enough (e.g. open short-lived, unauthorized safe injection sites in alleys) (Harati, 2015; Lupick, 2019; Campbell et al., 2009). This sustained push from inside and outside official corridors of power eventually moved the conversation among credentialed and mainstream policy actors, who accepted the harm reduction principles advanced by these activists.

Direct activism via protests and collaborative work with sympathetic health and policy officials by community advocates exposed the failures of the criminalization paradigm among important decision-makers in the city and province, which created space for the new lens of harm reduction to take root (Nowell et al., 2020; Lupick, 2019). Vancouver's chief coroner, Vince Cain, was one such individual, authoring a 1994 report on the alarming rise of overdose deaths, which concluded that society needed to shift how drug use was conceptualized. In particular, Cain was one of the first high-level officials to argue that drug use should be understood as a health, rather than criminal, issue and that life experiences over which many have little control, such as trauma, poverty, and discrimination, contribute to drug addiction (Campbell et al., 2009).

Cain recommended decriminalizing the possession of small amounts of drugs and suggested the adoption of a harm reduction philosophy for PWID. His report was not openly embraced at the political level in Victoria or Ottawa (though harm reduction as a general principle was first quietly endorsed in Canadian federal policy in the late 1980s), but it moved the conversation into new terrain at the local level. Indeed, while the first ministers at the provincial and federal orders of government were cool to these new ideas, line ministers and their top officials were increasingly warming up to new approaches, presenting an opportunity to take a few steps outside the previously dominant drug paradigm (Campbell et al., 2009).

In a 1996 report, Dr. Elizabeth Whynot, a Vancouver medical officer of health, called for various reforms to the city's approach to drug use and health. They included pioneering recommendations to create safe injection sites and allowing doctors to prescribe (clean) heroin to their patients (Campbell et al., 2009). Dr. Whynot's report had supporters and detractors in the medical community, and its two recommendations were too controversial for any elected political leader to support publicly. However, the report pushed the conversation onto the purview of the mainstream local medical community and policy officials.

With this type of work, the harm reduction movement in the DTES began to gain powerful and credentialed allies, such as Chief Coroner Larry Campbell, former Deputy Police Chief Ken Higgins, and Provincial Health Officer John Millar (Lessard, 2011). McGann (2007) likewise credits the development of innovative drug policy in Vancouver to an ongoing dance between grassroots activists and credentialed professionals, who aimed to advance ideas and solutions that gained the authorization and financial support of the government.

In this context, community organizations in the DTES began to position themselves for bolder action. The Portland Hotel Society (PHS), which would later create and operate Insite in partnership with the local health authority, had, from its creation in 1995, a different philosophy for its services to the community. In contrast to many other housing and support service providers at the time, the services of the PHS was firmly rooted in a harm reduction philosophy, which allowed for residents to use drugs in their rooms, prevented evictions on the basis of behaviour, and fostered the offering of medical services in their buildings (Lupick, 2019). The PHS and others in the community, such as the Vancouver Area Network of Drug Users (VANDU), took unilateral action where they could, but also displayed willingness to work with local officials in order to push harm reduction principles into the mainstream. For example, in 1996, Vancouver Mayor Philip Owen created the Coalition for Crime Prevention and Drug Treatment as a vehicle for various public, private and non-profit representatives to debate innovative solutions to tackle injection drug-related health and crime problems.

The Coalition, given its diversity, was quite divided in the initial phase of its work, but as the crisis continued unabated, minds opened to new avenues of action (Campbell et al., 2009). The Coalition would later endorse the Four Pillars approach to drug policies—prevention, treatment, enforcement, and harm reduction—after hosting many public forums, participating in international conferences, and undertaking site visits to Europe. An activist in the coalition, Bud Osborn of VANDU, was the DTES community representative on the Vancouver/Richmond Health Board, and is credited with persuading the board to declare a public health emergency in the DTES in 1997 (Lupick, 2019). The declaration of a public health emergency opened up debate and consideration of novel solutions and actions that could be taken by the government.

Local Political Leadership in the Drive for Reform

It would still be several years before a state-sanctioned SIS would appear in Vancouver. In the period between 1997–2003, efforts to establish harm reduction services, and a SIS in particular, either lost steam or were killed at the eleventh hour when proposed to political decision makers. One development that some credit with generating a broader base of public support (and therefore less political

62   INSITE IN VANCOUVER

risk) for the then-controversial harm reduction interventions was the early 2000s drug overdose crisis that began to reach middle class families in Vancouver. Members of these families mobilized around the issue—such as in the form of the group From Grief to Action—and brought these formerly controversial ideas further into the mainstream (Campbell et al., 2009).

Indeed, early political leadership that contributed to the movement towards a safe injection site was found in an unlikely source: the conservative Mayor Phillip Owen, who, for most of his political career had been an opponent of harm reduction ideas advocated by DTES activists (Harati, 2015). Some attribute his change in attitude to concerns over 'social decay' that drug addiction caused (Harati, 2015, 12). Others cite his changed attitude to his relationships with the DTES and community members (Lessard, 2011), and still others suggest he was persuaded by the report of his Chief Coroner, Vince Cain, diagnosing the problem and emphasizing the impact of the Mayor's participation in harm reduction conferences (Campbell et al., 2009).

Vancouver Mayor Owen, sufficiently confident that public education on harm reduction was building enough public support for a dramatic policy change, asked his drug policy team to prepare a policy paper for public comment. Politically, it was critical that harm reduction not be framed as a replacement for the enforcement of drug laws, but rather as a complementary approach to existing strategies. While this would rankle some activists, many of whom rejected any part of the existing criminal-legal regime (Lupick, 2019), Owen and others were clear that this was a new layer on an existing approach, not a wholesale paradigm replacement. It was Owen's stickhandling of the so-called Four Pillars Approach to Drugs— enforcement, prevention, treatment, and harm reduction—that legitimized harm reduction as a new, consensus position in Vancouver.

While there remained some community opposition (such as the neighbouring Chinatown Merchants Association), Mayor Owen's positionality as a right-of-centre leader helped legitimize the approach in circles who gave him the benefit of doubt. Yet one group that grew tired of his focus on the DTES was his own political organization, the Non-Partisan Association (which, in reality, is effectively a local political party). Although it voted to approve the Four Pillars policy, the Non-Partisan Association denied Owen its support in the next election because of his 'focus almost exclusively on drug policy' (Campbell et al., 2009, 167). Owen would have to compete to be the leader of the party; or in the words of ally and successor, Mayor Larry Campbell, they 'knifed' him politically (Campbell et al., 2009, 172). Owen's leadership in this area was politically costly, effectively ending his political career. Owen's decision not to run in the next election propelled Larry Campbell to jump into the mayoral race under the rival left-wing banner, Coalition of Progressive Electors (COPE).

By the time the more conservative members of the NPA engineered the defeat of their leader, the centre of gravity on the debate had moved such that the new NPA leader, Jennifer Clarke, and mayoral rival COPE's Larry Campbell, both advocated publicly and openly for the creation of a SIS in their 2002 campaign. The politics of the issue had shifted such that large majorities in Vancouver were ready for the previously unpopular and hence politically unthinkable policy, and Larry Campbell was elected on a clear mandate for a new approach in the DTES. An alignment had evolved among the Vancouver public, chief elected officials, and police, who now recognized the need for an alternative to the existing enforcement approach. Insite was a key part of that new direction (Paul, 2010). With little political space in the local political domain for those resisting harm reduction policies and programs, including a safe injection site, the focus of the struggle shifted to securing support from other orders of government. Vancouver MLAs and MPs, such as Libby Davies (New Democratic Party) and Hedy Fry (Liberal Party of Canada), were early advocates in the federal parliament (Lessard, 2011), but hardball strategies from advocates and local leaders, like new Mayor Larry Campbell, were also needed to push the federal government over the edge.

Building Momentum for Challenging Reforms

The development and implementation of Insite in Vancouver followed from the Vancouver Agreement (1999), under which city, provincial, and federal bureaucratic and political actors agreed to work collaboratively to address the complex intergovernmental issues in the DTES (Doberstein, 2011). What some conceptualize as a local issue of a neighbourhood in decline is in fact a shared responsibility by all three orders of government, who have authority over zoning, health, economic security, child welfare, criminal law, and drug enforcement, among other areas of policy. It was not so much that the municipal, provincial, and federal governments were inattentive to the needs of the neighbourhood, but rather that these problems were complex. They required a more collaborative approach not only to fund services, but also to settle the disputes around jurisdictional legalities and regulations associated with the new directions of policy and programs.

The governance context in this late 1990s to early 2000s period was thus characterized by government and nonprofit services delivered in a fragmented and, at times, contrasting fashion. For example, provincial health authorities were tacitly supporting community-driven, but formally unsanctioned, needle exchanges while local police were cracking down on them (Lupick, 2019). Local police leadership and rank and file police officers were historically hostile to the concept of a safe injection site (or any state response that implicitly or explicitly enabled drug use), but the new Police Chief, Jamie Graham, understood the link between mental health and addiction, and with some prodding from Vancouver's mayor, embraced the pilot safe injection site as long as it was legally authorized by the federal government (Campbell et al., 2009).

64   INSITE IN VANCOUVER

An unlikely ally was BC Premier Gordon Campbell, head of the BC Liberal Party, a free-enterprise political coalition, and also a former mayor of Vancouver, who was well versed in drug use issues. Premier Campbell had enabled and funded pioneering needle exchanges as mayor but 'needed no convincing to ante up provincial funding for the safe injection site ...[since] he saw it as a healthcare issue' (Campbell et al., 2009, 176). While some observers have stressed the importance of scientific evidence surrounding the crisis and the failures of the status quo as determinative to the creation of Insite, Fafard (2012) emphasizes that Insite emerged as a result of coalition-building and political struggle, whereby policy entrepreneurs took advantage of windows of opportunity for policy change. Area MLAs and MPs were likewise openly supportive of a safe injection site (Zhang, 2014), but the federal government was moving very slowly in finding a legal pathway for this initiative, given the immense pressure from the US government against going down this path.

The breakthrough came when newly elected Mayor of Vancouver Larry Campbell promised Vancouverites that a safe injection site would open in 90 days and put pressure on the federal government to forge a legal pathway. While the mandate of the Vancouver Agreement extended beyond public health matters, by the time Mayor Larry Campbell was elected in 2002, it already served as a vehicle to fund new health centres and creative harm reduction strategies to keep people alive. Insite was not in the initial plan of this work, but with a clear public mandate to pursue a SIS, Mayor Larry Campbell leveraged these collaborative relationships to get the legal and regulatory pieces in alignment, even as he pounded on tables in Victoria and Ottawa.

Furthermore, community activists, and Larry Campbell himself, were prepared to proceed without federal authorization (Lupick, 2019). The Portland Hotel Society (PHS) had already been preparing a site for a SIS and was seeking approvals from the local health authority. Behind the scenes, the local health authority was indicating financial support for the site, but stating that its support was contingent on political endorsements from the provincial and federal governments in Victoria and Ottawa, respectively (Lupick, 2019). Victoria was not going to be a problem, given BC Premier Gordon Campbell's long-standing philosophical (if not financial) support for harm reduction strategies. But the government of Canada still needed to be persuaded to take a leap on an issue that, in the rest of the country, remained very controversial and one that offered little electoral pay-off and considerable risk (Campbell et al., 2009).

The federal government was not prepared to radically reform drug policy in Canada to enable Insite to open, but it did agree to provide Insite with a temporary exemption from prohibitions on the sale, possession, and use of various drugs and substances in Canada's Controlled Drugs and Substances Act (CDSA). Section 56 of the Act gave the minister the ability to exempt persons from any part of the Act for medical or scientific purposes were Insite a research study.

This legal loophole made for a useful political strategy, enabling the government to exempt persons from any part of the Act for medical or scientific purposes. The minister was thus able to avoid a potentially controversial drug policy change that would affect most Canadians. Section 56 allowed the government to treat Insite as a scientific enterprise for a specific locality that was eagerly demanding a policy solution to a prevalent problem. The federal government provided $1.5 million over four years for the scientific evaluation of the pilot project, the provincial government provided $2 million to renovate the site, and another $2 million per year to cover staffing and other costs for the site (Smith and Stewart, 2006).

The political and public support for Insite remained robust in the early years when it was perhaps most vulnerable to challenge. Mayor Larry Campbell declined to run for reelection for personal reasons and an unrelated fraying of relations with his local political party COPE, but the two major candidates contesting the subsequent mayoral race were strong supporters of Insite—evidence of the local institutionalization of the concept and its implementation. The victorious Mayor Sam Sullivan, though the leader of the right-wing NPA, lent support to further innovations in this realm, such as the North American Opiate Medication Initiative (NAOMI)—a program to measure the impact of providing injectable (clean) heroin to deeply entrenched drug users. This project would lay the foundation for future debates over the safe supply of drugs when the fentanyl crisis emerged after his single-term tenure.

Overcoming an Existential Threat

Notwithstanding the powerful emerging coalition of drug users, activists, health professionals, bureaucrats, and key elected officials, there were citizen groups, professional interests, and a major national political party opposed to a safe injection site in Vancouver. First, a citizen group comprised of business and property owners in Vancouver, called Community Alliance, mobilized in an attempt to block development applications for PWID health care and support services, including Insite. It was unsuccessful at the council level and in legal venues (Zhang, 2014; Small et al., 2006). Second, the Royal Canadian Mounted Police's (RCMP) Drugs and Organized Crime Awareness Service attempted to mobilize RCMP and Vancouver Police Department (VPD) members to write letters to the prime minister opposing safe injection sites, and later the RCMP and the Canadian Police Association released statements (without supporting evidence) in 2006 that Insite was not successful and ought to be shut down (Wood et al., 2006). Third, while the right of centre party is a coalition of liberals and conservatives (and one that tends to suppress social conservative voices) in BC, at the federal level the Conservative Party of Canada is more traditional on social issues, including drug policy, and thus represented a major threat to the maintenance of Insite in Vancouver when they came to power in 2006.

Drug problems in the DTES were generally viewed as a local matter. Normally, this may have been shielded from federal government attention, however, the fact that the issue involved tolerating (and, in the view of the federal government, enabling) drug use elevated the matter to high-level attention in Ottawa. From a policy survival perspective, Insite's continued operation required a renewed positive decision by the new Conservative minister of health, which would exempt Insite from the provisions of the CDSA. That is, for Insite to continue to legally operate, the new Conservative government had to formally renew its exemption; simply ignoring it would not dissolve the legal basis for its operation. When the Harper government first came to power, the exemption was imminently due to expire. Although the Conservative government wanted to close Insite, it ended up renewing it until 2008, 'under duress' and in part as a response to their political ally BC Premier Gordon Campbell's strong urging (Campbell et al., 2009, 230).

The Conservative federal government, however, did send signals that they would not renew Insite in the future. This prompted the Vancouver Area Network of Drug Users (VANDU) and the Portland Hotel Society (PHS) to launch lawsuits against the Government of Canada to stop them from closing Insite through their regulatory power. The two cases were heard together in the BC Supreme Court, with the provincial government intervening in support of Insite, against the Government of Canada. Various legal arguments were made by the parties as the case snaked its way up the courts to the Supreme Court of Canada, but there were two main categories of arguments from the proponents, anchored in two powerful elements of the Canadian constitution. They were, first, that federalism, in particular healthcare is the exclusive jurisdiction of provincial governments whose policy choices on health services should have paramountcy over federal criminal laws. This argument is also known as the jurisdictional immunity doctrine. Second, closing Insite, against all of the evidence of its success, was inconsistent with the Charter of Rights and Freedoms, particularly the Section 7 guarantee of life, liberty, and security of person. While lower courts flirted with the jurisdictional immunity argument as possibly important, ultimately the Supreme Court of Canada (SCC) unanimously found that the ministerial discretion in issuing CDSA Section 56 exemptions must be in conformity with the Charter, and that the current minister's decision to not grant that waiver was arbitrary (against all the credible evidence), disproportionate in its effect, and inconsistent with the public interest (Boyd, 2013).

Many observers credit this legal success to the deep, grassroots, and addict-led movement that successfully reframed the narrative around addiction through a rights-based lens (Harati, 2015), as well as the careful and systematic accumulation of evidence of Insite's success in saving lives (Marshall et al., 2011; Boyd, 2013). It is important to note that the SCC logic was not entirely aligned with those of the proponents, who tended to be devoted to the jurisdictional argument and the unconstitutionality of the CDSA vis-à-vis the Charter. A decision hinging on those arguments would have major implications for federalism and public policy, and thus, perhaps, the SCC found the narrowest legal argument for intervention without causing major wakes in Canadian politics writ large (Ward, 2012). The minister was required to provide a CDSA exemption for Insite and the government was given a timeline to set a legislative and regulatory framework under which the minister would consider exemptions from future SIS applicants.

Growing Public Support and Pockets of Resistance

The programmatic success of Insite has thus contributed to its *political* success and its endurance as the leading response to a public health crisis facing many in Canada and abroad. As a result of a broad coalition of drug users and their advocates, health professionals, local and provincial government officials, and politicians putting pressure on federal officials, Insite became the first safe injection site in Canada with authority over controlled substances and criminal law.

Various public opinion polls suggest that a consistent majority of Canadians support safe injection facilities since Insite opened. A Government of Canada-commissioned study in 2006 showed that found 58 per cent of survey respondents endorse these facilities, with BC respondents highest at 70 per cent (Woods, 2006). Such levels of support were found in a similar survey by Research Co. in 2019 (CTV News, 2019). In 2017, Mainstreet Research found that majorities in Canada's largest four cities favoured opening safe injection sites in their own cities (Duggan, 2017). Support for SIS was well over 50 per cent among those who identified as voters of the Liberal Party of Canada, the New Democratic Party, and the Green Party of Canada, and nearly half of Conservative Party of Canada voters supported this intervention in the Research Co. survey conducted in 2019. With the programmatic and political success of Insite established, additional SIS opened across the country after receiving CDSA exemptions from the Government of Canada. As of early 2021, forty sites in five provinces were authorized in Canada (Government of Canada, 2020).

Notwithstanding the programmatic success and broad-based political legitimacy of SIS, its success remains somewhat contested. There remain critics of the approach from both the political right and the left. On the political right, Ontario Premier Doug Ford was 'dead against' them in his successful election campaign in 2018, claiming they encourage drug use; he favours traditional drug rehabilitation models instead (Canadian Press, 2018). The Ford government has also defunded recently opened SIS in Toronto and Ottawa due to neighbourhood concerns. The typical thrust of the conservative critique of SIS that it is inappropriate to 'use taxpayers' money to fund drug use' (Stephen Harper in 2005, as cited in Boyd, 2013) and that it is 'state-sponsored suicide', as stated by the US drug czar under President Bush (Elliot, 2014, 19). Yet, SIS approaches are well entrenched: today most conservative politicians in Canada are reluctant to take aggressive action against them, often promising to 'review the evidence' or 'listen to local concerns' rather than dismantle them.

Surprisingly, there is also critique among a small segment of the political (namely, academic) left, which views Insite and services like it as a 'site of surveillance, discipline, and regulation' (Elliot, 2014, 7). Authors such as Elliot (2014, 28–29) believe Insite has become 'fetishized in scientific and political discourse', falling into a neoliberal trap that individualizes drug use and reinforces frames of the 'disordered drug user' in need of 'regulation and surveillance' which obscures the fact that this problem is shaped by broader structural forces. The highly regulated environments in which SIS operate in Canada have prompted the creation of more peer-driven 'overdose prevention sites' (more on this below) in Vancouver and elsewhere. In recognition of some users' institutional resistance or suspicions, they are less medicalized by design.

Other commentators cite the continued public drug use in the DTES as evidence of the ineffectiveness of the harm reduction approach that Insite and associated services espouse. To some DTES residents, 'the quality of life in the community seems to have hit an historic low', with homelessness, poverty, and the opioid crisis ravaging the neighbourhood (Hernandez, 2019). Yet it is critical to keep in mind that a SIS, or even harm reduction policies broadly, were never conceived as solutions to systemic issues like poverty, mental health, homelessness, and unaffordable housing. The early advocates of Insite never envisioned that these services would cure the DTES of any of its perceived ills—the larger goal was to save the lives of PWID.

Policy Diffusion and Expansion

Following the constitutional challenge that limited the operational discretion of the federal minister of health around this issue, the harm reduction philosophy and associated programs have spread more widely across BC and Canada. Additional SIS opened across the country after receiving CDSA exemptions from the Government of Canada. Other similar services, such as Overdose Prevention Sites (OPS), have opened in Vancouver and elsewhere, as community (and often peer-led) initiatives that support safer drug use do not require Health Canada exemptions.

While the essential policy goals of Insite have remained robust and intact over nearly two decades, new problems in this realm reveal the limitations of SIS: the increasingly widespread presence of fentanyl and extreme drug potency and toxicity in 2015 (Kerr et al., 2017). The rise of fentanyl is often attributed to the delisting of OxyContin painkillers from western nations' pharmaceutical formularies (shifting demand to the illicit market) and the ease with which fentanyl can be manufactured and shipped into Canada. The illicit drug supply was becoming so tainted and unreliable that, in BC, deaths from injection drug use overdose rose from a relatively stable number of 300 fatal overdoses per year to a high of nearly 1,600 in 2018 (BC Coroners Service, 2021). While Insite and other SIS in Vancouver have successfully saved the lives of every client who has overdosed on their premises, only about 5 per cent of all injections in the DTES take place within Insite (Andresen and Jozaghi, 2012). With Insite at capacity in terms of users per day, additional sites have since opened in Vancouver. However, for various reasons ranging from geographic convenience to stigma, many continue to use these dangerous drugs in isolation, greatly risking their lives.

The BC government declared a public health emergency in 2016, which, like the emergency declaration related to HIV and Hepatitis C in the 1990s, broke down some walls and made room for more innovative responses from government and civil society (McKelvie, 2020). Nationally, small but important drug policy changes have also helped. For example, injectable naloxone—an antidote to opiate drug overdose—was removed from the Drug Schedules Regulation by Health Canada, allowing for its widespread distribution without prescription. As mentioned above, the public health emergency declaration facilitated the creation of various peer-driven Overdose Prevention Sites (OPC) around Vancouver without requiring Health Canada approvals. These can be mobile sites in vacant lots, tents in parks, or in modified or single-room occupancy (SROs) hotels, which allow users to inject without the supervision of medical professionals. Subject to oversight by peers with knowledge and tools to assist with overdose prevention, these OPCs, like Insite, have a 100 per cent survival rate (BC Coroners Service, 2021). These efforts showed promising results in reducing deaths from overdose by 37 per cent from 2018 to 2019, until the Covid-19 pandemic disrupted the illicit drug trade due to border closures and trade tumult. This returned deaths to an all-time high in 2020-22, as drug dealers further adulterated the illicit supply.

Tragically, while the harm reduction policies of Vancouver were saving the lives of their users, the population at risk of overdose expanded well beyond the capacity of these sites as the drug supply became highly unreliable and toxic. The BC government, with federal government cooperation, responded by approving the ability of primary care physicians and nurses to prescribe a safe supply of opioid alternatives to street drugs, such as hydromorphone.

The idea of a safe supply had been advanced as early as the late 1990s during the debate around SIS, but had been deemed too controversial by political decision makers. But as the Covid-19 crisis compounded the fentanyl overdose crisis in Vancouver, prior political constraints and risk calculations were dislodged. Thousands of BC residents were given access to hydromorphone as an opiate alternative

70 INSITE IN VANCOUVER

to the street supply. Early data from the BC CDC suggest fewer fatalities per month since this policy change, though spikes reemerged as the omicron wave of the Covid-19 pandemic further isolated folks (BC CDC, 2021). Facilitating the government distribution of free drugs to anyone at risk of overdose, once a deeply controversial proposition among Canadians, met no noticeable resistance among medical professionals, community interests, or political leaders. This response is indicative of the wide acceptance of harm reduction principles in BC and Vancouver in particular.

What Might Be Learned from Vancouver's Harm Reduction Journey?

The development of Insite in Vancouver and its associated harm reduction approaches across the country, as well as its endurance over time, is consistent with the dominant Canadian policy style, which is characterized by strong executive power and intergovernmental negotiation in the tradition of pragmatism. A signature feature of the Canadian administrative style is the dominance of first ministers—as opposed to legislators—as key players in policy-making. This is evident in the story of Insite, when key developments proceeded principally by persuading political executives. Many observers of Canadian policy-making styles point to a pragmatic approach that supports change-oriented governments (Gow, 2004). This is consistent with how, in the context of the DTES, the debate was centred around what new solutions could save lives as opposed to how or whether they aligned with ideological priors.

Furthermore, one cannot overstate the importance of federalism to the Canadian policy-making style, in particular the province-building dynamics that have resulted in more responsibility and legitimacy in many of the most important policy areas of the contemporary period (Howlett and Lindquist, 2004). This is critical in the case of Insite as the Province of British Columbia and the City of Vancouver muscled their way into a federal government space (criminal drug policy) under the auspices of their responsibilities to health and community development, and worked cooperatively through laborious intergovernmental negotiations and institutions (e.g. Vancouver Agreement) to drive change.

Finally, the case of Insite points to the post-Charter (1982) emergence of the courts as a check on executive-dominated government in Canada. While this may not be a central avenue in the overall Canadian policy style, it is nonetheless proven to be a critical one for issues that have rights-based dimensions, like Insite (Ward, 2012). The Canadian courts can be both bold in their rulings against Charter violations (particularly in the Harper era), but also, at times, deferential to governments to legislate a path out of the violations, which is present in the matter of Insite.

While there are various lessons that can be derived from the case of Insite in Vancouver, such as the importance of channelling grassroots activism to achieve policy success and establish political institutionalization, there are unique factors to this case that may limit how broadly those lessons ought to be applied. We should not forget that Insite was subject to a political challenge that it marginally survived thanks to its effective placement into a rights-based frame for which the powerful tool of the Charter of Rights and Freedoms was deployed and recognized. Not all issues can credibly be conceptualized in rights-based terms and are thus subject to the normal policy reversals or changes that come with partisan government turnover.

Also, the context of the DTES in the early 1990s was a genuine crisis of death and despair, which mobilized actors to build a movement. 'Crisis' is an elastic label that can be stuck on a social condition by anyone seeking to legitimize dramatic action or to increase their jurisdiction (Edelman, 1988 Spector, 2019), but this was (and is) killing people in large numbers; the urgency surrounding this issue was extreme and, even then, it took a decade to establish Insite. In this context, there were various idiosyncratic elements to the political leadership in the history of Insite that contributed to its development, such as otherwise conservative politicians (Mayor Philip Owen, Premier Gordon Campbell) being uniquely open-minded on this issue, and unconventional politicians (Mayor Larry Campbell) with higher political risk tolerances. Safe injection sites and safe supply measures, while perhaps morally controversial, do not threaten many powerful mainstream interests that might wish to mount a resistance campaign, even in the face of overwhelming evidence of their effectiveness. Perhaps the most powerful institutional interests initially opposed to Insite were police services, but in Vancouver (and indeed beyond) they became persuaded that the criminalization approach was not working.

Ultimately, the so-called harm reduction coalition displaced the criminalization coalition by mobilizing a diverse set of people and groups united by a belief system related to drug addiction that better fit with the continuing crisis that emerged in Vancouver in the 1990s. The members of the coalition engaged in strategic action in the streets and in the corridors of power to displace a coalition that did not have answers to the crisis of the day. They did this by using activism and evidence to generate broader public and political support for their preferred policy approach. The harm reduction coalition has remained dominant, as its members have adapted their beliefs as the problem shifted from one principally of needle sharing to extreme drug toxicity in recent years. The rival criminalization/abstinence coalition remains unable to respond in persuasive policy terms. While the rival coalition is by no means dead—in fact, it has considerable support among the general public— and can occasionally block SIS in particular locations around the country, it fails in fostering a larger belief system able to shape policy decisions and ameliorate the issue.

References

Andresen, M. A. and N. Boyd. 2010. "A Cost-Benefit and Cost-Effectiveness Analysis of Vancouver's Supervised Injection Facility." *International Journal of Drug Policy* 21 (1): pp. 70–76.

Andresen, M. A. and E. Jozaghi. 2012. "The Point of Diminishing Returns: An Examination of Expanding Vancouver's Insite." *Urban Studies* 49 (16): pp. 3531–3544.

Baum, D. 1996. *Smoke and Mirrors: The War on Drugs and the Politics of Failure*. Boston: Little, Brown.

Bayoumi, A. M. and G. S. Zaric. 2008. "The Cost Effectiveness of Vancouver's Supervised Injection Facility." *Canadian Medical Association Journal* 179 (11): pp. 1143–1151.

BC Centre for Disease Control (BCCDC). 2021. "Overdose Response Indicators." BCCDC. May. http://www.bccdc.ca/health-professionals/data-reports/overdose-response-indicators. Accessed on 24 February 2021.

BC Coroners Service. 2021. "Illicit Drug Toxicity Deaths in BC: January 1, 2010–December 31, 2020." BC Coroners Service. https://www2.gov.bc.ca/assets/gov/birth-adoption-death-marriage-and-divorce/deaths/coroners-service/statistical/illicit-drug.pdf. Accessed on 24 February 2021.

Boyd, N. 2013. "Lessons from INSITE, Vancouver's Supervised Injection Facility: 2003–2012." *Drugs: Education, Prevention and Policy* 20 (3): pp. 234–240.

Campbell, L., N. Boyd, and L. Culbert. 2009. *A Thousand Dreams: Vancouver's Downtown Eastside and the Fight for its Future*. Vancouver: Greystone Books.

Canadian Press. 2018. "Doug Ford Says He's 'Dead Against' Supervised Injection Sites." CBC News. 20 April https://www.cbc.ca/news/canada/windsor/doug-ford-says-he-s-dead-against-supervised-injection-sites-1.4628547

Compton, M. and P. 't Hart (eds). 2019. *Great Policy Successes*. Oxford: Oxford University Press.

CTV News. 2019. "Most Canadians Prefer Drug Treatment That Doesn't Rely on Opioid Replacement: Poll." CTV News. 15 August. https://bc.ctvnews.ca/most-canadians-prefer-drug-treatment-that-doesn-t-rely-on-opioid-replacement-poll-1.4551801

DeBeck, K., T. Kerr, L. Bird, R. Zhang, D. Marsh, M. Tyndall, J. Montaner, and E. Wood. 2011. "Injection Drug Use Cessation and Use of North America's First Medically Supervised Safer Injecting Facility." *Drug and Alcohol Dependence* 113 (2): pp. 172–176.

Des Jarlais, D., K. Kamyar Arasteh, and H. Hagan. 2008. "Evaluating Vancouver's Supervised Injection Facility: Data and Dollars, Symbols and Ethics." *Canadian Medical Association Journal* 179 (11): pp. 1105–6.

Doberstein, C. 2011. "Institutional Creation and Death: Urban Development Agreements in Canada." *Journal of Urban Affairs* 33 (5): pp. 529–548.

Duggan, K. 2017. "Poll Shows Where Canadian Cities Stand on Supervised Injection Sites." iPolitics. 18 January. https://ipolitics.ca/2017/01/18/where-canadian-cities-stand-on-supervised-injection-sites-poll/

Edelman, M. 1988. *Constructing the Political Spectacle*. Chicago: University of Chicago Press.

Elliott, D. 2014. "Debating Safe Injecting Sites in Vancouver's Inner City: Advocacy, Conservatism and Neoliberalism." *Contemporary Drug Problems* 41 (1): pp. 5–40.

Fafard, P. 2012. "Public Health Understandings of Policy and Power: Lessons from INSITE." *Journal of Urban Health* 89 (6): pp. 905–914.

Government of Canada. 2020. "Supervised Consumption Sites: Status of Applications." Health Canada. 12 April. https://www.canada.ca/en/health-canada/services/substance-use/supervised-consumption-sites/status-application.html#wb-auto-4. Accessed on 15 November 2020.

Gow, J. I. 2004. "A Canadian Model of Public Administration? Canada School of Public Service." http://www.publications.gc.ca/collections/Collection/SC94-108-2004E.pdf

Harati, D. F. 2015. "Inside Insite: How a Localized Social Movement Led the Way for North America's First Legal Supervised Injection Site." Harvard Law School, Irving Oberman Memorial Student Writing Prize: Law and Social Change. http://nrs.harvard.edu/urn-3:HUL.InstRepos:16386592

Hathaway, A. D., and K. I. Tousaw. 2008. "Harm Reduction Headway and Continuing Resistance: Insights from Safe Injection in the City of Vancouver." *International Journal of Drug Policy* 19 (1): pp. 11–16.

Hernandez, J. 2019. "It's Getting Worse and Worse: DTES Residents Say Neighbourhood Is Falling Apart." CBC News. 15 August. https://www.cbc.ca/news/canada/british-columbia/it-s-getting-worse-and-worse-dtes-residents-say-neighbourhood-is-falling-apart-1.5248298

Howlett, M. and E. Lindquist. 2004. "Policy Analysis and Governance: Analytical and Policy Styles in Canada." *Journal of Comparative Policy Analysis: Research and Practice* 6 (3): pp. 225–249.

Jozaghi, E. 2014. "The Role of Drug Users' Advocacy Group in Changing the Dynamics of Life in the Downtown Eastside of Vancouver, Canada." *Journal of Substance Use* 19 (1): pp. 213–218.

Kerr, T., S. Mitra, M. C. Kennedy, and R. McNeil. 2017. "Supervised Injection Facilities in Canada: Past, Present, and Future." *Harm Reduction Journal* 14 (1): pp. 1–9.

Lessard, H. 2011. "Jurisdictional Justice, Democracy and the Story of Insite." *Constitutional Forum* 19 (3): pp. 93–112.

Lupick, T. 2019. *Fighting for Space: How a Group of Drug Users Transformed One City's Struggle with Addiction.* Vancouver, BC: Arsenal Pulp Press.

Marlatt, G. A. 1996. "Harm Reduction: Come as You Are." *Addictive Behaviors* 21 (6): pp. 779–788.

Marshall, B. D. L., M.-J. Milloy, E. Wood, J. S. Montaner, and T. Kerr. 2011. "Reduction in Overdose Mortality after Opening of North America's First Medically Supervised Safer Injecting Facility: A Retrospective Population-Based Study." *The Lancet* 377 (9775): pp. 1429–1437.

McCann, E.J., 2008. "Expertise, Truth, and Urban Policy Mobilities: Global Circuits of Knowledge in the Development of Vancouver, Canada's 'Four Pillar' Drug Strategy." *Environment and Planning A* 40(4), pp. 885–904.

McConnell, A. 2010. *Understanding Policy Success: Rethinking Public Policy.* New York: Palgrave Macmillan.

McKelvie, S. 2020. "Smack in the Middle: Urban Governance and the Spatialization of Overdose Epidemics." *City and Community* 19 (3): pp. 704–725.

Mukherjee, I. and M. Howlett. 2015. "Who Is a Stream? Epistemic Communities, Instrument Constituencies and Advocacy Coalitions in Multiple Streams Subsystems." *Lee Kuan Yew School of Public Policy Research Paper* No. 15–18. http://dx.doi.org/10.2139/ssrn.2593626

74 INSITE IN VANCOUVER

Nowell, M., J. R. Masuda, and the Tenant Overdose Response Organizers. 2020. "You Need to Just Provide Health Services: Navigating the Politics of Harm Reduction in the Twin Housing and Overdose Crises in Vancouver, BC." *International Journal of Drug Policy* 82: pp. 102774–102793.

Paul, E.-A. 2010. *Harm Reduction and Supervised Safe Consumption Sites: Ideas and Policy in Toronto and Vancouver*. Doctoral dissertation. Department of Political Science-Simon Fraser University. http://summit.sfu.ca/system/files/iritems1/10083/etd5987.pdf

Sabatier, P. A. and H. C. Jenkins-Smith. 1993. *Policy Change and Learning: An Advocacy Coalition Approach*. Boulder, CO: Westview Press.

Small, D., A. Palepu, and M. W. Tyndall. 2006. "The Establishment of North America's First State Sanctioned Supervised Injection Facility: A Case Study in Culture Change." *International Journal of Drug Policy* 17 (2): pp. 73–82.

Smith, P. J. and K. Stewart. 2006. "Local Whole-of-Government Policymaking in Vancouver: Beavers, Cats, and the Mushy Middle Thesis." In *The State of the Federation 2004–Municipal-Federal-Provincial Relations in Canada*, edited by R. Young and C. Leuprecht, pp. 251–272. Montreal and Kingston: McGill-Queens University Press

Spector, M. 2019. "Constructing Social Problems Forty Years Later." *The American Sociologist* 50 (2): pp. 175–181.

Ward, C. 2012. "*Canada (A.G.) v PHS Community Services Society*—The Insite Decision." *Alberta Law Review* 50 (1): pp. 195–204.

Weible, C. M. and K. Ingold. 2018. "Why Advocacy Coalitions Matter and Practical Insights about Them." *Policy and Politics* 46 (2): pp. 325–343.

Wood, E., M. W. Tyndall, J. S. Montaner, and T. Kerr. 2006. "Summary of Findings from the Evaluation of a Pilot Medically Supervised Safer Injecting Facility." *Canadian Medical Association Journal* 175 (11): pp. 1399–1404.

Woods A. 2006. "Ottawa Ignores Support for Injection Sites." *The Vancouver Sun*. 6 November. A1–A2.

Zhang, K., 2014. *No easy fix: The Supervised Injection Site Debate in Canada*. Doctoral dissertation, University of Ottawa, Ottawa.

PART II
EDUCATION POLICY SUCCESSES

5

Schooling Successfully

The Elementary and Secondary Education Sectors in Canada

Jennifer Wallner

Introduction

Elementary and secondary education is one of the most significant areas of government-led activity in Canada. Setting aside the unprecedented interruption caused by the Covid-19 pandemic, each year, millions of students attend public schools from coast to coast to coast. Investments in public schooling constitute the second largest expenditure across the country, falling behind only health. According to Statistics Canada, the education arena is one of the largest general employment areas in the country, overshadowing many other sectors and industries (Statistics Canada 2018). Thanks to this policy activity, Canadian students record some of the highest achievements on international tests and realize high graduation rates relative to their counterparts in other countries.

In fact, activities in this area predate Confederation itself, with roots tracing back to early legislation enacted by colonial governments of British North America. Generally well-regarded by the public and education professionals working within the systems alike, it is an area that enjoys considerable popular approval throughout the country. Managed and overseen almost exclusively by the provinces and territories without direct intervention from the federal government, there is no singular education sector. There are instead 13 essentially independent systems operating in parallel without any hierarchically driven coordinative mechanisms. Despite their independence and autonomy, the 13 systems exhibit marked comparability, compatibility, and equity. Put together, elementary and secondary education in Canada constitutes a clear case of 'positive deviance' worthy of investigation.

To evaluate and document the successes of Canada's public elementary and secondary education sectors, this chapter advances in the following manner. First, I

Jennifer Wallner, *Schooling Successfully.* In: *Policy Success in Canada.*
Edited by Evert A. Lindquist et al., Oxford University Press. © Jennifer Wallner (2022).
DOI: 10.1093/oso/9780192897046.003.0005

open with a discussion of the programmatic successes recorded by international and national benchmark exercises. Using results from the Programme for International Student Assessment (PISA), and the Pan Canadian Assessment Program (PCAP), combined with graduation rates, I document the relatively high achievements secured by the 13 schooling systems. I then unpack how attributes of the broader institutional context, particular constellations of actors, and attributes of the sector itself both inadvertently and intentionally—through coincidence and design—worked to secure strong schooling practices. Using developments in teacher preparation as an exemplar, the third section details the ways in which provinces acted as literal laboratories of innovation, with one jurisdiction pioneering a new approach gradually adopted and translated into action by the others. The fourth section pulls the threads together, outlining the concrete components that have led to success.

As revealed in these pages, the elementary and secondary education arena in Canada is a case of enduring success and offers a remarkable alternative story to counter the pessimistic idea that many of our societies are 'ungovernable' (Compton and 't Hart, 2019, 1). A formidable, enduring yet evolving, consensus to fundamental paradigmatic and programmatic ideas about schooling, forged early in Canada's history, combined with positive spillover effects from fiscal federalism (see Béland et al., Chapter 12, this volume), have contributed to 13 successful systems of public elementary and secondary education. Canada's educational success story is nevertheless incomplete. While it has benefited the settlers to this country under the auspices of the 13 systems, the impact of education policies for Indigenous peoples in Canada has been calamitous. Consequently, it is necessary to first expose the ways in which the systems function very differently and generate markedly different results to gain a more complete understanding of the highs and lows of schooling in Canada.

A Settler Policy Success

Although it may seem an unusual choice to open with the counter narrative, a major stain on the otherwise remarkable performance of Canadian primary and secondary education must be immediately acknowledged: Canada's abysmal record in the schooling of Indigenous children. Despite intermittent efforts to correct them, many problems remain in place reinforcing inequality, marginalization, and discrimination for some in the country. It is a dark and continuing legacy that cannot be overlooked.

While it is accurate to say that many in Canada benefit from provincial and territorial schooling policies, past and present realities for many Indigenous peoples in the country are markedly different. The foundation of this difference rests first and foremost on the *Indian Act* and the fact that the formal responsibility for the schooling of 'Indians' falls to the federal government. Documented in the pages of the Truth and Reconciliation Commission (TRC 2014; see also Milloy, 1999), residential schools represent one of the largest and most destructive legacies of Canada's past. In operation for more than 100 years, residential schools existed to secure the assimilation of Indigenous peoples into settler society. Predominantly funded by the Government of Canada, and operated by the Anglican, Catholic, Methodist, and Presbyterian churches, it is estimated that approximately 150,000 Indian, Inuit and Métis children were separated from their families and communities to attend residential schools throughout the country. While at these schools, children 'were forced to abandon their language, cultural beliefs, and way of life. They were compelled to adopt the European languages of English or French, foreign religious denominations, and new habits' (Union of Ontario Indians, 2013, 5). The abuses endured at these schools included electrical shock, starvation, forcible confinement, exposure to freezing temperatures, exposure to contagious illnesses, forced labour, sexual assault, and physical beatings. Most horrifying, however, is the discovery in 2021 of the remains of 215 children on the site of a former residential school in BC. Former Senator and chair of the Truth and Reconciliation Commission, Murray Sinclair, issued an immediate and grim statement: 'We know there are lots of sites similar to Kamloops that are going to come to light in the future. We need to prepare ourselves for that' (quoted in Blum, 2021). While the last Indian residential school, located in Saskatchewan, closed in 1996, the Government of Canada has yet to conduct a fuller inquiry and investigation into the children who died in custody and uncover the location of deceased residential school children.

In 2008, on behalf of the Government of Canada, Prime Minister Stephen Harper issued an apology to Indigenous peoples, acknowledging Canada's direct role in the residential school system (Government of Canada, 2008). The social, cultural, and economic damages caused by the legacy of residential schools continues today. Until 2019, the funding provided by the federal government to support First Nations elementary and secondary schools in Canada was chronically behind that provided by provincial and territorial governments (Indigenous Services Canada, 2019). Consequently, Indigenous children receiving their schooling on-reserves have been significantly compromised due to official policy that perpetuated unequal funding.

As a result of the tireless efforts of Indigenous advocates working to strengthen and reshape the provision of schooling for their peoples, in recent years a series of important gains have been made in some Indigenous communities. Self-government agreements have seen improvements for certain First Nations' children living on and off reserves. For example, in 2017, the Anishnabek Nation Education Agreement was signed between the Anishinabek Nation in Ontario and the federal government, re-establishing control over the schooling of their children to the Nation. Indigenous children living off reserves who attend provincially or territorially run schools, moreover, have typically recorded better achievements than those living on reserves in schools run by the federal government.

80 SCHOOLING SUCCESSFULLY

However, the achievement gap between Indigenous and non-Indigenous students in Canada remains pernicious and requires extensive changes to be made by federal, provincial, and territorial governments in concert with Indigenous decision-makers.

For the settlers of Canada, what are the successes of Canada's education systems overall? One, albeit imperfect, measure of programmatic success are achievements reached on international and domestic assessment protocols. Launched more than two decades ago, the PISA, executed by the Organisation for Economic Cooperation and Development (OECD), is a powerful juggernaut in the education policy world. Measuring 15-year-olds' abilities in reading, mathematics, and science, PISA is billed as 'the world's most comprehensive and reliable indicator of students' capabilities', which provides governments with a powerful tool to 'fine-tune their education policies' (Schleicher, 2018). To be sure, large-scale assessments are not without their critics and are certainly only one kind of measure to gauge success (Mulford, 2002; Ryan, 2006). Despite their imperfections, assessments provide an initial indicator of achievements being realized in public programs.

According to the Council of Ministers of Education, Canada (CMEC, 2020, 1), information gathered through PISA 'enables a thorough comparative analysis of the performance of students near the end of their compulsory education. The assessment also permits exploration of the ways that achievement varies across different social and economic groups and the factors that influence achievement within and among countries.' 2018 marked the seventh iteration of PISA, where reading was the major domain and mathematics and science were the two minor domains. In total, 79 countries participated, with 5,000 to 10,000 students from at least 150 schools being tested in each country. To gain a representative sample from the provinces, 22,500 students from approximately 800 schools participated in Canada. This strategic over-sampling is said to produce reliable estimates of each province for both French and English-language school systems in Nova Scotia, New Brunswick, Québec, Ontario, Manitoba, Alberta, and British Columbia.

Significantly, Canada's proficiency levels are high *and* equitable. Canada was ranked eighth overall, ahead of such countries as Finland, the United Kingdom, New Zealand, Sweden, and Germany. Since the launch of PISA in the 2000s, Canada has consistently performed well, securing spots among the top 10 achievers, with high marks on equity of results measures. While socioeconomically advantaged students outperform socioeconomically disadvantaged students in Canada, the achievement gap is comparatively narrower in the country, indicating that 'disadvantage is not destiny' (OECD, 2019, 4). Consequently, this international assessment provides an indication of successful and equitable outcomes achieved by the 10 provincial education systems.

Maintaining a domestic complement to PISA, in partnership with Statistics Canada, the CMEC runs the PCAP. This cyclical test of 13-year-olds' achievements in reading, math, and science provides the provinces with a base-line for examining their respective curriculum and refining their individual assessment protocols.

In general, results from PCAP exhibit alignment with results from PISA. For example, results from the 2016 round of PCAP confirmed that Canadian students perform well in reading. As a result, the findings of Canada's domestic assessment protocol thus reinforce the assertion that in terms of programmatic aspects of the sector, education policies in Canada seem to be working

The final indicator of programmatic success are high school and post-secondary completion rates. According to 2015 data, 87 per cent of students across Canada graduated from high school (CMEC, 2020, 6). What is more, 54 per cent of the Canadian population aged 25 to 64 hold some form of tertiary education, one of the highest rates in the world. Whereas some of this high rate of tertiary education is a product of Canada's immigration policies that prioritize credential-holding migrants, it is nevertheless apparent that elementary and secondary schooling policies are enabling Canadians to pursue and successfully complete tertiary programs.

Together, these results have generated extensive commendation, with the BBC referring to Canada as 'an education superpower' (Coughlan, 2017). When asked to comment on Canada's success, the OECD's education director Andreas Schleicher implicates the commitment to equity throughout the country as a key factor accounting for high achievements (Ibid). As Anders and his colleagues write (2020, 2): 'despite its cultural, linguistic and historical similarities to many other Western nations, Canada achieves much higher average PISA scores than most OECD countries, while also apparently having a more equitable distribution of education achievement'. These results lead to a simple question: what are the concrete policies that have enabled such success?

Elementary and secondary education comprise a deep web of interconnected policies, programs, and strategies sorted into five categories: governance, finance, curriculum, assessment, and teacher preparation and certification. In each of these areas, policy-makers face a wealth of options, with the potential to encourage different trajectories in the design and delivery of public schooling (Wallner, 2014, 58–73). As Kauko (2019) details in his work, much of Finland's educational successes stem from the conscientious choice to introduce a comprehensive school system in the late 1960s, as opposed to a more rigid streamed or vocational approach that tends to characterize many other European nations. In regard to education finance, some models work to encourage parent choice and the expansion of private schooling, while others work to strengthen central control over a predominantly public schooling system (Wallner, 2018, 87–88). Given the considerable options and the sizable implications, Canada's 13 education systems could exhibit marked variability and incompatibility. Instead, a snapshot of contemporary arrangements reveals an image of considerable convergence.

Grounded on the principles of universality, such that all children and youths have access to public schooling, and situated within the macro-governance structure of parliamentary government, provinces and territories haveestablished relatively parallel administrative structures to oversee activities in the sector

(Wallner and Marchildon, 2019). In every jurisdiction, a minister is responsible for overseeing a department (or ministry) of education tasked with financing the system, setting curricula, hiring superintendents to oversee local education authorities, establishing examination and assessment protocols, and mandating requirements for the teaching profession.

For the most part, in every province and territory, intermediary bodies, known as school boards, oversee the day-to-day management and operation of local schools. The autonomy of these boards is nevertheless heavily circumscribed under the authority of the respective ministries of education. Public schools are essentially fully funded, with minimal local contributions drawn from municipal taxes at rates generally set by the provinces. The overwhelming majority of Canadians attend public schools, and those in private schools attend institutions that are heavily regulated by their respective provincial ministry. All provinces and territories generally adhere to the comprehensive (or composite) model of schooling, such that students have the chance to choose the tertiary program they wish to pursue as opposed to being streamed into designated programs according to academic measures taken early in their schooling careers. All provinces also administer some form of an internal assessment protocol (meaning standardized tests), although these do vary in terms of scope and impact (Wallner et al., 2020, 254). Finally, all teachers are required to hold a minimum of a university-level Bachelors' degree while also maintaining valid certification with the pertinent provincial or territorial authority.

Thus, all together, programs and practices in each of these areas culminate in a coherent policy framework that is shared from coast to coast to coast. This broad-based framework operates in all 13 jurisdictions and enables the provision of a baseline of reasonably high-quality, publicly-provided schooling that is available for most who wish to access it. Policy choices in individual categories have thus set the stage for the realization of successful outcomes.

Context, Challenges, and Agents

For many, the programmatic successes recorded by provincial and territorial elementary and secondary education sectors come as a surprise. Relative to many other federations, Canada is regarded as highly decentralized, with provinces enjoying considerable autonomy and independence compared to their subnational counterparts elsewhere (Bakvis and Skogstad, 2002, 4; Lecours, 2019). In the eyes of some, autonomy, without hierarchical coordination, is likely to produce variability.

One reason for this autonomy lies in Canada's fiscal architecture. Ottawa assuredly holds the lion's share of fiscal power; however, provinces' own source revenues out of total provincial revenues are nevertheless high and conditions associated with federal grants are generally restrained (Lecours, 2019, 65).

Provinces have therefore been able to allocate funds largely to their own discretion and have not faced the challenges of unfunded mandates as experienced in other federations, like the United States (Simeon and Radin, 2010).

Additionally, Canada's federal and provincial leaders have long been attuned to the detrimental effects of regional economic inequalities (Bryden, 2019, 34). For provinces to meet their responsibilities in different policy fields, they need sufficient revenues—but fiscal capacities vary considerably. In the 1950s, a means to share revenues was devised (see Béland et al., in this volume). Known as equalization and constitutionally entrenched in 1982, this 'fundamental principle' of Canadian federalism provides 'the necessary fiscal scaffolding for any universal social policy – either present or future' (Bryden, 2019, 41). Despite significant variations in revenue-raising capacities across the provinces, per student spending in public schools is relatively comparable ranging from the lower end in Québec ($11,543) to the higher end in Saskatchewan ($15,423) (Hill, Li, and Emes 2020, 8). Without equalization, it is unlikely that such a feat could be achieved.

Decentralization also emerges from the allocation of key policy sectors, including education, to the provinces (Wallner, 2018). The 13 provincial and territorial jurisdictions operate their respective elementary and secondary schooling systems largely free from one another and the federal government. Aside from the constitutionally guaranteed provision of minority language education, there are no overarching mandates or regulations, and only minimal explicit federal funding is dedicated to elementary and secondary education in the country. In contrast to other federations like Australia, Germany, and the United States, there is no 'national' department of education overseen by the federal government (Wallner et al., 2020). Furthermore, unlike almost all other major Canadian policy areas falling under provincial purview—like healthcare and post-secondary education—there is no formal 'national' policy space or some similar singular locus of policy activity. An intergovernmental body, known as the Council of Ministers of Education, Canada (CMEC), provides a voluntary forum for information exchanges and some coordinative initiatives. However, the CMEC neither affords federal representation nor imposes provincial and territorial compliance on initiatives.

Institutional decentralization would seem to lay a foundation for marked variations in programs, policies, and strategies deployed in the 13 systems. Despite the foundation for variation, however, contemporary arrangements in elementary and secondary education exhibit a relatively high degree of comparability and compatibility achieved through longstanding practices of interjurisdictional learning, emulation, and adaptation.

The roots of Canada's contemporary schooling systems can be traced back before Confederation itself in 1867. The new colonies of British North America proved fertile ground for fresh educational ideas percolating since the beginning of the 1800s. A growing number of advocates were increasingly promoting a novel vision of schooling—one that encouraged the democratization and expansion of

84   SCHOOLING SUCCESSFULLY

knowledge literacy throughout an entire population to ameliorate class inequality, minimize the influence of religious institutions in the provision of learning, and further the role of the state in fostering a collective identity (Wallner, 2014, 120). In pursuit of these goals, statutes establishing small local schools were enacted in Upper Canada[1] and Lower Canada.[2] This activity by the small colonies inadvertently assured that the responsibility for education would fall to the provinces when they came together to form Canada.

For much of Canada's early history, the country was sparsely populated, with salient divisions appearing along linguistic and religious lines. Communications among and even within the embryonic provinces was a challenge at best. Where many were unified around the revolutionary educational goals and ideas that had emerged in the 1800s, the revolution did not advance without conflict and controversy. One of the most salient fault lines in these early years appeared between religious leaders and those who wished to assert largely secular control. This produced different configurations of authority within the various provinces (Sissons, 1959). In Ontario, Egerton Ryerson (who played a major role in developing the model of residential schools adopted throughout the country to assimilate Indigenous peoples, e.g. Knight, 2021) managed to establish a civic authority, known as the Council of Public Instruction, under which Catholic education authorities were enabled to operate a parallel system to that of public authorities (Wallner, 2014, 130). Under the common umbrella, Catholic authorities were subject to the same rules and regulations as the common schools, including those relating to curriculum protocols, teacher training, and funding requirements—a legacy that persists today. This arrangement was intentionally mirrored in many Western provinces as they worked to establish early schooling systems.

In the independent colony of Newfoundland (which would eventually join Confederation in 1950) and Québec, however, a different path was pursued. It was a path that saw the establishment of religious trusteeship with responsibilities conferred to ecclesiastical leaders. In Newfoundland, seven different denominations gained authority and remained in place well into the twentieth century. The churches deeply established themselves into the system and successfully blocked any attempt to impose public control of the sector (Wallner, 2014, 137). This arrangement was long-lived, lasting until 1968 (Wallner, 2014, 189). In Québec, a dual system emerged, with Protestant-English authority on one side and Catholic-French authority on the other. The Catholic Church had cast itself as a defender of French Québec, solidifying its authority in that majority portion of the population. Furthermore, similar to Newfoundland, the Church rebuffed many educational innovations and any effort to exert public control (Wallner, 2014, 161). The dualist system persisted right up until the 1960s, when a revolution swept the

---

[1] Now known as Ontario (1807), Nova Scotia (1811), New Brunswick (1816)
[2] Now known as Québec (1825) and Prince Edward Island (1825)

province under the leadership of Georges-Émile Lapalme, head of the Québec Liberal Party.

One of the key innovations in education governance that has enabled education success in the country nevertheless emerged in the late 1800s, with Ontario once again leading the way (Wallner, 2014, 136). Notwithstanding the achievements recorded under the guidance of the Council of Public Instruction, two critical weaknesses remained in place. First, the Chief Superintendent—namely Ryerson—could easily circumvent the desires of elected officials by using his formidable regulatory powers. Second, under the rules of parliamentary government, only elected ministers were allowed to answer questions on the floor of the legislature, which meant the Chief Superintendent of the Council of Public Instruction could not address questions in this public forum or account for his actions. Ryerson's retirement in 1876 opened a window of opportunity through which Ontario Liberal Premier Oliver Mowat jumped, creating the post of minister of education directly responsible to the elected legislature.

By the opening years of the twentieth century, all provinces west of Ontario had emulated the change, permanently adopting the post of minister of education with a seat at the cabinet table. The eastern provinces, in the meantime, took longer to introduce the change, as other governance arrangements had a firmer hold in those respective systems. Despite the stickiness of previous institutional choices, the alternative models were nevertheless dislodged and replaced by individual ministerial responsibility in the 1960s. Consequently, in all the jurisdictions, the mainstay of policy-making occurs within each ministry of education, in concert to varying degrees with teachers' associations and local school boards. Decisions are driven by ministers of education, who are supported by their hierarchically structured, professional, and somewhat isolated bureaucracies. In-house expertise is a hallmark of most Westminster bureaucracies (Campbell and Pedersen, 2014), a characterization confirmed by these ministries tasked with overseeing elementary and secondary education throughout the federation. The core commonality eventually eased the way forward in another area that helped foster success in elementary and secondary education: the realization of a dedicated intergovernmental organization.

In 1891, not long after Confederation, education professionals from a number of provinces met in Montréal to found a new organization, known as the Dominion Education Association (DEA). One of the earliest formal interprovincial bodies, the DEA set itself out to help government and non-government leaders in the respective education systems to come together and forge a general plan for education (Wallner, 2014, 123). Over the years, the DEA evolved into the Canadian Education Association (CEA), and secured membership from all provinces. This organization helped establish some early—if tenuous, imperfect, and fragile—bonds to connect what would become Canada's education policy community.

86 SCHOOLING SUCCESSFULLY

With inclusive membership practices, the CEA welcomed the participation of all involved in the education policy community, including elected and appointed officials, superintendents, school trustees, principals, and teachers. The organization, however, never established a permanent secretariat, which hampered its capacity to meaningfully support extended exchanges or further coordinate policy initiatives. What is more, the inclusivity of the body made it challenging to set clear agendas or establish priorities. Consequently, in tandem with provincially-based teachers' unions and school board associations, other pan-Canadian organizations targeting specific types of agents in the sector thus started to proliferate.

Seeing these organizational weaknesses, in 1945, the provinces forged a collective agreement to finance a permanent secretariat for the CEA based in Toronto. In exchange for the funds, the provinces demanded that each of their respective deputy ministers of education would sit on a committee to head the organization. This new committee immediately set out to drive a major interprovincial research agenda and worked to better integrate the governmental members of the policy community. Between 1945 and the 1960s, pan-Canadian conferences on education increased dramatically, nurturing exchanges and lesson-drawing across the country, which assisted the processes of universalizing the provision of elementary and secondary schooling across the country. In the meantime, the 1950s and 1960s, saw an explosion in enrollments, technological advancements, and an intensification in international activities in the education arena.

This intensification in activity generated some strife in the sector that subsequently affected the Association. Specifically, the interests of government officials were not always in line with the interests of teachers, superintendents, and principals, creating rifts within the CEA (Wallner, 2014, 159). The president of the Canadian Teachers' Federation, for example, launched a highly public campaign in the 1960s demanding that the federal government establish national standards for schools and start intervening more directly in the sector. To combat this campaign, and protect their jurisdiction in the field, the provinces decided it was time to formally break away from the CEA and create the Council of Ministers of Education, Canada (CMEC) in 1967.

As one of the first formal intergovernmental bodies in Canada, the CMEC has evolved into one of its most permanent and institutionalized. With its dedicated secretariat based in Toronto (a legacy thanks to the CEA), the CMEC successfully oversees the creation of the ongoing, low-stakes, pan-Canadian assessment protocol, assures Canada's participation in the OECD's PISA, and represents Canada abroad on the international arena. It offers a focal point for exchanges among politicians and officials, while preserving and protecting provincial and territorial autonomy in the field. Each province and territory remains responsible for all interactions, consultations, and engagements with the various members of their respective policy communities, so as not to inadvertently create some form of 'national policy space' that could potentially undermine the balance and synergies established in the field. It was through this diffuse space that specific programmatic ideas and broader paradigmatic norms took hold, gradually translating into what has emerged as a successful policy framework in Canadian elementary and secondary education.

Seeding Success: Leaders, Innovators, and Champions

While Canada's successes rest on a culmination of choices in various components of education policy, those made in the specific area of teacher education provide a compelling example of the ways in which one province could act as a laboratory of innovation for the others, instituting a policy change the others watched, learned from, and subsequently emulated. Furthermore, substantively, as the direct providers of schooling programs, teachers play a critical role interpreting and executing the policies designed by the respective Ministries of Education. If they were poorly trained, underpaid, and lacking in prestige and professionalism, it is unlikely that the 13 systems would be securing such strong results.

As Canada expanded westward, 'Sons and daughters of the Maritimes and Central Canada migrated to the plains and built up the West, thus forging innumerable links between the older Canada and the new' (Royal Commission on Dominion-Provincial Relations, quoted in Wallner, 2014, 122). Early education leaders were highly attuned to the potential benefits to be reaped from commonalities in schooling programs. To quote George Ross, Ontario's Minster of Education in 1892:

If there was a unity of feeling, then the same stuff that makes a good teacher in Prince Edward Island is what we want in Ontario, and if we could here by some means ascertain what would be a suitable common standard for all and work up to that standard, then the citizens of Canada would be citizens indeed.
(quoted in Wallner, 2014, 145–146).

The story once again starts in Ontario when Ryerson was head of the Council of Public Instruction. Inspired by the arrangement of 'normal schools'—which were dedicated institutions to prepare teachers for the classroom—that he had examined during his travels through Europe, Ryerson opened the doors of the Toronto Normal School in 1847, the first of its kind in British North America (Love, 1978). New Brunswick followed suit in 1848, Nova Scotia in 1854, then Prince Edward Island in 1850, and in Québec, two separate normal schools were created, one for the French Catholics and the other for the English Protestants. Ryerson's model then 'set the pattern for elementary teacher-training across western Canada for almost a century' (Johnson, 1966, 18).

Individuals trained and working in Ontario were particularly instrumental as physical conduits of diffusion, bringing the normal school model to the new provinces. John Jessop, to provide one example, was the first Superintendent of Education in British Columbia. An early graduate of the Toronto Normal School, Jessop had been exposed to Ryerson's ideas and used them when developing an approach to teacher preparation on the Pacific coast (Child, 1978, 279–301). These individual entrepreneurs were also assisted by the DEA. The first conference of the DEA featured an extensive discussion on teacher training and, in 1919, the DEA hosted the Conference on Teacher Education in Edmonton, which explained the features and benefits of the normal school system, reinforcing processes of policy diffusion across the country (Wallner, 2014, 146). Consequently, early in Canada's history, a common choice was somewhat seamlessly made across all the jurisdictions in this critical area of education policy.

Mid-twentieth century, a major change occurred in teacher preparation, this time emerging from the province of Alberta and inspired by innovations that had been happening south of the border. Throughout the United States, universities had started offering programs to train prospective teachers as a Bachelor's degree. Stimulated by these emergent ideas, Dr. H.M. Tory founded the School of Education at the University of Alberta in 1928. Supported by Dean Ezra LaZerte, the school evolved into a formal Faculty of Education in 1942, offering the first degree in Bachelor of Education in Canada. The Alberta Teachers' Association (ATA) applauded this change and welcomed the inception of university-led teacher preparation, as a marker of a new era of professionalization, authority, and standing for the occupation.

Despite enthusiasm from various parts of the Alberta education policy community, politically, it took some time for this change to curry favour. The normal school system was cheap and expedient, as training only took four months. Because normal schools were also under the exclusive purview of the Department of Education, the minister of education enjoyed complete control over the structure and delivery of the program. If responsibility for teacher preparation was transferred to universities, the cost and duration of the programs would invariably increase. What is more, due to the principle of academic freedom preserved and protected by university administrators, the minister would lose control. Consequently, such a change was politically unpalatable and unlikely to succeed, but for a change in electoral fortunes.

In 1935, William Aberhart became premier of the province. A former educator, Aberhart had first-hand experience in the classroom and knew the challenges poorly trained teachers faced. He decided to take it upon himself to hold the post of minister of education and then appointed long-time supporter of university-led teacher preparation, Dr. Fred McNally, as his deputy minister. As a result, the senior leadership of the Department of Education was now firmly supportive of the idea and worked to change minds within the bureaucracy to assure it gained the necessary acceptance. Thanks to these efforts, three years after the University of Alberta launched the bachelor's degree in education, the Government of Alberta transferred responsibility for teacher preparation to the University. Within short order, BC, Saskatchewan, and Manitoba all followed suit and allowed universities to take over this dimension of the education sector.

East of Manitoba, however, the change took longer to take hold. As early adopters of the normal school model, this policy was more firmly entrenched in these other provinces and far more difficult to dislodge. Furthermore, where western education policy-makers often looked favourably on American-inspired ideas, the response was far more critical in eastern Canada (Wallner, 2014, 176; Fullan and Connelly, 1987). Finally, the older—and more traditional—universities of eastern Canada were not as receptive to the notion of offering teacher preparation programs, snubbing the idea on the grounds that teaching was neither a 'real' profession nor an academic discipline. In Ontario, for example, when first encouraged by the then-minister of education (and future premier), William Davis, to start offering a Bachelor of Education, faculty members and administrators adamantly pushed back and refused to see teacher training as a legitimate component of university education.

Similar dynamics were seen elsewhere in Nova Scotia and Prince Edward Island. Major provincial inquiries, commissioned by various governments in the 1960s and 1970s, nevertheless were united behind the idea of university-led teacher preparation. Throughout the eastern provinces, these commissions helped to send cogent and dedicated messages encouraging political leaders of the day to transform teacher preparation programs. Furthermore, teachers themselves—including the CTF—championed the idea, recognizing that such a change to university-led teacher preparation would elevate the status and professionalism of the occupation. Together, these efforts enabled the dislodgement of the normal school system and the inception of university-led teacher preparation throughout the country.

Enduring Success: Broad and Robust Commitment

The development of education policy in Canada can be broken down into four periods according to the goals and priorities that tended to preoccupy educational leaders and members of the wider policy communities of the day (Wallner, 2014, 31). The first period, between 1840 and 1945, featured the foundation and consolidation of public schooling. Then, from 1945 to 1967, policy-makers worked to assure the universalization of schooling, enabling access for all Canadians, regardless of where they lived in the country. The 1960s marked the beginning of the third period, which stretched up to 1982. Here, newer ideas about 'child-centred learning' took hold, encouraging some individualization of programs and reinforcing the choice to institute the composite form of secondary schooling across the country. Finally, from 1982 up to the present, we have witnessed the continued and ongoing standardization of schooling practices. Overarching programmatic goals and paradigmatic ideas helped inform the choices being made by decision-makers through each of these periods.

While paradigms and norms have transformed, the bedrock of provincial schooling practices have exhibited remarkable durability over time. In contrast to other areas of policy activity, there is a strong and transnational consensus on the value, necessity, legitimacy, and effectiveness of publicly-provided education, particularly at the elementary level. Seen as an instrument to foster economic development, further social cohesion, and support community improvements, as well as a means to enhance individual achievements, governments around the world remain dedicated to providing a baseline of schooling for all citizens. For example, in 2017, the Government of Québec stated:

> As a vital part of everyday community life, schools and educational childcare centres cater to a wide variety of people from different socioeconomic and cultural backgrounds and with different needs. They offer a living environment that transmits the values of Québec society, which fosters identity formation and equips Quebecers to be active citizens.

> (Government of Québec 2017, 12).

Such sentiments are reflected among all the 13 systems.

Provinces and territories demonstrate a similar, if not in many cases more robust, commitment to providing quality education to all residents in their respective jurisdictions. In some countries, the private, independent, or charter schools are more prominent, particularly at the secondary level. In Australia, for example, more than 40 per cent of secondary students and almost 30 per cent of primary students attend a private school (Burke and Yan, 2019). In Canada, despite growing in some provinces over the past two decades, the private or independent school share remains relatively small in comparison to the rates of participation in the public sector, even at the secondary level.

Key stakeholders within the policy community reinforce this broad-based commitment to public schooling, made universally available at the elementary and secondary levels (Wallner and Marchildon, 2019). Teachers, who are well-organized and highly professionalized within each province and territory, are strong supporters of universal public schooling. The Alberta Teachers' Association, for example, states that public education must be 'free and accessible to every child; delivered by certified, highly skilled and knowledgeable teaching professionals; appropriately funded to ensure that every child learns, every child succeeds; and a responsibility shared by all Albertans' (ATA, 2017). Teachers' unions also further the interests of their members before the respective governments, lobbying and pressing for the continuation of robust public funding to assure the provision of quality schooling within each system. As the Nova Scotia Teachers' Union affirms, the union is committed to 'leadership in education change by: maintaining and promoting excellence in teaching; encouraging life-long learning; influencing education trends through research and evaluation; disseminating information' (Nova Scotia Teachers Union, 2020).

The principles of public schooling have also been defended by the Supreme Court of Canada. In 2016, the Court ruled in favour of the BC Teachers' Federation, overturning legislation passed in 2002 reinstating the right of the union to negotiate classroom conditions, practices for inclusive education, and class sizes. In another case that also pertained to British Columbia, the Supreme Court explicitly mobilized the discourse of universal public provision of education when it declared:

> Adequate special education, therefore, is not a dispensable luxury. For those with severe learning disabilities, it is the ramp that provides access to the statutory commitment to education made to *all* children in British Columbia (*Moore vs. British Columbia (Education), [2012] 3 SCR 360 at section 5, emphasis in original).

Finally, across Canada, the public remains dedicated to the idea and provision of universal, high quality, public elementary and secondary education. While pan-Canadian data on attitudes towards public schooling are not systematically collected, various provincial-level surveys and election coverage reveal the extent to which Canadians are committed to public schooling policies and practices. In Ontario, for example, the twentieth Ontario Institute for Studies in Education Survey of Educational Issues exposed a series of interesting trends. While satisfaction with the school system in general has been declining in the province, parents with children in schools have a generally more favourable view of education than the public as a whole (Hart and Kempf, 2018, 10). Also, the majority of the public and parents in the province have at least some to quite a lot of confidence in schools and education policy (Hart and Kempf, 2018, 12). A poll conducted in British Columbia, in 2019, found that the overwhelming majority of parents in the province are 'content' with their children's education. According to Research Co., 83 per cent of respondents indicated that the experience of their child with the education system has been 'very positive' or 'moderately positive' and a majority of parents indicated that they were 'very satisfied' or 'moderately satisfied' with the quality of instruction (Canseco, 2019, n.p.). Public support therefore offers positive reinforcements, furthering the broad-based commitment and enduring success of elementary and secondary education in Canada.

Analysis and Conclusions

Together, the overall success of provincial and territorial education systems rests in large part on the mutually reinforcing nature of many of the choices made in each individual category of the education sector. For example, throughout the country, ministries of education are responsible for providing clear leadership and consistent funding to the school districts managing the individual schools. Curriculum and large-scale assessments are developed by the ministries and all teachers are required to hold university-level education and pre-service training. These core building blocks, used to fashion a robust universal social program, have been in place since the late 1980s, enabling remarkable net benefits and realizing positive results for Canadians throughout the federation.

The legacy of learning, emulation, and adaptation that have generated success can be attributed to four factors. The first is *institutional incentives*. Due in part to what could be labelled as happenstance, Canada's education sectors indirectly and inadvertently benefited from certain constraints imposed by the rules of parliamentary government. Specifically, the fact that only a minister of the crown may speak in the legislature and that only cabinet as the political executive may create a budget, helped to encourage the creation of similar governing arrangements in each of the jurisdictions (Wallner, 2014). Instead of separate provincial level boards of education, that operate outside of the formal executive as is the case throughout the United States, early provincial education leaders opted to create formal ministries of education headed by a dedicated member of the political executive and supported by a professional public service (Wallner et al., 2020). While the complete realization of this model consistently throughout the country took many decades, by the late 1960s, all of the provinces had converged on this approach. Consequently, ministries of education, headed by a Cabinet minister and supported by professional civil servants, oversee all the major decisions and activities of the elementary and secondary schooling sector.

Dispersed yet concerted public management is the second factor that served to facilitate success. The powerful bureaucracies share similar types of authority and influence such that it is fit to describe Canada's schooling sector as *de-concentrated* as opposed to decentralized (Wallner, 2018). Ministries establish the fundamental parameters of schooling policies that are subsequently implemented by locally elected school boards. Robust public funding helps assure that all boards in large part adhere to ministry edicts, including curricular standards, hiring certified teachers, and participating in provincially mandated large-scale assessment programs. This is not to suggest or claim that conditions within provinces do not vary both among boards and across schools under a specific local jurisdiction.

To be sure, the assertion of technocratic and centralized management has certainly been contested in various jurisdictions and by some observers (Bennett, 2020). Such technocratic control has nevertheless eased the movement of ideas across the country, enabling a relatively high degree of consistency of practices for the majority of Canadian students since the 1990s. Officials working within each ministry are part of a close-knit policy community that maintains considerable authority over practices at work within each of their systems. The CMEC further helps to facilitate this work, bolstering opportunities for interjurisdictional exchanges on education policy (Wallner and Marchildon, 2019, 77). As such, in contrast to fragmented systems like the United States where the configuration and extent of authority exercised by public officials among states varies considerably, Canadian provinces and territories have managed to coordinate in elementary and secondary education without a proverbial 'Leviathan' (Wallner, 2017).

The third factor of success is found in Canada's *fiscal architecture*. First introduced in 1957, and entrenched in the Constitution Act of 1982, equalization is intended to reduce differences in revenue-generating capacity across Canada's 10 provinces. Financed entirely from Government of Canada's general revenues, equalization is entirely unconditional, enabling provinces to make decisions for their residents and remain accountable to the voters for whom they provide services, including elementary and secondary education. 'By compensating poorer provinces for their relatively weak tax bases or resource endowments, equalization helps to ensure that Canadians residing in provinces have access to a reasonably similar level of provincial government services at reasonably similar levels of taxation, regardless of which province they call home' (Roy-César, 2008, 1). Due to their increased fiscal challenges, the territories are the beneficiaries of a separate, more enhanced, Territorial Formula Financing, that is similarly free from federally-set mandates or conditions. These arrangements that form the cornerstone of Canada's fiscal architecture assist provinces and territories to maintain robust social programs—including education—securing relatively equal and highly successful achievements.

The fourth factor stems from the *characteristics of education as a policy area itself*. A field of developmental policy, centred on investing in the general well-being of a population while simultaneously providing the critical infrastructure for economic growth and human capital, the politics of education are markedly different than those appearing in other policy areas (Wallner, 2014, 239). Where areas of redistributive policy—and particularly those with targeted as opposed to universal benefits—may experience a race to the bottom, weak commitments, and pitched conflicts over resource allocation, as an area of developmental policy, education tends to witness unrelenting demands for more investments and strong commitments that translate into a positive competitive dynamic, as each jurisdiction endeavours to race to the top. Citizens consistently demand high-quality schooling systems from their governments, and always rank education as a high issue on the policy agenda (Wallner and Marchildon, 2019, 68). Those employed within the education sector are also crucial stimulants of policy choices, and are similarly committed to securing high quality programs. While this characteristic of the

94   SCHOOLING SUCCESSFULLY

education sector is shared across all countries and schooling systems, in Canada, this feature is enhanced and more influential due to the compounding facilitating factors listed above.

References

Anders, J., S. Has, J. Jerrim, N. Shure, and L. Zieger. 2020. "Is Canada Really an Education Superpower? The Impact of Non-Participation on Results from PISA 2015." *Educational Assessment, Evaluation and Accountability* 33 (1): pp. 229–249.

ATA (Alberta Teachers' Association). 2017. *A Mission and Vision for Public Education.* Edmonton: Alberta Teachers' Association. Available online at: https://www.teachers.ab.ca/SiteCollectionDocuments/ATA/Publications/Albertas-Education-System/Vision%20and%20Mission%20for%20Public%20Eudcation.pdf   Accessed on 7 January 2021.

Bakvis, H. and G. Skogstad. 2002. "Canadian Federalism: Performance, Effectiveness, and Legitimacy." In *Canadian Federalism: Performance, Effectiveness, and Legitimacy*, edited by H. Bakvis and G. Skogstad, pp. 3–23. Don Mills: Oxford University.

Bennett, P. 2020. *The State of the System: A Reality Check on Canada's Schools.* Montreal and Kingston: McGill-Queen's University Press.

Blum, B. 2021. "Canadians Should Be Prepared for More Discoveries Like Kamloops, Murray Sinclair Says." *CBC.* 1 June. Available online: https://www.cbc.ca/news/canada/sinclair-kamloops-residential-remains-1.6049525

Bryden, P. E. 2019. "Equalization and the Fiscal Foundation of Universality." In *Universality and Social Policy in Canada*, edited by D. Béland, G. P. Marchildon, and M. J. Prince, pp. 31–47. Toronto: University of Toronto Press.

Burke, M. and Y. Yan. 2019. "The Debate over Private Schooling Has Missed its Impact on City Traffic." *The Conversation.* 28 October. Available online: https://www.abc.net.au/news/2019-10-29/australia-private-schooling-hidden-impact-on-city-traffic/11646918#:~:text=In%20Australia%20today%2C%20just%20over,children%20attend%20a%20private%20school

Campbell, J. L. and O. K. Pedersen. 2014. *The National Origins of Policy Ideas: Knowledge Regimes in the United States, France, Germany, and Denmark.* Princeton, NJ: Princeton University Press.

Canseco, M. 2019. "Class Sizes, Teacher Shortage Worry Parents in British Columbia" *Research Co.* 5 June. Available online at: https://researchco.ca/2019/06/05/strong-words-in-the-staffroom-the-accusations-fly/

Child, A. H. 1978. "The Ryerson Tradition in Western Canada, 1871–1906." In *Egerton Ryerson and his Times*, edited by N. McDonald and A. Chaiton. Toronto: Macmillan.

Compton, M. E. and P. 't Hart. 2019. "How to 'See' Great Policy Successes: A Field Guide to Spotting Policy Successes in the Wild." In *Great Policy Successes*, edited by M. E. Compton and P. 't Hart, pp. 1–20. Oxford: Oxford University Press.

Coughlan, S. 2017. "How Canada Became an Education Superpower." *BBC News.* 1 August. Available online at: https://www.bbc.com/news/business-40708421. Accessed 11 December 2020.

Council for Ministers of Education Canada. 2018. *PCAP 2016: Report on the Pan-Canadian Assessment on Reading, Mathematics, and Science.* Toronto: Council for Ministers of Education, Canada. Available online at: https://www.cmec.ca/publications/lists/publications/attachments/381/pcap-2016-public-report-en.pdf. Accessed 11 December 2020.

Council for Ministers of Education Canada. 2019. *Measuring up: Canadian Results of the OECD PISA 2018 Study*. Toronto: Council for Ministers of Education, Canada. Available online at: https://www.cmec.ca/Publications/Lists/Publications/Attachments/396/PISA2018_PublicReport_EN.pdf. Accessed 11 December 2020.

Council for Ministers of Education Canada. 2020. *Ensuring Inclusive and Equitable Quality Education: Sustainable Development GOAL 4 in Canada*. Toronto: Council for Ministers of Education Canada. Available online at: https://www.cmec.ca/Publications/Lists/Publications/Attachments/407/Sustainable%20Development%20Goal%204%20in%20Canada%20EN.pdf. Accessed 11 December 2020.

Fullan, M. and F. M. Connelly. 1987. *Teacher Education in Ontario: Current Practice and Options for the Future: A Position Paper*. Toronto: OISE.

Government of Canada. 2018. "Anishinabek Nation Education Agreement." Government of Canada. 29 March. Available online: https://www.rcaanc-cirnac.gc.ca/eng/1517588283074/1542741544614 Accessed on 14 December 2020.

Government of Canada. 2008. "Prime Minister Harper Offers Full Apology on Behalf of Canadians for the Indian Residential Schools System." Government of Canada. 11 June. Available online at: https://www.rcaanc-cirnac.gc.ca/eng/1100100015644/1571589171655 Accessed on 11 December 2020.

Government of Quebec. 2017. "Policy on Educational Success: A Love of Learning, A Chance to Succeed." Quebec: Government of Quebec. Available online at: http://www.education.gouv.qc.ca/fileadmin/site_web/documents/PSG/politiques_orientations/politique_reussite_educative_10juillet_A_1.pdf. Accessed 7 January 2021.

Hart, D. and A. Kempf. 2018. *Public Attitudes towards Education in Ontario 2018: The 20th OISE Survey of Educational Issues*. Toronto: Ontario Institute for Studies in Education of the University of Toronto. Available online at: https://www.oise.utoronto.ca/oise/UserFiles/Media/Media_Relations/OISE-Public-Attitudes-Report-2018_final.pdf. Accessed 7 January 2021.

Hill, T., N. Li, and J. Emes. 2020. *Education Spending in Public Schools in Canada, 2020 Edition*. Vancouver: The Fraser Institute. Available online at: https://www.fraserinstitute.org/sites/default/files/education-spending-in-public-schools-2020.pdf. Accessed on 5 January 2021.

Indigenous Services Canada. 2019. *Backgrounder—New Funding and Policy Approach for First Nations Kindergarten to Grade 12 Education*. Available online at: https://www.afn.ca/wp-content/uploads/2019/01/2019.01.21_BG-Word_K-12Education-EN.pdf. Accessed on 11 December 2020.

Johnson, F. H. 1966. "Teacher Education in Historical Perspective." In *Teacher Education at the University of British Columbia*, pp. 1–25. Vancouver: Faculty of Education, University of British Columbia.

Kauko, J. 2019. "The Finnish Comprehensive School: Conflicts, Compromises, and Institutional Robustness." In *Great Policy Successes* edited by M. E. Compton and P. 't Hart, pp. 122–142. Oxford: Oxford University Press.

Knight, H. 2021. "Egerton Ryerson: Racist Philosophy of Residential Schools Also Shaped Public Education." *The Conversation*. 22 February. Available online at:

https://theconversation.com/egerton-ryerson-racist-philosophy-of-residential-schools-also-shaped-public-education-143039. Accessed on 8 March 2021.

Lecours, A. 2019. "Dynamic De/Centralization in Canada, 1867–2010." *Publius: The Journal of Federalism* 49 (1): pp. 57–83.

Love, J. 1978. "The Professionalization of Teachers in the Mid-Nineteenth Century Upper Canada." In *Ryerson and his Times*, edited by N. McDonald and A. Chaiton, pp. 109–198. Toronto: Macmillan.

McConnell, A. 2010. "Policy Success, Policy Failure and Grey Areas In-Between." *Journal of Public Policy* 30 (3): pp. 345–362.

Milloy, J. S. 1999. *A National Crime: The Canadian Government and the Residential School System, 1879 to 1986.* Winnipeg: University of Manitoba Press.

Mulford, B. 2002. "Sorting the Wheat from the Chaff: Knowledge and Skills for Life: First Results from the OECD's PISA 2000." *European Journal of Education* 37 (2): pp. 211–221.

Nova Scotia Teachers Union. 2020. "Our Beliefs." NSTU. Available online at: https://nstu.ca/the-nstu/about-us/our-beliefs. Accessed on 7 January 2021.

Organization for Economic Cooperation and Development (OECD). 2019. *Country Note: Programme for International Student Assessment (PISA) Results from PISA 2018.* Available online at: https://www.oecd.org/pisa/publications/PISA2018_CN_CAN.pdf. Accessed on 8 March 2021.

Paradkar, S. 2020. "New StatCan Data Shows How Canada Is Failing New Generations of Black Youth." Toronto Star. 29 February. Available online at: https://www.thestar.com/opinion/star-columnists/2020/02/29/how-canada-is-failing-new-generations-of-black-youth.html. Accessed on 14 December 2020.

Roy-César, É. 2008. *Canada's Equalization Formula in Brief.* Ottawa: Library of Parliament. Available online at: https://lop.parl.ca/sites/PublicWebsite/default/en_CA/ResearchPublications/200820E. Accessed on 16 December 2020.

Ryan, T. G. 2006. "Performance Assessment: Critics, Criticism, and Controversy." *International Journal of Testing* 6 (1): pp. 97–104.

Schleicher, A. 2018. *PISA 2018: Insights and Interpretations.* OECD. Available online at: https://www.oecd.org/pisa/PISA%202018%20Insights%20and%20Interpretations%20FINAL%20PDF.pdf. Accessed on 17 December 2020.

Simeon, R. and B. A. Radin. 2010. "Reflections on Comparing Federalisms: Canada and the United States." *Publius: The Journal of Federalism* 40 (3): pp. 357–365.

Sissons, C. B. 1959. *Church and State in Canadian Education: An Historical Study.* Toronto: Ryerson Press.

Statistics Canada. 2018. "Back to School … by the Numbers." *Government of Canada.* 7 September. Available online at: https://www.statcan.gc.ca/eng/dai/smr08/2018/smr08_220_2018 Accessed on 11 December 2020.

Truth and Reconciliation Commission. 2015. *Honouring the Truth, Reconciling for the Future: Summary of the Final Report of the Truth and Reconciliation Commission of Canada.* Truth and Reconciliation Commission of Canada. Available online at: http://nctr.ca/assets/reports/Final%20Reports/Executive_Summary_English_Web.pdf. Accessed on 11 December 2020.

Union of Ontario Indians. 2013. *An Overview of the Indian Residential School System.* Union of Ontario Indians. Available online: http://www.anishinabek.ca/wp-content/uploads/2016/07/An-Overview-of-the-IRS-System-Booklet.pdf. Accessed on 11 December 2020.

Wallner, J. 2014. *Learning to School: Federalism and Public Schooling in Canada.* Toronto: University of Toronto Press.

Wallner, J. 2017. "Cooperation Without the Leviathan: Intergovernmental Policymaking in Canadian Education." *Regional and Federal Studies* 27 (4): pp. 417–440.

Wallner, J. 2018. "Federalism and Education: The Canadian Case." In *Federalism and Education: Ongoing Challenges and Policy Strategies in Ten Countries*, edited by K. K. Wong, F. Knüpling, and M. Kölling, pp. 81–99. Charlotte, NC: Information Age Publishing.

Wallner, J. and G. P. Marchildon. 2019. "Elementary and Secondary Education: The First Universal Social Program in Canada." In *Universality and Social Policy in Canada*, edited by D. Béland, G. P. Marchildon, and M. J. Prince, pp. 63–82. Toronto: University of Toronto Press.

Wallner, J., G. C. Savage, S. Hartong, and L. C. Engel. 2020. "Laboratories, Coproducers, and Venues: Roles Played by Subnational Governments in Standards-Based Reforms in Four Federations." *Comparative Education Review* 64 (2): pp. 249–268.

6
Québec's Subsidized Childcare Network

Nathalie Burlone

Introduction

Children are our first wealth; they are the future of Québec society. Our responsibility is to do everything we can to provide them with the best possible starting conditions and to ensure that they benefit, as much as possible, from the same chances of success and achievement in life.

(Gouvernement du Québec 1997).[1]

It was on this strong stand in defence of children's development that, on 23 January 1997, the then Québec premier Lucien Bouchard revealed the family policy White paper '*Les enfants au coeur de nos choix*',[2] under which the Centres de la petite enfance (CPEs)[3] would be created. Nine months later, in the autumn of 1997, Québec's CPE network, a cornerstone of its family policy, was implemented. This chapter provides insight into the policy success that the development and implementation of subsidized childcare in Québec represents. Described as *Québec exceptionalism* (Arsenault et al., 2018), the provincial system, still in place, is unique in Canada. For more than twenty years, it has outlived changes in governing political parties, withstood policy changes, survived budgetary crises, and adapted to harsh criticisms.

A number of factors have influenced the evolution of family trends in Canada and Québec (Baker, 1994), leading to different family policy decisions. Arguably, a chief factor is the decline in Québec's fertility rate. Although Canada experienced a baby boom between 1945 and the early 1960s, the province's fertility rate has since fallen sharply to 1.5 children per woman, below the population replacement rate set by demographers at 2.1 children per woman. Other changes, such as rising divorce and common-law union rates, sharp increases in the number of

---

[1] Author's translation
[2] 'Children at the heart of our choices' (Author translation)
[3] 'Early Childhood Centres' (Author translation)

Nathalie Burlone, *Québec's Subsidized Childcare Network*. In: *Policy Success in Canada.*
Edited by Evert A. Lindquist et al., Oxford University Press. © Nathalie Burlone (2022).
DOI: 10.1093/oso/9780192897046.003.0006

single-parent families (from 289,000 in 1976 to 698,000 in 2014)[4] and family debt (176.9 per cent of disposable income in 2020) have contributed to the changing face of Canadian families over the years and brought the problems facing families and governments into sharper focus. For instance, while declining fertility rates are not necessarily a problem per se, they have direct consequences for how society is organized, and they impact the provision and diversity of public services. They also raise important public policy challenges (permanent closure of some schools, for example). Changes in the labour market, such as the increased participation of mothers with young children in the workforce and the rise of single-parent families, challenge governments to develop concrete measures to ensure a work-family balance. The level of family debt highlights important concerns about individuals' purchasing power, and its effects on intergenerational transfers and the erosion of the middle class. The increased participation of women in the labour market brings attention to the heavy burden of women's dual responsibilities and questions the role of governments in this regard (Mathieu, 2016; Bergeron, 2005; Jenson and Sineau, 2001; Porter, 2003; O'Connor et al., 1999). These transformations shape government conceptualizations regarding families and parental roles, while raising questions around how to best integrate the market, the family, and the state into policy (Burlone and Couture, 2011) through pertinent instruments (Burlone, 2009).

The 1997 Québec family policy acknowledges these transformations. The proposed measures were grounded in the then budgetary constraints (objective of zero deficit) and social, economic, and labour market changes. With an initial announcement of the soon-to-be enacted policy at the 1996 *Sommet sur l'emploi et l'économie*,[5] the provincial government took a clear stand on recognizing the primary responsibility of parents to provide for their children and suggested that any such policy should be integrated into the family life course (Burlone, 2013). The government's duty was to support this responsibility with programs that would better address poverty, bring mothers and welfare recipients into the workforce, and promote equality of opportunity for both parents and children. Consistent with education and income security reforms under way at the time, the policy, implemented a year after the Summit, contained several provisions. One was the long-term creation of 200,000 childcare places available to all Québec children under the age of five at a flat daily rate of $5 through a single-window system. These services, certainly the most important provision of the policy, are still delivered today in CPEs facilities (as non-profit organizations) or in family settings (under the supervision of CPEs), where parents play an important role on boards of directors.

The creation and implementation of childcare services in 1997 have since been the subject of criticisms that pertain to rising expenses, the gradual move away

---

[4] https://www150.statcan.gc.ca/n1/pub/75-006-x/2015001/article/14202/parent-eng.htm
[5] Summit on the Economy and Employment

from an initial universality principle[6] due to problems of accessibility (ameliorated partly by the Liberal government with the decision to include subsidized and non-subsidized commercial childcare centres in 2003), and consecutive increases in the daily parental contribution (to $7 in 2003 and the addition of an annual contribution based on family income between 2015 and 2019). Nevertheless, the fact remains that the creation of CPEs largely meet the criteria for policy success proposed for this volume (see also McConnell, 2010, 2017), which shall be discussed further below. To better situate its programmatic, process, political, and endurance successes, the story of the program's creation, substance, and evolution will be presented first.

The Journey towards Childcare Services

Developing family policy in Québec

Family policies consist of many types. Baker's typology (1994) embraces policies related to issues of marriage/divorce, adoption, reproduction, income support (such as family allowances, maternity and paternity benefits), and direct service provisions including, but not exclusively, childcare. The policy success that the creation of CPEs represent must be appreciated in light of the broader transformations brought on by the development of the 1997 family policy package. By substantially transforming the range of services and benefits available to Québec families, the policy introduced a somewhat revolutionary approach to childcare, which was unprecedented within Canada. CPEs were able to break with several decades of programs exclusively focused on financial benefits.

This new policy package did not materialize in a vacuum. In fact, as early as the 1960s, Québec had improved the universal family allowance granted by the Canadian federal government after World War II by offering school allowances for 16- and 17-year-olds. This measure was proposed to ensure the extended education of children and to provide access to education for all, at all levels of instruction (at the time, under-education of French-Canadian students was striking compared to English-speaking ones). The province later adopted additional measures, such as childcare allowances for children under 16 years of age (1967) and the first tax credits for childcare expenses (1972). Moreover, the first childcare policy, introduced in 1974, was limited to start-up grants and funded a portion of childcare costs for disadvantaged parents in order to increase accessibility (Baillargeon, 1996). The 1979 Child Care Act recognized the importance of developing daycares without, however, providing the means to address the underfunding of such services.

---

[6] Some authors have, however, criticized the claim that subsidized childcare is universal, arguing that no government since the program's inception has been able to meet the demand for spaces.

With two organizational structures specifically devoted to families, the *Secrétariat à la famille* and the *Conseil de la famille,* 1987 marked a turning point for recognizing the need for innovative government action for families (Le Bourdais, 1989). Both structures had been given joint responsibility for managing the measures included in this revision of Québec's family policy. The family support programs offered in 1987 were mainly developed to address the low fertility rate of Québec families. At that time, the province was experiencing a serious birth crisis, going from being the most fertile province to one with the fewest children in under 30 years (Baker, 1990). Duly characterized as pro-natalist, the 1987 programs consisted of financial allowances in the form of birth benefits (relatively generous from the third child on) and tax credits, the amount of which varied according to income. While the 1987 programs compensated for the expense of bringing additional children into the family, the sole pursuit of a generational renewal objective provided only partial and targeted assistance over time. Measures of this type do not increase birth rates or necessarily encourage families to have *more* children than initially planned. This was also the case for Québec. Between 1988 and 1990, the number of births increased by 13 per cent but then fell back to the 1988 level (Dandurand, 2020). The 1987 provisions were also rather inefficient in addressing the new realities of parents. The long-term issues of reducing family income inequalities, integrating and reintegrating parents into the workforce, and ensuring the physical and psychological development of children, which were specific problems arising from transformations within Québec society, were left unaddressed. Moreover, the challenge of reconciling family and work responsibilities remained a strong theme for social advocates.

Ultimately, the 1997 family policy reform turned its back on natalist goals and, instead, it was guided by a logic of financial stability for families (especially for women), which was expected to improve the well-being of children. As Pauline Marois, the then minister of education and head of the *Office des services de garde à l'enfance*[7] in 1997, recalls on the twentieth anniversary of the policy:

> For us, it was a huge equality of opportunity policy, a fight against poverty. By offering childcare services at a reduced price, we allowed many families and many single mothers to enter the job market because the income they earned was still enough to cover the costs, since childcare costs were very low.
>
> (Bertrand, 2017. Author's translation)

The new family policy recognized the transformation of Québec society. By 1997, the composition of households had changed considerably, and the traditional family structure had lost its dominance. The number of single-parent families (with women as the responsible parent in most cases) and reconstituted families had

---

[7] Childcare Services Office

increased, representing respectively 20 per cent and 10 per cent of all families in the province. This transformation created significant economic pressure for some families who, forced into a situation of poverty, struggled to find assistance to cover their basic needs within existing government responses. In addition, there was also little incentive for families on welfare to work, leading to situations of inequity and unequal opportunities for children. Finally, the extended years of schooling and the consequential postponement of socio-professional integration also had a significant impact on social programs. The 1997 family policy sought to respond to these new realities by proposing a substantial reconfiguration of the programs offered to families based on innovative principles.[8] The policy also had the goal of reaching a significant number of individuals and inducing a positive long-term impact on diverse social groups.

In addition to the historical developments outlined above, the 1997 Québec family policy must be understood within the governmental budgetary context, the evolution of the labour market, and social and economic transformations. Surprisingly, the development of Québec's family policy was carried out in a context of significant budgetary restrictions (Dandurand, 2020). In the spring of 1997, Lucien Bouchard's PQ (Parti Québécois) government was committed to returning to a balanced budget to avoid the province's credit rating being reduced further. The government announced its intention to eliminate the deficit through a series of program cuts and rationalization of resources. Among other things, achieving the zero-deficit objective required curbing the fragmented and inefficient expenditure of $2.2 billion on existing social programs. Work incentive programs for income security recipients were not working (Bouchard et al., 1996), and early childhood services were insufficient and scattered. This required the new family policy to be coordinated with ongoing reforms in education and income security (the new policy would eventually replace some of these programs), as well as with other existing policies. In 1996, two thirds of Québec mothers were working outside the home with insufficient childcare options and the *Office des services de garde à l'enfance* had not created enough places to solve the problem (Dandurand, 2020). While the PQ government sought to ensure greater coherence between existing measures in childcare and parenthood support, it also wanted to provide Québec with a flagship family policy.

The *Secrétariat du Comité des priorités*,[9] which was reporting to the Cabinet, was responsible for drafting a three-part policy as early as the spring of 1996, and

---

[8] Some authors argue, however, that the 1997 provisions, although important, don't represent a complete turnaround but a foreseeable evolution due to the national and international trends prevailing in the 1990s. See, for example, Dandurand and Saint-Pierre (2000).

[9] Priority Committee Secretariat (now named the *Secrétariat aux priorités et aux projets stratégiques/ Strategic Priorities and Projects Secretariat*). In 1997, the Secretariat was the body that supported the Priority committee composed of the premier and key ministers including the Finance and Education ministers.

was also tasked with validating its content with an interdepartmental ministerial committee created specifically for this purpose (Burlone, 2001). This committee, responsible for harmonizing policy proposals with the expertise provided by the departments of Education, Social Solidarity, Pensions, and Finance, worked to prepare the new policy announcement to be made at the *Sommet sur l'emploi et l'économie* in the autumn of 1996. The mandate of this working group was to examine all programs directly or indirectly related to families, and administered by different sectors, in order to gain a comprehensive overview of their scope, objectives, costs, actual outcomes, and problems encountered. This analysis revealed a serious lack of harmonization across programs. The committee quickly came to the conclusion that the patchwork of disparate measures and programs only reached the surface of existing problems and were not integrated into a coherent vision. More importantly, these programs and measures no longer responded to the needs of Québec families.

It would be misleading to believe that the desire to provide the province with an innovative family policy only came from governmental reflection and political will. When it comes to family matters, Québec can count on a history of organized groups, such as family associations, social workers, and experts, (Lemieux, 2011) as well as on the 'dual action of the family movement and the women's movement' (Dandurand and Kempeneers, 2002, 68). Indeed, as far back as the 1930s, under the impetus of the Catholic youth movement, several issues affecting families were brought forward by the clergy as well as medical and educational experts. The period between the early 1960s and the end of the 1970s was marked by the strong contribution of social movements for more appropriate childcare in Québec. Although emancipation of married women in the workforce had been growing, some issues remained unaddressed by the government. For instance, the absence of paid maternity leave and the lack of access to childcare services continued to marginalize women in Québec (Baillargeon, 1996). It is in this context that groups such as the *Fédération des unions des familles,*[10] women's groups, feminist activists, and single-parent family associations joined forces to promote changes in family policy—namely the creation of a few non-profit daycares. Their actions also led to numerous public consultations resulting in the creation of a *Conseil supérieur de la famille*[11] in 1964 (Lemieux, 2011). The 1970s were marked by the rise of the unionization of women's movements, which put forth ideas around the universalization of childcare services through different courses of action, such as protests and advertisements (Bellemare and Briand, 2012). Present and powerful since the 1960s, such movements have been more influential in bringing about change in family services in Québec than in the rest of Canada:

[10] Federation of Family Unions (Author translation)
[11] Higher Council of the Family

During the 1980s, family associations, especially through the creation of the Re-
groupement interorganismes pour une politique familiale au Québec *(RIOPFQ),*
were undoubtedly the strongest lobby in the establishment of the 1987 family policy.
In the process of implementing or transforming family policies, however, the fam-
ily movement was not the only civil society player to be involved. This movement
is, as with family associations, represented within a (consultative) Council on the
Status of Women, which has repeatedly expressed its views on family issues, from
alimony, poverty in single-parent families, parental leave, to balancing family and
work responsibilities.

(Dandurand and Kempeneers, 2002, 68. Author's translation).

The Provisions of the 1997 Family Policy

Aligned with the recommendations and proposals made at the Taxation Review Committee (2015) and at the *États généraux sur l'Éducation*[12] (2016), Québec's family policy was officially announced at the November 1996 Summit. Two months later, on 23 January 1997, the white paper containing the new family policy provisions was officially released (Secrétariat du Comité des priorités du ministère du Conseil exécutif, 1997), and the policy was implemented the following autumn. The new family policy consisted of three major components: the introduction of the *Unified Child Allowance,* the development of a new *Parental Insurance Plan,* and the development of *Early Learning and Childcare Services.*

The *Unified Child Allowance* (UCA) proposed to consolidate a dozen existing measures that were to be redistributed. This non-taxable benefit, based on income and number of children, was included in a new income security policy. It intended to bring the benefits received by welfare recipients in line with those received by low-income families as a means to create a new incentive for welfare recipients to join the workforce. The UCA replaced the package introduced in 1987—the Family Allowance, the Youth Allowance, and the Birth Allowance (the Child Tax Credit was maintained)—and came into effect in July 1997.

The purpose of the *Parental Insurance Plan* was to respond more adequately to the new demands of the workplace. Parental insurance was to increase leave benefits by guaranteeing 75 per cent of net income. The Parental Insurance Plan was also designed to restore equity between salaried and self-employed workers, the latter being excluded from maternity or compensated parental leaves. This provision did not come into effect until 2006 due to lagging negotiations with the federal government over the amounts that would be transferred to Québec.

The *Early Learning* provisions included the creation of preschool classes for children aged 4 and 5 (full time and mandatory for 5-year-olds). Already called

[12] National Education Forum

for in the Parent Report in the 1960s,[13] the establishment of preschool classes was based on the direct and documented relationship between the duration of preschool attendance and the decrease in the repetition rate in elementary school. While available to all children, this provision was intended to target children from disadvantaged regions or neighbourhoods. Compulsory full-time preschools for 5-year-olds were implemented in 1998,[14] while the first preschools (not compulsory) for 4-year-olds were introduced in low-income areas in 2013. Access to preschools for all 4-year-old Québec children is projected for 2023.

If the creation of preschools for 4- and 5-year-olds was an important proposal of the 1997 family policy—and indeed these contributed to the development of children, better prepared them for elementary school, and generated positive social and economic outcomes (White et al., 2015)—the development of a network of subsidized childcare services through *Centres de la petite enfance* (CPEs) is without a doubt the policy's signature measure (Dandurand and Kempeneers, 2002).

The CPEs Then and Now

The benefits of subsidized CPE-like programs on children have been widely documented (Vandenbroeck, 2020; White et al., 2015):

> *An expanding research corpus demonstrates that high quality ECEC programmes can improve children's well-being, which we conceptualize broadly to include cognitive, social/emotional and physical development. These effects appear to be strongest for children who come from disadvantaged backgrounds including low family incomes, or having very young, single and poorly educated parents.*
>
> (White et al., 2015).

However, the payoffs do not stop with the children. Subsidized childcare generally improves the well-being of parents, and especially mothers (Schmitz, 2020). What the Bouchard government proposed in 1997 amounted to a complete revamping of the childcare system aimed specifically at these outcomes. On the one hand, the government designed the creation of free childcare services for children from disadvantaged backgrounds in existing preschools. On the other hand, for non-disadvantaged neighbourhoods, it promised the long-term creation of 200,000 affordable single daily rate childcare places available to all Québec children under the age of five, regardless of family income. These services would be offered in public facilities and family settings through CPEs, bringing Québec's service levels up to that of world-leading countries: '*While low-cost (or even free) child care is a*

---

[13] The Parent Report was the result of the Royal Commission on Education set up in 1961 by the Québec Liberal government to examine the province's education system.

[14] Non-mandatory 5-year-old preschools have been established in Québec since the 1960s.

common reality in countries such as France and Sweden, in North America this is unique and an enviable measure for many Canadian provinces and some US states' (Dandurand and Kempeneers, 2002. Author's translation).

The family policy needed an organizational structure responsible for its implementation and sustainability, and the simultaneous creation of the *Ministère de la Famille et de l'Enfance*[15] met that need and ensured a rapid deployment of the new provisions. The Department oversaw the implementation of the policy, including childcare services, and replaced the less powerful *Office des services de garde à l'enfance*, which was abolished. CPEs were created as non-profit organizations responsible for delivering childcare services. Meeting the promise of creating 200,000 places proved challenging. According to data from the Québec Department of the Family,[16] between 1998 and 2006, the number of places in CPEs increased by around 9 per cent every year but growth rates decreased considerably thereafter. In 2006, the target of 200,000 childcare places was nonetheless reached. Most of these places were subsidized and offered through CPEs (37 per cent in a facility and 45 per cent in home-based childcare settings) and private subsidized childcare centres (17 per cent). The difference was made up by places in non-subsidized but government-recognized childcare facilities. By 2020, Québec had a total of 306,152 childcare places, of which 235,731 were subsidized (41 per cent offered in CPEs, 39 per cent in home settings and 20 per cent in private subsidized facilities). The single daily rate of $5 was maintained until 2004, one year after the election of Jean Charest's Liberal Party. From that year until 2015, the rate increased to $7 per day. Between 2015 and 2019, a means-tested and family-size dependent annual contribution (a user fee) was applied.

Although the 1997–2003 period under the Parti Québécois government was one of expansion with the initial weekly rate maintained, Mathieu (2019) refers to the gradual transformation of childcare as a 'breach in the collectivization of social reproduction care' brought on by neoliberal ideology. The 2003–2012 Liberal government under Jean Charest showed a clear preference towards for-profit childcare. In 2008, the government substantially increased the tax credit for childcare expenses, which allowed families to pay for non-subsidized childcare places at a rate almost equivalent to that of CPEs. This decision is partly explained by the insufficiency of places in CPEs to meet public demand and the pressure to develop places that would ensure adequate coverage of family needs to accommodate a work-family balance. Starting in 2015 (under the liberal government of Philippe Couillard), the childcare program was significantly modified by the modulation of daily rates. The attractiveness of a CPE place over one in a non-subsidized private childcare facility began to diminish for some families:

---

[15] Department of the Family and Childhood
[16] https://www.mfa.gouv.qc.ca/fr/services-de-garde/portrait/places/Pages/index.aspx

In 2018, the cost of a subsidized GDS place is $8.05 for families with an income of less than $51,340, while families with an income of more than $165,005 must pay $21.95 for a place for the first child (basic contribution of $8.05 per day + additional contribution of $13.90).

(Mathieu, 2019, 217. Author's translation).

In 2019, after a change of government, the newly elected Legault government (Coalition Avenir Québec) abolished the annual contribution and announced a plan to improve access to early learning and childcare services that included catching up on the number of places created.

Despite these policy shifts and the gradual adaptations to the CPE program, the fact remains that the public popularity of subsidized childcare has not waned. To date, Québec is the only province to have adopted such work-family balance measures. The province also invests more in childcare services than other Canadian provinces, resulting in the higher affordability of such services in Québec when compared to the rest of the country. In a recent study, Arsenault et al. (2018) show the unique nature of Québec's subsidized childcare system in Canada.[17] Indeed, despite the attractiveness and success of the program, no other Canadian province has followed in Québec's footsteps to *massively* invest in childcare services:

When comparing the social policies of the different Canadian provinces, one of them stands out for its audacity: Québec's childcare policy. No other social policy so clearly distinguishes one province from the others. Indeed, while there are notable differences between childcare services in other Canadian provinces, they all have in common low public funding, high fees and lower utilization rates than in other Western countries.

(Arsenault et al., 2018, 2. Author translation)

A Policy Success: Assessing the CPE System

From a *programmatic* point of view, the childcare services network put in place in 1997 is a policy innovation and a huge success. The PQ government identified a need and decided to devote important funds to support families. The CPEs replaced what was considered a scattered and fragmented set of governmental measures and programs targeting families with limited impact. Prioritizing social investment and collectivization of care work (Mathieu, 2019), the development of CPE offerings has attracted a significant number of children to services that allow

---

[17] The author points, however, to the fact that Québec's uniqueness fades away when compared to other Welfare states or OECD countries.

108   QUÉBEC'S SUBSIDIZED CHILDCARE NETWORK

them to be better prepared for elementary school. The creation of a network of subsidized childcare services has yielded various positive results. The most obvious is the important diminution in the parental contribution to the cost of childcare services. Baker et al. (2008) valued this decrease at more than 60 per cent for two-parent families and 40 per cent for single-parent families, who are also able to benefit from other subsidies. To put it another way, while families were subsidized at a rate between 47 per cent and 80 per cent for the cost of a childcare place, the average rate was 32 per cent in the rest of Canada (Fortin et al., 2013). The number of subsidized places has also tripled between 1997 and 2012, from 79,000 in 1997 to 245,000 in 2012 (Fortin et al., 2013).

The rapid implementation of CPEs provided incentives for young parents to seek or stay in work, bolstered assistance to low-income families, and afforded labour integration or reintegration opportunities for mothers. Fortin et al. (2013) note that the employment rate of Québec women aged 20–44 increased substantially in the province between 1996 and 2011, reaching levels twice as much as the rest of Canada (whereas it was lower than the Canadian average in 1996). CPEs have facilitated a family-work balance. Moreover, single-parent families are known to be the poorest Canadian households. In 2016, 39 per cent of female lone-parent families in Canada were considered low-income (Harding, 2018). Therefore, enabling single female parents to have access to quality services at a reduced cost helped lower the poverty rate. For instance, between 1996 and 2017, the number of single-parent families on welfare dropped by 64 per cent. Poverty rates decreased from 38 per cent in 1998 to 23 per cent in 2014 (Bertrand, 2017). Compared to the rest of Canada, the implementation of the Québec family policy and particularly, the CPEs provision, also helped reduce the revenue gap between mothers and women with no children:

> Indeed, Québec mothers who gave birth to their first child in 2001 or later saw their incomes increase more rapidly in subsequent years compared with mothers in the rest of Canada and to mothers in Québec whose first child was born before 2001. This effect of Québec family policies is significant: the long-term wage gap, 10 years after the birth of the first child, is reduced by 39 percentage points for Québec mothers, going from 49 per cent to 10 per cent. In comparison, the gaps for women in the rest of Canada have narrowed from 48 per cent to 41 per cent; this is an improvement, but not of the same order of magnitude as the change in Québec. The net effect of Québec's family policies is therefore 32 percentage points.
>
> (Conolly et al., 2020. Author's translation)

Finally, extended public provision of childcare services has improved the quality of services, with CPEs meeting higher requirements than for-profit or unregulated home care settings (Japel et al., 2005) and receiving far fewer complaints than public daycares (Couturier and Hurteau, 2016). Related to quality, in 2018, more than

90 per cent of CPEs complied with the required qualification ratio of educators (two-thirds of qualified staff)—which represents more than 80 per cent of qualified staff—compared to around 33 per cent of non-subsidized private childcare providers (Vérificateur général du Québec, 2020). The number of qualifications doubled with the mobilization of childcare representatives, and such mobilization efforts also resulted in considerable improvements in working conditions since 1999, including wage increases (Couturier, 2017). For example, in 2011, the unions won a '44 per cent increase in the base stipend that family childcare providers receive, retroactively' (Bellemare and Briand, 2012, 129. Author's translation) as well as improved pensions. This outcome is significant considering that a majority of CPEs workers are women. The improvement of living conditions remains at the heart of union priorities, particularly during the Covid-19 pandemic. Indeed, the *Centrale des syndicats du Québec*[18] fought for salary increases and consistent measures for at-risk educators to ensure their return to work (Colpron et al., 2020).

The policy *process* leading to the development and implementation of the CPEs should be appraised in conjunction with the development of the family policy as a whole. Once the White Paper was made public, an interdepartmental committee was formed, bringing together several important departments and agencies (Revenue, Treasury, Finance, Education, Intergovernmental Affairs, Office des services de garde à l'enfance) with the task of translating the government's orientations into operational mandates (Burlone, 2001). This committee, divided into three subcommittees (one for each of the components of the new policy), was still almost exclusively overseen by the executive branch, namely the *Secrétariat du Comité des priorités* and the Premier's Office. While this approach may seem authoritarian and imposed, it had the merit of speeding up the decision-making process, leading to a swift implementation of the policy.

The involvement of the Department of Finance and the Treasury Board is important to note because of the substantial funding involved. Their role was to ensure that the measures to be implemented complied with the agreed tax relief, the overall budget available, and the rationalization of existing programs, while also being consistent with the objective of achieving a zero deficit. This financial logic, although compatible with the objectives of coherence and simplification central to the policy, was an extremely important consideration that put the finance minister, Bernard Landry, and Premier Bouchard at odds at different points. The education minister, Pauline Marois, was also a key player in the development of the policy (Burlone, 2001). An experienced politician, respected by her colleagues and the premier, she had the necessary perspective to evaluate the proposed reforms in light of past struggles that challenged families and

---

[18] Québec Labour Congress

women.[19] Other ministerial actors involved, who for the most part were recruited by the *Secrétariat du Comité des priorités*, had a secondary role in the deliberations, and mainly focused on providing the interministerial committee with information from their respective sectors of activity (Burlone, 2001).

The time between the drafting of measures, and their implementation, took only a year. This narrow timeframe, unusual for a policy with such a broad scope, posed a major challenge for the actors involved, but was made possible by the underlying collaborative work involved in preparing for the implementation. The interdepartmental committees responsible for developing the policy framework in time for its announcement at the autumn 1996 *Sommet sur l'emploi et l'économie* and for formulating the various instruments played a crucial role, together with a coordinating body directly connected to the premier (Secrétariat du Comité des priorités). These structures, which were activated within a short period of time, facilitated information sharing, informal exchanges, broader consultation of experienced actors, and an ongoing drafting of bills. Québec's organizational structure was transformed with the creation of the *Ministère de la Famille*, the body responsible for implementing the policy. The province had not seen a department dedicated solely to the family unit since the 1960s.

From a *political* perspective, given the scope of the proposed reform and the budgetary context, one might have expected the government to engage in extensive public consultations before or after its announcement, but that was not the case for the 1997 family policy. The impetus behind the work that led to the new family policy came straight from the government, and was rooted in a political commitment towards families in the province (Burlone, 2001). The sector was not in crisis; families were not otherwise being overlooked by the government. Premier Lucien Bouchard, however, insisted on developing an integrated family policy out of personal conviction that a government like Québec's had a duty to have one. The premier was convinced that support for families should be substantial and that the sector as a whole had to be re-examined in order to present a clear direction to Québec families. The matter quickly became a priority and he continued to monitor its progress closely.

Another political element for assessing the success of the implementation of subsidized childcare is the key role played by central agencies in the development of the policy. The fact that the *Secrétariat du Comité des priorités* led the development was an unusual practice. Typically, sector departments develop first drafts, submit them for consultation with stakeholders, and make amendments based on the feedback received. However, not only was the family policy development initiated by the highest political level (the premier), but the draft was prepared by

---

[19] Twenty years earlier, Pauline Marois was the chief of staff to Lise Payette, then minister of state for Social Development and the Status of Women.

professionals from a body that does not engage in policy-making. The Secrétariat du Comité des priorités played an instrumental role in initiating and driving policy development, and in acting as an intermediary between departments and the Privy Council. It was also responsible for drafting the White Paper and integrating the interdepartmental committee's discussions into a comprehensive family policy framework.

As mentioned earlier, the role of the central agencies and the premier in initiating the development of the new family policy came to fruition at an announcement during the *Sommet sur l'emploi et l'économie* in the autumn of 1996. This announcement affirmed the premier's commitment to provide Québec with new measures to help families. Not only did Lucien Bouchard announce new provisions, he also promised to implement them in less than a year. Validated by the entire Executive and Council of Ministers, the principles set out in the policy were made public. Turning back was no longer an option. The strong leadership of the executive in developing the family policy, which was necessary for its rapid implementation (in all, only eight months separated the publication of the White Paper and the implementation of the policy), generated some tension and resistance. The departments involved were all important and, in theory, were of equal status. In practice, however, some, such as the Department of Finance, dictated the rules of the game. Prime-ministerial leadership, backed by strong public support for the proposed policy, transformed the policy development processes and, in this instance, helped secure cabinet and parliament backing.

In terms of an *endurance* assessment, the system has flourished across the province. There were 993 CPEs in Québec in 2020, spearheading a set of complementary measures that have proven to be appropriate instruments for achieving initial policy objectives. Over the years, the number of CPE places increased (either in facilities or in home care settings) up until the change in government in 2003, where the proportion of CPEs developed in relation to the entire range of childcare services diminished to the advantage of for-profit facilities. CPEs still benefit from very strong public support and have been maintained (albeit transformed) under the three successive governments since the defeat of the Parti Québécois in 2003. Their popularity has also not vanished since the early 2000s, as they continue to be victims of their own success: supply cannot meet the demand, extending wait times for families to obtain a subsidized place.

Under the Charest Government, CPEs were subjected to budget cuts of approximately $260 million between 2006 and 2014, and tax credits were offered to users of commercial childcare centres. And as discussed earlier, in 2015, the Couillard Government imposed means-tested user contribution fees while delaying the creation of new childcare places until 2021. At that point, the future of the policy looked uncertain. Yet, the political pendulum swung again, and the newly elected Legault government abolished the users' annual contribution in 2019 and announced a plan in 2021 to improve access to early learning and childcare services,

112 QUÉBEC'S SUBSIDIZED CHILDCARE NETWORK

which included streamlining the construction CPEs to address the shortage of subsidized spaces.

Conclusion: The Driving Forces of Success

With the development of its 1997 family policy, and particularly the establishment of a network of subsidized childcare services, Québec reaffirmed its characteristic support for the social economy. It is this commitment to social innovation that makes Québec a leading province in several areas and sets it apart from other Canadian provinces (Vaillancourt, 2002). Arsenault et al. (2018) propose three explanations as to why Québec's childcare measures have not extended beyond the province's borders. The first one has to do with the party in power at the time the family policy was developed. Indeed, the PQ, a leftist party, put forward social measures that couldn't be implemented by a Liberal government. The second explanation relates to the fact that, in Québec, interest groups are more focused on the provincial level than groups in other provinces, who prefer targeting the federal government. As seen in this chapter, groups have been, and still continue to be, very active in the development of affordable childcare services. Finally, the fact that the province of Québec's political party system is less polarized contributed to the endurance of the policy, as both the Liberal government and the current CAQ (Coalition Avenir Québec) government have maintained and invested in the program.

The prevailing context also had a role to play in the success of CPEs. The pro-natalist provisions established under the 1987 policy had not yielded the expected results. Active women in the labour market were demanding work-life balance measures, existing childcare services were no longer meeting demand, and women's and family movements were pressuring the government to implement programs that would facilitate labour market integration or reintegration (Dandurand, 2020). The context was therefore conducive to change. As premier, Lucien Bouchard was able to take advantage of a window of opportunity. The political momentum, the socio-economic context, and the specific actors called upon to participate in the policy development were all favourable to the introduction of a major reform for Québec's families. Childcare services were specifically what parents wanted. The system in place was ripe to be transformed. The abolition and rationalization of some existing programs from the previous policy also allowed the government to immediately allocate large budgets to an ambitious program (around 40 per cent of the budget for families was allocated in direct subsidies).

While political leadership in the shape of direct involvement by the premier was certainly a factor propelling the policy forward, the minister leading the project, Pauline Marois, also had an important role to play. Her presence, status, and authority within the PQ government and her strong commitment to seeing family policy become a reality must be factored into the success of the policy. Mrs. Marois was given responsibility over the new *Ministère de l'Enfance et de la Famille* created with the policy, and she used this responsibility to allow the implementation of the new system to proceed apace.

Another driving force, both of a political and process nature, was the interoganizational structure that was set up to craft the policy and administer the system. The *Secrétariat du Comité des priorités*, by bringing together strategic actors from relevant departments, made it possible to swiftly materialize the premier's wishes. This political will translated into clear objectives: equal opportunities for young Québecers and access to the labour market for women. CPEs provided the structure for a better work-family balance. Sometimes, very clear, definite, and somewhat imperative political will can help push forward issues that, at other times, would take too long to succeed (Anderson, 1997). This case shows that when governments have a firm intention to accomplish something, no matter how many departments and agencies are involved, and no matter how compressed the time frame is, policy objectives can be realized.

The 1997 policy and its childcare services offered in CPEs were transformed by successive governments that followed the Parti Québécois. Today, private childcare centres are more present, parents' daily contribution has increased, and the number of CPEs and available places still does not meet the demand. Nevertheless, Québec's CPE remains an exceptional service in Canada, providing affordable and quality childcare. While it has not been adopted by other Canadian provinces, the federal government intends to draw inspiration from this policy to create a national network of affordable childcare services (Lafontaine-Émond, 2021). Indeed, the 2021 federal budget includes $4 billion in funding to help Canadian provinces build similar services. This important decision reinforces the idea that quality, affordable, and accessible childcare is a cornerstone of effective family policy. Programs such as CPEs are key instruments that have multiple effects, including fostering equal opportunity and educational success, reducing obstacles to women's integration into the workforce, addressing poverty issues, and supporting economic growth.

References

Anderson, G. 1997. "The New Focus on the Policy Capacity of the Federal Government." *Canadian Public Administration* 39 (4): pp. 469–488. https://doi.org/10.1111/j.1754-7121.1996.tb00146.x

Arsenault, G., O. Jacques, and A. Maioni. 2018. "Les services de garde subventionnés : l'exception du Québec dans le contexte fédéral." *Étude IRPP* 67. https://doi.org/10.26070/76ah-vk19

Baillargeon, D. 1996. "Les politiques familiales au Québec. Une perspective historique." *Lien social et politiques* 36: pp. 21–32. https://doi.org/10.7202/005052ar

Baker, M. 1990. "Family Policy in Québec." Library of Parliament, BP-226E 167.

Baker, M. 1994. *Tendances et politiques relatives aux familles : les politiques gouvernementales face aux familles canadiennes en transition.* Institut Vanier de la famille.

Baker, M. 2001. *Families: Changing Trends in Canada,* 4th edn. Toronto: McGraw-Hill Ryerson.

Baker, M., J. Gruber, and K. Milligan. 2008. "Universal Child Care, Maternal Labor Supply, and Family Well-Being." *Journal of Political Economy* 116 (4): pp. 709–745. doi:10.1086/591908.

Bellemare, G. and L. Briand. 2012. "La syndicalisation des services de garde au Québec : à pratiques innovatrices, des concepts nouveaux." *La revue de l'Ires* 4 (5): pp. 117–141. doi:https://doi.org/10.3917/rdli.075.0117.

Bergeron, J. 2005. "Femmes, mères et travailleuses devant l'absence d'une politique nationale de garde des enfants." In *Femmes et politiques: L'État en mutation,* edited by D. Masson, 105–136. Ottawa: Les Presses de l'Université d'Ottawa.

Bertrand, M. 2017. "Les CPE ont permis de faire reculer la pauvreté au Québec." Radio-Canada, 2 May 2017. https://ici.radio-canada.ca/nouvelle/1031407/cpe-enfants-garderies-permis-recul-pauvrete-femmes-marche-travail

Bouchard, C., V. Labrie and A. Noël. 1996. *Chacun sa part. Rapport de trois membres du comité externe de réforme de la sécurité du revenu.* Montréal: ministère de la Sécurité du revenu, Gouvernement du Québec. https://www.emploiquebec.gouv.qc.ca/publications/pdf/SR_chacun_sa_part_rapport.pdf

Bouchard, J., M. Fortin, and M. Hautval. 2017. "Des droits des mères à ceux des enfants? Les réformes du régime québécois de pensions alimentaires pour enfants." *Droit et société* 95 (1): pp. 13–26. https://doi.org/10.3917/drs.095.0013

Burlone, N. 2001. *L'impact de la coordination interministérielle sur l'élaboration des politiques publiques: une exploration des facteurs de performance.* Thèse de doctorat École nationale d'administration publique.

Burlone, N. 2009. "Le sens de la famille: Réflexion autour du choix des instruments de politique familiale." *Économie et Solidarité* 38 (2): pp. 105–121.

Burlone, N. 2013. "Linéarité des politiques publiques et temporalités individuelles." In *Repenser la famille et ses transitions. Repenser les politiques publiques,* edited by S. Gaudet, N. Burlone, and M. Lévesque, pp. 181–201. Québec : Les Presses de l'Université Laval.

Burlone, N. and J.-P. Couture. 2011. "Gouvernance et choix des instruments de politique familiale: De la logique des systèmes au monde vécu." In *L'État et la société civile sous le joug de la gouvernance,* edited by C. Rouillard and N. Burlone, pp. 120–151. Québec :Les Presses de l'Université Laval.

Clavet, N.-J., J.-Y. Duclos. 2014. "Le soutien financier à la garde d'enfants: les effets sur le travail des femmes, le revenu des familles et les finances publiques." *Canadian Public Policy/Analyse de Politiques* 40 (3): pp. 224–244.

Colpron, S., L. Leduc, and H. Pilon-Larose. 2020. "CPE: Hier encore, j'étais à risque et là, je ne le suis plus?" *La Presse.* 7 May 2020. https://www.lapresse.ca/covid-19/2020-05-07/cpe-hier-encore-j-etais-a-risque-et-la-je-ne-le-suis-plus

Conolly, M., M. M. Fontaine, and C. Haeck. 2020. *Les politiques familiales du Québec évaluées à partir des trajectoires de revenus d'emploi des parents et des personnes sans enfant.* Montréal: Cirano. http://cirano.qc.ca/files/publications/2020RP-05.pdf

Couturier, E.-L. 2017. *De gardienne d'enfant à éducatrice en garderie.* Montréal: IRIS. http://www.aqcpe.com/content/uploads/2017/03/2017-iris-de-gardienne-denfants-a-educatrice-en-garderie.pdf

Couturier, E.-L. and P. Hurteau. 2016. *Les services de garde au Québec : champ libre au privé*. Montréal: IRIS. https://cdn.iris-recherche.qc.ca/uploads/publication/file/Services_de_garde_WEB.pdf

Dandurand, R.-B. 2020. "La politique québécoise *Les enfants au cœur de nos choix :* un pari audacieux néanmoins gagnant." *Enfances Familles Générations* 35. http://journals.openedition.org/efg/10191

Dandurand, R.-B. and M. Kempeneers. 2002. "Pour une analyse comparative et contextuelle de la politique familiale au Québec." *Recherches sociographiques* 43 (1): pp. 49–78. https://doi.org/10.7202/009446ar

Dandurand, R.-B. and M.-H. Saint-Pierre. 2000. "Les nouvelles dispositions de la politique familiale québécoise. Un retournement ou une évolution prévisible ?" In *Comprendre la famille (1999) : Actes du 5e symposium québécois de recherche sur la famille*, edited by M. Simard and J. Alary, pp. 59–80. Quebec City: Les Presses de l'Université du Québec.

Fortin, P., 2017. "Twelve Flawed Statements of the Fraser Institute on Quebec's Childcare Program." OISE. April. https://www.oise.utoronto.ca/atkinson/UserFiles/File/Policy%20Commentaries/PFortin_Twelve_Flawed_Statements_of_the_Fraser_Institute.pdf

Fortin, P., L. Godbout, and S. St-Cerny. 2013. "L'impact des services de garde à contribution réduite du Québec sur le taux d'activité féminin, le revenu intérieur et les budgets gouvernementaux." *Revue Interventions économiques* 47. https://doi.org/10.4000/interventionseconomiques.1858

Gingras, L., A. Lavoie, and N. Audet. 2015a. *Enquête québécoise sur la qualité des services de garde éducatifs—Grandir en qualité 2014, tome 2 : Qualité des services de garde éducatifs dans les centres de la petite enfance (CPE)*. Montréal: Institut de la statistique du Québec.

Gingras, L., A. Lavoie, and N. Audet. 2015b. *Enquête québécoise sur la qualité des services de garde éducatifs—Grandir en qualité 2014, tome 3 : Qualité des services de garde éducatifs dans les garderies non subventionnées*. Montréal: Institut de la statistique du Québec.

Gouvernement du Québec. 1997. "Note pour une allocution du premier ministre du Québec monsieur Lucien Bouchard à l'occasion de la nouvelle politique familiale." AQCPE. January. https://www.aqcpe.com/actualites/2017/01/allocution-de-lucien-bouchard-23-janvier-1997/

Harding, A. 2018. "The Effect of Government Transfer Programs on Low-Income Rates: A Gender-Based Analysis, 1995 to 2016". Ottawa, ON: Statistics Canada, no. 75F0002M. https://www150.statcan.gc.ca/n1/en/pub/75f0002m/75f0002m2018003-eng.pdf

Japel, C., R. E. Tremblay, and S. Côté. 2005. "Quality Counts! Assessing the Quality of Daycare Services Based on the Quebec Longitudinal Study of Child Development." *IRPP Choice* 11 (4): pp. 1–44.

Jenson, J. 2002. "Against the Tide. Childcare in Quebec." In *Child Care Policy at the Crossroads: Gender and Welfare State Restructuring*, edited by S. Michel and R. Mahon, pp. 61–78. New York: Routledge.

Jenson, J, M. Sineau, F. Bimbi, A. Daune-Richard, V. Della Sala, R. Mahon, B. Marques-Pereira, O. Paye, and G. Ross. 2001. *Who Cares? Women's Work, Childcare, and Welfare State Redesign*. Toronto: University of Toronto Press. doi:10.3138/9781442683389

Lafontaine-Émond, I. 2021. *Early Childhood and Care in Canada*. Library of Parliament, Background paper 2021-07-E. https://lop.parl.ca/staticfiles/PublicWebsite/Home/ResearchPublications/BackgroundPapers/PDF/2021-07-e.pdf

Le Bourdais, C. 1989. "Politique familiale ou politique nataliste : un enjeu de taille pour les femmes." *Revue canadienne de santé mentale* 8(2): pp. 83–102. https://doi.org/10.7202/031543ar

Lemieux, D. 2011. "La revendication d'une politique familiale : un mouvement québécois forgé dans le creuset de la Révolution tranquille, 1960–1990." *Enfances, Familles, Générations* 15: pp. 23–44. https://doi.org/10.7202/1008144ar

Mathieu, S. 2016. "From the Defamilialization to the "Demotherization" of Care Work." Social Politics 23 (4): pp. 576–591. https://doi.org/10.1093/sp/jxw006

Mathieu, S. 2019. "La transformation de l'offre de services de garde au Québec : une brèche dans la collectivisation du travail de reproduction sociale ?" *Revue canadienne de sociologie* 56 (2): pp. 204–223. https://doi.org/10.1111/cars.12243

McConnell, A. 2010. "Policy Success, Policy Failure and Grey Areas In-Between." *Journal of Public Policy* 30 (3): pp. 345–362. doi:10.1017/S0143814X10000152

McConnell, A. 2017. "Policy Success and Failure." In *Oxford Research Encyclopedia of Politics*, https://oxfordre-com.proxy.bib.uottawa.ca/politics/view/10.1093/acrefore/9780190228637.001.0001/acrefore-9780190228637-e-137

O'Connor, J. S., A. S. Orloff, and S. Shaver. 1999. *States, Markets, Families: Gender, Liberalism, and Social Policy in Australia, Canada, Great Britain, and the United States*. Cambridge: Cambridge University Press.

Porter, A. 2003. *Gendered States: Women, Unemployment Insurance and the Political Economy of the Welfare State in Canada, 1945–1997*. Toronto: University of Toronto Press.

Schmitz, S. 2020. "The Impact of Publicly Funded Childcare on Parental Well-Being: Evidence from Cut-Off Rules." *European Journal of Population* 36: pp. 171–196. 10.1007/s10680-019-09526-z

Secrétariat du Comité des priorités du ministère du Conseil exécutif. 1997. *Nouvelles dispositions de la politique familiale : Les enfants au cœur de nos choix*. Quebec City: Gouvernement du Québec.

Vaillancourt, Y. 2002. "Le modèle québécois de politiques sociales et ses interfaces avec l'union sociale canadienne." *Institut de recherche en politiques publiques, Enjeux publics*, 3 (2). https://irpp.org/wp-content/uploads/assets/research/canadian-federalism/new-research-article-2/pmvol3no2f.pdf

Vandenbroeck M. 2020. "Early Childhood Care and Education Policies That Make a Difference." In *The Palgrave Handbook of Family Policy*, edited by R. Nieuwenhuis and W. Van Lancker, pp. 169–191. London: Palgrave Macmillan. https://doi.org/10.1007/978-3-030-54618-2_8

Vérificateur général du Québec. 2020 . *Accessibilité aux services de garde éducatifs à l'enfance. Audit de performance et observations du commissaire au développement durable*. Quebec City: Ministère de la Famille. https://www.vgq.qc.ca/Fichiers/Publications/rapport-annuel/165/vgq_ch02_cpe_web.pdf

White, L. A., S. Prentice, and M. Perlman. 2015. "The Evidence Base for Early Childhood Education and Care Programme Investment: What We Know, What We Don't Know." *Evidence and Policy: A Journal of Research, Debate and Practice* 11 (4): pp. 529–546. doi: 10.1332/174426415X14210818992588

7

Early Years Policy Innovations Across Canada

A Policy Success?

Adrienne Davidson and Linda A. White

Introduction

The Canadian welfare state was largely built on male-breadwinner/female-caregiver norms regarding employment policy, and morally regulative 'cause of need' rather than 'fact of need' social policy provision that discriminated against particular groups of women, especially those marginalized by race, sexuality, and class (Brodie, 2008, 166; Little, 1998; Valverde, 1991). The dominance of the 'worker-citizen' paradigm of a working father and stay-at-home mother as the ideal meant that policymakers tended to cast childcare as a 'women's issue' and primarily as a family responsibility (Dobrowolsky and Jenson, 2004). For those who fell outside the norm of male-breadwinner/female-caregiver norms, such as single mothers, state assistance 'often involved surveillance, conditionality, social stigma, and low levels of provision' (Brodie, 2008, 169).

While this gendered institutional order (Ritter, 2007) embodied by male-breadwinner norms and stigmatized social assistance has largely been replaced by gender equality norms in labour markets and in some social policies, vestiges of the previous gendered institutional order continue to linger in government policies and programs. Gendered understandings of the appropriateness of certain government interventions and, in the case of early years policy, the norms of care, have become embedded within governing structures. As such, despite progressively shifting narratives about early years policy—from family-oriented, to women's rights oriented, to children's rights oriented—these entrenched norms continue to persist in policies and institutions, even as the original political logics behind existing early years policy have broken down. Reforms have also been resisted by socially conservative actors, including Conservative-led federal and provincial governments supportive of the traditional gendered division of responsibility for care (White, 2017).

Adrienne Davidson and Linda A. White, *Early Years Policy Innovations across Canada.*
In: *Policy Success in Canada.* Edited by Evert A. Lindquist et al., Oxford University Press.
© Adrienne Davidson and Linda A. White (2022). DOI: 10.1093/oso/9780192897046.003.0007

Given this context, it is perhaps not surprising that on several important measures, Canada's record on early years policy cannot be claimed as a resounding success. Canada measures well behind its counterparts in the OECD with respect to government investments in children (UNICEF Canada, 2020). Canada has developed a fairly middling policy approach to maternal and parental leave policies. UNICEF (2020, 6) ranks Canada 24th among rich countries, and 26th in terms of support for child poverty. It ranks Canada 28th among rich countries in terms of investments in children and families, including early childhood education and care (ECEC). However, these aggregate indicators mask some important policy diversity within the Canadian federation. Bright spots within the early years landscape—at both the federal and provincial orders of government—warrant exploration, and deserve to be cast as successes in policy development that can either be replicated across other provincial jurisdictions or explored further by other national governments.

Canada's federal system has both created opportunities for and, in some cases, impeded the successful evolution of early years policy. Federal government investment in early years programs is limited by the constitutional division of powers, which grants substantive jurisdiction over social policy to provincial governments. The federal government's use of its spending power for early years policy has waxed and waned over the decades and the federal government has mainly relied on tax instruments and intergovernmental transfers to incentivize provincial action. Ultimately, the bulk of early childhood care and education (ECEC) programming lies with provincial governments, which regulate care provision, make determinations over social assistance for care (e.g. public subsidies), and develop policy around early learning.

To capture the resultant complexity, this chapter covers early years policy innovations across both the federal and provincial orders of government in Canada. We examine the federal Child Tax Benefit (CTB) program, first introduced in 1992, and expanded and consolidated in the Canada Child Benefit (CCB) in 2016; Ontario's full-day kindergarten (FDK) model introduced in 2011; and Québec's maternity and parental leave benefits introduced in 2006. We touch briefly on Québec's subsidized childcare model as part of the larger suite of family policies introduced by Québec in the 1990s and early 2000s, but as this policy is given a much fuller exploration by Burlone in Chapter 6 in this volume, we have condensed our analysis of it. We investigate the political and policy design features that have contributed to these varied policy successes, both within the jurisdiction adopting the innovation, and across jurisdictions. In each of the three policies profiled in this chapter, we begin by reviewing the ideational and institutional evolution of early years policy.

We highlight the role of the federal government in leading the ideational shifts seen throughout the decades (through several commissions and task forces on the issue), while also illustrating how, and in what ways, the federal and provincial governments have innovated on institutional design and implementation.

In providing this history, we consider the scope and limits of policy paradigm change around children and families and maternal employment. Our chapter pays particular attention to post-1990 reforms that entailed a paradigm shift in policy-making to focus on the child rather than mothers (Dobrowolsky and Jenson, 2004) and human capital development concerns (Prentice, 2009) as part of an anti-poverty and child school readiness strategy; to use tax instruments directed to families rather than funding program development; and to ignore feminist arguments around gender equality in care and employment (with the important exception of policy developments in Québec in the 1990s).

A Broadly Based Policy Success

In exploring questions of policy success, federal systems such as Canada offer an opportunity to examine several jurisdictions for examples of promising policy innovations. Literature that examines the role of veto points and veto players on policy innovation notes that federalism is one of the key institutionally generated veto points that can make it difficult to construct a win-set to alter the status quo (Stepan and Linz, 2011, 844). Scholars have argued that federalism is gendered; federal structures, practices, policy arrangements, and intergovernmental relations often affect men and women differently, and provide these groups with different opportunities to make change (Vickers, 2012; Gray, 2010). Nonetheless, federalism maintains the potential to advance policy innovation (Chappell and Curtin, 2012), and is a key factor shaping the dynamics of government investment in early years policy development.

In order to measure policy success, we look to both provincial and federal orders of government to identify potential policies for analysis. We apply the same set of metrics across both orders of government, exploring the degree to which our cases of provincial and federal policy innovation meet the metrics of success regarding programmatic, process, and political features, as well as policy consolidation over time (see Table 7.1). These ratings are grounded in an analysis of the empirical case studies that follow. While we indicate our overall assessment in dichotomous (success/not) terms, our case analysis examines the degrees of success on each of these dimensions.

This chapter examines the political and policy design features that explain these varied policy successes. As one of the clear promises of federalism is the potential of 'successful' policies to be taken up and emulated, we conclude with an exploration of policy emulation. We discuss the relatively uneven experience of policy emulation of these policies across provinces. While Ontario's 2011 FDK policy has seen considerable emulation, Québec's suite of family policies, including subsidized childcare and a more robust parental leave program, have seen a much more limited uptake across the Canadian federation. We trace this variability to

120 EARLY YEARS POLICY INNOVATIONS ACROSS CANADA

Table 7.1 Metrics of Success

Case	Jurisdiction	Metrics of Success—'Performance'			
		Programmatic	Process	Political	Endurance
Canada Child Benefit	Federal	✓	✓	✓	✓
Full-Day Kindergarten	Ontario	✓	✓	✓	✓
Maternity/Parental Leave	Québec	✓	✓	✓	✓
Subsidized Childcare	Québec	✓	✓	✓	~

important differences in the policy ideas and narratives that shaped provincial policy debates and explore the implications for the future evolution of early years policy in Canada.

Case Study 1: Canada Child Benefit

Despite playing an important role in shaping the evolving narrative around early years policy, the federal government has largely been reticent to engage in the development of early childhood education and care (ECEC). Instead, the federal government has relied primarily on its tax and transfer capabilities to carve out a more limited role in early years policy, but one which nonetheless affects the lives of children and families throughout Canada. Prime Minister Trudeau's 2016 announcement of the Canada Child Benefit (CCB) marked the consolidation (and enrichment) of federal early years policy. The CCB combined several existing cash transfers, both income-tested and universal, into a cash transfer for parents of young children. The existing benefit itself is a tax-free payment of up to $6,400 per child under the age of 6, and $5,400 per child for children aged 6–17. Total payments begin phasing out at net household incomes above $30,000, but with the enhanced benefit structure, most families found themselves better off under the new CCB. The CCB—like its predecessors—was aimed at reducing child and family poverty and improving the lives of lower- and middle-income families. Yet, in consolidating and expanding the existing framework (both eligibility and the progressivity of benefits), the federal government—once again—largely left the provision of ECEC to the provinces.

Contexts, Challenges, and Agents

Calls for a more comprehensive policy approach to reconciling work and family life date back to the Royal Commission on the Status of Women, which released its report in December 1970 (Bégin, 1992). Among its 167 recommendations, the Royal Commission recommended that the federal government establish a national maternity leave program and that 'the federal government immediately take steps to enter into agreement with the provinces [and territories] leading to the adoption of a national Day-Care Act' (Government of Canada, 1970, 411). The Commission specifically recommended a cost-sharing model to build and run childcare centres that met a minimum standard threshold for quality, including cost sharing for operating costs, and (for the first seven years) cost-sharing of capital expenses, as well.

While the recommendations did not lead to immediate political uptake or implementation, they cemented childcare as a policy issue worthy of the national spotlight and childcare became a fixture on political agendas over the next several decades. In 1984, Prime Minister Pierre Trudeau set up a federal Task Force on Childcare. Like the Royal Commission before it, the Task Force recommended that the federal government develop a national and universal childcare program, to be designed and managed provincially (Status of Women Canada, 1986). However, the timing of the report was less than ideal; a recent federal election had resulted in a change in the governing political party, and the report was shelved. The new government under Prime Minister Mulroney convened a Special Parliamentary Committee on Childcare whose recommendations led to the introduction of Bill C-144, The Canada Childcare Act. However, the proposed legislation was opposed by childcare groups, such as the Canadian Day Care Advocacy Association (1988), for a number of reasons, including the funding of commercial childcare. Thus, following the 1988 federal election, the issue once again fell off the agenda. Federal investments to increase childcare spaces were part of the Liberal Party's 1993 election platform (the 'Red Book'). However, once elected, the new government faced significant deficits which, combined with the politics of a post-referendum Québec, pushed the creation of a comprehensive childcare policy to the back of the federal political agenda.

Design and Choice

Throughout the 1990s, the childcare policy debate at the federal level experienced a broad narrative shift about the nature of the policy problem. Whereas the 1970s and 1980s focused on childcare as a feminist and women's equality issue, the 1990s focused increasingly on the child, with solutions designed to supplement the incomes of low-income families and reduce child poverty (Dobrowlowsky and Jenson, 2004). Additionally, a growing consensus amongst federal policy actors asserted that ECEC was primarily a provincial problem, one which the federal government could supplement in part through intergovernmental transfers, and more directly through federal tax relief for families. This jurisdictional divide, combined with the changing nature of the policy narrative, saw the federal government increasingly focus its attention on child poverty as the 'problem' worth solving. Moreover, the government addressed the problem through relatively straightforward tax credits and tiered income benefits, policy designs that could be implemented without raising jurisdictional concerns, and which would easily build on its existing policy capacity and history within this field. Thus, in 1992, the federal Conservative government under Prime Minister Mulroney eliminated the universal family allowance and created a more targeted Child Tax Benefit (CTB). The CTB was designed for low- and middle-income parents of children aged 0–17, delivered as a refundable tax credit, which was means tested, and based on the number of eligible children in a family. The CTB also included a supplement for low-income working parents (the Working Income Supplement).

Financial restructuring by the federal Liberal government in the mid-1990s led to the elimination of the Canada Assistance Plan (CAP). CAP had treated childcare like other welfare services, stipulating that federal funds only be used for services for low-income families. Under the CAP, the federal government had funded 50 per cent of provincial subsidies to provide regulated and non-profit childcare for low-income families (Friendly and White, 2007, 187). However, the 1995 federal budget introduced the Canada Health and Social Transfer (CHST), a block funded program that replaced a number of programs including the CAP. The move to the CHST eliminated federal targeted childcare funding, leaving provincial governments wholly funding childcare subsidy programs.

In 1998, the federal government expanded family benefits by transforming the CTB into the more comprehensive Canada Child Tax Benefit (CCTB). Compared to the CTB, the new CCTB increased benefits to all low-income families and removed work requirements associated with the Working Income Supplement. The CCBT also included the Child Disability Benefit for low- and moderate-income families caring for children with disabilities. The CCTB was also augmented with a new program—the National Child Benefit (NCB) Supplement—designed to specifically target low-income families with children. Under the NCB, the federal government provided low-income families with a cash benefit supplement.

In its earliest form, the NCB was ill-received by social groups as being both too little, in terms of the amount of the benefit, and too targeted in nature. Additionally, there was very little consciousness about the program itself (Battle and Mendelson, 1998). Another downside of the NCB was that provinces could—at their discretion—subtract the dollar value of the NCB benefit from provincial social assistance (welfare) supports to families (Milligan and Stabile, 2009). While those cost 'savings' could then be applied to other provincial programs and child benefits, provinces turned those savings into a variety of provincial approaches and supports (Milligan and Stabile, 2011). By the end of the 1990s, federal policymakers and provincial policymakers alike had largely turned their attention away from ECEC policy, and instead focused on the development and introduction of tax mechanisms to support low-income families.

Delivery and Endurance

The federal policy focus continued to shift during the early 2000s, as the scientific community began to consolidate around a social investment framework for early childhood programming (and as federal finances began to stabilize after years of hawkish deficit reduction policies) (White, 2017). In response, political discourse moved briefly beyond the tax and transfer system and the discussion at the federal level became less about whether to create a national childcare program and more about how to do so.

Intergovernmental dynamics remained paramount, with questions around financing and whether provinces would agree to any strings. Nonetheless, in the early 2000s, the federal Liberal government under Jean Chrétien signed two major funding agreements with provincial governments: the Early Childhood Development Initiative in 2000, and the Multilateral Framework Agreement on Early Learning and Childcare in 2004. That latter agreement committed provincial governments to invest in childcare that met the 'QUAD' principles: that is, of high quality, universally inclusive, accessible, and developmentally appropriate (Friendly and White, 2007, 189). The minority Liberal government under Paul Martin committed to expanding early learning and childcare financing, striking bilateral deals with provincial governments in 2004–2005 to spend $5 billion over five years on registered childcare (Collier and Mahon, 2008, 111).

This investment frame, however, was highly politicized and contested. In the lead-up to the 2006 election, Conservative Leader Stephen Harper took aim at the bilateral accords, casting them as out of touch with the needs and wants of Canadian parents. He accused the government as wanting to make childcare choices for parents by ploughing 'all available money into one option, that of supporting institutional day care centres' (White, 2017, 211). When the 2006 federal election toppled the Liberal government, the new Conservative minority government withdrew from the bilateral agreements. Instead, the Conservative government diverted the intergovernmental transfers into the creation of yet another cash transfer to parents in the form of the Universal Child Care Benefit (UCCB). The UCCB distributed a taxable benefit of $100 per month per child under the age of six (Collier and Mahon, 2008, 110). Meanwhile, the NCB and CCTB remained intact. In 2015, the UCCB was increased to $160 per month per child under six, with an additional $60 per month for children aged 6–17 (Government of Canada, 2018).

The most recent iteration of this policy has been expansionary in nature. In 2016, under the frame of assisting the 'middle class and those seeking to join it', the newly elected Liberal government of Prime Minister Justin Trudeau introduced the Canada Child Benefit (CCB). The new CCB replaced the Universal Child Care Benefit (UCCB), Canada Child Tax Benefit (CCTB), and National Child Benefit (NCB)—streamlining all three federal programs into a single means-tested cash

124 EARLY YEARS POLICY INNOVATIONS ACROSS CANADA

payment to parents of children aged 0–17. In removing the universality of the UCCB, Trudeau commented that the only parents who would be 'losing out' under the new benefits scheme were those at the highest household incomes.

Conclusion

Despite moments of federal political interest in supporting provinces in ECEC delivery (most notably the bilateral federal-provincial agreements under Prime Minister Paul Martin), for the most part (and until very recently), the federal government has 'stayed in its lane' and limited its engagement in early years policy to cash transfers. The CTB, first introduced in 1992, has been added onto, transformed, supplemented, and ultimately consolidated over successive Liberal and Conservative governments. Its bipartisan support suggests a policy framework that is relatively robust and unlikely to see significant retrenchment in the future. While the 2016 CCB suggested that the current government was content to stay within the cash transfer realm, hints of a more interventionist federal government approach became more visible in federal spending priorities. In 2017, under the Multilateral Early Learning and Child Care Framework the federal and provincial and territorial governments developed bilateral agreements. Through these agreements, the federal government provided $1.2 billion over three years to provinces to make ECEC enhancements and increase licensed childcare spaces (Government of Canada, 2020a). In the April 2021 federal budget, the Liberal government pledged $30 billion over five years of conditional grants to finance a national ECEC system (Government of Canada, 2021a). This pledge became a cornerstone proposal in the 2021 federal election, which the Liberal party won, forming a minority government. The 2021 federal budget committed $30 billion over five years, with $9.2 billion every year thereafter, with the funds directed at reducing fees for ECEC to an average of $10 per day in regulated care, increasing the number of regulated childcare spaces across provinces, and supporting training and wage enhancements for ECEC workers (Government of Canada, 2021b). As of writing, ten provinces and three territories have signed bilateral agreements with the federal government, with details regarding implementation to follow.

Case Study 2: Ontario Full-Day Kindergarten

Provinces have substantive responsibility for the development and implementation of childcare and education policies. The ideational shifts present in the evolving federal policy focus were, in many ways, mirrored at the provincial level as provincial governments recognized the need for what have been labelled as social investment policies and programs (Garritzmann et al., 2018; Häusermann, 2018).

As the federal government eschewed more interventionist means of engaging in the policy space, relying primarily to cash-transfer mechanisms for policy alleviation, provincial policy actors have played an important role in reforming early years policy, subject to the vagaries of provincial politics. Provinces have developed a range of programs aimed at subsidizing the cost of childcare for low-income parents, invested in free early-years programming for families, and in some cases (Québec, and increasingly British Columbia) engaged in significant investments in creating high quality and low cost childcare. One area that has seen provincial-level policy innovation in early years policy through the lens of social investment is the expansion of public education systems to include full-day kindergarten. While provincial funding for *childcare* has been fairly modest (with the notable exception of Québec), provincial governments have moved progressively to expand public education programming to include younger children.

Contexts, Challenges, and Agents

Until the early 2000s, only three provinces provided full-day kindergarten programming for five-year-olds. New Brunswick had developed a voluntary program in 1992, while Québec and Nova Scotia introduced voluntary programs in 1997. Both Nova Scotia and New Brunswick transformed their programs into mandatory full-day kindergarten in 1998 (CNLEEC, 2010). Interest in early learning of this form largely stalled until the 2000s, as provincial governments began to take up the new policy narrative around the social investment frame, tapping into the emerging scientific consensus around the long-range social and economic benefits associated with early childhood education (White, 2017). Leading the way on this new form of early years investment was the Province of Ontario, which launched a provincial commission to study full day kindergarten in 2007, and implemented its FDK program for four- and five-year-olds in 2010.

The election of a Liberal government under Dalton McGuinty in 2003 marked the start of an important shift in early learning investments. After years of political strife between educators and the former Conservative government of Mike Harris (and briefly Ernie Eves), McGuinty styled himself as the 'education premier' looking to reinvest in public education, improve provincial literacy and numeracy rates, improve high school graduation rates, and mend relations with the teachers' unions (Campbell, 2020)

While childcare investments did not make up much of its first election platform, once elected, the McGuinty government took a more expansive view towards early years policy. It began by creating a new Ministry of Children and Youth Services, which was tasked with developing Ontario's Best Start strategy. Introduced in 2005, the Best Start Plan included investments in quality and affordable childcare, a new policy around childcare subsidies—moving from a means assessment to an income assessment—and a new college of early childhood educators to establish and maintain professional standards. Importantly, Best Start marked a notable shift in the provincial narrative of policy interventions, moving from anti-poverty to a narrative of social investment (including the need to invest in children to improve the future economy, address school readiness, and promote equal educational opportunities for children from all backgrounds). Government communications announcing the strategy noted that 'Best Start will provide many more families with easy, affordable access to services and supports, so that all Ontario children can arrive in Grade 1 healthy, ready, and eager to learn' (Government of Ontario, 2005). Largely missing from the conversation, however, was any mention of closing the gap in maternal labour force participation and women's equality in the workplace; moreover, the plan still took on a mostly targeted approach, with the identification of priority neighbourhoods and communities for early policy implementation.

While Best Start was introduced in 2005, it was not until the 2007 provincial election that the McGuinty government began to move substantively on full-day kindergarten. Unlike in 2003, the 2007 election campaign foregrounded early years policy as an election issue: in its provincial election platform, the government committed to 'appoint an Early Learning Advisor to advise the Premier on developing and funding a full-day pre-school program' (Ontario Liberal Party, 2007, 18). Immediately after the government's re-election in October 2007, the premier appointed Dr. Charles Pascal as the special advisor on early learning.

Design and Choice

While the Best Start Plan indicated some early design ideas regarding early years learning for four- and five-year-olds (noting an expansion of early learning using junior and senior kindergarten), the government remained open to a range of policy instruments for implementation. Throughout 2008, Dr. Pascal travelled throughout the province convening 83 community fact-finding roundtables. In interviews, Pascal floated 'trial balloons' and raised design ideas such as whether children should be taught by early childhood educators or by teachers, or whether kindergarten classes could be located 'off-site' in non-school buildings such as community centres, childcare centres, churches, and workplaces (Mahoney 2008a). Groups of parents, community organizers, and the broader policy community—including the Elementary Teachers Federation and the Ontario Public School Boards' Association—responded. They favoured a model in which young children would receive 'the best quality education at a school with fully certified teachers delivering the program' (Mahoney 2008b).

Dr. Pascal issued his final report in June 2009; in it, he recommended the implementation of a play-based learning model of full day kindergarten for four- and five-year-olds. He recommended that kindergarten classes be taught by a certified teacher, with an early childhood educator (ECE) in the classroom to assist with learning. Finally, he recommended that the new full-day expansion be located in schools, to enable seamless services for before and after school care. Shortly following the release of the report, the McGuinty government announced its full support of the recommendations. Implementation began in September 2010 with schools in priority low-income neighbourhoods and areas where capital development was not needed (Ontario Office of the Premier, 2009). By 2014, full implementation of full-day kindergarten was largely complete.

Delivery and Endurance

Within the province of Ontario, full-day kindergarten has proven remarkably resilient, both programmatically and politically. The engagement of both experts and the public in the process of designing the program resulted in a policy design that has proven to be both enormously popular and quickly institutionalized (Millar et al., 2020). While technically voluntary in nature, parental take-up of the program has been very high, with over 90 per cent of eligible children enrolled in the Ontario FDK program. Given its popularity, the program's design and price tag have been able to withstand both political and administrative attempts to undermine it.

The first attempt to undermine the program came just one year into the five-year implementation schedule, during the 2011 provincial election. The election campaign began with then-Opposition leader (and Progressive Conservative party leader) Tim Hudak promising to end the program and associated spending. Facing strong public support for the program, Mr. Hudak reversed his position part way through the election campaign, although the reversal ultimately did not save his campaign (Cohn, 2011). In 2012, the province's commission on public service reform recommended cancelling (or at least delaying) the program as a cost-saving measure for a province facing fiscal tightening after the 2008 financial crisis; Premier McGuinty rejected the suggestion. Most recently (in 2019), current Conservative Premier Doug Ford and his education minister, Lisa Thompson, backtracked on comments that suggested full-day kindergarten for four- and five-year-olds was at risk of cancellation under the new government. The suggestion received significant backlash from Ontario parents and teachers' unions, and any changes were seemingly sidelined from the agenda (Rushowy, 2019). Thus, with over a decade now elapsed following the initial roll-out of the FDK program, funding, program design, and delivery are both intact and largely entrenched.

Conclusion

While the voluntary FDK program is a clear case of both political and programmatic success, provincial governments have been reluctant to move beyond FDK and radically expand regulated childcare in the province. The social investment frame, while successfully utilized for the expansion of *education* to include children age four and five, has not been significantly activated as a rationale for investing in *care* opportunities of younger children. Even the Liberal government under Premier Kathleen Wynne, following a spate of child deaths in unlicensed care in 2015, shied away from implementing a universal licensing system for Home Child Care (HCC) as part of its modernization of childcare legislation and regulations (White et al., 2018). It continues to allow unlicensed HCC facilities to operate in a virtually unregulated manner. Some more recent provincial investments in expanding the availability of public subsidies for low-income families and wage enhancements for childcare workers (under the Wynne government) were largely retracted following the 2018 election of the Conservative government under Doug Ford (Monsebraaten and Rushowy, 2019).

Case Study 3: Québec Maternity and Parental Leave and Investments in Early Childhood Education and Care (ECEC)

While most provincial governments in Canada mirrored the ideational shifts of the evolving federal policy narrative, a notable exception—both narratively and programmatically—is Québec. Like other provinces in the 1990s, the Québec government faced similar financial pressures and demands for deficit reduction; yet, it introduced significant early years and family policy investments which have expanded and endured as a policy regime. As Burlone's chapter in this volume assesses the endurance of Québec's childcare policy, our primary focus is on the maternity and parental leave policies which, along with childcare, labour economists have praised as generally bolstering maternal employment (Baker, Gruber, and Milligan, 2008; Zhang, 2007). However, we will reflect on some of the endurance challenges associated with the entirety of the family-focused policy framework in recent years.

Contexts, Challenges, and Agents

After the defeat of the sovereignty referendum in 1995, the provincial Parti Québécois looked for ways to distinguish itself from the rest of Canada and built a distinct set of social programs reflecting what Arsenault (2018) calls a 'social economy' approach. While the federal and other provincial governments focused their attention on anti-poverty policies and targeted spending to the poorest, most 'deserving' children and families, the Parti Québécois government under Premier Lucien Bouchard responded instead to shifting labour markets and growing demands for policies to balance work and family life. In 1996, Premier Bouchard convened employers, labour union representatives, and other nongovernmental groups at a Summit on the Economy and Employment. The attendant task force's work, along with a 1997 White Paper on family policy, shifted the provincial government's approach away from traditional pro-natalist approaches to family policy (Jenson, 2002; Maroney, 1992) to instead support maternal employment as part of a larger provincial labour market strategy and to improve child development (Arsenault, 2018; Fortin, 2018). Jenson (2002, 312) notes the influence of 'feminists, the family movement, anti-poverty activists, social workers, and experts on development and early childhood education, as well as municipal government and the provincial public sector'.

The pillars of reform included a provincial family allowance in the form of a refundable tax credit that varies by income; government financing of childcare programs for children aged 0–4 years so that parents paid a flat fee of $5 per day; and an expanded system of paid parental leave (Tougas, 2002). The $5 per day scheme rolled out over four years, and was fully implemented in 2000 (Fortin, 2018, 2). A precursor to the reforms in Ontario, the Québec government expanded its voluntary kindergarten program from part- to full-day for all five-year-olds (as well as a small portion of four-year-olds from disadvantaged backgrounds, mostly in the city of Montréal). In advancing a nationalist and feminist policy agenda within the province of Québec, the provincial government largely stepped outside ideational trends in the rest of Canada and began developing policy separate from the federal government. With regard to child benefits, the province elected to stay outside the National Child Benefit (NCB) program introduced by the federal government, instead instituting major reforms to its own child benefits system in 1997 and 2005 (Milligan and Stabile, 2011). Until the 1997 reforms, families were eligible for a family allowance, a young child allowance, and a newborn allowance (Milligan and Stabile, 2011). The allowance increased with the number of children and did not depend on family income. In 1997, these programs were combined into a new family allowance with a minimum level for all families and a claw back for higher income families (Milligan and Stabile, 2011).

Québec's maternity and parental leave was similarly built separate from the federal model. Québec's Parental Insurance Plan (QPIP) program built on, and expanded from, the federal Employment Insurance (EI) architecture. However, the program faced a rockier implementation that involved a protracted battle with the federal government over whether the federal government would agree to reduce its share of EI premiums collected in Québec so the Québec government could collect its own premiums to finance a more generous scheme (White, 2006, 331). The federal and Québec governments finally reached an agreement in 2006 to allow Québec residents to access regular EI and special benefits but held the province responsible for its own maternity and parental leave program (Mathieu et al., 2020, 174). Thus, the program is not severed completely from the federal EI program. And eligibility for both programs rests on labour market attachment (Mathieu et al., 2020, 175).

Design and Choice

QPIP has two components. Parents can choose between a 'basic plan' that covers a longer leave period but at a lower remuneration rate, or a 'special plan' that comprises a shorter number of weeks at a higher wage replacement rate. The basic maternity leave benefits plan pays 70 per cent of average weekly earnings for up to 18 weeks. The special plan pays 75 per cent of average weekly earnings for up to 15 weeks. Parents are also eligible for an additional 32 weeks of parental leave paid at 70 per cent of average weekly earnings for the first 7 weeks, and 55 per cent of average weekly earnings for the other 25 weeks; or 25 weeks at 75 per cent of average weekly earnings. The Québec government also encourages fathers to take up to five weeks of leave paid at 70 per cent of average weekly earnings, or three weeks paid at 75 per cent of average weekly earnings. Additionally, it provides adoption benefits and maternity termination benefits (Government of Québec, 2020).

Québec's plan is thus far more generous than federal EI benefits; as of 2020, parents can receive up to $1,103 per week compared to $573 under federal EI (Mathieu et al., 2020, 175). Moreover, QPIP covers a larger share of workers, including employers, those who are self-employed, engaged in part-time or contract work, and even some students, and there is no unpaid two-week waiting period (McKay et al., 2016). Qualifications are based on flat-rate earnings from the previous year rather than accumulated hours, which means those who may not qualify for benefits under federal EI are eligible for QPIP (Mathieu, 2020, 175). Outside the province of Québec, stricter eligibility requirements mean that many parents are ineligible for paid leave. McKay et al. (2016) found nearly four in ten mothers outside Québec do not qualify, either because they are not employed in jobs that are EI eligible, or they did not accumulate 600 hours of insurable employment prior to applying for leave. Meanwhile in one in three families with a new child, neither parent claims EI family benefits (Robson, 2017, 20).

Delivery and Endurance

While it is difficult to assess the likelihood of policy endurance around QPIP, to date, there have been no significant political or programmatic threats to its maintenance within Québec. One likely factor supporting its endurance is the relatively anemic federal policy framework that exists as the alternative. Québec parents know that they are better off under the current policy regime, fulfilling both the nationalist and feminist visions of the program's early creation.

Other parts of Québec's family policy framework, however, have been more contested. In particular, Québec's record in terms of childcare is more mixed. The universal childcare subsidy program is comprehensively covered in Chapter 6 so we only briefly mention it here. But, as we note below, problems with Québec's childcare model—notably poor quality overall that tracked with the expansion of the commercial sector and family childcare—have emerged. The original coalition of actors who supported educational childcare broke down with the election of provincial Liberal governments in 2003. While the $5 per day flat fee was increased to $7 per day in 2003 by the new Liberal government (Jenson, 2009), the more substantive shift was in how the Liberal government responded to growing demand for care services. Instead of continuing to build capacity through increased public investments in cooperative and not-for-profit models, the Liberal Party responded to increased demand for spaces by permitting the growth of for-profit centres. The government also enabled the expansion of family childcare providers, including unlicensed providers, which has also meant more varied quality of childcare (Fortin, 2018). Access to high quality care is stratified, with higher income families tending to have greater access to the centre-based nonprofit programs and disadvantaged families having to rely on lower quality and unlicensed care (Fortin, 2018; Japel, 2008; Japel et al., 2005). Politically, however, the program remains quite popular, and families in Québec have pushed back against some programmatic changes. In 2015, the flat fee was replaced by a sliding fee scale based on parental income (Fortin, 2018, 2) but in 2019 the CAQ provincial government returned to a flat fee system of $8.35 per day (Famille Québec, 2020).

Conclusion

Québec policy investments are largely successful within-jurisdiction but have faced more narrow success in terms of emulation outside of its borders. We attribute this limited success to divergence in norms and attendant policy frameworks since the 1990s. Both disrupted the liberal welfare model typical to the rest of Canada in favour of a social economy model (Arsenault, 2018; Jenson, 2002), and resulted in very different gendered institutional orders in Québec vs. the rest of Canada currently. Perhaps as work-family norms shift in the rest of Canada, Québec may prove to be a source of policy learning and emulation. Indeed, the recent federal investments reference using the Québec childcare system as a model for affordable and accessible care (Government of Canada, 2021).

Analysis: Lessons from Canada's Early Years Policies

What lessons can be drawn from the case of early years policy development in Canada? And to what extent can we declare Canada to demonstrate policy success? In terms of Canada's economic and social well-being, gender equality norms have not been fully institutionalized although there is evidence that gender equality norms have emerged in Québec. Furthermore, new social investment norms and programs that have been tracked in other OECD countries have been less fully implemented in Canada (Garritzmann et al., 2018; Häusermann, 2018). Some have, though, as we have tracked in the cases examined in this chapter.

The mix (and variety) of provincial and federal action on early years policy draws attention to the fact that solutions to policy problems usually entail more than one policy. This is particularly true in federal states where opportunities for government action may be available at both federal and subnational orders of government, even where jurisdictional boundaries limit action. Federal systems foster opportunities for policy innovation, as well as opportunities for policy learning. The innovations seen at the federal government level have been in areas where the government holds exclusive jurisdiction and has mainly relied on tax instruments and intergovernmental transfers to incentivize provincial action, the most successful being the CTB and variants, most recently the CCB. Policy-makers outside Canada have touted it as a model to the world about how to support families through the federal tax system (Sherman, 2018). We rate this program in its current form a policy success.

With jurisdiction over early years policy held predominantly at the provincial level, we might expect that early years policy would be a space for emulation across the federation. On the question of policy emulation—that is, the degree to which a successful provincial policy framework is adopted or adapted by other governments within the federal system—early years policy suggests that learning is contingent and tied to the narrative frames associated with the different policy proposals put forward, as constituent governments have responded to their population's distinctive values. In this case, 'good ideas' have been left on the table, at the expense of policy effectiveness (Bakvis and Skogstad, 2020).

Of the provincial policies profiled in this chapter, we observe highly variable experiences of policy emulation. On the 'successful' side of policy emulation, the introduction of full-day kindergarten in Ontario triggered uptake by other provinces; its diffusion was likely enabled by its reliance on the narrower framing of the policy goal of education, which built on existing institutions. The policy has been taken up both politically—being advanced as a successful model for improving education and early learning—and programmatically. Whereas FDK was limited to only three provinces in the 1990s, today seven provinces and one territory offer full-day kindergarten for children age five and up, namely: British Columbia, Ontario, Québec, New Brunswick, Nova Scotia, Newfoundland, PEI, and the Northwest Territories (Pelletier, 2017). We are also seeing program expansion by age. The Northwest Territories adopted a similar program to Ontario with FDK beginning age four, and both Québec and Nova Scotia have announced plans to expand early learning through kindergarten and universal preschool programs, also beginning at age four (Lau, 2019; McIsaac and Turner, 2019).

More on the side of 'failed' emulation are the innovative family policies coming out of Québec. Despite the relative success—both politically and programmatically—of the policies that Québec adopted in the 1990s, these policies have largely not diffused outside provincial borders. In terms of horizontal emulation (that is policy uptake by other provinces), only now, over 25 years after Québec's policies were introduced, are we beginning to see steps towards universal government-subsidized childcare. Prior to the federal government's commitments following the 2021 election, the most significant steps had been in British Columbia and Newfoundland, as well as a since-cancelled pilot project in Alberta (CBC News, 2020; CBC News, 2021). However, several of these pilots and programs have primarily emulated the flat-fee portion of the Québec model, ignoring many of the strategic investments in capacity and quality that were so important to the early successes seen in Québec. The Province of British Columbia shows the most promise as a case of policy learning, moving beyond the fee structure to forthcoming investments to assist unlicensed providers in becoming licensed, training early childhood educators, and creating new funds for operating and maintenance costs (Government of British Columbia, 2018; Saltman, 2019). Meanwhile, no other province or territory has shown interest in emulating the parental leave policy introduced by Québec in 2006.

We are also beginning to see evidence of vertical emulation, as the federal government also stands to learn from elements of Québec's early years policy. In the 2020 Fall Economic Update, the federal government announced its intention to invest in early childhood education noting that as 'Saskatchewan once showed Canada the way on healthcare and British Columbia showed Canada the way on pricing pollution, Québec can show us the way on childcare' (Government of Canada, 2020b). The federal government has also emulated aspects of QPIP, although it still leaves many gaps for parents in terms of eligibility and generosity. Compared to the QPIP program, federal benefit rates under both standard and extended benefits, as well as the shared benefit, remain low. Nonetheless, building from the QPIP model, and in an effort to encourage fathers to take parental leave, as of 2019, the federal government added five weeks of a 'Parental Sharing Benefit', providing 'use it or lose it' additional time for a second parent.

Until very recently, outside of Québec, most early years policy has been guided by instrumentalist arguments about preparing children for school (school readiness) and the labour market (job readiness) and as part of anti-poverty strategies. That social investment focus has meant a successful consolidation of only a narrow range of programs. This has meant that institutional arrangements (outside

134 EARLY YEARS POLICY INNOVATIONS ACROSS CANADA

Québec) were predominantly guided by norms about what we can do for kids, not women (Dobrowolsky and Jenson, 2004), a feature well-exposed by the Covid-19 pandemic that has forced mothers to absorb the care and work responsibilities in the home (Johnston et al., 2020). However, with the historical narrowness of federal involvement in childcare now in flux, how these institutional norms and structures intersect with a newly expansionist federal policy will be ripe for exploration and evaluation.

References

Arsenault, G. 2018. "Explaining Québec's Social Economy Turn." *Canadian Journal of Nonprofit and Social Economy Research* 9 (1): pp. 58–75.

Baker, M., J. Gruber, and K. Milligan. 2008. "Universal Childcare, Maternal Labor Supply, and Family Well-being," *Journal of Political Economy*, 116(4): pp. 709–745.

Bakvis, H. and G. Skogstad (eds). 2020. *Canadian Federalism: Performance, Effectiveness, and Legitimacy.* 4th edn. Toronto: University of Toronto Press.

Battle, K. and M. Mendelson. 1998. "The National Child Benefit: Another Hiccup or Fundamental Structural Reform?" Paper prepared for the CSLS Conference on the State of Living Standards and the Quality of Life in Canada, Ottawa, Canada, 30–31 October. Available from: http://www.csls.ca/events/oct98/batt.pdf

Bégin, M. 1992. "The Royal Commission on the Status of Women in Canada: Twenty Years Later." In *Challenging Times: The Women's Movement in Canada and the United States*, edited by D. Flaherty and C. Backhouse, pp. 21–38. Montreal and Kingston: McGill-Queen's University Press.

Brodie, J. 2008. "Putting Gender Back In: Women and Social Policy Reform in Canada." In *Gendering the Nation State: Canadian and Comparative Perspectives*, edited by Y. Abu-Laban, pp. 165–185. Vancouver: University of British Columbia Press.

Campbell, C. 2020. "Educational Equity in Canada: The Case of Onatio's Strategies and Actions to Advance Excellence and Equity for Students. *School Leadership and Management* 41(4-5): pp. 409–428.

Canadian Day Care Advocacy Association. 1988. *Bill C-144: A Critique of the Proposed Canada Child Care Act.* Available from: https://riseupfeministarchive.ca/wp-content/uploads/CDCAAcritiqueofBillC144-1988-1.pdf. Accessed: 24 April 2021.

Canadian Network for Leadership in Education and Early Learning and Care (CN-LEEC). 2010. Early Learning/Kindergarten Programs and Ministry/Department Integration of Education and Child Care in Canada. Vancouver: CECD

CBC News. 2020. "End to Alberta's $25/day Child-Care Program Creates 'Double Blow' for Families." *CBC News.* 2 July. Available from: https://www.cbc.ca/news/canada/edmonton/end-to-alberta-s-25-day-child-care-program-creates-double-blow-for-families-1.5635310. Accessed: 24 April 2021.

CBC News. 2021. "$25-a-Day Daycare Begins in N.L., a 'Weight off our Shoulders' to Lucky Parents." *CBC News.* 7 January. Available from: https://www.cbc.ca/news/canada/newfoundland-labrador/25-a-day-daycare-begins-newfoundland-labrador-1.5862890. Accessed: 24 April 2021.

Chappell, L. and J. Curtin. 2012. "Does Federalism Matter? Evaluating State Architecture and Family and Domestic Violence Policy in Australia and New Zealand." *Publius* 43 (1): pp. 24–43.

Cohn, M. R. 2011. "The Education of Tim Hudak on Full-Day K," *The Toronto Star*, 24 August 2011.

Collier, C. and R. Mahon. 2008. "One Step Forward, Two Steps Back: Child Care Policy from Martin to Harper." In *How Ottawa Spends: A More Orderly Federalism?* edited by A. Maslove, pp. 110–133. Montreal and Kingston: McGill-Queen's University Press.

CRRU (Childcare Resource and Research Unit). 2018. *Early Childhood Education and Care in Canada 2016: Key Findings*. Toronto: CRRU.

Dobrowolsky, A. and J. Jenson. 2004. "Shifting Representations of Citizenship: Canadian Politics of 'Women and Children." *Social Politics* 11 (2): pp. 154–180.

Famille Québec. 2020. "Childcare Services." Government of Quebec. Available from: https://www.mfa.gouv.qc.ca/en/services-de-garde/Pages/index.aspx. Accessed: 24 April 2021.

Fortin, P. 2018. "Québec's Childcare Program at 20." *Inroads: The Canadian Journal of Opinion* 42. Available from: https://inroadsjournal.ca/author/pierre-fortin/. Accessed: 24 April 2021.

Friendly, M. and L. A. White. 2007. "From Multilateralism to Bilateralism to Unilateralism in Three Short Years: Child Care in Canadian Federalism 2003–2006." In *Canadian Federalism: Performance, Effectiveness and Legitimacy*, edited by G. Skogstad and H. Bakvis, pp. 182–204. 2nd edn. Toronto: Oxford University Press.

Garritzmann, J. L., M. R. Busemeyer, and E. Neimanns. 2018. "Public Demand for Social Investment: New Supporting Coalitions for Welfare State Reform in Western Europe?" *Journal of European Public Policy* 25 (6): pp. 844–861.

Government of British Columbia. 2018. "Child Care B.C. Caring for Kids, Lifting up Families: The Path to Universal Child Care. Government of British Columbia. Available from: https://www.bcbudget.gov.bc.ca/2018/childcare/2018_Child_Care_BC.pdf. Accessed: 24 April 2021.

Government of Canada. 1970. *Royal Commission on the Status of Women*. Ottawa: Government of Canada. Available from: http://publications.gc.ca/site/eng/9.699583/publication.html. Accessed: 24 April 2021.

Government of Canada. 2018. *Backgrounder: Strengthening the Canada Child Benefit*. Department of Finance. Available from: https://www.canada.ca/en/department-finance/news/2018/03/backgrounder-strengthening-the-canada-child-benefit.html. Accessed: 24 April 2021.

Government of Canada. 2020a. "Early Learning and Child-Care Bilateral Agreements." Government of Canada. 16 April. Available from: https://www.canada.ca/en/early-learning-child-care-agreement/agreements-provinces-territories.html. Accessed: 24 April 2021.

Government of Canada. 2020b. *Supporting Canadians and Fighting COVID-19: Fall Economic Statement*. Department of Finance. Available from: https://budget.gc.ca/fes-eea/2020/report-rapport/FES-EEA-eng.pdf. Accessed: 24 April 2021.

Government of Canada. 2021a. *Budget 2021: A Recovery Plan for Jobs, Growth, and Resilience*. Department of Finance. Available from: https://www.budget.gc.ca/2021/pdf/budget-2021-en.pdf. Accessed: 24 April 2021.

Government of Canada. 2021b. *Economic and Fiscal Update 2021*. Department of Finance. Available from: https://budget.gc.ca/efu-meb/2021/report-rapport/EFU-MEB-2021-EN.pdf. Accessed: 20 January 2022.

Government of Ontario. 2005. "Three Communities to Showcase McGuinty Government's Best Start Plan." Ontario News Room. 11 March. Available at: https://news.

ontario.ca/archive/en/2005/03/11/three-communities-to-showcase-mcguinty-government039s-best-start-plan.html. Accessed: 24 April 2021.

Government of Québec. 2020. "Québec Parental Insurance Plan." Quebec Government. 22 September. Available at: https://www.rqap.gouv.qc.ca/en/what-is-the-Québec-parental-insurance-plan. Accessed: 24 April 2021.

Gray, G. 2010. "Federalism, Feminism and Multilevel Governance: The Elusive Search for Theory?" In *Federalism, Feminism, and Multilevel Governance*, edited by M. Haussman and J. Vickers, pp. 19–33. Vermont: Ashgate.

Häusermann, S. 2018. "The Multidimensional Politics of Social Investment in Conservative Welfare Regimes: Family Policy Reform between Social Transfers and Social Investment." *Journal of European Public Policy* 25 (6): pp. 862–877.

Japel, C. 2008. "Factors of risk, vulnerability, and school readiness among preschoolers: Evidence from Quebec." *IRPP Choices* 14 (16): 1–42

Japel, C., R.E. Tremblay and S. Coté. 2005. "Quality counts! Assessing the quality of daycare services based on the Quebec longitudinal study of child development." *IRPP Choices* 11 (5): 1– 42

Jenson, J. 2002. "Against the Current: Child Care and Family Policy in Québec." In *Child Care Policy at the Crossroads: Gender and Welfare State Restructuring*, edited by S. Michal and R. Mahon, pp. 309–331. New York: Routledge Press.

Jenson, J. 2009. "Rolling out or Backtracking on Québec's Childcare System? Ideology Matters" In *Public Policy for Women*, edited by M. G. Cohen and J. Pulkingham, pp. 49–70. Toronto: University of Toronto Press.

Johnston, R. M., A. Mohammed, and C. Van Der Linden. 2020. "Evidence of Exacerbated Gender Inequality in Child Care Obligations in Canada and Australia during the COVID-19 Pandemic." *Politics and Gender* 16 (4): pp. 1131–1141.

Lau, R. 2019. "Québec Government Pushes on with Plan to Enroll 4-Year-Olds in Preschool." *Global News*. 14 February. Available from: https://globalnews.ca/news/4960838/Quebec-government-pushes-on-with-plan-to-enroll-4-year-olds-in-preschool/. Accessed: 24 April 2021.

Little, M. 1998. *No Car, No Radio, No Liquor Permit: The Moral Regulation of Single Mothers in Ontario, 1920–1996*. Toronto: Oxford University Press Canada.

Mahoney, Jill. 2008a. "Teach kindergarten outside school, advisor says." *The Globe and Mail*, 22 April.

Mahoney, Jill. 2008b "Kindergarten plans would be second rate, teachers' union says." *The Globe and Mail*, 23 April.

Maroney, H. J. 1992. "'Who Has the Baby?' Nationalism, Pronatalism and the Construction of a 'Demographic Crisis' in Québec 1960–1988." *Studies in Political Economy* 39 (1): pp. 7–36.

Mathieu, S., A. Doucet, and L. McKay. 2020. "Parental Leave Benefits and Inter-Provincial Differences: The Case of Four Canadian Provinces." *Canadian Journal of Sociology* 45 (2): pp. 169–194.

McIsaac, J. and J. Turner. 2019. "Nova Scotia's New Pre-Primary Class Gives Kids a Head Start through Play-Based Learning." *The Conversation*. 29 April. Available from: https://theconversation.com/nova-scotias-new-pre-primary-class-gives-kids-a-head-start-through-play-based-learning-115444. Accessed: 24 April 2021.

McKay, L., S. Mathieu, and A. Doucet. 2016. "Parental-Leave Rich and Parental-Leave Poor: Inequality in Canadian Labour Market-Based Leave Policies." *Journal of Industrial Relations* 58 (4): pp. 543–562.

Millar, H., A. Davidson, and L. A. White. 2020. "Puzzling Publics: The Role of Reflexive Learning in Universal Pre-Kindergarten Policy Innovation in Canada and the US." *Public Policy and Administration* 35 (3): pp. 312–336.

Milligan, K. and M. Stabile. 2009. "Child Benefits, Maternal Employment, and Children's Health: Evidence from Canadian Child Benefit Expansions." *American Economic Review, Papers & Proceedings* 99 (2): pp. 128–132.

Milligan, K. and M. Stabile. 2011. "Do Child Tax Benefits Affect the Well-Being of Children? Evidence from Canadian Child Benefit Expansions." *American Economic Journal: Economic Policy* 3 (3): pp. 175–205.

Monsebraaten, L. and K. Rushowy. 2019. "Ontario Cancels $50M Fund That Helped Child-Care Centres Keep Parent Fees down." The Star. 1 May. Available from: https://www.thestar.com/politics/provincial/2019/05/01/ontario-cancels-50m-fund-that-helped-child-care-centres-not-pass-on-costs-to-parents.html. Accessed: 24 April 2021.

Ontario Liberal Party. 2007. Moving Forward Together: The Ontario Liberal Plan 2007. Toronto: Ontario Liberal Party.

Ontario Office of the Premier. 2009. "Ontario Moves Forward with Full-Day Learning: McGuinty Government Putting Kids and Parents First." *News Release* 27 October.

Pelletier, J. 2017. "Children Gain Learning Boost from Two-Year, Full-Day Kindergarten." *The Conversation*. 2 August. Available from: https://theconversation.com/children-gain-learning-boost-from-two-year-full-day-kindergarten-79549. Accessed: 24 April 2021.

Prentice, S. 2009. "High Stakes: The 'Investable' Child and the Economic Reframing of Childcare." *Signs* 34 (3): pp. 687–710.

Ritter, G. 2007. "Gender and Politics over Time." *Politics and Gender* 3 (3): pp. 386–397.

Robson, J. 2017. "Parental Benefits in Canada: Which Way Forward?" *IRRP Study* 63: pp.1–46.

Rushowy, K. 2019. "Doug Ford Government Says Full-Day Learning Is Here to Stay in Ontario." The Toronto Star. 1 February. Available from: https://www.thestar.com/politics/provincial/2019/02/01/ford-government-says-full-day-kindergarten-is-here-to-stay-in-ontario.html. Accessed: 24 April 2021.

Saltman, J. 2019. "B.C. Budget 2019: Increase to Child-Care Funding, New Child Benefit Introduced." Vancouver Sun. 20 February. Available from: https://vancouversun.com/news/local-news/b-c-budget-2019-minor-increase-to-child-care-funding-new-benefit-introduced. Accessed: 24 April 2021.

Sherman, A. 2018. "Canadian-Style Child Benefit Would Cut U.S. Child Poverty by More Than Half." *Off the Charts*. 24 May. Available from: https://www.cbpp.org/blog/canadian-style-child-benefit-would-cut-us-child-poverty-by-more-than-half. Accessed: 24 April 2021.

Status of Women Canada. 1986. *Report of the Task Force on Child Care*. Cooke Report. Ottawa: Minister of Supply and Services.

Stepan, A. and J. Linz. 2011. "Comparative Perspectives on Inequality and the Quality of Democracy in the United States." *Perspectives on Politics* 9 (4): pp. 841–856.

Tougas, J. 2002. *Reforming Québec's Early Childhood Care and Education: The First Five Years*. Working Paper. Toronto: Childcare Resource and Research Unit.

UNICEF Canada. 2020. *Worlds Apart: Canadian Companion to UNICEF Report Card 16*. Toronto: UNICEF Canada.

Valverde, M. 1991. *The Age of Light, Soap, and Water: Moral Reform in English Canada 1880s–1920s*. Toronto: University of Toronto Press.

Vickers, J. 2012. "Is Federalism Gendered? Incorporating Gender into Studies of Federalism." *Publius: The Journal of Federalism* 43 (1): pp. 1–23.

White, L. A. 2006. "Institutions, Constitutions, Actor Strategies, and Ideas: Explaining Variation in Paid Parental Leave Policies in Canada and the United States." *ICON: International Journal of Constitutional Law* 4 (2): pp. 319–346.

White, L. A. 2017. *Constructing Policy Change: Early Childhood Education and Care in Liberal Welfare States.* Toronto: University of Toronto Press.

White, L. A. 2020. "Does Federalism Support Policy Innovation for Children and Families? Canada in Comparative Context" In *Handbook on Federalism, Diversity and Gender*, edited by J. Vickers, C. Collier, and J. Grace, pp. 32–47. Cheltenham: Edward Elgar.

White, L. A., M. Perlman, A. Davidson, and E. Rayment. 2018. "Risk Perception, Regulation, and Unlicensed Child Care: Lessons from Ontario." *Journal of Risk Research* 22 (7): pp. 878–896.

Zhang, X. 2007. "Returning to the Job after Childbirth." *Perspectives on Labour and Income* 8 (2): pp.18–24.

8

Modernizing Canada's Research Universities

Allan Tupper

Introduction

This chapter examines the impressive university research policies undertaken by the federal Liberal government of Prime Minister Jean Chrétien between 1997 and 2003. Armed with $11 billion from a new-found federal budget surplus, the Liberals undertook several important policies that modernized Canada's research universities, established Canada's large research universities as world leaders, and solidified Ottawa's dominance of university research policy. In succession, the federal government developed the Canada Foundation for Innovation (CFI), established the Canadian Institutes for Health Research, launched an ambitious program of 2,000 Canada Research Chairs at Canadian universities and, importantly, provided funding for the indirect costs of federal research grants. These major policies were Canada's most important responses to growing international competition for talented individuals specializing in the sciences and medical field.

Federal university research policies of this period are good examples of successful public policies in terms of the assessment framework used in this volume. Interestingly, they are successful across all dimensions of public policy—program, process, politics, and endurance. In 2021, at time of writing, Chrétien's university research policies continue to provide the foundations of Canada's research capacity, establish Ottawa as the dominant actor in university research policy, and provide a basis for other successful research policies to unfold.

Federal university research policies raise interesting questions about the determinants of successful public policies. For one thing, they point to the importance of public finance as a source of policy innovation. After a period of severe fiscal restraint in the early 1990s, the Chrétien Liberals saw the first substantial fiscal surplus in several decades. The government was determined to allocate those funds for a variety of important political and public policy purposes.

Allan Tupper, *Modernizing Canada's Research Universities*. In: *Policy Success in Canada*.
Edited by Evert A. Lindquist et al., Oxford University Press. © Allan Tupper (2022).
DOI: 10.1093/oso/9780192897046.003.0008

140 MODERNIZING CANADA'S RESEARCH UNIVERSITIES

Equally, these policies raise interesting questions about elements of good policy processes. One lesson is that policies can be undertaken by good processes, but that such processes need not engage large numbers of people, interest groups, or even Parliamentarians in order to be successful. The federal research policies studied here were a successful 'inside job' par excellence. The Chrétien revolution in university research policies also highlights the range of forces at work in the establishment and endurance of successful public policies. The policies studied raise 'big picture' policy questions about the possible impact of the knowledge economy on Canada. The policies were also based on guesses about the impact of the Internet and other emerging technologies on workplaces, on firms, and on governments themselves. Canada's compelling university research policies also show the impact of Chrétien's personal style and his views about why federal leadership in university research was essential if Canada was to thrive.

And finally, federal research policies are a fascinating case of a policy area where, for several reasons including luck, no major counter narratives emerged. A hegemonic view of what constitutes good university research, and indeed, a good university, prevailed. As this chapter shows, policy critics like the Canadian Association of University Teachers (CAUT) were sidelined and little engaged. And for several reasons, Canada's provincial governments, armed with constitutional power in education including post-secondary education, decided by the early 2000s not to contest Ottawa's dominance in the important policy area of university research.

The chapter proceeds with a fleshed out argument about why Chrétien's university research policy is an example of a successful public policy in all dimensions, and equally, why no powerful opposition to such policies emerged. It then probes how Canadian federalism provides a distinctive context that shapes university research policy. The federal government, armed with superior financial resources, undertook to consolidate its leadership in university research policy. It thereby extended itself deeply into post-secondary education, regardless of the extensive involvement and exclusive jurisdiction of the provinces in this area (Bakvis, 2008; Cameron, 1991; Cameron, 2002). The chapter next moves to the policy process and to the substance of the policies themselves. A section on 'who got what' builds on McConnell, Greely, and Lea's (2020) recent framework that provides a tool to assess the impact and success of different actors. Finally, it evaluates how and why the federal university research policy of 1997–2003 has stood the test of time and allowed a strong partnership between the federal government and Canada's major research universities to emerge.

A caveat is required. As McConnell (2010) noted, in the 'real world' of policy and public management, a completely successful policy, especially one that prevails over time, is a rare, probably non-existent phenomenon. Likewise, in federal research policy, problems and controversies abound. No actor or interest group completely prevailed on all matters or got everything it wanted. Mistakes were made and some aspects of the underlying policy process were disputed to a degree. But none of these problems were, or are, major or insurmountable. Successful policies are always imperfect undertakings that should be seen and understood as such.

A Policy Success

This section outlines my claim that university research policy in the 1997–2003 period is an excellent example of a successful policy across program, process, and political dimensions. First, the policies, when seen together, are underpinned by a coherent view of what is needed to increase the amount and quality of Canadian university research. They rest on a clear sense of how modern, high quality university research infrastructure (through Canada Foundation for Innovation) will attract, retain, and appeal to excellent researchers (recruited through the Canada Research Chairs program) and increase the number of excellent graduate students. At the same time, the policies added considerable new research funding and finally engaged the Government of Canada in a program of financial assistance for the indirect costs of federal research funds. An impressive package of interrelated, well-financed programs was achieved.

Second, the underpinning policy process was not merely acceptable, but also probably necessary to the achievement of the policy and its subsequent success. In a nutshell, Prime Minister Chrétien believed that a wide-open debate about the use of Ottawa's new found budget surplus would likely be slow, potentially divisive, and almost certainly hostile to research policies that, while important for Canada's future well-being, brought long-term benefits that would probably be received in the distant future (and certainly after the life of the current government). To prevent this situation, he decided to keep the debate to an inhouse one that ultimately engaged senior federal public servants with considerable policy experience and legitimacy, key officials at the Association of Universities and Colleges of Canada, and the presidents of a few major research universities.

The provincial governments were not engaged directly either. One argument, probably better called a rationalization, was to justify these major federal expenditures in post-secondary education as legitimate uses of the federal government's 'spending power'. A more compelling reason not to engage the provincial governments was that they were then moving to new positions regarding federal engagement in university research. The new provincial position was one that reflected indifference towards university research in some provinces, such as British Columbia. At the same time provincial governments in Alberta, Ontario and, for several important reasons, Québec, saw the value of university research but also saw that the Government of Canada was better equipped financially to engage this policy area. Whatever their views, no provincial government publicly criticized

142 MODERNIZING CANADA'S RESEARCH UNIVERSITIES

Chrétien's initiatives (Cameron, 2002). Although unimpressive in the breadth or diversity of interests engaged, Ottawa's process was appropriate to the context and to a unique policy area that, while costly and important, garnered attention from few Canadians.

The policy process in this case also had important strengths. The federal government put a substantial amount of money on the table and ensured that universities would be well equipped to move forward. The process also sped up policy-making and put interesting, efficacy-driven administrative structures in place. The machinery succeeded in allowing university and business elites to dominate the administrative process, and kept deliberations about the research priorities of particular universities away from politicians who might try to push them towards perennial questions about local and provincial benefits.

The politics of university research policies undoubtedly increased the reputations of those at the centre of the action. The few fully engaged participants—a handful of very senior federal officials, key people in the Prime Minister's Office, and some university presidents—were, by definition, widely seen as major forces. The prime minister's stock rose among the elites involved in this process; they commended his willingness to undertake important policies that would take a long time to show their benefits, and thus, unlikely to yield electoral benefits. In short, the politics were oddly favourable to Chrétien's major university research policies. To engage the old cliché, good policy generated good politics.

Probably the most difficult test of policy success is to establish a policy that has a lasting contribution to the national interest. The university research policies of 1997–2003 are examples of policies with lasting positive impacts. For one thing, they undertook, and achieved, two major structural changes. First, the research policies solidified Ottawa's increasingly close relations with Canada's large research universities. The federal government recognized the research universities' sense of themselves as national, increasingly international, institutions that had outgrown meddlesome, penny-pinching provincial governments. Second, the federal research policies also established Ottawa as the focal point of research, and certainly, university research policy. The provincial governments were relegated to the role of managing controversial topics, like student tuitions, and questions of university governance, including boards of governors. A quiet constitutional change had been undertaken.

Ottawa's university research policy also endured a change of government after the Liberal prime minister, Paul Martin, was defeated by Stephen Harper's fledgling Conservative Party. Harper formed two minority governments before finally achieving a majority in 2010. Interestingly, the Conservatives maintained, and in some areas, increased expenditures on Liberal university research policy, whose principles they felt were sound. The Canada Foundation for Innovation, the Canada Research Chairs, the Canadian Institutes of Health Research, and a permanent federal program of support for the indirect costs of federally funded research were all maintained. Moreover, in 2020 Ottawa's role in university research continues to expand. For example, in its response to the Covid-19 pandemic, the federal government established programs that provided emergency assistance to university researchers and graduate students.

The next section describes the Chrétien government's key university research policies. It notes some of the interesting features of their administration and funding, which are central to their long-term success. Equally, the focus on the policy's features allow the reader to get inside the black box and watch a prime minister and his key advisors at work. Finally, a further (unsuccessful) effort is made to crack a key issue—why did Jean Chrétien insist that a substantial portion of Ottawa's new-found budget surplus be allocated to strengthening the research capacity of Canadian universities?

How the Initiatives Unfolded

The heart of Ottawa's university research initiatives were: the Canada Foundation for Innovation (CFI), the Canadian Institutes for Health Research (CIHR), the Canada Research Chairs (CRC), and federal funding for the indirect costs of federal research (Tupper, 2003). The Canada Foundation for Innovation was established by statute in 1997 with an initial endowment of $800 million. Its administration was unusual and unique among Ottawa's arsenal of administrative structures. As a foundation, the CFI was governed by a board of directors, only a minority of which was selected by the Government of Canada. As an endowed body, the CFI was not responsible to the auditor general and was not reliant on annual appropriations. Moreover, the Foundation had a strong sense of its accountability to the research community and to Canadians more generally. Importantly, the CFI's structure evoked strong controversy about whether it achieved adequate levels of public accountability. Canada's auditor general criticized endowed funds as a serious insult to Canadian norms. Her position was that endowed foundations were excessively autonomous. They were, in fact, private bodies financed through considerable public money, which undertook important policy roles. Professor Peter Aucoin, a leading scholar of public management, wrote powerfully in support of the auditor general's attacks on funds like the CFI (2003). He argued that the CFI's powerful supporters were indifferent to issues of public accountability. Such indifference allowed Ottawa to proceed on its course.

At the heart of its mandate, the CFI was to provide funding for important, new research infrastructure principally at universities and research hospitals (normally linked with universities). As noted, the formation of the CFI was logically seen as the first major policy to be undertaken. A rigorously modernized research infrastructure was seen as central to the attraction of 'knowledge workers' who

144   MODERNIZING CANADA'S RESEARCH UNIVERSITIES

would drive the Canadian economy forward. The CFI could only fund 40 per cent of a worthy project. The balance had to be found elsewhere and, in practice, the remaining funds generally came from provincial governments and from recipient institutions themselves. Since 1997, Canada's universities have rebuilt their research infrastructure with CFI funding. Importantly, the CFI was the first federal government program to require recipient institutions to provide a major research plan that made a compelling case for federal money and located particular infrastructure projects within a coherent, long-term institutional plan.

The CFI's structure has been controversial (Aucoin, 2003). Its status as an endowed foundation raised the ire of critics, who felt that its operations were not compatible with established norms of responsible government within Canada. The foundation was criticized as having too much freedom from government direction and, more loosely, as being too much like a 'private' foundation. Ottawa held firm against such criticisms and argued that, to be effective, research funding decisions were best insulated from the ebbs and flows of partisan politics. My point is not to judge which argument or accountability vision is better than the other. Rather, I seek to point out that Ottawa has viewed a more independent form of administration as central to the CFI's success. And broadly speaking, the university research community has accepted that claim wholeheartedly.

The restructuring of the health sciences research administration featured the termination of the Medical Research Council of Canada, which was later replaced by the Canadian Institutes of Health Research (CIHR). The CIHR reshaped key features of Canada's new university research landscape. First, health science funds were now allocated to interdisciplinary networks of strong researchers. Second, these networks encouraged research teams to embrace researchers from different Canadian universities. Third, networks were funded for longer periods, thereby removing the need for researchers to complete time consuming requests for short-term grants from the former Medical Research Council. Fourth, the CIHR was very interested in the commercialization of research. It received a substantial boost in federal funding with an increase to its base funding of $175 million, a large amount by the standards of the time.

The most publicized federal university research initiative was the Canada Research Chair program. Canada Research Chairs (CRCs) are endowed chairs funded by the Government of Canada. They were launched in 1999 by an initial federal commitment of $900 million for the first 2,000 chairs. The chairs were to provide Canadian universities a capacity to attract and retain world leading researchers. The program was seen as an effort to prevent the loss of top Canadian researchers, who could be enticed by better opportunities abroad. Equally, the CRCs would enable Canadian universities to repatriate talented Canadians, who had been attracted by better research opportunities in other countries, notably the United States. Two types of CRC were provided. Tier I CRCs were provided to distinguished scholars with proven research records. They were provided for a once-renewable seven-year term and were initially funded with $200,000 (about $300,000 in 2020 dollars). A Tier II CRC provided promising scholars with a single five-year term. Tier II CRCs were each provided with $100,000.

Like the CFI, the CRC program was structured to limit political interference in the allocation of the chairs. For example, for a CRC application to be successful, the individual had to be nominated by an eligible university and approved by an internationally recognized College of Reviewers. Equally, the CRC program was not originally expected to allocate chairs on the basis of provincial quotas. And there was also federal government concern that too much attention would be paid to particular disciplines. Interestingly, some adjustments were made by the federal government to allow for a wider basis of university support to emerge. All universities would be provided at least one chair and a specific number of chairs were allocated to social scientists and humanists. Such adjustments retained Ottawa's core objective of building a few world class universities, while also accommodating smaller universities who had modest natural sciences and engineering programs and, in many cases, no medical faculties at all.

The precise source of the CRC idea is not really known. In conversations with senior federal government officials, Martha Piper, the president of the University of British Columbia, and her colleagues had often stressed the long-term recruitment and retention challenges of Canadian universities. But the author of the precise CRC initiative was probably Robert Lacroix, rector of the Université de Montréal. In his insightful analysis of the Chrétien years, Eddie Goldenberg, Chrétien's senior policy advisor, shares a Sunday morning meeting with Chrétien, Lacroix, and himself to discuss university hiring (2007). Chrétien was sold on the CRC concept when Lacroix argued that Canadian universities could, like the Montréal Expos baseball team, field a decent team but were unable to recruit and retain superstars. Interestingly, Lacroix made the remark unaware that Chrétien was an Expos fan, who agreed wholeheartedly with Lacroix's assessment both of the Expos and of Canadian universities!

The program of federal financial support for the indirect costs of research is one of the most important of the Chrétien university initiatives. Such a policy had been intermittently advocated for by universities since 1949. The program is not really linked by the rhetoric of other Chrétien university research initiatives. Indirect costs are probably better understood as research overhead. They refer to the substantial costs of research like the wear and tear on university infrastructure, researcher and support staff salaries, and library books and periodicals. The Government of Canada's long standing refusal to fund such overhead was seen to fundamentally weaken Canadian universities compared with major American research universities, whose indirect costs had long been well-funded by governments. More importantly, Canadian universities argued that unfunded indirect costs forced them to transfer money from teaching to pay such bills. And in the Chrétien years, the universities particularly sought federal funding for their

146 MODERNIZING CANADA'S RESEARCH UNIVERSITIES

indirect costs. The more successful a university was in undertaking research that attracted federal government research funding, the greater was its indirect costs deficit. Therefore, unfunded indirect costs were a particular problem for major research-intensive universities, which were the prime targets of Chrétien's other research initiatives. In many ways, they were the major problem facing Canadian universities as they intensified their links with Ottawa.

This brief review of the initial content and structure of Ottawa's very successful university research initiatives highlights several important stories. First, the meeting between Prime Minister Chrétien and Rector Lacroix reveals how a major, highly successful federal program—the Canada Research Chairs—was sold to the prime minister by an off-the-cuff remark about Montréal's professional baseball team. Second, the CRC and CFI were structured by a federal government determined to protect the integrity of sponsored university research by insulating it from the vagaries of partisan electoral politics. Third, federal government adjustments to the CRC program, which paid some attention to provincial and discipline-based allocations, won university and political support at little cost to the federal government. This suggests how a clever government can institute small, symbolic changes to ensure the success and longevity of major flagship programs. Fourth, the new federal programs stressed ideas like interdisciplinary research and the commercialization of university research.

As mentioned, the Government of Canada's impressive group of university research programs was funded in the 1997–2003 period by budget surpluses. The chapter has already noted how the prime minister insisted that there be no wide-ranging caucus discussion, let alone a public debate, about priorities for spending the surplus. Chrétien worried that such debates might be divisive and slow. His deeper worry was that scarce public monies might be squandered as if small funds were provided to many different needs. At the end of the day, all that would be achieved was incrementally increased spending in established program areas.

All that said, no clear answer emerges to the question of why Chrétien was persuaded by the cause of universities and their research. One line of reasoning suggests that the prime minister, late in a long and successful career, was looking for a lasting legacy. But again, why university research? Another line of thought focuses on Chrétien's deeper ideas about where public policy really mattered and where government played an essential role in a modern society. He was from a large working-class family and his parents stressed the importance of education for both personal and societal advancement. One of his brothers, Michel Chrétien, was a distinguished university researcher. And his wife, the late Aline Chrétien, also came from a working-class background in Chrétien's home town of Shawinigan. She, too, was an avid supporter of education, and even urged the prime minister to fully support the Canadian Millennium Scholarship Fund as an important avenue for upward mobility.

The key policy question about why well-funded university research was a pressing national priority for Chrétien thus remains without a precise answer. That unanswered question and the story about the Montréal Expos stress how the making of complex highly successful public policies remains a subtle, very human process, that is almost certainly shaped by many forces that political scientists may not immediately identify as important.

The Larger Context of Policy-Making

To this point, Canada's successful university research policies have been situated in the actions of the Liberal government under Chrétien between 1997 and 2003. Like all important policies, however, they are underpinned by long standing debates and policy concerns. In this case, Ottawa's university research policy initiatives reflect perennial debates about the structure of the Canadian economy. Writing in 1975, Donald V. Smiley argued that a tight alliance between Canadian universities, certain segments of Canadian business, and the Government of Canada increasingly anchored federal policy thinking (1975).

Smiley noted that federal governments in Canada have sometimes pursued national economic policies, which has resulted in an 'integrated and autonomous' economy (1975, 42). Canadian governments, as manifest by the famous Macdonald-Laurier National Policy, were determined to build a distinctive economy from their powerful American neighbour down south. Canada was also engaged in building a prosperous economy that defied strong natural economic impulses and built an east-west economy that was independent of the American economic superpower. Such nationalistic Canadian impulses have ebbed and flowed since Confederation. They have faced strong competition from many policy-makers and business leaders, who have preferred tighter links with the United States, as manifested by the current tri-lateral free trade agreement with the United States and Mexico. And as Smiley notes, Canada has pursued a number of 'surrogate' national policies, including Keynesian economic policies and Ottawa's post-war construction of a national welfare state (1975). However, such major initiatives were indifferent to the economy's structure and, thus, were not national policies in the sense of being a part of deliberate federal efforts to shape the structure of the overall Canadian economy.

Smiley and others have noted policy prescriptions and ambitions similar to those which inspired Chrétien's university research initiatives (1975). Universities, especially large research universities, have been at the heart of important federal policies that, together, form a new technological nationalism. Important policy goals include building an economy with capacity for Indigenous economic innovation, and for developing dynamic secondary industries. Equally, to the extent that natural resource industries remained important, Canadian resources were to

148 MODERNIZING CANADA'S RESEARCH UNIVERSITIES

be upgraded (processed) prior to export. Resource businesses were to be driven by sophisticated processes that were themselves the products of research partnerships between governments, business, and universities. And key sectors of the new economy, notably aerospace, computing hardware and software, and research-driven renewable resource industries were to be preserved for Canadian ownership and control. All such goals are echoed in, or dealt with explicitly, by Chrétien's university research policies. Interestingly, Chrétien, given his long service in Canadian government, had engaged in many debates about Canadian economic nationalism. He never mentioned these debates in his comments about university research. But the range of policy elites engaged in the development of university research policies from the senior public service, senior university leaders, and among advocates of tighter business-government-university links almost certainly contained those quiet economic nationalists.

In the 1970s and 1980s, commentators thought strong economic provincialism, a phenomenon with deep historical roots in Ontario, was also flourishing in Alberta and Québec. Ottawa's nascent nation building was increasingly challenged by province building. University research was one area, however, where Ottawa was untouched by aggressive provincial government policy. University research was a costly undertaking whose impacts were hard to assess, whose politics had little purchase for mass politics, and whose benefits were long beyond the normal four-year term of a Canadian provincial government. On the other hand, the new economic nationalism appealed to major Canadian research universities and their leadership, to Canadian governments notably under Liberal leadership, and to segments of Canadian industry that relied on sophisticated research and needed skilled workers.

Success for Whom? Winners and Losers

Recent work by Allan McConnell, Liam Grealy, and Tess Lea (2020) extends McConnell's (2010) well known framework from the policy level to the level of individual actors in the larger policy process. The actor-specific perspective opens up important new avenues of analysis. As the authors note, an actor-specific approach almost certainly demands analysis of forces external to government. Consideration of the success of such interests like industry associations, public private partnerships, and other governance alliances weakens the strong 'government centric' focus of whole-system assessments. Moreover, analysis of winners and losers may highlight important questions about the capacity of policy critics to develop important counternarratives. Equally, the framework for analysing specific policy actors uses the same language and definitions as McConnell's original analysis. Such commonality allows actor-specific assessments to dovetail with broader analysis of policy success. On the other hand, McConnell et al.'s framework provides latitude for subjective assessment of competing actors' relative influence over the process, precise program content, and the politics. For example, McConnell (2010) allows influence in each area to be graded as 'low, medium or high'. Policy success remains therefore an open question whose answer can be hotly debated by policy participants and observers.

Accordingly, the next section briefly reviews the relative success of several key groups involved in the development of Ottawa's university research policies. The key groups are: identifiable forces in the Government of Canada, the presidents of major Canadian research universities, the Association of Universities and Colleges of Canada (AUCC), and the Canadian Association of University Teachers (CAUT). The AUCC (now Universities Canada) is the body responsible for developing a common cause among Canada's universities, and for representing these institutions to garner favourable policies from Ottawa. The CAUT is an organization that, like the AUCC, was dedicated to seeking favourable policy responses from Ottawa. Its interests and policy views differed considerably from those of the AUCC.

The federal government tightly controlled the policy process, the program content, and funding around university research policies. Key central federal government institutions dominated the process's construction, its timing, and its major participants. Key actors in the Prime Minister's Office, the Privy Council Office, the Department of Finance, Industry Canada, and selected other senior officials, including David Dodge (the deputy minister of health) and Alex Himmelfarb (the deputy minister of human resources Canada) shaped the agenda for debate. Such central control flowed from the prime minister's desire to ensure that major new university research policies were not sacrificed to widespread political participation. The format of the policy process and final decisions about policy content, policy financing, and policy timing were squarely in Ottawa's court.

An interesting issue is Ottawa's willingness to surrender some control of program delivery and management to outsiders in both the Canada Foundation for Innovation and the Canada Research Chair Program. As mentioned, the CFI was established as an endowed fund whose affairs were governed by a board of directors, only a minority of whom were selected by Ottawa. Ultimately, policy control rested with the federal government. However, with the exception of major policy changes, the CFI ran independently to ensure that 'expert' decisions prevailed about its funding priorities and choices. Equally the CRC program also had an interesting administrative structure, where an expert College of Reviewers advised on all decisions. Such structures cannot really be considered a loss of government control. These arrangements also had the further impact of keeping the federal funds well beyond any provincial government control, as would have been the case under more traditional federal-provincial structures. As mentioned, key federal policy-makers, such as Eddie Goldenberg, the prime minister's chief policy advisor, sought to ensure that important decisions made under Chrétien's flagship

150 MODERNIZING CANADA'S RESEARCH UNIVERSITIES

university research policies were made on the basis of scholarly excellence. Provincial allocations, formulas dividing up funds across all universities, and other such schemes were antithetical to Ottawa's ambition of making Canadian universities centrepieces of the emerging knowledge economy.

The reputations of key federal officials were raised by their role in the design of Ottawa's research programs. The capacity and influence of the finance department, the Privy Council Office, and the Prime Minister's Office were again highlighted by their ability to work hand-in-hand with an ambitious prime minister armed with a fiscal surplus. Equally, the weight of an official like David Dodge was further acknowledged by his inclusion in the inner circle. On the other hand, officials at the federal research granting councils, previously key forces in the policy area, were not major players in the design of Ottawa's new university research programs.

A body whose influence was substantially increased by Chrétien's university research policies was the Liberal Party's Government Caucus on Post-Secondary Education and Research. Established in 1994 by two Liberals MPs who were former university professors, Peter Adams and John English, the party caucus became an important policy participant. It emerged as a body tasked with finding a common cause among different universities to urge these institutions—a policy community known as notoriously decentralized and internally competitive—to work together in gathering valuable policy feedback on federal policy initiatives. The caucus held annual meetings, hosted important university interest groups, like the AUCC, and annually presented an overview of priority university needs to the minister of finance. Moreover, it built a welcoming constituency within Liberal ranks for Prime Minister Chrétien's politically risky university research policies that consumed a large portion of Ottawa's new-found, much sought-after budget surplus. In short, the Liberal Party caucus is an interesting example of an unplanned and unanticipated policy force that did good work at a fortuitous time for the government.

Interesting developments also transpired outside government circles. Presidents of major research universities were often consulted as Ottawa considered the details of new research policies. Robert Prichard, president of the University of Toronto, Robert Lacroix, rector of the Université de Montréal, and Martha Piper, president of the University of British Columbia, were seen as persons of consequence in Ottawa. They were sometimes consulted about the desirability of new federal university research policies and for ideas to put flesh on the bones of federal initiatives. Their personal stocks, and those of their universities, rose appreciably through their roles in federal policy-making. Interestingly, particular presidents assumed insider status for various reasons. For example, Goldenberg met Robert Lacroix, who would ultimately convince the prime minister to proceed with CRCs, in a chance meeting in Montréal. Lacroix later went on a skiing vacation to British Columbia, where he broke a leg, and while convalescing in Vancouver, spoke to Piper at length about her views on how to deal with the brain drain.

The Association of Universities and Colleges of Canada emerged as an influential force in national policy-making. Its reputation rose dramatically in Ottawa. In the mid 1990s the AUCC decided to engage federal policy-making aggressively. It concluded that federal funding for universities needed to increase substantially, and set about to learn how to better wield policy influence. To that end, the AUCC hired Robert Giroux as president to guide the way of the organization in Ottawa. Giroux was previously an influential, well-respected senior federal official, who held such important posts as Secretary to Treasury Board. He undertook to build AUCC's policy capacity. As Clara Morgan noted: 'With Robert Giroux on board, the AUCC had a savvy leader who could navigate the federal landscape and translate the AUCC's interests into federal policy language' (2009, 68).

Giroux quickly won the respect of university presidents, especially those of the research universities, who became his key constituency within the AUCC. The AUCC also made the strategic decision to lessen its commitment to student financial assistance, and to instead focus its efforts on university research. Equally, it successfully curbed the ambitions of the so-called G-10 group of major research universities that was urging the AUCC to accelerate its research funding message. In this respect, the AUCC played the classic role of articulating a common cause for all universities in the labyrinth of policy-making in Ottawa.

In a variety of submissions in the late 1990s, the AUCC articulated a strong message about the need for more federal government support of university research (Morgan, 2009). These submissions were general and tended to support, not lead, federal thinking. The AUCC agenda urged federal support for infrastructure spending and more funding for professorial positions. The AUCC also echoed universities' long-standing complaints about the lack of federal funding for the indirect costs of federally provided research grants. In this sense, the AUCC became a player in Ottawa policy-making by allowing the federal government to craft its own university research policy agenda with almost certain university support. As influential federal officials began to generate the necessary university research programs, the AUCC became a strong supporter, whose opinion was often sought as program details became clearer. In this regard, the AUCC has been criticized for being uncritically supportive of Chrétien's suite of university research policies. In other words, Ottawa got strong public support for its successful policies from the AUCC in exchange for enhancing the organization's reputation and granting it access to the process of policy-making in this arena.

While the AUCC had policy access and some input into federal policy thinking, the other major university group in Ottawa, the Canadian Association of University Teachers (CAUT), played a modest role. The CAUT was never able to articulate a 'counter narrative' with enough purchase on federal policy-makers to force its admission into the policy process. The only commonality between the AUCC and CAUT was their shared interest in having a strong federal government as a force in post-secondary education. The CAUT was much more critical than the AUCC about emerging federal research policies. It complained that Ottawa's largesse offered too little support to humanists and social scientists. The federal government's strong desire for private sector involvement in research and the commercialization of research were seen as wrongful violations of long-standing principles of university neutrality when selecting and implementing research initiatives. The CAUT also lamented the uneven, sometimes unfair, impact of federal research policy on smaller universities and on smaller urban centres. What, though, accounts for its inconsequential role? And what explains its failures compared to AUCC's successes?

No single answer emerges to these questions. The following possibilities arise. First, the CAUT, regardless of the merits of its criticisms, was voiceless in a policy area that was characterized by support for federal initiatives among all major political parties. Its comments realized little media coverage and were relegated to the status of afterthoughts. Second, the CAUT had little support from university presidents and other leaders, who saw it primarily as a voice for faculty unionization. The AUCC, and individual universities, had no strong incentives to partner with the CAUT. Indeed, if anything the CAUT was seen as a negative force in policy-making, whose criticisms might weaken the lobbying initiatives of universities through the AUCC. Its positions were found especially lacking by the larger universities, who saw Ottawa's research initiatives as essential to their ambitions to become world-class universities on par with major American institutions. Third, university research policy-making was undertaken by a very few elite players. Put simply, it was a policy area that offered little space for critics, whose views could easily be responded to or ignored by other universities and by the government itself. The CAUT at best offered interesting debating points and was never capable of advancing a compelling counterpoise to Ottawa's dominant policy position.

Intended and Unintended Policy Impacts

At time of writing in early 2021, Chrétien's university research policies remain central features of the Canadian government, Canadian universities, and Canada's overall research capacity. How have policies that were launched two decades ago shaped Canadian universities? What accounts for their longevity?

The Canada Foundation for Innovation has been a boon for Canadian universities. Canadian university research infrastructure has been renewed in large measure and continues to flourish. The CFI, in providing a workable structure to finance essential research infrastructure, has provided Canada a continuing advantage over other OECD countries where university infrastructure is dependant on the ebbs and flows of annual budget cycles. Equally, Canada Research Chairs continue to provide Canadian universities with ongoing opportunities for the renewal of their cadre of outstanding researchers. CRCs have also proven to be a flexible policy instrument that can respond to and accommodate changing conditions. For example, the positions have been adapted to changing demands for diversity by including a more balanced representation of different races, disabled persons, and Indigenous people. CRS's original objective to prevent 'brain drain' by repatriating impressive Canadian researchers, and attracting talented young people to university careers, remain important.

Ongoing rankings of major world universities give evidence of the positive impact of Chrétien's policies. All such respectable rankings note three Canadian universities—University of Toronto, McGill University and University of British Columbia—in the world's top 50 universities, with University of Toronto routinely being placed in the world's top 25. For example, the Times 2019 rankings placed University of Toronto at 18, University of British Columbia at 34, and McGill University at 42. Equally, McMaster University, University of Montréal, and sometimes, University of Alberta are in the world's top 100. When rankings examine only public universities, Canadian performance is even more impressive.

More subjectively and subtly, Canadian universities appear ambitious and self-confident in the 2020s. They still have important problems including high operating costs, burgeoning faculty salaries, and concerns about student debts and tuition fees. But consider, for example, the CAUT's message to the Chrétien government in the 1990s. It asserted that social sciences and humanities would be weakened and universities would become the handmaidens of corporations. Those messages had little traction in the 1990s and seemed even less relevant in 2020. To the contrary, social sciences and humanities are strong, and complaints about corporate takeover seem exaggerated. Indeed, closer links between Canadian firms and universities are probably viewed as positive developments. They were pursued by Chrétien and subsequent federal governments as Canada struggled to cope with a changing world economy.

Ottawa's dominance of university research has, however, changed universities substantially in unplanned and unanticipated ways. The large university research enterprise requires a noteworthy increase of administrative personnel and expenditure. Technology transfer activities and spin off companies, for example, raise complex questions that demand skilled administrative staff with specialized financial and legal knowledge. To be eligible for federal funding, university research projects require ethics approval, which leads to controversies and high compliance costs. Research vice presidents, once occupants of sleepy offices with essentially clerical duties, are now forces in university deliberations. Their forte is such matters as intellectual property and the management of complex relations with governments and corporations.

Increased complexity and costs have generally been accepted by universities as necessary to their undertaking of complex research programs. Interestingly, one

154 MODERNIZING CANADA'S RESEARCH UNIVERSITIES

well-rehearsed faculty complaint in a large Canadian research university in 2020 is that administrative staff are increasing more quickly than faculty. Ironically, such a hiring pattern, if true, is an almost inevitable response to the research enterprise that is widely supported by the contemporary faculty themselves. Equally, as driven by Chrétien's research policies, Canadian universities now pay more explicit and transparent attention to the better treatment of animals used in university research. Serious problems, such as conflicts of interest between faculty and students in the use and control of research findings, are now governed by clearer rules. In these and many other ways, it can be suggested that Ottawa's research policies have improved universities, albeit at a considerable expense.

A major, and probably intended, consequence of Chrétien's successful university research policies has been the intensification of research in Canada's larger universities and tightening links between these institutions and the federal government. The larger universities, especially University of British Columbia, University of Toronto, and McGill University have long seen themselves as national assets. As this chapter has noted, they have applauded and pursued a close identification with Ottawa—an identification that has been considerably deepened by Chrétien's research policies and by the growing 'internationalization' of post-secondary education. In broad measure, Ottawa's research program, as structured, also serves the interests of the larger universities for the simple reason that they are the site of the most substantial research undertakings. Moreover, to the degree that Chrétien's government sought advice about its university research initiatives, it did so primarily from senior leadership of the larger universities. As well, the AUCC came to serve the larger universities, although it was always aware of the need to maintain a common cause among all Canadian universities.

Is Ottawa's close relationship with larger Canadian universities a good or a bad thing? David M. Cameron (2002) argued strongly that it was probably a good thing. He criticized the view that universities, despite major differences between them, should be treated similarly, especially in matters of research policy. His case is that Canada would be well served by a greater differentiation of university research mandates. Large universities with substantial science, engineering, and medical faculties should be the site of most frontier research. Other universities could then concentrate on teaching and a few specialized research niches. Cameron (2002, 171) put it this way:

One thing that is likely to result from continued federal government support of the indirect costs of research is a widening of the distance between research-intensive universities and the others. This is probably good. It invites each institution to find its own place. This is already happening. Both Ontario and British Columbia, for example, have recently established new universities with a specifically technical focus.

Conclusions: Lessons about Success

This chapter argues that Prime Minister Jean Chrétien's major, well-funded university research policies of the 1997–2003 period are examples of successful public policies. The Canada Foundation for Innovation, the Canada Research Chairs program, and a permanent program of financial support for the indirect costs of federally funded research achieved an important public purpose, were strongly supported by university leaders and, two decades later, remain cornerstones of Canadian university research. A few of the interesting points raised by university research policies are summarized here.

First, this case shows how lasting policy success is achieved by the policy's core characteristics and, interestingly, by small program adjustments early in the policy's life. The Chrétien government saw changes to the CRC program that established quotas for different disciplines as necessary to calming worries from social scientists and humanists about their possible exclusion. Equally, Ottawa provided extra funding to the Atlantic Opportunities Agency to facilitate that region's participation in the funding of CFI projects that were beyond the wherewithal of Atlantic provincial governments. Ottawa had not wanted to undertake these changes but judged them as necessary compromises that provided greater long term support for the policy's objectives.

Second, dimensions of Ottawa's university research policies raise issues that cannot be judged categorically as either good or bad. A good example is the early debate about the accountability of the foundation structure that Ottawa employed to fund and administer the Canada Foundation for Innovation. Is an endowed fund that operates independently from direct Parliamentary control through an annual budget process a serious policy problem? The government's view was that the auditor general's criticisms were misguided. The auditor general failed to see that the foundation structure allowed it to be responsive to the Fund's users.

A third interesting feature of Ottawa's university policies was the policy process used to achieve them. As noted, Chrétien believed that upgraded research universities with strong government backing were essential to Canada's economic future. His related view, however, was that few Canadians were interested in the content of university research policies. Canadians interests lay in federal policies for student financial assistance and in the important tax expenditures that, for example, allowed parents to transfer portions of student tuition fees to their own income tax forms. Ottawa would address ongoing partisan politics through policies such as those. At the same time, university and government elites would hammer out the research policies. Chrétien and his close advisors also worried that widespread political engagement would weaken the chance that costly research policies with uncertain, long term benefits would be accepted when pitted against pressing short

156 MODERNIZING CANADA'S RESEARCH UNIVERSITIES

term expenditure needs. The public interest thus demanded a closed policy process that allowed for direct engagement and control from the prime minister (Simpson, 2002).

A fourth interesting point is how Chrétien's research initiatives contributed to an important federalism goal. By design, they achieved Ottawa's dominance of university research policy, an area that gave the federal government enduring control over universities that were key to Canada's long-term prosperity. They tied universities closely to Ottawa and, given the financial resources employed, put funds on the table that no provincial government was willing to match. The universities were pleased and the provincial governments, whether pleased or not, accommodated the federal initiatives.

A final point is the various interesting winners and losers generated. Ottawa's major university research policies increased the reputations of key federal officials and several presidents of major research universities. The AUCC's stock also rose after its decision to stand as a firm supporter of Chrétien's initiatives. The CAUT, whose position was much more critical of the new university research policies, was excluded and became a weak, marginalized outsider. The organization had the potential to develop an interesting counter narrative, but lacked the capacity to engage the federal government. 'Who gets what' is, again, shown to remain at the heart of all politics.

References

Aucoin, P. 2003. "Independent Foundations, Public Money and Public Accountability: Whither Minister Responsibility as Democratic Governance?" *Canadian Public Administration* 46 (1): pp. 1–26.

Bakvis, H. 2008. "The Knowledge Economy and Post-Secondary Education: Federalism in Search of a Metaphor." In *Canadian Federalism: Performance, Effectiveness and Legitimacy*, edited by H. Bakvis and G. Skogstad, pp. 205–222. Don Mills, ON: Oxford University Press.

Cameron, D. M. 1991. *More Than an Academic Question: Universities, Government and Public Policy in Canada*. Halifax: Institute for Research on Public Policy.

Cameron, D. M. 2002. "The Challenge of Change: Canadian Universities in the 21st Century." *Canadian Public Administration* 8 (2): pp. 145–174.

Compton, M. and P. 't Hart. 2019. "How to See Great Policy Successes: A Field Guide to Spotting Policy Successes in the Wild." In *Great Policy Successes*, edited by M. Compton and P. 't Hart, pp. 1–20. Oxford: Oxford University Press.

Goldenberg, E. 2007. *The Way It Works: Inside Ottawa*. Toronto: Douglas Gibson Books.

Levasseur, K. 2009. "Universities and the Regulation of Research Ethics." In *Research and Innovation Policy: Changing Federal Government—University Relations*, edited by G. B. Doern and C. Stoney, pp. 242–264. Toronto: University of Toronto Press.

McConnell, A. 2010. *Understanding Policy Success: Rethinking Public Policy*. Basingstoke: Palgrave Macmillan.

McConnell, A. 2010. "Policy Success, Policy Failures and Grey Areas In-Between." *Journal of Public Policy* 30 (3): pp. 345–362.

McConnell, A., L. Grealy, and T. Lea. 2020. "Policy Success for Whom? A Framework for Analysis." *Policy Sciences* 54 (4): pp. 589–608. http.doi.org/10.1007/s11077-020-09406-y

Morgan, C. 2009. "Higher Education Funding and Policy Trade-Offs: The AUCC and Federal Research in the Chrétien-Martin Era." In *Research and Innovation Policy: Changing Federal Government–University Relations*, edited by G. B. Doern and C. Stoney, pp. 59–86. Toronto: University of Toronto Press.

Simpson, J. 2002. "There's At Least One Chrétien Legacy: Universities." Globe and Mail. 9 November. https://www.theglobeandmail.com/news/politics/theres-at-least-one-Chrétien-legacy-universities/article757642/

Slaughter, S. and G. Rhoades. 2004. *Academic Capitalism and the New Economy: Markets, States and Higher Education*. Baltimore, MD: Johns Hopkins University Press.

Smiley, D. V. 1975. "Canada and the Quest for a National Policy." *Canadian Journal of Political Science* 8 (1): pp. 40–62.

Tupper, A. 2003. "The Chrétien Governments and Higher Education Policy: A Quiet Revolution in Public Policy." In *How Ottawa Spends, 2003–2004: Regime Shift and Policy Change*, edited by G. B. Doern, pp. 105–117. Don Mills: Oxford University Press.

Tupper, A. 2009. "Pushing Federalism to the Limit: Post-Secondary Education Policy in the Millennium." In *Research and Innovation Policy: Changing Federal Government*, edited by G. B. Doern and C. Stoney, pp. 35–58. Toronto: University of Toronto Press.

PART III
SOCIAL POLICY SUCCESSES

9

Good and Lucky

Explaining Canada's Successful Immigration Policies

Triadafilos Triadafilopoulos

Canadian immigration policy is widely considered successful, with respect to McConnell's (2010) criteria of endurance, process, programs, and politics. The major aims of Canadian immigration policy—responding to demographic and labour market needs, enabling family reunification, and meeting Canada's international humanitarian obligations regarding refugees—have been in place since the Immigration Act of 1976, and continue to orient policy under the 2001 Immigration and Refugee Protection Act (IRPA). With respect to process, Canadian governments have introduced and amended policies efficiently and effectively, with the support of key stakeholders. In the sphere of programs, Canadian governments have enacted policies that achieved their aims. In the estimation of the Organisation for Economic Cooperation and Development (OECD):

> *Canada has the most carefully designed and longest-standing skilled migration system in the OECD. It is widely perceived as a benchmark for other countries, and its success is evidenced by good integration outcomes. Canada also boasts the largest share of highly educated immigrants in the OECD as well as high levels of public acceptance of migration. In addition, it is seen as an appealing country of destination for potential migrants.*

> (OECD, 2019).

The United Nations High Commissioner for Refugees, Filippo Grandi, referred to Canada's refugee resettlement program as an 'exemplary' model worthy of emulation (CBC Radio, 2016). In politics, Canada's success in generating a broad consensus in support of expanding its immigration program, in an era in which immigration has become deeply politicized, has made it an object of intense scrutiny on the part of academics, journalists, international organizations, and foreign governments. A thriving literature has emerged, dedicated to pondering how Canada has managed to avoid the nativist surge all too common in other advanced liberal democracies (Triadafilopoulos, 2021).

Triadafilos Triadafilopoulos, *Good and Lucky*. In: *Policy Success in Canada*.
Edited by Evert A. Lindquist et al., Oxford University Press.
© Triadafilos Triadafilopoulos (2022). DOI: 10.1093/oso/9780192897046.003.0009

Canada's successes in terms of immigration policy processes, programs, and politics are based on a combination of purposeful and contingent factors. Canada has been good, but it has also been lucky. Decisions taken in the late-1980s and early-1990s to focus immigration policy squarely on recruiting large numbers of well-educated, highly skilled economic immigrants were successful in a programmatic sense. Policymakers also maintained the support of key stakeholders, enabling process success, while addressing political debates, enhancing political success. Similarly, the decision to favour resettlement over asylum in refugee policy addressed concerns over the abuse of the immigration system, while maintaining the support of stakeholders that benefited from the policy's innovative inclusion of private sponsorship provisions. Finally, Canada's policy of official multiculturalism (see Chapter 10 by Banting in this volume) has also resulted in a public ideology supportive of immigration (Bloemraad, 2012; Reitz, 2011).

Effective policy design is, however, only part of the story. Three contingent factors also stand behind Canada's successful immigration policy. First, Canada's isolated geography—akin to what Reese and Ye (2011) refer to as 'place luck'—limits flows of asylum seekers and other unwanted immigrants. Second, the substantial power vested in the federal executive branch, and the de facto dominance of the federal government in immigration policy, has enabled Canadian governments to respond to flows of unplanned, unwanted migrants quickly (Triadafilopoulos, 2013b; Ellermann, 2021). The fact that both the 1976 Immigration Act and the IRPA are framework laws has further enabled the exercise of executive power and discretion. Third, the pro-immigration consensus among Canada's major political parties is based on a fortuitous concatenation of immigration settlement patterns, citizenship policy, and Canada's Single Member Plurality (SMP) electoral system (Triadafilopoulos and Taylor, 2021; Taylor, 2021). The overwhelming majority of Canada's immigrants settle in the most densely populated parts of the country, also home to the greatest concentration of federal electoral ridings. Canada's efficient citizenship regime transforms almost all of them into enfranchised voters, whose electoral weight is amplified by Canada's SMP electoral system. Pro-immigration positions are therefore in the interest of all major parties.[1]

This chapter is organized as follows. It begins by tracing the development of Canada's approach to immigration from the era of racial selection to adoption of the 'points system' in 1967, the Immigration Act of 1976, and IRPA in 2001, highlighting policymakers' use of executive power to shift Canadian immigration policy in the 1980s and 1990s to privileging selected economic immigration. This

---

[1] Consensus on pro-immigration positions is the norm for provincial politics as well, with the conspicuous exception of Québec, where parties have competed to demonstrate their willingness to uphold secularism by imposing limits on religious expression (Laxer, 2019). That being said, Québec continues to welcome a significant number of immigrants every year; none of Québec's major political parties comes near to expressing the sorts of anti-immigration positions that have become sadly normal in Western Europe and the United States (Joppke, 2021).

allowed Canada to maintain its commitment to economic, family, and humanitarian/refugee immigration to further national interests, while defusing political conflict and generating public support. The chapter then surveys the evolution of Canada's most important immigration and refugee programs. In doing so, the chapter notes the continued success of immigration policies in attracting economic immigrants, responding to changing labour market demands, and overcoming other challenges through innovative policies. Similarly, shifts in refugee policy, which have narrowed access to asylum seekers while adjusting resettlement programs to enhance the role of private sponsorship, are also highlighted. The chapter then turns to the politics of immigration and refugee policy, noting popular support and cross-party political consensus for a robust immigration system, and highlights the role of effective policy design, executive power, fortuitous geography, and other contingent factors that have contributed to this political success. The chapter concludes by reflecting on how the Canadian case speaks to the wider challenge of regulating international migration in liberal-democratic states. If success in immigration policy is premised on the effective use of executive power to develop efficient systems that privilege selected economic immigrants and effectively deter unwanted migrants, is 'success' compatible with fundamental standards of liberal justice and legitimacy? This dilemma is particularly acute with respect to process success. Immigration policy starkly highlights how satisfying the interests of political insiders (stakeholders, citizens) may involve diminishing those of outsiders (migrants) who lack standing or are otherwise disadvantaged and marginalized in policy deliberations.

From White Canada to the Canadian Model: Executive Power and Process Success

Immigration has always played an important role in Canada's development. The National Policy, introduced by Canada's federal government in 1878, included the promotion of immigration to stimulate domestic demand for goods and services and meet the labour needs of industry (Kelley and Trebilcock, 2010, 62–63). Using immigration policy to satisfy economic ends is thus not new. The standards used to select immigrants have, however, changed radically over the course of Canada's history.

For most of the nineteenth and twentieth centuries, Canada based its immigration admissions policies on racial criteria. Immigration policy was designed with an eye to maintaining Canada's status as a 'white man's country' (Triadafilopoulos, 2004; Lake and Reynolds, 2008; Fitzgerald and Cook-Martín, 2014). In terms of occupational preferences, Canadian policy skewed heavily towards farmers, as immigration was aimed at facilitating western expansion and settlement (Kelley and Trebilcock, 2010, ch. 3).

164 CANADA'S GOOD AND LUCKY IMMIGRATION POLICIES

Canada's discriminatory immigration policies were challenged after World War II. The discrediting of scientific racism, emergence of a global human rights regime, and acceleration of the decolonization movement drove this process (Triadafilopoulos, 2012; also see Thompson, 2020). Racially discriminatory immigration policies enacted before the war presented a problem for liberal democracies that had fought to defeat Nazism and advance the cause of human dignity. Emboldened by this shift in prevailing norms, aggrieved domestic constituencies, foreign governments, and international organizations vigorously challenged Canada's discriminatory immigration policies (Triadafilopoulos, 2012). Their pressure campaigns were effective. Changes to immigration policy in the 1950s granted some access to previously excluded groups (Triadafilopoulos, 2012; Fitzgerald and Cook-Martín, 2014). In 1962, the Diefenbaker government publicly announced that Canada would no longer refer to race in its admissions decisions (Simmons, 2010, 73). This move was strengthened in 1967, with the introduction of the 'points system' (Triadafilopoulos, 2013a).

The points system established a standard set of measures for weighing applicants' qualifications. Prospective immigrants received a score based on their age, education, training, occupational skill in demand, knowledge of English or French, relatives in Canada, arranged employment, and employment opportunities in area of destination. A personal assessment by an immigration officer was added to the tally. Applicants meeting the threshold set by the government (initially 50 assessment points) would be admitted as independent immigrants, and would enjoy the right to sponsor dependents as well as 'nominated relatives'. The points system made human capital the principal criterion for determining the suitability of immigrants, universalizing immigrant admissions and aligning immigration policy with Canada's transformation into an increasingly urban, industrialized society (Simmons, 2010, 76–77; Kelley and Trebilcock, 2010, 360–362).

The elimination of racial considerations in immigration selection, through the Diefenbaker Progressive Conservative government's 1962 statement on immigration policy and the Pearson Liberal government's introduction of the points system in 1967, reflected the significant power and discretion of the executive branch (Ellermann, 2021). Although the House of Commons and Senate were consulted, there was no formal parliamentary debate or vote on the points system. One of the most profound shifts in the history of Canadian public policy was enacted through a modification of existing regulations.

The changes to immigration policy introduced through the 1950s and 1960s were entrenched in the Immigration Act of 1976. In contrast to the process leading to the introduction of the points system, the government engaged in extensive consultations led by a Special Joint Committee of the Senate and the House of Commons. The inclusion of many of the Committee's recommendations enhanced the legitimacy of the new law. The fundamental principles and objectives of Canadian immigration policy set out in the 1976 Immigration Act endure to this day. They include:

1. Promotion of economic, social, demographic, and cultural goals
2. Endorsement of family reunification
3. Fulfilment of Canada's international obligations under the United Nations Convention and 1967 Protocol relating to refugees (Knowles, 2007, 169)

The Immigration Act defined three classes of immigrants: the economic class, selected through the points system; the family class, recruited through sponsorship by Canadian citizens and permanent residents; and the refugee class, which included individuals resettled by the Canadian state and authorized private sponsors, and individuals claiming asylum after arriving in Canada ('in-land' claimants/asylum seekers). The Immigration Act also called for the government to set an annual immigration target, determined through consultation with the provinces, and present an annual report to parliament summarizing yearly immigration planning. As with previous immigration acts, the detailed operation of Canada's immigration system would be determined by regulations.

By the mid-1980s, the mix between economic and family class immigrants was skewed towards the latter (Ellermann, 2021, 217). Whereas family class immigrants accounted for 35 per cent of the total immigration intake in 1975, their share had grown to 55 per cent in 1983. Conversely, economic class immigrants had declined from 73 per cent of total admissions in 1971 to 31 per cent in 1983. These outcomes were due both to the expansive provisions governing sponsorship at the time of the enactment of the 1976 Act and wariness regarding the admission of economic immigrants during a period of relative economic decline. A decision was taken in 1982 to admit only individuals with arranged employment (Green and Green, 1999, 432).

Policymakers began to address this programmatic shortcoming in the economic/family class balance of immigrants from the mid-1980s onward. The Mulroney Progressive Conservative government increased immigration levels, from 84,000 in 1985 to 161,600 in 1988 and 191,600 in 1989 (Statistics Canada, 2016). To increase the share of economic class immigrants, the prerequisite of arranged employment for economic class applicants was dropped in 1986 (Green and Green, 1999, 433) and programs aimed at attracting entrepreneurs and investors were introduced (Simmons, 2010, 79). The number of economic immigrants tripled between 1985 and 1989 'expanding the economic class relative significance from 31 to 47 per cent of total admissions' (Ellermann, 2021, 222). The proportion of family class admissions was reduced by reallocating resources for processing family class applications to the administration of business and investor programs.

In 1990, the Mulroney Conservatives tabled a five-year plan calling for immigration to continue to rise to an annual intake of 250,000 individuals by 1995.

Future immigration levels would remain at 250,000 per year, regardless of prevailing economic conditions; the longstanding 'tap-on/tap-off' approach, which tied economic immigration to the state of the economy, was abandoned. A 1992 report, *Managing Immigration: A Framework for the 1990s*, justified the decision to increase immigration levels independently of labour market conditions by pointing to Canada's transition to a 'globalized, highly competitive, knowledge-based economy' (Simmons, 2010, 82–83). The report also called for further reductions to family class immigration. Policymakers obliged by reducing the age limit for sponsored children from 21 to 19 and eliminating sponsorship provisions for extended relatives. These moves shifted the mix of annual admissions: 'By 1995 ... the percentage of family immigrants had dropped from 50 percent in 1984, when Mulroney took office, to 36 percent' (Ellermann 2021, 224).

The transition begun by the Mulroney Conservatives to an immigration program aimed squarely at attracting large numbers of highly skilled economic immigrants was completed by the Liberal governments of Jean Chrétien and Paul Martin. By the late-1990s, political parties, civil servants and key stakeholders, most notably employers, agreed on the need for Canada's immigration system to complement a labour market that prized flexibility. Their consensus reflected the influence of neoliberal ideas in the 1990s (Abu-Laban and Gabriel, 2002). But there was more to the shift. Critics of immigration policy, led by the Reform Party, decried the size of family class admissions, arguing that too many sponsored immigrants lacked the tools needed to succeed in a knowledge-based economy. Elderly parents and grandparents and sponsored family members, more generally, were framed as unproductive consumers of welfare benefits (Abu-Laban and Gabriel, 2002, 63). The shift to an immigration program focused on the recruitment of highly skilled immigrants was aimed at defusing these criticisms.

The politics of immigration policy were also marked by controversy over asylum seekers. As a signatory to the 1951 Refugee Convention and its 1967 Protocol, Canada was required to consider all applications for asylum made on Canadian territory (Labman, 2019, 35). This obligation was reinforced by the 1976 Immigration Act's acknowledgement that Canada would fulfil its 'international legal obligations with respect to refugees and ... uphold its humanitarian tradition with respect to the displaced and persecuted' (Labman, 2019, 40). As Shauna Labman has argued, there is an important distinction contained in this statement. Whereas Canada's legal obligations under the Refugee Convention pertained to its treatment of asylum seekers who made a refugee claim upon landing in Canada, Canada's 'humanitarian tradition' referred to a history of resettling refugees through discretionary acts of kindness, typically exercised in an ad hoc manner, and very much based on a degree of self-interest (Labman, 2019, 44).

Canadian governments elided this distinction for a brief time. Indeed, the UNHCR awarded Canada the Nansen Refugee Award for its contribution to the refugee cause in 1986, in response to Canada's resettlement of over 60,000 Indochinese refugees between 1978 and 1982 (Knowles, 2007, 223). Changes in the dynamics of international migration in the late-1980s and 1990s forced Canadian policymakers to reconsider their approach to refugees. The low number of asylum claims in the 1970s rose steadily in the 1980s and precipitously in the 1990s. As the number of in-land asylum claims increased steeply, the adjudication system through which refugee status was extended came under intense pressure. By the end of 1988, the backlog of claims exceeded 100,000 (Simmons, 2010, 80). The Supreme Court of Canada's decision in *Singh v Minister of Employment and Immigration* (1985) exacerbated this challenge by mandating that asylum claimants in Canada were entitled to an oral hearing (Simmons, 2010, 80). The government established the Immigration and Refugee Review Board in 1988 to speed up the status determination process and reduce the backlog, which nevertheless remained persistently high. Indeed, asylum claims increased in the early-1990s with the end of the Cold War (Keely, 2001).

Experts broadly agreed that the problems related to refugee status determination was a programmatic failing. Yet the asylum issue went well beyond programmatic concerns. The arrival of asylum seekers by boat, often with the assistance of human smugglers, generated intense media coverage and raised concerns about the integrity of Canada's system of border control (Labman, 2019, 41). The Reform Party 'raised the spectre of "illegal immigration" and "bogus refugees" to further demonstrate [its] contention that Canadian immigration policy and immigration regulations were too lax' (Abu-Laban and Gabriel, 2002, 64).

Canadian governments responded to these criticisms with legislation to discourage refugees. After 173 asylum seekers arrived by boat off the coast of Nova Scotia in July 1987, the Mulroney government amended the Immigration Act to 'deter refugee claimants, impose more stringent detention provisions, and expand inadmissibility provisions' (Kelley and Trebilcock, 2010, 406). It also passed Bill C-86 in 1992 to (among other things) prohibit refugee claimants from 'seeking employment until a final determination of their claim' had been made (Kelley and Trebilcock, 2010, 408). When four ships containing some 600 migrants from China arrived on Canada's shores in the summer of 1999, many of the immigrants, including children, were detained until their identities could be confirmed. Most of these individuals were returned to China, and only about 5 per cent of those who claimed refugee status were granted asylum or allowed to remain on a Minister's Permit (Kelley and Trebilcock, 2010, 422).

By the end of the 1990s, the basic parameters of the Canadian model of immigration and refugee policy were in place. Immigration aimed first-and-foremost at meeting Canada's economic needs through the recruitment of well-educated and highly skilled immigrants. While family class immigration would continue to be an important part of Canada's immigration program, its standing as compared to economic migration was decidedly inferior. While Canada was obliged to consider claims for asylum by uninvited migrants that managed to gain a foothold in Canadian territory, measures would be taken to reduce their numbers and streamline the status determination process. Refugee policy would emphasize resettlement, which was also based on selection. These fundamental positions reflected prevailing ideas concerning competitiveness in a globalizing world, and the imperatives of security in a geostrategic environment marked by asymmetrical threats and transnational criminal organizations involved in human smuggling and trafficking (Irvine, 2011). Henceforth, immigration policy would be primarily oriented towards enhancing Canadians' prosperity and security.

These core components of Canada's refugee policy were clear in the 2001 IRPA. Introducing the first version of the legislation to the House of Commons in April 2000, minister of immigration and citizenship, Elinor Caplan, described it as a 'tough bill' designed to enable the government to close 'the back door to those who would abuse the system' so as to ensure 'that the front door will remain open … to genuine refugees and to the immigrants our country will need to grow and prosper in the years ahead' (cited in Kelley and Trebilcock, 2010, 425). While the IRPA maintained the 1976 Immigration Act's three distinct immigration classes, its 'skeletal' structure enabled the government to continue favouring carefully selected economic immigrants as against family class immigrants and refugees. The IRPA established a broad framework for immigration policymaking, 'leaving the details to the executive to design and implement through regulation, with minimal parliamentary scrutiny' (Kelley and Trebilcock, 2010, 425).

Assessing the Program Success of Canada's Immigration and Refugee Policies

Robust Admissions and Striking Diversity

Canada has succeeded in attracting high numbers of immigrants. Annual admissions averaged 250,000 through the 1990s and early 2000s, regardless of the state of the economy (Statistics Canada, 2016). Immigration levels have increased since the 2015 election, from 296,368 in 2016 to 336,499 in 2019 (Immigration, Refugees and Citizenship Canada, 2019, 2020). The Trudeau government's current targets call for 401,000 immigrants to be admitted in 2021, 411,000 in 2022, and 421,000 in 2023 (Harris, 2020). Canadian immigration levels have remained robust despite the disruptions prompted by the 9/11 terrorist attacks, the 2008–9 global economic crisis, and the Covid-19 pandemic.

Canada's foreign-born population increased from 17.4 per cent in 1996 to 21.9 per cent in 2016. Based on projections by Statistics Canada, this figure could rise to 30 per cent by 2036 (Statistics Canada, 2017). The combination of immigrants and second-generation individuals (the children of immigrants) could climb to half of Canada's total population in the same timeframe.

Canada's decision to eliminate racial criteria from its immigrant selection system significantly shifted the source regions of the country's immigrants. Whereas the vast majority of immigrants hailed from Europe until the introduction of the points system in 1967, by 2016, 48.1 per cent of Canada's foreign-born population was born in Asia, as against 27.7 per cent born in Europe (Statistics Canada, 2016). The top five source countries in 2017 were India, the Philippines, the People's Republic of China, Syria, and the United States of America (Immigration, Refugees and Citizenship Canada, 2017). Canada's visible minority population—those individuals neither white nor Indigenous—increased from 4.7 per cent in 1981 to 22.3 per cent in 2016. This figure is estimated to increase to 35.9 per cent in 2036.

Adapting Economic Immigration Policies to Meet New Demands

As Canadian decision-makers intended, annual admissions since the early-2000s have skewed heavily towards economic immigrants. In 2019, 196,658 of Canada's 336,499 immigrants (58.4 per cent) were in the economic class (Immigration, Citizenship and Refugees Canada, 2020). The Trudeau government's most recent targets aim to have economic immigrants make up 60 per cent of total annual admissions (Harris, 2020). Family class immigrants presently account for a little more than a quarter of annual admissions (Immigration, Citizenship and Refugees, Canada 2020).

The Federal Skilled Worker Program (FSWP) has been a key part of Canada's immigration system since the 1970s. Through the late-1990s and early-2000s, the FSWP favoured the admission of immigrants with advanced degrees, professional designations, and extensive foreign work experience (Reitz, 2004). Paradoxically, these immigrants experienced worrying rates of unemployment and falling earnings relative to native-born Canadians and previous immigrant cohorts, despite having satisfied more stringent admissions requirements (Boyd, 2013; Hawthorne, 2013). The FSWP, which traditionally operated on a first-come-first-served basis, was also beset by backlogs, with applicants typically waiting several years to have their cases decided.

The Conservative government of Prime Minister Stephen Harper sought to address these problems through several reforms. One, among the most important, was the introduction of 'two-step' immigration programs: certain classes of Temporary Foreign Workers (TFWs) and international students could convert their temporary status to permanent residency (Hennebry, 2010, 62–67). Two-step immigration was pursued through the retooling of the Provincial Nominee Program (PNP) and creation of the Canadian Experience Class (CEC). A second improved the outcomes of the FSWP by introducing the Express Entry system.

The PNP, introduced by the Liberals in 1995, aimed to assist low-immigrant provinces by enabling them to select a limited number of economic immigrants in accordance with their demographic and labour market needs (Banting, 2010, 9). This process began with Manitoba in 1998 and, by 2007, all the provinces (with the exception of Québec) and two of Canada's three northern territories had enacted PNP agreements (Banting, 2012, 88–89). Québec had already been granted extensive power to select immigrants through the 1978 Cullen-Couture Agreement and the 1991 Canada-Québec Accord (Kelley and Trebilcock, 2010, 387–388). Although immigrant admissions under PNP began modestly, by 2019 they constituted over a third of total economic immigration (Immigration, Refugees and Citizenship Canada, 2019, 2020).

The PNP became a central component of Canada's economic immigration system due to the expansion of TFW migration under the Conservative Harper governments (Foster, 2012). The PNP enables the provinces to satisfy regional labour needs by nominating TFWs, including lower skilled TFWs who would otherwise not satisfy the conditions of the FSWP. The CEC also plays a role in this regard, as it allows international students and highly skilled TFWs with Canadian work experience and a job to convert their temporary status to permanent residency.

The Express Entry System also gives employers a more prominent role in selecting immigrants (Triadafilopoulos, 2015). Applicants submit a 'preliminary expression of interest' for admission under the FSWP and the CEC, and are screened through a points-based system. Successful candidates apply for permanent residency and applications are processed within six months. The Express Entry System's success in broadening the range of candidates for admission under the economic class, and eliminating application backlogs, has contributed to its durability.

Canada's economic immigration programs are considered effective, legitimate, and innovative. However, some recent changes have raised concerns. While expanding two-step migration has benefited provinces and employers, its longer term consequences are unclear. All immigrants admitted through traditional one-step measures qualify for settlement assistance upon landing in Canada (Andrew, 2011; Banting, 2012). Between 2000 and 2015, the share of economic class migrants admitted under one-step measures fell from 90 to 40 per cent (Ellermann, 2019, 154–155). Conversely, economic immigrants initially arriving as TFWs or international students only qualify for settlement assistance after they become permanent residents. Whether this discrepancy in access to settlement assistance leads to shortfalls in the integration outcomes of immigrants selected through two-step programs is an open question.

The introduction of the Express Entry system came at some cost to process. Tens of thousands of applications received under the previous system and languishing in the backlog were returned without processing, despite applicants having waited several years for a decision on their file (Levitz, 2012). In a cruel irony, the cost of resolving the backlog problem was paid for by those that had been its chief victims.

Refugee Policy: Program Success in Restricting Asylum and Adapting Resettlement

Canada's refugee system is made up of two parts: the In-Canada Asylum Program and the Refugee and Humanitarian Resettlement Program. The asylum program provides protection to people in Canada unable or unwilling to return to their home country because they have a well-founded fear of persecution (as per the Refugee Convention) or are at risk of torture, or cruel or unusual punishment (as per the United Nations Convention Against Torture and Other Cruel, Inhuman or Degrading Treatment or Punishment). Successful claimants receive Convention refugee status or are deemed a 'person in need of protection' (in cases that fall under the UN Convention on Torture) and are eligible to apply for permanent residency. Failed claimants receive a conditional removal order and must leave Canada within 30 days of their decision. However, rejected claimants may seek a stay of removal and apply for leave for judicial review; apply for a temporary resident permit; apply for a pre-removal risk assessment; apply for permanent residency on humanitarian and compassionate grounds; appeal their decision to the Refugee Appeal Division (RAD); or seek judicial review through the Federal Court.

Asylum policy has long generated political controversy. Public dissatisfaction has tended to spike during periods when groups of asylum seekers have landed in Canada without prearranged authorization, usually by boat. These events have raised public concern that the complex system of rules and procedures in place to protect the rights of refugees are being exploited by economic migrants, who would otherwise not qualify for admission to Canada. Immigration officials share these concerns. The immigration officials Sandy Irvine interviewed in 2005 and 2006 also believed that 'an overly fair refugee determination system, too many opportunities to appeal decisions, and long delays in processing claims [made] the Canadian system more susceptible to abuse' (Irvine, 2011, 186).

Recent changes in Canada's asylum policies have been undertaken with the aim of assuaging these worries by demonstrating Canada's commitment to the Refugee Convention but also to mitigating potential abuse of the system. In March 2010, less than six months after two ships carrying Tamil migrants landed off the coast of British Columbia, the Harper government introduced Bill C-11, the Balanced Refugee Reform Act. An amended version of the bill was passed by the House and Senate in June 2010. In August of 2010, a second ship carrying Tamil migrants landed in British Columbia. Before the ship had even anchored, a spokesperson for Citizenship and Immigration Canada promised Canadians that the government was committed to 'cracking down on bogus refugees, while providing protection to those that truly need our help' (cited in Labman, 2019, 48). In October 2010, the government introduced Bill C-49, the Preventing Human Smugglers from Abusing Canada's Immigration System Act (Labman, 2019, 49). The bill, which died on the order paper when the 2011 election was called, was reintroduced after the Conservatives won a new mandate in a majority parliament. Bill C-31, the Protecting Canada's Immigration System Act came into effect on 28 June 2012.

According to the rules in place since 2012, asylum seekers arriving from 'designated countries of origin' (DCOs) that generally do not produce refugees have their applications decided on a fast-track basis. Refugees who arrive in a group of two or more fall under the 'irregular arrivals' category and are termed 'designated foreign nationals' (DFNs) (Labman, 2019, 49). They may be detained while their applications are considered and cannot appeal if their claims are rejected. Even when they receive Convention refugee status, DFNs face a 'five-year suspension before being eligible to apply for permanent residency, temporary residency, or permanent residency on humanitarian and compassionate grounds' (Labman, 2019, 50).

Asylum claims fell between 2012 and 2016 but rose sharply in 2017 and 2018, as a result of changes to immigration and refugee policies in the United States. Many asylum seekers in the United States crossed the Canada-US land border irregularly, bypassing official points of entry in order to avoid being sent back under the terms of the 2002 Canada-US Safe Third Country Agreement (which holds that asylum seekers must make their claim in the country of first arrival) (Macklin, 2004). As in the past, the entry of irregular migrants drew significant press attention, raising concerns regarding the Canadian government's ability to control its borders (Angus Reid, 2018; Boyd and Ly, 2021).

The Trudeau government introduced legislation to check the flow of asylum seekers in its 2019 omnibus budget bill. Changes included an amendment to the IRPA 'denying refugee claimants the right to a hearing if they ever sought asylum in any country "holding information sharing agreements" with Canada' (Boyd and Ly 2021). The budget also included 'substantial funding for enhanced law enforcement' and a 'comprehensive Border Enforcement Strategy to "better detect and intercept individuals who cross Canadian borders irregularly and *who try to exploit Canada's immigration system*"' (Boyd and Ly 2021, emphasis added).

Whereas asylum seekers select Canada as a potential site of refuge, Canada's Refugee and Humanitarian Resettlement Program endows the Canadian state and authorized private sponsors with the power to decide who merits sanctuary. Government Assisted Refugees (GARs) are referred by the UNHCR and already meet the conditions of the Refugee Convention. The Government of Canada facilitates their travel to Canada, grants them permanent residency upon arrival, and covers the costs of their resettlement for one year. GARs are entitled to services such as orientation sessions and life skills training through the Resettlement Assistance

Program (Elgersma, 2015). After their first year in Canada, all resettled refugees are eligible for means-tested government social programs.

Privately Sponsored Refugees (PSRs) are sponsored by groups of private individuals in Canada. Private Sponsorship Agreement Holders (SAHs) are organizations that have a signed agreement with the Canadian government to sponsor a refugee or refugees, or to assist other sponsoring 'constituent groups' with their applications. Faith-based organizations play an outsized role in private sponsorship, accounting for 75 per cent of SAHs (Hyndman, Payne and Jiminez, 2017, 58). Refugees can also be sponsored by 'Groups of Five', whereby five or more Canadian citizens and/or permanent residents, who demonstrate their financial means and sponsorship ability, enter into an agreement to support a refugee or refugees. Private sponsors provide settlement assistance to the refugees under their care for one year.

While annual admissions to Canada's refugee resettlement program have remained relatively stable over the past twenty years, the share of resettled refugees falling under private sponsorship has increased significantly. The 2012 federal budget shifted 1,000 refugees from the GAR program to private sponsorship and created the Blended Visa Office-Referred (BVOR) Program. BVOR matches Convention refugees identified by the UNHCR with private sponsors in Canada, splitting settlement costs over one year between the government and private sponsors (Labman, 2019, 56). PSRs have outnumbered GARs since 2017. In 2019, 19,130 PSRs were resettled in Canada, as against 9,940 GARs and 990 refugees falling under the BVOR program (Martani, 2021, 3).

How might we judge the success of Canada's refugee programs? On the one hand, Canada has emerged as the world's top resettlement country (in terms of refugee numbers), surpassing the United States in 2018 (Radford and Connor, 2019). Canada's unique system of private sponsorship has also been applauded and efforts are underway to 'export' it (Smith, 2020). Canadian governments refer to their records in resettlement to demonstrate that they consistently meet their humanitarian obligations to refugees.

On the other hand, Canada's contribution to meeting the needs of the world's refugees is paltry. Refugees account for the lowest share of annual immigration admissions. Even in 2016, which featured a one-time expansion of Canada's resettlement program to fulfil a Liberal Party election pledge to resettle 25,000 Syrian refugees, refugees accounted for less than 16 per cent of Canada's total immigration admissions. Of the 58,435 refugees admitted to Canada in 2016, 79.3 per cent came through resettlement programs; barely one fifth came through the asylum program (Immigration, Citizenship and Refugees Canada, 2017).

Even if Canada's commitment to settling 30,000 refugees per year places it atop the resettlement standings, it is a modest gesture in a world in which the UNHCR designates approximately one million refugees in urgent need of resettlement (Lenard 2021). Nonetheless, Canadian governments have successfully cast their refugee resettlement policies as evidence of their willingness to assist the 'truly' desperate. Resettlement provides a useful means of satisfying domestic humanitarian groups (that benefit from private sponsorship) while deflecting attention away from Canada's stingy asylum policies.

An Exceptional Country? Success in the Politics of Immigration Policy

Canadian success in immigration policy is most conspicuous when we consider politics. Canadians expressed the most positive view on immigration in the Pew Research Center's 2018 Global Attitudes Survey (Gonzalez-Barrera and Connor, 2019, 3). Public opinion has become more supportive of immigration over time (Banting and Soroka, 2020). The 2020 iteration of the Environics Institute for Survey Research's long-running 'Focus Canada' survey found that 'strong and increasing majorities of Canadians express comfort with current immigration levels, see immigrants as good for the Canadian economy ... and believe that immigration is essential to building the country's population ... By a five-to-one margin, the public believes immigration makes Canada a better country' (Environics, 2020).

Support for immigration extends beyond public opinion to include the media, business and labour organizations, and civil society more broadly. Most remarkably, all three of Canada's major political parties agree on the fundamental features of Canada's immigration system. Anti-immigrant campaigns are rare. The People's Party of Canada's attempt to politicize immigration in the 2019 federal election ended with the party polling under 2 per cent and its leader, Maxime Bernier, losing his seat in the House of Commons (Ling, 2019).

Support for Canada's immigration policy is based in part on Canadian governments' long standing efforts to highlight its beneficial effects. As Daniel Hiebert (2016, 5) has noted, 'framing immigration in economic terms and presenting it as a solution to the nation's problems has led to a mutually reinforcing set of outcomes: Canadians expect immigration to be coordinated with economic need and, as a result, they have typically supported immigration mainly when it is aligned with economic concerns.' Multiculturalism policy has played a complementary role, encouraging the development of a national identity that 'embraces immigration, diversity, and tolerance' (Bloemraad, 2012, 8).

The flipside of this emphasis on coordination and openness is the rigorous suppression of uncoordinated and unselected migration. Canadian governments have benefited from Canada's distinctive geography in this regard: 'that Canada has no direct land connection to less developed nations and that it is separated from them by very wide oceans helps explain why fewer unauthorized immigrants enter Canada' (Simmons, 2010, 105). Those who make it to Canada confront a gauntlet of measures devised since the late-1980s to limit their numbers. Substantive executive power, aided by legislation that facilitates discretion, enables Canadian governments to quickly respond to challenges as they arise.

Cross-party consensus on the benefits of managed immigration rests on the contingent interplay of immigrant settlement patterns, an efficient citizenship regime, and Canada's SMP electoral system. Over 70 per cent of Canada's foreign-born population has settled in the provinces of Ontario, British Columbia, and Québec, concentrated in and around the cities of Toronto, Vancouver, and Montréal (Triadafilopoulos and Taylor, 2021, 25). At the same time, 38 per cent of Canada's federal electoral ridings are located in the greater Toronto, Vancouver, and Montréal regions. Immigrants make up a substantial proportion of the population in a considerable number of federal electoral ridings (Griffith, 2017).

Canada's liberal and highly efficient citizenship regime quickly transforms immigrants into voters. Canada's citizenship acquisition rate has long stood at or above 80 per cent (Xu and Golah, 2015, ii). The 2011 National Household Survey found that Ontario 'had the largest eligible immigrant population and the highest proportion of immigrants who had obtained citizenship (87.0 Percent)'. Québec's and British Columbia's proportions of eligible immigrants who had obtained citizenship stood at 85.1 and 84.3 per cent, respectively (Statistics Canada, 2013, 4).

As Alan Cairns (1968) has pointed out, Canada's SMP electoral system rewards regionally concentrated support while heavily discounting territorially dispersed support. SMP systems reward winning parties and punish losers, regardless of the difference in vote share. Small swings in the vote preferences of regionally concentrated groups can translate into large swings in the seat counts of competing parties, particularly when those groups are concentrated in areas with a significant share of competitive seats (Linzer, 2012). Immigration since the 1990s has amplified this basic effect of the electoral system (Westlake, 2018; Taylor, 2021). The growth and concentration of immigrant and visible minority voters in urban Canada, generally, and the Greater Toronto Hamilton Area (GTHA), in particular, has transformed these ridings into electoral battlegrounds that no party interested in governing can afford to ignore. Consequently, Canadian parties have avoided politicizing immigration during and between elections.

Conclusion

Canada's immigration policies meet the standard of success in terms of endurance, process, programs, and politics. The fundamental principles underlying Canadian immigration policy have been in place since the passage of the 1976 Immigration Act and, despite changes in emphasis, remain the pillars of the 2001 IRPA. With regard to process, Canadian governments have taken advantage of the significant power and discretion at their disposal to quickly adapt policies to address administrative and political shortcomings. These moves have been supported by key stakeholders and buttressed by the support of the Canadian public. In terms of programs, Canada's system of managed immigration focuses on the recruitment of economic immigrants, while meeting its obligations with respect to family sponsorship. Canada also maintains its commitment to the Refugee Convention but has narrowed access to asylum seekers, while emphasizing its more popular resettlement programs. Political support for immigration has steadily increased since the mid-1990s, as reflected in ever more positive public opinion and consensus among Canada's major political parties on the benefits of a selective system of managed immigration. While populist anti-immigration politics is present in Canada, it remains marginal.

Canada's success in immigration policy has been based on a combination of effective design, executive power, and contingent factors. As other countries cannot move into better neighbourhoods or easily change their electoral systems, the range of 'lessons' to be learned from Canada is limited to policy design and techniques of policymaking. With respect to policies, there has been a noteworthy turn to managed migration policies along Canadian lines in Britain, Germany, and other European countries (Triadafilopoulos, 2013b). Even former American president Donald Trump, perhaps the world's most infamous nativist, spoke favourably of Canada's selective immigration policies (Kwong, 2019).

Other jurisdictions have also followed Canada's lead in terms of process. Unwanted flows of unselected migrants are dealt with quickly, often through rights-restrictive measures. This is evident in Australia's move to 'off-shore' its asylum system (Castles, Vasta, and Ozkul, 2014), the radical cuts to refugee admissions in the United States (Waslin, 2020), and ongoing efforts in Europe, at the national and supranational levels, to strictly police asylum through a bewildering array of rapidly proliferating initiatives (Geddes, 2018). Interventions along these lines are defended with reference to enabling the efficient administration of immigration systems and maintaining the political support of fickle publics wary of uncontrolled migration.

These trends raise deeper questions: do managed migration policies that enjoy the support of democratic publics require the vigorous exercise of coercive state power to quickly plug gaps and preserve the smooth functioning of administrative systems? If so, how can successful policy processes be reconciled with basic human rights and due process? Canada has demonstrated that the strictures imposed by the Refugee Convention and domestic law do not advance the interests of asylum seekers very far. If democratic politics pulls governments towards drawing ever sharper distinctions between wanted and unwanted immigrants, what countervailing forces will check this trend? To what degree can a world of effective and successfully managed immigration be legitimate, in terms of fundamental standards of justice?

The Canadian case suggests that success in immigration policy comes at a cost. Yet, even McConnell's relatively nuanced approach to determining policy success, failure, and the 'grey areas in-between' has difficulty registering such costs. Indeed, 'a successful policy that achieves the goals its proponents set out' with little in the way of criticism and 'virtually universal support' may still be open to question on normative grounds (McConnell, 2010, 351). This is especially true with regard to how 'process' is conceptualized in McConnell's framework. Given their status as aliens without presence (let alone standing) in Canadian politics, migrants' positions on policies that directly affect them have generally not been taken into consideration. As Arash Abizadeh (2008, 37–38) has noted, this is true of immigration policy as a rule: 'According to the state sovereignty view—the dominant ideology of the contemporary interstate system—entry policy ought to be under the unilateral discretion of (the members of) the state itself, and whatever justification is required for a particular entry policy is simply owed to members: foreigners are owed no justification and so should have no control over a state's entry policy.' Indeed, it is not hard to see how process success might require limiting the range of opinions included in policy deliberations. In a representative democracy, satisfying the demands of stakeholders and voters necessarily comes before attending to the interests of outsiders. While this failure of the 'all affected' principal (Koenig-Archibugi, 2017) is starkest with respect to immigration policy, it is also relevant in other policy areas where insiders enjoy a marked advantage in terms of advancing their positions in political deliberations and outsiders' voices are either muted or ignored altogether. This suggests that determinations of policy success and failure must be careful to consider the interests of all affected parties, especially those that are easily neglected by policymakers and academics.

Acknowledgements

I thank Keith Banting, Grace Skogstad, Paul 't Hart, Rob Vipond, and an anonymous reviewer for their very helpful comments on earlier drafts of this chapter. Thanks also to Michael Howlett, Evert A. Lindquist, and Geneviève Tellier.

References

Abizadeh, A. 2008. "Democratic Theory and Border Coercion: No Right to Unilaterally Control Your Own Borders." *Political Theory*, 36 (1): pp. 37–65.

Abu-Laban, Y. and C. Gabriel. 2002. *Selling Diversity: Immigration, Multiculturalism, Employment Equity, and Globalization*. Toronto: Broadview Press.

Adams, M. and D. Norris. 2018. "Sanctuary Cities: Why it's Harder for Trumpism to Take Root in Urban Canada." *Globe and Mail*, 19 January.

178 CANADA'S GOOD AND LUCKY IMMIGRATION POLICIES

Alboim, N. and K. Cohl. 2012. *Shaping the Future: Canada's Rapidly Changing Immigration Policies.* Toronto: Maytree.

Andrew, C. and R. A. Hima. 2011. "Federal Policies on Immigrant Settlement." In *Immigrant Settlement Policies in Canadian Municipalities,* edited by E. Tolley and R. Young, 49–72. Montreal and Kingston: McGill-Queen's University Press.

Angus Reid Institute. 2018. "Two-Thirds Call Irregular Border Crossings a 'Crisis'." Angus Reid Institute. 3 August. https://angusreid.org/safe-third-country-asylum-seekers/

Banting, K. and S. Soroka. 2020. "A Distinctive Culture? The Sources of Public Support for Immigration in Canada, 1980–2019." *Canadian Journal of Political Science* 53 (4): pp. 1–18.

Banting, K. 2010. "Federalism and Immigrant Integration in Canada." Unpublished paper for the conference on Immigrant Integration: The Impact of Federalism on Public Policy. Brussels, Belgium. November 2010.

Banting, K. 2012. "Canada." In *Immigrant Integration in Federal Countries,* edited by C. Joppke and F. L. Seidle, pp. 79–112. Montreal and Kingston: McGill-Queen's University Press.

Béchard, J. and S. Elgersma. 2013. *Refugee Protection in Canada. Background Paper.* Ottawa: Library of Parliament.

Bloemraad, I. 2012. *Understanding 'Canadian Exceptionalism' in Immigration and Pluralism Policy.* Washington, DC: Migration Policy Institute.

Boyd, M. 2013. "Accreditation and the Labor Market Integration of Internationally Trained Engineers and Physicians in Canada." *In Wanted and Welcome? Policies for Highly Skilled Immigrants in Comparative Perspective,* edited by T. Triadafilopoulos, pp. 165–198. New York: Springer.

Boyd, M. and N.T.B. Ly. 2021. "Unwanted and Uninvited: Canadian Exceptionalism in Migration and the 2017-2020 Irregular Border Crossings." *American Review of Canadian Studies* 51 (1): pp. 95–121.

Cairns, A. 1968. "The Electoral System and the Party System in Canada, 1921–1965." *Canadian Journal of Political Science/Revue canadienne de science politique* 1 (1): pp. 55–80.

CBC Radio. 2016. "Canada's Refugee Model Praised by UN High Commissioner." CBC News. 22 March. https://www.cbc.ca/radio/asithappens/as-it-happens-tuesday-edition-1.3502370/canada-s-refugee-model-praised-by-un-high-commissioner-1.3502379

Castles, S., E. Vasta, and D. Ozkul. 2014. "Australia." In *Controlling Immigration: A Global Perpsective,* edited by J. F. Hollifield, P. L. Martin, and P. M. Orrenius, pp.128–150. 3rd edn. Stanford, CA: Stanford University Press.

The Economist. 2016. "Liberty Moves North: Canada's Example to the World." *The Economist.* 29 October. https://www.economist.com/weeklyedition/2016-10-29

Elgersma, S. 2015. *Resettling Refugees: Canada's Humanitarian Commitments.* Ottawa: Library of Parliament.

Ellerman, A. 2019. "Fifty Years of Canadian Immigration Policy." In *Policy Transformation in Canada: Is the Past Prologue?* edited by C. Hughes Tuohy, S. Borwein, P. John Loewen, and A. Potter, pp. 151–158. Toronto: University of Toronto Press.

Ellermann, A. 2021. *The Comparative Politics of Immigration: Policy Choices in Germany, Canada, Switzerland, and the United States.* New York: Cambridge University Press.

Environics. 2019. *Focus Canada—Fall 2019: Canadian Public Opinion about Immigration and Refugees*. Environics. 5 November. https://www.environicsinstitute.org/docs/default-source/project-documents/focus-canada-fall-2019---immigration-refugees/focus-canada-fall-2019-survey-on-immigration-and-refugees---final-report.pdf?sfvrsn=56c2af3c_2

Environics. 2020. *Focus Canada—Fall 2020: Canadian Public Opinion about Immigration and Refugees*. The Environics Institute for Survey Research. 7 October. https://www.environicsinstitute.org/docs/default-source/project-documents/fc-fall-2020---immigration/focus-canada-fall-2020---public-opinion-on-immigration-refugees---final-report.pdf?sfvrsn=bd51588f_2

Fitzgerald, D. S. and D. Cook-Martín. 2014. *Culling the Masses: The Democratic Origins of Racist Immigration Policy in the Americas*. Cambridge, MA: Harvard University Press.

Flynn, D. 2005. "New Borders, New Management: The Dilemmas of Modern Immigration Policies." *Ethnic and Racial Studies* 28 (3): pp. 463–490.

Foster, J. 2012. "Making Temporary Permanent: The Silent Transformation of the Temporary Foreign Worker Program." *Just Labour* 19: pp. 22–46.

Geddes, A. 2018. "The Politics of European Union Migration Governance." *Journal of Common Market Studies* 56 (S1): pp. 120–130.

Global Refugee Sponsorship Initiative. 2021. "Who We Are." GRSI. https://refugeesponsorship.org/who-we-are

Gonzalez-Barrera, A. and P. Connor. 2019. "Around the World, More Say Immigrants Are a Strength Than a Burden." Pew Research Center. 14 March. https://www.pewresearch.org/global/2019/03/14/around-the-world-more-say-immigrants-are-a-strength-than-a-burden/

Green, A. G., and D. A. Green. 1999. "The Economic Goals of Canada's Immigration Policy: Past and Present." *Canadian Public Policy/Analyse de politiques* 25 (4): pp. 425–451.

Griffith, A. 2017. "The Growing Diversity within Federal Ridings." *Policy Options*. 15 December. https://policyoptions.irpp.org/magazines/december-2017/the-growing-diversity-within-federal-ridings/

Harris, K. 2020. "Federal Government Plans to Bring in More Than 1.2m Immigrants in Next 3 Years." CBC News. 30 October. https://www.cbc.ca/news/politics/mendicino-immigration-pandemic-refugees-1.5782642

Hawkins, F. 1988. *Canada and Immigration: Public Policy and Public Concern*. 2nd edn. Kingston and Montreal: McGill-Queen's University Press.

Hawthorne, L. 2013. "Skilled Enough? Employment Outcomes for Recent Economic Immigrants in Canada Compared to Australia." In *Wanted and Welcome? Policies for Highly Skilled Immigrants in Comparative Perspective*, edited by T. Triadafilopoulos, pp. 219–256. New York: Springer.

Hennebry, J. 2010. "Who Has their Eye on the Ball? Jurisdictional Fútbol and Canada's Temporary Foreign Worker Program." *Policy Options* 31 (7): pp. 62–67.

Hiebert, D. 2016. *What's So Special about Canada? Understanding the Resilience of Immigration and Multiculturalism*. Washington, DC: Migration Policy Institute.

Hyndman, J., Payne, W., and Jimenez, S. 2017. "Private refugee sponsorship in Canada". *Forced Migration Review* 54, 56–59.

Immigration, Refugees and Citizenship Canada. 2017. 2017 Annual Report to Parliament on Immigration. Ottawa: Government of Canada. https://www.canada.

ca/en/immigration-refugees-citizenship/corporate/publications-manuals/annual-report-parliament-immigration-2017.html#sec1_1

Immigration, Refugees and Citizenship Canada. 2019. 2019 Annual Report to Parliament on Immigration. Ottawa: Government of Canada. https://www.canada.ca/en/immigration-refugees-citizenship/corporate/publications-manuals/annual-report-parliament-immigration-2019.html#s5

Immigration, Refugees and Citizenship Canada. 2020. *2020 Annual Report to Parliament on Immigration*. Ottawa: Government of Canada. https://www.canada.ca/en/immigration-refugees-citizenship/corporate/publications-manuals/annual-report-parliament-immigration-2020.html#permanent

Irvine, S. 2011. "Canadian Refugee Policy: Understanding the Role of International Bureaucratic Networks in Domestic Paradigm Change." In *Policy Paradigms, Transnationalism, and Domestic Politics*, edited by G. Skogstad, pp. 171–201. Toronto: University of Toronto Press.

Joppke, C. 2021. *Neoliberal Nationalism: Immigration and the Rise of the Populist Right*. New York: Cambridge University Press.

Keely, C. B. 2001. "The International Refugee Regime(s): The End of the Cold War Matters." *International Migration Review* 35 (1): pp. 303–314.

Kelley, N. and M. Trebilcock. 2010. *The Making of the Mosaic: A History of Canadian Immigration Policy*. Toronto: University of Toronto Press.

Knowles, V. 2007. *Strangers at our Gates: Canada, Immigration and Immigration Policy, 1540–2006*. Toronto: Dundurn Press.

Koenig-Archibugi, M. 2017. "How to Diagnose Democratic Deficits in Global Politics: The Use of the 'All-Affected Principle'." *International Theory* 9 (2): pp.171–202.

Kwong, M. 2019. "Trump Wants an Immigration System 'Like They Have in Canada.' Would a Merit-Based Plan Work in the U.S.?" CBC News. 30 April. https://www.cbc.ca/news/world/trump-immigration-system-canada-merit-based-points-1.5115475

Labman, S. 2019. *Crossing Law's Border: Canada's Refugee Resettlement Program*. Vancouver: University of British Columbia Press.

Lake, M. and H. Reynolds. 2008. *Drawing the Global Colour Line: White Men's Countries and the International Challenge of Racial Equality*. Cambridge: Cambridge University Press.

Laxer, E. 2019. *Unveiling the Nation: The Politics of Secularism in France and Quebec*. Montreal and Kingston: McGill-Queen's University Press.

Lenard, P.T. 2021. "How Exceptional? Welcoming Refugees the Canadian Way." *American Review of Canadian Studies* 51 (1): pp. 78-94.

Levitz, S. 2012. "Would-Be Immigrants Take Ottawa to Court over Cancelled Applications." *Toronto Star*. 16 May.

Ling, J. 2019. "How Maxime Bernier Lost his Seat: Canada's Nationalist People's Party Has Run a Familiar Populist Playbook—and Ended up a Joke." *Foreign Policy*. 20 October. https://foreignpolicy.com/2019/10/20/canada-maxime-bernier-populism-peoples-party/

Linzer, D. 2012. "The Relationship between Seats and Votes in Multiparty Systems." *Political Analysis* 20 (3): pp. 400–416.

Macklin, A. 2004. "Disappearing Refugees: Reflections on the Canada-US Safe Third Country Agreement." *Columbia Human Rights Law Review* 36: pp. 365–426.

Martani, E. 2021. "Canada's Private Sponsorship Program: Success, Shortcomings, and Policy Solutions." *Ryerson Centre for Immigration and Settlement, Canada Research Excellence Chair in Migration and Integration Working Paper*. No. 2021/6.

McConnell, A. 2010. "Policy Success, Policy Failure and Grey Areas In-Between." *Journal of Public Policy* 30 (3): pp. 345–362.

OECD. 2019. "Canada Has the Most Comprehensive and Elaborate Migration System, But Some Challenges Remain." OECD. 13 August. https://www.oecd.org/canada/canada-has-the-most-comprehensive-and-elaborate-migration-system-but-some-challenges-remain.htm

Radford, J. and P. Connor. 2019. "Canada Now Leads the World in Refugee Resettlement, Surpassing the U.S." Pew Research Center. 19 June. https://www.pewresearch.org/fact-tank/2019/06/19/canada-now-leads-the-world-in-refugee-resettlement-surpassing-the-u-s/

Reese, L. A. and M. Ye. 2011. "Policy versus Place Luck: Achieving Local Economic Prosperity." *Economic Development Quarterly* 25 (3): pp. 221–236.

Reitz, J. 2011. *Pro-Immigration Canada: Social and Economic Roots of Popular Views.* Montreal: Institute for Research on Public Policy. https://munkschool.utoronto.ca/wp-content/uploads/2012/07/Reitz_Pro-ImmigrationCanada_2011.pdf

Reitz, J. G. 2004. "Canada: Immigration and Nation-Building in the Transition to a Knowledge Economy." In *Controlling Immigration: A Global Perspective*, edited by W. A. Cornelius, P. L. Martin, J. F. Hollifield, and T. Tsuda, pp. 97–133. 2nd edn. Stanford, CA: Stanford University Press.

Silverman, S. 2014. "In the Wake of Irregular Arrivals: Changes to the Canadian Immigration Detention System." *Refuge* 30 (2): pp. 27–34.

Simmons, A. B. 2010. *Immigration and Canada: Global and Transnational Perspectives.* Toronto: Canadian Scholar's Press Inc.

Smith, C. 2020. "A Model for the World? Policy Transfer Theory and the Challenges to Exporting' Private Sponsorship to Europe." In *Strangers to Neighbours: Refugee Sponsorship in Context*, edited by S. Labman and G. Cameron, pp. 286–302. Montreal and Kingston: McGill-Queen's University Press.

Smith, C. D., T. Hadziristic, and L. Alipour. 2017. "Private Sponsorship Is Not Panacea for Refugee Integration." *The New Humanitarian.* 4 April. https://deeply.thenewhumanitarian.org/refugees/community/2017/04/04/private-sponsorship-not-panacea-for-refugee-integration-researchers

Stasiulis, D. and Y. Abu-Laban. 2004. "Unequal Relations and the Struggle for Equality: Race and Ethnicity in Canadian Politics." In *Canadian Politics in the 21st Century*, edited by M. Whittington and M. Williams. 6th edn., pp. 284–311. Toronto: Thompson-Nelson.

Statistics Canada. 2013. "National Household Survey: Immigration and Ethnocultural Diversity in Canada." Statistics Canada. 8 May. Catalogue no. 99-010–X2011001.

Statistics Canada. 2016. "150 Years of immigration in Canada." Statistics Canada. 29 June. https://www150.statcan.gc.ca/n1/pub/11-630-x/11-630-x2016006-eng.htm

Statistics Canada. 2017. "Study: A Look at Immigration, Ethnocultural Diversity and Languages in Canada up to 2036, 2011 to 2036." Statistics Canada. 25 January. https://www150.statcan.gc.ca/n1/daily-quotidien/170125/dq170125b-eng.htm

Statistics Canada. 2019. "Just the Facts: Asylum Claimants." Statistics Canada. 17 May. https://www150.statcan.gc.ca/n1/pub/89-28-0001/2018001/article/00013-eng.htm

Taylor, Z. 2021. "The Political Geography of Immigration: Explaining Party Competition for Immigrants' Votes in Canada, 1997–2019." *American Review of Canadian Studies* 51(1): pp. 18–40.

Thompson, D. 2020. "Race, the Canadian Census, and Interactive Political Development." *Studies in American Political Development* 34: pp. 44–70.

Triadadilopoulos, T. 2004. "Building Walls, Bounding Nations: Migration and Exclusion in Canada and Germany, 1870–1939." *Journal of Historical Sociology* 17 (4): pp. 385–427.

Triadafilopoulos, T. 2012. *Becoming Multicultural: Immigration and the Politics of Membership in Canada and Germany*. Vancouver: University of British Columbia Press.

Triadafilopoulos, T. 2013a. "Dismantling White Canada: Race, Rights, and the Origins of the Points Sytem." In *Wanted and Welcome? Policies for Highly Skilled Immigrants in Comparative Perspective*, edited by T. Triadafilopoulos, pp. 15–38. New York: Springer.

Triadafilopoulos, T. (ed). 2013b. *Wanted and Welcome? Policies for Highly Skilled Immigrants in Comparative Perspective*. New York: Springer.

Triadafilopoulos, T. 2015. "Fairness in einem klassischen Einwanderungsland—erfahrungen aus Kanada." In *Migration gerecht gestalten. Weltweit Impulse für einen fairen Wettbewerb um Fachkräfte*, edited by B. Stiftung, pp. 181–190. Gütersloh: Verlag Bertelsmann Stiftung.

Triadafilopoulos, T. 2019. "Germany's Post-2015 Immigration Dilemmas." *Current History* 118 (806): pp. 108–113.

Triadafilopoulos, T. 2021. "The Foundations, Limits, and Consequences of Immigration Exceptionalism in Canada." *American Review of Canadian Studies* 51 (1): pp. 3–17.

Triadafilopoulos, T. and Z. Taylor. 2021. "The Political Foundations of Canadian Exceptionalism in Immigration Policy." In *International Affairs and Canadian Migration Policy*, edited by Y. Samy and H. Duncan, pp. 13–40. New York: Palgrave Macmillan.

Waslin, M. 2020. "The Use of Executive Orders and Proclamations to Create Immigration Policy: Trump in Historical Perspective." *Journal on Migration and Human Security* 8 (1): pp. 54–67.

Westlake, D. 2018. "Multiculturalism, Political Parties, and the Conflicting Pressures of Ethnic Minorities and Far-Right Parties." *Party Politics* 24 (4): pp. 421–433.

White, S., N. Nevitte, A. Blais, J. Everitt, P. Fournier, and E. Gidengil. 2006. "Making Up for Lost Time: Immigrant Voter Turnout in Canada." Electoral Insight. December. https://www.elections.ca/content.aspx?section=res&dir=eim/issue19&document=p3&lang=e

Xu, L. and P. Golah. 2015. *Citizenship Acquisition in Canada: An Overview Based on Census 1986 to 2006*. Ottawa: Citizenship and Immigration. http://publications.gc.ca/collections/collection_2016/ircc/Ci4-146-2015-eng.pdf

10

Multiculturalism Policy in Canada

Conflicted and Resilient

Keith Banting

Introduction

The year 2021 represented the 50th anniversary of the adoption of multiculturalism in Canada. Clearly, multiculturalism policy has stood the test of time. However, more than sheer longevity testifies to its success. In programmatic terms, the multiculturalism approach has clearly advanced the goals that animated its introduction in 1971. The immediate goal was to change the terms of integration for immigrants, laying to rest ideas of assimilation and creating space for minorities to celebrate aspects of their traditional culture and customs while participating in the mainstream of life in the country. Inherent in this immediate goal, however, was a larger, long-term mission. Multiculturalism was also part of a broad state-led redefinition of national identity, an effort to diversify the historic conception of the country as a British/French society, and to build a more inclusive nationalism reflective of Canada's cultural complexity.

As we shall see, multiculturalism has met with considerable success in advancing these goals. It has changed the terms of integration for immigrants, which has helped strengthen their sense of attachment to the country, their embrace of a Canadian identity, and their engagement in political life. In terms of its implicit symbolic goal, the idea of multiculturalism has become deeply embedded in Canadian culture, at least in English-speaking Canada, and has contributed to a more inclusive form of Canadian national identity. Admittedly, multiculturalism has not eliminated racial discrimination in Canada, and the commitment to diversity seems fragile at times, most recently in the case of Muslims. Nonetheless, judged against the experience of other democratic countries generally, multiculturalism policies have succeeded in enhancing the attachment of immigrants to Canada and contributed to a more inclusive sense of national identity. More speculatively, multiculturalism has arguably helped forestall the type of anti-immigrant backlash we have seen elsewhere.

Keith Banting, *Multiculturalism Policy in Canada*. In: *Policy Success in Canada*.
Edited by Evert A. Lindquist et al., Oxford University Press. © Keith Banting (2022).
DOI: 10.1093/oso/9780192897046.003.0010

184 MULTICULTURALISM POLICY IN CANADA

Multiculturalism has had sufficient political support to survive and adapt to change for over half a century. Unlike some European countries, Canada has never rejected the multicultural approach to diversity. However, multiculturalism is not embedded in a deep and comprehensive political consensus. Political challenges have emerged from several directions, the most potent of which have been rooted in social conservatism and Québec nationalism. The multicultural approach has largely survived social conservatism at the national level, but Québec nationalism proved potent. Canadian multiculturalism now lives in a secondary position in diversity management in that province.

To advance this assessment, this chapter proceeds in four sections. We first specify more clearly the nature of multiculturalism policies as they are understood in Canada. We then examine the political drivers and the policy process, which have been deeply entwined. Next, we assess the programmatic impact of multiculturalism policies, in terms of both immigrant integration and the wider terrain of Canadian culture and identity. The final section pulls the threads of the argument together.

Multiculturalism Policy: What is it and what is it not

How should states respond to growing ethno-racial and religious diversity? During the nineteenth and early twentieth centuries states engaged in nation-building projects, seeking to reinforce their status in the international political order by nurturing a robust nationalism among their populations (Weber, 1976; Hobsbawm, 1992). This process of nation-building left little room for minorities. In their efforts to build a common culture and identity, states sought to assimilate or marginalize internal ethnic minorities, and were hostile to immigration flows that would diversify their populations. Starting in the 1960s, however, we see a shift towards a more accommodating approach to state-minority relations. The new approach was part of a broader liberalization of the normative order in the West. World War II was a watershed in attitudes towards ethnicity, race, and human rights, as manifested in decolonization, the American civil rights movement, and similar movements elsewhere. This new normative order underpinned the widespread adoption of anti-discrimination instruments to protect the individual rights of citizens. It also gave life in many countries to a multicultural approach to diversity, including a more accommodating approach to immigrants (Triadafilopoulos, 2012).

Historically, Canada, like many states, had an assimilationist approach to immigration. Immigrants were encouraged and expected to assimilate to the mainstream culture, with the hope that they would become indistinguishable from the native-born population over time. Indeed, groups that were seen as incapable of this sort of cultural assimilation (e.g. Asians, Africans) were prohibited from immigrating to Canada. This assimilationist approach was slowly discredited in the post-war period, and officially repudiated in the late 1960s and early 1970s

(Kelly and Trebilcock, 2010). The first step was the implementation of race-neutral admissions criteria in immigration policy in 1967, after which immigrants increasingly came from non-European and non-Christian societies. The second step was the adoption of a more multicultural conception of integration, one that expects that many members of immigrant communities will wish to visibly express their ethnic identity, and that accepts an obligation on the part of public institutions to accommodate their distinctiveness. This multicultural accommodation is afforded not only to recent immigrants, but to all members of minorities that owe their presence in the country to immigration, including those born in Canada.

The concept of multiculturalism is widely debated, and there is no universally accepted definition of the concept. For our purposes here, the defining feature of multiculturalism policies is that they go beyond the protection of the basic civil and political rights guaranteed to all individuals in a liberal-democratic state, to also extend some level of recognition, accommodation, and support for minorities to express their distinct identities and practices. Multiculturalism, therefore, is not just about ensuring the non-discriminatory application of laws in a diverse context, but about changing the laws and regulations themselves to accommodate the distinctive needs and aspirations of minorities.

Conceptually, multiculturalism policies for immigrants have three basic purposes: to recognize, accommodate, and support cultural diversity (Banting and Kymlicka, 2006). Recognition implies that the state acknowledges immigrant minorities as legitimate components of the wider population, that the state 'sees' them as they see themselves and accepts them as part of 'us'. Accommodation involves the adjustment of existing laws and policies to facilitate the participation of immigrants in economic, social, and political life. Inevitably, immigrants make the biggest adjustments during the integration process, but the idea of accommodation implies that the host society also makes adjustments in its institutions to facilitate their inclusion. Finally, support involves the provision of concrete services or regulatory changes that enable immigrant groups to preserve their distinctiveness.

These three purposes imply a whole-of-government approach. Too often, Canadians assume that federal multiculturalism policy is the small program of grants provided to immigrant groups. In fact, it is much broader. For example:

> *Recognition* can be seen in section 27 of the Charter of Rights and Freedoms, which directs that the rights guaranteed by the Charter are to be 'interpreted in a manner consistent with the preservation and enhancement of the multicultural heritage of Canadians.' Recognition can be seen at work in the educational curricula of schools that incorporate the history and contributions of immigrants to Canada. Recognition is also entrenched in the Broadcasting Act, which requires that broadcasters 'reflect the multicultural and multiracial nature of Canada'. Minorities should see themselves, and be seen on television screens.

186 MULTICULTURALISM POLICY IN CANADA

Accommodation involves changes in laws and regulations, such as acceptance of dual citizenship and exemptions from official dress codes. Such accommodations have always been the most controversial part of multicultural strategies, and have represented flashpoints in the last decade.

Support to assist immigrant minorities to preserve their distinctive cultures can be seen in the funding of ethnic organizations and associations, public funding to support mother-tongue instruction, or the inclusion of racialized immigrant minorities in employment equity programs to assist disadvantaged minorities.

Historically, Canada was a leader among countries in adopting such policies and initiatives, as can be seen with the help of the cross-national Multiculturalism Policy Index. This Index ranks the strength of multiculturalism policies across 21 democratic countries over the four decades between 1980 and 2020 (Appendix 1 provides details of the construction of the Index. For a fuller discussion, see Banting and Kymlicka, 2013).

Table 10.1 presents the ranking for the full set of countries. Two conclusions stand out. First, Canada, along with Australia, was an early leader in the adoption

Table 10.1 Multiculturalism Policy Index, 1980–2020

	1980	1990	2000	2010	2020
Australia	5.5	8	8	8	8
Austria	0	0	1	1.5	1.5
Belgium	1	1.5	3.5	5.5	5.5
Canada	5	6.5	7.5	7.5	7
Denmark	0	0	0	0	1
Finland	0	0	1.5	6	7
France	1	2	2	2	1.5
Germany	0	0.5	2	2.5	3
Greece	0.5	0.5	0.5	2.5	2.5
Ireland	1	1	1.5	4	4.5
Italy	0	0	1.5	1.5	1.5
Japan	0	0	0	0	0
Netherlands	2.5	3	4	2	1
New Zealand	2.5	5	5	6.5	6.5
Norway	0	0	0	3.5	4.5
Portugal	0	1	3	3.5	3.5
Spain	0	1	1	3.5	3
Sweden	3	3.5	5	7	7
Switzerland	0	0	1	1	1
United Kingdom	2.5	5	5	5.5	6
United States	3.5	3	3	3	3.5

Source: www.queensu.ca/mcp/

of a multicultural approach to immigrant diversity. Second, a range of other countries increasingly adopted a measure of multiculturalism policies, which suggests a process of emulation across countries.

Political and Process Assessment: A Contested Project

The political drivers of multiculturalism policy, and the policy process through which it evolved, have been deeply entwined from the outset. In the early years, a multi-party political consensus protected the program, allowing it to evolve through a relatively deliberative process. In the 1990s and 2000s, however, the multi-party consensus weakened. Since then, policy development has been driven increasingly by party ideology and partisan electoral objectives, with very different implications for the policy process. Over time the politics of the policy has become more conflicted (McConnell, 2010).

At its origins, multiculturalism was an unanticipated by-product of efforts to accommodate the rise of Québec nationalism during the 1960s. When a royal commission recommended a policy of bilingualism and biculturalism, privileging people of British and French heritage, well-established immigrant minorities, including Ukrainians, Portuguese, Italians, and others, pushed back against a dualist definition of the country that did not include them. The result was the policy of multiculturalism within a bilingual framework, which was announced in 1971, embedded in the constitution in 1982, codified in legislation in 1988, and confirmed after a major review in 1997. Although the multiculturalism policy was adopted in response to pressure from groups who were largely European and Christian (with the addition of the Jewish community), it became a policy template that could be rolled forward to incorporate new immigrants who were racially and religiously more distinct from traditional Canada.

The initial policy was announced in 1971 by a Liberal prime minister, Pierre Elliot Trudeau. The integrationist intent of the initiative was clear in the four goals he outlined:

- to 'assist all Canadian cultural groups that have demonstrated a desire and effort to continue to develop a capacity to grow and contribute to Canada';
- to 'assist members of all cultural groups to overcome cultural barriers to full participation in Canadian society';
- to 'promote creative encounters and interchange amongst all Canadian cultural groups in the interest of national unity';
- to 'assist immigrants to acquire at least one of Canada's official languages in order to become full participants in Canadian society'. (Trudeau 1971).

The traditional brokerage style of Canadian political parties provided considerable protection for both immigration and diversity in the late stages of the twentieth

188   MULTICULTURALISM POLICY IN CANADA

century. Debates over immigration proceeded within 'an unprecedented political and public consensus' on a generally liberal policy, a pattern highlighted by the near-unanimous passage of the 1976 Immigration Act (Kelley and Trebilcock, 2010, 379). This consensus largely extended to multiculturalism as well. It was the Progressive Conservative government led by Brian Mulroney that embedded multiculturalism in legislation in 1988. Political debates in this period tended to focus on program details rather than fundamentals.

In this politically protected context, the policy process engaged a relatively small sector, operating through interactions among bureaucratic officials and leaders of ethnic organizations, with external consultants providing occasional reviews and ministers providing intermittent direction (Pal, 1993). This executive-dominated system facilitated a deliberative and consultative process and an evolutionary approach to policy change. Within a year of the announcement of the program in 1971, the Multiculturalism unit had rolled out nine programs, the most important of which was the grants program. Reviews and adjustments occurred in 1975 and 1981, without significant political conflict.

In these early days, the emphasis in the grants program was on cultural celebration and retention. However, tensions soon emerged between established ethnic organizations and groups representing new arrivals from Asia, Africa, and the Caribbean, who 'were less interested in celebrating their cultures than in battling discrimination and racism' (Pal, 1993, 137). Over time, the focus of the program shifted from cultural retention to equality, tolerance, and antiracism, an orientation codified when the Conservatives introduced the Canadian Multiculturalism Act the following year. However, this focus was soon short-circuited. During the 1990s and 2000s, a crisis in Québec-Canada relations and the prospect of a second Québec referendum on independence shifted priorities in the multiculturalism program from anti-racism and accommodation towards a more explicit focus on integration (Griffith, 2103; Abu-Laban and Gabriel, 2002).

Multiparty consensus clearly facilitated a deliberative policy process. However, that process also tended to insulate the program from growing latent unease. During the 1990s, criticisms of multiculturalism emerged in intellectual circles, media commentary, and parliamentary debates (Ryan, 2010). More importantly, two serious ~~political challenges,~~ political challenges moved to centre stage, driven by social conservatism and Québec nationalism.

Challenges (I): Social Conservatism

Anxieties about multiculturalism burst into the political domain in the election of 1993, which saw the breakthrough of the populist Reform Party. The Reform Party articulated a potent social conservatism and a highly individualist approach to diversity. The party opposed 'special' status for Québec, spending on Aboriginal peoples, gender equality, multiculturalism and affirmative action, all of which they saw as catering to 'special interests' (Harrison, 1995). Reform activists occasionally criticized the levels of non-white immigration that had emerged in the previous two decades, and in 1990 the party officially criticized immigration policy for changing the ethnic makeup of Canada (Laycock, 2012, 90). Following their electoral breakthrough, party leaders tried to tone down anti-immigrant views in official party positions (Flanagan, 1995, 197–198). However, the party did not hold back on multiculturalism. The Reform Party's 1996–97 Blue Book of policies stated that the party 'opposes the current concept of multiculturalism and hyphenated Canadianism pursued by the Government of Canada. We would end funding of the multicultural program and support the abolition of the Department of Multiculturalism' (as quoted in Griffiths, 2013, 8–9). Their 1997 election manifesto was less comprehensive, but pledged to lead a campaign to repeal the multicultural section of the Charter of Rights and Freedoms, which is part of the constitution of the country (Reform Party, 1997).

Although the Reform Party did not last, its views on immigration and diversity became one stream of opinion that flowed into the restructured Conservative Party in the early 2000s (Farney, 2012; Thomas and Sabin, 2019; Wilkins-Laflamme and Reimer, 2019). The result was a complicated balancing act. When the Conservatives came to power in 2006, they adopted a multi-track approach. For economic reasons, the government continued to support existing levels of immigration. However, in the domain of multiculturalism and citizenship, the government struggled with two conflicting imperatives: to build long-term electoral support among immigrant groups, and to appeal to social conservatives among its electoral base. This tension between these imperatives has been dubbed the 'populists' dilemma' in Canada (Marwah et al., 2013).

The arrival of a Conservative government at the federal level disrupted the policy process. The new government moved the multiculturalism program from the Department of Canadian Heritage to the department responsible for immigration, implicitly indicating that multiculturalism was about newcomers and not the multiple generations within minority groups, let alone the attitudes of all Canadians. The Conservatives also reduced funding for the grants program. More importantly, ideology became the primary driver of policy direction, and the role of public servants narrowed to issues of implementation, rather than broad policy (Griffith, 2013). The new government distrusted research-based approaches and relied on opinion polls and personal contacts with their supporters. As a result, the principal connection with immigrant groups shifted from bureaucratic to political channels. The government's determination to build electoral support among immigrant voters produced energetic ministerial engagement with immigrant groups across the country, and grants represented a useful political tool to realize this

190 MULTICULTURALISM POLICY IN CANADA

goal. In the cautious words of a former official, the program was reshaped in part to find 'ways to deliver grants and contributions funding that met Ministerial requirements' (Griffith, 2013, 18; see also Tolley, 2017).

Policy content also shifted. The Harper government never explicitly attacked multiculturalism, relying on a more stealthy strategy to shift the balance from accommodation to integration, and to send symbolic reassurance to social conservatives (Abu-Laban, 2014; Carlaw, 2021). Symbolically, their 2009 revisions to the citizenship guide, given to immigrants preparing for the citizenship tests, sought to rejuvenate an earlier conception of Canada by downplaying multiculturalism in favour of Canada's military history and its legacy of British institutions and traditions (Citizenship and Immigration Canada, 2009). The Conservatives also questioned the loyalty of dual citizens, and toughened standards for the citizenship test, driving down the success rate, especially among immigrants with low family income, low proficiency in official languages, and low educational levels (Hou and Picot, 2020). In addition, the Conservatives repeatedly targeted Muslims, the least popular minority in the country (Triadafilopoulos and Rasheed, 2020). They symbolically denounced 'barbaric cultural practices' in the revised citizenship guide and countless ministerial speeches, and, in 2011, Jason Kenney, the then minister for citizenship, immigration, and multiculturalism, announced that those wishing to become Canadian citizens would have to uncover their face during the citizenship oath. In 2015, the government legislated on a range of its complaints in its *Zero Tolerance for Barbaric Cultural Practices Act.*

This complicated juggling act of appealing simultaneously to immigrant voters and to social conservatives seemed to work during the election of 2011 (Bricker and Ibbitson, 2013; Kwak, 2019). However, the strategy fell apart during the election campaign of 2015. The pre-campaign period had been marked by the Syrian refugee crisis, and the Conservative government adopted a historically cautious policy of admitting only 10,000 refugees. This position imploded politically early in the election campaign when pictures of the lifeless body of three-year-old Alan Kurdi, washed up on a Turkish beach, flashed around the world. Conservatives pivoted quickly to an anti-Muslim trope, campaigning hard on a promise to protect Canadian values against the alleged threat posed by Muslim women wearing the niqab. In the middle of the campaign, the courts struck down their ban on the niqab during citizenship ceremonies. Rather than conceding, the Conservatives doubled-down, appealing the judgment to the Supreme Court, promising a 'barbaric cultural practices' tipline on which Canadians were encouraged to inform on their neighbours, and suggesting a ban on the niqab not only during the oath of citizenship but also in the civil service. These measures proved a step too far (Kymlicka, 2021). Support for the Conservatives dropped in the last weeks of the campaign, and the Liberals won the election and immediately raised the target intake of Syrian refugees, with the new prime minister personally handing out winter coats to the first arrivals at the airport. Later, the former Conservative immigration minister admitted that their emphasis on 'barbaric cultural practices' made many immigrants, including non-Muslims, nervous. 'It's why we lost ... we allowed ourselves to be portrayed in the last election as unwelcoming. That was a huge mistake.' (CTV News, 2016).

In time, the Liberal government also reversed a number of policies. They accepted the court's decision on the niqab and amended the Canadian Citizenship Act to make it easier to gain citizenship and to eliminate revocation provisions introduced by the Conservatives. They modified the barbaric practices legislation, established several anti-racism initiatives, and launched a revision of the citizenship guide. In addition, they returned the multiculturalism program to the Department of Canadian Heritage and reversed the decline in funding. The most dramatic imprint of social conservatism was thus diluted. Nonetheless, while sympathetic to multiculturalism, the Liberal government also moved cautiously in the politicized environment, and it is notable that the revised citizenship guide did not emerge before the 2019 election. Indeed, it still had not appeared at the time of the 2021 election.

Challenges (II): *Québec Nationalism*

Meanwhile, Québec was developing its own approach to diversity, known as interculturalism, with two features that set it apart from the federal approach. First, while federal multiculturalism promotes the choice of two official languages, English and French, the Québec model defines French as the language of public life in the province. Beginning in the 1990s, Québec also developed a distinct approach to diversity, announced in a policy document entitled *Let's Build Québec Together: Policy Statement on Integration and Immigration* (Quebec, 1990). While federal multiculturalism assumes integration into either the English- or French-speaking language communities, it was seen as otherwise implying the equal recognition of all cultures, negating the centrality of any particular culture. In contrast, Québec's intercultural approach defines the majority culture in the province as the central hub towards whichminority cultures are expected to move (Gagnon and Iacovino, 2007; Labelle and Rocher, 2009).

In the early years, there was considerable debate about whether federal multiculturalism and Québec interculturalism actually differed much on the ground. In the 2000s, however, the differences were magnified by the growing salience of religion. Commentators in Québec increasingly define secularism as a central feature of Québec culture, and many Québecers fear that this commitment to *laicité* is undermined by the greater religiosity of some minorities, especially the Muslim and Sikh communities. The result has been a series of increasingly intense controversies around the wearing of religious symbols. In an attempt to calm the waters, the Liberal government of Jean Charest appointed a consultative commission led

192 MULTICULTURALISM POLICY IN CANADA

by two senior scholars of diversity, Gérard Bouchard and Charles Taylor. Their report failed to resolve the tensions (Bouchard and Taylor, 2008). In 2013, a *Parti Québécois* government proposed a Québec Charter of Values that would restrict wearing all religious symbols in the public space, but the government was defeated in an election before their proposal passed. In 2017, a Liberal government passed milder legislation, which was quickly challenged in the courts. Finally, in 2019, the government of the *Coalition Avenir Quebec* succeeded in passing the *Loi sur la laïcité de l'État,* which prevents new employees in the public sector from wearing religious symbols, and requires members of the public to uncover their face when receiving public services. To preempt legal challenges, the government took the dramatic step of invoking the notwithstanding clause, which shields the legislation from review under the Charter of Rights for five years.

As a result, two diversity models prevail in the province of Québec, reflecting two distinct nation-building projects. The federal multicultural approach continues to apply in federal areas of jurisdiction in Québec with respect to the granting of citizenship and the conduct of citizenship ceremonies. However, Québec's less accommodating model dominates most of the public space within which Québecers live.

Hence the assessment of multiculturalism as a conflicted political project. It has stood the test of time for half a century and has survived challenges from social conservatism that have proved potent elsewhere. But multiculturalism has had to concede ground to a different approach in Québec, home to one-quarter of the Canadian population. Although the implementation of Québec's legislation limiting religious dress has resulted in a reduction in the overall ranking of Canada in the Multiculturalism Policy Index from 7.5 out of 8 in 2010 to 7 out of 8 in 2020, it is important not to overstate the impact of this one provincial dimension on an overall assessment of the multicultural experience. Other dimensions continue to apply across the country and, as Table 10.1 confirms, Canada remains one of the most multiculturalist members of the Organisation for Economic Co-operation and Development (OECD).

Programmatic Assessment: Resilient Success

In assessing the programmatic success of multiculturalism, we focus on its explicit and implicit goals: adjusting the terms of immigrant integration, and building a more inclusive conception of Canadian culture and identity. The assessment draws primarily on evidence about the impact of Canadian programs. However, given the problems inherent in drawing inferences about causality from a single case, the discussion also draws on studies that compare the experience of countries that adopted multicultural strategies with countries that rejected the approach.

Immigrant Integration

As we have seen, multiculturalism policies are designed to change the terms of integration, to enable immigrant minorities to participate in Canadian life without having to fully surrender their own culture. The underlying assumption has been that easing the cultural costs of integration will encourage immigrant minorities to embrace the country more fully. Some critics have worried that such policies have the opposite effect of encouraging social segmentation, with minorities living separately in parallel societies. The evidence, however, is consistent with the view that multiculturalism policies enhance the integration of immigrants in political and social life.

We begin with immigrant identity. Immigrants tend to retain their ethnic identity in virtually all countries, but the extent to which they also embrace the national identity of their host society varies. In the Canadian case, immigrants are comfortable with multiple identities and embrace a Canadian identity, with their levels of commitment to Canada on some measures higher than those of the population as a whole (Soroka et al., 2007). Recently, Bilodeau and his colleagues (2019) found that the sense of belonging among first-generation immigrants is strong. They conclude that 'immigrants' perception of their relationship with Canada appears overwhelmingly positive and is thus consistent with the claim that Canada represents a success story when it comes to immigrant inclusion' (Bilodeau, 2019, 5; see also Hou et al., 2016, and White et al., 2015).

Feelings of acceptance and attachment enhance political engagement. The rate at which immigrants become citizens remains high by international standards. In her classic study of naturalization in Canada, Bloemraad argued that multiculturalism policies in Canada help immigrants to feel accepted, increasing their interest in formally joining the country's national community (Bloemraad, 2006). Bilodeau and his colleagues also find that feelings of attachment and acceptance are strongly related to political participation, including interest in politics, turning out to vote, and confidence in legislative institutions (Bilodeau et al., 2019). Immigrant voter turnout is similar to the native born population, although turnout among racial minority immigrants is lower (Gidengil and Roy, 2016), a point to which we return in the next section.

Many factors undoubtedly shape these patterns, and it is difficult to disentangle the distinct role of multiculturalism policies. However, comparative analysis provides supplementary support. An obvious comparison is between Québec and the rest of Canada, since the two parts of the country have different approaches to diversity. A study based on data from the early 2000s found a lower sense of belonging among racial-minority immigrants in Québec than elsewhere in the country, especially among the second generation (Banting and Soroka, 2012). Additional evidence comes from a recent study examining the impact of major changes in integration policies in Québec, the proposed Québec Charter of Values in 2014, and the banning of religious dress in 2019. These policy shifts, and the divisive politics surrounding them, further weakened immigrants' sense of attachment to Québec generally, but this effect was especially prevalent among Muslims (Bilodeau and Turgeon, 2021).

Cross-national comparative analysis also finds that immigrant identification with the host country is stronger in countries that have adopted multiculturalism policies than in countries that have shunned the approach (Wright and Bloemraad, 2012; Citrin et al., 2012). Social psychologists have long argued that there is no automatic trade-off between attachment to minority and majority identities, and that the benefits of hyphenated or nested identities are easier to achieve in multicultural settings (Berry, 2005; Nguyen and Benet-Martinez, 2013; Guimond et al., 2014). Cross-national evidence on political participation points in the same direction. There is a strong positive relationship across democratic societies between multiculturalism policies and immigrant acquisition of citizenship (Liebig and Von Haaren, 2011, 27–28).

This relationship may reflect easier access to citizenship in countries that have also adopted strong multicultural policies, but it also likely reflects greater symbolic support for immigrants becoming citizens in more multicultural states. In addition, an early study by Koopmans and colleagues concluded that immigrants in more multicultural settings are more likely to engage in nonviolent activities, and their activism focuses more on the host country than the country of origin (Koopmans et al., 2005, 128, 137). Finally, the representation of immigrants and ethnic minorities in national legislatures is higher in multicultural countries. In a detailed analysis, Alba and Foner conclude:

> In Britain, Canada and the United States, state models of multiculturalism or ethnic pluralism have reinforced the effects of the electoral, political and party systems in providing scope for ethnic minority candidates.... In contrast, the ways in which France and Germany have defined immigrants and their integration into the state have hindered ethnic minorities' ability to gain electoral office.
>
> (Alba and Foner, 2015, 165).

Nonetheless, there are limits to multiculturalism policies. The approach has clearly not eliminated racial *economic* inequality in Canada. Although there are considerable differences across racial minorities, poverty levels among some racialized communities are much higher than across the population as a whole. Among Blacks, Arabs, and West Asian communities in particular, high poverty rates persist into the second and even the third-plus generations (Banting and Thompson, 2021). There is also evidence that job applicants with foreign-sounding names face discrimination in the labour market (Oreopoulos, 2011). Defenders of multiculturalism might reply that, as in the case of political representation, multiculturalism policies reduce the levels of discrimination that would otherwise prevail. Support for this view comes from a comparative study of the 'ethnic penalties' in the labour market faced by second-generation racial-minority individuals, that is, people who were born and educated in the country and speak the local language. Although racialized minorities in all of the countries included in the study earn less than one would expect given their levels of education, the penalties were considerably smaller in Canada; indeed, the authors conclude that in comparison with ten major democratic countries, racial minority groups tend to be most successful in Canada (Heath, 2007, 658). While a variety of factors are undoubtedly responsible for this outcome, the multiculturalist context is undoubtedly a part of the mix.

Defenders of multiculturalism might further argue that expecting multiculturalism to fully offset racial economic inequality inflates the original promise of multiculturalism, which was about the equality of cultures more than equality of incomes. The policy tools relevant to economic inequality, including income redistribution and labour market regulation, have seldom been defined as central to the multicultural mandate. However, critical race theorists worry that by focusing attention on cultural recognition, multiculturalism serves to reassure Canadians that their country has a progressive response to diversity, deflecting attention from the realities of racial discrimination and racial economic inequality (Thobani, 2007; Galabuzi, 2006; Bannerji, 2000).

The debate over the impact of multiculturalism on racial inequality echoes broader debates about 'recognition versus redistribution', in which the central question has been whether focusing on cultural recognition deflects concern for material inequality (Fraser, 1995). One form of this debate has asked whether multiculturalism undercuts support for redistribution and weakens the coalitions sustaining the welfare state. However, the accumulated cross-national empirical evidence is now clear that countries that adopted multiculturalism policies have not had greater difficulty in sustaining redistribution. Indeed, if anything, the relationship between multiculturalism and support for redistribution is positive (for a summary of the recent evidence, see Banting et al., 2022). We should, therefore, not assume too quickly that Canada's policies of multicultural recognition have weakened efforts to reduce racial inequality. The politics of inequality are not necessarily zero-sum, and societies can tackle different forms of inequality at the same time.

In the end, the failure to eradicate racial inequality does point to the limits of multiculturalism. Nonetheless, when judged against its explicit goals, multiculturalism policies have been a comparative success. They have adjusted the terms of integration, helping immigrant minorities to retain elements of their culture and traditions while joining the social and political mainstream. Measured against experience in other countries on this dimension, the Canadian record suggests that multiculturalism represents part of a successful response to diversity.

Canadian Attitudes and Culture

Inherent in the multicultural goal of changing the terms of integration for immigrant minorities has been the implicit goal of redefining Canadian identity (Uberoi, 2008). Multicultural norms were expected to help to 'normalize' diversity, especially for younger generations, slowly reshaping embedded collective memories (Harell, 2009; also Esses et al., 2006).

For Canadians, especially younger Canadians, multiculturalism has become a defining feature of their national identity. As Figure 10.1 indicates, almost all Canadians consider multiculturalism to be very important or somewhat important to Canadian national identity. Of course, it is unclear how Canadians conceive of multiculturalism when answering such questions, and some respondents may simply be celebrating the ethnic diversity of the population. However, the import seems to go further. Support for multiculturalism reflects a culture of acceptance of diversity, which in turn undoubtedly contributes to the sense of acceptance registered by immigrants that we saw earlier.

This interpretation finds support in survey evidence about public attitudes towards the different types of multiculturalism policies. Using the terms of our earlier grouping of multiculturalism policies, Canadians seem strongly committed to policies that *recognize* diversity as a legitimate feature of Canadian life, as Table 10.2 suggests. In contrast, Table 10.3 suggests Canadians are less enthusiastic about changing policies or providing additional services to *accommodate* difference. The tables also highlight the differences between respondents in Québec compared to the rest of the country (ROC), especially on accommodation issues, although it should be noted that this survey was conducted in 2014 during an intense debate over the proposed Québec Charter of Values, which may have influenced responses in Québec.

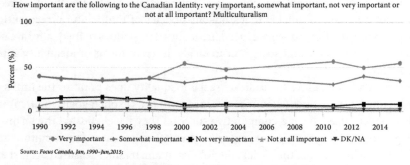

Fig. 10.1 How Important Is Multiculturalism to Canadian Identity?
Source: Focus Canada, January 1990–June 2015.

Table 10.2 Public Attitudes towards Multiculturalism Policies: Recognition

	Pass law declaring ethnic and cultural diversity to be fundamental to national identity		Ensuring schools teach about the role of minorities and immigrants		Requiring that the media represent minorities fairly	
	ROC	Québec	ROC	Québec	ROC	Québec
Str. Support	14	15	27	15	26	13
Support	24	21	33	32	30	31
Neither	35	31	27	36	34	40
Oppose	13	17	8	8	7	9
Str. oppose	15	16	5	10	3	6

Table 10.3 Public Attitudes towards Multiculturalism Policies: Accommodation

	Allowing police and armed forces to wear religious headgear while on duty		Allowing immigrants to keep their citizenship after becoming Canadian citizens		Requiring public schools to offer classes in immigrant language	
	ROC	Québec	ROC	Québec	ROC	Québec
Str. Support	10	3	16	10	5	3
Support	17	3	17	18	10	4
Neither	18	9	26	30	17	10
Oppose	17	18	16	17	25	23
Str. oppose	38	68	25	25	44	61

Source: Data for Tables 10.2 and 10.3 from the Identity Diversity and Social Solidarity (IDSS) survey, February 2014. In both tables, "ROC" reefers to the rest of Canada.

The limits of multiculturalism are also evident in other ways. Despite the public's embrace of multiculturalism as a symbol, racial discrimination persists. Since the early 2000s, comprehensive evidence has been available on immigrants' sense of discrimination: 35 per cent of racialized minorities reported having experienced discrimination or unfair treatment, with Blacks, South Asians, and Chinese having the highest rates (Statistics Canada, 2003, 18–19; also Reitz and Banerjee, 2007). In the contemporary period, anti-Muslim sentiments have flourished, not just in Québec; data from 2014 found that 20 per cent of Muslims had experienced discrimination during that year (Wilkins-Laflamme, 2018). The contradiction between broad public support for multiculturalism and considerable Islamophobia defies easy explanation (Donnelly 2021). Muslims have emerged as the least-favoured religious minority in the country, and Islam has been framed internationally as an illiberal, intolerant, and at times, a violent religion. Evidence to the contrary about Muslims in Canada—a 2016 Environics Institute survey of

198   MULTICULTURALISM POLICY IN CANADA

Canadian Muslims revealed their relatively liberal outlook (Environics, 2016)—does not break through such perceptions. As discourse during the 2015 election campaign demonstrated, opposition to Islam is justified as protecting a tolerant, liberal-democratic order, leading Triadafilopoulos and Rasheed to speculate that 'in a peculiar way,... support for multiculturalism may inform opposition to Islam' (2020, 1).

Despite the limits to Canadians' embrace of multiculturalism, the ethos remains important. Multiculturalism has helped sustain public support for one of the largest immigration programs among democratic countries. In the words of one analyst, 'popular multiculturalism creates a positive political environment for the development of Canada's expansionist immigration policy and helps immigrants integrate into the economy and society' (Reitz, 2014, 108; see also Gonzalez-Barrera and Connor, 2019). Moreover, Canadian support for immigration has remained remarkably stable throughout the turmoil of the 2000s. Canada is not immune to the tensions that exist in other countries, and about 30 per cent of Canadians worry that immigrants do not embrace Canadian values. Moreover, in recent years attitudes have become more polarized between supporters of the Conservative Party and supporters of the Liberal and New Democratic parties (Banting and Soroka, 2020). Nonetheless, the stability in general support for immigration is impressive, and the pervasive multicultural identity helps sustain this distinctive feature of Canada.

The implications likely go further. Canada also stands out as a country whose politics have not been transformed by anti-immigrant backlash and authoritarian anti-system politics. Certainly, there are populist strains in Canadian politics. A radical-right party, the People's Party of Canada, participated in the 2019 and 2021 federal elections; and in the winter of 2022 truckers' protest conveys pararalyzed the capital city for close to a month and blocked several border crossings. Nonetheless, Canadian populism has a distinctive hue. Analysts of populist backlash elsewhere have debated the extent to which such reactions are driven by economic factors, such as growing precarity and inequality, or cultural factors such as immigration and diversity. The consensus seems to be that both are involved, but that cultural drivers predominate (Norris and Inglehart, 2019; Bonikowski, 2017; Sides et al., 2018). Along with other democratic countries, Canada has experienced a growth of inequality and precarious employment. However, potential anti-system populists cannot also tap into a deep public hostility to immigration and are thereby deprived of a major ingredient that has fuelled backlash elsewhere. As a result, recent populist mobilization has centred on anti-government attitudes and opposition to public health manadates. The People's Party of Canada received a derisory 1.6 per cent of the vote in 2019 when it ran on an anti-immgrant platform; but it captured almost 5 percent of the vote in 2021 when it ran on opposition to public health mandates. Similarly, despite xenophobic tinges to the trucker conveys, it was opposition to public health mandates, not immigration, that fueled the protest. Undoubtedly, other factors are important in explaining the limited electoral impact of populist backlash, including the electoral system, which punishes small protest parties whose support is evenly distributed across the country (Triadafilopoulos and Taylor, 2021). Nevertheless, multiculturalism undoubtedly helps reduce the impact of anti-immigrant populism in Canada.

Conclusions

The strongest evidence of the success of Canadian multiculturalism lies in a *programmatic* assessment. The launch of the multiculturalism strategy was a highly ambitious initiative. Governments know how to transfer income and deliver services. By contrast, efforts to transform cultures, identities, and the symbolic ordering of a society represent sensitive and potentially dangerous political terrain. Yet the evidence suggests that multiculturalism policies have succeeded in their two major goals: facilitating the social and political integration of ethnic and racial minorities and contributing to a more inclusive sense of Canadian identity and culture.

Multiculturalism has programmatic limits. It may have reduced levels of racial inequality in political and economic life, but it has not eliminated racism's corrosive effects. Nonetheless, the benefits of multiculturalism should not be discounted. Given the demographic realities of Canada, some form of multicultural identity would seem to be the only basis on which a reasonably integrated and peaceful society could persist on the northern half of the North American continent. Yet the emergence of such an identity was not inevitable. Experience elsewhere suggests that not all countries have transitioned as successfully to an identity consistent with contemporary diversity.

Any assessment of the policy *process* through which multiculturalism policies are shaped must be more qualified. In the early decades, multiculturalism policies evolved in a deliberative process of bureaucratic-group relations, with occasional political interventions. That process was able to adapt the program to successive changes in the demography of minorities and the problems they faced. However, the idea of an evidence-based, consultative policy process has been undermined by the politicization of multiculturalism in recent decades. Policy has been increasingly driven by ideological conflicts, and at times multiculturalism seems becalmed, too hot to touch even by a government that in principle is sympathetic.

In *political* terms, multiculturalism has been conflicted. It has persisted for half a century, including in recent decades when the concept became controversial in many other countries, especially in Europe. Despite its remarkable longevity, however, the policy strategy is not sustained by a deep and comprehensive political consensus. Elements in the conservative movement in Canada are uncomfortable

200 MULTICULTURALISM POLICY IN CANADA

with the celebration of difference implicit in the concept; and Québec has rejected multiculturalism in favour of a different conception of state-minority relations.

In the end, however, multiculturalism's greatest political contribution may be found in what has *not* happened. Canada stands out in the international community, not only as a distinctly multicultural country but also as a country that has avoided the anti-immigrant backlash which has reshaped the political terrain in many countries, weakening the sinews of democracy as it goes. Radical-right populism exists in Canada, but it is not energized by anti-immigrant themes. While we may debate the relative importance of multiculturalism policies in that outcome, its role cannot be easily dismissed. That alone is a singular mark of success.

Appendix A The Multiculturalism Policy Index

The eight indicators used to build the MCP Index for immigrant minorities are:

(1) constitutional, legislative, or parliamentary affirmation of multiculturalism, at the central and/or regional and municipal levels;
(2) the adoption of multiculturalism in the school curriculum;
(3) the inclusion of ethnic representation/sensitivity in the mandate of public media or media licensing;
(4) exemptions from dress-codes, either by statute or by court cases;
(5) allowing of dual citizenship;
(6) the funding of ethnic group organizations to support cultural activities;
(7) the funding of bilingual education or mother-tongue instruction;
(8) affirmative action for disadvantaged immigrant groups.

These eight indicators capture the main ways in which states express multiculturalist commitments, which we earlier described as 'recognition' (indicators 1–3), 'accommodation' (indicators 4–5), and 'support' (indicators 6–8). To build the index, countries are scored on each indicator as 0 (no such policy), 0.5 (partial), or 1.0 (clear policy). The component scores are then aggregated, with equal weighting for each indicator, producing a country score ranging from 0 to 8. (For the empirical evidence supporting the rankings, see Wallace et al, 2021.)

References

Abu-Laban, Y. 2014. "Reform by Stealth: The Harper Conservatives and Canadian Multiculturalism." In *The Multiculturalism Question: Debating Identity in 21st-Century Canada*, edited by J. Jedwab, pp. 149–172. Montreal: McGill-Queen's University Press.

Abu-Laban, Y., and C. Gabriel. 2002. *Selling Diversity: Immigration, Multiculturalism, Employment Equity, and Globalization*. Toronto: University of Toronto Press.

Alba, R. and N. Foner. 2015. *Strangers No More: Immigration and the Challenges of Integration in North America and Western Europe*. Princeton, NJ: Princeton University Press.

Bannerji, H. 2000. *The Dark Side of the Nation: Essays on Multiculturalism, Nationalism and Gender*. Toronto: Canadian Scholars Press.

Banting, K. and W. Kymlicka. 2006. *Multiculturalism and the Welfare State: Recognition and Redistribution in Contemporary Democracies*. Oxford: Oxford University Press.

Banting, K. and W. Kymlicka. 2013. "Is There Really a Retreat from Multiculturalism Policies? New Evidence from the Multiculturalism Policy Index." *Comparative European Politics* 11 (5): pp. 577–598.

Banting, K. and S. Soroka. 2012. "Minority Nationalism and Immigrant Integration in Canada." *Nations and Nationalism* 18 (1): pp. 156–176.

Banting K. and S. Soroka. 2020. "A Distinctive Culture? The Sources of Public Support for Immigration in Canada, 1980–2019." *Canadian Journal of Political Science* 53 (4): pp. 821–838. doi:10.1017/S0008423920000530

Banting, K. and D. Thompson. 2021. "The Puzzling Persistence of Racial Inequality in Canada." *Canadian Journal of Political Science* 54 (4): pp. 870–891. doi:10.1017/S0008423921000585.

Banting, K., D. Westlake, and W. Kymlicka. 2022. "The Politics of Multiculturalism and Redistribution: Immigration, Accommodation and Solidarity in Diverse Democracies." In The Edward Elgar Handbook on Migration and Welfare, edited by M. M. L. Crepaz. Cheltenham: Edward Elgar, pp. 210–229.

Berry, J. 2005. "Acculturation: Living Successfully in Two Cultures." *International Journal of Intercultural Relations* 36 (6): pp. 697–675.

Bilodeau, A. and L. Turgeon. 2021. "Critical Events and Ethnocultural Minorities' Sense of Belonging: Exploring the Impact of the Charter of Quebec Values and Bill 21" Presentation to the School of Policy Studies, Queen's University, 19 March.

Bilodeau, A., S. White, L. Turgeon, and A. Henderson. 2019. "Feeling Attached and Feeling Accepted: Implications for Political Inclusion among Visible Minority Immigrants in Canada." *International Migration* 58 (2): pp. 272–288.

Bloemraad, I. 2006. *Becoming a Citizen: Incorporating Immigrants and Refugees in the United States and Canada*. Berkeley, CA: University of California Press.

Bonikowski, B. 2017. "Ethno-Nationalist Populism and the Mobilization of Collective Resentment." *The British Journal of Sociology* 68: pp. S181–S213.

Bouchard, G. and C. Taylor. 2008. *Building the Future: A Time for Reconciliation, Abridged Report*. Québec: Gouvernement du Québec.

Bricker, D. and J. Ibbitson. 2013. *The Big Shift: The Seismic Change in Canadian Politics, Business, and Culture and What It Means for our Future*. Toronto: Harper Collins.

Carlaw, J. 2021. "Unity in Diversity? Neoconservative Multiculturalism and the Conservative Party of Canada". *Working Papers* Series, Ryerson Centre for Immigration and Settlement (RCIS) and the CERC in Migration and Integration: Ryerson University.

Citizenship and Immigration Canada (CIC). 2009. *Discover Canada: The Rights and Responsibilities of Citizenship*. Ottawa: Government of Canada.

Citrin, J., R. Johnston, and M. Wright. 2012. "Do Patriotism and Multiculturalism Collide? Competing Perspectives from the U.S. and Canada." *Canadian Journal of Political Science* 45 (3): pp. 531–552.

CTV News. 2016. "Chris Alexander on 'Barbaric Cultural Practices': 'It's Why We Lost'." *CTV News*. 9 October. https://www.ctvnews.ca/politics/chris-alexander-on-barbaric-cultural-practices-it-s-why-we-lost-1.3106488

Donnelly, M. 2021. "Discrimination and Multiculturalism in Canada: Exceptional or Incoherent Public Attitudes?". *American Review of Canadian Studies* 51 (1): pp. 166–188.

Esses, V., M. U. Wagner, C. Wolf, M. Preiser, and C. J. Wilbur. 2006. "Perceptions of National Identity and Attitudes toward Immigrants and Immigration in Canada and Germany." *International Journal of Intercultural Relations* 30 (6): pp. 653–669.

Farney, J. 2012. *Social Conservatives and Party Politics in Canada and the United States.* Toronto: University of Toronto Press.

Flanagan, T. 1995. *Waiting for the Wave: The Reform Party and Preston Manning.* Toronto: Stoddart.

Fraser, N. 1995. "From Redistribution to Recognition? Dilemmas of Justice in a 'Post-Socialist' Age." *New Left Review* 1 (212): pp. 68–93.

Gagnon, A.-G. and R. Iacovino. 2007. *Federalism, Citizenship and Quebec: Debating Multinationalism.* Toronto: University of Toronto Press.

Galabuzi, G.-E. 2006. *Canada's Economic Apartheid: The Social Exclusion of Racialized Groups in the New Century.* Toronto: Canadian Scholars' Press.

Gidengil, E. and J. Roy. 2016. "Is There a Racial Divide? Immigrants of Visible Minority Background in Canada" In *Just Ordinary Citizens? Toward a Comparative Portrait of the Political Immigrant,* edited by A.Bilodeau, pp. 149–65. Toronto: University of Toronto Press.

Gonzalez-Barrera, A. and P. Connor. 2019. *Around the World, More Say Immigrants Are a Strength Than a Burden: Public's Divided on Immigrants' Willingness to Adopt Host Country's Customs.* Washington: Pew Research Centre. Available from: https://www.pewresearch.org/global/wp-content/uploads/sites/2/2019/05/Pew-Research-Center_Global-Views-of-Immigrants_2019-03-14_Updated-2019-05-02.pdf

Griffith, A. 2013. *Policy Arrogance or Innocent Bias: Resetting Citizenship and Multiculturalism.* Ottawa: Anar Press.

Guimond, S., R. de La Sabionnière, and A. Nugier. 2014. "Living in a Multicultural World Intergroup ideologies and the Social Context of Intergroup Relations." *European Review of Social Psychology* 25 (1): pp. 142–188.

Harell, A. 2009. "Majority-Minority Relations in Canada: The Rights Regime and the Adoption of Multicultural Values," Paper presented at the Canadian Political Science Association Annual Meeting, Ottawa.

Harris, K. 2019. "Revamped Citizenship Guide Still a Work in Progress as Election Nears." CBC. 19 May. www.cbc.ca/news/politics/citizenship-guide-liberal-mandate-1.5137126

Harrison, T. 1995. *Of Passionate Intensity: Right-Wing Populism and the Reform Party of Canada.* University of Toronto Press.

Heath, A. 2007. "Cross-National Patterns and Processes of Ethnic Disadvantage" in *Unequal Chances: Ethnic Minorities in Western Labour Markets,* edited by A. Heath and S. Y. Cheung. Proceedings of the British Academic 137. Oxford: Oxford University Press, pp. 643–663.

Hobsbawm, E. J. 1992. *Nations and Nationalism since 1780: Programme, Myth, Reality.* 2nd edn. Cambridge: Cambridge University Press.

Hou, F. and G. Picot. 2020. "The Decline in the Naturalization Rate among Recent Immigrants in Canada: Policy Changes and Other Possible Explanations." *Migration Studies* 9 (3): pp. 1030–1053. https://doi.org/10.1093/migration/mnaa010

Hou, F., G. Schellenberg, and J. Berry. 2016. *Patterns and Determinants of Immigrants' Sense of Belonging to Canada and to their Source Country.* Ottawa: Ministry of Industry.

Environics Institute. 2016. *Survey of Muslims in Canada: Final Report*. Toronto: Environics Institute for Survey Research.

Kelley, N. and J. Trebilcock, 2010. *The Making of the Mosaic: A History of Canadian Immigration Policy*, 2nd edn. Toronto: University of Toronto Press.

Koopmans, R., P. Statham, M. Guiugni, and F. Passy. 2005. *Contested Citizenship: Immigration and Cultural Diversity in Europe*. Minneapolis: University of Minnesota Press.

Kwak, L. J. 2019. "New Canadians Are Neo Conservatives: Race, Incorporation and Achieving Electoral Success in Multicultural Canada." *Ethnic and Racial Studies* 42 (10): pp. 1708–1726. https://doi.org/10.1080/01419870.2018.1508734

Kymlicka, W. 2021. "The Precarious Resilience of Multiculturalism in Canada." *American Review of Canadian Studies* 51 (1): pp. 122–142. Available at: doi.org/10.1080/02722011.2021.1878544

Labelle, M. and F. Rocher. 2009. "Immigration, Integration and Citizenship Policies in Canada and Quebec: Tug of War between Competing Societal Projects." In *Immigration and Self-Government of Minority Nations*, edited by R. Zapata-Barrero, pp. 57–86. Brussels: P.I.E. Peter Lang.

Laycock, D. 2012. *The New Right and Democracy in Canada: Understanding Reform and the Canadian Alliance*. Don Mills: Oxford University Press.

Liebig, T. and F. Von Haaren. 2011. "Citizenship and Socio-Economic Integration of Immigrants and their Children: An Overview across EU and OECD Countries." In OECD. 2011. *Naturalization: A passport for Better Integration of Immigrants?*, OECD. Paris: OECD Publishing., pp. 24–81.

Marwah, I., T. Triadafilopoulos, and S. White. 2013. "Immigration, Citizenship, and Canada's New Conservative Party" In *Conservatism in Canada*, edited by J. Farney and D. Rayside, pp. 95–119. Toronto: University of Toronto Press.

McConnell, A. 2010. "Policy Success, Policy Failure and Grey Areas In-Between." *Journal of Public Policy* 30 (3): pp. 345–362.

Nguyen, A.-M. D. and V. Benet-Martinez. 2013. "Biculturalism and Adjustment: A Meta-Analysis." *Journal of Cross-Cultural Psychology* 44 (1): pp. 122–159.

Norris, P. and R. Inglehart. 2019. *Cultural Backlash: Trump, Brexit, and Authoritarian Populism*. New York: Cambridge University Press.

Oreopoulos, P. 2011. "Why Do Skilled Immigrants Struggle in the Labor Market? A Field Experiment with Thirteen Thousand Résumés." *American Economic Journal: Public Policy* 3 (4): pp. 148–171.

Pal, L. 1993. *Interests of State: The Politics of Language, Multiculturalism, and Feminism in Canada*. Montreal: McGill-Queen's University Press.

Quebec. 1990. *Let's Build Quebec Together: Policy Statement on Integration and Immigration*. Montreal: Ministere des Communautes Culturelles et de l'Immigration du Quebec.

Reform Party of Canada. 1997. "A Fresh Start for Canadians: A 6 Point Plan to Build a Brighter Future Together." PolText. https://www.poltext.org/en/part-1-electronic-political-texts/electronic-manifestos-canada

Reitz, J. and R. Banerjee. 2007. "Racial Inequality: Social Cohesion and Policy Issues in Canada." In *Belonging? Diversity, Recognition, and Shared Citizenship in Canada*, edited by K. Banting, T. J. Courchene, and F. Leslie Seidle, pp. 489–546. Montreal: Institute for Research on Public Policy.

Reitz, J. G. 2014. "Multiculturalism Policies and Popular Multiculturalism in the Development of Canadian Immigration." In *The Multiculturalism Question: Debating Identity in 21st-Century Canada*, edited by J. Jedwab, pp. 107–126. Montreal: McGill-Queen's University Press.

Ryan, P. 2010. *Multicultiphobia*. Toronto: University of Toronto Press.

Sides, J., M. Tesler, and L. Vavreck. 2018. *Identity Crisis: The 2016 Presidential Campaign and the Battle for the Meaning of America*. Princeton, NJ: Princeton University Press.

Soroka, S., R. Johnston, and K. Banting. 2007. "Ties That Bind? Social Cohesion and Diversity in Canada." In *Belonging? Diversity, Recognition, and Shared Citizenship in Canada*, edited by K. G. Banting, T. J. Courchene, and F. Leslie Seidle, pp. 561–600. Montreal: Institute for Research on Public Policy.

Statistics Canada. 2003. *Ethnic Diversity Survey: Portrait of a Multicultural Society*. Ottawa: Statistics Canada. Catalogue no. 89-593-XIE.

Thobani, S. 2007. *Exalted Subjects: Studies in the Making of Race and Nation in Canada*. Toronto: University of Toronto Press.

Thomas, P. and J. Sabin. 2019. "Candidate Messaging on Issues in the 2016–17 Conservative Party of Canada Leadership Race." *Canadian Journal of Political Science* 52 (4): pp. 801–823.

Tolley, E. 2017. "Political Players or Partisan Pawns? Immigrants, Minorities, and Conservatives in Canada." In *The Blueprint: Conservative Parties and their Impact on Canadian Politics*, edited by J. Lewis and J. M. Everitt, pp. 101–128. Toronto: University of Toronto Press.

Triadafilopoulos, T. 2012. *Becoming Multicultural: Immigration and the Politics of Membership in Canada and Germany*. Vancouver: University of Britiah Columbia Press.

Triadafilopoulos, T. and J. Rasheed. 2020. "A Religion Like No Other: Islam and the Limits of Multiculturalism in Canada." Ryerson Centre for Immigration and Settlement (RCIS) and the CERC in Migration and Integration Working Paper No. 2020/14.

Triadafilopoulos, T. and Z. Taylor. 2021. "The Political Foundations of Canadian Exceptionalism in Immigration Policy." In *International Affairs and Canadian Migration Policy*, edited by S. Yiagadeosen and H. Duncan, pp. 13–40. London: Palgrave Macmillan.

Trudeau, P. 1971. "Statement to the House of Commons on Multiculturalism." House of Commons, Official Report of Debates, 28th Parliament, Third Session, 8 October: 8545–8546.

Uberoi, V. 2008. "Do Policies of Multiculturalism Change National Identities?" *The Political Quarterly* 79 (3): pp. 404–417.

Wallace, R., E. Tolley and M. Vonk. 2021. *Multicuturalism Policy Index: Immigrant Minority Policies*. Third Edition. Kingston: The Multiculturalism Policy Index Project, Queen's University. https://www.queensu.ca/mcp/

Weber, E. 1976. *Peasants into Frenchmen: The Modernization of Rural France, 1870–1914*. Stanford, CA: Stanford University Press.

White, S., A. Bilodeau, and N. Nevitte. 2015. "Earning their Support: Feelings towards Canada among Recent Immigrants." *Ethnic and Racial Studies* 38 (2): pp. 292–308.

Wilkins-Laflamme, Sarah. 2018. "Islamophobia in Canada: Measuring the Realities of Negative Attitudes Toward Muslims and Religious Discrimination." *Canadian Review of Sociology* 55 (1): 86–110.

Wilkins-Laflamme, S. and S. Reimer. 2019. "Religion and Grass Roots Social Conservatism in Canada." *Canadian Journal of Political Science* 52 (4): pp. 865–881.

Wright, M. and I. Bloemraad. 2012. "Is There a Trade-off between Multiculturalism and Socio-Political Integration: Policy Regimes and Immigrant Incorporation in Comparative Perspective." *Perspectives on Politics* 10 (1): pp. 77–95.

11

The Magic Is in the Mix

How the Guaranteed Income Supplement and Old Age Security Interact in Canada's Pension System to Tackle Successfully Poverty in Old Age

Daniel Béland and Patrik Marier

Introduction

A policy mix that comprises of several major social programs, Canada's pension system is among the best in the world in reducing poverty in old age and providing a high replacement rate for low-income retirees (RRQ, 2004). To this day, this continues to puzzle most policy analysts and scholars, who routinely compare the Canadian pension system to the likes of the United States and the United Kingdom when, in fact, it should be compared to countries providing generous public pensions, such as Sweden (for example see Wiseman and Yčas, 2008).

In this chapter, we focus on the interaction between two closely related components of Canada's pension system as a policy mix that is particularly successful at reducing old-age poverty: the Guaranteed Income Supplement (GIS) and the Old Age Security (OAS) program. More specifically, we analyse the primary root of this policy success: the 'failure' to dismantle a program that was meant to be temporary, the Guaranteed Income Supplement (GIS); and its complementarity to the Old Age Security (OAS) program. The GIS was introduced in 1967, as a transitory measure to expediently tackle the prevalent poverty amongst Canadian seniors, and was expected to disappear with the maturation of the Canada Pension Plan/Québec Pension Plan. Not only was this program never abolished, it failed to generate the kind of stigma associated with social assistance benefits, as it was linked with the quasi-universal OAS program. As a result of this policy design, it is an income-tested program—not to be confused with a means-tested program where assets are also taken into consideration—which makes older adults feel thet're entitled OAS beneficiaries. The combination of OAS and GIS provides a relatively generous floor for retirees with limited resources. This points to the close and complementary relationship of key elements within the public pension policy mix in Canada.

Daniel Béland and Patrik Marier, *The Magic Is in the Mix*. In: *Policy Success in Canada.*
Edited by Evert A. Lindquist et al., Oxford University Press. © Daniel Béland and Patrik Marier (2022).
DOI: 10.1093/oso/9780192897046.003.0011

This case study focuses on how, within Canada's pension system, the GIS interacts with OAS to help achieve the policy objective of curbing poverty among older adults (65+) along the four dimensions of success proposed by McConnell (2010), and Compton et al. (2019). In a nutshell, the GIS and its interaction with the OAS program is distinctive because, together, they form a potent targeted instrument to reduce poverty, cover a large portion of the older adult population, and reduce the level of stigma traditionally attached to social assistance programs such as the GIS. In the last section, we discuss some of the weaknesses of the policy mix by, for example, shedding light on why poverty alleviation gradually becomes less effective as one gets older. We also stress disadvantages facing immigrants and older single women within Canada's public pension policy mix. We conclude with some of the key challenges facing this policy mix moving forward and with a discussion about how success in poverty reduction does not mean that other key objectives of Canada's public pension system, namely providing a high replacement rate for middle income retirees and rising inequalities in retirement income, are addressed. This means that it is possible to further improve our relatively successful public pension policy mix.

A (Surprising) Policy Success

Programmatic Success

Perhaps one of the most interesting features of this success is its unique design and its relative obscurity in the international literature on pension systems. In the comparative welfare state literature, when it comes to Canada's system, predominant studies on pensions paint a bleak picture of generosity and universality. In Gøsta Esping-Andersen's (1990) now classic *Three Worlds of Welfare Capitalism*, Canada's low score on pensions (7.7) is consistent with a liberal welfare regime, above only the United States (7) and Ireland (6.7) among the 18 industrialized countries studied in the book. It also lies at the opposite end from Social Democratic countries such as Denmark (15) and Sweden (17.7) (50). John Myles and Paul Pierson (2001) also depict Canada as a classic latecomer in the provision of a mandatory and public earnings-related pension program. With rising concerns over the costs of many public programs and the growing availability of occupation pensions, latecomers adopted public programs with limited replacement rates, such as the adoption of the Canada Pension Plan (CPP)/Québec Pension Plan (QPP)[1] in the late 1960s with a 25 per cent replacement rate for the average worker.

---

[1] There are slight differences between the Canada Pension Plan and the Québec Pension Plan, but the core features are essentially the same with the noticeable exception of higher contribution rates for Québec. For the purpose of this chapter, we treat them as the same.

208 SUCCESSFULLY TACKLING OLD AGE POVERTY

These assessments are at odds with, for instance, the then *Régie des rentes du Québec's* conclusion that Québec's pension system is one of the best performers in the world along with those of Scandinavian countries (RRQ, 2004, 2)[2] with respect to poverty alleviation. The generosity of Canada/Québec's public pension system was also a point of contention in Scruggs and Allan's (2006, 892) replication of Esping-Andersen's study. Canada's score of 13.5 was above the median, and relatively closer to the most generous countries.

The source of these widely divergent assessments lies with how one defines social outcomes, which has been at the heart of welfare state debates with regards to both the conceptualization and measurement of social policies (Green-Pedersen, 2004). There are studies using entitlements as the core dependent variable (Esping-Andersen, 1990; Scruggs and Allan, 2006), studies focusing simply on spending (Tepe and Vanhuysse, 2010), and studies focusing specifically on policy outcomes such as redistributive capacities (Gál et al., 2018), or poverty alleviation (Kaida and Boyd, 2011). Studies on welfare state retrenchment even include the underlying policy infrastructure, such as the institutions responsible for providing benefits (Pierson, 1994). These differences matter greatly when it comes to the validation of existing social policy theories. For instance, a recent meta-analysis on quantitative studies about retrenchment demonstrates that studies using entitlements were four times more likely to denote a partisanship effect than those using social spending (Bandau and Ahrens, 2020).

In terms of the programmatic criteria of this volume, the GIS and, more generally, the non-contributory portion of its retirement income system (i.e. OAS and GIS), satisfies the core criterion of a purposeful and valued action when it comes to poverty reduction. One would be hard pressed to find a better value proposition. By providing poverty alleviation outcomes associated with generous welfare states at a lower cost and without the presence of a generous earnings-related pension program (CPP/QPP), Canada is performing a balancing act. Benefits have been deemed 'cheap and effective' and are a potent reminder that a pension system does not have to be encompassing to alleviate poverty (Myles, 2013, 315). In a recent US article, proponents of a Targeted Minimum Benefit Plan to replace the highly ineffective Social Security Supplemental (SSI) draw their inspiration from the GIS, which they depict as a 'cost-effective method for reducing elder poverty to very low levels' (Herd et al., 2018, 74).

In terms of achievement, the continuous presence and importance of the GIS in the Canadian pension system is actually an unintended consequence, as the program was originally designed to be temporary during the implementation phase of the C/QPP in the late 1960s and early 1970s (see discussion on the context below). It is now a highly popular program, which contributes to the establishment of an enhanced basic pension that is non-contributory in nature. Indicative of its

---

[2] Following an administrative reform, this office is now called Retraite Québec.

popularity across the country, eight provinces include a top-up ranging from $30 to over $200 per month (Marier and Séguin, 2015).

Finally, based on the latest data from the Organization for Economic Co-operation and Development (OECD), Canada is fourth among OECD countries when it comes to the percentage of gross average earnings originating from non-contributory pension programmes at 30.1 per cent (2019). This is well above the OECD average of 20.4 per cent (135). This percentage would likely be higher if one focused on net earnings because, in contrast to OAS benefits, the GIS is a non-taxable benefit. The GIS remains a classic redistribution program offering benefits targeting lower-income seniors, which are financed through general revenues of the federal government.

Process Success

The process behind the adoption of the GIS features a deliberate selection of policy instruments that one would expect to find in a temporary program to boost retirement income for seniors during the implementation of the C/QPP. The proposal retained by the federal government in 1966, which would eventually become the GIS, was shaped by a special committee on the socio-economic issues related to aging within the Senate. The committee rejected the idea of increasing the generosity of OAS benefits to create a more comprehensive universal pension—something that was hotly debated in the political arena—because it would generate highly noticeable inequities between current retirees relying mostly on universal pensions and younger cohorts who would benefit from both a universal pension and the C/QPP. The committee also feared that a universal pension would be too costly. These concerns led to the proposal of a new temporary supplement with a phase-out period, income eligibility based on tax revenues, and a 10-year residency test. It drew immediate positive reviews, in contrast to the polarizing debate on universal pensions, prompting the government to build on this proposal (Bryden, 1974, 153). Cost concerns and typical considerations associated with social assistance programs, such as disincentives to save, were prominent. Still, the equality of treatment across generations, nowadays frequently mentioned in the context of intergenerational equity, was an important argument deployed against the adoption of a larger universal pension and in favour of introducing the GIS alongside OAS.

With the original aim of being a temporary program, the punishing policy tools and administrative burdens associated with traditional (means-tested rather than income-tested) social assistance programs are notoriously absent from the GIS. The focus was clearly on providing additional income to a cohort of older adults while they awaited the maturity of the C/QPP. As such, the use of income tax filings to calculate eligibility represents an optimal tool requiring minimal administrative capacity, and it does not lead to the negative consequences traditionally associated with means-tested programs.

For the most part, this conceptualization of the GIS, and the policy design to alleviate poverty by combining both the GIS and OAS programs, have ensured its effectiveness and stability over the years. At first glance, the GIS also represents a classic case of positive policy feedback (Pierson, 1994) with unintended consequences, which has allowed it to survive beyond the original 1967–1977 period to become a permanent fixture of Canada's public pension system. Still, the fact that the GIS became permanent in the mid-1970s is as much a reflection of the popularity of the program as it is a reflection of the need to grant additional income support because, after 10 years of existence, the C/QPP had failed to lift many older people out of poverty.

As originally designed, the GIS remains an income-tested policy instrument—as opposed to a classic means-tested benefit—and its coupling with OAS has far reaching consequences. Programmes targeting the poor tend to be ineffective in achieving their goal of poverty alleviation. Filled with administrative burdens and a source of stigma for their recipients, these programs tend to be unpopular and are an easy target for cutbacks (Rothstein, 2002). In many ways, these programmes are constructed as much to discourage—or even punish—potential beneficiaries who access them as to help them (Schneider and Ingram, 1993). For instance, in the UK, there are 23 types of state pension benefits for seniors and more than a third of poor older adults do not claim the Pension Credit despite being eligible to do so (Moffatt and Scambler, 2008, 875-6). Hence, universal welfare states tend to achieve much better results in terms of poverty alleviation *by not targeting the poor* and providing substantial benefits to the middle class (Korpi and Palme, 1998). Canada has the distinction of achieving the opposite outcome by targeting the poor and providing comparatively limited benefits to middle income earners (Myles, 2013).

The GIS avoids these familiar issues. The uptake rate is 90 per cent and those most in need, such as women, individuals with income below $15,000, and older adults aged 80 and above, access it at a higher rate (Employment and Social Development Canada, 2019). Other groups frequently marginalized by means-tested benefits access the benefit at a higher rate than the average. For instance, immigrants and indigenous seniors have an uptake rate of 96 per cent and 91 per cent respectively (Employment and Social Development Canada, 2019, 9).

Political Success

Both OAS and GIS qualify strongly as a political success. First, voices opposed to the OAS/GIS programs in tandem are quite rare. Suggestive of this broad support across a wide range of stakeholders, a recent meta-study indicates a weaker probability of finding partisanship effects in this policy area compared to other social policy areas, most notably those associated with class conflicts, such as unemployment and sick benefits (Bandau and Ahrens, 2020). The OAS/GIS structure benefits from positive policy feedback (Pierson, 1994; Patashnik, 2008), as large pan-Canadian age-based networks such as the FADOQ and CanAge, play a crucial role in maintaining the political pressure to sustain, via proper indexation, and increase the financial support for these programs. Provinces are also notable stakeholders who are constantly pushing for a sustained and more generous OAS and GIS. This is typically part of their aging action plan commitments (Marier, 2021). The latter is a clear illustration that policy actors enhance their reputation by being linked to both OAS and GIS, a core feature of political success in the policy success framework, even though these federal programs receive very marginal input from the provinces.

Second, both GIS and OAS benefit from strong popular support across a wide range of social, political, and administrative actors. The sizable constituency of GIS and OAS recipients, who also represent potential voters, looms large in political debates surrounding pension policies in Canada. They are highly visible federal programs whose impact is accentuated since social policies are typically a provincial responsibility. There is strong support from within the public administration as well. As illustrated regularly by actuarial reports, the GIS and OAS are not expensive to administer, and projections indicate that these are sustainable in the long run (Béland and Marier, 2019, 114).

These elements make Canada unique by international standards. Non-contributory components of pension systems are more vulnerable to change, especially in the liberal welfare state. For instance, in a comparative analysis of pension retrenchment (in Australia, Canada, New Zealand, United Kingdom, and the United States), Bridgen (2018) demonstrates that pension expenditures for those over 65 in New Zealand dropped by 126 per cent between 1980 and 2010. This is highly notable because New Zealand's public pension system consists primarily of a large, non-contributory public benefit, which remains the most generous non-contributory pension scheme in the OECD, replacing 40 per cent of the average wage (OECD, 2019). In the United States, the Supplemental Security Income (SSI) covers a wide range of individuals, including people with disabilities, who constitute a larger majority of recipients. It is as a result of its indexation mechanism and its strict means-test that the program has continuously covered a small population of older adults (currently, less than 5 per cent) (Duggan et al., 2015). In contrast with the GIS in Canada, the SSI is not well integrated with state policies, as it interacts poorly with myriad welfare programs offered at the state level. On average, every dollar transferred to the states results in only 50 cents in actual cash benefits to recipients (Goodman-Bacon and Schmidt, 2020).

Endurance: A Resilient Policy Mix

The GIS and the GIS/OAS policy mix has lifted many Canadians out of poverty. Until recently, the OAS/GIS policy mix had steadily achieved outstanding results relative to its peers in other industrialized countries. Still, a cohort of older adults find themselves near or below the poverty line. The latest figures from the OECD indicate a noticeable increase in the poverty rate for all older adults, which currently stands at 12.2 per cent. This remains below the OECD average of 13.5 per cent and is substantially better than the US figure of 17.8 per cent, another country with a relatively modest public earnings-related pension scheme (OECD, 2019: 187). Still, this actually represents a 74 per cent increase from the data reported in Myles (2013) and 600 per cent increase from the Canadian figures of 2 per cent provided by the RRQ around 15 years ago (2004, 74). The sources of this gradual decline, and recent initiatives that will alleviate this decline, are discussed in the last section of this chapter.

Contexts, Challenges, Agents

In Canada, aside from military and public service pensions, the development of public pensions took place slowly, in part because of the dominance of economic liberalism and the idea of self-reliance, which pushed governments to emphasize personal responsibility and personal savings. In 1908, this context led Ottawa to create a federal government annuities program, which would remain in place until the mid-1970s (Bryden, 1974). Yet, voluntary savings, even when mediated by the state, had a limited effect in fighting old-age poverty. This was already apparent in Europe, where a growing number of countries, including the United Kingdom, had already enacted major public pension programs by the early-mid-1920s to ameliorate the problem.

The history of the modern Canadian public pension system began in earnest in 1927 with the enactment of the Old Age Pensions Act. The federal legislation created a framework for Ottawa to reimburse half of the federally approved provincial spending on flat, means-tested old-age assistance pensions for poor citizens or people with at least two decades of residency aged 70 and older. 'Administration was entirely a federal responsibility, but an administrative scheme and any changes to it had to have federal approval in advance' (Bryden, 1974: 61). Politically, the enactment of the Old Age Pensions Act was largely the product of electoral calculus on the part of William Lyon Mackenzie King's Liberals, who campaigned in favour of creating a public pension scheme during the 1926 federal campaign. After King's Liberals formed a minority government prompted by Liberal-Progressive MPs, they moved forward with the idea of a federal pension framework, despite the opposition of those who thought the federal government should not get involved in the field of social welfare, as this was seen as a purely provincial area at the time. The main rationale to move forward with this decision was based on the idea that, on their own, provinces could not address the issue of old-age security, which had become the most important social policy issue of the decade (Bryden, 1974: 74).

The implementation of the new federal old-age assistance framework faced three major challenges (Bryden, 1974, 82). First, it took nearly a decade for all the provinces to accept to participate in the federal framework created by the federal legislation. In 1931, to make the framework more attractive to the provinces in the context of the Great Depression, which further increased concerns about old-age poverty across the country, the federal government increased its contribution to provincial old-age pensions from 50 to 75 per cent. Finally, in 1936, Québec became the last province to (reluctantly) agree to participate in the federal old-age pension framework created nine years earlier (Banting, 2005, 100). Second, disparities among provinces appeared over time. For instance, some provinces paid supplementary benefits while others did not. This meant that the level of pension benefits actually varied from province to province. Simultaneously, administrative differences among provinces led to variance in how the means test was implemented on the ground, making it either easier or harder for poor older people to access benefits, depending on their province of residence (Bryden, 1974). This issue was addressed in 1951 with the federalization of old-age assistance, which took place at the same time as the creation of Old Age Security. Finally, 'rising living costs immediately before and after the outbreak of World War II gave rise to a politically significant demand for increased benefits' (Bryden, 1974, 81).

These demands, combined with calls to both lower the age of eligibility and reduce the reliance on the means test, were instrumental in the post-war push to pension reform that led to the enactment of new federal pension legislation in 1951. That year, in the context of the post-war expansion of the federal welfare state, the Old Age Security Act and the Old Age Assistance Act transformed Canada's pension system. The Act eliminated the means test and extended public pension coverage to all people aged 70 and over who met specific residency requirements. Old Age Security (OAS) was the new program created with the enactment of this legislation. At the same time, the Act extended means-tested benefits to people aged 65–69. Old Age Assistance remained in place until 1970 when eligibility for OAS had been lowered to 65 years (Béland and Myles, 2005).

OAS universalized access to public pensions in Canada while beginning a process of federalizing pension policy. A constitutional amendment was required to allow the provinces to let Ottawa directly enter the field of old-age pensions. After its enactment, OAS only paid out a modest universal pension of up to a mere $40 per month. A key rationale for such a low amount was the apparent necessity to incentivize personal savings and the explicit reliance on voluntary, employment-based private pensions. In an era of unprecedented economic security, there was

214   SUCCESSFULLY TACKLING OLD AGE POVERTY

much optimism about the expansion of both personal savings and employment-based pensions. This is reflected in the introduction of the tax-subsidized Registered Retirement Savings Plans (RRSPs) in 1957, only six years after the creation of OAS.

This move did not satisfy the Co-operative Commonwealth Federation (CCF) which, in tandem with labour unions, pushed for much higher OAS benefits in the late 1950s and early 1960s. Ultimately, in the context of growing electoral competition between the CCF (and later the NDP) and the Liberal Party of Canada, the push for more generous public pensions led the latter to include the creation of an earnings-related Canada Pension Plan in their electoral platform (Bryden, 1997). Soon the idea of adding a new, earnings-related layer to Canada's pension system gained ground. Since provincial consent was necessary for the enactment of a federal earnings-related pension program, negotiations with the provinces took place during the first couple of years of the Liberal minority government under Lester B. Pearson (1963–1968). During these negotiations, Québec decided to opt out of the proposed Canada Pension Plan (CPP) to create the Québec Pension Plan (QPP), a program nearly identical to the CPP that would help the province invest in provincial economic development through what would become the Caisse de dépôt et placement du Québec (CDPQ). All in all, the creation of the CPP and QPP led to an expansion of Canada's public pension system, as new earnings-related pensions financed through contributions of workers and employers would complement and add to the OAS (Béland and Myles, 2005).

Despite the creation of the CPP and QPP, old-age poverty remained high in Canada. This was especially the case because, as earning-related schemes, these two programs would not pay out benefits immediately, which delayed their positive socio-economic effects. Simultaneously, a growing gap between people who retired before the creation of the CPP and QPP, and younger people who would qualify for earnings-related benefits after at age of 65, raised some equity concerns. It is in this context that the Guaranteed Income Supplement emerged. The idea of a 'guaranteed income program' for older people was first raised by a Senate Special Committee on Aging created in 1963. The idea of a guaranteed income seemed like a much cheaper fiscal alternative for the federal government than an across-the-board expansion of OAS. This option would also avoid the means-test, which was perceived as 'utterly unacceptable', except to address 'special circumstances' (report of the Special committee on Aging as quoted in Bryden, 1974, 153).

In the end, in 1967, the federal government implemented the Guaranteed Income Supplement (GIS), an income-tested social assistance program meant to support poorer older people aged 65 and over during the ramping up of both the CPP and QPP. In this context, GIS was meant to be a temporary program conceived as a 'bridge' between the 'old' public pension system and the 'new', post-CPP and QPP system. Closely related to OAS, the GIS rapidly became popular with both older people and government officials, as it developed into an effective tool to fight old age poverty (Béland and Myles, 2005). Therefore, a temporary program meant to last for only one decade was made permanent in the mid-1970s. As historian Dennis Guest (2013) explains:

> Although the Guaranteed Income Supplement (GIS) was initially seen as a transitional program to be phased out when the C/QPP began paying full benefits in 1976, it was found that a sizable portion of C/QPP beneficiaries qualified for less than a maximum pension. This, coupled with the fact that only a minority of workers had an employer-sponsored pension, meant that the GIS remained a critical element in reducing the incidence of poverty among the elderly. Thus the program was maintained, increased in value, and indexed quarterly to the cost of living.

This is how a temporary program became a permanent and essential feature of Canada's public pension system. By the time OAS had been made permanent in the mid-1970s, the architecture of Canada's modern public pension system had been completed and its general organization has remained the same ever since. In the next section, we take a closer look at the specific design and features of this system and its different components.

A Resilient Success

Contrary to policy successes where there was a clear intent to alter specific outcomes, the GIS, and its interactions with OAS, is a case of a minor—and in this case, even initially temporary—program that eventually became permanent and grew in importance. Interestingly, this also occurred with another program within the pension policy of Canada: the Registered Retirement Savings Plans (RRSPs). RRSPs were created in 1957 to complement occupational pension plans and have since been the de facto retirement savings vehicle for individuals without access to occupational pensions, known as Registered Pension Plans (RPPs).

As discussed above, adopted in 1967, the GIS aimed to facilitate the transition of workers while they began to accrue entitlements within the C/QPP. However, the first wave of C/QPP payments resulted in many individuals falling significantly short of the maximum benefits, a situation that accentuated the political pressures to maintain the GIS and make it a permanent program. Regarding the GIS, there are several design features that facilitated such a strong, positive policy feedback effect. One is that 32 per cent of OAS recipients receive—in part or in full—the GIS (Employment and Social Development Canada, 2019). This is a substantially higher level of coverage (nearly one senior out of three) than a typical social assistance.

Moreover, the GIS is not means-tested but income-tested. Access to the benefit is relatively easy to obtain and focuses solely on taxable income and, as such, foregoes many traditional features of means-tested benefits, such as asset tests. This is

216   SUCCESSFULLY TACKLING OLD AGE POVERTY

highly cost efficient in terms of administering the program and makes it easy for provinces to offer a top up because all provinces, with the exception of Québec, utilize the joint (federal/provincial) personal income tax declaration. This policy design is also highly impersonal (i.e. only income and not other characteristics are considered when assessing eligibility), which is a major advantage because it removes the welfare stigma associated with these benefits.

Also, as a result of its original design, the GIS has been integrated within the Old Age Security Act from the time of its conception. This has multiple implications, such as the provision of a single OAS/GIS cheque, which reinforces the apparent symbiosis between the two programs, as they have almost become a joined-up 'brand' for their recipients, while also blurring the line between universality (OAS) and targeting (GIS).

Fourth, the ones who benefit the most from the GIS tend to be women and adults over 75. In stark contrast to the United States, where seniors are referred to as net beneficiaries of public programs, Canadian media typically construe older adults as frail and vulnerable (Marier and Revelli, 2017). Thus, in Canada, this segment of the population is seen as 'deserving' of state assistance, making it difficult for any government to justify cuts.

Finally, the structure of this program and the clear division of pension responsibilities in Canada result in the provinces being proponents of a generous OAS/GIS, as it allows them to offer other types of benefits for older adults. These five elements result in the GIS benefiting from a wide constituency, consisting most notably of seniors' groups and provincial leaders. In fact, provincial action strategies/plans for seniors typically emphasize the importance for the federal government to maintain generous OAS and GIS benefits (Marier, 2021).

GIS Today

The GIS is available to citizens—or legal residents—aged 65 and above, who have resided at least 10 years in Canada since the age of 18. To qualify for the GIS, an individual living alone must be at least 65 and have an income below $18,600. The maximum benefit for this category of recipients is $10,997 and, to achieve the latter amount, one must not have any taxable income revenues (Table 11.1). This would include, for instance, revenues from the C/QPP, occupational pension income, withdrawals from an RRSP, and employment income. However, it excludes OAS benefits and withdrawals from a Tax-Free Savings Account (TFSA). The GIS amount begins to decline as soon as one earns $24 at a 50 per cent rate. Following a recent reform, there is also a GIS top up for seniors living alone with an income below $8,400, but with a recapture rate slightly below 75 per cent for additional income (Shillington, 2019).

Table 11.1 GIS, by Family Types, 2020

Household Composition	Maximum Annual Income to Qualify	Maximum Benefit	Clawback income greater than
Living Alone	$18,600	$10,997	$24
Couple, both receive OAS	$24,576	$13,239	$48
Couple, one receiving OAS, other does not receive OAS	$44,592	$10,997	$4,096

Source: Authors' calculations with data from the Guaranteed Income Supplement Webpage[3]

Beyond the number of years of residency and income, the GIS eligibility criteria feature two other forms of exclusions. First, there are some barriers for immigrants depending on an individual's status. Sponsored immigrants must terminate their sponsorship period to qualify. For non-sponsored immigrants, the 10-year residency requirement can be waived if the country of origin has a social security agreement with Canada. Second, incarceration in a federal penitentiary over a period of two years results in a suspension of the GIS benefit.

An important component of the GIS design remains its simplicity and the ease upon which provinces can add benefits targeting low income seniors. Eight provinces offer such benefits, with Nova Scotia and Québec being the two exceptions (Marier and Séguin, 2015). These benefits operate along similar parameters as the GIS, but typically feature additional conditions. There are noticeable provincial variations. For instance, in New Brunswick, older adults can qualify for the Low-Income Seniors Benefit—an annual cheque of $400—if they receive one of the three benefits from the Old Age Security Act (GIS, Allowance for Survivor, Allowance Program). This amount is per household and applies regardless of whether one is living alone or with a spouse or partner. In Saskatchewan, the Seniors Income Plan (SIP) features an income test targeting older people living with very limited retirement income beyond OAS and GIS (see Table 11.2). The top up is much more generous than New Brunswick's and the monthly amount varies according to the type of accommodation and living arrangements (see Table 11.2). In addition, the SIP is used as a qualifier for targeted programs such as free eye examinations, a reduced prescription drug plan, and a home care subsidy.

Surviving Challenges

The enduring popularity of the GIS is related to its policy design emphasizing income-testing rather than means-testing, which has eliminated, or at least considerably reduced, the stigma associated with this social assistance. Simultaneously,

[3] See https://www.canada.ca/en/services/benefits/publicpensions/cpp/old-age-security/guaranteed-income-supplement.html

218 SUCCESSFULLY TACKLING OLD AGE POVERTY

Table 11.2 Seniors Income Plan (Saskatchewan), by Family Types and Living Situations, 2020

Household Composition	Maximum Annual Income to Qualify	Maximum Benefit
Living at Home		
Living Alone	$4,560	$3,240
Married, both pensioners	$7,440	$5,640
Married, spouse less than 60 of age	$10,320	$3,240
Living in Special Care Home		
Living Alone	$912	$600
Married, both pensioners	$1,776	$600
Married, spouse less than 60 years of age	$7,872	$600

Source: Authors' calculations drawn from Seniors Income Plan (SIP) webpage[4]

OAS, which is closely related to the GIS, has remained in place even in a context of an increasingly aging population, and despite the politics of retrenchment, which has increased pressures to control costs since the early 1980s. To understand the resilience of both programs over time, it is helpful to survey key attempts at reforming OAS and GIS that took place between 1985 and 2012.A first major challenge to OAS and GIS emerged in the aftermath of the 1984 federal electoral campaign, during which the soon-to-be Progressive Conservative prime minister Brian Mulroney questioned the legitimacy of OAS as a universal program, claiming that the wealthy should not be entitled to OAS benefits. Although criticisms from the labour movement and organizations representing older people forced Mulroney to back away from this discourse, his promise to fight large federal deficits transformed OAS and GIS, two programs financed through general revenues, into potential retrenchment targets (Myles, 1988, 49).

The following year, in May 1985, approximately nine months after the election, Progressive Conservative finance minister Michael Wilson proposed the 'partial deindexation' of OAS benefits as a cost-saving measure. In part because the Progressive Conservatives had explicitly opposed deindexation during the 1984 federal campaign, and in part because the measure would have affected both current and future beneficiaries, the announcement triggered an unprecedented political mobilization from older people, as well as political and civil society organizations seeking to defend their interests. In the end, the Mulroney government withdrew this proposed measure in what constituted a humiliating political defeat (Battle, 1997).

Considering this public opposition to pension cutbacks, the Mulroney government decided to adopt a less visible form of retrenchment that took the shape of

[4] See https://www.saskatchewan.ca/residents/family-and-social-support/seniors-services/financial-help-for-seniors

a fiscal claw back of OAS benefits adopted as part of the 1989 federal budget. This claw back effectively took away money from higher income OAS recipients, until the entire pension disappeared at approximately $89,000 per year. Over time, because of the limited indexation of the cut-off point for the claw back, the percentage of people excluded from OAS benefits altogether was set to increase (Béland and Myles, 2005). Despite this, because most older people were not affected by the claw back and because this low-profile change did not attract much media and political attention, it was widely understood as a form of 'social policy by stealth' (Battle, 1990).

In 1996, the Liberal government of Jean Chrétien launched a more explicit attempt at targeting pension benefits funded through general revenues. The Liberal proposal announced by Finance Minister Paul Martin was to replace both OAS and GIS with a new program called the Seniors Benefit. This new program would have ended universality by creating a single income-tested scheme that would exclude higher-income older people, while offering more generous benefits to middle- and low-income seniors. In contrast to the OAS claw back adopted in 1989, which was calculated based on individual income, the Seniors Benefit would have been based on family income. This situation generated feminist opposition to the proposal, as it appeared to threaten the independence of women who could lose their benefits because of their husband's income. Simultaneously, other political actors, especially those on the right of the political spectrum, criticized the benefit because they believed it would further weaken the incentives workers had to save for retirement. In the end, attacked by both the left and the right, the Seniors Benefit was never enacted, especially because the advent of large federal surpluses reduced short-term fiscal pressures and further reduced the apparent legitimacy of the proposed program (Béland and Myles, 2005).

The last major political challenge to OAS and GIS came in early 2012, when Prime Minister Harper announced that the eligibility age for these benefits would gradually increase from 65 to 67 between 2023 and 2029. Justified by growing fiscal concerns stemming from demographic aging, this measure, if enacted, would have directly penalized low-income older people who need OAS and GIS to retire. This is partly why the Liberals and the NDP promised that if they formed government, they would reverse that decision before the change in eligibility age was set to increase. This is exactly what the new Liberal government of Justin Trudeau did shortly after the 2015 federal elections, thus cancelling the Conservative plan altogether (Béland and Marier, 2019).

This short historical overview suggests that both OAS and GIS are popular, politically entrenched (Patashnik, 2008) programs that have survived retrenchment attempts, which have weakened the universality of OAS but not the overall architecture of the Canadian public system. The fact that this system has proved effective at fighting poverty among older people while maintaining public pension spending significantly below the OECD average has further increased the support for this basic architecture and for the preservation of the GIS, a program initially meant to exit only on a temporary basis.

Analysis and Conclusions

How can we explain the relative stability of the Canadian pension system over the last 50 years? The answer is two-fold. First, as the best international scholarship on pension systems suggests, pension programs are among the hardest to retrench and dismantle, because they generate large and politically active constituencies (Campbell, 2003) and because they involve long-term expectations and commitments on the part of citizens and governments, respectively (Myles and Pierson, 2001). Second, specific characteristics of the Canadian pension system, such as comparatively low pension spending and payroll contributions, have weakened the 'need to reform' (Cox, 2001, 463) and made incremental changes more likely. Simultaneously, the relatively modest nature of Canada's public pensions and the key role of the GIS made it possible to reduce poverty among older people, while keeping most of this demographic in the second and third income quintiles rather than in the top two income quintiles. This situation made it harder for reformers to claim that Canada's public pensions were too generous, and that older people were 'greedy', which is what took place in the United States and some European countries (Béland and Myles, 2005).

These factors help explain why, since the consolidation of Canada's modern public pension system in the mid-late-1960s, programmatic change has proved quite limited in scope, both in OAS and GIS. For instance, looking at the six policy elements identified by Howlett and Cashore (2009, 39) in their seminal article on policy change (goals, objectives, settings, instrument logic, mechanisms, and calibrations), only calibrations have been significantly altered in OAS and GIS. This is the case because changes to both programs have proved relatively limited and incremental adjustments to benefit, indexation, and tax levels. Yet, changes to OAS have been consequential, as the program's universal nature has been diminished through the introduction of the claw back. Simultaneously, because of the indexation system used, the real value of OAS benefits is slowly declining over time. This situation reduces long-term fiscal budgetary and fiscal pressures while further increasing the importance of the GIS in the fight against old-age poverty in Canada (Béland and Marier, 2019).

The surprising longevity of the GIS, its design, and its close relationship to OAS have produced a potent policy mix to alleviate poverty in Canada. As a result, the Canadian pension system has had far more in common with European countries, even flirting with Scandinavian-like poverty alleviation outcomes for a while, when compared to other countries in the so-called Liberal welfare regimes, like the United States and the United Kingdom (Wiseman and Yčas, 2008).

Current developments indicate that the OAS/GIS programs are likely to remain crucial in the years to come. First, the Canadian pension system continues to perform poorly when it comes to wage replacement (i.e. maintaining the income of older people after they retire), especially with those earning the median wage and above (OECD, 2019). Low income individuals and those with interrupted careers obtain a high replacement rate because of the coverage and generosity of the OAS/GIS programs. The continued weakening of occupational pensions in the private sector, and the meagre efforts to introduce potent alternatives to boost retirement savings, suggest that OAS and GIS will play a similar, if not more important, role in the future (Curtis and McMullin, 2018).

The indexation mechanism of both OAS and the GIS is currently the biggest threat to their potency as a tool for poverty alleviation. Indexing on prices, as opposed to wage growth, gradually erodes the value of these benefits as they relate to the median income. This is the primary reason why poverty rates among older adults, which was at an impressive 2 per cent in the early 2000s (RRQ, 2004), has grown above 12 per cent (OECD, 2019, 187). This is still below the OECD average of peer liberal countries, but still relatively far from leading industrialized countries when it comes to poverty alleviation. The indexation of both OAS and GIS is, in fact, a source of constant criticism from seniors' interest groups, as it also represents a powerful (and barely visible) policy tool to constrain the cost evolution of both programs.

Despite this real threat to both programs and to Canada's pension policy mix more generally, it is clear from our analysis that the combination of GIS and OAS has produced positive social policy outcomes through relatively targeted public spending. What are the lessons of the story told in this chapter for policy scholars and policymakers who might not be interested in pension reform per se? First, our analysis suggests that, as far as policy instruments are concerned, 'success' is not only the design of each element on its own. This is the case because the relationship among different policy instruments can prove crucial for policy success, as the 'magic' can be in the mix. Such remarks suggest that the intersection between policy designs and policy mixes is an important issue both scholars and practitioners should pay closer attention to moving forward (on policy mixes and their relationship to policy design see Howlett and Rayner, 2007).

Second, our analysis suggests that temporary programs such as the GIS can become permanent over time as they build stronger constituencies and/or become perceived as a policy success in terms of socio-economic outcomes. This points to the need for policymakers to pay closer attention to temporary programs, while keeping in mind they might become permanent some day. Such an awareness of the possibility that explicitly temporary policies can become permanent is especially crucial in the aftermath of major crises such as the Covid-19 pandemic, which has witnessed the enactment of a host of temporary public policies that could last longer than originally intended. This is why temporary policies should be designed with an eye on the possibility that they may become permanent, which increases the above-mentioned need to take policy design, policy mixes, and their interaction more seriously, even when creating policies perceived as short-lived and/or transitory.

References

Bandau, F. and L. Ahrens. 2020. "The Impact of Partisanship in the Era of Retrenchment: Insights from Quantitative Welfare State Research." *Journal of European Social Policy* 30 (1): pp. 34–47.

Banting, K. G. 2005. "Canada: Nation-Building in a Federal Welfare State." In *Federalism and the Welfare State*, edited by H. Obinger, S. Leibfried, and F. G. Castles, pp. 89–137. Cambridge: Cambridge University Press.

Battle, K. (under the pseudonym of Grattan Gray), 1990. "Social Policy by Stealth." *Policy Options* 11 (2): 17–29.

Battle, K. 1997. "Pension Reform in Canada." *Canadian Journal of Aging* 16 (3): pp. 519–552.

Béland, D. and P. Marier. 2019. "Universality and the Erosion of Old Age Security." In *Universality and Social Policy in Canada*, edited by D. Béland, G. P. Marchildon, and Michael Prince, pp. 103–120. Toronto: University of Toronto Press.

Béland, D. and J. Myles. 2005. "Stasis amidst Change: Canadian Pension Reform in an Age of Retrenchment." In *Ageing and Pension Reform around the World*, edited by G. Bonoli and T. Shinkawa, pp. 252–272. Cheltenham: Edward Elgar.

Bridgen, P. 2018. "The Retrenchment of Public Pension Provision in the Liberal World of Welfare during the Age of Austerity—and its Unexpected Reversal, 1980–2017." *Social Policy and Administration* 53 (1): pp. 16–33.

Bryden, K. 1974. *Old Age Pensions and Policy-Making in Canada*. Montreal: McGill-Queen's University Press.

Bryden, P. E. 1997. *Planners and Politicians: Liberal Politics and Social Policy, 1957–1968*. Montreal: McGill-Queen's University Press.

Campbell, A. L. 2003. *How Policies Make Citizens: Senior Political Activism and the American Welfare State*. Princeton, NJ: Princeton University Press.

Compton, M. E., J. Luetjens, and P. 't Hart. 2019. "Designing for Policy Success." *International Review of Public Policy* 1 (1–2): pp. 119–146.

Cox, R. H. 2001. "The Social Construction of an Imperative: Why Welfare Reform Happened in Denmark and the Netherlands But Not in Germany." *World Politics* 53: pp. 463–498.

Curtis, J. and J. McMullin. 2018. "Dynamics of Retirement Income Inequality in Canada, 1991–2011." *Journal of Population Ageing* 12 (1): pp. 51–68.

Duggan, M., M. S. Kearney, and S. Rennane. 2015. "The Supplemental Security Income Program." In *Economics of Means-Tested Transfer Programs in the United States*, edited by R. A. Moffitt, 2nd edn. Chicago: University of Chicago Press.

Employment and Social Development Canada. 2019. *Evaluation of the Guaranteed Income Supplement.* Ottawa: Government of Canada.

Esping-Andersen, G. 1990. *The Three Worlds of Welfare Capitalism.* Princeton, NJ: Princeton University Press.

Gál, R. I., P. Vanhuysse, and L. Vargha. 2018. "Pro-Elderly Welfare States within Child-Oriented Societies." *Journal of European Public Policy* 25 (6): pp. 944–958.

Goodman-Bacon, A. and L. Schmidt. 2020. "Federalizing Benefits: The Introduction of Supplemental Security Income and the Size of the Safety Net." *Journal of Public Economics* 185: pp. 104–174.

Graebner, W. 1980. *A History of Retirement: The Meaning and Function of an American Institution, 1885–1978.* New Haven, CT: Yale University Press.

Green-Pedersen, C. 2004. "The Dependent Variable Problem within the Study of Welfare State Retrenchment: Defining the Problem and Looking for Solutions." *Journal of Comparative Policy Analysis: Research and Practice* 6 (1): pp. 3–14.

Guest, D. 2013. "Old-Age Pension." *The Canadian Encyclopedia.* https://www.thecanadianencyclopedia.ca/en/article/old-age-pension

Herd, P., M. Favreault, M. Harrington Meyer, and T. M. Smeeding. 2018. "A Targeted Minimum Benefit Plan: A New Proposal to Reduce Poverty among Older Social Security Recipients." *RSF: The Russell Sage Foundation Journal of the Social Sciences* 4 (2): pp. 74–90.

Horner, K. 2008. "Saving Incentives and OAS/GIS Costs." *Canadian Public Policy* 34 (4): pp. 119–135.

Howlett, M. and B. Cashore. 2009. "The Dependent Variable Problem in the Study of Policy Change: Understanding Policy Change as a Methodological Problem." *Journal of Comparative Policy Analysis* 11 (1): pp. 33–46.

Kaida, L. and M. Boyd. 2011. "Poverty Variations among the Elderly: The Roles of Income Security Policies and Family Co-Residence." *Canadian Journal on Aging* 30 (1): pp. 83–100.

Kesselman, J. R. 2015. *Behind the Headlines: Who's Really Benefitting from Higher TFSA Limits?* Ottawa: Broadbent Institute.

Korpi, W. and J. Palme. 1998. "The Paradox of Redistribution and Strategies of Equality: Welfare State Institutions, Inequality, and Poverty in Western Countries." *American Sociological Review* 63: pp. 661–687.

Marier, P. 2021. *The Four Lenses of Population Aging: Planning for the Future in Canada's Provinces.* Toronto: University of Toronto Press.

Marier, P. and M. Revelli. 2017. "Compassionate Canadians and Conflictual Americans? Portrayals of Ageism in Liberal and Conservative Media." *Ageing and Society* 37 (8): pp. 1632–1653.

Marier, P. and A. Séguin. 2015. "Aging and Social Assistance in the Provinces." In *Perspectives on Provincial Social Assistance in Canada,* edited by D. Béland and P. Daigneault, pp. 339–352. Toronto: University of Toronto Press.

McConnell, A. 2010. "Policy Success, Policy Failure and Grey Areas In-Between." *Journal of Public Policy* 30: pp. 345–362.

Michael H. and J. Rayner. 2007. "Design Principles for Policy Mixes: Cohesion and Coherence in 'New Governance Arrangements'." *Policy and Society* 26 (4): pp. 1–18.

Moffatt, S. and G. Scambler. 2008. "Can Welfare-Rights Advice Targeted at Older People Reduce Social Exclusion?" *Ageing and Society* 28 (6): pp. 875–899.

Myles, J. 1988. "Social Policies for the Elderly in Canada." In *North American Elders: United States and Canadian Perspectives*, edited by E. Rathbone-McCuan and B. Havens, pp. 37–54. New York: Greenwood Press.

Myles, J. 2013. "Income Security for Seniors: System Maintenance and Policy Drift." In *Inequality and the Fading of Redistributive Politics*, edited by K. Banting and J. Myles, pp. 312–334. Vancouver: University of British Columbia Press.

Myles, J. and P. Pierson. 2001. "The Comparative Political Economy of Pension Reform." In *The New Politics of the Welfare State*, edited by P. Pierson, pp. 305–334. New York: Oxford University Press.

OECD. 2019. *Pensions at a Glance 2019: OECD and G20 Indicators*. Paris: OECD.

Patashnik, E. M. 2008. *Reforms at Risk: What Happens after Major Policy Changes Are Enacted*. Princeton, NJ: Princeton University Press.

Pierson, P. 1994. *Dismantling the Welfare State? Reagan, Thatcher, and the Politics of Retrenchment*. Cambridge: Cambridge University Press.

Rothstein, B. 2002. "The Universal Welfare State as a Social Dilemma." In *Restructuring the Welfare State*, edited by B. Rothstein and S. Steinmo, pp. 213–233. New York: Palgrave.

RRQ [Régie des rentes du Québec]. 2004. *Adapter LE RÉgime de RENTES AUX NOUVELLES RÉalités du Québec : étude présentant les impacts des propositions de modification sur les rentes des futurs bénéficiaires*. Quebec City: Régie des rentes du Québec.

Schneider, A. L. and H. Ingram. 1993. "Social Construction of Target Populations: Implications for Politics and Policy." *American Political Science Review* 87: 334–347.

Scruggs, L. and J. Allan. 2006. "Welfare-State Decommodification in 18 OECD Countries: A Replication and Revision." *Journal of European Social Policy* 16 (1): pp. 55–72.

Shillington, R. 2019. "Are Low-Income Savers Still in the Lurch? TFSAs at 10 Years." *IRPP Insight:* pp. 1–20.

Tepe, M. and P. Vanhuysse. 2010. "Elderly Bias, New Social Risks and Social Spending: Change and Timing in Eight Programmes across Four Worlds of Welfare, 1980–2003." *Journal of European Social Policy* 20 (3): pp. 217–234.

Vettese, F. 2014. "Even the Rich Can Qualify for Guaranteed Income Supplement—Here's How". *National Post,* 11 November. https://financialpost.com/personal-finance/tfsa/even-the-rich-can-qualify-for-guaranteed-income-supplement-heres-how

Wiseman, M. and M. Yčas. 2008. "The Canadian Safety Net for the Elderly." *Social Security Bulletin* 68: 53–67.

12

The Federal Equalization Program as a Controversial and Contested Policy Success

Daniel Béland, André Lecours, and Trevor Tombe

A Policy Success?

Featuring the federal equalization program in a volume about policy successes in Canada could sound counter-intuitive, at least considering the barrage of criticisms the program faced over the last two decades. Equalization in Canada involves the federal government making annual payments to provinces whose fiscal capacity—that is, how much revenue the province could generate at national average levels of taxation—falls below the national average. The criticisms directed at equalization are related to economic and political changes, as well as to the zero-sum nature of equalization whereby larger transfers for some provinces mean smaller transfers for others. Such a situation can create political animosity on the part of non-recipient and recipient provinces alike, especially when equalization is understood in a broader economic and political context that triggers debates about the efficiency and the fairness of Canada's federal system. Criticism is also related to the fact the federal government does not need to consult with the provinces to alter the equalization formula and the decision-making process is not arms-length but rests with the federal government alone (Béland et al., 2017).

Yet, even while recognizing this governance issue and the inevitable nature of debates over the efficiency and fairness of equalization, this program can be assessed as both programmatically and politically successful. First, from a *programmatic* standpoint, equalization produces positive economic, social, and policy outcomes by reducing interprovincial inequality while preserving provincial autonomy. Without equalization, Canada would likely not only face greater consequences for its regional inequalities, but provinces would also have less autonomy. In the United States, where there is no stand-alone equalization program (Béland and Lecours, 2014), the federal government usually intervenes more directly to solve pressing issues in areas under state jurisdiction. From this perspective, equalization is a central and necessary component of Canada's decentralized

---

Daniel Béland, André Lecours, and Trevor Tombe, *The Federal Equalization Program as a Controversial and Contested Policy Success*. In: *Policy Success in Canada*. Edited by Evert A. Lindquist et al., Oxford University Press.
© Daniel Béland, André Lecours, and Trevor Tombe (2022). DOI: 10.1093/oso/9780192897046.003.0012

welfare state. In his detailed comparison between Canada and the United States, economist Bruno Théret (1999, 483) suggests the following:

> *A federation without equalization payments — a rare situation, where the archetype is the USA—tends to promote economic competition between territories, regions and towns in the form of tax war, social dumping etc. This competition then does little to promote the emergence of a true welfare state that might protect the social bond on the federal level: on the contrary, it increases the risks of federalism disintegrating through centralization or break-up. A contrario, the presence of equalization programmes, as in Canada, directs rivalry between the orders of government into the political arena, favours the emergence and the resilience of a developed welfare state, and allows the social and the territorial bonds to be maintained at the same time.*

This discussion points to the need to imagine what Canada would look like without an equalization program, which is closely tied to the advent of the welfare state and social citizenship. In fact, the federal equalization policy plays a key role in Canadian social policy because it helps poor provinces reduce the potential negative impact of lower fiscal capacity in areas such as education and healthcare. This is especially the case now because, in contrast to the situation prevailing before the Harper government (2006-2015), the Canada Health Transfer (CHT) and Canada Social Transfer (CST) both operate on a per capita basis—a situation that has reduced horizontal fiscal redistribution through health and social transfers. This suggests that the redistributive role of equalization is even more central today, as this program is the only explicitly redistributive major federal transfer to the provinces (Béland et al., 2017).

Second, equalization can be considered a *political* success because, despite criticisms of its specific design details, there is a broad consensus behind its core principles, which have been constitutionally entrenched. These principles, involving the notion that provinces should not have to resort to above-average rates of taxation to deliver public services and that the quality of these services should be comparable across provinces, have roots that span nearly a century. Moreover, the constitutionalization of the federal government's commitment to making equalization payments makes the dismantlement of the program highly unlikely despite the harsh criticisms it faces, especially in non-recipient provinces like Alberta. Simultaneously, the provinces that receive equalization strongly support the program, in which they have a strong stake. Such a situation creates powerful vested interests that would make significant changes to equalization a risky political proposition for the federal government.

Similar to other popular welfare state programs, the federal equalization program is subject to self-reinforcing feedback effects, which strengthen the policy over time (Jacobs and Weaver, 2015). As politicians and voters in transfer-receiving provinces defend equalization at all costs, the program becomes further entrenched into the policy framework of Canada. Also, some provinces that do not currently receive equalization know they might become entitled to payments in the future, a situation likely to reduce their short-term political grievances towards it. Perhaps more importantly, Ottawa has full control over equalization policy, just has it has over health and social transfers. This means that the federal government can revise the equalization formula at will, without having to seek provincial support for changes. And when provinces do complain about equalization, they seldom agree among themselves on reforms because of its zero-sum nature.

Notwithstanding equalization's policy and political success, there is no denying that this success remains somewhat contested and thus precarious (McConnell, 2010). Equalization is a controversial program that perennially faces considerable criticism. Moreover, misleading perceptions about how equalization works have exacerbated controversy, providing ideological ammunition to politicians in non-recipient provinces, such as Alberta, who attack the very legitimacy of this program.

Misperceptions about equalization are widespread in Canada, in part because it is a complex program that few Canadians understand (Marchildon, 2005). One particularly popular misperception is the false claim that equalization policy involves a direct financial transfer from non-recipient to recipient provinces. Widely present in media reports, this inaccurate representation suggests that some provinces pay for equalization while others do not. In fact, equalization is financed exclusively through federal revenues extracted across all the provinces and territories. This reality does not prevent politicians in Alberta, and other non-recipient provinces, to describe equalization as a program that reduces the fiscal capacity of their province, which is not the case (Lecours and Béland, 2010).

The misleading idea that Québec is the main beneficiary of the federal program also fuels controversies over equalization. Those who adhere to this false idea claim that equalization payments are being used primarily for political aims, such as quelling the nationalist movement in the province to keep the federation together. For instance, in 1971, British Columbia Premier W. A. C. Bennett stressed that Québec was the main beneficiary of equalization as he called for the dismantlement of the program: 'The Government of Canada has paid out over $5,500,000,000 in equalization payments since their introduction in 1957, and they continue to increase substantially each year. One province, Quebec, received 47 per cent of this amount' (Bennett, cited in Resnick, 2000, 23). Although it is true that Québec received more from the equalization program in absolute terms, it is not the case that it is the largest per capita recipient; proportionally, Atlantic provinces and Manitoba rely significantly more on equalization than Québec. However, politicians critical of equalization and most media outlets prefer to look at absolute numbers rather than per capita figures, which reinforces the narrative (especially popular in Alberta) that equalization is primarily a tool to please Québec and a mere reflection of the province's 'excessive' political influence in the Canadian federation (Lecours and Béland, 2010).

In the media and political discourse, the narrative that equalization is deeply problematic rather than successful is amplified by these perceptions about the nature and purpose of this contested federal program. Equalization is perceived by its opponents as being unfair towards non-recipient provinces, such as Alberta. In this province, claims about the unfairness of equalization are typically grounded in broader frustrations about the functioning of Canadian federalism. For example, as discussed below, Alberta Premier Jason Kenney's criticisms of equalization are explicitly tied to frustrations with pipeline building and federal environmental regulations, as well as to open opposition to pipeline projects coming from Québec, the province perceived as the main benefactor of equalization for political reasons. In this context, direct attacks against equalization are also attacks against both the federal government and the province of Québec. Such criticisms are grounded in long-standing grievances associated with Western alienation, and past struggles regarding the National Energy Program and provincial control over national resources in Western Canada (Janigan, 2012). To fully understand contemporary political criticisms of equalization grounded in regional resentment, we must take this history into consideration (Lecours and Béland, 2010).

Alongside these political attacks on equalization, we find more technical, economic criticisms, such as the argument that the program creates perverse economic incentives in recipient provinces. In other words, these provinces would fall into a 'welfare trap' they cannot escape because of their long-standing dependency upon the federal government. Indeed, transfers to provincial governments may increase expenditure on public services more than an equivalent increase in personal income would, mainly because the local political and economic costs of raising revenues through direct taxation are higher. This 'flypaper effect', as it is known, has both empirical and theoretical support (Dahlby, 2011). There may also be macroeconomic effects of equalization transfers, both positive and negative. On the one hand, individuals may move to provinces with significant source-based revenues (natural resources, investment income, and so on) even if such moves are marginally worse for the individual in terms of their pre-tax incomes. Such fiscally induced migration may lower overall economic efficiency, and equalization serves to offset this adverse migration. But, on the other hand, when all federal revenue and spending are considered, equalizing transfers may overcompensate and distort migration and employment across provinces (Albouy, 2012; Tombe and Winter, 2021). Finally, by compensating for smaller tax bases, equalization transfers may lessen the cost of raising provincial tax rates and, therefore, potentially induce inefficiently high taxes in recipient provinces (Smart, 2007).

In short, the fact that equalization is a political and policy success should not prevent us from addressing criticisms formulated against it, in the name of both fairness and efficiency, as some of these criticisms raise legitimate issues policy-makers could tackle to make the program even stronger. At the same time, we recognize that while equalization is successful in both political and policy terms, the *process* side of the program related to its governance requires much attention, as its current governance structure, centred in Cabinet and within the Department of Finance, is problematic in terms of public optics and policy legitimacy. Therefore, Canada could consider the creation of a permanent, arms-length fiscal commission that would make regular and transparent recommendations to the federal government on payments and on how to improve the program (Béland et al., 2017).

Context, Challenges, Agents

Equalization programs are the norm in federations. Most advanced industrialized federations implement some type of equalization program, with the United States being the most prominent exception (Béland and Lecours, 2014). Because they de-centralize political power, federations may aggravate the policy consequences of existing territorial disparities. For example, in absence of equalization, poorer constituent units having to run their own education and/or health systems have fewer resources to put towards these expensive services than their wealthier counterparts, thereby resulting in lower quality of services or higher subnational taxation. Such a situation may produce an inequality of treatment amongst citizens depending on their constituent unit of residence. Equalization represents a tool for mitigating such inequality.

Context

Wealth disparities between provinces have always been a political issue in the Canadian federation (Janigan, 2020). For roughly the first hundred years of the federation's life, the major economic cleavage was between Ontario and the rest of the provinces. Therefore, although implementing an equalization program in Canada did not constitutionally require provincial support, it necessitated, from a political perspective, the support of Ontario. There was precedent for special transfers to provinces with unique fiscal needs but not for a stand-alone equalization program.[1]

---

[1] New Brunswick received a special temporary transfer, within the original terms of the creation of the Canadian federation, to address unique fiscal strains. In 1869, the federal governments offered an additional grant (so called 'Better Terms') to Nova Scotia where opposition to the new federation was strong. Finally, when Prince Edward Island entered the federation in 1873, it received a disproportionately high debt allowance.

Today, a significant aspect of Canada's equalization program is that its principles and objectives are enshrined in the Canadian constitution. Such enshrinement did not occur at the creation of the program in 1957, happening much later in 1982. Three contextual elements account for the constitutionalization of equalization's principles and objectives in the Constitution Act 1982. First, because of a spike in the price of oil in the late 1970s, territorial disparities in Canada had increased. This outcome reinforced the importance of equalization. Second, the Pierre Trudeau governments that were in power through the 1970s (except for nine months of a Progressive Conservative minority government in 1979–1980) and the early 1980s were particularly keen to reduce inequality to make Canada a 'just society'. Third, the federal and provincial governments began negotiating to change the Canadian constitution starting in the early 1970s,[2] opening the door for equalization to find its way into the Constitution (Lecours et al., 2020).

Enshrining equalization in the Canadian constitution was surprisingly uncontroversial. Consensus was aided by the fact that Alberta, which was primarily focused on strengthening provincial powers on natural resources after having experienced the National Energy Program (NEP), accomplished its goal in section 92A (the so-called resource amendment). The consensus among the provinces resulted in section (36) in the Constitution Act 1982 entitled 'Equalization and regional disparities'. This section does not constitutionalize a particular equalization program, but only its general principles and objectives, which are to ensure provincial governments have the fiscal capacity to deliver comparable public services at comparable rates of taxation.

Multiple provinces have complained about equalization through the history of the program, but the attacks of the Alberta government over the last few years have perhaps been the most serious. In fact, at the time of writing, the Conservative provincial government has denounced the program as unfair to Alberta, as has the 'Fair Deal Panel' (2020), a body mandated by the province to make recommendations on how to get a better deal in the federation. Following the Panel's recommendation, the government announced it could hold a referendum on equalization in 2021 to compel the federal government to reform the program. The recent escalation of Alberta's grievances around equalization are due to the drop in the price of oil after 2014 and the perceived insufficiency of pipeline expansions to take the province's oil to the East and West coasts for export to European and Asian markets, respectively. The Alberta government considers greater pipeline capacity an essential condition for stimulating an economy that has been labouring for several years. Alberta, still a non-recipient province due to its high fiscal capacity, has blamed the federal government for issues that have

---

[2] The 1971 Victoria Charter (which was never implemented) did not mention equalization but contained a section on regional disparities.

arisen with the development of these pipelines. The Alberta government has also targeted Québec, arguing that some of its wealth is transferred to this province through equalization to finance generous provincial social programs, like subsidized childcare. It has denounced Québec's opposition to pipelines on its territory as selfish and ungrateful. Hence, an ongoing struggle about pipelines is being partially fought through discussions of equalization, which is why the Alberta Conservative government tied its referendum on equalization to progress made in the area of pipeline development.

Challenges

Equalization was created to tackle two specific challenges. The first was horizontal and referred to *interprovincial inequality*. Provinces have different fiscal means at their disposal, affecting their ability to provide quality public services at a given level of taxation. In the post-World War II period, as welfare state development led to the expansion of social citizenship, discrepancies in the quality of public services across provinces, or in the level of taxation required to reach similar quality in provincial public services, were increasingly seen as a major problem. Moreover, inequality in provincial fiscal capacity could result in out-migration from poorer provinces to wealthier ones. Equalization represented a potential solution to the inequality problem, as it was designed to bring provinces that fell below a fiscal capacity standard up to a standard in line with the national average. Yet, because equalization is a completely unconditional transfer in the name of provincial autonomy, provincial governments are not compelled to put equalization money towards the financing of public services.

The enshrinement of equalization in the Constitution Act 1982 reflects this concern with inequality. In subsection (1), which is titled 'Commitment to promote equal opportunities', federal and provincial governments commit to '(a) promoting equal opportunities for the well-being of Canadians; (b) furthering economic development to reduce disparity in opportunities; and (c) providing essential public services of reasonable quality to all Canadians.' Subsection (2) states that 'Parliament and the government of Canada are committed to the principle of making equalization payments to ensure that provincial governments have sufficient revenues to provide reasonably comparable levels of public services at reasonably comparable levels of taxation.'

Unsurprisingly, equalization has always been received positively in traditionally recipient provinces (Manitoba, New Brunswick, Nova Scotia, Prince Edward Island, Québec and, to a lesser extent, Newfoundland and Labrador), for whom the program has represented a partial solution to weaker fiscal capacity. Equalization payments occupy a non-negligible part of these provinces' budget (20 per cent in the case of Prince Edward Island), which suggests the program has represented an important contribution to the ability of many provincial governments to deliver quality public services at a reasonable level of taxation.

The second challenge equalization was designed to tackle was *national unity and solidarity*. Québec opting out of the tax rental system in the mid-1950s threatened to institutionalize an asymmetry in fiscal federalism. The centralizing nature of the tax rentals, where provinces would give up taxation in exchange for fixed sum payments from the federal government, was unsustainable in the long term, particularly as nationalism in Québec was picking up steam. The federal government looked for an alternative way to achieve redistribution in the federation through a system that would include all provinces. A stand-alone equalization program could achieve this objective, and it presented potential for tackling the challenge of national unity. In fact, not only would Québec be fully integrated within Canadian fiscal federalism, but it would be a recipient province due to its lower-than-average fiscal capacity, which could generate sentiments of Canadian solidarity in Québec and show Québecers that federalism was, at the very least, a good practical arrangement for the province (Béland and Lecours, 2014; Bryden, 2009). Economic, financial, and fiscal issues turned out to be the Achilles' heel of the independence movement, and secessionist politicians sought to avoid discussions of equalization, which put them on the defensive. Equalization has often been called the glue that holds the federation together (Boadway and Shah, 2009, 552) but, at the same time, many provincial governments have criticized the program over the years, including British Columbia in the first two decades or so of the program; Alberta, starting roughly in the 1990s; Ontario, in the 2000s, when the province's manufacturing sector and overall economy was declining; and Newfoundland and Labrador, as well as Saskatchewan, also in the 2000s, as oil and gas exploitation transformed these provinces into non-recipients (Lecours and Béland, 2010).

Actors

The driving agent behind the creation of the federal equalization program in 1957 is a relatively unheralded prime minister: Louis St-Laurent. Early on, he saw the potential for the long-term fragmentation of the tax rental system and sought to devise an alternative fiscal arrangement that would support poorer provinces while favouring national unity (Janigan, 2020). St-Laurent personally spearheaded the process for creating a stand-alone equalization system, with the assistance of Finance Minister Walter Harris (Janigan, 2020). Perhaps aided by his personal biculturalism, he skilfully bridged the gap between Québec, which was concerned with preserving provincial autonomy, and other poorer provinces that did not have similar concerns—a process that included difficult negotiations with Québec's *Union Nationale* (UN) Premier Maurice Duplessis. St-Laurent chose to place the management of equalization in the hands of the civil servants at the Ministry of Finance.

A quarter of a century later, the constitutionalization of equalization's principles and objectives was pioneered by another prime minister, Pierre Trudeau, who led government from 1968 to 1979, and again from 1980 to 1984. Trudeau was keenly interested in constitutional reform, primarily to enshrine a Charter of Rights and Freedoms, but also to afford protection to equalization. Equalization was coherent with Trudeau's notion of Canada as a 'just society', where rights are protected and equality is fostered (Lecours et al., 2020).

Across the decades, equalization has been criticized by many provincial premiers, including British Columbia's W.A.C. Bennett, and Alberta's Ralph Klein and Jason Kenney. More generally, Alberta premiers have been the most aggressive in mobilizing the historical sentiments of Western alienation to denounce equalization as too generous and unfair to their province. Jason Kenney, although a former member of the Stephen Harper Cabinet that implemented the current equalization formula, has demanded the reform, if not the outright abolition, of equalization. Frustrated by what he views as inadequate federal action on pipeline development and by Québec's outright opposition to the project, Premier Kenney, supported by his counterpart Scott Moe in Saskatchewan (another oil and gas producing province), has launched multiple attacks on equalization. His strongest political move against equalization in decades is his promise to hold a provincial referendum on the program in 2021 (presumably to then exercise some type of leverage on the federal government) if he deems progress on pipelines by then to be unsatisfactory.

Design and Choice

A more detailed look at the history of Canada's equalization program can complement this review of the broad context, challenges, and actors involved. As we will see, this history reveals the pressures that equalization in Canada must necessarily confront, and it demonstrates how policymakers in Canada have continued to adapt as necessary to ensure the program's success. Despite regular challenges and pressures for reform, the core principles that underpin the program have remained remarkably stable. In addition, the design process historically involved continual intergovernmental negotiations but also relied heavily on rigorous analysis and review. From oil price spikes and financial crises to adverse incentives for resource development and inter-regional equity, the processes of design, analysis, negotiation, and ultimately decision-making are the source of equalization's success to this day. To be sure, the road from initial idea to Canada's current equalization program was long and difficult. Spanning nearly three decades, connecting the Great Depression to the late 1960s, the very creation and early development of equalization as it occurred was not a foregone conclusion. During this period, numerous alternative approaches were proposed, evaluated, and sometimes implemented (Perry, 1997). But starting in 1967, ten years after the creation of the program, (nearly) full equalization of provincial revenues began.

The origins of equalization as an explicit program to support provincial governments may be traced to the 1940 report of the Royal Commission on Dominion-Provincial Relations (more commonly known as the Rowell-Sirois Commission). The Commission proposed fundamental changes to the structure of the Canadian federation, including explicit support to provinces with more limited means to ensure they could provide 'normal services' with 'no more than normal taxes'. The Commission's approach, however, was based on ad hoc calculations of fiscal needs and capacity that were never adopted. World War II prevented any action on this or other recommendations, and the Commission's approach to National Adjustment Grants was set aside. Nevertheless, the principles it proposed to guide such a policy ultimately motivated the language adopted in the Constitution Act 1982; namely, the program should ensure that provinces have the capacity to deliver comparable public services at comparable levels of taxation.

The early post-war years are notable. During the war, provincial governments ceded to the federal government their entire personal and corporate income tax fields and all succession duties (i.e. inheritance taxes) to support the broader war effort. Afterwards, the federal government wanted to maintain its dominant presence and offered provinces generous cash transfers in exchange. Most agreed, but Ontario and Québec did not. These provinces prioritized autonomy over their own revenues and were therefore willing to forego the short-term cost of rejecting the offered cash transfers from Ottawa. This scenario was not sustainable either fiscally or politically, but nevertheless, the issue was not quickly resolved. Once it became clear to the federal government that Québec would reject any arrangement that did not facilitate its ability to collect income taxes, regardless of how generous the terms were, the federal government recognized that it needed to design a system that left provinces equally well off fiscally whether they accepted federal arrangements or did not.

Equalization was the answer. Provinces that agreed to not raise their own income taxes were provided with generous cash transfers while provinces that did not agree were provided top-up cash transfers alongside their own income tax revenues, which equalled to what the agreeing provinces received. Either way, provincial governments had (roughly) equivalent per capita fiscal resources. More precisely, the original formula credited provinces with 10 per cent of federal personal income taxes, 9 per cent of corporate income taxes, and half of succession duties, and then it topped up provinces to the average per capita yield of those taxes in the top two provinces. This scheme immediately faced two fundamental design challenges: it was insufficiently generous to lower-income provinces, and it was narrow in scope.

Under the new equalization program, lower-income provinces were, roughly speaking, little better off than they had been in any of the prior arrangements. The program was not materially more redistributive and therefore offered little additional support to provinces in greater need. Instead, it merely separated into two components (tax points plus equalization) what was previously only one. These issues gained electoral salience in the 1957 federal election campaign when the Progressive Conservative leader, John Diefenbaker, campaigned (in part) on a *New Deal for the Provinces*. 'How can there be national unity,' asked the PC Platform, 'with Provinces and Municipalities handcuffed by inadequate sources of revenue...?' (Progressive Conservative Party of Canada, 1957). After winning a narrow victory, in no small part because of the party's position on fiscal transfers, Prime Minister Diefenbaker soon delivered on some of his campaign commitments. He boosted the share of income taxes given to the provinces and created a special (generous) grant for Atlantic provinces. The 'Atlantic Provinces Adjustment Grant' attempted to achieve, in an ad hoc manner, what equalization at the time did not. And while the initial changes to equalization design did not expand the set of revenues included in the calculation of provincial fiscal capacity, it was not long until subsequent changes did.

Pressure to expand the coverage of provincial revenues started from the very beginning of the federal equalization program. The exclusion of natural resource revenues from the program implemented in 1957 was particularly notable. Only the standard taxes on personal income, corporate income, and inheritances were equalized, as these were the taxes ceded to the federal government during the war. Moreover, under the top-two province standard, whereby provinces were equalized up to the average revenues of Ontario and British Columbia, even Canada's rich oil producing province of Alberta received equalization payments: more than $12 million that first year. However, the latter became a source of controversy that same year, when Alberta announced a one-time payment of $22 per person to half a million Albertan adults (roughly $200 in today's dollars), which totalled $11.5 million. Though nominally framed as returning resource revenues to Albertans (equivalent to roughly one-third of such revenues), its magnitude meant that, in effect, the government accepted the $12 million equalization payment and passed $11.5 million of it through to Albertans directly. In a pointed editorial, *The Globe and Mail* at the time called the move 'mass bribery of the electorate' (Alberta's Dividends, 1957). 'More blessed it is to give, than to receive,' the paper noted, 'but Alberta is in the happy situation of doing both.' 'If such a Province is a "have-not",' they observed, 'what on earth is a "have"?' Then, as now, treatment of resource revenues was a continual challenge for equalization design. Pressure mounted for reform, and the federal government soon acted.

In 1962, resource revenues were included for the first time in the equalization formula. This fundamental change shifted equalization away from a mechanism to ensure provincial governments rejecting federal tax rentals were no worse off than

236 THE FEDERAL GOVERNMENT'S EQUALIZATION PROGRAM

those accepting a program designed to achieve greater fiscal equality among the provinces. The trouble was that merely including resource revenues would have dramatically increased the size of the program. Equalization payments, after all, topped provinces up to some 'benchmark' level. The benchmark under the original formula was the average of the two richest provinces (Ontario and BC). Including resource revenues would make BC and Alberta the top two and dramatically raise the bar to which each province is compared. It would, roughly speaking, quadruple the total cost of the program for the federal government. The solution to avoid a dramatically expanded program was simple: instead of a top two standard, the federal government adopted a 'national average' standard, which was significantly lower. Including resource revenues meant Alberta and British Columbia would no longer be entitled to equalization, while moving to a national standard meant lower payments to all, particularly Québec.

This strategic design choice left British Columbia particularly incensed. 'A Separatist, West-Coast Style' boomed a *Globe and Mail* headline from September 1963. On the campaign trail during that year's BC provincial election, the newspaper coverage reported that Social Credit Premier W. A. C. Bennett complained equalization payments 'are nothing more than straight subsidies out of the pockets of the people of British Columbia', and suggested 'British Columbia is carrying the rest of the nation on its back, and he [Bennett] is tired of it' (Bolwell, 1963). Bennett was not alone in opposing the change. The federal Liberal Party under Lester Pearson also campaigned against the new arrangements in 1963, and it won.

Following through on their campaign commitments, the federal Liberals took resources out of the formula and moved back to a top-two standard upon forming the new government. But to ensure payments were not made to resource rich provinces, a new deduction was added. If a province had above-average resource revenues, then half of its 'excess' resource revenues above that average were deducted from any equalization payment it would receive. The principal consequence of these changes was to significantly increase payments to Québec (Tombe 2018, 894). While this solution achieved its short-term objectives, it was not sustainable in the long run. Perceptions of unfairness in some provinces could not be solved by ad hoc reforms, and the government started a comprehensive review of the program that ultimately led to the 1967 overhaul that created Canada's modern equalization formula.

These first few years of equalization featured moves and countermoves by competing interests that were ultimately somewhat reconciled. No perfect solution existed, but balancing perceptions of unfairness found within both high- and lower-income provinces was accomplished by gradually expanding the scale of the program. The reform of 1967, which followed a rigorous examination and study of the program, put equalization on solid ground—economically and politically— and provided a formula that largely remains in place today. Nearly all provincial revenues are captured by the formula, and the provincial revenue-raising capacity is measured by the per capita revenues that each province could raise if it had national average tax rates. Provinces with below-average capacities can then be topped-up to the national average level. In short, if a province has a lower share of national fiscal capacity than it has a share of the national population, then it receives a top-up payment under equalization. This new approach has withstood the test of time.

This period also reveals a cycle that is seen throughout equalization's history: ad hoc adjustments that are followed by fundamental review and reform. The process of design that led to the 1967 formula was one such cycle, but there would be at least two more leading to significant change in 1982 and 2007. These latter two cycles illustrate well the practical application, delivery, and endurance of the equalization formula. But no discussion of equalization choices would be complete without evaluating whether the specific design adopted in 1967, which last to this day, successfully achieved the program's stated goals.

By including almost all revenue sources, and by comparing provinces to a representative benchmark, equalization succeeds in ensuring provinces have access to average levels of revenue per person. The representative benchmark to which all provinces are compared has changed over time, sometimes using a ten-province standard and other times using a five-province one. However, the benchmark's overall objective has always stayed the same: to capture 'normal tax rates'. To be sure, provinces have full autonomy to decide whether to access these revenue sources or not, but the formula leaves them with no less than average per capita capabilities to raise provincial revenues. The formula accomplishes this task by estimating average tax rates and the per capita revenues provinces would raise at those averages. Provinces are free to set actual tax rates above or below this level. Over time, there are regular adjustments to the formula details—such as whether property taxes are included, how to calculate specific tax bases, and so on— but the program's core functioning captures relative fiscal capacity of provincial governments extremely well.

While Canada's equalization program is somewhat smaller than similar programs in other federations—which range between 0.5 to 3.7 per cent of GDP, with Canada's being at less than 1 per cent (Blöchliger et al., 2007)—it is nonetheless critical for the fiscal position of several provinces. Without the equalization program, lower-income provinces would require significantly higher tax rates to fund comparable public services—or they would be forced to have lower than average spending on such services. For perspective, we estimate that total equalization payments in 2020 to recipient provinces were at one-quarter of total taxation revenues. That is, those provinces would require (at least) 25 per cent higher tax rates to deliver their public services. For New Brunswick and Prince Edward Island, equalization payments exceed 40 per cent of their taxation revenues. Expressed as general sales tax rates, Prince Edward Island would require an additional 14 percentage points to generate similar revenues as those received through equalization.

238 THE FEDERAL GOVERNMENT'S EQUALIZATION PROGRAM

Similarly, New Brunswick would need 12.5 additional percentage points, Nova Scotia 10, and Québec and Manitoba just under 8. Nationally, the equivalent increase in Canada's general sales tax to fund the program is just over 2 per cent. Equalization provides, and has always provided since its inception, material fiscal support to lower-income provinces to enable them to deliver public services of comparable quality, should they choose to do so.

Delivery and Endurance

Though the 1967 equalization formula established a program that remains largely in place today, it has nevertheless faced significant structural challenges, both external and internal. Through the 1970s, because of rising oil prices, equalization delivery faced severe practical challenges in the form of rising program costs. As federal governments coped with these pressures, they adopted several ad hoc solutions that eventually led to a wholesale reform in 1982. This external challenge to equalization was significant, but so too was a later internal one. While the relative economic positions of Canada's various provinces were relatively stable at time, Newfoundland and Labrador's dramatic growth in the early 2000s was a notable exception. The province's offshore resource developments, which began in the late 1990s, led to an incredible reversal of fortune for the traditional equalization recipient. This created challenges for equalization delivery, and motivated various ad hoc responses under successive federal Liberal governments in the 1990s and early 2000s that, once more, ultimately led to wholesale program reform. Both episodes are examples of Canada's success in delivering equalization through rapidly changing economic and fiscal realities. Flexibility in the delivery of equalization, combined with periodic fundamental examinations and reforms, is how the program has endured.

Beginning in October 1973 with the OPEC (Organization of the Petroleum Exporting Countries) oil embargo, the price of oil rose substantially. By early 1974, the price of West Texas Intermediate (a key North American benchmark) rose from $4.31 per barrel to $10.11. And later that decade, starting in 1979, production declined following the Iranian Revolution, which led prices to increase even further—peaking just shy of $40 per barrel by early 1980 (Federal Reserve Bank of St. Louis, n.d.). With rising oil prices came rising oil royalty revenues for certain provinces in Canada, most notably Alberta. There, total non-renewable resource revenues increased from $332 million in 1972/73 to $3 billion by 1977/78—equivalent to over 70 per cent of the total provincial government revenue that year (Alberta Energy, 2018). With resource revenues included in the equalization calculation, this situation led to dramatic increases in measured inequality across Canada's provinces. Without changes to the original formula, this would have produced large equalization entitlements and additional costs to the federal government.

Due to this situation, many changes to the equalization program's instrument settings occurred through the 1970s. The federal government gradually decreased the share of resource revenues included in the calculation of provincial fiscal capacity; excluded land lease sales; introduced ad hoc restrictions to ensure Ontario (the largest province) did not receive equalization payments; and, most significantly, directly intervened in energy markets to lower the price of oil within Canada through its National Energy Program. Had no federal policy reforms been enacted in response, and if resource revenues have been fully included in the calculation of provincial fiscal capacity, potentially as much as one-third of the federal budget would have been required to fund equalization in 1980/81 (Tombe, 2018). To illustrate the effect of energy price swings on the program, Figure 12.1 displays the actual equalization program costs against what the 1967 formula would have paid out without reforms to its delivery over time.

Following these years of continuous ad hoc reforms to keep costs in check, the federal government undertook a comprehensive review of the program to ensure it could endure. The 1981 Parliamentary Task Force on Federal-Provincial Fiscal Arrangements conducted an in-depth examination of fiscal federalism in Canada, with a particular focus on equalization. It represented the most ambitious and thorough review since the Rowell-Sirois Commission over four decades earlier. The Task Force proposed fundamental reforms, with an eye towards limiting the extent to which high energy prices would affect equalization payments. Specifically, the 1982 reform excluded Alberta (and, for balance, the Atlantic Provinces) from the calculation of the equalization standard. This 'five-province' model worked for some time in ensuring a more stable program, and it allowed for the full inclusion of resource revenues once again.

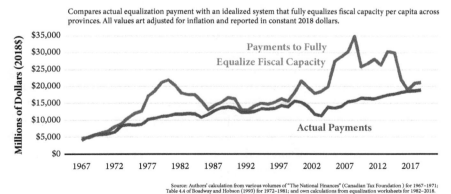

Fig. 12.1 Actual vs. 'Full' Equalization Payments in Canada

240   THE FEDERAL GOVERNMENT'S EQUALIZATION PROGRAM

The Task Force's analysis and recommendations were based on rigorous research conducted both inside the government and by external experts. The work of the Task Force not only helped overcome challenges that came up through the 1970s, but it was also central to reaching a political compromise with Ontario. This province was arbitrarily restricted from receiving payments in the late 1970s through what was called the 'personal income override'. Provinces with above-average per capita personal income levels could not receive equalization, regardless of the formula's determination. This only affected Ontario and was retroactively implemented in 1981 to cover prior years (Bill C-24, 1981). The Ontario government accepted this override, but this acceptance was 'conditional on the program being reformed in 1982' (Canada, 1981, 168). The Task Force worked to deliver these reforms. Although it advocated technical changes, the Task Force was strongly supportive of the underlying principle of equalization to ensure all provinces had sufficient fiscal capacity to deliver public services of comparable quality at comparable tax rates. While the reforms succeeded in ushering in the longest period of relative program stability, equalization was eventually confronted with new challenges in the late 1990s.

Newfoundland and Labrador's rise as an oil producer created an internal challenge to the delivery and operation of equalization. In 1997, the offshore Hibernia oil field started production, ushering in a dramatic rise in provincial income. Reforms to equalization became necessary as a result. Under the formula established in 1982, an increase in Newfoundland and Labrador's revenues through offshore oil royalties would, over time, be fully offset by a lower equalization entitlement. The net gain to the provincial treasury from offshore development would therefore be nil, and the government's incentive to proceed would be dramatically lowered. Recognizing this already in the mid-1980s, the Atlantic Accord (extended by later agreements) provided offset payments to effectively shelter some resource revenues from equalization clawbacks. A 1994 reform, entitled the 'generic solution', effectively capped the total clawback rate to 70 per cent. Still, this implicit clawback of incremental resource revenues for Newfoundland and Labrador was significant. As revenues to the province grew, equalization payments declined.

From 1957 to 2000, equalization payments to the province averaged 28 per cent of its total revenues, but by 2008 the province was no longer a recipient. Following pressure from the provincial government, this situation led to a comprehensive review by an Expert Panel in 2005. Many reforms were proposed, but the Panel most notably suggested that no more than 50 per cent of resource revenues be included in the calculation of provincial fiscal capacity. Accepting the Expert Panel's overall recommendations, a new Conservative federal government formed in 2006 went one step further: either 0 per cent or 50 per cent of resource revenues would be included, whichever was better for a province.

This partial inclusion approach remains a feature of the program today. Overall, the tension between including all revenues, and mitigating the adverse incentives that full inclusion creates, is a central challenge for equalization design in Canada. With oil price spikes in the 1970s, price crashes in the 1980s, and large-scale developments offshore, the equalization formula bent and creaked but never cracked. Ad hoc reforms were quickly adopted when necessary, and broader reviews and redesigns were undertaken when needed. In this way, the program endures.

More important than detailed design choices is the fact that *equalization's core objectives have remained largely intact over time*. A program that ensures all provinces have sufficient fiscal ability to deliver public services of comparable quality at comparable rates of taxation is a constant in the modern Canadian federation. And despite significant reversals in the economic fortunes of some provinces, substantial swings in the level of territorial fiscal inequality, intense strain on federal finances through the financial crisis, and a complete overhaul of the equalization formula in 2007, public support for the program remains strong. Polling work by Environics for the Confederation of Tomorrow Survey (a joint initiative of numerous reputable think tanks and research groups in Canada), shows that 83 per cent of Canadians supported equalization in 2001, and 74 per cent continued to do so in 2020 (Environics, 2020). Most of the decline in support is due to an increase in the number of respondents who are unsure, rather than in the number of those who oppose it. Even in Alberta and Saskatchewan, where support fell the most, the program still enjoys 57 per cent and 60 per cent backing, respectively.

Across the country, Canadians share the belief that each provincial government should have the capacity to deliver quality public services. Equalization has successfully ensured that this capability exists. And while the equalization formula is complex and often misunderstood, it is broad, objective, predictable, and—critically—adaptable. When circumstances change, so too does the program. These are not easy transitions, but they are manageable. The 1981 Task Force's report wisely noted that 'the one constant in intergovernmental relations in Canada is the need to adjust ... and to meet new challenges' (Canada, 1981, 76). Adaptability and flexibility in equalization delivery, while ensuring its key components remain intact, make the program a genuine Canadian policy success.

Analysis and Conclusions

Equalization is a federal program, but it is also one component of a system of federal fiscal transfers to the provinces (Béland et al., 2017). As such, its nature is unique, which means it is neither emblematic of a Canadian policy style nor can it be viewed as atypical. The administration of equalization resembles that of the two other major transfers (CHT and CST), in that it is solely under federal government responsibility. While the model of an arms-length agency, like Australia's Commonwealth Grants Commission, was considered to manage equalization in

Canada, it was always rejected by the federal government and the provinces (Béland and Lecours, 2011). The federal government has been loath to relinquish one of the few tools it possesses to manage a decentralized federation. The provinces are more comfortable having the federal government rather than a technocratic independent agency as an interlocutor on equalization. As a result, federal executive discretion is the basic structure for decision-making on the equalization program. In short, the federal government has the last word on equalization, CHT, and CST. It may consult provinces, or it may not. Indeed, sometimes it does, and sometimes it does not.

This discretionary approach to equalization design and delivery creates both opportunities and challenges. On the one hand, it enables the federal government to respond flexibly, and sometimes rapidly, to changing economic, fiscal, and social conditions. Unforeseen developments are often addressed with minor tweaks to the formula. Yet, over time, as such minor changes accumulate, and occasional wholesale reforms are required to ensure equalization fulfils its primary objectives. The option to commit to such reforms provides an effective means to alleviate political pressures on occasion, as we saw with the 1982 reform that addressed concerns raised by Ontario. However, on the other hand, and unlike the intergovernmental dynamics surrounding the two other major transfers, provinces can seldom unite on anything related to equalization. The program, after all, involves a zero-sum game. This situation contributes to further empowering the federal government in its management of equalization, and potentially sustains the frequent criticism it faces from some provinces in its crafting and administration of the program.

Because of the unique nature of Canadian equalization, it is difficult to draw specific lessons from this success story; no other policy or major transfer compares easily with a program for which only certain provinces are recipients. Even as we look at how other federations could gain insight from equalization in Canada to design or reform their own program of horizontal redistribution, we have to keep in mind that the balance between provincial autonomy and territorial redistribution embodied in the Canadian equalization program reflects the multinational nature of a federation, whose provinces fiercely defend their independence but at the same time accept broad principles of equality in the access to quality public services for all Canadian citizens.

Yet, both in Canada and abroad, scholars and practitioners may look at Canada's equalization program for lessons about how the constitutional entrenchment of a particular public policy can shape its politics. Specifically, the decision to embed the principles and objectives of equalization in the Constitution Act 1982 reinforced the political standing of the program and made it harder for opponents to call for its dismantlement, an issue that speaks to the long-term political sustainability of this public policy (on this issue see Patashnik, 2008). Scholars interested in the relationship between public policy and constitutional law could benefit from examining equalization in Canada, a controversial yet successful policy. More generally, the case of equalization policy in Canada draws attention to the constitutionalization of policy principles, a rather neglected issue that deserves more attention within the field of public policy research.

References

"Alberta's Dividends." 1957. *Globe and Mail.* 4 March.

Alberta Energy, Government of Alberta. 2018. "Historical Royalty Revenue." Government of Alberta. https://open.alberta.ca/opendata/historical-royalty-revenue

Albouy, D. 2012. "Evaluating the Efficiency and Equity of Federal Fiscal Equalization." *Journal of Public Economics* 96 (9–10): pp. 824–839.

Béland, D. and A. Lecours. 2014. "Fiscal Federalism and American Exceptionalism: Why Is There No Federal Equalization Program in the United States?" *Journal of Public Policy* 34 (2): pp. 303–329.

Béland, D., A. Lecours, G. P. Marchildon, H. Mou, and R. Olfert. 2017. *Fiscal Federalism and Equalization Policy in Canada: Political and Economic Dimensions.* Toronto: University of Toronto Press.

Bill C-24. 1981. *An Act to Amend Laws Relating to Fiscal Transfers to the Provinces*, 1st Sess., 32nd Parl., 1981 (assented to 19 February 1981), S.C. 1981, c. 46.

Blöchliger, H., O. Merki, C. Charbiti, and L. Mizelli. 2007. *Fiscal Equalisation in OECD Countries.* OECD Working Papers on Fiscal Federalism 4.

Boadway, R. and A. Shah. 2009. *Fiscal Federalism: Principles and Practices of Multiorder Governance.* Cambridge: Cambridge University Press.

Bolwell, E. 1963. "A Separatist, West-Coast Style." *Globe and Mail.* 16 September.

Bryden, P. E. 2009. "The Obligations of Federalism: Ontario and the Origins of Equalization." In *Framing Canadian Federalism: Historical Essays in Honour of John T. Saywell*, edited by D. Anastakis and P. E. Bryden, pp. 75–94. Toronto: University of Toronto Press.

Canada. 1981. *Fiscal Federalism in Canada: Report of the Parliamentary Task Force on Federal-Provincial Fiscal Arrangements.* Ottawa: Parliament, House of Commons. pp. 168.

Dahlby, B. 2011. "The Marginal Cost of Public Funds and the Flypaper Effect." *International Tax and Public Finance* 18 (3): pp. 304–321.

Environics Institute for Survey Research. 2020. *Report 2: The Division of Powers and Resources.* Toronto: Environics.

Federal Reserve Bank of St. Louis. n.d. "Spot Crude Oil Price: West Texas Intermediate (WTI)." FRED. https://fred.stlouisfed.org/series/WTISPLC. Accessed: 29 September 2020.

Fair Deal Panel. 2020. *Report to Government.* Edmonton: Fair Dear Panel.

Janigan, M. 2012. *Let the Eastern Bastards Freeze in the Dark: The West versus the Rest since Confederation.* Toronto, ON: Knopf.

Janigan, M. 2020. *The Art of Sharing. The Richer versus the Poorer Provinces since Confederation.* Montreal and Kingston: McGill-Queen's University Press.

Jacobs, A. M. and R. K. Weaver. 2015. When Policies Undo Themselves: Self-Undermining Feedback as a Source of Policy Change, *Governance,* 28(4): 441–457.

Lecours, A. and D. Béland. 2010. "Federalism and Fiscal Policy: The Politics of Equalization in Canada." *Publius: The Journal of Federalism* 40 (4): pp. 569–596.

Lecours, A., D. Béland, and G. Marchildon. 2020. "Fiscal Federalism: Pierre Trudeau as an Agent of Decentralization." *Supreme Court Law Review* 99: pp. 77–99.

Lecours, A and Daniel B. 2011. "The Ideational Dimension of Federalism: The 'Australian Model' and the Politics of Equalization in Canada." *Australian Journal of Political Science* 46 (2): pp. 199–212.

Marchildon, G.P. 2005. Understanding Equalisation: Is it Possible? *Canadian Public Administration* 48(3): 420–428.

McConnell. A. 2010. *Understanding Policy Success: Rethinking Public Policy.* Basingstoke: Palgrave.

Patashnik, E. M. 2008. *Reforms at Risk: What Happens after Major Policy Changes Are Enacted.* Princeton, NJ: Princeton University Press.

Perry, D. 1997. *Financing the Canadian Federation, 1867 to 1995: Setting the Stage for Change.* Toronto: The Canadian Tax Foundation.

Progressive Conservative Party of Canada. 1957. "A New Deal for Provinces and Municipalities." *A New National Policy: Highlights of Progressive Conservative Policy in Verbatim Quotations from Speeches by John Diefenbaker*, p. 2.

Resnick, P. 2000. *The Politics of Resentment: British Columbia Regionalism and Canadian Unity.* Vancouver: UBC Press.

Smart, M. 2007. "Raising Taxes through Equalization." *Canadian Journal of Economics* 40 (4): pp. 1188–1212.

Tombe, T. 2018. "Final and Unalterable—But Up for Negotiation: Federal-Provincial Transfers in Canada." *Canadian Tax Journal* 66 (4): 871–917.

Tombe, T. and J. Winter. 2021. "Fiscal Integration with Internal Trade: Quantifying the Effects of Federal Transfers in Canada." *Canadian Journal of Economics* 54 (2): 522–556 https://doi.org/10.1111/caje.12491

PART IV
ECONOMIC AND INDUSTRIAL POLICY SUCCESSES

13

Regulating Canada's Banking System

Tackling the 'Big Shall Not Buy Big' Problem

Russell Alan Williams

Introduction

While judging policy success is often complicated by the limitations of the values policy actors place on subjective, preferred outcomes, in the case of Canadian banking regulation, success is easy to see for all involved. Policymakers have achieved both highly valued public goods enjoying broad political support in the form of industry stability and public access, and widespread political consensus, a key standard for defining success (cf. Compton and 't Hart, 2019). They have also managed to sustain this over a considerable period of time, throughout a period of intense across-the-board volatility for the financial services industry.

Indeed, Canada's Banking and financial system has developed a reputation for being one of the more stable and secure systems in the world (Williams, 2012). During the 2007–2009 financial crisis, Canadian institutions successfully navigated a global crisis with minimal market disruption. No institutions required formal bailouts, and the savings and investments of depositors were protected. In part, the stability of the Canadian financial sector amidst the turbulent world of globalized finance is a product of policy choices made by governments in response to globalization. Canada's success in navigating the financial crisis is part of a broader strategy to ensure that the country could 'play along' in global finance (Porter and Coleman, 2003), albeit in an environment of successful regulatory oversight—a 'policy success' long in gestation, but much admired in other jurisdictions.

When global banking markets first threatened to break down the barriers between different kinds of financial activities, and the emerging threat posed by the ability of large foreign financial firms to directly offer financial services to Canadian firms and consumers, the Federal government ushered in a decade of regulatory changes, starting in the mid 1980s, which reorganized the Canadian industry in preparation for new forms of financial services. These changes helped

---

Russell Alan Williams, *Regulating Canada's Banking System*. In: *Policy Success in Canada*.
Edited by Evert A. Lindquist et al., Oxford University Press. © Russell Alan Williams (2022).
DOI: 10.1093/oso/9780192897046.003.0013

248 REGULATING CANADA'S BANKING SYSTEM

produce a small number of large financial firms, better equipped to manage the increased complexity of global financial markets. In combination with this, the government also took steps to strengthen political oversight of the sector, ensuring major policy changes that might destabilize the industry in the future would receive ample political scrutiny. Both changes have served to establish a well-organized financial sector that has successfully navigated global finance for the last three decades.

As this chapter will illustrate, the process chosen to manage deregulation has created important feedback mechanisms. It is precisely these mechanisms that have allowed Canada to avoid the excessive levels of industry concentration (the 'big buying big problem') that has radically increased the risks and costs of industry bailouts in other jurisdictions.

A Policy Success Rooted in Good Process

Advancing the policy sciences requires some idea of what constitutes good public policy. Policy subsystem participants, partisan politicians, the media, and the broad public all have strong, and frequently very different views of what constitutes good policy—what can appear as a success story to one observer is a failure to another. Therefore, on one level, policy evaluation and learning are always political (Bovens and 't Hart, 1996).

This is a problem, both from the perspective of theory development, but also from the perspective of how policy research can inform governments—without clearer stories of success and failure, it is hard to offer strategic wisdom about both what governments should do, and how they should do it.

While much work has recently been done to try to overcome this problem, Allan McConnell's (2010, 351) central idea, that a policy is successful if it, 'achieves the goals that proponents set out to achieve and ... support is virtually universal' helps operationalize a test of 'success'. From this, McConnell, Grealy, and Lea (2020) give us a range by which 'success' can be categorized across four realms—processes, programs, politics, and time. The challenge then being to apply a plausibility test to assess whether policy has been a success for those actors.

For example, in the case of process, a successful policy is one where governments have managed to preserve government goals while also building a sustainable coalition of support for the policy. At the other extreme, policy process failure is illustrated by widespread evidence of opposition to the policy and termination of the process. In this sense, McConnell and colleagues suggest that policy success in process terms is not something that it is measured in relation to what the policy actually 'does'. Rather, policy success is based ultimately on whether policy subsystem participants agree with a process that de facto reinforces the government's ability to achieve its goals.

Building on McConnell, Grealy, and Lea (2020), this chapter argues that the Canadian government, working closely with the financial sector, has engineered such a success in the design and management of its bank deregulation efforts – see table 13.1. Not only did the government foster the development of a small number of globally competitive 'national champions' in the Canadian financial industry, but it increased the regular review of banking policy, creating an expectation of ongoing political oversight of the sector. While this has provided legitimacy to the goals and instruments of federal regulatory policies and institutions, it has also helped shape the process by which deregulation has unfolded. The inclusive process has allowed a wide range of policy participants to 'tweak' the regulation of financial services and it has helped the Canadian industry avoid many of the pitfalls that have occurred in other states as they have struggled with the twin dilemmas of globalization and industry deregulation.

Changing the Future of Canadian Banking: The Era of Deregulation

In the 1980s the Canadian financial industry, working under the legacy of a pillarized financial system which separated firms into different kinds of financial activities (banking, insurance, and securities trading), fostered a diverse and competitive domestic marketplace where there was considerable regulatory ambiguity—only banks and their traditional banking activities were fully subject to federal oversight and regulation. During major changes to the Bank Act in the 1980s and again in the 1990s, the Federal Government radically re-worked an often-crisis-prone industry by allowing the large federally-regulated banks to progressively enter other market segments and to engage in aggressive strategies of conglomeration.

What emerged from these changes was a smaller cadre of large, federally-regulated firms that were not only better prepared to compete with the threat posed by the potential entry of larger American firms into the Canadian market (Porter and Coleman, 2003), but also better able to cooperate in a new style of prudential regulation under the guidance of the newly-created Office Superintendent of Financial Institutions (OSFI). Most importantly, these firms, now subjected to an informal but more careful scrutiny of their underlying prudential soundness, took over a volatile securities sector, at a time when financial instruments were becoming more complex and the scope for industry failures and corruption was more pronounced (Harris, 2010). Despite complaints about conglomeration, high fees and an oligopolistic lack of competitiveness, these changes produced an integrated financial industry that has provided Canadian markets with stable and sound financial practices for the last two and a half decades.

Table 13.1 Evaluating Policy Success—Preparing the Canadian Financial Services Industry for Globalization

Realm	Core Issue	Success measures for the Federal Government	Degree of Actor Success		
			High	Medium	Low
Policy-making Process	*Ensuring the Federal Government's ability to oversee the financial sector*	Degree of control over problem construction	X		
		Degree of control of policy development			X
		Degree of control over final decision	X		
		Ability to shape legitimacy of policy development	X		
Program	*Degree of congruence between government's goals and program outcomes*	Degree to which outputs match Governments' goals	X		
Politics	*The political benefits of the program for government*	Degree to which policy enhances Federal authorities' reputation	X		
		Degree to which the policy helps the Federal Government control the short-term agenda			X
		Degree to which the policy helps the Federal Government control the long-term agenda	X		
Time	*The sustainability of policy benefits*	Degree to which the policy benefits are sustainable over time	X		

Adapted from Table 13.1: McConnell, A., Grealy, L., Lea, T. (2020)

Politically, the existing system of 'pillarization' had divided industry participants not only by market sector, but also by jurisdiction, with the federal government exclusively overseeing the banking industry, while much of the insurance, mortgage and trust, and securities industries were subject to provincial jurisdiction. De-pillarizing and allowing different financial service providers (FSPs) into other sectors effectively eroded the divide between jurisdictions, creating considerable confusion. As Coleman (1996, 205) notes, 'once embarked along these policy paths, Canadian policy-makers would come to face broader questions about the very governance of financial services, questions that promised to add to frictions already existing between the federal and provincial levels of government.'

Prior to the formal process of deregulation, federal-provincial disagreements in financial services tended to work to the benefit of industry participants, as provincial governments competed to attract the financial service industry by offering incentives and deregulation. However, as deregulation shifted the focus of policy-making to the federal government, there has been a move away from a federal 'banking policy sector' to a national 'financial services policy sector', which boasts a wider range of participants. More actors have a stake in federal government policy than was the case in the past.

Deregulation has also expanded the role of Parliament in this sector. In the past, policy-making in financial services, as in most other countries, had been the isolated preserve of major financial services companies and key state agencies (Williams, 2012). The sector was thought to be too complex or too important for Parliament and the public to play a role. However, since deregulation, by design, Parliament has become a more important venue for debating key policy choices.

When the government allowed Canada's banks to take over the financial services sector and emerge as federally-regulated 'national champions' of Canadian markets, the government also strengthened Cabinet and Parliamentary oversight of the industry. At the same time as OSFI was created, the Federal government committed to more regular parliamentary reviews of the Bank Act (every five years) which has fostered significant, regular opportunities for parliamentarians and critics of Canada's big banks to demand regulatory changes. Bank Act reviews have provided recurrent 'Groundhog Day' opportunities for consumer groups to seek regulation of bank service fees, small business organizations to seek improved access to lending and investment, and financial watchdogs to draw attention to industry conflicts of interest.

Furthermore, by allowing Canada's banks to become the key actors in Canadian financial services, and thereby, effectively, centralizing policy-making in Ottawa, the Federal government also ensured debates about some of the most core aspects of deregulation—namely, whether foreign firms would be able to enter the Canadian market and whether industry conglomeration, which threatened to reduce market competition, would be subject to the OSFI and the national Competition

252 REGULATING CANADA'S BANKING SYSTEM

Bureau. Reports by those bodies to Parliament would be politically important events.

The result of this has been an increased politicization of the sector, in which Parliament at times has resisted the kinds of industry demands made in other jurisdictions that may have destabilized the sector and fostered more aggressive financial practices that have led to disaster elsewhere. Successive governments, under pressure from Parliament, have rejected mergers amongst large financial institutions, limited the direct access of foreign firms to Canadian markets, established new industry watchdogs focused on protecting consumers from poor financial advising, and perhaps quixotically, demanded that banks maintain an expansive local branch network—as both a kind of industrial strategy and a mechanism to ensure the availability of finance in smaller centres. Regardless of the specific implications of any of these interventions, Parliament crucially has retained some control over the pace and nature of industry change—this is notably different than many other jurisdictions. Such control has fostered a different culture of financial services—more risk averse and more attuned to meeting national economic goals.

There have been many policy developments in the thirty years since government first made these choices that illustrate the robustness of the sector's commitment to broad public scrutiny and oversight of the industry. Examples include the recurring attention to bank user fees and the successful management of Canada's response to the 2008 financial crisis. Yet, the handling of the 'too big to fail' problem, including the question of how much conglomeration was 'too much', is perhaps most illustrative, and therefore takes centre stage in this case study.

The Politicization of Bank Mergers and the 'Too Big to Fail' Question

Between 1987 and 1997, deregulation unfolded in the way intended by federal policymakers. In a rapid process of conglomeration, federally regulated banks took over much of the existing provincially regulated securities sector. This set the stage for a still-ongoing debate between the federal government and the provinces over who should regulate this sector. Notwithstanding these discussions within the governmental system, these moves rested upon a high level of consensus in the sector—which was dominated by the five major banks and the Department of Finance—around the necessity to respond to the rapidly changing global environment that financial services providers were encountering. The banks, government regulators, and the Department of Finance believed that increased conglomeration offset by increased international competition was inevitable and, thus, industry participants should be set free from any regulatory overhang of pillarization in order to meet that competition. Most of the key participants in sectoral policy-making supported domestic deregulation and industry concentration.

By 1997, this process was largely completed. The government was then confronted with a serious follow-up question: what to do about potential mergers between the big banks themselves? Such 'big shall buy big' mergers could threaten the level of domestic competition and raise the risks of what would happen if such merged mega-institutions were to run into financial trouble. The government initially chose to address the issue by submitting it to a special Task Force (the Task Force on the Future of the Canadian Financial Services Sector, or the MacKay Task Force) as a part of a broad policy review process for the next round of Bank Act changes. This took control of the policy formulation process out of the hands of the Department of Finance, which in the past had only privately consulted with the leading firms in the sector. Moving away from the inner-circle approach that had produced the initial move to deregulation in the 1980s, government was now essentially delivering on the other half of the plan for deregulation—enhanced, political oversight of key decisions.

During the work of the Task Force, the big five banks themselves, and the Canadian Banker's Association (CBA) working on their behalf, repeatedly raised the concern that the WTO (World Trade Organization) and NAFTA (North American Free Trade Agreement), by removing barriers to trade in financial services internationally, required the reduction of remaining regulatory burdens, particularly the restrictions on the range of services they could offer (Roberge, 2004, 135). Their submission emphasized globalization, along with the trend towards conglomeration elsewhere, and suggested that Canadian banks were facing a surge in competition from larger foreign competitors *inside* the Canadian market. Facing these threats, the CBA asked the MacKay Task Force to recommend abolishing the 'big shall not buy big' policy, which held that the federal government would not allow existing big banks to merge with one another. Furthermore, the Association argued that the system for approving mergers should be amended so that bank mergers could be judged by the general legislation governing corporate mergers. Their proposal would mean that mergers would only be reviewed by the Competition Bureau and that Office of the Superintendent of Financial Institutions (OSFI), and subsequent 'ministerial reviews' would automatically result in the approval of a merger if it satisfied the Competition Bureau guidelines (Roberge, 2004, 54-55). Perhaps anticipating that the greatest opponent to such mergers would be MPs, who might pressure Cabinet to block any attempt to further reduce competition in the sector, the CBA was trying to minimize the role of Parliament and the government in any decision.

In their submissions to the MacKay Task Force and their releases to the media, smaller financial institutions, credit unions, trust companies, small business

254 REGULATING CANADA'S BANKING SYSTEM

associations, and consumer groups frequently rejected the ideas of the larger banks, arguing that further mergers between big players would allow the resultant mega-banks to shut down competition and squeeze out smaller market participants. The Trust Companies Association of Canada (TCAC), the Independent Investment Dealers Association (IIDA), and a number of other non-bank financial service industry groups and firms argued that more effort needed to be made to ensure that there was a healthy second tier of competition for the banks, since the banks had become too big and threatened competition. There was a widespread sense that the process of de-pillarization had consistently favoured the banks as Independent Investment Dealers Association argued:

> *The result has been the creation of a single super-pillar. This, independent dealers believe, has led to a lessening of competition, innovation and efficiency within the financial services sector and higher prices for Canadian consumers, with no discernible benefit for the Canadian economy.*
>
> (quoted from Schacter, 1998, 20)

Indeed, even extremely wealthy companies argued that banks' domination of financial services was rapidly increasing. In response to MacKay's investigation, they presented data suggesting that the banks accounted for a staggering 64 per cent of profits by TSE 300 companies between 1992 and 1996 (Schacter, 1998, 21). Power Financial Corporation (often called Power Corp), like some of the other major insurance companies, was not a political lightweight; it owned the largest mutual fund company in Canada, the Investors Group, and several insurance companies. The company was large and politically well connected, particularly to Finance Minister Paul Martin.

While the Task Force listened to these highly public arguments, the banks were already formulating their merger proposals. They believed that increased international competition would sway the MacKay Task Force to ultimately endorse the idea of mergers between big banks. As such, the Royal Bank and Bank of Montréal (Canada's second and third largest institutions at that time) decided to 'build a globally-competitive' financial institution through a 'merger of equals' (Kingston, 1998, 1). Perhaps failing to read the tea leaves, the two banks believed that the government would back the merger proposal.

Before the MacKay Task Force could finish its deliberations, the banks announced their proposed merger to a surprised public. In a joint press conference, the two bank chairmen framed the central argument they would put forward over the next year—that 'size mattered' in banking circles. The new mega-bank would have $453 billion in assets, making it the tenth largest bank in North America and the twenty-second largest in the world. They argued that competition from globalization required this to be able to compete with their large US competitors. During the press conference, Bank of Montréal Chairman Matthew Barrett argued that:

What we don't plan to be is the corner hardware store, waiting for Home Depot to put us out of business. What we do plan is to give the financial equivalents of Home Depot or Wal-Mart the stiffest competition that we can ... Like Alcan, Bombardier or Nortel, the new bank will be a Canadian champion abroad. It will have the resources to lead any financial deal large or small.

(Quoted from Depalma, 1998)

Understandably, given the fact that the industry had not witnessed a merger between two of Canada's big banks in living memory, the merger was big news. The public was shocked and the government seemed to be caught off-guard. The news even surprised the industry. Many experts and participants had been expecting merger proposals, none thought one would happen so soon. Analysts were surprised not by the banks' desire to merge but rather by their announced intention to do so prior to the government's approval of the plan (Kingston, 1998). Many assumed that there would have to be a lengthy dialogue with the government about how a proposed merger would be handled prior to any formal announcement.

This seems to have been the prevalent attitude in Ottawa in the hours after Cleghorn and Barrett's press conference. According to many sources, Finance Minister Paul Martin was upset by the proposed merger, irked that the government had not been given appropriate forewarning on what the banks were doing, and displeased that the MacKay Task Force's process was being disrupted (Greenspon, 1998). The banks' plans might have also affected Martin's long-standing ambition to become Canada's next prime minister. Eager to lure progressive-liberals to his leadership campaign, Martin had been trying to shake his image as a fiscally-conservative supporter of corporate Canada. Given how Canadians felt about the banks, Martin believed that if he accepted the merger, it would raise credibility problems for him in any leadership contest (Greenspon, 1998).

Paul Martin's concerns framed the problems the banks would encounter in the sector after their merger announcement. In the lead up to the merger, the banks were widely known to be highly profitable. Both banks were breaking profit records; RBC was the most profitable company in Canada. In 1997 RBC posted a $1.68 billion profit, while the Bank of Montréal made $1.31 billion. RBC's return on shareholder equity was 19.5 per cent—very high by global industry standards. The public, angered by the proliferation of new service fees and believing that those fees were the basis of the banks' recent success, were sceptical that the banks faced impending doom unless they were allowed to merge. Given the public's feelings, any minister that would approve the merger ran the risk of appearing to be too cozy with big business.

Even officials at the CBA argued that the banks' decision to proceed at that time, and in the way that they did, was poorly thought out. One senior lobbyist, aware of the huge public relations problems the banks had, and the views of many MPs, suggested that an approval for a merger at that time was extremely unlikely. Indeed, the CBA was in the midst of an initiative by CEO Ray Protti to improve the banks' relations with MPs. The CBA knew that, on some level, parliamentary approval would be required—that had clearly been the intention of the government since the first steps towards deregulation. While throwing out the 'big shall not buy big' policy was not a hill the government was going to die on politically, doing it without a rigorous, transparent, comprehensive policy review was still deemed unacceptable. Indeed, at a hurriedly organized press conference held after the merger announcement, Paul Martin stated that any approval of the merger would have to await a full investigation by both the Competition Bureau and the OSFI, as well as the completion of the MacKay Task Force; thereby setting the stage for a year-long, highly political, and highly public, struggle over the merger.

The perceived unpopularity of the RBC/BMO merger was intensified a few months later. Prior to any serious government work on the evaluation of that merger, on 13 April, Toronto Dominion (TD) and the Canadian Imperial Bank of Commerce (CIBC) (the first and fourth largest banks, respectively) announced similar merger plans. The new bank would have assets worth $460 billion, which would have made it the ninth largest bank in North America and the twenty-first largest in the world. It would also be slightly larger than the RBC/BMO merged entity. As well, through the merger of their mutual discount brokerage services, TD Green Line Investor Services and CIBC's Investor's Edge, they would become the world's second largest discount brokerage. The second merger proposal only intensified the struggle over the first as, considered jointly—as Martin would insist that they be—the combined proposals would reduce the number of big banks from five to three, with two superbanks dominating the industry.[1]

Parliament and the Public Interest in Canadian Banking

From April of 1998 onwards, the arduous process of evaluating the mergers began behind closed doors in Ottawa. Both the Competition Bureau and the OSFI launched detailed examinations. However, outside these processes, there was also public evaluation of the mergers. Both in the press, and before the various parliamentary committees and task forces that would examine the issue, the four

---

[1] Source: Confidential Interviews, 2005. While the two banks argued that the move was a response to the same pressures confronting RBC/BMO, many said that they had more 'strategic' motives. Experts felt that the approval of two such mergers was unlikely, thus some argued that the second merger was simply a 'spoiler' designed to ensure that both mergers were rejected, preventing the RBC/BMO entity from becoming the dominant Canadian bank. Other insiders suggested that the motive for the TD/CIBC merger was more defensive. Either both mergers would be approved and the TD/CIBC marriage would emerge as the largest company, or having raised the stakes, both mergers would be rejected, thereby blocking the surprise proposals from RBC/BMO. TD and CIBC had nothing to lose.

involved banks, the CBA, and other supporters would argue that the mergers were in (what they considered to be) the public interest. Industry insiders duly expected that despite the initial unpopularity of the mergers, ultimately, they would receive government approval.

Some factors worked in the banks' favour. The proposed mergers did seem to jibe with the general deregulatory trajectory of government policy since the 1980s. The banks argued that the merger could help them to deal with the increased cost of new technologies and achieve the efficiencies of economies of scale that would put them in a better position to compete globally. Their view was often endorsed by the various investigations into the industry. Indeed, the MacKay Task Force was largely sympathetic. Furthermore, the banks' lobby had a great deal of political clout. Aside from being the dominant players in a crucial economic sector, the banks were quite simply some of Canada's largest and richest companies; they also made large direct contributions to party finances generally, and to the governing Liberals in particular. According to Elections Canada's disclosure of political party contributions for 1997, Canada's major banks accounted for a significant portion of campaign financing, as the Liberals received abnormally large donations from major financial service companies. In fact, over this period, there was an attempt to obscure this relationship, as the banks' securities subsidiaries often made donations that equalled those coming from the much larger parent bank, hiding the size of the banks' political donations to casual observers. Based on factors like these, some experts predicted that, despite the political unpopularity of the mergers, they would be approved.

However, the banks faced a serious challenge from the outset. The mergers clearly threatened to upset the policy overhaul of the sector. They also posed serious policy questions around how the government should regulate the industry in the future. The government had intended to resolve these questions in a public and deliberative way. Abandoning the 'big shall not buy big' rule would be a major change, paving the way for the kind of giant banks that dominated domestic financial sectors in other smaller financial centres. Furthermore, the government would have to consider these issues amid considerable public controversy as, from the outset, a large array of organizations and competing firms began to exert pressure, both public and private, on the government to reject the mergers. Small business groups, consumer organizations, the opposition parties in Parliament, provincial governments, and many industry participants in the financial services sector all campaigned fiercely against the mergers throughout 1998. Trust companies, competing securities dealers, credit unions, other banks, as well as large and influential financial services companies like Power Corporation, all opposed the mergers. This sprawling 'anti-bank' advocacy supported the new, more 'public' style of policy-making in the sector.

Indeed, while many groups and interests weighed in on various policy concerns, some of the most compelling arguments focused on the issue of process

258 REGULATING CANADA'S BANKING SYSTEM

itself. As the Centre for Policy Alternatives, a popular left-leaning think tank, argued:

> ... *beyond these economic and financial consequences, the merger controversy reveals the enormous political arrogance of these behemoths. So confident that their political power is greater than the democratic authority of the Canadian government, they simply pronounce the new reality in the midst of a parliamentary review of banking regulations. This is a deliberate attempt to pre-determine government policy.*
>
> (Dobbin, 2001).

The fact that the banks were acting pre-emptively, and effectively dictating the agenda of regulatory reform, was perceived as manifestly unfair.

Small business groups such as the Canadian Federation of Independent Business (CFIB), emerged as a major thorn in the Banks' side during the review process. Indeed, the CFIB had been persistently appearing before parliamentary committees since the 1980s, any time financial services regulation was at issue. The CFIB wanted the government to increase the pool of financing available to small businesses, and suggested that these mergers would only reduce the access of small businesses to a competitive market for financial services, particularly in smaller centres. In its own research analysis of the mergers, CFIB argued that it was 'imperative' for the interests of small business that parliamentarians block the proposals. Political constituencies like the CFIB were hard for Liberal MPs to ignore. They represented the small business people who often formed the backbone of local constituency organizations.

The anti-competitive impact of the mergers, in terms of branch closings and the availability of credit, were particularly important considerations and would be addressed in the Competition Bureau's review of the proposals. Indeed, polemics aside, the opinion of the financial markets themselves on the super-merger proposals was clear. Announcements of mergers initially drove the stock prices of the banks upwards as investors believed that the ensuing increase in market power would allow the new banks to set artificially high prices, not because it made the banks more efficient or globally competitive (Baltazor and Santos, 2003).

Some experts on banking also argued that the merger proposals potentially created the conditions for reckless bank behaviour—the kind of recklessness which would be exposed during the 2007–2009 financial crisis in jurisdictions that chose to embrace more radical ideas about conglomeration and deregulation. Bob Jenness (1998), a senior research director at the Economic Council of Canada, argued this in a *Monthly Economic Review* article, suggesting bank profits were closely tied to macroeconomic policy and that low interest rates, coupled with low inflation, produced higher bank profits. There was a thus a risk that the merged banks, with increased power in relation to the government, might force it to adopt inappropriate macro-economic policies in order to shield themselves from the mistakes of 'aggressive' overseas lending that globalization engenders. Rather than being prudent, the banks, secure in their ability to pressure the government to change policies, might also themselves pursue inappropriate business opportunities.

Ironically, the debate also took place within the banking sector itself. As the head of the only major bank to not have a merger partner, Scotiabank Chairman Peter Godsoe had strong reasons to oppose the proposed mergers; however, the fact that he was the head of a bank also lent his analysis a great deal of credibility. Constantly speaking against government approval of the mergers, he used strong rhetoric to argue that the resulting 'superbanks' would 'kill competition' and would 'dynamite' the existing banking system (Cole, 1998).

The Politics of Reports and the Importance of Process

Beginning in September of 1998 the results of a series of government evaluations of the mergers and a report by the MacKay Task Force were released, ensuing a host of parliamentary responses. The MacKay Task Force made myriad complex recommendations. In the short term however, due to its chief focus on the challenges of globalization, the Task Force recommended virtually everything that the banks had been asking for. It endorsed the CBA's recommendation that the 'big should not buy big' rule needed to be abandoned, suggesting that, in theory, the big banks should be allowed to merge. This fit well within the broader thrust of the Report, which embraced more rapid deregulation of the industry.

The Task Force also supported the CBA's demands that financial services companies ought to be allowed to offer a full range of services, recommending that the banks should be allowed to provide automobile leasing and insurance, lucrative sectors from which the banks are still excluded. Appearing before a Senate Banking Committee hearing on the results of the Task Force, the CBA framed the recommendations as a victory for the banks, which were seeking more deregulation. The problem for the merger proposals themselves was that the MacKay Task Force, made up of banking veterans, was always going to be the process that most favoured the banks.

Opinion was moving a different direction in the House of Commons. On 4 November, Tony Ianno, a backbench Liberal MP from Ontario who was particularly concerned with the problems small businesses faced in dealing with the banks, released his own 'Task Force' report on the mergers. The 'Ianno Report' was drawn up by an ad hoc parliamentary committee that conducted its own hearings on the merger proposals. Seen as a somewhat unfair show trial by the banks, the

260 REGULATING CANADA'S BANKING SYSTEM

hearings focused on submissions from groups like the Canadian Federation of Independent Business. The committee's report was signed by fifty Liberal MPs and four Senators. It recommended that the finance minister reject the mergers, arguing that they were not in-line with the public interest (Whittingdon and Eggerston, 1998). Ianno and his colleagues argued the mergers would lead to large scale job losses, branch closures, and reduced consumer choice, and would also make it harder for small businesses to get financing. Furthermore, the report suggested that the banks had failed to make a clear case about why they needed mergers.

Indeed, the Ianno Report did not stop its analysis at the merger issue. It also touched on a number of other bank regulatory concerns, which had been popular in Parliament for some time. Jumping ahead of the formal legislative response to the MacKay recommendations, Ianno and his fellow MPs also suggested that Paul Martin should reject a number of other ideas put forward by the Task Force. Bill C-8, the subsequent legislation in response to the review conducted by the MacKay Task Force, endorsed almost all of the Ianno Report's recommendations, and broke with the MacKay recommendations on a number of important items, such as allowing the banks to sell insurance.

Ianno's report also generated a great deal of public interest, as it was very unusual for a committee of government backbenchers to put this kind of public pressure on the government. The problem was that Parliament expected a role and its members worried that the House of Commons Finance Committee and Senate Committee on Banking Reports in response to the MacKay Task Force would be stacked against their concerns.[2]

Many in the financial industry, most importantly, insurance brokers and automobile dealers, applauded the report. Richard Gauthier, president of the Canadian Automobile Dealers Association labelled it 'a victory for Main Street over Bay Street' (Whittington and Eggerston, 1998). Indeed, the response by those opposed to the mergers was celebratory. The Council of Canadians argued that the banks had been given the opportunity in the Ianno hearings to justify why the mergers were necessary and that they had failed to do that. The Council's executive director, Peter Bleyer, argued that 'the whole discussion about bank mergers is—or should be—a non-starter. The real discussion that needs to take place is about how to make banks more accountable to the public through better regulation. The banks hijacked that discussion earlier this year when they announced their proposed mergers.'[3]

The reception of the report emphasized the political problems the mergers had become. Even the opposition Reform Party, aware of the publics' anti-merger sentiments, which Ianno had tapped into, began to suggest a 'middle way' strategy.

---

[2] Source: Confidential Inrterviews, 2006. This was a concistent concern amongst backbench members of the Liberal Party that wanted a "say" over the decision.

[3] Source of quote: Council of Canadians, http://www.canadians.org/campaings/campaigns-bankmedia06.html.

Ironically the Reform Party's stance was the one the government would eventually embrace. Reform Party critic Dick Harris, uncomfortable with the anti-business overtones of the report, suggested that the government should simply place a moratorium on such mergers until there was a policy process in place to deal with them (Whittington and Eggerston, 1998). The immediate problem for the government was even more pronounced. Regardless of what happened in either of the parliamentary committees that were going to review the MacKay recommendations, or at OSFI and the Competition Bureau, one third of the government's sitting members had signed a report calling for a rejection of the mergers.

In effect, the Ianno committee had expanded parliamentary oversight of the sector. MPs had directly reviewed the merger proposals and rejected them. This was a privilege which Parliament had legally surrendered in the 1910 Bank Act (Darroch, 1992). Before 1910 it required an act of Parliament for two banks to merge. After, it was up to the minister of finance. Having removed Parliament from the process after 1910, the number of banks dwindled.

The events of 1998 reflected a re-assertion of Parliament's direct role in regulating levels of competition in the sector. Of course, legally, Paul Martin could have ignored the Ianno Report since no vote was required in the House to approve the mergers. Therefore, in theory, Ianno and his 50 members were not needed but, in practice, this was politically risky, particularly for someone who wanted to become prime minister. Indeed, in private meetings with consumer and small business groups, Martin asked if they would consider changing their position on mergers if he put in place a temporary guarantee against branch closings and moved to regulate service fees.[4]

In December, both parliamentary committees—the Standing Committee on Finance and the Senate Committee on Banking—released their reports. Both committees were careful to support the idea that mergers could be allowed in theory, but that these specific proposals could not be judged prior to the release of the Competition Bureau and OSFI reports. However, the Commons Committee argued that while mergers could be allowed, there should be a clearer process in place for evaluating their economic and prudential impact before government approval was granted. In effect, the position of the Commons Finance Committee was that, while they had no opposition in principle to proposals for mergers, they wanted a regularized system by which they would be given a role in evaluating the proposals.[5] All four opposition parties released dissenting opinions in the report, much of which expressed opposition to the mergers and support for new regulations of bank practices.

---

[4] Source: Confidential Interviews 2006. The finance minister clearly had sympathy for the merger proposal throughout the process, but he was under considerable preasure from his own caucus.

[5] It should also be noted that when they limited their analysis to this point, they were already aware that the Competition Bureau was going to reject these mergers. Source: Confidential Interviews, 2006.

262   REGULATING CANADA'S BANKING SYSTEM

On 10 December, within days of the two parliamentary committee reports, the OSFI report to Paul Martin was publicly released. The OSFI report concluded there were prudential reasons to be concerned about the impact of the mergers on the Canadian financial market. Given its mandate, OSFI had been instructed by Martin to investigate whether the mergers would have an adverse impact on the financial safety and soundness of either merged bank, and whether the mergers increased the risk to the public if one of the institutions ran into financial trouble. On the second question, in an eerie foreshadowing of the 2007–2009 financial crisis, OSFI reached the obvious conclusion that it would, stating that: '... given the relative size of the institution in relation to potential buyers and investors ... a "least cost" resolution may be more difficult to achieve' (OFSI, 1998). Essentially, OSFI said that if one of these large banks ran into trouble, it would be harder for the government to manage the process of rescuing it. OFSI hinted that such rescues would inevitably involve further difficult public policy decisions, as it was likely that only some sort of international partner would have the ability to buy out a troubled Canadian post-merger 'superbank'.

The following day the Competition Bureau's report to Paul Martin was released to the public. The Competition Bureau had not been called on to investigate competition in the financial sector in the past, but given parliamentary concerns over this issue, their analysis generated a great deal of attention. In the case of the bank mergers, the bureau was guided by a set of Merger Enforcement Guidelines, which laid out specifically how it should evaluate the likely effects of a large merger on levels of competition. Under the existing legislation, if the commissioner found that there were problems with a proposed merger, the Bureau had the authority to demand remedies through a competition tribunal. It could inhibit the merger or demand changes to the merger proposal to limit its effect on competition. However, in the case of a merger between entities regulated by the Bank Act, the process was more immediately political. In the case of a merger between two or more of the banks, the merger requires the ultimate approval of the minister of finance. Indeed, the minister has authority under Section 94 of the Competition Act to set aside the normal process if he or she rules in favour of a merger between banks. Furthermore, neither the Bank Act, nor the Competition Act, spells out how the commissioner and the finance minister should interact in evaluating a bank merger. Thus, while the Competition Bureau was required to evaluate the proposed mergers between Canada's largest banks, it was not straightforward what role its investigation would play in approving or disallowing such mergers (see Competition Bureau, 2003). In fact, the government chose to view the Competition Bureau's investigation of the mergers as a recommendation.

The Bureau argued that the mergers would undermine competition. The investigation was substantially different from the one conducted by OSFI. In particular, the Bureau argued that competition for basic banking services would be drastically affected. Given the legacy of de-pillarization, securities dealing and the credit card business would also see reduced competition. The Bureau also questioned how the remaining smaller banks and credit unions would be able to compete. Noting the cost efficiencies of the new superbanks, the Bureau suggested that even the Bank of Nova Scotia, which was huge in relation to most smaller institutions, but would be less than half the size of either merged bank, would be '... at a significant cost disadvantage and would not be able to compete effectively unless it also merged with another major bank' (Competition Bureau, 1998).

The Bureau's assessment confirmed what analysts and pundits in the financial services industry had been saying about the heads of those financial institutions that opposed the mergers: that they were 'dead men walking'. It confirmed some of the worst fears of merger opponents—that rather than ending up with two super-banks and a host of smaller traditional and new competitors, Canada might end up with only two big banks.

The two regulators' reports further fuelled parliamentary opposition to the mergers. At the end of the year, Paul Martin did what had become inevitable: he announced to the public that given the reports that he had received, it was not possible for the proposed mergers to go forward at that time. Indeed, while it would normally have been possible to revise the merger proposals to satisfy the concerns raised, Martin cut the entire process short. He had decided that the mergers were unacceptable, and instead would have to await the legislative overhaul of Canada's banking regulations that was due in response to the MacKay Report. Martin promised that this overhaul would include new guidelines to govern the process for evaluating large mergers in the banking sector.

Despite this promised potential window for mergers in the future, the 'big shall not buy big' rule has been entrenched. Subsequent rumours of possible merger proposals under the Conservative government in the following decade never amounted to anything serious. Mergers between large banks in Canada that would result in creating the kind of globally competitive banks that had emerged elsewhere, have been deemed to be anti-competitive and too risky by Parliament. No bank has been willing to brave the political process of removing those remaining barriers to a more deregulated market. And the fallout from the 2007–2008 financial crisis has only provided ample evidence of the wisdom of the decision.

It is important to emphasize here that had Canada adopted the regulatory policy style of other jurisdictions, one where expectations of parliamentary oversight of major policy changes like this were not required, the events of 1998 would have been very different. The merging banks convinced the MacKay Task Force (made up of the kind of financial industry experts that dominate policy-making in other settings), that their proposals were sound. But parliamentary oversight, at times informal, and at times required by the system established after deregulation, opened these discussions to a wider array of actors and the result was very different. The fact that parliamentary oversight served to entrench the government's early policy

264 REGULATING CANADA'S BANKING SYSTEM

goal that 'big shall not buy big' during deregulation illustrates how much process matters.

In the 1980s the government delivered a rapid program of deregulation in exchange for the promise that there would be more regular and ongoing oversight of the sector by Canada's parliament. That process has generated significant support for the policies that govern the financial services sector—a safer and more competitive banking system than might have otherwise been the case.

Conclusions

McConnell, Grealy, and Lea (2020) suggest that we use plausibility tests of policy success across various realms (process, program, politics, and time) to judge impacts on the key actor—here the federal government and its plans for the banking sector. Judging a 'process success' rests less on the extent to which outcomes have met the overarching and subjective policy goals of the government, and more on the degree to which the choices about process serve to reinforce the government's ability to meet those goals over time. While government's broad goals for the industry also seem to have been a 'success', what really stands out in this case is the extent to which governments' choice to widen the politization of policy-making in this sector helped entrench those goals from powerful lobbyists.

As has been illustrated above, the 'big shall not buy big rule', Canada's response to the risks posed by the 'too big to fail' problem emerging in global finance, was challenged by the big banks. Had they got their way, the fallout of the 2007–2008 financial crisis might have been very different; indeed the Canadian financial services industry in general would be very different today. Instead, by ensuring that major regulatory changes in banking would be subjected to orderly policy deliberations, thereby including a role for parliamentary committees, the government stacked the deck against the banks. Their choices in the period of deregulation enhanced the capacity of future governments to 'stick to the program', ensuring the Canadian industry remained competitive and stable amid the uncertainties generated by globalization.

In the bank mergers debate, the process used by the government to oversee the deregulation and Canada's response to globalization in banking, opened the private club of policy-making to many new participants. 'Anti-bank' groups and other large financial service providers (including both the influential insurance industry as well as one of the banks), as well as expert reports from within government about the risks of excessive conglomeration, acted to turn Parliament into a key site of struggle for policy-making in the sector. The individual banks were understandably upset about the rejection of their mergers, but the fact that the debate has not recurred is illustrative of the extent to which the goals of the deregulatory period, which sought to create a stable group of federally regulated, one-stop-shop financial institutions, operating under a regulatory umbrella enjoying broad political legitimacy, remains soundly in place.

Since the deregulation era there have been two major global financial crises that severely strained policy goals in other jurisdictions. Domestically, Canadian governments have had to manage significant interjurisdictional disputes over the regulation of the securities sector (Roberge, 2013) and sustained political pressure to allow increased industry concentration after deregulation. Despite these turbulent challenges, the Canadian financial sector has remained sound and internally competitive (at least as competitive as it was prior to deregulation), while a variety of smaller public interest goals have been successfully pursued. Process matters.

References

Baltazor. R. and M. Santos. 2003. "The Benefits of Banking Mega Mergers: Event Study Evidence from the 1998 Failed Mega Merger Attempts in Canada." *Canadian Journal of Administrative Sciences* 20 (3): pp. 196–208.

Bovens, M. and P. 't Hart. 1996. *Understanding Policy Fiascos*. Piscataway, NJ: Transaction Publishers.

Canadian Bankers Association. 1998. *CBA's Preliminary Response to the MacKay Task Force Report—Submitted to the Standing Senate Committee on Banking Trade and Commerce*. Toronto: CBA. http://www.cba.ca/eng/CBA_on_the_Issues/Submissions/980929-a.htm

Cleghorn, J. and M. Barrett. 1998. "Remarks at the Announcement of the Agreement to a Merger of Equals with the Royal Bank of Canada." Press Release, 28 January.

Cole, T. 1998. "Waiting for Godsoe." *Report on Business Magazine*. September.

Coleman, W. D. 1996. *Financial Services, Globalization and Domestic Policy Change: A Comparison of North America and the European Union*. Basingstoke: Macmillan.

Competition Bureau. (1998). The Competition Bureau's Letter to the CIBC and TD Bank. 11 December. https://www.competitionbureau.gc.ca/eic/site/cb-bc.nsf/eng/01601.html

Competition Bureau. 2003. *The Merger Enforcement Guidelines as Applied to a Bank Merger*. Ottawa: Competition Bureau.

Compton, M. and P. Hart 2019. *Great Policy Successes*. Oxford University Press.

Darroch, J. 1992. "Global Competitiveness and Public Policy: The Case of the Canadian Multinational Banks." *Business History* 34 (3): pp. 153–175.

Depalma, A. 1998. "Two of Canada's Biggest Banks in a Surprise Merger Plan." *New York Times*. January 24.

Dobbin, M. 2001. "Are the Bank Mergers Good for the Country?" Canadian Centre for Policy Alternatives. 21 November. http://www.policyalternatives.ca/bc/opinion12.html

Greenspon, E. 1998. "St. Paul among the Philistines." *Report on Business Magazine*. March.

Harris, S. 2010. "The Global Financial Meltdown and Financial Regulation: Shirking and Learning—Canada in an International Context." In *How Ottawa Spends,*

2010–2011, edited by G. Doern and C. Stoney, pp. 68–86. Montréal and Kingston: McGill-Queens University Press.

Jenness, B. 1998. "Current Issues in Canadian Banking." *Monthly Economic Review*. 26 October.

Kingston, A. 1998. "Stealth Banker." ROB Magazine. April.

McConnell, A. 2010. "Policy Success, Policy Failure and Grey Areas In-Between." *Journal of Public Policy* 30 (3): pp. 345–362.

McConnell, A., L. Grealy, and T. Lea. 2020. "Policy Success for Whom? A Framework for Analysis." *Policy Sciences* 53 (4): pp. 589–608.

Office of the Superintendent of Financial Institutions (OFSI). 1998. *Proposed Mergers between the Royal Bank of Canada and the Bank of Montreal, and the Canadian Imperial Bank of Commerce and the Toronto-Dominion Bank—Report to the Minister of Finance*, 10 December.

Porter, T. and W. D. Coleman. 2003. "Playin' Along: Canada and Global Finance." In *Changing Canada: Political Economy as Transformation*, edited by W. Clement and L. F. Vosko, pp. 241–264. Montreal and Kingston: McGill-Queens University Press.

Roberge, I. 2004. *The Internationalization of Public Policy and Multi-Level Governance: A Comparison of Financial Services Sector Reform in Canada and France*. Doctoral dissertation, McMaster University.

Roberge, I. 2013. "Politics Over Policy: Multilevel Public Management of the Financial Services Sector in Canada." In *Making Multilevel Public Management Work: Stories of Success and Failure from Europe and North America*. Edited by D. Cepiku. D. Jesuit and I. Roberge. Pp. 103–118. CRC Press.

Schachter, H. 1998. "The Great Debate." Canadian Banker. May/June.

Whittington L. and L. Eggerston. 1998. "Liberal Caucus Says No to Piggy Bank Mergers: Ball in Paul Martin's Court." *Toronto Star*. http://www.flipside.org/vol1/nov98/n98w1013.htm

Williams, R. A. 2012. "The Limits of Policy Analytical Capacity—Canadian Financial Regulatory Reform." *International Journal of Public Sector Management* 25 (6/7): pp. 455–463.

14

Supply Management in Canada's Dairy and Poultry Sectors

Grace Skogstad

Introduction

Born during a period of economic crisis, the supply management systems established in Canada's dairy and poultry sectors in the late 1960s and early 1970s have proved resilient. Their combination of domestic production controls and administered pricing has endured, even while their third policy instrument, import controls, has weakened under international pressures. Judged by McConnell's (2010) criteria, supply management is a *political* success insofar as it enjoys the support of both federal and provincial governments, Canada's major political parties, and the Canadian public. The coalition that supports supply management has remained intact. Judgements of its *programmatic* success differ according to the weight placed on its different objectives. Supply management has achieved the foremost goal of its founders; that is, stabilizing domestic production and increasing the bargaining power of producers. At the same time, supply management is credited with higher costs for Canadian consumers and future farmers, and criticized for impeding the change needed to allow the system to adjust to a policy context much different from that wherein it originated. On *process* success criteria, the conflicted and even precarious success that jeopardized supply management in its early days has largely, but not entirely, given way to resilient success. By way of evidence, the administrative agencies responsible for implementing supply management have demonstrated their capacity for problem-solving, adjusting policy instruments under the exigencies of pressure from the domestic and international political economy. At the same time, criticisms remain regarding the overrepresentation of producer interests in poultry supply management, and the hurdles posed by existing administrative practices to developing innovative products in alignment with the tastes and needs of downstream customers.

The *durability* of dairy and poultry supply management to date provides instructive lessons into the dynamics that shape national policy-making in Canada.

Grace Skogstad, *Supply Management in Canada's Dairy and Poultry Sectors.* In: *Policy Success in Canada.*
Edited by Evert A. Lindquist et al., Oxford University Press. © Grace Skogstad (2022).
DOI: 10.1093/oso/9780192897046.003.0014

They are a composite of interests and ideas at the systemic level of the international political economy, the macro-level of Canadian federal and parliamentary institutions, and the meso-level of administration. At the international level, supply management reveals the initially permissive but later constraining impact of the international trade regime on Canadian public policy and Canada's international commercial relations. At the macro-level of Canada's federal system, supply management demonstrates the requisite of intergovernmental cooperation to solve problems that transcend the jurisdiction of a single order of government, but equally as well, the status-quo bias of policies that require the unanimous consent of federal and provincial governments. At the macro-level of the parliamentary system, supply management reveals the power of coalitions across Canada's two most populous provinces, Ontario and Québec. And finally, at the meso-level, supply management highlights the significance of administrative policy subsystems as mechanisms of policy continuity and policy change.

To illustrate these dynamics, and the success of Canadian supply management within them, the chapter proceeds as follows. I first describe the international and domestic federal and parliamentary context, within which national supply management emerged in the early 1970s as a solution to the economic problems experienced in the dairy and poultry sectors. I then provide an account of the evolution of supply management and its performance on programmatic, process, and political success criteria over time, as it has been forced to adjust to a changing economic and political context. I conclude with an assessment of the insights supply management provides on evaluations of policy successes, including in the Canadian policy-making context.

The Origins and Instruments of Supply Management

Marketing boards with supply management powers exercise delegated authority from governments to regulate the total amount of a product sold by all farmers within a given territory, over a specified period. Its champions view supply management as a solution to the problems created by imperfect competition in agriculture. Individual farmers, large in number, find themselves in a weak position to secure fair prices from the far fewer purchasers of their products. To augment their marketing power, from the early twentieth century onward, farmers formed cooperatives to sell their produce.

When cooperatives proved inadequate in redressing the imbalance of market power between producers and buyers, over the 1950s and 1960s farmers turned to their provincial governments to use their authority over intraprovincial marketing to establish compulsory marketing boards (Hiscocks, 1970). Provincial marketing boards, acting as the sole seller for a farm product, could negotiate a higher price for it than could farmers individually, providing the board could control the total supply of the product that entered a given market. Their price-setting effectiveness was circumscribed, however, when buyers had recourse to supplies from other provinces or countries. Insofar as regulating inter-provincial and external shipments of produce falls within the jurisdiction of the government of Canada, establishing and operating national marketing agencies with supply management powers has required the cooperation of federal and provincial governments.

The Dairy Sector

The establishment of supply management in the Canadian dairy sector followed a history of federal government intervention (Skogstad, 1987; 2008). Like its counterparts in several other countries, the Canadian government deployed price supports, export subsidies, and import restrictions to address oversupplies of milk and offset low prices for milk producers. As early as the 1930s, the Government of Canada began supporting the prices of cheese and butter, the surplus products of which were exported. Beginning in 1959, it also paid a direct subsidy to industrial milk producers, which had the effect of increasing industrial milk production. Entering the 1960s, the problem of low prices was especially acute for the Canadian farmers who produced the industrial milk that accounted for three-quarters of all milk marketed (Scullion, 2006, 4). Industrial milk, which is not drunk fresh but processed into dairy products like butter and cheese, fetched a lower price than the perishable fluid milk—fresh table milk and cream—purchased by dairies and consumed locally.

In this context of economic distress, dairy supply management emerged as a solution that served the common interests of producers, the processors who purchased their product, and federal and provincial governments. For producers, supply management offered the promise of higher and more stable returns and the market security they needed to invest for the long-term. By merging marketing organizations and pooling milk revenues across dairy producers, supply management was also a means to address inequities between large versus small producers and between fluid versus industrial milk producers. In addition, supply management also helped dairy farmers to promote their interests through a shared identity as a professional industry. For processors, although import controls on the main processed dairy products already protected them to some degree from foreign competition, supply management assured them of the supplies they needed to survive and expand in the Canadian market. And for governments, supply management offered the opportunity to unburden themselves of the uncontrolled costs of supporting dairy product prices. Indeed, between 1958–9 and 1967–8, 80 per cent of federal expenditures on price and income maintenance had gone to the dairy sector (Skogstad, 1987, 47). It also offered a way to consolidate the dairy sector into more efficient production units (Skogstad, 1993, 3).

Leadership on dairy supply management came first at the provincial level, where several provincial governments established marketing boards with powers to regulate fluid milk sales and negotiate prices. In 1965, acting on the recommendation of a commission that had been asked to address the chaotic marketing conditions and discord in the industry, the Ontario government established the first province-wide marketing board in Canada to control fluid milk production by distributing quotas to individual producers. By 1968, it had empowered the Ontario Milk Marketing Board to purchase all fluid milk in the province, establish minimum prices for its sales to dairies/processors, pool the revenues received from all fluid milk sales, and distribute them across producers in proportion to their individual sales (Nurse-Gupta, 2017). The regulation of fluid milk sales, however, did nothing to solve the problem of oversupplies and low prices in the industrial milk sector, where producers dumped milk excess to their fluid milk quota.

Owing to the jurisdictional limits of provincial legislation and its historic role in supporting prices of industrial milk, the Government of Canada also faced persistent pressure to remedy the instability and oversupplies in the dairy sector. Throughout the 1960s, the well-organized farm lobby, with the support of MPs in all federal political parties, called for federal action. At the urging of the Canadian Federation of Agriculture (CFA), which represented farm organizations in every province, and under pressure from provinces, the federal minister of agriculture convened a national conference on the state of the dairy industry in February 1963. Attended by the Dairy Farmers of Canada representing dairy producers, the National Dairy Council representing dairy processors, the CFA, the National Farmers Union, and representatives of federal and provincial governments, it called for a national dairy policy and the formation of a Canadian Dairy Advisory Committee to agree on its details. Acting on that recommendation in June 1963, federal Minister of Agriculture Harry Hays appointed representatives of farm federations, dairy producers, dairy processors, provincial governments, and one federal appointee to the Advisory Committee.

The Report of the Advisory Committee served as a blueprint for the policy instruments and institutions of national dairy supply management (Scullion, 2006, 23). It recommended the formation of a 'national dairy authority' which would, in cooperation with provincial governments, have powers to negotiate and administer national marketing quotas. It also recommended this authority assume responsibility from the minister of agriculture for support of industrial milk prices, as well as for the export and import of dairy products. These recommendations took effect with the passage of the Canadian Dairy Commission Act (CDC Act) in 1966. The Act provided the legislative basis for the implementation of supply management of industrial milk, creating a federal body, the Canadian Dairy Commission (CDC), and a Consultative Committee that would assist the Commission in setting policies for milk production, dairy price supports, and dairy product exports.

The institutions and instruments of supply management—production controls, administered pricing, and import controls—were put in place over the next years. Implementing nation-wide production controls on industrial milk—necessary to stabilize domestic milk production—was challenging and required cooperation across provinces. This cooperation materialized only when Ontario and Québec, which together accounted for almost three quarters of Canadian milk production and processing (Scullion, 2006, 14), brought their industrial milk under a market-sharing quota system. By 1974, the other nine provinces with a dairy sector (excluding Newfoundland) had done so as well. In 1975, the task of recommending the annual national market sharing quota and its allocation among provinces was given to the Canadian Milk Supply Management Committee (the CMSMC). Chaired by the CDC, the CMSMC's other members are the provincial milk marketing boards, and ex-officio delegates from Dairy Farmers of Canada, and the organization representing dairy processors. On the advice of the CMSMC, CDC sets national production quota levels. Provincial milk boards then allocate their provincial share among farmers, negotiate prices with buyers, and set quota transfer rules.

The CDC assumed responsibility for the other two instruments of supply management: administered pricing and import controls. With respect to administered pricing, the CDC establishes support prices for dairy products (cheese, butter, skim milk powder), which are then used as a reference by provincial marketing boards to determine prices paid by dairy processors for milk. Until 1995, countries were allowed under the General Agreement on Tariffs and Trade, (GATT) to control the quantities of imports, providing they controlled domestic production. Until 2002, when they were ruled illegal by the World Trade Organization, subsidies of dairy exports were also an important safety valve to keep domestic milk supplies in equilibrium with domestic demand (Skogstad, 2008, 262–264).

The Egg and Poultry Sectors

Similar problems and concerns explain the establishment of supply management in the egg, chicken/broiler, and turkey sectors: that is, domestic production in excess of domestic demand, low returns to producers, conflicts between producers and processors, rising government payments to support poultry prices, smaller processors facing financial problems, and the threatened loss of the Canadian market to vertically integrated American companies. An additional element was the 1970 chicken and egg wars, occasioned when the Québec egg board and the Ontario chicken board erected, respectively, barriers to the entry of these products from other provinces. National supply management emerged as the only effective mechanism of production controls when, in the so-called Manitoba Egg

Reference Case, the Supreme Court of Canada ruled provincial restrictions on interprovincial trade illegal in 1971.

In advance of the Supreme Court ruling, the Canadian Federation of Agriculture and organizations representing the poultry industry had called for national marketing board legislation. So had the Federal Task Force on Agriculture (1969, 328), commissioned by the federal minister of agriculture, Bud Olson, to recommend policies to improve the viability of Canadian agriculture. Bud Olson agreed that national marketing boards with supply management powers were needed to rectify Canadian farmers' recurring low incomes and dwindling economic clout (Skogstad, 1980, 91-92).

Although it was opposed by the official Opposition, the legislation Olson introduced in 1970 to enable national marketing agencies was assured passage by the Liberal government's majority. That majority included a significant bloc of Québec and Ontario MPs whose constituents included the majority of Canadian egg and poultry producers. Still, passage of the legislation was delayed until Olson made amendments to secure the approval of provincial governments; these amendments strengthened the role of provinces and producers in the establishment and administration of national supply management plans (Skogstad, 1987, 90). At the same time, vigorous opposition from the cattle sector and the official Opposition Conservative Party led to the reduced scope of the legislation.

Following the passage of the Farm Products Marketing Agencies Act in 1972, national marketing agencies with supply management powers were established in 1972 for eggs, in 1973 for turkeys, in 1978 for chickens, and in 1986 for chicken hatching eggs. The national marketing agencies are overseen by a national supervisory body appointed by the government of Canada. Called the Farm Products Council of Canada since 2009, this body has authority to approve national marketing agency regulations with respect to quota allocations and producer levies (to finance their operations), as well as to investigate any complaints that arise with respect to marketing agency operations. The national agencies establish the total amount of a product that can be produced and allocate production quotas for each province. The latter quotas are, in turn, allocated by provincial marketing boards to individual producers. Provincial marketing boards exercise authority delegated to them by the federal government to regulate interprovincial shipments of poultry/egg products and to fix and collect levies for interprovincial and export sales. Provincial marketing boards also determine the prices individual producers receive, using a formula based on their costs of production and market conditions. As with dairy supply management, the quantity of poultry/egg imports entering Canada is controlled under the terms of international agreements Canada has signed.

As illustrated above, Canadian supply management would not have come into being without the pressures of an economic crisis in Canadian agriculture; the political mobilization of farm organizations in response to it; and, above all, the support of federal and provincial agriculture ministers who believed, out of conviction or self-interest, that the state had a role to play in stabilizing the agricultural sector.

Implementation: From Precarious to Resilient Success

The discussion of the success of supply management is usefully divided into two periods based on the source and nature of the challenges to its success over time. During the first period, when the institutions and policy instruments of supply management were being established, the success of supply management hinged overwhelmingly on its demonstration that it could bring domestic supply into alignment with domestic demand. During the second period, whose beginning dates roughly from the late 1980s onward, the capacity of supply management to secure its objectives has been contingent not only on domestic events, but also events emanating from the international political economy.

The discussion below provides a brief assessment of the precarious success of supply management during its early start-up years. A fuller assessment of its long-term success, discussed later in the paper, is one of either resilient or conflicted success, depending upon the success criterion used and the assessor.

Starting Up: Precarious Success

The foremost and earliest challenge for supply management was demonstrating its ability to bring supplies of dairy and poultry products into equilibrium with demand for them. This task proved especially difficult in the early years. By 1975, dairy production exceeded the initial allocation of national dairy quotas and domestic demand. As the federal government's costs of supporting dairy prices and purchasing surplus dairy products rose, Minister of Agriculture Eugene Whelan saw the need to intervene directly to reduce the total dairy quota by 18 per cent and freeze the dairy subsidy in 1976. His decision brought 10,000 angry dairy farmers to Parliament Hill (Scullion, 2006, 54). Growing pains also occurred in the egg sector where production exceeded demand/quota and costs mounted for the storage and disposal of excess products. Twenty-eight million (surplus) eggs purchased by the Canadian Egg Marketing Agency (CEMA) had to be destroyed in 1974 when they rotted in storage (Skogstad, 1987, 99).

These visible programmatic failures to manage supplies and stabilize the supply-managed sectors attracted the attention of the media and critics of regulated marketing. Reports prepared by the federally funded Economic Council of Canada in the early 1980s were highly critical of the chicken and egg marketing agencies, accusing them of 'unduly' raising consumer prices, providing 'excessive' returns to farmers, and failing 'to balance the public interest and the specific interests of other participants in the food system against those of producers' (Arcus, 1981; Forbes et al., 1982, 113).

The precarious programmatic success of supply management during its earliest decade was accompanied by its conflicted success on policy process grounds. The national marketing agencies and provincial boards responsible for the administration of egg and poultry supply management publicly challenged one another's authority with respect to establishing and enforcing regulations regarding crucial matters, like the allocation of provincial market shares/quotas and pricing formula. Provincial marketing boards threatened to, and sometimes did, leave the national marketing agency when they did not get what they believed was their fair market share. For example, British Columbia withdrew from the national dairy supply management system in 1983, returning a year later only once its demands for a larger share of the national quota were met (Scullion, 2006, 83-86). British Columbia also served withdrawal notices from the national chicken marketing agency in the 1980s, and Alberta remained outside it for a time (Skogstad, 1987, 97; Skogstad, 2008, 151). In addition, national marketing agencies also openly defied the orders of the national supervisory agency (Skogstad, 1987, 97-103).

Political intervention and support were crucial to supply management resolving these disputes, some of which pitted Ontario and Québec against one another in the early 1980s. Federal and provincial ministers of agriculture warned administrators responsible for supply management that they had to cooperate in order to silence critics of supply management (Skogstad, 1987, 100–102). At the same time, federal Minister of Agriculture Eugene Whelan, under whose watch egg and poultry marketing boards were created, remained committed to orderly marketing. In fact, such was his commitment that on his induction into the Ontario Hall of Agricultural Fame, a nomination supported by organizations representing all the supply managed sectors, the eulogy heaped praise on Whelan for his 'unwavering belief in orderly marketing' (Ontario Agricultural Hall of Fame, n.d.) He rebuffed critics of poultry and egg supply management by arguing that supply management was 'an efficient way of protecting domestic producers' as it guaranteed them 'a fair price for their product' even while stabilizing prices for processors and consumers (Whelan and Archbold, 1986, 149). The support of Whelan, and his counterparts in the governments of Ontario and Québec, where the supply managed sectors are concentrated, enabled supply management to weather the early programmatic and process failures that put it in jeopardy.

Adapting to New Realities: Towards Resilient Success

Since the mid-1980s, Canada's negotiation and signing of market-liberalizing international trade agreements has required supply management to succeed in a context that differs appreciably from that in which it was conceived and set up. The latter context, as defined by the GATT trading regime, gave national governments a relatively free hand to protect their agricultural producers and spend on their behalf. The new context, and the extent of its pressures on supply management, have built up gradually. Neither the 1989 Free Trade Agreement between Canada and the United States, nor the 1994 North American Free Trade Agreement (NAFTA), that included Mexico directly, imperilled supply management. Nor did the 1995 implementation of the World Trade Organization (WTO) Agreement on Agriculture. Like NAFTA, the Agreement on Agriculture did not immediately circumscribe Canadian agricultural policies, including those for supply management. The GATT prohibition on imports (given domestic supply management) was replaced in the Agreement on Agriculture with bound tariffs and tariff rate quotas (TRQs). The latter allowed small amounts of imports to enter Canada at low tariffs but imposed high tariffs on imports above these quotas. The TRQs that Canada successfully negotiated for supply managed products, facilitated by the extensive lobbying of organizations representing dairy and poultry producers, were set at a sufficiently high level that they continued to protect the supply managed sectors from foreign competition.

Nonetheless, the WTO Agreement on Agriculture, like NAFTA and subsequent regional trade agreements Canada has signed, have constrained the country's independence with respect to supply management policies. All three instruments of supply management have been affected. Import barriers that protected the domestic market for Canadian supply managed producers have been most visibly affected; the most recent agreements signed by Canada in 2017 and 2018 increased the quantities of Canadian imports of supply managed products.

Although no trade agreement has jeopardized the powers of Canadian poultry and marketing boards and the CDC to negotiate or set prices, Canada's right to regulate domestic production—a crucial instrument of supply management—has been indirectly affected by Canada's entry into international trade agreements. NAFTA's phasing out of tariffs on food products containing less than 50 per cent supply managed products and tariff exemptions on some consumer-ready foods containing supply managed products have put pressure on cost-of-production administered pricing. Canadian food processors and manufacturers argue the prices they pay for these inputs need to be competitive (lower) with those of like imports into Canada. Domestic production controls have also been affected by restrictions on export subsidies by the WTO Agreement on Agriculture, as noted earlier. With options for surplus disposal significantly limited, milk supplies have had to be more closely regulated so as not to exceed demand. The international trade agreements signed by Canada in the past five years, which have permitted more dairy and poultry products to enter Canada, have required reductions in the production quotas of Canadian farmers.

The effectiveness and legitimacy of supply management and its policy instruments have also been affected by other factors. Some of these are exogenous to supply management, like shifting consumer preferences for more processed foods, and technological developments, most apparent in the dairy sector, that create substitutes for milk (Doyon, 2011). Others are endogenous to supply management, like the inflation of quota values (as expressed by the cost of dairy herds, for example) that create significant financial hurdles for successive generations of farmers to enter supply managed sectors. Amidst 'reform-or-else' exhortations from federal ministers of agriculture, and pressures from external trading partners, the success of supply management has been contingent upon its ability to evolve. The discussion below evaluates its success in doing so.

Process Assessment

Using McConnell's (2010, 353) process success criteria, administrative processes with respect to supply management are successful when they are: (a) effective in addressing problems that threaten its goals and/or instruments; (b) perceived as legitimate by affected stakeholders; (c) preserve intact the coalition supportive of supply management; and (d) encourage innovation. The last criterion (d) is dealt with below in the evaluation of the programmatic success of supply management.

Evaluated across the first three criteria, supply management is arguably a case of conflicted success on the first criterion. On the one hand, those responsible for the administration of dairy and poultry supply management have sought ways to address the challenges to policy instruments posed by international trade agreements and endogenous developments. Reforms to an administered pricing formula that are more responsive to the economic interests of those further down the supply value chain seeking lower cost inputs are a successful example of such efforts. On the other hand, attempted reforms have not always been effective, and have occasioned sufficient international backlash to be abandoned. For example, when a special class of milk created to give Canadian dairy processors incentives to purchase Canadian milk rather than a US milk substitute not produced in Canada met with the ire of the United States, Canada agreed to eliminate it as part of its concessions to conclude the renegotiated NAFTA.

The legitimacy of national supply management marketing agencies has been enhanced (criterion b) but, again, not to the degree needed to completely silence their critics. Among producers themselves, interprovincial conflicts over market share that prompted exits of provinces from national marketing agencies in their start up years no longer occur. Relations between national poultry marketing agencies and the federal Farm Products Council of Canada have improved, as has the capacity of the latter to monitor the performance of the national agencies. The legitimacy of poultry supply management processes has also been beefed up by reforms to national marketing agencies to provide representation for the processors, further processors and restaurants who use supply managed products as an input.

These reforms have weakened, but not eliminated, perceptions of producer domination of the institutions that administer poultry and supply management. This perception of a producer bias does not apply to dairy supply management to the same degree. Dairy processors have enjoyed representation, alongside producers, on the Canadian Dairy Commission since the outset, and milk producers and processors appear to have a good working relationship at the provincial level. As the chair of Québec Milk Marketing Board recently stated: 'Our relationship with processors has aged well … It is stronger and less confrontational. Even though we each have our own interests, we have common threats' (Letendre, 2019, 5). However, there have been recent calls for the Canadian Dairy Commission to be more transparent and accountable (Charlebois et al., 2020).

On the final criterion of process success, there can be no dispute that the coalition in support of dairy and poultry supply management has been remarkably durable. This durability, which owes much to the shared interest of supply managed farmers in retaining the appreciable equity and wealth they hold in quotas, has enabled the five organizations representing poultry and dairy supply management to present a united front in defence of supply management during trade negotiations that jeopardize its existence.

Programmatic Assessment

Programmatic success is measured by a) implementation of the policy in line with its objectives; b) achievement of intended policy goals and/or other beneficial social outcomes; c) the achievement of benefits for target groups; and d) a perception of a fair distribution of the benefits and costs of the policy across institutional and community stakeholders (McConnell, 2010; McConnell et al., 2020).

Recall that those who established supply management saw it as a way to deal with problems of cycles of overproduction, price instability, economic dislocation, inequities among farmers, and inequities in the market power of farmers and downstream purchasers of their commodities. The legislation enabling the establishment of dairy and poultry supply management plans identified objectives consistent with solutions to these problems. As defined by the Canadian Dairy Commission Act, the objectives of the Commission were a) to provide efficient producers of milk and cream the opportunity to obtain a fair return for their labour and investment; and b) to provide consumers of dairy products with a continuous and adequate supply of high-quality dairy products. The Farm Products Marketing Agencies Act (Section 21) renamed the Farm Products Agencies Act in 1993, stated the objectives of national poultry marketing agencies were '(a) to promote a strong, efficient and competitive production and marketing industry; and (b) to have due regard to the interests of producers and consumers of the regulated product' (Farm Products Agencies Act, n.d).

When supply management is assessed with respect to its intended goals and benefits for targeted producers, it can be rated a *success*. It enjoys the support of dairy and poultry farmers who today earn much higher and more stable revenues than did their pre-supply management predecessors. Indeed, their incomes are among the highest of Canadian farmers (Canadian Dairy Information Centre; Farm Products Council of Canada, 2019a; 2019b). The organizations that represent the supply managed sectors and the politicians that support supply management also cite the economic and societal benefits to the rural communities in which supply managed production and processing is based.

While there is little disagreement that current supply management producers are beneficiaries of supply management, future generations of dairy and poultry farmers face high entry costs owing to the appreciation of quota and other asset values. Although this unintended consequence has not deterred new farmers from entering the sectors, the inequity between current and future generations is a failure recognized by not only critics but also those who want the supply management system to survive, and believe reforms are needed for it to do so (Girouard, 2014).

Assessed on its policy goals with respect to consumers, supply management has achieved some but not all of its goals. On the one hand, it has provided consumers (including processors) of both dairy and poultry products with a continuous and adequate supply of high-quality products at non-volatile prices (Mussell et al., 2011). On the other hand, most economic analyses indicate Canadian consumers pay more for supply managed products than do their counterparts in the United States, where prices of dairy and poultry products are not administratively determined (cf. Cardwell et al., 2015; Dumais and Chassin, 2015; Findlay, 2012; Grant et al., 2014). As noted below in the assessment of the political success of supply management, higher consumer prices are not the concern for Canadian consumers that they are for free-market economists.

As mandated in its enabling legislation, poultry supply management was also expected 'to promote a strong, efficient, and competitive production and marketing industry'. The same objective could reasonably be expected of dairy supply management. Has this objective been achieved? The supply managed sectors have consolidated into fewer and larger units. Charlebois et al. (2020, Figure 8, p.15) report a decline from 145,000 dairy farms in 1971 to roughly 11,000 dairy farms in 2018 who produce slightly more milk—one possible indicator of efficiency. At the same time, critics as well as sympathizers argue the need to make changes to the quota allocation system, administered pricing, and import barriers to enhance efficiency and spur the innovation needed for growth in the domestic and export markets (Doyon, 2011; Mussell, 2011: 42; Girouard, 2014).

Efficiency and competitiveness criteria of programmatic success have acquired elevated importance in the wake of trade agreements, which have increased quantities of tariff-free imports of poultry and dairy products. As a result of Canada's new trade agreements with Europe and Asia and the renegotiated NAFTA (CUSMA), Canada's 11,000 dairy producers have lost 18 per cent of the domestic market (Dairy Farmers of Canada, 2020); its 1,100 egg producers, 7 per cent (Egg Farmers of Canada, 2018, 25); and its 3,000 chicken producers, 11 per cent (Chicken Farmers of Canada, 2018, 42). For supply managed products—like dairy, chicken, and eggs—where Canadian consumer demand is growing, Canadian producers will have to share that market growth with imported products. Where consumer demand is not growing—turkey products—imports will displace Canadian producers' current market share. While the eventual consequences of CUSMA remain unclear, some observers warn that it 'could accelerate the unwinding' of the dairy market (McKenna and Atkins, 2018, B10) unless there are major reforms to domestic quota allocations and administered pricing (Charlebois et al., 2020).

Depending upon how one weights the different indicators of programmatic success—and the seriousness of the current challenges facing supply management—it is a case of either resilient or conflicted programmatic success. It has achieved its foremost goals of bringing order to the Canadian poultry and dairy markets, raising the incomes of producers within them, and ensuring Canadian consumers receive a steady supply of high-quality dairy and poultry products. Whether one describes it as a resilient or conflicted success depends upon how significant one finds its shortfalls: higher consumer prices, barriers to entry for future generations of farmers, and regulatory rigidities that impede innovation and create inefficiencies.

Political Assessment

Policies with respect to supply management ordinarily stay out of the political limelight, and do not perturb the business of governing. Their low profile, one of McConnell's (2010, 335) success criteria, is however disrupted by periodic trade conflicts with Canada's most important trading partner, the United States, over Canada's import restrictions, especially on dairy products. Canadian efforts to negotiate liberalizing trade agreements have also elevated the political salience of supply management and drawn media attention to the critiques of market-oriented policy institutes that detail supply management's costs (as noted above). During these times, supply management becomes a matter of high politics, engaging not just trade negotiators, but also first ministers, who wrestle publicly with the challenge of reconciling Canada's broader protection of supply managed products with the country's overall interest in liberalized trade (including for the 90 per cent of Canadian farms whose incomes depend upon access to export markets).

When confronted with having to reconcile supply management with the international trade policy interests of Canada, national Conservative and Liberal governments alike have publicly remained committed to maintaining supply management. In practice, they have made concessions in the trade agreements signed in the past five years that open up the Canadian poultry, egg, and dairy markets to greater foreign competition, and have agreed to financially compensate supply managed farmers for domestic market losses. Prime Minister Stephen Harper described as 'limited' the concessions he negotiated under the Trans-Pacific Partnership (eventually signed as the CPTPP) to allow additional duty free access amounting to 3.25 per cent of Canada's current dairy production, and introduced a compensation package for supply managed farmers' domestic market losses (*National Post*, 2015). The Liberal Government raised the compensation package to $1.75 billion over eight years to compensate for additional domestic market losses under USMCA (AAFC, 2020). Both Conservative and Liberal governments defended the compensation package as necessary to support rural economies and family farms. Whether these market-opening concessions undermine the programmatic success of supply management has been discussed above. Here the question is why Canadian governments have felt it necessary to resist major reforms to the policy instrument of border protection.

McConnell's (2010, 353) other three criteria of resilient political success provide answers. Supply management, including its defence during international trade negotiations, is supported by the major political parties. For example, in the early years of the Doha Round of WTO negotiations a motion introduced by the Bloc Quebecois on 23 November 2005 to preserve supply management passed unanimously in the House of Commons. During the NAFTA renegotiation talks, a similarly worded motion introduced by the NDP on 11 June 2018 also received all party support. Parties seeking to capture office nationally, as well as all Québec-based parties, have calculated that support for supply management is favourable to their electoral prospects and/or consistent with their values. Although supply management is ideologically at odds with parties opposed to government restrictions on the freedom of individuals and market forces, these considerations are offset for conservative and liberal parties by their electoral calculus, as supporting supply management enhances their electoral prospects (Skogstad, 2021).

In supporting supply management, Canadian political parties do so with the permissive consensus of the Canadian public. In a 2017 survey undertaken by the Angus Reid Institute (2017), while a full majority of Canadians said they know 'nothing at all' about supply management, they were nonetheless sympathetic to supply-managed farmers and believed that the system should be protected (Charlebois et al., 2020). Most Canadians believe they pay a fair price for milk in Canada (Charlebois et al., 2020) and are willing to compensate farmers financially so they can recover losses endured through trade agreement concessions (Kurl, 2017). These public opinion data lend support to Peta's (2019) argument that organizations representing Canadian dairy farmers have successfully promoted the narrative that the Canadian dairy industry is a distinct Canadian cultural commodity, and one that requires supply management to defend it against threat of foreign (US, EU) markets.

Groups representing the supply managed sectors have been extremely well organized, not only on Parliament Hill but also at the venues of international trade negotiations. They have been adroit at drawing attention to the programmatic success of supply management, and the high costs that would be incurred were it to be dismantled. A widely-circulated report commissioned in 2015 by Agropur, a farmer-owned dairy cooperative based in Québec, concluded that a total and immediate opening of the dairy sector (abolition of import controls, farm production quotas, and support prices) would put 24,000 jobs at risk and reduce Canada's GDP by $3.5 billion (Boston Consulting Group, 2015). The economy of Québec would be most affected, with 50 per cent of Québec dairy farms at risk (Boston Consulting Group, 2015). During trade negotiations, including the 2018 renegotiation of NAFTA, Québec politicians of all partisan stripes have presented a united front to warn the government of Canada not to trade off supply management and the interests of the province of Québec for those of other economic sectors and provinces (Arsenault, 2018).

Although the supply managed sectors are found in every province, they are concentrated in Ontario and Québec. Québec and Ontario together account for 75 per cent of the total market sharing quota for dairy and two-thirds of dairy processing plants (Canadian Dairy Information Centre, n.d.). Ontario and Québec account for 60 per cent of chicken production, 55 per cent of egg production, and two-thirds of the poultry processing plants (Girouard, 2014, 23). The economic significance of supply management to these two vote-rich provinces is undoubtedly an important component in its resilient political success.

Conclusions and Lessons

The endurance of Canadian dairy and poultry supply management for almost fifty years is a story of policy success. But it also constitutes a puzzle when viewed from the perspective of domestic and international paradigms of appropriate models of state-market relationships. In terms of international paradigms, the logic and instruments of state assistance embodied in supply management are a vestige of the post-World War II period of embedded liberalism (Ruggie, 1982; Skogstad, 2008) and anomalous with the current orthodoxy of market liberalism in the international trade regime. Canada is at odds with other countries, such as Australia and New Zealand, that deregulated their dairy markets in the late twentieth century. Supply management is also a domestic exception in cross-provincial state-regulated marketing. The single other example, the Canadian Wheat Board, which was the sole export marketing agency for prairie grown wheat and barley for over seventy years, fell prey to the free-market ideology of the Harper Conservative government and was eliminated by it in 2011 (Skogstad and Whyte, 2015). Today, Canada's 15,000 Canadian dairy, egg, and poultry farmers are a small minority of the roughly 200,000 Canadian farmers and whose market returns vary with the vagaries of supply and demand price fluctuations. Nor is the model of state-market relations in supply management one that prevails in Canadian economic policy more generally.

Given that supply management policies are a Canadian economic policy outlier, what lessons, if any, do they offer about the dynamics of successful public policy-making in Canada? Relatedly, what do they suggest about the relative importance of the three categories of programmatic, process, and political success? Four lessons can be drawn.

First, supply management suggests that during the policy innovation phase, when the operational details of a policy are still being worked out, programmatic or process success is by no means assured and political support is crucial to a policy's survival. During this early phase, new policies are likely to lean heavily on the ideological conviction of political and institutional veto players. In the case of supply management, the decisive veto players were the ministers of agriculture in the provinces of Ontario and Québec, and the government of Canada. Without these politicians' ideological commitment to the goals they believed supply management could achieve, supply management would likely not have survived its critics. Although political support remains important thereafter, once policies have established their workability—ability to achieve their foremost programmatic objectives—they are in a position to garner support on other instrumental grounds, including electoral calculations in the case of politicians.

Second, supply management demonstrates the possibility for a collaborative model of intergovernmental relations in Canadian policy-making, and the central role that Canada's two largest provinces play in its political viability. Amidst the manifold examples of intergovernmental conflict in the Canadian federal system, national marketing agencies are a rare example of intergovernmental cooperation: that is, of provinces and Ottawa pooling their respective jurisdictional authority over intraprovincial trade, and interprovincial and export trade. Governments' willingness to cooperate has undoubtedly been influenced by pressure from farm organizations to do so and ongoing producer support for supply management.

Third, supply management highlights the significance of administrative policy subsystems as mechanisms of both policy continuity and change. In the case of supply management, producer and processor interests have considerable power in administrative decision-making. As such, while the institutions that administer supply management have sometimes been a mechanism for brokering the compromises needed to adjust policies to contextual changes over time, they have also been a brake on policy change by embedding policy ideas about appropriate state-market relationships as well as powerful organized interests.

Finally, supply management demonstrates that, in the area of economic policy-making, policy success criteria need to pass muster not only with domestic politicians and industry stakeholders but also with powerful international actors. The latter pose a threat to the continuing durability of supply management insofar as they force Canadian governments to grapple openly and directly with the political and programmatic benefits and costs of supply management.

References

Agriculture and Agri-Food Canada. 2020. "Government of Canada Announces Investments to Support Supply-Managed Dairy, Poultry and Egg Farmers." Government of Canada. 28 November. https://www.canada.ca/en/agriculture-agri-food/news/2020/11/government-of-canada-announces-investments-to-support-supply-managed-dairy-poultry-and-egg-farmers.html

Angus Reid Institute. 2017. "Supply Management: Most Canadians Say Scrapping System Should Be on the Table during NAFTA Talks." Angus Reid Institute. 2 August. http://angusreid.org/supply-management-nafta-renegotiation/

Arcus, P. L. 1981. *Broilers and Eggs*. Ottawa: Economic Council of Canada.

Arsenault, J. 2018. "Quebec's Political Parties Announce Common Front in Favour of Supply Management." CTV News. 31 August. https://www.ctvnews.ca/canada/quebec-political-parties-announce-common-front-in-favour-of-supply-management-1.4075573

Boston Consulting Group. 2015. *Analysis of the Political Impacts of the End of Supply Management in the Canadian Dairy Industry*. BCC and Agropur. https://www.agropur.com/sites/default/files/documents/Analysis_of_%20impacts_of_supply_management_Canadian_dairy_inudstry-EN.pdf

Canadian Dairy Information Centre. n.d. *Canada's Dairy Industry at a Glance*. Government of Canada. Available at https://www.dairyinfo.gc.ca/eng/about-the-canadian-dairy-information-centre/canada-s-dairy-industry-at-a-glance/?id=1502465180911. Accessed 2 February 2021.

Cardwell, R., C. Lawley, and D. Xiang. 2015. "Milked and Feathered: The Regressive Welfare Effects of Canada's Supply Management Regime." *Canadian Public Policy* 41 (1): 1–14.

Charlebois, S., J.-L. Lemieux, and S. Somogyi. 2020. *Supply Management 2.0*. Halifax, Nova Scotia: Dalhousie University Agri-Food Analytics Lab and Arrell Food Institute.

Chicken Farmers of Canada. 2018. *Annual Report*. Ottawa: CFC. https://www.chickenfarmers.ca/wp-content/uploads/2019/03/2018-Annual-Report-ENG-WEB-v1.pdf

Dairy Farmers of Canada. 2020. "Throne Speech: Government's Intention to Meet its Commitment to Dairy Farmers a Positive Step, says DFC." CISION. 23 September. Available at: https://www.newswire.ca/news-releases/throne-speech-government-s-intention-to-meet-its-commitment-to-dairy-farmers-a-positive-step-says-dfc-869009495.html

Doyon, M. 2011. *Canada's Dairy Supply Management: Comprehensive Review and Outlook for the Future*. CIRANO. https://www.cirano.qc.ca/pdf/publication/2011DT-01.pdf

Dumais, Mario and Yuri Chassin. 2015. Canada's Harmful Supply Management Policies. Montreal: Montreal Economic Institute. URL: https://www.iedm.org/files/lepoint0515_en.pdf

Egg Farmers of Canada. 2018. *Annual Report*. Ottawa. Accessed: 2 February 2020.

Farm Products Council of Canada. 2015. *2015–2018 Strategic Plan: Leadership in Changing Times*. Ottawa: FPCC https://www.canada.ca/content/dam/fpcc-cpac/documents/20161101-2-en.pdf

Farm Products Council of Canada. 2019a. *Egg Industry Profile*. Ottawa: FPCC.

Farm Products Council of Canada. 2019b. *Chicken Industry Profile*. Ottawa: FPCC.

Farm Products Marketing Agencies Act. (n.d.). Ottawa. Available at: https://laws-lois.justice.gc.ca/eng/acts/F-4/index.html

Findlay, M. H. 2012. "Supply Management: Problems, Politics—and Possibilities." *SPP Research Papers* 5 (19). https://www.policyschool.ca/wp-content/uploads/2016/03/supply-management-hall-findlay.pdf

Forbes, J. D., R. D. Hughes, and T. K. Warley. 1982. *Economic Intervention and Regulation in Canadian Agriculture*. Ottawa: Economic Council of Canada and the Institute for Research on Public Policy.

Geloso, V. and A. Moreau. 2016. *Supply Management Makes the Poor Even Poorer*. Montreal: Montreal Economic Institute.

Girouard, B. 2014. *Toward Supply Management 2.0 in Canada: A Discussion Paper*. Lachute, Quebec: Union Paysanne.

Grant, Michael, Richard Barichello, Mark Liew and Vijay Gill. 2014. Reforming Dairy Supply Management: The Case for Growth. Ottawa: The Conference Board of Canada.

Heppner, K. 2017. "Dairy Farmers Made a Difference in Scheer's Surprise Win over Bernier." Real Agriculture. 29 May. https://www.realagriculture.com/2017/05/dairy-farmers-made-difference-in-scheers-surprise-win-over-bernier/

Hiscocks. G.A. 1970. "Supply Management—Definition, Techniques and Implications." *Canadian Farm Economics* 5 (2): pp. 20–26.

Kesteman, J.-P., G. Boisclair, and J.-M. Kirouac. 1984. *Histoire du syndicalisme agricole au Québec*. Montreal: Boréal Express.

Kurl, S. 2017. "Canadians' Opinions Mixed on Supply Management." Policy Options. 15 August. https://policyoptions.irpp.org/magazines/august-2017/canadians-opinions-mixed-supply-management/

Letendre, B. 2019. *"Message from the Chair"*. Les producteurs de lait du Québec Annual Report 2019. Longueuil, Quebec

McConnell, A. 2010. "Policy Success, Policy Failure and Grey Areas In-Between." *Journal of Public Policy* 30 (3): pp. 345–362.

McConnell, A., L. Grealy, and T. Lea. 2020. "Policy Success for Whom? A Framework for Analysis." *Policy Sciences* 53 (4): pp. 589–608. https://doi.org/10.1007/s11077-020-09406-y

McKenna, B. and E. Atkins. 2018. "Ottawa Promises Farmers Full Compensation for Concessions." *Globe and Mail*. 2 October. pp. B1, B10.

Mussell, A. 2011. "Supply Management: Advantage vs. Challenge." In *Advancing a Policy Dialogue*, pp. 39–43. Guelph: George Morris Centre for the Canadian Agri-Food Policy Institute. https://capi-icpa.ca/wp-content/uploads/2011/02/Understanding-the-Structure-of-Canadian-Farm-Incomes-2011.pdf

National Post. 2015. "A future of participation over isolation: Harper praises vast Trans-Pacific Partnership Trade Deal." October 5, 2015. https://nationalpost.com/news/world/trans-pacific-partnership-deal-reached-official

Nurse-Gupta, J. 2017. ""Milk Is Milk": Marketing Milk in Ontario and the Origins of Supply Management." *Journal of the Canadian Historical Association* 28 (1): pp. 127–156.

Ontario. 1965. *Report of the Ontario Milk Industry Inquiry Committee.* Toronto: Government of Ontario.

Ontario Agricultural Hall of Fame. n.d. "Hon. Eugene Whelan." Available at: https://www.oahf.on.ca/inductee/hon-eugene-whelan/

Peta, C. 2019. "Canada's Supply Management System and the Dairy Industry in the Era of Trade Liberalization: A Cultural Commodity?" *American Review of Canadian Studies* 49 (4): pp. 547–562.

Ruggie, J. G. 1982. "International Regimes, Transactions, and Change: Embedded Liberalism in the Post-War Order." *International Organization* 36 (2): pp. 379–415.

Scullion, E. 2006. *The Canadian Dairy Commission: A 40-Year Retrospective.* Ottawa: Canadian Dairy Commission.

Skogstad, G. 1980. "The Farm Products Marketing Agencies Act: A Case Study of Agricultural Policy." *Canadian Public Policy*: 6(1): pp. 91–100.

Skogstad, G. 1987. *The Politics of Agricultural Policy-Making in Canada.* Toronto: University of Toronto Press.

Skogstad, G. 1993. "Policy under Siege: Supply Management in Agricultural Marketing." *Canadian Public Administration* 36 (1): pp. 1–23.

Skogstad, G. 1998. "Canadian Federalism, Internationalization and Quebec Agriculture: Dis-Engagement, Re-Integration?" *Canadian Public Policy* 24 (1): pp. 27–48.

Skogstad, G. 2008. *Internationalization and Canadian Agriculture: Policy and Governing Paradigms.* Toronto: University of Toronto Press.

Skogstad, G. 2021. "Political Parties and Policy Change in Canadian Agricultural Marketing Institutions." *Journal of Comparative Policy Analysis* 23(5–6): pp. 561–575. https://doi.org/10.1080/13876988.2020.1749519

Skogstad, G. and T. Whyte. 2015. "Authority Contests, Power and Policy Paradigm Change: Explaining Developments in Grain Marketing Policy in Prairie Canada." *Canadian Journal of Political Science* 48 (1): pp. 79–101.

Whelan, G. E. and R. Archbold. 1986. *Whelan: The Man in the Green Stetson.* Toronto: Irwin.

15

From R&D to Export

Canola Development as a 'Resilient Success'

Matt Wilder

Introduction

Canola was not always the successful crop it is today. Rather, its development and commercialization are relatively recent. The 'canola' moniker was coined in 1978 as a means of differentiating plants that produce oilseeds with desirable attributes from traditional rapeseed. Since then, canola has evolved from a limited-use crop, the oil and meal of which was objectionable to the senses and possibly hazardous to human health, to one of the most popular, versatile, and healthy oilseeds. Canola is also one of a handful of crops that has been subject to genetic engineering.

This chapter proceeds in two steps. The first step traces the evolution of canola from its war-time use as a marine engine lubricant to a popular edible oil with novel industrial applications. The second step evaluates the success of Canadian policy towards canola in light of the programmatic, political, process, and endurance (PPPE) criteria laid out in the introduction to this volume. The thesis is that Canadian policy towards canola constitutes a 'resilient success'. This evaluation stems from the fact that, although policy towards canola encountered some modest opposition and some incidence of programmatic failure, neither has been sufficient to seriously undermine the overall track record of the policy or its continuation. Accordingly, Canadian canola development serves as an example of successful and resilient innovation and industrial policy in a liberal setting.

What accounts for the resilient success of Canadian canola policy? On one hand, canola development has been successful because policy in support of the crop has been consistent with Canada's institutional comparative advantage (cf. Hall and Soskice, 2001). Specifically, Canadian institutions permit governments and firms to pursue risky policies and radically-innovative technologies relatively unencumbered by opposing forces in society. The same cannot be said for many countries in Europe and East Asia, where opposition to transgenic crops has been both more pronounced and more effective than in North America. Moreover, to the extent that liberal institutions create potential pitfalls—namely opportunities

Matt Wilder, *From R&D to Export*. In: *Policy Success in Canada.*
Edited by Evert A. Lindquist et al., Oxford University Press. © Matt Wilder (2022).
DOI: 10.1093/oso/9780192897046.003.0015

for policy-makers to impose unreasonable costs on society—Canadian policy towards canola also benefited from co-production and private regulation, which has internalized considerable cost and risk within the beneficiary group. Government involvement has been largely limited to a supportive role, which has encouraged industry actors to take the initiative in steering the development of the technology.

On the other hand, lack of effective political representation on the part of environmentalists and organic producers created policy losers of these groups. In response, opposition groups have engaged in venue shifting tactics intended to bring potential drawbacks of canola policy to the attention of the media and the courts. While opposition groups have been unsuccessful in achieving policy change, their tactics have entailed costs for commercial interests invested in transgenic crops.

From R&D to Export

Following Phillips (2018), I document four stages of the Canadian canola industry from genesis to maturation (see also Gray et al., 2001). The first stage spanned the 1943–1967 period and was dedicated to basic research conducted predominantly in government and university labs. The second stage, from 1967 to 1973, witnessed the organization of industry associations dedicated to branding, market research, outreach, and extension. In the third stage, between 1974–1990, the initial product was perfected, transgenic processes were introduced, and private actors became noticeably active in the industry. The fourth and final stage, from 1990 to the present time, saw the clearing of regulatory hurdles and concomitant exploitation of canola's potential with respect to herbicide-tolerance, yield improvement, hardiness, genomics, gene editing, and novel applications. The fourth stage also culminated in the vertical integration of the industry in private multinational corporations.

Basic Research in the Public Sector, 1943–1967

The first phase of canola development was characterized by basic research in public laboratories. Basic research takes the form of a public good whenever circumstances prevent private firms from capturing adequate returns on investment (Arrow, 1962; Nelson, 1959). Early canola varieties were not conducive to private investment due to small acreage and because returns were not sufficiently appropriable. The seeds from newly discovered plants with novel traits could be harvested and sown free of charge. It was only with the advent of hybrid canola and technology stewardship agreements in the 1980s and 1990s that private research and development became profitable (Gray et al., 2006).

288 DEVELOPING CANOLA: FROM R&D TO EXPORT

Canadian production of rapeseed began with a garden crop planted in Shellbrook, Saskatchewan in 1936. In the early years, given its unpalatable flavour, colour, and odour, rapeseed oil was used primarily as a marine engine lubricant, while its meal was used as animal feed and fertilizer. Allied naval demand for Canadian rapeseed oil spiked during World War II when European and Asian supplies were cut off. To supply the war effort, the first commercial scale rapeseed crops were planted in 1942 in Saskatchewan and Manitoba. The effort was overseen by the Forage Crop Division of the Federal Department of Agriculture.

Scientific research on rapeseed began shortly after the wartime scale-up at federal government laboratories in Saskatoon and the University of Manitoba in Winnipeg. The development of a new method of analysing rapeseed oil by B.M. Craig at the National Research Council lab in Saskatoon led to the discovery by Keith Downey and B. Stefansson of plants that exhibited low erucic acid (McLeod, 1974). This was a major breakthrough, as erucic acid is one of two characteristics that make conventional rapeseed nutritionally undesirable, the other being high levels of sulphur compounds called glucosinolates (Boulter, 1983).

Quality improvements regarding erucic acid content created the necessary conditions for largescale commercialization. Although early entrants in the rapeseed business did not have much commercial success, those that remained enjoyed first mover advantages. This group included the Prairie Pool cooperatives, United Grain Growers, Western Canadian Seed Processors, and Canada Packers (now Maple Leaf Foods). The Prairie Pools had a marketing arrangement with Sweden's Svalöf (later acquired by BASF) dating back to the 1950s, which facilitated seed marketing on the part of the Pools. To increase oil production and assist officials in the war effort, crushing operations were established in the late 1940s. Through a joint commercial venture, the Saskatchewan, Manitoba, and Alberta Pools entered the commercial crushing business in 1956 with the establishment of Agra Vegetable Oil (later CSP and Canamera). The same year, rapeseed production spread to Alberta and, in 1960, Western Canadian Seed Processors opened a crushing plant in Lethbridge.

During this period, federal and provincial governments also started offering extension services related to rapeseed, which entailed relaying information to farmers based on results obtained on demonstration farms set up to field test new varieties. In time, universities and agriculture colleges in Alberta, Saskatchewan, and Manitoba joined federal and provincial governments in their research and extension efforts. Extension work was necessary for the success of the crop, as the farm acreage devoted to rapeseed was meagre, amounting to less than 1 per cent market share in the years following World War II (Phillips, 2018, 102).

In the late 1950s, Canada Packers' Toronto and Montréal facilities began producing bleached and deodorized shortening and salad oils from rapeseed supplied by the Prairie Pools. Obtaining regulatory approval for human consumption of rapeseed oil proved challenging, however. To that end, Canada Packers developed a relationship with the Edible Oils Institute, a Washington-based trade association, to lobby the Canadian government for product approval of margarine and shortening made from rapeseed oil against countervailing pressure from the dairy industry.

In 1965, examination of oil samples from four Western Canadian crushers led to the establishment of initial quality standards by the Edible Oils Institute, which were adopted by the Canadian Government Specification Board (McLeod, 1974). The establishment of quality standards for rapeseed coincided with the formation of the Rapeseed Association of Canada. The emergence of an official organization focused solely on the development of the rapeseed industry marked a new chapter in the story of canola development. Up to that point, industry actors were primarily interested in other agricultural products, having entered the rapeseed business as a means of diversifying their product lines. By 1965, conditions were right for the establishment of a dedicated industry.

Collaboration in Research and Development, 1967–1973

Two objectives defined the second stage of canola development. One objective involved the continuation of basic research in pursuit of plants with novel traits, including improved yield. The other objective entailed an acceleration of applied research on the amenability of novel rapeseed varieties to field conditions. Both basic and applied research involved collaboration between government, the newly formed Rapeseed Association of Canada, and universities. The major policy objective during this period was to convert rapeseed production to low erucic acid varieties, while the major research objective was to develop 'double-low' varieties that exhibited both low erucic acid content and low levels of glucosinolates. Urgency surrounding conversion to low erucic acid varieties followed from an alarming 1970 study that found conventional rapeseed oil caused heart and kidney damage in young animals. Although the findings were rebuffed by subsequent studies, the alarm created sufficient doubt in overseas markets about conventional varieties to accelerate action by government and industry towards low erucic acid varieties.

Following its establishment in 1965, the Rapeseed Association of Canada collected levies from producers on a voluntary basis and directed them towards product and market development, research, and extension. Saskatchewan and Manitoba established provincial associations shortly after the formation of the national association, followed by Alberta in the 1970s and Ontario in the late 1980s. The provincial associations were focused on extension, agronomy, and policy development, leaving the bulk of market development and pre-commercial research to the national association (Gray et al., 2001).

From 1971 to 1991, the Rapeseed Association of Canada's budget was also supplemented by a $12.5 million Rapeseed Utilization Assistance Program dedicated to pre-market research. The program was financed through the Federal Department of Industry on a matching basis with the Rapeseed Association of Canada. The federal government contributed between $200,000 and $350,000 per year, matched on a per dollar basis by the Rapeseed Association of Canada, the latter of which administered the research program in partnership with universities (Darcovich, 1973).

Two programs followed the discovery of low erucic acid producing plants in 1960. One program, undertaken between 1971 and 1974 by the Federal Department of Agriculture and the Federal Department of Health and Welfare, involved a concerted effort to convert rapeseed production to low erucic acid varieties. The other program was dedicated to the discovery and development of double-low varieties containing both low levels of erucic acid and low levels of glucosinolates, which was accomplished in 1974 when University of Manitoba scientists, B.R. Stefansson and Z.P. Kondra, developed the variety *Tower* using low glucosinolate material developed by researchers in Saskatoon. The development of *Tower* prompted the Rapeseed Association of Canada to register the canola trademark in 1978 as a designate for rapeseed containing less than 5 per cent erucic acid and less than 3mg per gram of glucosinolate. With the registration of the canola trademark, the association changed its name to the Canola Council of Canada and began researching and promoting the health benefits of canola.

There remained work to be done, however. Although initial canola varieties exhibited desirable double-low characteristics, there was a price to pay in terms of diminished yield. This 'yield drag' was not in any way related to the plant's double-low characteristics but was rather a consequence of other genetic baggage inherited from varieties in the plant's genetic lineage. It was often the case that improvements on one dimension, such as oil quality, involved trade-offs on other dimensions, such as yield and disease resistance. For instance, the high-yield variety *Westar*, developed by Agriculture Canada, dominated canola acreage for a period in the 1980s but was susceptible to blackleg fungus, which later migrated from Australia.

After the introduction of double-low rapeseed in the mid-1970s, overcoming the next obstacle required finding ways to select and exploit desirable traits without the accompanying genetic frailties. Hybrid plant breeding and transgenics were two means of achieving this objective. Although public sector research continued play a role in hybrid development and genomics, the economics surrounding these varieties were conducive to private sector research and development as well. Whereas conventional canola plants produce seeds that can be harvested and planted year after year, hybrid seed must be purchased by producers every season. For non-hybrids, the advent of licensing agreements also enabled commercial entities to capture returns on investment. Transgenic varieties were especially well-suited to licensing agreements, as seed could be sold to producers as part of a package containing broad-spectrum herbicide and seed specifically engineered to tolerate it.

Public–Private R&D Partnerships, 1974–1990

Public-private research and development partnerships characterized the third stage of the canola saga. As a consequence of decades of public sector canola research at Agriculture Canada and the National Research Council laboratories, the federal government owned substantial stocks of canola germplasm. This publicly-owned genetic material came to be valued by private sector actors looking to invest in canola. Private research on hybridization and transgenic techniques made strides in the 1980s, but required canola germplasm held by the government to become commercially viable. Public-private partnerships were thus forged with the purpose of bringing together the fruits of basic research conducted by the public sector with new discoveries made in private labs. During this period, government's role shifted from in-house plant breeding and commercialization to industry support and partnerships.

As Canadian researchers were busy developing the first double-low canola varieties, a world-changing event took place in 1973 when American scientists, Stanley Cohen and Herbert Boyer, successfully transplanted recombinant DNA between bacteria *in vitro*. Following the Cohen-Boyer discovery, initial success in transgenic agricultural biotechnology revolved around four plants: carnations, petunias, tobacco, and canola. As one confidential interviewee put it, 'canola was the only food crop, so it got a lot of people's attention.'[1]

In response to the emergence of transgenics, the Government of Canada convened a private sector taskforce in 1980 to assess the industry's potential to exploit new avenues in biotechnology. The taskforce reported favourably in 1981 and a national biotechnology strategy focused on food, forestry, and energy was implemented in 1983. The National Research Council was the lead entity for the national biotechnology strategy. The Government of Saskatchewan assembled its own council on biotechnology in 1981, and a provincial biotechnology policy was announced in 1985. Alberta, Manitoba, and Ontario announced their own provincial biotechnology policies shortly thereafter.

At the federal level, Agriculture Canada put in place complementary programs at its Ottawa and Saskatoon labs, whereby the Ottawa group focused on inserting genes and recovering transgenic plants while the Saskatoon group concentrated on the acceptance of new varieties to field conditions. Researchers from the Saskatoon and Ottawa groups met once a year to compare notes and communicate priorities.

---

[1] Confidential telephone interview conducted by the author, 2 January 2017.

292 DEVELOPING CANOLA: FROM R&D TO EXPORT

Agriculture Canada's Ottawa labs also hosted several industrial scientists from multinational corporations as part of the Foreign Investment Review Agency (FIRA) mandate put in place by the government of Pierre Elliot Trudeau in 1973.

At the Ottawa lab, Agriculture Canada researchers worked with a visiting industrial scientist from the German agrochemical firm, Hoechst, on inserting a herbicide-resistant gene owned by Hoechst into canola germplasm. The effort was a success, resulting in the first transgenic herbicide-tolerant variety, *Innovator*. This discovery set the stage for Agriculture Canada plant breeders in Saskatoon to transfer herbicide-tolerance to superior germplasm. The partnerships between Hoechst and Agriculture Canada's Ottawa and Saskatoon labs ultimately led to the commercialization of the herbicide-tolerant *Liberty Link* system in 1995, which was produced by Hoechst's successor company, AgrEvo, and marketed through the Prairie Pools as a package consisting of glufosinate herbicide and seed engineered to withstand it. Meanwhile, two other herbicide-tolerant systems were developed by American seed and chemical companies. One was Monsanto's *Roundup Ready* system, which employed transgenics and the herbicide glyphosate. The other was Pioneer Hi-Bred's *Pursuit* system, which was based on a non-transgenic process called mutagenesis, and compatible with both imidazolinone and sulfonylurea herbicides.

The transgenic technology required to develop Monsanto's *Roundup Ready* canola originated at Calgene, a southern California start-up that had patented agrobacterium transgenic processes in the early 1980s. From the beginning, researchers at Calgene were interested in developing transgenic plants resistant to glyphosate, the active ingredient in Monsanto's *Roundup* herbicide, which had been used as a general purpose weed-killer and for chemical fallowing since 1976. Yet, according to interview respondents, Calgene began working on canola after discussions with investigators affiliated with Agriculture Canada's Ottawa lab.[2] In 1989, Calgene researchers filed a patent for the 'transformation and foreign gene expression in brassica species'. This, and a similar patent filed in 1992, led to the commercialization of *Roundup Ready* canola in 1996, which was marketed by Monsanto as it completed its acquisition of Calgene.

Regarding Pioneer Hi-Bred's *Pursuit* system, the story began in Ontario with the establishment of a provincial biotechnology strategy and a company called Allelix in 1983. Allelix started out as a joint venture between Labatt Ltd., the Canadian Development Corporation, and the Government of Ontario. Although the company's initial strategy was consistent with government objectives to pursue biotechnology in agriculture, forestry, and energy, Allelix dropped energy and forestry from its portfolio in 1984 and focused its attention on specialty chemicals, fermentation, and plant breeding involving corn and potatoes. After consulting

---

[2] Confidential telephone interview conducted by the author, 22 February 2021.

with Wallace Beversdorf, a plant scientist at the University of Guelph, Allelix adjusted its plant breeding program towards canola. Shortly thereafter, Allelix hired Larry Sernyk from B.R. Stefansson's lab at the University of Manitoba, which had acquired cytoplasmic male sterility technology, useful for cultivating hybrids, from China.

Although more costly to grow, hybrid canola is superior to open-pollinating varieties in terms of yield and potential for specialty oil development. According to one interviewee, even if one could get open pollinated seed for free, it would still be more economical to purchase hybrid seed every season.[3] In 1985, Allelix entered a joint venture with the United Grain Growers marketing cooperative to develop canola hybrids. The following year, Allelix entered into an agreement with Weibull AB of Sweden to diversify its stock of canola germplasm, exchanging germplasm held by Weibull for a hybridization system owned by Allelix. Although production of specialty oil was not perfected until later, Allelix was an early mover in specialty oil and had entered negotiations in 1987 to supply Frito Lay with high stability oil engineered to extend the shelf-life of packaged fried foods.

Production of specialty oil depended on a process called mutagenesis, which involves chemically treating plants for the purpose of altering genetic composition. Mutagenesis technology gave Allelix an early edge over competitors working with transgenes, as transgenic canola did not obtain regulatory approval until the mid-1990s. By contrast, mutagenesis was a well-established and accepted process in both North American and overseas markets. In 1987, Allelix entered into an agreement with the multinational chemical company Cyanamid to develop, through mutagenesis, canola resistant to its imidazolinone herbicide compound.

Allelix staff had some prior experience in non-transgenic herbicide-tolerance. Although discovered as a natural mutation—not via mutagenesis—the first herbicide-tolerant canola was developed in the late 1970s by the same University of Guelph researchers who ended up consulting with, or working for, Allelix. However, this 'triazine-tolerant' canola, which was commercialized by the University of Guelph in 1984, had unavoidable trade-offs regarding photosynthetic efficiency that diminished yield to such an extent that triazine-tolerant varieties were of little value.

Labatt and the Canada Development Corporation divested their shares in Allelix in 1990, and the company was sold to Pioneer Hi-Bred as part of the latter's effort to diversify its investment portfolio. Up to that point, Pioneer Hi-Bred had specialized in hybrid corn. The purpose of acquiring Allelix was to tap into hybrid canola and the specialty oils that could be produced from its seeds. The imidazolinone-tolerant system that materialized from the Allelix-Cyanamid venture was trademarked *Pursuit* by Pioneer in 1990. The complementary seed

---

[3] Confidential telephone interview conducted by the author, 6 September 2020.

294 DEVELOPING CANOLA: FROM R&D TO EXPORT

was marketed as *Delta* by United Grain Growers, which maintained its former marketing relationship with Allelix after its acquisition by Pioneer.

Besides providing canola germplasm as a public good, the government also provided infrastructure and absorbed costs associated with coordinating the industry. In 1983, as part of the national biotechnology strategy, the federal government expanded the National Research Council Prairie Regional Lab to establish the National Research Council Plant Biotechnology Institute at the University of Saskatchewan, which incubated several commercial start-ups. In 1987, the Saskatchewan Research Council opened Genserv, a public genetics lab oriented towards commercialization. In 1989, the Saskatchewan government established Ag-West Biotech Inc, a government-subsidized, independent, not-for-profit company with a mandate to coordinate the sector. The Saskatchewan Economic Development Corporation (SEDCO) also invested several hundred million dollars in Innovation Place. Originally built in the late 1970s to attract and incubate an information technology industry in Saskatchewan, Innovation Place was reoriented towards agricultural biotechnology in the early 1980s. Innovation Place continues to house the core of the Saskatchewan agricultural biotechnology cluster.

While government provision of public goods was a major factor in canola development, the importance of a favourable regulatory environment should not be discounted. Phillips (2001) attributes the emergence of the Canadian agricultural biotechnology industry to the amenability of Canadian law to the new technology, namely intellectual property rights, and Canada's regulatory approval of transgenic crops. Although intellectual property rights for whole plants were not established in Canada until 1990, and although regulatory clearance for transgenic crops was not granted until 1995, Phillips argues that expressed intentions from the late 1970s onward were sufficient to both stimulate private activity in agricultural biotechnology and attract private firms to Canada. While a favourable regulatory environment may have been necessary to prompt investment, regulation alone was insufficient to mobilize the industry. Whereas the third stage was predominantly characterized by voluntary partnerships, the fourth phase of canola development was marked by active policy measures to attract firms with competence in hybridization, transgenic processes, and agrochemicals to Canada.

Regulation and Consolidation, 1990–Present

Buoyed by early success with herbicide-tolerant and hybrid canola, the Saskatchewan government arranged for several foreign firms to establish operations in Saskatoon by offering grants, loans, and equity financing as part of its Partnership for Renewal (Saskatchewan, 1992). According to interviewees, this policy of enticing firms with technical know-how to locate in Canada was encouraged by the scientific community, which believed that geographic dispersion of technical expertise hindered the uptake of innovation in the canola sector.[4] This foreign investment strategy coincided with the push among industry actors to obtain regulatory approval for new plants and agrochemicals. Consistent with the argument from Phillips (2001) summarized above, federal amenability to transgenic crops was signalled, first, by the 1983 National Biotechnology Strategy and, subsequently, by the government's Agricultural Policy Framework and Growing Forward strategies (Canada, 2008). These policies also permitted the consolidation of the industry in a limited number of multinational corporations.

Financing came from a variety of sources. The Royal Bank of Canada (RBC) and the Canadian Imperial Bank of Commerce (CIBC) partnered with the federal Department of Western Economic Diversification in the early 1990s to supply seed money to knowledge-based industries. Provincial funding was also funnelled through government investment entities, like the Saskatchewan Economic Development Corporation (SEDCO), and Crown Investment Corporation (CIC), as well as the government-subsidized but private not-for-profit organization, Ag-West Biotech Inc. Ag-West has operated as a coordinating, networking, and investment entity since 1989, and absorbed the International Centre for Agricultural Science and Technology (ICAST) investment portfolio in 1997. There were also direct government subsidies from various funds administered by government ministries. Although investments made through government investment bodies and Ag-West were not expected to be lucrative, the fact that investments were extended as loans (as opposed to subsidies) allowed some expenses to be recouped. Of the $11.97 million invested by Ag-West from 1989 to 2012, Smyth et al. (2013) found $4.75 million had been repaid. With ICAST write-offs omitted from the calculations, Ag-West's investment recovery rate was 50 per cent.

The Pool cooperatives and growers' associations also devoted significant portions of their budgets to research and development partnerships. Producer associations ramped up their involvement in research and development just as large agrochemical businesses turned their attention to canola in the late 1980s. To finance their research and development efforts, producer associations in Alberta, Saskatchewan, and Manitoba implemented mandatory levies of $0.50 per tonne of canola seed for growers, crushers, and exporters in 1989, 1991, and 1996, respectively (Gray et al., 2001, 100–101).

Whereas investments by producer associations were primarily oriented towards pre-commercial research and development, investments undertaken by government, Ag-West, banks, and the Prairie Pools were directed mainly towards commercial production. Four investments in particular attracted firms with competence useful to the industry to locate their operations to Saskatchewan. The first

---

[4] Confidential telephone interview conducted by the author, 22 November 2018.

296 DEVELOPING CANOLA: FROM R&D TO EXPORT

was an investment in Plant Genetic Systems of Belgium organized by the government through the Royal Bank in 1993. The purpose of this investment was to access proprietary genetic markers owned by Plant Genetic Systems. The second investment, the following year, transferred $6 million from SEDCO to French seed giant, Groupe Limagrain, which located its $13 million global canola research centre in Innovation Place as a result. The third major investment was a $500,000 ICAST and Ag-West enticement to US-based Mycogen, owner of several *Bt* genes, in 1997. The fourth investment, executed in 1999, transferred $7.6 million from SEDCO and CIC to the Canadian plant acclimation firm, Performance Plants.

Other notable investments included a ten year strategic alliance between Dow Agrosciences and the National Research Council's Plant Biotechnology Institute to enhance canola seed quality; a 1996 Saskatchewan Wheat Pool partnership with Calgene to exploit complementarities between the former's proprietary germplasm and the latter's transgenic patents; a follow up 1997 investment in Plant Genetic Systems worth $600,000 undertaken by Ag-West for hybrid development; and a 1992–1996 partnership between Ag-West, Western Economic Diversification, Saskatchewan Wheat Pool, and Canamera to develop *Brassica juncea*—a tame mustard species closely related to canola. Hoechst and its successor, AgrEvo, also channelled funding through Western Economic Diversification and the North American Biotechnology Initiative (NABI) to its Saskatoon operations, which is reported by an anonymous interviewee to have 'propelled [Hoechst-AgrEvo] into becoming a significant player in canola development'.[5] Other companies, such as Allelix, DuPont, Ciba-Geigy, Procter and Gamble, and Zeneca have also received assistance through government ministries. Meanwhile, efforts to entice Pioneer and Cargill to set up operations in Innovation Place were unsuccessful, although both established operations in Saskatoon.

This is not to say that all investment in the fourth phase of the industry's development ended up in Saskatchewan. As already discussed, Pioneer Hi-Bred's operations were concentrated in Southern Ontario following its acquisition of Allelix in 1990. Moreover, as Monsanto began its acquisition of Calgene in the early 1990s, Calgene's top canola scientist, Maurice Moloney, was attracted to the University of Calgary in Alberta. Moloney went on to establish a company called SemBioSys Genetics at the University of Calgary, which focused on medical applications using canola and safflower. Limagrain and Performance Plants have also since relocated to Ontario.

Not all of the investments undertaken by government and industry paid dividends, either. For instance, a partnership between Rhone Poulenc, Svalof, and the University of Manitoba to develop varieties resistant to bromoxynil herbicides fell short of commercial success. For its part, *Brassica juncea* never gained much of a foothold in terms of acreage, despite a concerted effort to develop varieties.

---

[5] Confidential telephone interview conducted by the author, 28 May 2021.

Likewise, *Brassica rapa* continued to command significant research attention even though it was crowded out by *Brassica napus* varieties in the 1990s owing to the latter's favourable characteristics regarding amenability to Canada's production intensive regions, input cost, yield, and disease resistance.

Regarding novel applications, Corteva, which was born from a merger of Dow and Dupont, has commercialized oil for use a wide range of food, industrial, and consumer products. Prior to the merger, Dow developed *Nexera* high stability fry oil for Frito Lay, after acquiring, through a series of mergers and acquisitions, mutagenesis technology originally developed by Allelix. Cargill has also emerged as a major player in specialized oil profiles derived through mutagenesis. University Technologies and Biomira, both associated with the University of Calgary, along with Mycogen, began exploring the use of canola in industrial oil and plastics in the early 1990s. Biomira was also involved in plant protein research for medical applications. Procter and Gamble, in partnership with Canamera and Calgene, began production of high-laurate canola under the trademark *Laurical* in 1997, which was used to make plant-based detergents. While high-laurate canola was abandoned on the basis that it could not compete with detergent made from palm oil, both industrial grade canola oil made from high erucic acid rapeseed (HEAR) and high-oleic fry oil have emerged as non-transgenic niche products.

Whereas commercial seed was traditionally handled as a bulk commodity, the development of 'boutique varieties' with novel traits meant that systems had to be created to segregate seeds destined for different markets. A major impetus for identity preserved production and marketing (IPPM) stemmed from the fact that European and Japanese markets had not registered transgenic canola varieties by the time these varieties became commercially available in North America (Smyth and Phillips, 2002). Consequently, continued access to overseas markets required systems for differentiating transgenic canola from conventional and non-transgenic boutique varieties, like HEAR and high-oleic fry oil. To that end, AgrEvo and Monsanto coordinated with the Canola Council of Canada to devise an IPPM system to prevent contamination of non-transgenic seed during shipping and handling (Smyth and Phillips, 2001).

While the IPPM system entailed significant costs for commercial actors, it proved insufficient due to severely restrictive tolerances being put in place by foreign regulators regarding trace amounts of transgenic material in imports of non-transgenic canola. As with any pollen-producing plant, pollen from transgenic canola can contaminate conventional canola crops, even when distances between transgenic and non-transgenic fields are great (Belcher et al., 2005). The general sentiment among industry representatives is that zero tolerance regulations exist primarily for protectionist purposes. This issue has not posed much of a problem for HEAR or high-oleic boutique varieties because the seed is crushed in North America before it is exported as oil or processed food products. Organic

298 DEVELOPING CANOLA: FROM R&D TO EXPORT

producers, by contrast, have suffered as a consequence of externalities associated with transgenic canola. Yet, in 2003, when the Saskatchewan Organic Directorate launched a class action lawsuit against Monsanto and Aventis (later Bayer) for damages from crop contamination, the Saskatchewan Court of Appeal dismissed the application to certify the class and the Supreme Court of Canada declined to hear the case.

Although mergers and acquisitions have characterized agribusiness since its beginnings, the advent of biotechnology introduced a dose of competition to agricultural industries, as start-ups began to appear and as multinationals restructured their operations towards the emerging industry. Development of the know-how to exploit the potential of hybrid and transgenic canola led to the acquisition of start-ups by large multinationals and, subsequently, mergers and acquisitions among the large firms that remained. The Pool cooperatives also witnessed consolidation and privatization in the late 1990s. The Saskatchewan Wheat Pool severed its co-operative roots to become a publicly traded company in 1996. The Alberta and Manitoba pools merged in 1998 to form Agricore Cooperative Ltd. In 2001, United Grain Growers joined Agricore under the banner of Agricore United, at which point the venture ceased to be a farmer-owned cooperative. The Saskatchewan Wheat Pool then took over Agricore United, forming Viterra.

Consolidation of the industry was not entirely without critics. Some small farmer associations have lobbied against the federal government's Growing Forward policy for permitting the seed industry to become dominated by a few multinational corporations (National Farmers Union, 2013). Indeed, as of 2010, following the acquisition of Limagrain by Monsanto and the obsolescence of *Pursuit* (Pioneer has since licensed Monsanto's *Roundup Ready* gene), 47 per cent of the Canadian canola crop was seeded with *Roundup Ready* canola, while 46 per cent was seeded for use with the *Liberty Link* system, leaving only 7 per cent of the market to other varieties (Canola Council of Canada, 2010). Moreover, after acquiring controlling interest in Plant Genetic Systems in the late 1990s, AgrEvo was itself acquired by Aventis CropScience, which was then acquired by Bayer in 2002. Bayer's acquisition of Monsanto in 2018 would have given Bayer a virtual monopoly in the Canadian seed and chemical business were it not for a remedy ordered by the Canadian Competition Bureau that Bayer divest a portion of its assets related to research and seed production, which were acquired by BASF (Canada, 2018).

Some environmental critics have also been vocal opponents of Canadian policy towards canola. While unsuccessful in effecting major policy change, these critics have proven apt at drawing negative attention to the industry by appealing to the media and the courts. In 1998, upon being sued by Monsanto for violating its *Roundup Ready* licensing agreement, Saskatchewan canola farmer, Percy Schmeiser, launched a vigorous defence and $10 million countersuit with the support of Greenpeace. The case drew considerable media attention and public debate about the perceived dangers of biotechnology, but ultimately ended with the Supreme Court of Canada ruling in Monsanto's favour.

More recently, emboldened by jury verdicts in the United States, several class action lawsuits have been launched against Monsanto and Bayer under the auspices that the *Roundup* glyphosate compound causes non-Hodgkin's lymphoma—a claim bolstered by the World Health Organization's controversial classification of glyphosate as 'probably carcinogenic to humans' (World Health Organization, 2015). As food companies and political jurisdictions consider restrictions or outright bans on glyphosate, it remains to be seen what damage may befall the many seed and chemical companies that license *Roundup Ready* canola.

A 'Resilient Success'

Canadian policy towards canola constitutes a 'resilient success' according to the programmatic, political, process, and endurance (PPPE) framework set out in the introduction to this volume. As per the following subsections, dimensions for evaluation include process success, program success, and political success. McConnell (2010) suggests ascertaining process success against four criteria: the extent to which government's policy goals and favoured instruments are preserved throughout the policy process; the extent to which the policy process is legitimate according to accepted norms of legitimacy; the extent to which policy is sustained by a durable coalition of supporting actors; and the extent to which the policy process encourages innovation. Program success reflects the extent to which outcomes are consistent with the objectives of government and stakeholders. Political success represents the extent to which political benefits of policy outweigh political costs, which entails 'marginalizing critics' and maintaining the 'broad values of government' (McConnell, 2010, 353).

Process Success

On the process dimension, although there have been refinements to the policy instruments surrounding canola development, changes have not seriously undermined policy objectives. For instance, certification of canola varieties was initially handled by a division within Agriculture Canada but was transferred to the newly created Canadian Food Inspection Agency in the early 1990s. This change arguably slowed, but did not stop, the approval process for new varieties. Previously, the agriculture policy community monopolized the agenda with a strong focus on the science of quality improvement. Relinquishment of this policy monopoly ushered in a more cautious approach, which coincided with the loss of autonomy for scientists and a concomitant increase in management. As one interviewee lamented, 'science in the government labs used to be driven quite heavily by the scientists, but

300 DEVELOPING CANOLA: FROM R&D TO EXPORT

somewhere a decision was made that you need managers ... consequently, Canada has a lot of bureaucratic inertia, and a lot of it has to do with the fact that the people in charge are general managers, not specialists, so they can't decide—they need committees, so you get all this gridlock.[6]

While changes to policy instruments surrounding approvals detracted from the consistency and expediency of the policy process, these changes arguably bolstered legitimacy. Although canola policy was contested by environmental groups, organic producers, and marginal farmer associations, opponents have thus far been unsuccessful in challenging the policy in either political or judicial forums. This suggests Canadian canola policy is sufficiently consistent with accepted norms to prevent reform via normal institutional channels. Moreover, although government has been criticized by some for permitting the industry to lead the sector with public backing, collaboration led by a durable coalition of stakeholders arguably encouraged adaptability and innovation (cf. Kneen, 1992; Pitsula and Rasmussen, 1990). In the words of a veteran member of the policy community:

> There are about ten of us who meet monthly to discuss what's hot, what's emerging, and what's not working ... Nobody's there because they're assigned by their company. They're there because they're part of this community. It's membership by merit, rather than membership by authority. I don't think anybody's there because they have a job. They're there because they have a vocation.[7]

Programmatic Success

At the program level, success has similarly been resilient. Recall that the 1983 National Biotechnology Strategy identified agriculture, energy, and forestry as target sectors. Yet, energy and forestry were dropped early on by the Allelix public-private partnership, as was its work on corn and potatoes, when the company reoriented its focus towards canola. Although such programmatic alterations may be interpreted as failures, the ability to 'fail fast' may be virtuous if it frees up resources to pursue more promising projects.

Regarding biotechnology specifically related to canola, although undoubtedly successful overall, several 'programmatic failures' can be identified. Research and development related to triazine and bromoxynil tolerance, high-laurate canola, and Brassica juncea did not yield high returns. Moreover, the IPPM and distancing systems designed to prevent contamination of organic and other non-transgenic varieties fell short of their objectives to maintain access to overseas markets, where many transgenic varieties remain uncertified. Yet, to the previous point, programmatic failure is considered by many to be a necessary evil of innovation, as

---

[6] Confidential telephone interview conducted by the author, 2 October 2018.
[7] Confidential telephone interview conducted by the author, 22 November 2018.

achieving success almost inevitably requires some incidence of failure (Alchian, 1950). Had government required industry actors to sustain programs that were failing, the cost of programmatic failure could have been much greater.

Political Success

Although policy towards canola has been criticized in some quarters, disenchantment has not been sufficient to mobilize serious political opposition. Every major Canadian political party has presided over canola policy at either the provincial or federal level, and none has implemented major reforms. The general thrust in favour of hybrids and transgenic varieties has proven resilient. This feature of Canadian public policy contrasts with the experience in Europe and Asia, where moratoria on transgenic crops and their accompanying herbicides have been issued under the aegis of the 'precautionary principle', which states that a product need not be demonstrably unsafe for regulators to deny its certification. Although sources indicate that progress is being made in a liberalizing direction in these markets, it is reported to be taking place 'at glacial speed'.[8]

Interviews with former politicians and bureaucrats suggest that opposition to agricultural biotechnology was not anticipated initially. Rather, political backing was premised on the assumption that investment in biotechnology would pay off, even if it was unclear at the outset what would be produced. In the words of one interviewee 'the early biotech strategies were pretty nebulous and undifferentiated; they were saying "this is important technology ... we're not quite sure how it is going to be used, but there are about a thousand different ways it could change the world, so we're going to support it" '.[9] This is not to say that government actors were naïve in their enthrallment with the emerging technology. On the contrary, Grant Devine, the premier of Saskatchewan who presided over the third stage of canola development, was an agricultural economist familiar with Keith Downey's research on canola and the advances being made at Agriculture Canada's Ottawa and Saskatoon labs.

Accounting for Policy Success

What explains Canada's amenability to agricultural biotechnology? According to Hall and Soskice (2001), Canada and other liberal countries possess a 'comparative institutional advantage' when it comes to the commercialization of

---

[8] Confidential telephone interview conducted by the author, 28 May 2021.
[9] Confidential telephone interview conducted by the author, 2 January 2017.

302 DEVELOPING CANOLA: FROM R&D TO EXPORT

radically-innovative technologies, like biotech. Indeed, Canadian institutions governing both public and corporate policy permit decision-makers to pursue high-risk, high-return ventures unencumbered by opposing forces in society, such as coalition partners, strong unions, and shareholders. On the political side, Canada's first-past-the-post electoral system tends to produce both centrist parties and one-party governments capable of pursuing policy objectives without compromise (Duverger, 1954; Savoie, 1999). On the business side, corporate law in North America permits executives to quickly adapt corporate strategy by facilitating stock trading, mergers, and acquisitions (Whitley, 2007).

As stated by McConnell (2010, 357) 'striving for success in one realm can mean sacrificing, intentionally or through lack of foresight, success in another... such trade-offs and tensions are at the heart of the dynamics of public policy.' While it is true that liberal institutions permit decision-makers to externalize costs and risk onto unwilling segments of society, in this case, co-production and private regulation served to internalize much of the cost and risk associated with Canadian canola policy within the beneficiary group.

For instance, the IPPM system put in place to segregate transgenic and non-transgenic varieties was financed almost entirely by industry. Government, industry, universities, producer associations, the Prairie Pools, and United Grain Growers also cultivated mutually-beneficial collaborative schemes, which gave private interests with valuable capital access to university and government research, as well as the marketing networks controlled by the Prairie Pool cooperatives and United Grain Growers. As but one example, Agriculture Canada worked with Hoechst-AgrEvo to develop the first transgenic herbicide-tolerant system, *Liberty Link*, which was marketed through the Prairie Pools. Yet, access to marketing networks was not always sufficient to elicit private investment. Allelix began as a private-public partnership, after all, which worked with University of Guelph scientists to develop the hybrids that eventually led to its buyout by Pioneer Hi-Bred. Government and university scientists were also the ones to develop triazine-tolerant canola, the precursor to canola tolerant to the imidazolinone-based *Pursuit* herbicide.

Although some criticized the focus on hybrids in the 1980s, it was not until the fourth phase (1990–present) that opposition to Canadian canola policy garnered much attention (cf. Kneen, 1992). Even so, the use of public money to attract private firms to Canada did not draw much fire, which may be explained by the fact that many such investments were scrutinized by arms-length entities like Ag-West Biotech, major banks, CIC, and SEDCO. By resisting the temptation to externalize excessive costs and risk onto the public, Canadian governments avoided political liabilities at a time when fiscal discipline was a major priority among Canadian voters (MacKinnon, 2003). To be clear, not all costs associated with canola development were internalized by its beneficiaries. Rather, the level of cost internalization was arguably sufficient to prompt wise investments and avoid waste that might otherwise have galvanized greater opposition to government policy towards canola.

Social and environmental costs cannot be so easily internalized in a liberal system, however. Consequently, opponents like Greenpeace, the National Farmers Union, the Saskatchewan Organic Directorate, and other litigants against agrochemical companies are incentivized to seek out venues in which their gripes may be heard (Baumgartner and Jones, 1991). Besides provoking media attention, in Canada, opposition strategies typically involve recourse to the courts (Pralle, 2006). Although the Supreme Court of Canada has been dismissive of opposition claims to this point, support of the courts does little to undo the negative publicity that has coincided with litigation, as Bayer's shareholders can attest.

Insofar as liberal institutions are equated with free markets, it is important to keep in mind that unregulated markets do not lend themselves to providing public goods, the likes of which the success of Canadian canola policy depended upon. Nor do markets enshrine private property rights necessary for their proper functioning. Rather, governments must enforce competition policy and guarantee property rights, both tangible and intellectual. Likewise, governments or some other non-market entity must step in to provide public goods (Picciotto, 1995). Government, Pool cooperatives, producer associations, the Edible Oils Institute, and Ag-West Biotech are examples of non-market coordination in an otherwise liberal market economy, as was the alliance between Monsanto, AgrEvo, and the Canola Council of Canada to put in place the IPPM system required to differentiate canola destined for different markets. Although industrial policy can be very wasteful, encouraging rent-seeking and moral hazard on the part of recipients of government subsidies, the approach to co-production taken in the canola industry has largely checked such tendencies (cf. Atkinson and Coleman, 1989). As discussed above, financing via producer levies and repayable loans has had the effect of internalizing some of the costs and risk associated with canola development within the beneficiary group.

Whereas Canada's liberal institutions are largely entrenched, counterweights are not automatic. Rather, checks against negative aspects of liberal institutions must be consciously designed by entrepreneurial actors. Blood, sweat, and tears went into forging cooperative marketing networks, finding ways to analyse oil composition, implementing producer levies for research and development, and striking alliances between firms, cooperatives, producer associations, government labs, and universities. Moreover, to the extent that Canada's institutional comparative advantages were realized, it must be kept in mind that institutions constrain and enable actors by specifying rules; institutions cannot act themselves (Granovetter, 1985). Thus, although Canada's regulatory environment may have been conducive to agricultural biotechnology, agency was required on the part of entrepreneurial actors to see canola's development through to fruition.

Conclusion

The story of canola development is one of taking positive steps towards ensuring the core of the industry was located in Canada and that as much value as possible was captured within the country. The protagonists were a motley group consisting of government labs, private firms, associations, cooperatives, government ministries, and universities. Achievement of these actors' objectives was facilitated by Canada's liberal institutions, which permitted risk-taking necessary to develop, commercialize, and certify radically-innovative biotechnology. Yet, to the extent that Canada's liberal institutions encourage excessive risk-taking and cost-shifting, these tendencies were blunted by the implementation of co-production schemes that internalized much of the risk in the beneficiary group, while fostering coordination necessary to bring the industry to fruition.

Not all groups in society were on-side with Canadian policy towards canola, however, making the case a 'resilient' rather than a complete success. Environmental groups opposed to genetically-modified organisms used the Supreme Court case *Monsanto Canada Inc. vs. Schmeiser* to advertise a contrary position via media outlets. Although the Supreme Court of Canada ruled in favour of Monsanto in both the Schmeiser case and the following class action suit brought on by the Saskatchewan Organic Directorate, opposition to genetically-modified crops has not gone away. While Canadian policy has been steadfast in upholding certification for transgenic crops and the herbicides that complement them, moratoria abroad and legal challenges at home have damaged the share value of agricultural biotech companies.

Against the charge that corporate concentration would lead to farmer dependence on large multinational seed and chemical corporations, Canadian policy towards canola has been similarly resilient. Although marginal groups like the National Farmers Union have aired their concerns about corporate concentration following the privatization of the cooperatives in the late 1990s, they have been unsuccessful in prompting policy change. Indeed, every major political party has sustained the general direction of Canadian policy towards canola at either the federal or provincial level, despite having the means and opportunity to change it.

The previous point draws attention to the fact that, although institutions are important, institutions do not accomplish anything on their own. Rather, entrepreneurial actors must navigate institutional channels that specify constraints and opportunities in order to realize their objectives. Without the innovative ideas of entrepreneurial actors and their willingness to pursue them, there would be no canola industry in Canada. As we have seen, Canada's liberal institutions permitted entrepreneurial actors to pursue daring positive-sum projects unhindered by forces in society that would otherwise prevent them from doing so. At the same time, policy has been designed in such a way that society was spared from bearing excessive costs. Government's role was largely limited to supporting industry-led development, which gave private actors incentive to adapt as circumstances warranted. The case serves as an example of successful innovation and industrial policy in a liberal setting. Although disaffected groups have also navigated the Canadian institutional environment to have their grievances heard, dissatisfaction has thus far been insufficient to reverse Canadian policy towards canola.

References

Alchian, A. A. 1950. "Uncertainty, Evolution, and Economic Theory." *Journal of Political Economy* 58 (3): pp. 211–221.

Arrow, K. J. 1962. "Economic Welfare and the Allocation of Resources for Invention." In *The Rate and Direction of Inventive Activity: Economic and Social Factors*, edited by R. Nelson, pp. 609–626. Princeton, NJ: Princeton University Press.

Atkinson, M. and W. Coleman. 1989. *The State, Business, and Industrial Change in Canada*. Toronto: University of Toronto Press.

Baumgartner, F. R. and B. D. Jones. 1991. "Agenda Dynamics and Policy Subsystems." *The Journal of Politics* 53 (4): pp. 1044–1074.

Belcher, K., J. Nolan, and P. Phillips. 2005. "Genetically Modified Crops and Agricultural Landscapes: Spatial Patterns of Contamination." *Ecological Economics* 53 (3): pp. 387–401.

Boulter, G. S. 1983. "The History and Marketing of Rapeseed Oil in Canada." In *High and Low Erucic Acid Rapeseed Oils*, edited by J. Kramer, F. Sauer, and W. Pigden, pp. 62–84. Don Mills: Academic Press.

Canada. 2008. *Growing Forward: A Federal-Provincial-Territorial framework Agreement on Agricultural, Agri-Food and Agri-Based Products Policy*. Ottawa: Agriculture and Agri-Food Canada.

Canada. 2018. Competition Bureau Statement regarding Bayer AG's Acquisition of Monsanto Company. Competition Bureau. 8 June. https://www.competitionbureau.gc.ca/eic/site/cb-bc.nsf/eng/04374.html

Canola Council of Canada. 2010. Estimated percentage of HT and conventional canola. https://www.canolacouncil.org/markets-stats/statistics/estimated-acreage-and-percentage/

Darcovich, W. 1973. *Rapeseed Potential in Western Canada: An Evaluation of a Research and Development Program*. Ottawa: Canada Department of Agriculture.

Duverger, M. 1954. *Political Parties: Their Organization and Activity in the Modern state*. London: Methuen.

Granovetter, M. 1985. "Economic Action and Social Structure: The Problem of Embeddedness." *American Journal of Sociology* 91 (3): pp. 481–510.

Gray, R., S. Malla, and P. Phillips. 2001. "Industrial Development and Collective Action ." In The Biotechnology Revolution in *Global Agriculture: Innovation, Invention and Investment in the Canola Industry*, edited by P. Phillips and G. Khachatourians, pp. 83–104. Wallingford: CABI Publishing.

Gray, R., S. Malla, and P. W. Phillips. 2006. "Product Innovation in the Canadian Canola Sector." *Supply Chain Management* 11 (1): pp. 65–74.

Hall, P. A. and D. W. Soskice (eds). 2001. *Varieties of Capitalism: The Institutional Foundations of Comparative Advantage*. Oxford: Oxford University Press.

Kneen, B. 1992. *The Rape of Canola*. Toronto: NC Press.

MacKinnon, J. 2003. *Minding the Public Purse: The Fiscal Crisis, Political Trade-offs, and Canada's Future*. Montreal and Kingston: McGill-Queen's University Press.

McConnell, A. 2010. "Policy Success, Policy Failure and Grey Areas In-Between." *Journal of Public Policy* 30 (3): pp. 345–362.

McLeod, A. (ed.). 1974. *The Story of Rapeseed in Western Canada*. Saskatchewan Wheat Pool.

National Farmers Union. 2013. *Growing Forward 2: Accelerating Globalization, Stalling Food Sovereignty*. Guelph: National Farmers Union.

Nelson, R. R. 1959. "The Simple Economics of Basic Scientific Research." *Journal of Political Economy* 67 (3): pp. 297–306.

Phillips, P. 2001. "Regulating Discovery." In *The Biotechnology Revolution in Global Agriculture*, edited by P. Phillips and G. Khachatourian, pp. 197–212. Wallingford: CABI Publishing.

Phillips, P. 2018. "Private–Public R&D in the Development of the Canola Industry in Canada." In *From Agriscience to Agribusiness: Theories and Practices in Technology Transfer and commercialization*, edited by N. Kalaitzandonakes, E. G. Carayannis, E. Grigoroudis, and S. Rozakis, pp. 101–118. Switzerland: Springer.

Picciotto, R. 1995. *Putting Institutional Economics to Work: From Participation to Governance*. Washington, DC: World Bank.

Pitsula, J. M. and K. A. Rasmussen. 1990. *Privatizing a Province: The New Right in Saskatchewan*. Vancouver: New Star Books.

Pralle, S. 2006. "The 'Mouse That Roared': Agenda Setting in Canadian Pesticides Politics." *Policy Studies Journal* 34 (2): pp. 171–194.

Saskatchewan. 1992. *Partnership for Renewal: A Strategy for the Saskatchewan Economy*. Queen's Printer.

Savoie, D. 1999. *Governing from the Centre: The Concentration of Power in Canadian Politics*. Toronto: University of Toronto Press.

Smyth, S. and P. Phillips. 2002. "Product Differentiation Alternatives: Identity Preservation, Segregation, and Traceability." *AgBioForum* 5 (2): pp. 30–42.

Smyth, S. and P. Phillips. 2001. "Competitors Co-operating: Establishing a Supply Chain to Manage Genetically Modified Canola." *The International Food and Agribusiness Management Review* 4 (1): pp. 51–66.

Smyth, S., P. Phillips, W. and C. Ryan. 2013. *Economic and Networking Impact Assessment for Ag-West Bio Inc: 1989-2012*. Saskatoon: Ag-West Bio Inc.

Whitley, R. 2007. *Business Systems and Organizational Capabilities: The Institutional Structuring of Competitive Competences*. Oxford: Oxford University Press.

World Health Organization. 2015. "Evaluation of Five Organophosphate Insecticides and Herbicides." *IARC Monographs, 112*.

16

Developing the Canadian Wine Industry

A Contested Success

Andrea Riccardo Migone

Introduction

While the Canadian wine industry's roots go back to the 1860s in Ontario, its most evident successes date to the late-twentieth century, when a mix of policy learning from the Australian and Californian experiences, and targeted policy measures from Canadian jurisdictions allowed it to develop into its current shape. Concentrated in British Columbia and Ontario, Canadian winemakers have, over time, developed a series of products that have enjoyed commercial and critical success. This chapter argues that the success of the Canadian wine sector over the past three decades has been quite remarkable. However, the industry may have reached a plateau, which will soon require a change of policy approach at the interprovincial level if the industry is to increase its international footprint.

Canada is a small player in the global wine landscape. However, the industry has grown substantially in terms of production and size over the last two decades. At the beginning of the twenty-first century Canada had 170 wineries (Agriculture and Agri-Food Canada, 2002), which increased to 470 in 2012 (Agriculture and Agri-Food Canada, 2012) and to 746 in 2019 (Industry Canada, 2020). Geographically, most wineries tend to be concentrated in British Columbia and Ontario, with Québec following in third place and a smattering in the Atlantic Provinces. An enduring feature of the industry is the split among producers in terms of company size (Hope-Ross, 2006). The large majority are relatively small (under 100 employees) with few very large players, such as Constellation Brands Inc., Andrew Peller Limited, and Treasury Wine Estates Ltd., often connected to global multinational corporations. Notwithstanding its small size, the Canadian wine sector has garnered important economic success. A recent economic impact report commissioned by the industry's associations estimated that each dollar spent in the sector generates $3.42 in GDP, and the overall annual value of the Canadian wine industry is $8 billion (Rimerman, 2017). Some of that success is reflected in the output

Andrea Riccardo Migone, *Developing the Canadian Wine Industry.* In: *Policy Success in Canada.*
Edited by Evert A. Lindquist et al., Oxford University Press. © Andrea Riccardo Migone (2022).
DOI: 10.1093/oso/9780192897046.003.0016

308 DEVELOPING THE CANADIAN WINE INDUSTRY

of the industry: according to the Organisation Internationale de la Vigne et du Vin (OIV), between 1995 and 2019 vineyard surface areas grew by 72 per cent to over 12 thousand hectares and per capita wine consumption rose from 7.8 litres to 14.9 litres. However, sales of Canadian products, which include wines produced in Canada or Canadian products blended with imported ones, fell from 37 per cent to 31 per cent of total wine sales (Canadian and imported). The industry also progressively expanded its export capacity, which now has a yearly value around $80 million. These figures climbed dramatically starting in 2010, immediately following the first export strategy supported by the federal government. An important percentage of export value is represented by sales of ice wine, of which Canada is one of the most stable producers. Exports for ice wine and other wines are highly concentrated in a few target countries, with China, the United States, and South Korea taking the lion's share.

This chapter applies the framework from Compton and 't Hart (2019) and Luetjens et al. (2019) to analyse the wine industry as involving two distinct policy subfields: a 'sector development' one, which comprises federal and provincial interventions to support the producers, and a 'retail and trade' one, which touches upon the framework for managing sales of both domestic and foreign wines and the attendant international trade facets of the market. The analyses in this chapter will discuss these two stages of sector development by covering three periods: an emergence stage from the 1970s to the first half of the 1990s; a growth period roughly from 1995 to 2005; and a maturity stage from the mid-2000s to the present. The first section of the chapter presents a brief sketch of the Canadian wine industry through these three stages and situates the industry within the dynamics of the global wine industry. The second section of the chapter examines in more detail how Canadian agri-food and trade policy are related to the sector, especially in terms of the increased relevance of Canada in the global wine market. The third section of the chapter offers reflections on the lessons to be drawn for policy success from the case of the Canadian wine industry.

This chapter relies on McConnell's (2010) definition of policy success, which looks at process (how a policy is designed and implemented), programs (its content), and politics (what political effects it has). Ascertaining policy success for the Canadian wine sector is complex because it is about sector development, the retail and trade of wine, and the policies of federal and provincial governments. Measuring the success of a wine industry is relatively straightforward (higher production and revenue, more sustainable winemakers, better quality product), but determining what constitutes a successful policy framework is more complicated: it depends on the actors' perspective and the stage of the wine industry's evolution. Key success indicators might be policies that enable the winemakers and vintners to thrive, along with technical and financial support. But from other new world vintners, we know that developing a clear identity for the products is crucial for asserting the value proposition of a wine-making region and, here, the industry must lead while also working with governments. From a process perspective, policies to promote the Canadian wine industry must be developed in the context of the legal, policy, and regulatory layering of the Canadian federation. Decision-makers must balance their support for the nascent wine industry with considerations around international and domestic trade rules, retail and tax revenue calculations, and consumer protection. Finally, although the wine industry has been a relatively benign policy area, generally producing win-win policies, recent conflict has emerged in the two areas of wine quality and retail practices.

Context: History and Structure of Government Activity in the Sector

The early success of the Canadian wine industry depended on small, local producers and large international corporations adapting some core lessons from other new world producers to the Canadian situation, particularly by focusing on cool climate products. This included a strategy that mostly focused on satisfying the domestic market while targeting very specific niches, such as ice wine, for export. The sector established itself relatively early as a major contributor to the agri-food business in both Ontario and British Columbia (Hope-Ross, 2006). Recently, two major trends have emerged: first, Canadian producers dramatically have increased their exports in those niche markets—albeit remaining minor global players—and, second, the Canadian market has become an important one for wine consumption.

While the success of the wine industry at large depends on a variety of complex variables, like the available *terroir* (which is relatively limited), the quality of the products, the nature of marketing, and so forth (Dana et al., 2016), in North America, government policy has been important (Carew and Florkowski, 2012a, Doloreux and Lord-Tarte, 2012, Lee and Gartner, 2015). In Canada, despite fragmented and multi-layered regulatory and legislative frameworks, the wine industry has received increasing support. Historically, governments have been important players in its development. The Government of Canada remains a relatively arms-length player in the field, mostly focusing on supporting the scientific and practical development of the sector, but also on managing barriers to international and domestic sales. Provincial governments have more direct impact through supporting the agri-food industry in their jurisdictions and by managing the retail, taxation, and trade of alcoholic beverages using similar but distinct regulations and approaches. Provincial policy for the wine sector, which grants the province with a retail monopoly, dates back to the early-twentieth century—a model found across the country except Alberta. In 1927, Ontario established the Liquor Control Board of Ontario (LCBO) after the end of prohibition (Mytelka and Goertzen, 2004), which along with the Ontario Grape Growers Marketing Board (now the Grape Growers of Ontario—GGO) created a layer of mediation between clients and suppliers. The GGO establishes bottom prices for the grape varieties marketed to end users, while the LCBO effectively has a monopoly on wine sales in the province and can control market access, especially for smaller producers. Initially, the LCBO restricted the sales of alcohol and the production of wine, and the Ontario wine industry shrank dramatically between the late 1920s and the mid-1970s (Mytelka and Goertzen, 2004, 47).

In British Columbia, as in Ontario, wineries are permitted to sell directly to the public through their own stores and to restaurants and hotels; however, most wine sales take place though the BC Liquor Distribution Board (BCLDB). Unlike its Ontario counterpart, the BCLDB aggressively promoted the sale of BC wines early on (Hickman and Padmore, 2005). Alongside the BCLDB, the Liquor and Cannabis Regulation Branch in British Columbia grants licenses for the operation of wineries and breweries. These provincial organizations have long distributed and managed alcoholic beverages in Canada, often with divergent outcomes (Bird, 2010; 2015). While parallel sales channel through supermarkets and private liquor stores have recently been allowed in many provinces, such outlets represent only a small portion of total sales. This fits the federal government's general approach to inter-jurisdictional policy-making: Ottawa is comfortable with allowing a high degree of policy latitude to each subnational jurisdiction but with the proviso that this latitude is bound by a general policy framework that is set cooperatively at an inter-jurisdictional level by all actors (Howlett and Migone, 2019).

Another characteristic of the Canadian wine sector is its diversity and fragmentation. Producers vary along two dimensions: company size and location. A majority of companies are small, or very small, in terms of acreage and production, while several are large international wine makers. Ontario and BC producers rely on local grape growers (who must compete for scarce land with other cash crops like cherries and peaches) to meet the local content requirements set by regulation and, therefore, have an important connection to agricultural policy. Geographically, the wine industry is concentrated in Ontario and British Columbia, but producers in various areas approach production and marketing differently. For example, a dispute on grape handling standards led to a split over ice wine appellation between Québec producers on one side and Ontario and BC producers on the other.

The smaller producers are unable to compete with cheaper imported wines, hence their focus on the Vintners Quality Alliance (VQA). The larger producers approached the challenge by blending domestic grapes with imported ones at the lower end of the market and/or focused on VQA products. However, the survival of smaller wineries remains an ongoing concern. Complex regulations, unclear marketing strategies by provincial retailers, high tax burdens and increased competition (VanSickle, 2020) threaten their survival in a context generally better suited for larger actors. Amidst these challenges, industry associations do not appear to be capable of playing a bridging role in what still remains a largely regionalized system, as Figure 16.1 shows.

National Organizations
• Wine Growers Canada • Canadian Grapevine Certification Network • Canadian Association of Liquor Jurisdictions

Research Organizations
• Atlantic Wine Institute • Wine Research Centre • Okanagan College • Vineland Research and Innovation Centre • Guelph Grape and Wine Research Group • Niagara College Teaching Winery • Cool Climate Oenology and Viticulture Institute

Industry Organizations				
• New Brunswick Grape Growers Association	• Wine Growers Nova Scotia	• Conseil des vins du Québec • Vignerons Indépendants du Québec	• VQA Ontario • Grape Growers of Ontario • Wine Growers Ontario • Wine Country Ontario • Ontario Craft Wineries	• Wine Growers British Columbia • British Columbia Grapegrowers Association • British Columbia Wine Authority

Fig. 16.1 Major Wine and Grape Associations in Canada

Finally, the playing field also includes consumers, who have increased in number and represent an important global market, and foreign producers, who supply the largest proportion of wines consumed in Canada and have recently become more active in lobbying for fair access. Canada has no shortage of policy actors in this area, but they are not well aligned. For example, provincial sales and retail practices have consistently run afoul of international trade rules under the General Agreement on Tariffs and Trade (GATT), and its successor, the World Trade Organization (WTO). What international trade standards deem as discriminatory practices have traditionally been seen—with some reason—by the provinces as a necessary tool to support the growth of local winemakers.

Emergence: Early Developments to Mid-1990s

The 1960s were a stepping-stone for new world producers. The BC government acted as a trailblazer when it required local products to contain at least 25 per cent local grapes (Carew and Florkowski, 2012b). As North American demand moved towards more sophisticated table wines, the industry began restructuring in this direction. Large companies began investing in new world producers, introducing better technology, and centring production on European grape varietals. Producers in California and Australia moved onto the world stage (Banks and Overton, 2010). The changes drew public support in those jurisdictions and research centres began to appear, often attached to local universities. Canada generally lagged behind until the 1970s when new boutique wineries, generally small and medium sized, started to emerge in Ontario and BC. In 1974, Donald Ziraldo and Karl Kaiser founded Inniskillin Wines in Ontario and, five years later, Harry McWatters opened Sumac Ridge Estate Winery in the Okanagan Valley. These two companies

312 DEVELOPING THE CANADIAN WINE INDUSTRY

were trailblazers in Canada's modern wine sector (Hickton and Padmore, 2005; Mytelka and Goertzen, 2004).

In the 1970s the industry began to restructure in terms of the range of products and the number and type of wineries, and moving into the early 1980s various research and adaptation initiatives were launched. For example, the Becker Project in the Okanagan, showed that properly managed *Vitis Vinifera* would produce excellent wine in this climate. The approach was replicated in Ontario and elsewhere in the country, and Canadian wines began winning international awards (Hickton and Padmore, 2005). This was at the early stage of developing an effective model for the agri-business side of the wine industry. The industry was still nascent (mostly in the area of vineyard management) and select provincial policies (especially subsidies and protective regulations) provided key support to growers and winemakers taking their first steps.

However, what pushed the Canadian wine industry 'from a weak, inward-looking industry to a prize-winning international competitor' (Hart, 2005, 6) were the many technical innovations first implemented in the early 1990s (Bramble et al., 2007; Doloreaux, 2015). An important impetus for those shifts came from external policy regime shocks. The first was the signing of the North American Free Trade Agreement (NAFTA) in 1988: grandfathered into this agreement were provisions in the Canada-U.S. Free Trade Agreement that allowed Canada to retain some protections for domestic wines in return for better access to its domestic market for US ones. However, NAFTA began to undermine the highly restrictive provincial regimes surrounding alcoholic products (Heien and Sims, 2000). A subsequent GATT decision eliminated much of the tariff protection that the industry had enjoyed, but left provinces with substantial latitude in managing wine retail. Both events stimulated the production of much higher quality wines since price was less of a factor (Hickton and Padmore, 2005; Kingsbury and Hayter, 2006). Along with trade policy change came the large-scale replacement of native grapes with the obviously successful *Vinifera* (Hope-Ross, 2006, Sharpe and Currie, 2008), which was supported by important risk-mitigation programs managed by provincial governments like the Ontario Wine Assistance Programme (OWAP) or the Grape and Wine Adjustment Assistance Program (GWAAP) in British Columbia (Carew, 1998).

Finally, wine quality standards were introduced in Ontario with the 1988 Vintners Quality Alliance (VQA), with BC adopting a variation in 1990 (Rabkin and Beatty, 2007) via the BC Wine Act of 1990. The latter act also created the BC Wine Institute (Kingsbury and Hayter, 2006), which rebranded itself as the Wine Growers British Columbia in 2021. Provincial legislation was introduced to allow for the production of Canadian wine from imported grapes and grape products. For example, the Ontario Wine Content Act, R.S.O. 1990 and the attendant regulation *R.R.O. 1990, Reg. 1099: Wine Blending Requirements*, required a minimum content of 25 per cent Ontario grapes or grape products for a wine to be labelled an Ontario-produced wine.

Sales of Canadian wines increased dramatically in the 1990s. The blending wave was both a testament to their success and an attempt from the industry to enter this lucrative market and maximize profits in the face of limited production capacity. Two major wine research centres were founded at the University of British Columbia (Wine Research Centre) and at Brock University (Cool Climate Oenology and Viticulture Institute).

By the mid-1990s, the Canadian wine industry had established itself nationally, with the help of both federal and provincial authorities supporting the sector's development. There was a clear focus, however, on increasing sales of wines even if those products were liberally blended with internationally sourced grapes, which cost much less than locally-produced ones, to increase profit margins (Cartier, 2014). By 1993, for example, the Ontario regulatory framework allowed for up to 90 per cent of non-Ontario grapes to be added to wines produced there (Carew and Florkowski, 2012a). This regulation was later reversed and requirements for Canadian content have been progressively increased. Ontario returned to 25 per cent with the Wine Content and Labelling Act, S.O 2000, and current regulations require up to 40 per cent, as per *Ontario Reg. 659/00: Content of Wine*.

From a policy perspective, Canadian governments had been crafting a relatively open and supportive policy environment. It was initially focused on ensuring that Canadian vintners could cultivate *Vitis Vinifera* as a first step in an emerging domestic market from which they could later enter the world market where they would be compared, not only to Old World brands, but also to Australian and Californian wines. This early period for the Canadian wine industry represented a cohesive approach by the industry and different levels of government. Canadian winemakers worked very hard to redefine their product as a high quality one— even if sales were maximized in the bourgeoning domestic market by blending Canadian products with imported ones. Ottawa mainly focused on supporting the agricultural efforts of the industry, while BC and Ontario mostly targeted business development, industry protection, and the large-scale planting of *Vitis Vinifera*. In short, we have fairly good indications (larger sales, better quality product, more entrants in the sector) that there was programmatic success and a high degree of process success with a relatively limited scope of policies, which targeted a small number of players. The field meets the bar for political success, but the policy goals were uncontroversial in the country insofar as they targeted a very small segment of the agri-food industry.

Growth: Mid-1990s to Mid-2000s

Two major trends dominate the policy field during this period: increased recognition of the rising relevance of the Canadian wine industry at the global level, and a progressively stronger focus on consolidating the domestic industry and growing the actual and perceived quality of its products. Between 1997 and 2005, the

314 DEVELOPING THE CANADIAN WINE INDUSTRY

Canadian wine industry's contribution to the national GDP grew at a very high yearly rate of 7.1 per cent, double the national average of other country's wine consumption. Still, the Canadian wine industry accounted for a small section of the national economy, representing only 2,500 workers in 2004 and 0.03 per cent of the gross domestic product in 2005 (Hope-Ross, 2006, 6–7). In most other successful new world producers of wine, companies had been targeting the export market. This did not occur in Canada, where expansion went hand in hand with a focus on developing higher quality wines (Carew and Florkowski, 2012a) and satisfying the growing domestic demand. As the industry changed (Cho et al., 2007), Canadians consumed a lot more wine: the average adult went from drinking 7.8 litres of wine in 1995 to drinking 14.1 litres in 2005.

Government and industry representatives from Australia, Chile, New Zealand, and the United States of America created the World Wine Trade Group (WWTG) in 1998 to wrest open domestic markets to international competition. Canada joined soon after, and today, the group also includes Argentina, Georgia, South Africa, and Uruguay. Membership in the WWTG, which highlighted the increased need for the actors involved to come to the global wine trade table and play by the rules that the major players had developed, put pressure on Canadian provincial regulations that apply differential treatment to international and local wine products. Policy consolidation for the industry passed through diverse areas such as agricultural and local planning, tourism and food sector policies (Caldwell, 2000), as well as product quality requirements. The latter was partly based on dynamics related to the increased consumption noted earlier. Part of that increased consumption was fuelled by the 'Cellared in Canada' approach, which favoured larger producers rather than boutique ones (Carew and Florkowski, 2012a). However, by the end of the 1990s, in response to a backlash against loose labelling of these blended products, more and more focus was placed on increasing the quality perception of Canadian wines. This was accomplished with legislation like the Ontario Vintners Quality Alliance Act (1999), which transformed the VQA from a voluntary tool into the formal appellation standard.

In BC, the VQA approach was supported by a shift in how the government regulated wineries in 1998. Before, three classifications existed: major (commercial wineries), estate, and farm wineries, with the estate group producing the most VQA products while the major/commercial wineries were able to produce wine without owning vineyards. But the shift to a single system, and the purchase of smaller wineries by giants like Vincor, introduced producers to the higher end of the market, increasingly coterminous with VQA (Carew and Florkowski, 2012b). In 2005, BC formalized its VQA system—which had been modelled on the Ontario one—taking responsibility for operating the appellation system through the Wines of Marked Quality Regulation (2005) enforced by an independent agency, the British Columbia Wine Authority. This formalization, aside from being an evident step towards ensuring higher quality products, marked an important step in the policy trajectory of the industry. As the quality of the products and the economic relevance of the wine sector improved, governments increasingly reframed their policy to support the quality appellation system. This made economic sense since a VQA certification enabled producers to charge higher wine prices and, while larger wineries seemed better positioned to access the VQA certification, it was also critical for smaller producers who wanted to increase their market share (Ugochukwu et al., 2017). Domestic labelling rules supporting VQA products, for example, are a boon to smaller wineries which can charge a premium for their products and can better compete with foreign products and cheaper blended wine produced in Canada.

This period showcases two different dynamics in the sector. First, the producers and the provincial governments attempted to develop a value proposition that would increase the perceived quality of Canadian wines—chiefly through the VQA model. Second, some producers—especially the larger ones—found that the Cellared in Canada (CIC) model opened an extremely profitable market. Most actors seemed to cooperate in only a loosely connected fashion, as different producers had different paths to commercial success. Governments in the key producing provinces backed the strategy of introducing the VQA model pioneered in Ontario, but were not particularly sanguine about combating the Cellared in Canada model because it ensured sales for Canadian companies and increased revenues of the liquor distribution branches. Nor were they in a hurry to dismantle the frameworks that supported the industry's development, often by tax exemptions and privileged access to the points of sale for domestic products. The federal government during these years operated mostly at arm's length from the industry: stimulating the wine sector was not a top priority at this stage.

Maturity: Mid-2000s Onwards

The mature phase of the Canadian wine industry showcases three important trends: first, compared to 25 years ago, Canadians now drink more than double the volume of wine at more than triple the value; second, the Canadian wine industry became a commercial success marked by its growth and increased focus on niche exports; and, third, global producers increased their penetration in the Canadian market. According to OIV, among the new world producers, Canada trailed only New Zealand in the growth rate of its market between 1995 and 2019 (201 per cent increase in consumption versus 159 per cent) but its wine consumption was five times as large. Underpinning this growth is a continued focus on better quality, which has come with increasing the required content of domestic grapes in wines, more stringent labelling rules, and doing away with the 'Cellared in Canada' label

316 DEVELOPING THE CANADIAN WINE INDUSTRY

in 2018. The growth in Canadian domestic consumption has triggered challenges to the policies that affect domestic and international trade of wines.

By the mid-2000s both the Okanagan and the Niagara wine clusters were established (Wolfe et al., 2005) and showcased innovative elements (Hickton and Padman, 2005; Mytelka and Goertzen, 2004). Until then, neither Canadian cluster focused much on increasing exports with innovative technology, like the Australian sector had (Aylward, 2004, 2006). However, exports—especially of ice wine—became a lot more relevant over the years. Sustained lobbying from select producers like Inniskillin (Hirasawa, 2008) and industry associations (Canadian Vintners Association, 2014) led to more attention from both Canadian governmental authorities and the producers.

The federal government stepped up its efforts in the area. In 2006, to support the growing number of wineries and vintners the government introduced legislation that exempted Canadian wines from paying excise taxes and, in March 2009, it produced its inaugural export strategy for Canadian wines (O'Dell, 2009). The strategy set the ambitious goal of doubling exports for ice wines and premium table wines by looking at other countries' export models, where partnerships between governments and the producers, alongside a more centrally delivered export strategy, proved effective in building foreign market penetration. Ottawa also decided to provide a total of up to $1.2 million in financial incentives (matching federal funds) to wineries that would participate in a collective effort to promote high-quality Canadian vintages abroad. The geographical focus for the export strategy was Asia, towards which 50 per cent of the effort would be directed, with the United States following at a close 40 per cent, and the EU at 10 per cent (O'Dell, 2009, 22). Another indicator of the new engagement with governments came in September 2009 when Agri-Food Canada granted $318,100 towards the foreign marketing of Canadian wines, and over $11 million to support the Canadian Grapevine Certification Network (CGCN) in 2018 as one of the Canadian Agricultural Partnership's Agri-Science Clusters. However, Canada believes it is necessary to honour free trade agreements and therefore, in late 2008, it agreed to WTO tax exemptions and reductions for wine and beer of Most Favoured Nations, including the EU.

At the provincial level, policy tended to focus more on industry support and development. Falling within the increasingly relevant trend towards improving the quality of the wine, for example, in 2010 the Ontario government started to provide $6 million per year worth of grants to local wineries to defray the cost of obtaining a VQA certification. Since the 2015/2016 fiscal year, the program has been managed by Agricorp for the province. In December of 2013, the government announced a provincial Wine and Grape Strategy.

The success of the industry, and the growing relevance of Canada as a consumer market, seems to be another reason for the increased provincial support to domestic producers, which is at times supplemented with direct support from Ottawa. In

2020, an export strategy was designed by the BC Wine Institute (British Columbia Wine Institute, 2020) with cooperation from all actors, and significant financial support from Ottawa. Following the examples of Australia and New Zealand, the industry increasingly looks at complex and long-term strategic approaches (British Columbia Wine Institute, 2019) and attempts to break into the large yet complex European market (Balogh, 2019). While Ontario and British Columbia remain the strongest players, the Québec government also increased its support policies starting in 2013 when it bolstered financial support to wine makers from $125,000 per year to $300,000. The province also worked with the Société des Alcools (SAQ) to increase the percentage of provincial wines in its stores.

These policies are not always well coordinated, and—as with wine trade and retail—different actors often have contrasting goals and priorities. On the one hand, there are a series of policies—often backed by funding—aimed at supporting the industry's growth and development, which are largely driven by provincial actors, with the Government of Canada actively engaged. On the other hand, there has been an ongoing process, played out on the international and interprovincial tables, of removing protectionist measures for the retail and trade legislative and regulatory frameworks for wines. At the international level, the federal government has a dominant interest in maintaining free trade, while provincial governments fight rearguard battles to retain the discriminatory rules they apply to wine sales. At the interprovincial level, where domestic movements of alcoholic beverages are concerned, the provinces have more leverage in restricting trade. Moreover, the international search for common ground on wine quality has accelerated under the WWTG. Its members have achieved important results, including agreements on labelling (2007); a memorandum of understanding on certification (2011); a further agreement on reducing unnecessary labelling barriers (2013); arrangements on analytical methodology and regulatory limits impacting trade (2014); and on information exchange, technical cooperation, and counterfeiting (2017).

Policy Dynamics in a Fragmented Landscape

The increased internationalization of the wine industry has put pressures on the Canadian wine industry to transition. The increased appetite of Canadians for wine, including imported wines, and the increase in Canadian exports of niche products such as ice wine, have put Canada's alcoholic beverages sector under increasing scrutiny and created incentives for regulatory reform. At home, provincial governments have been working to eliminate some trade barriers and restrictions. This exercise is part of a broader effort to reduce internal trade barriers that culminated in the 2017 Canadian Free Trade Agreement (CFTA), which in turn built on the Agreement on Internal Trade (AIT). A specific focus of the CFTA is the sale

318 DEVELOPING THE CANADIAN WINE INDUSTRY

and distribution of alcoholic beverages: a testament to the economic relevance of consumer interest in this sector.

Provincial liquor management boards have traditionally preferred to restrict and manage access to their jurisdiction of alcohol produced in other Canadian locations. Until 2012 this was backed up by Ottawa through the Importation of Intoxicating Liquor Act (IILA) of 1985, which forbid individuals from moving alcohol across provincial borders for personal use. The sector remains somewhat hampered by domestic trade regulations that generally place restrictions on interprovincial alcohol sales and imports, even in the face of increasing efforts to develop a more integrated domestic market. Recently, two developments framed the issue.

First, in *R. v Comeau* (2018 SCC 15 (CanLII), [2018] 1 SCR 342), the Supreme Court of Canada reaffirmed the right of provinces to limit individuals and companies from moving alcohol across provincial borders, provided that the explicit primary goal of their legislation was not to restrict inter-provincial trade.[1] The court, however, noted that a constitutionality issue might arise were provincial legislation to treat 'in-Province' producers differently from 'out of Province' ones.[2] The SCC also noted that S.121 of the Constitution Act (guaranteeing free movement within Canada of goods) should be interpreted within the broad scope of the federalism principle. In their view, insofar as the federalism principle enables diverse legal and regulatory regimes, the effective way to resolve interprovincial trade conflicts is political negotiation rather than top-down decisions. There are signs that this is what has been done at the policy level.

Second, in April 2019, Ottawa removed the remaining federal impediments to the movement of alcoholic beverages among provinces and territories by amending S. 3(1) of the IILA. Subsequently, many provinces—including BC, Ontario, Manitoba, Alberta, Saskatchewan, Nova Scotia and Prince Edward Island— removed limits to carrying personal amounts of alcohol across their borders. However, remaining differences in provincial regulations prompted the CFTA to create a dedicated website (alcohollaws.ca) highlighting critical information for consumers and businesses.

The legal and regulatory landscape remains fragmented. For example, although Ontario amended its regulations in 2019 to remove interprovincial personal exemption limits for alcohol, direct sales from producers to out-of-province consumers are not covered and the products must be ordered through the monopsony

---

[1] The decision follows the logic established in *Air Canada v Ontario (Liquor Control Board), [1997] 2 SCR 581*, where the SCC affirmed that provinces have the right to regulate the supply and demand of alcoholic beverages.

[2] Later that same year the Court of Queen's Bench of Alberta in *Steam Whistle Brewing Inc v Alberta Gaming and Liquor Commission, [2018] ABQB 476* noted, following the reasoning of *R. v Comeau*, that favourable treatment of Alberta beer brewers compared to out of province ones did constitute a 'trade restriction' and was therefore not permissible.

Liquor Control Board of Ontario. BC, which also eliminated interprovincial personal exemption limits, has allowed interprovincial shipping of 100 per cent Canadian wines since 2012. In general, however, direct-to-consumer sales are still not permitted and the various liquor control boards retain a tight hold on the sector. In this area, the different programmatic approaches to the wine trade of federal and provincial authorities affect the international negotiation process. In particular, Ottawa is closely aligned with international free trade models, while the provinces are tied to supporting the industry, even if doing so breaks WTO rules.

In the early 2000s, the increased relevance of the Canadian market for foreign wines led to a heightened scrutiny of the policy framework underpinning the industry's retail side. Over the years, provincial authorities have tended to manage this very closely, often introducing different regulatory regimes for Canadian wines and for imported wines, and, in the process, triggering various challenges to their practices in the multilateral trade regime (Lacombe, 2019). Québec introduced differential policies for provincial wines by imposing a higher administrative burden on out-of-province wines. Ontario imposed different taxation levels on out-of-province wines and restricted their shelf space. Similarly, British Columbia relegated international wine sold in its stores to specific areas, and only allowed BC wines to be sold in grocery stores. These limitations triggered a US WTO dispute (DS 520–2017), joined by Australia and later Argentina, the European Union, and New Zealand. Australia also launched an independent claim in 2018 (DS 537–2018) against procedures undertaken by British Columbia, Ontario, Québec, and Nova Scotia that it deemed were in breach of fair competition rules.

In 2020, the Canadian and Australian governments reached a partial agreement that will repeal Canadian wines from the 2006 exemption from excise payments by June 2022. The agreement also stipulated that Nova Scotia and Ontario will align their regulatory and legislative frameworks to the WTO national treatment model. This new focus is not surprising: the US note supporting DS 520 highlights that Canada is the second largest wine export market for the United States. Similarly, the Australian formal request to join the consultation states that Canada is the fourth largest export market for Australian wines and constitutes the highest value bilateral export between the two countries. Policy success will be defined differently here by various actors: while some degree of convergence will likely be imposed through WTO challenges, there is a lot more work to be done to align different visions.

Conclusion: Policy Success in the Canadian Wine Sector

Government policies for the Canadian wine sector have entailed supports for industry development as well as for the retail and distribution of wines. The former

320 DEVELOPING THE CANADIAN WINE INDUSTRY

measures were largely concentrated in the earlier period, and they, quietly but effectively, supported the establishment of a modern wine industry in Canada. These polices achieved programmatic, process, and political success, at least in BC and Ontario, and, more recently, in Québec. This policy success was built not just by government policies, like the federal support given to research and development centres, or provincial legislation and financial aid to the budding industry, but also by the active role of winemakers who—over time and with purpose—moved towards the VQA model and ensured their products were perceived as high quality by consumers. This engagement has paid substantial dividends for the wine industry across the country.

Where retail and management of wines is concerned, provincial authorities have a powerful hold, which they have used to effectively set domestic (or in some cases provincial) products on a preferential footing with respect to the competition. In terms of trade and retail of wines, international protections based on tariffs were eliminated after the last GATT round. Other provincial regulatory and policy choices—such as limiting the space where imported or non-provincially produced wines can be displayed, or where they can be sold—sought to boost the sector but ran afoul of the interests of large importers of wines into Canada, leading to WTO complaints. Trade disputes have surged in recent years as the Canadian market has become more lucrative. Opening up interprovincial trade in alcoholic beverages remains a stickier issue, but one that is on the agenda through the Federal-Provincial-Territorial Action Plan for Trade in Alcoholic Beverages.

Actors in complex policy sectors like this have different policy goals and strategies. In Canada, the progressive alignment of most actors in the industry development field has led to policy success. We can say that not only programmatic, process, and political success were achieved, there are also signs of consolidation and endurance in the system (McConnell, 2010).

The federal government has been interested in reducing market distortions in the retail of alcoholic beverages while the provinces, especially the wine producing ones, have changed their regulatory approach only under duress from WTO challenges and court decisions. The current approach to wine retail has proven commercially successful for the industry: Canadian producers focused first on satisfying domestic demand and then on ice wine as a niche—a high-return export in which they had a strong comparative advantage. This made sense, since Canada wine production emerged at the tail end of the arrival of new world producers on the global market. It also aligned well with the provincial strategy in Ontario and British Columbia of supporting the nascent sector—among other things— through the distribution chains it controlled. So, the early stages of this approach achieved programmatic, process, and political success. By favouring local products through non-tariff approaches, provincial authorities were able to use straightforward and effective policy and regulatory tools that made sense to the sector and were flexible enough to support the development of the industry (consider the retail management of both Cellared in Canada and VQA wines). This approach was enabled by the fact that Canadian production was small enough to leave ample space to imported products.

However, the increased relevance of Canada as a market for foreign wines attracted increased attention to it, making these approaches unsustainable in the long-run. The policy approach will need to change, as various provinces have recognized. However, a comprehensive policy approach has not yet emerged: a patchwork of similar, but still fragmented, regulatory and legislative landscapes is in place across the country. In this sense, changes to the process phase of policy seem to align with the spheres of competence exhibited by various actors. Ottawa favours its free trade programmatic policy approach, compatible with its longstanding commitment to support the wine industry by supporting scientific knowledge and helping frame business opportunities, like with the recent funding of export strategy analyses. In contrast, the programmatic policy approach of wine-producing provinces still relies on a number of ad hoc terms to support the industry. Where these conflict with international rules, and where Ottawa has a larger capacity, process changes have been forced that will necessarily affect the programmatic dimension. Where the negotiations are less influenced by external actors, the provinces have continued to maintain more policy autonomy. While these challenges do not constitute a failure in the Canadian wine industry retail and distribution management policy area, they flag important challenges that need to be addressed.

References

Agriculture and Agri-Food Canada. 2002. *The Canadian Wine Industry*. Ottawa: Agriculture and Agri-Food Canada.

Agriculture and Agri-Food Canada. 2012. *The Canadian Wine Industry*. Ottawa: Agriculture and Agri-Food Canada.

Aylward, D. K. 2004. "Innovation-Export Linkages within Different Cluster Models: A Case Study from the Australian Wine Industry." *Prometheus* 22 (4): pp. 423–437.

Aylward, D. K. 2006. "Global Pipelines: Profiling Successful SME Exporters within the Australian Wine Industry." *International Journal of Technology, Policy and Management* 6 (1): pp. 49–65.

Balogh, J. M. 2019. "Pricing Behaviour of the New World Wine Exporters." *International Journal of Wine Business Research* 31 (4): pp. 509–531.

Banks, G. and J. Overton. 2010. "Old World, New World, Third World? Reconceptualising the Worlds of Wine." *Journal of Wine Research* 21 (1): pp. 57–75.

Bird, M. G. 2010. "Alberta's and Ontario's Liquor Boards: Why Such Divergent Outcomes?" *Canadian Public Administration* 53 (4): pp. 509–530.

Bird, M. G. 2015. "Canadian State-Owned Enterprises: A Framework for Analyzing the Evolving Crowns." *Policy Studies* 36 (2): pp. 133–156.

Bramble, L., C. Cullen, J. Kushner, and G. Pickering. 2007. "The Development and Economic Impact of the Wine Industry in Ontario, Canada." In *Wine, Society, and*

Globalization: Multidisciplinary Perspectives on the Wine Industry, edited by G. R. Campbell and N. Guibert, 63–86. New York: Palgrave Macmillan.

British Columbia Wine Institute. 2019. *Wine BC 2030 Long-Term Strategic Plan.* Kelowna: British Columbia Wine Institute.

British Columbia Wine Institute. 2020. *2021–2023 BCWI Wine Export Strategy.* Kelowna: British Columbia Wine Institute.

Caldwell, W. J. 2000. *Planning for the Future Development of Ontario's Wine Industry.* Guelph: School of Rural Planning and Development, University of Guelph.

Canadian Vintners Association. 2014. *Red and White Export Strategy: Canadian Wine Industry Long-Term International Trade Strategy.* Ottawa: Canadian Vintners Association.

Carew, R. 1998. "The British Columbia Wine Sector and the Canada–U.S. Free Trade Agreement: Strengths and Opportunities." *Review of Agricultural Economics* 20 (1): pp. 248–258.

Carew, R. and W. J. Florkowski. 2012a. "Regulatory and Institutional Developments in the Ontario Wine and Grape Industry." *International Journal of Wine Research* 4: pp. 34–45.

Carew, R. and W. J. Florkowski. 2012b. "Wine Industry Developments in the Pacific Northwest: A Comparative Analysis of British Columbia, Washington State, and Oregon." *Journal of Wine Research* 23 (1): pp. 27–45.

Cartier, L. 2014. "The British Columbia Wine Industry: Can It Compete with the Big Guys?" *American Association of Wine Economists*, Working Paper No. 147.

Cho, D. I., M. Permyakov, and T. Ogwang. 2007. "Structural Changes in the Demand for Wine in Canada." *International Journal of Wine Business Research* 19 (4): pp. 311–326.

Compton, M. E. and P. 't Hart. 2019. "How to 'See' Great Policy Successes: A Field Guide to Spotting Policy Successes in the Wild." In *Great Policy Successes*, edited by M. Compton and P. 't Hart, pp. 1–20. Oxford: Oxford University Press.

Dana, L.-P., R. Grandinetti, and M. C. Mason. 2016. "International Entrepreneurship, Export Planning and Export Performance: Evidence from a Sample of Winemaking SMEs." *International Journal of Entrepreneurship and Small Business* 29 (4): pp. 602–626.

Doloreux, D. 2015. "Use of Internal and External Sources of Knowledge and Innovation in the Canadian Wine Industry." *Canadian Journal of Administrative Sciences* 32 (2): pp. 102–112.

Doloreux, D. and E. Lord-Tarte. 2012. "Context and Differentiation: Development of the Wine Industry in Three Canadian Regions." *The Social Science Journal* 49 (4): pp. 519–527.

Hart, M. 2005. *Great Wine, Better Cheese—How Canada Can Escape the Trap of Agricultural Supply Management.* Backgrounder no. 90. Toronto: C. D. Howe Institute.

Heien, D. and E. Sims. 2000. "The Impact of the Canada–United States Free Trade Agreement on U.S. Wine Exports." *American Journal of Agricultural Economics* 82 (1): pp. 173–182.

Hickton, C. and T. Padmore. 2005. "The Okanagan Winemaking Cluster." In *Global Networks and Local Linkages: The Paradox of Cluster Development in an Open Economy*, edited by D. A. Wolfe and M. Lucas, pp. 83–118. Montreal and Kingston: McGill-Queen's University Press.

Hirasawa, J. G. 2008. *Inniskillin and the Globalization of Icewine.* Harvard Business School Case Study No. 9-805-129. Cambridge, MA: Harvard Business School.

Hope-Ross, P. 2006. *From the Vine to the Glass: Canada's Grape and Wine Industry.* Ottawa: Statistics Canada.

Howlett, M. and A. Migone. 2019. "Over-Promising and Under-Delivering: The Canadian Policy Style." In *Policy Styles and Policy-Making: Exploring the Linkages*, edited by M. Howlett and J. Tosun, pp. 137–156. London: Routledge.

Industry Canada. 2020. *Summary—Canadian Industry Statistics—Wineries.* Ottawa: Industry Canada.

Kingsbury, A. and R. Hayter. 2006. "Business Associations and Local Development: The Okanagan Wine Industry's Response to NAFTA." *Geoforum* 37 (4): pp. 596–609.

Lacombe, M. 2019. "More Problems with Wine Regulation in Canada." *Michigan Journal of International Law Online* 41.

Lee, W. F. and W. C. Gartner. 2015. "The Effect of Wine Policy on the Emerging Cold-Hardy Wine Industry in the Northern U.S. States." *Wine Economics and Policy* 4 (1): pp. 35–44.

Luetjens, J., M. Mintrom, and P. 't Hart (eds). 2019. *Successful Public Policy: Lessons from Australia and New Zealand.* 1st edn. Canberra: ANU Press.

McConnell, A. 2010. "Policy Success, Policy Failure and Grey Areas In-Between." *Journal of Public Policy* 30 (3): pp. 345–362.

Mytelka, L. K. and H. Goertzen. 2004. "Learning, Innovation and Cluster Growth: A Study of Two Inherited Organizations in the Niagara Peninsula Wine Cluster." In *Clusters in a Cold Climate: Innovation Dynamics in a Diverse Economy*, edited by D. A. Wolfe and M. Lucas, 43–72. Montreal and Kingston: McGill-Queen's University Press.

O'Dell, S. 2009. *A National Export Strategy for Canadian Wines.* Ottawa: The National Export Working Group and Foreign Affairs and International Trade Canada.

Rabkin, D. E. and T. K. M. Beatty. 2007. "Does VQA Certification Matter? A Hedonic Analysis." *Canadian Public Policy* 33 (3): pp. 299–314.

Rimerman, F. A. 2017. *The Economic Impact of the Wine and Grape Industry in Canada 2015. Canada's Wine Economy—Ripe, Robust, Remarkable.* St. Helena: The Wine Business Center.

Sharpe, A. and I. Currie. 2008. *Competitive Intensity as Driver of Innovation and Productivity growth: A Synthesis of the Literature.* CSLS Research Report No. 2008–3. Ottawa: Centre for the Study of Living Standards.

Ugochukwu, A. I., J. E. Hobbs, and J. F. Bruneau. 2017. "Determinants of Wineries' Decisions to Seek VQA Certification in the Canadian Wine Industry." *Journal of Wine Economics* 12 (1): pp. 16–36.

VanSickle, R. 2020. "Grapes of Wrath: Trouble in Ontario Wine Country." Wines in Niagara. 9 October. https://winesinniagara.com/2020/10/grapes-of-wrath-trouble-in-ontario-wine-country/. Accessed 7 January 2021.

Wolfe, D. A., C. Davis, and M. Lucas. 2005. "Global Networks and Local Linkages: An Introduction." In *Global Networks and Local Linkages: The Paradox of Cluster Development in an Open Economy*, edited by D. A Wolfe and M. Lucas, pp. 1–23. Montreal and Kingston: McGill-Queen's University Press.

PART V
ENVIRONMENTAL POLICY SUCCESSES

17

Managing Canada's National Parks

Integrating Sustainability, Protection, and Enjoyment

Robert P. Shepherd, Diane Simsovic, and Alan Latourelle

Introduction

When Bill 85: Respecting Forest Reserves and Parks was introduced in the House of Commons in 1911, it was a low priority policy relative to mining and timber rights (Globe, 1911). The idea of 'parks' was considered a fanciful innovation that did not require much action, other than the appointment of a bureaucrat 'to oversee the forest reserves and to make any decisions necessary for the 'protection, care and management' of public parks' (Campbell, 2011, 2).

However, Alexander Haggart, an MP from Winnipeg, understood the intrinsic worth of parks and the role they could hold for future generations, but questioned how they would be managed under Bill 85. He asked whether it was wise to 'divest ourselves [Canadians] of the power of governing a kingdom', by handing stewardship to an unknown 'hired official' (House of Commons, 1911). He could not have foreseen that what was thought a minor bureaucratic decision would come to 'convince Canadians that in their national parks resided the true wealth of a kingdom ... [and that] we [Canadians] prize our national parks because they are places of physical beauty, snapshots of the incredible diversity of the Canadian landscape' (Campbell, 2011, 2). Despite early debates, Canada became the first country to dedicate a relatively independent office, Dominion Parks Branch within the Department of the Interior, to manage national parks (Hart, 2010).

Haggart's question merits review: has Parks Canada, by virtue of its dedication to conserving Canada's natural heritage, achieved 'mission mystique'? (Goodsell, 2011a, 3). Has it become a veritable public institution? (t'Hart et al., 2021) In broad terms, this chapter defines policy success regarding this policy area in the following manner: a) Parks Canada achieves highly valued social outcomes and enjoys a broad base of public support through accepted processes and costs; and b) it has sustained performance for a long time despite political and economic change. We attribute policy success to several enabling institutional features: its

---

Robert P. Shepherd, Diane Simsovic, and Alan Latourelle, *Managing Canada's National Parks*. In: *Policy Success in Canada*. Edited by Evert A. Lindquist et al., Oxford University Press. © Robert P. Shepherd, Diane Simsovic, and Alan Latourelle (2022). DOI: 10.1093/oso/9780192897046.003.0017

328 MANAGING CANADA'S NATIONAL PARKS

ability to remain non-partisan; its responsiveness to the needs and aspirations of its various stakeholder communities including Indigenous voice; and its ability to act as an independent steward, enjoying political and bureaucratic commitment to its mission.

Assessing Parks Canada: Policy Success and Mission Mystique

Charles Goodsell (2011b) proposes that some highly regarded public agencies develop *mission mystique* over time, an institutional legitimacy that results both from their clear mission to contribute to the collective good, and from how well they deliver on their mandate. Highly influenced by Selznick's (1957) classic distinction between an organization and an institution, it suggests that the intrinsic value of an institution with *mystique* is recognized both internally and externally, and that there is wide public agreement on the societal importance of its mandate. A *mystique-infused public institution* is a *policy success* because it remains true to its core purpose and consistently achieves its goals, even as it adapts and renews its activities and focus over time ('t Hart et al., 2021). It remains responsive to changing political and societal imperatives, and it is transparent in its operations subject to public scrutiny. It is an enduring success because its organizational culture imbues the institution with a shared sense of purpose, enables receptiveness to challenge, celebrates policy innovation, and supports continuous learning.

There are three main descriptors of success in mission mystique: purpose, energy, vitality. The model is not applied linearly, but rather suggests a framework that in sum identifies key archetypal elements that are needed. The mission mystique framework (Figure 17.1) aligns well with Compton and 't Hart's (2019) PPP framework for identifying policy success, with its emphasis on program, process, and political success, as well as endurance. The PPP model requires a multi-dimensional, multi-perspective, and multi-criteria approach to assessment and presumes that policy success cannot be measured without a detailed examination of its evolution and impact. Evaluating the policy success of Parks Canada benefits from both frameworks because it has a long history with many successes and failures, including that its purpose was not defined or agreed on for some time. But, its journey towards purpose, free in many ways of partisan motivations, allowed the agency to build the arrangements needed to find its place. Throughout its history, Parks Canada has reflected the political and social norms of the times and carefully integrated the needs of people with environmental protection, development, and sustainability (Kopas, 2000, 1–11). It has adapted to shifting public interest in preserving marine and terrestrial ecosystems, while at the same time satisfying economic and social considerations. Early exclusions of Indigenous peoples, and restrictions on their traditional use of national park lands, have given way to recognition of Indigenous rights, active collaboration in interpreting and

	Direction Aspects	Environment Aspects	Time Aspects
Charged with Purpose	**1** A Central Mission Purpose Permeates the Agency	**2** The Societal Need Met is Seen as Urgent	**3** Distinctive Reputation Based on Achievement
Charged with Energy	**4** Personnel Are Intrinsically Motivated	**5** The Culture Institutionalizes the Belief System	**6** Agency History Is Known and Celebrated
Charged with Vitality	**7** Beliefs Are Open to Contestation and Opposition	**8** Qualified Policy Autonomy to Permit Innovation	**9** Agency Renewal and Learning are Ongoing

Fig. 17.1 The Mission Mystique Framework
Source: Goodsell (2011b, 6).

managing cultural, historic, and natural places and co-management of parks. The function of Parks Canada as a national symbol of Canadian identity allows it to integrate heritage aims with commitments to biodiversity and climate sustainability. Its evolving ability to juggle competing imperatives is critical to its mystique and policy success.

This chapter mainly follows the mission mystique framework, but inherently considers how this illustrates programmatic, process, and political success. It is organized using the major headings of purpose, energy, and vitality, and concludes with thoughts that integrate the characteristics of policy success, as highlighted in the introduction to this volume.

From Policy Decisions to Institution-Building

Canada's First National Parks' Management System: An Economic Purpose

The story of Canada's first national park set the foundation for park creation and management. The Department of the Interior was established on 1 July 1873 under the Dominion Lands Act 1872 to open settlement in Western Canada, and worked alongside the Canadian Pacific Railway (CPR) to connect the east and west of Canada. While mapping a rail route in 1883, workers for the CPR accidently discovered hot springs in the rocky foothills of Alberta and tried to establish a claim to profit from commercial development. The federal government denied the claim, and in 1885 established twenty-five square kilometres of protected forest reserve around the springs.

330 MANAGING CANADA'S NATIONAL PARKS

Federal surveyors indicated that the site had 'features of the greatest beauty and was admirably adapted for a national park' (Campbell, 2011, 3). In 1886, the deputy minister of the interior stated that the hot springs were to become, 'the greatest and most successful health resort on the continent' (Lothian, 1976, 23). George Stewart became the first superintendent of Rocky Mountain Forest Park in 1886, reporting directly to the deputy minister, and thus, the Department of the Interior. Few understood what a national park was, nor its purpose, other than to create public wealth (Kopas, 2000, 69–71). The federal government partnered with CPR to build a new railway and hotel on the forest reserve. When the minister wanted to enlarge the hot springs reservation and establish a national park, special legislation was required 'to cope with the complexities of national park administration which ... involved municipal affairs as well as natural resources' (Parks Canada, 2013a). This set the stage for the first national park legislation.

In June 1887, Parliament passed the Rocky Mountain Park Act, creating 'a public park and pleasure ground for the benefit, advantage and enjoyment of the people of Canada' (Department of the Interior, 1887; Parks Canada, 2013a). The Act provided authorities to preserve the landscape, protect wildlife, and lease lands for residences and trades. Indigenous communities advocated for a 'natural environment' around the hot springs, but they were largely ignored. Although they were asked to appear at 'Indian Days', an annual festival that called on Indigenous people to perform for the tourists from 1907 to 1976, they were not invited to participate in the establishment of Canada's national parks (Mason, 2008, 226).

Four additional 'dominions', later named 'national' parks, were created under the Dominion Forest Reserves and Parks Act 1911 (replacing the Rocky Mountain Park Act 1887): Yoho, Glacier, Jasper, and Waterton Lake. Elk Island Park, and Buffalo Dominion Park were created in 1913, from former forest or wildlife reserve lands. The Act also created the Dominion Parks Branch in the Department of the Interior, where it would remain until 1921.

Formalizing Management of Parks (1921): A Temporary Home

The first commissioner of the Parks Branch was James Bernard Harkin (1911–1936) who, knowing little about parks, directed his staff of seven people to find out everything about them (MacEachern, 2011, 22). His first task was to reconcile the role of the Forest Branch and the Parks Branch whose roles over the 1910s had overlapped. Eventually, the Canadian National Parks Branch was constituted in 1921, formally separating the responsibilities of the Dominion Parks Branch from the Forest Branch. The Parks Branch set out to consolidate the five parks into a single structure and framed a new management culture around internal and external collaboration to achieve a national purpose (Harkin, 1957). It was a forward-thinking culture for the country, encouraging partnership (MacEachern, 2011, 27).

During his 25 years as commissioner, Harkin built roads and highways throughout the western park system to facilitate the emerging trend of motoring tourists. The roads opened the way for the Banff-Jasper Highway in 1940, and many CPR hotels, trails, and businesses were established in or near parks to support visitors. He advocated for the protection of historic sites, convincing Arthur Meighen, Minister of the Interior, to create the Historic Sites and Monuments Board of Canada in 1919. Harkin oversaw the expansion of the park system over his tenure, including the creation of Kootenay National Park in 1920 and Vidal's Point in Saskatchewan in 1921. He also created or expanded several wildlife and forest reserves, including Nemiskam Wildlife Park in 1922, Prince Albert National Park (created out of Sturgeon Lake Forest Reserve) in 1927, Georgian Bay Island Park (Ontario) and Riding Mountain Park (Manitoba) in 1929 (MacEachern, 2011, 28).

Several initiatives involved the active collaboration of provinces and territories, with processes established between 1919 and 1930. They required boundary negotiation, and the construction of highways needing provincial/territorial agreement. Agreements, such as completing the Banff-Windermere Highway in 1919 between Canada and British Columbia (i.e. connecting British Columbia and Alberta), spearheaded the harmonization of jurisdiction between the federal and provincial government within the national parks, including the collection of automobile fees, granting liquor licenses in parks, sharing fee revenues with parks residents, and game management (Parks Canada, 2013a).

Institutionalizing Collaboration: The 1930 National Parks Act

The most significant shift in forest reserves and parks authorities in the Harkin era was the enactment of the National Parks Act 1930, which expanded the purpose of parks from preserving space for enjoyment to include the preservation of lands and resources for future generations: 'to provide for the benefit, education and enjoyment of the people' (Taylor, 1991, 128). The Act removed the authorities for creating and managing parks from the Dominion Forest Reserves and Parks Act 1911. The Deputy Minister of the Interior, W. W. Cory, recognized in 1919 that this was necessary given conflicting legislative authorities. Between 1926 and 1929, agreements were reached with BC, Alberta, Saskatchewan, and Manitoba that paved the way for the National Parks Act 1930. The Act changed the name of dominion parks to national parks (Parks Canada, 2013a; Sandlos, 2011, 56), and made explicit the protection of game, wildlife, and historic sites, prohibiting the granting of new mineral exploration and development rights, and restricting timber harvesting to park use only. Park lands were administered solely by the federal government under a separate agency: the precursor to the current Parks Canada agency regime.

Creation of an Independent Agency: Parks Canada (1995–2000)

In 1994, Parks Canada was moved from Environment Canada to the newly formed Department of Canadian Heritage under Minister Sheila Copps. Thomas Lee, Assistant Deputy Minister of Parks Canada (1993–2002), found that the majority of his employees would not report to him and that budgets were still unstable. However, the reorganization signalled revitalized government interest in Parks Canada's responsibilities, including the launch of new initiatives that would reaffirm its primary mandate, purpose, and responsibilities, provide necessary structure and policy direction, and support flexibility, responsiveness, and grass-roots innovation (Kopas, 2000, 272–288).

Responding to concerns from environmental groups and citizen advocates, particularly those affiliated with Banff National Park, the first initiative set out to reduce commercial development in parks. Minister Sheila Copps launched the Banff-Bow Valley Study in 1994 to improve decision making in the park. An independent task force was launched to consult about federal responsibilities in parks locally and across Canada. The final report (Banff-Bow Valley Task Force, 1996) included more than 500 recommendations, and the resulting Banff Management Plan (Heritage Canada, 1997) and Banff Community Development Plan (1997) reflected many of these. They limited new commercial development, reduced the Banff townsite boundaries and sent a clear signal that the Government intended to honour its commitment to ecological integrity in Banff and elsewhere in its parks system. Permanent limits on commercial development were set for all western national park townsite communities. Environmental groups were pleased (Canadian Parks and Wilderness Society, 2016), as were the majority of permanent residents of Banff (Eisler, 1997).

Following the launch of the Banff-Bow Valley Study, the Parks Canada Agency was created in 1998, fulfilling a commitment made in the 1996 Federal Budget to transition Parks Canada into a quasi-arm's-length special operating agency. Parks Canada was to have more operational and resource flexibility, as well as stable budgets and resources. The Secretary of State for Parks Canada and the Heritage Minister initiated public consultations on ways to ensure public accountability, financial and human resources flexibility, and strong ministerial oversight.

Consolidating Governance Arrangements: The 2000 National Parks Act

The Canada National Parks Act 2000 (Justice Canada, 2000, Section 4(2)) echoed the dedication in the National Parks Act 1930 by reconfirming the core purpose of national parks: that they be unimpaired for the benefit of future generations. The Parks Canada Agency Act 1998 establishes the management of parks through the mandate of Parks Canada as 'ensuring that Canada's national parks, national historic sites and related heritage areas are protected and presented for this and future generations' (Justice Canada, 1998, Preamble). It also established that overall broad policy direction for Parks Canada would remain the responsibility of the Minister and Cabinet, while a chief executive officer (CEO) accountable to the Minister would have control over managing and operating the new organization, including providing policy proposals and advice. To allow for innovation, efficiency, and nimbleness in responding to new opportunities, the Agency would have financial, staffing, and organizational flexibility, and be flatter, with field superintendents responsible directly to the CEO (Kopas, 2000, 282–284).

Multiple accountability mechanisms were included through the Minister and Parliament and directly to Canadians. Biennial forums, chaired by the Minister, were mandated, giving individuals and groups the opportunity to evaluate the Agency's performance and provide input on future priorities. Also, individual park management plans were to be created and reviewed every five years, with input from local stakeholder groups, before final approval by the House of Commons (Kopas, 2000, 283). Park superintendents are expected to develop highly localized plans for the unique needs of their park's ecosystems, reflecting the knowledge, input, and concerns of local populations. Parks Canada is required to submit an annual plan and annual performance review (internally completed) through the minister to Parliament.

Charged with Purpose: Parks Canada Mission Mystique

Crafting Resilient Success: Policy Adaptation and Responsive Leadership

As of 2020, Parks Canada managed a portfolio of 38 national parks, 10 park reserves, one urban park, five national marine conservation areas, and 171 national historic sites covering 31 of 39 terrestrial regions (Parks Canada, 2020a, 2). This success can be attributed to visionary prime ministers and ministers, dedicated Parks Canada leaders, officials working across the country, tourism operators who respect the value of parks, Indigenous and provincial/territorial partners, and the many volunteers who contribute to the collaborative management of these iconic places. Such commitment did not occur overnight, but rather through a shared sense of value and purpose, and the belief that parks are the 'soul' and 'wealth' of the nation. Parks Canada leaders struggled to harmonize the competing interests in parks by building the conditions for effective management: mission became linked with management systems and processes, critical relationships with provinces/territories and various publics, and a sense of self as the steward of a valued public good.

334   MANAGING CANADA'S NATIONAL PARKS

James B. Harkin developed and sustained a national parks service that would last more than a century, establishing Parks Canada's role 'to render the best possible services to Canada and Canadians' (Harkin, 1914, 2). He set a *national* purpose for parks and historic sites that informed the leadership of Frank H. H. Williamson, who served as Controller of the National Parks Bureau (equivalent to commissioner) from 1936 to 1941. After serving for many years as Harkin's Assistant Commissioner, he oversaw the expansion of the parks system in the Atlantic region, and developed several historic sites, including the transfer of Green Gables and Dalvay-by-the-Sea in Prince Edward Island to the bureau. He classified several larger historic sites, such as the Fortress of Louisbourg, Fort Chambly, and Prince of Wales Fort as National Historic Parks, thereby stabilizing appropriations to these sites and solidifying Parks Canada's place as the national steward (MacEachern, 2001).

James Smart (1941–1953) led the National Parks Service through the war years, spearheading major construction projects such as the Trans-Canada Highway through Banff National Park, expanding the campground system in Banff, Jasper, and Mt. Revelstoke, and developing golf courses in the three maritime parks, equating protection with enjoyment. J. A. Hutchison (1953–1957) spent considerable effort rebuilding the Historic Sites Program, despite negligible funding for more than two decades. The Royal Commission on National Development in the Arts, Letters and Sciences (Massey Commission) released its report in 1951, and it was Hutchison who advocated for introducing the Historic Sites and Monuments Act in 1953, providing a legislative base for designating and protecting historic sites with architectural significance.

J. R. B. Coleman, director of National Parks Branch (1957–1968) under Indian Affairs and Northern Development, instituted new administrative units in 1959 to promote understanding of the purpose of national parks: 'to preserve for all time areas which contain significant geographical, geological, biological or historic features as a natural heritage … [for] the people of Canada' (Parks Canada, 2013b, n.p.). Due to Coleman's efforts, visits to national parks and sites increased from 4 million in 1957 to 13 million by the late 1960s, and the annual budget grew from $17 million to $37 million (Parks Canada, 2013b). However, such success manifested in park overcrowding, resulting in a growing number of voices from the science community advocating for restricting park access to protect sensitive wildlife, flora, and fauna (Needham et al., 2016, 125). Coleman responded with several park policies, including restrictive zoning to localize human use within parks, but tempered such branch decisions by instituting regular public consultations on park use (Indian Affairs and Northern Development, 1964). He streamlined decision processes through a restructuring plan that reduced regional headquarters, led by regional directors, from six to three (Parks Canada, 2013b; Kopas, 2000, 84–108).

In 1975, John I. (Jack) Nicol (1968–1978) mandated consultation with provincial/territorial and local Indigenous governments, and emerging environmental groups through a renewal plan. The plan adopted the principle of ecological integrity and divided the country into 39 natural regions. It committed to creating at least one national park in each region (Parks Canada, 2013b), stipulating that natural and historic qualities would be protected, that Canadians would be involved and consulted, and that an orderly framework would be provided for adding new heritage areas. The plan called for a renewed emphasis on partnership and co-operation with other levels of government, local and Indigenous communities, and the private sector (Parliament of Canada, 1976), which depoliticized parks creation (Campbell, 2011, 8). The period marked a 'coming of age' for Parks Canada, highlighted by greater sophistication and rational management in program development and historic site protection.

Fully incorporating these initiatives into a management policy was the hallmark of Al Davidson's tenure (1978–1985), who realized Harkin's vision of a national purpose: 'to protect for all time those places which are significant examples of Canada's natural and cultural heritage and also to encourage public understanding, participation, and enjoyment of this heritage, which will leave it unimpaired for future generations' (Parks Canada History, 2020).

Charged with Energy: Building Relationships

A Passion for Service

This mystique agency has achieved a resilient policy success (McConnell, 2010) through the motivation and dedication of its staff. Goodsell (2011a) notes that an organization 'charged with energy' shares common values that guide leaders and employees in creating policies and programs that amplify its core purpose. This starts at the top: whether through serendipity or design, Canada has benefited from a succession of Parks Canada leaders skilled at translating political direction and societal trends, and incorporating emerging ecological and conservation science. Many of its most visionary leaders did not come from a conservation or tourism background yet became ardent champions of Parks Canada and its aims, expanding its reach through establishing new parks, preserving built heritage, strengthening commitment to conservation, and sustainably broadening access to Canadians and tourists alike. Regardless of the many shifts of governance Parks Canada experienced prior to becoming an arm's-length agency, its public-service professionals remained steadfast to the idea of creating and preserving national parks and historic sites (Taylor, 2011).

Although a mystique agency must first meet a recognized societal need, its ongoing legitimacy is a function of how well its core values are translated into policy, and how they are reflected in the routine actions and commitment of employees. Parks Canada recognized early on the importance of attracting knowledgeable and enthusiastic specialists, creating the position of Chief Park Naturalist in 1959

336　MANAGING CANADA'S NATIONAL PARKS

to lead the hiring of seasonal naturalists who developed nature trails, field excursions, exhibits, and lecture series to explain local wildlife and nature to park visitors.

The Parks Canada Agency Act 1998 furthered empowered employees at all levels. Recognizing that Parks Canada staff were disheartened after years of staff and budget cuts in the 1990s, a top priority of CEO Thomas Lee (1993–2002) was to establish a decentralized and inclusive management structure. Widely regarded as an inspirational and effective leader, Lee infused new energy into Parks Canada, creating a corporate culture (Parks Canada History, 2020) reflected in its statement of values enshrining competence, fairness, and mutual respect (Parks Canada, 2017c). Today, drawing on the expertise of local staff, individuals working for Parks Canada are encouraged to create innovative programs to engage Canadians and enhance ecological integrity at their respective parks. For example, the popular Red Chair program, which places red Adirondack chairs at scenic locations, was conceived by staff in one park and then spread to others.

In the 2019 Public Service Employee Survey, a high percentage of Parks Canada staff consistently report liking their job (86 per cent) and taking pride in their work (88 per cent), higher than the average for the federal public service often by three to five percentage points. In addition, more than 71 per cent of employees believe Parks Canada communicates its mission, vision, and goals clearly, and 83 per cent understand how their work contributes to these objectives (TBS, 2020: Parks Canada). This is a remarkable level of cohesiveness, given that so many of the agency's employees are seasonal and stationed across the country.

A Rocky History: Indigenous Participation Contested

Part of Parks Canada history was not always exemplary: public demands for environmental protection, and increased interest in Canada's North coincided when the Trudeau Liberals were elected in 1968. However, the government's commitment to creating 40 to 60 national parks by 1985 meant that park boundaries increasingly encroached on Indigenous communities and conflicted with land claims. This included the creation of Forillon (Quebec in 1970) and Kouchibouguac (New Brunswick in 1969), leading to significant outcry from Indigenous communities and the public. In response, Minister of Indian Affairs and Northern Development Jean Chrétien announced in 1971 that all future park management plans would be developed through public consultation and giving formal voice to local communities by instituting regular Indigenous consultations on major policy changes with the aim of balancing power relations—a major shift in protocols and ultimately organizational culture that led to successful consultations with Indigenous groups to establish Kluane National Park Reserve (1972), Nahanni (1974), and Auyuittuq (1974).

The National Parks Act 1974 further provided the basis for protecting traditional hunting and fishing practices and embedded requirements to negotiate settlements with provincial, territorial, and Indigenous governments when creating future parks, particularly in disputed areas with unresolved land claims. A major policy innovation, developed with Indigenous input, was the option to create park reserves: land set aside for a future national park pending settlement of land claims. For the first time, Parks Canada recognized the role of people in shaping the design of national parks, how their environments would be designated, and the land's cultural significance (Neufeld, 2011). These initial steps to recognize the input of Indigenous voice was central to building policy success in its relationships with Indigenous communities.

The 1999 *Gwaii Haanas National Park and Haida Heritage Site: Management Plan for the Terrestrial Area*, followed on from the historic 1993 Gwaii Haanas National Park Act and reflected a further step-change in Canada–First Nations collaboration. It showed how both parties could work together for a common purpose, even without resolving disagreements on sovereignty and rights to the lands themselves. Featuring parallel statements of purpose, objectives, and process, and a commitment to consensus decision-making, the Management Plan was a policy innovation, informed by multiple sources of information, including traditional Haida knowledge and scientific data (Canada and Council of Haida Nation, 1999, par 1.6). Since 1999, the agreement has been a template for collaborating with Indigenous communities to create or amend legislation on national parks or national park reserves through formalized management processes. Agreements are now in place for all parks located in Canada's three territories. The template was also adapted for federal-provincial co-management in areas such as the Saguenay-St. Lawrence Marine Park in Quebec.

Improving relations between Parks Canada and Indigenous people was formally institutionalized by Thomas Lee, who established the Aboriginal Consultative Committee, consisting of 12 chiefs and elders from across Canada each providing unfiltered advice to the CEO. To further embed the importance of Indigenous relations, Lee established an Aboriginal Affairs Secretariat and held executives to account for ensuring meaningful progress in Indigenous representation at all levels in their management plans, and the development of the Parks Canada Agency charter in 1998.

These commitments were consolidated by Alan Latourelle (2002–2015), who entrenched a culture of openness, particularly with Indigenous communities. Working with Parks Canada has become synonymous with respect and transparency, reflected in designating Canada's largest historic site, Sahoyúé-§ehdacho and creating Torngat Mountains National Park with Indigenous peoples. Today, 20 national parks are co-managed collaboratively with First Nations or Inuit partners, up from 10 in 1998, and all have individualized impact and benefit agreements in place based on indicators identified by Indigenous partners (Brown-John, 2006).

338 MANAGING CANADA'S NATIONAL PARKS

In addition, the Indigenous Guardians and Watchmen initiative 'provides training and career opportunities for Indigenous Peoples to work as equal partners with government and industry on the protection and management of land and resources' (Parks Canada, 2017b, n.p.). As of 2017, four Watchmen/Guardian programs were in place (Parks Canada, 2017b).

Listening to Local Government in Parks: A Challenging Journey to Process Success

Early on, Parks Canada was noted for its lack of consultation with parks' residents. Because national parks are under federal jurisdiction, towns in them were not afforded the delegated authorities afforded provincially chartered municipalities. Instead, they were administered by local and regional Parks Canada officials. Recognizing that residents should have a voice in matters of local jurisdiction, in 1921 the Minister of the Interior created a *citizen advisory council* for Banff residents. The Banff Citizens Association of nine elected representatives, met annually with the Minister or Commissioner of National Parks to discuss routine matters like traffic control, local employment, appointment of local magistrate, and camping regulations.

Given this experience, the policy innovation was extended to Jasper (1924) and Waterton Park (1959). Today, modern municipal arrangements, including taxation powers, are in place in Banff and Jasper, although governance is shared, and limits are placed on growth and development. Governance remains a highly contested issue in many national parks.

Charged with Vitality: Integrating Emergent Values

Managing Change: A Bifurcated Mandate

Implementing the core mandate of Parks Canada requires integrating two conflicting priorities: balancing public enjoyment of parks along with limiting overuse and preserving important ecosystems. The 1960s witnessed the emergence of an 'era of public participation' (Kopas, 2008, ch. 3), including the establishment of influential environmental lobby groups such as the Canadian Parks and Wilderness Society in 1963. At 'Parks for Tomorrow', its first conference in 1968, 'scholars leveled pointed criticism at user-oriented development' (Campbell, 2011, 8). Lobby groups grew in influence after 1970, with the 'second wave' (Taylor, 2011, 139) of activism attracting university students with ties to wilderness advocacy groups. Today, various environmental groups are regularly and formally included in policy-making processes.

Creating Parks Canada as a stand-alone agency provided the opportunity to reform the National Parks Act 1930, in response to criticism from environmental and Indigenous groups about the tension between Parks Canada's bifurcated mandates. Key objectives of the revised Canada National Parks Act 2000 included streamlining the Parliamentary process for creating and enlarging parks, strengthening the ecological integrity clause, extending measures to protect wildlife and other park resources, adding several new parks and park reserves to the Act, and establishing legislative limits on development for the seven communities located in the national parks system (Parliamentary Research Branch, 2000).

In 2000, the Expert Panel on the Ecological Integrity of Canada (2000b) consulted extensively with diverse stakeholder groups, producing a two-volume report and recommendations (2000a). It confirmed that many park ecosystems were under serious threat. In response to the report and agency advice, Minister Copps modernized the national parks legislation and endorsed the Action Plan developed by Thomas Lee.

A third related legislative initiative was launched in response to global concerns about protecting marine biodiversity and resources. The National Marine Conservation Act 2002 provided the policy framework to establish and manage national marine parks. Together, the three new pieces of legislation strengthened the Government of Canada's capacity to preserve and protect the ecological integrity of its natural heritage.

Policy Learning and Ongoing Agency Renewal

The Parks Canada Agency Act 1998, Canada National Parks Act 2000, and National Marine Conservation Act 2002 consolidated the ongoing learning processes concerning the interconnectedness between ecological integrity and human enjoyment. The Acts empowered Parks Canada to develop detailed management plans to address the government's policy priorities: healing broken connections with Indigenous peoples; increasing visits to parks outside the Rocky Mountain corridor; establishing at least one park in each of Canada's 39 terrestrial regions; creating marine protected areas in all 29 marine regions; improving ecological integrity within each park; and conserving, protecting, and interpreting cultural heritage assets. Parks Canada also leads on delivering Canada's international commitments concerning biodiversity and the preservation of natural heritage, key components addressing climate change.

Successfully delivering on these priorities posed a major challenge, made more difficult by competing federal budget priorities and the chronic underfunding of maintenance and conservation of established parks and heritage sites. Thomas Lee fearlessly pointed out the challenges hindering fulfilment of Parks Canada's legislated mandate. Despite the agency's new ability to retain revenues generated from

340   MANAGING CANADA'S NATIONAL PARKS

its activities and to use proceeds from gifts, endowments, and the sale of excess assets to create new parks, funding became a critical issue. In a remarkable *Globe and Mail* interview in 2001, Lee highlighted that two-thirds of Parks Canada infrastructure was in fair or poor condition, and an immediate investment of $1 billion was needed to bring physical and ecological assets into acceptable condition (Mitchell, 2001). By 2019, a consultant reported that 40 per cent of built assets remained in poor or very poor condition, requiring an estimated initial investment of $9.5 billion, and subsequently, $825–$900 million annually to maintain assets once restored (Parks Canada, 2020b).

Insufficient budget for maintaining Parks Canada's assets (natural and cultural heritage and built infrastructure) has been a common theme in audit and consultant reports, regardless of whether Liberal or Conservative governments were in power. Notwithstanding, both parties made significant budget allocations to address the backlog of critical maintenance and support ecological integrity. For example, Liberal Prime Minister Chrétien announced a $75 million annual investment in 2003 to improve ecological integrity; in 2014 Conservative Prime Minister Harper announced a five-year, $3.2 billion capital investment for infrastructure in parks and heritage sites.

When Alan Latourelle replaced Thomas Lee in 2002, he focused initially on engaging Parks Canada employees and external stakeholders to develop a strategic plan. The plan aimed to: restore ecological integrity within the parks; meet Species at Risk obligations; establish a leading-edge ecological program to monitor ecosystems health; and, oversee the development of results-oriented accountability mechanisms. Management plans for each park were established, and Latourelle focused on his 'One Team—One Vision' approach to meet system-wide objectives. As a result, the footprint of land and water areas protected under Parks Canada stewardship grew by 50 per cent. He also developed strategies to increase Parks Canada's relevancy to an increasingly urban and immigrant population (Parks Canada History, 2020).

In 2005, Environment Minister Stephane Dion hosted the bi-annual multistakeholder ministerial roundtable required by legislation. Visitor numbers were falling with independent national surveys showing that 73 per cent of Canadians in 2000 who valued national parks as important to national identity fell to 62 per cent in 2003. Roundtable participants made several recommendations to improve public appreciation of Canada's iconic spaces and highlighted the need for new visitor programming to respond to changing demographics, Canadian diversity, and evolving tourism trends (Commissioner of the Environment and Sustainable Development 2005). An extensive program of visitor research was launched to determine the expectations and behaviours of current and potential visitors, identify key markets, and effectively target visitor opportunities. The research informed the creation of new outreach programs, participatory experiences, and activities that steadily and sustainably boosted visitor numbers and encouraged discovery of sites outside of the Rocky Mountain parks corridor. By 2018–19, annual visits had increased to 25.1 million, up from 21.6 million in 2006–07 (Parks Canada, 2020b).

Progress on other key federal commitments, particularly increasing the number of parks and establishing at least one park or park reserve in each of Canada's 39 terrestrial regions and 29 marine regions, lagged despite repeated promises. In the mid 1990s, the federal government promised that almost all terrestrial regions would be represented by parks or reserves by the year 2000. At the 2002 United Nations World Summit on Sustainable Development, Prime Minister Chretien pledged to create ten new national parks, increase the size of the national park system by 50 per cent, and create five new marine conservation areas, all within five years (Chase, 2002). Parks Canada's Corporate Plan for 2005/06 to 2009/10 included the goal that 34 out of 39 terrestrial regions and 8 out of 29 marine regions would be represented by national parks or marine conservation areas. The current government continues to set 'stretch' goals for Parks Canada. Its 2020–21 Departmental Plan includes a commitment by the Minister of Environment and Climate Change to protect and conserve 25 per cent of Canada's land and 25 per cent of Canada's oceans by 2025, working towards protecting 30 per cent of each by 2030 (Parks Canada, 2020b).

Haggart's early concerns about placing parks' management in the hands of public officials have been largely disproved, as has been the fear that granting agency status would diminish Parks Canada's legitimacy, accountability, and responsiveness to Canadians (Senate of Canada, 1998). Parks Canada has consistently worked with local residents and stakeholder groups to develop *idiosyncratic policy networks* (Brown-John, 2006) that inform each park management plan. The agency reports on its activities and progress publicly and regularly conducts internal performance audits. It is responsive to new Cabinet directives, including requiring environmental impact assessments in all new policies. Although the political preferences of the government of the day still influence Parks Canada's activities, these tend to be limited to few instances such as the 2012 approval of the Glacier Skywalk project (a private venture in Jasper National Park) and providing free admission to all parks and historic sites during Canada's 150th birthday celebrations in 2017 (Parks Canada, 2017a).

Concerns that the agency would become overtly entrepreneurial, prioritizing revenue generation over conservation and ecological integrity, have also been largely unfounded. For example, despite a $30 million annual budget cut imposed by the Conservative government in 2012 and 600 staff being declared surplus, Latourelle preserved Parks Canada's most critical and high priority functions: the ecological restoration, fire management, and Species at Risk programs were spared from budget cuts. In 2013, the Auditor General concluded that the agency honoured its obligations for maintaining or restoring ecological integrity in national parks 'through a solid framework of policies, directives and guidelines for fulfilling its responsibilities' (OAG, 2013, par 7.75).

342 MANAGING CANADA'S NATIONAL PARKS

One significant outcome of agency status is the emergence of an organizational culture of experimentation that has resulted in innovative solutions for improving operational and service outcomes in parks (Parks Canada, 2020b). For example, the Learn to Camp program, initiated as a pilot program in 2011, proved a popular and effective way to introduce urban dwellers and new Canadians to the Parks experience and to build appreciation for Canada's natural environment. This program attracted 111,000 participants in 2019. A 2019 survey found 80 per cent of youth respondents aged 18–34 supported Parks Canada's mandate (Parks Canada, 2020b). In 2020–21, Parks Canada used 'internal crowdsourcing' to identify, design, and implement novel conservation projects to accelerate ecological improvements in its parks (Parks Canada, 2020a).

Policy Legitimacy and Agency Reputation

Parks Canada has earned a reputation as a global leader in parks' management, advising governments in China, Mexico, Chile, and Colombia on effective management policies and practices. It is known for effective consultation with critical stakeholders and jurisdictions to identify, create, and co-manage parks, particularly with Indigenous communities. In 1978, two Parks Canada sites (L'Anse aux Meadows and Nahanni) were among the first 12 in the world to be designated UNESCO (United Nations Educational, Scientific and Cultural Organization) World Heritage sites. In 1986, UNESCO invited Canada (CEO J. D. Collinson) to chair the World Commission on Protected Areas of the International Union for Conservation of Nature (IUCN). Parks Canada is also well known for its ability to balance the various purposes for parks, something few jurisdictions do well. In the 2016 *National Geographic Guide to the National Parks of Canada* (Locke, 2017, 382–383), the IUCN World Commission on Protected Areas member Harvey Locke identified Parks Canada as a pioneer in endangered species and landscape conservation, and in applying the principles of ecological integrity to parks' management.

According to Compton and 't Hart (2019), a key feature of the political success of a policy is legitimacy, such that the policy enjoys high levels of social and political support. Regarding conserving and protecting natural spaces, a 2017 National Conservation Survey found that 88 per cent of Canadians polled believed environmental protection was 'very important' and 79 per cent supported increased federal funding for new national parks and protected areas (Earnscliffe, 2017). Similarly, an Environics *Focus Canada* Survey found that 'the beauty of the land' ranked fourth out of nine reasons for pride in being Canadian (Environics Institute, 2012).

Due to its dedication to conservation, sustainability, and protection, Parks Canada has been identified by Canadians as one of the top three most trusted government agencies (*Reader's Digest Canada*, 2012). A 2018 public opinion survey found that 9 out of 10 Canadians supported its mandate (Parks Canada, 2019), and a 2017 Dalhousie University survey of 1,641 Canadians on dimensions of Social License to Operate, found that Parks Canada placed third amongst 17 Canadian government departments and agencies, ranking high on trust and environmental responsibility (Howard et al., 2017).

The reputation and history of Parks Canada is also celebrated amongst Canadians and internationally largely because it is kept alive by both current and former employees, and by important conservation and ecological organizations. Many books, articles, and web resources celebrate and disseminate Parks Canada's history and achievements, including a comprehensive historical e-library developed and maintained by friends of the agency (e.g. Canadian Parks and Wilderness Society, and the Canadian Parks Council), and a Canadian National Parks Wardens alumni group that commemorates and maintains oral histories, journals, and achievements.

Conclusions: Ingredients for Effective Policy Success

Canadian national parks governance is a policy and agency success, facilitated by decades of experimentation and strong commitment from political decision-makers to the bifurcated aims inherent in creating and maintaining parks and historic sites. At least four key factors have contributed to this success. First, federal parks policy has been constituted with non-partisan and non-political aims since the Dominion Parks Branch was created in 1911. Although there has always been politics when creating and implementing policies, partisan aims have largely been avoided, thereby minimizing pet projects and capture by special interests. Led by strong Parks Canada leaders and key partners, the interpretation of the Parks Canada mandate (2018) has evolved over time, integrating enjoyment, environmental protection, and economic sustainability (Theberge et al., 2016). Room to allow strong vision and leadership to develop in the institution has been fiercely defended and championed by ministers, supported by strong civil-society and Indigenous advocates who stand with Parks Canada leaders.

Second, national parks policy-making has been highly responsive and flexible to the needs and demands of various external users and stakeholder groups and communities. Mechanisms were constructed in legislation and conventional management practice to ensure ongoing consultation and collaboration with provinces/territories, Indigenous peoples, parks-based communities, and myriad non-profit and advocacy organizations. The Parks Canada Agency now provides a forum for environmental and conservationist non-governmental organizations (NGOs) to participate in creating ecological best practices, and has built-in mechanisms to actively engage local groups, especially Indigenous communities, regarding the creation and delivery of park management plans. National dialogues and legislated minister-led roundtables engage much more widely on various topics including the designation and establishment of new protected sites. Many Indigenous leaders are highly supportive of parks' management processes because they are actively included in decision-making through formalized management agreements and internal Parks Canada decision-making arrangements. Such regular consultation endows the agency with a prevailing legitimacy that is unparalleled in other federal departments, reflecting a legacy of high confidence in management processes that emphasize openness and transparency.

Third, Parks Canada enjoys considerable independence in its day-to-day operations, human resources, and financial management. Effective and ongoing independent oversight of its operations is provided by the Office of the Auditor General (OAG). The OAG has robust internal management processes, including high degrees of coordination with its regional operations: a feature Harkin wanted but did not get in his mandate. The value of this independence, both in legislation and by the commitment of political decision-makers, cannot be understated. It is an indicator and a product of *mission mystique* that the Agency has earned a reputation for fair and representative decision-making with various stakeholder groups. The Agency has established a culture of results-based management, whereby key indicators of policy success, such as ecological integrity, have been ingrained in management decision-making (OAG, 2013, par 7.35).

Finally, Parks Canada has long enjoyed the strong commitment of its staff to its mission mystique. Its culture reaffirms and reinforces its core mandate to ensure that national parks, historic sites, heritage and marine conservation areas are protected and presented for current and future generations. This passionate defence of parks and historic sites is rooted in its history traced to James B. Harkin, who created the public-good orientation staunchly defended by all leaders since. A culture of strong leadership permeates the agency and is celebrated in its various programs, visitor centres, websites, and routine maintenance of parks. The uniform of Parks Canada employees is well known: a symbol of trust and integrity, and a reputation that places the agency in a leadership position worldwide. There is no better testimony of the agency's enduring success than the commitment to its mission by its people and unwavering national support by citizens.

References

Banff-Bow Valley Task Force. 1996. *Banff-Bow Valley: At the Crossroads Summary Report*. Ottawa: Minister of Supply and Services. https://search.library.utoronto.ca/details?1266315

Brown-John, C. 2006. "Canada's National Parks Policy: From Bureaucrats to Collaborative Managers." Canadian Political Science Association. https://www.cpsa-acsp.ca/papers-2006/Brown-John.pdf

Campbell, C. E. 2011. "Governing a Kingdom: Parks Canada, 1911–2011." In *A Century of Parks Canada: 1911–2011*, edited by C. E. Campbell, pp. 1–20. Calgary: University of Calgary Press.

Canada and Council of Haida Nation. 1999. *Gwaii Haanas/South Moresby Agreement*. CCHN. March. https://www.haidanation.ca/wp-content/uploads/2017/03/GwaiiHaanasAgreement.pdf

Canadian Parks and Wilderness Society. 2016. *Protecting Canada's National Parks: A Call for Renewed Commitment to Nature Conservation*. Ottawa: CPAWS. https://cpaws.org/wp-content/uploads/2019/07/CPAWS-Parks-Report-2016.pdf

Chase, S. 2002. "Chretien Vows to Create 10 New Park Sites." *The Globe and Mail*. September 3. https://www.theglobeandmail.com/news/national/chretien-vows-to-create-10-new-park-sites/article1026128/

Commissioner of the Environment and Sustainable Development. (2005). *2005 September Report of the Commissioner of the Environment and Sustainable Development*. Ottawa: Supply and Services. Retrieved from https://www.oag-bvg.gc.ca/internet/English/parl_cesd_200509_02_e_14949.htm

Compton, M. and P. t'Hart. 2019. *Great Policy Successes*. Oxford: Oxford University Press.

Department of the Interior. 1887. *Annual Report of the Department of the Interior: 1886*. Ottawa: Supply and Services.

Earnscliffe. 2017. "National Conservation Survey." Ernscliffe. November. https://earnscliffe.ca/wp-content/uploads/2017/11/National-Conservation-Survey.pdf

Eisler, D. 1997. "The Battle over Banff: Millions of Tourists May Be Threatening a Treasured National Park." Maclean's. 4 August. https://archive.macleans.ca/article/1997/8/4/the-battle-over-banff

Environics Institute. 2012. *Focus Canada 2012*. Toronto: Environics Institute. https://www.environicsinstitute.org/docs/default-source/project-documents/focus-canada-2012/final-report.pdf?sfvrsn=1ef1218_2

Globe, The. 1911. "Government Bills Put through the Commons." The Globe. 29 April.

Goodsell, C. T. 2011a. *Mission Mystique: Belief Systems in Public Agencies*. Washington, DC: CQ Press.

Goodsell, C. T. 2011b. "Mission Mystique: Strength at the Institutional Center." *American Review of Public Administration* 20 (10): pp. 1–20.

Harkin, J. B. 1914. *Memorandum re National Parks—Their Values and Ideals*. Ottawa: Library and Archives Canada. Harkin Papers, MG30 E169, 2.

Harkin, J. B. 1957. *The Origin and Meaning of the National Parks of Canada*. Saskatoon: H. R. Lawson Publishing Co. http://parkscanadahistory.com/publications/origin_meaning.pdf

Hart, E. J. 2010. *J. B. Harkin: Father of Canada's National Parks*. Edmonton: University of Alberta Press.

t'Hart, P., A. Boin, and L. Fahy, 2021. *Guardians of Public Value: How Public Organisations Become and Remain Institutions*. New York: Palgrave-Macmillan.

Heritage Canada. 1997. *Banff National Park Management Plan, Summary*. Ottawa: Parks Canada. http://parkscanadahistory.com/publications/banff/mgt-plan-summary-1997.pdf

House of Commons. 1911, May 9. An Act Respecting Forest Reserves and Parks. *Debates, Geo. V (Chapter 10), Statutes of Canada 1–2*. Ottawa.

Howard, V., A. Kader, T. Lightfoot, M. Adams, P. Cunningham, P. Friesen, and T. Walker. 2017. *Social License to Operate Rankings—Key Findings*. Halifax: Dalhousie University School of Management.

346 MANAGING CANADA'S NATIONAL PARKS

Indian Affairs and Northern Development. 1964. *National Parks Policy.* Department of Northern Affairs and National Resources. Ottawa: National Parks Branch.

Justice Canada. 1998, 12 March. "Parks Canada Agency Act." Justice Laws Website. 3 December. https://laws-lois.justice.gc.ca/eng/acts/P-0.4/page-1.html#h-388901

Justice Canada. 2000. "Canada National Parks Act. s. 4(1)." Justice Laws Website. 20 October 20. https://laws-lois.justice.gc.ca/eng/acts/n-14.01/page-1.html#h-360258

Kopas, P. 2000. "Taking the Air: Canadian National Parks Policy and Contextualizing Ideas." PhD Thesis. University of Toronto. Retrieved from Collections Canada: https://www.collectionscanada.ca/obj/s4/f2/dsk2/ftp03/NQ49980.pdf

Kopas, P. 2008. *Taking the Air: Ideas and Change in Canada's National Parks.* Vancouver: UBC Press.

Locke, H. 2017. "Parks Canada's International Leadership Role on National Parks." National Geographic Guide to the National Parks of Canada. pp. 382–383.

Lothian, W. F. 1976. *History of Canada's National Parks.* Ottawa, ON: Parks Canada: Mnister of Indian and Northern Affairs.

MacEachern, A. 2001. *Natural Selections: National Parks in Atlantic Canada, 1935–1970.* Montreal and Kingston: McGill-Queen's University Press.

MacEachern, A. 2011. "M. B. Williams and the Early Years of Parks Canada." In *A Century of Parks Canada: 1911–2011*, edited by C. E. Campbell, pp. 21–52. Calgary: University of Calgary Press.

Mason, C. W. 2008. "The Construction of Banff as a 'Natural' Environment: Sporting Festivals, Tourism, and Representations of Aboriginal Peoples." *Journal of Sport History* 35 (2): pp. 221–239.

McConnell, A. 2010. "Policy Success, Policy Failure and Grey Areas In-between." *Journal of Public Policy* 30 (3): pp. 345–362.

Mitchell, A. 2001. "Our Parks Crumbling, Chief Says." *The Globe and Mail.* 22 January.

Needham, M. D., W. Haider, and R. Rollins. 2016. "Protected Areas and Visitors: Theory, Planning, and Management." In *Parks and Protected Areas in Canada: Planning and Management*, edited by P. Dearden, R. Rollins, and M. Needham, pp. 104–140. 4th edn. Don Mills, ON: Oxford University Press.

Neufeld, D. 2011. "Kluane National Park Reserve, 1923–1974: Modernity and Pluralism." In *A Century of Parks Canada, 1911–2011*, edited by C. E. Campbell, pp. 235–272. Calgary: University of Calgary Press.

OAG. 2013. *2013 Fall Report of the Commissioner of the Environment and Sustainable Development: Ch. 7, Ecological Integrity in National Parks.* Ottawa: Supply and Services Canada. https://www.oag-bvg.gc.ca/internet/English/parl_cesd_201311_07_e_38677.html

Panel on the Ecological Integrity of Canada. 2000a. *Report of the Panel on the Ecological Integrity of Canada's National Parks: A Call to Action.* Ottawa: Supply and Services. https://www.pc.gc.ca/en/docs/pc/rpts/ie-ei/report-rapport_1

Panel on the Ecological Integrity of Canada's National Parks. 2000b. *Unimpaired for Future Generations: Volume II: Setting a New Direction for Canada's National Parks.* Ottawa: Supply and Services. http://parkscanadahistory.com/publications/R62-323-2000-2E.pdf

Parks Canada. 2013a. "A History of Canada's National Parks: Volume 1: The Early Years (Up to 1900)." Parks Canada. 11 March. http://parkscanadahistory.com/publications/history/lothian/eng/vol1/chap1.htm

Parks Canada. 2013b. "A History of Canada's National Parks: Volume II, Chapter 4: National Parks Administration (1885 to 1973)." Parks Canada. 11 March. http://parkscanadahistory.com/publications/history/lothian/eng/vol2/chap4.htm

Parks Canada. 2017a. *Let's Talk Parks, Canada!: Minister's Roundtable on Parks Canada 2017 Progress Report*. Ottawa: Public Works and Government Services. Retrieved from https://www.pc.gc.ca/en/agence-agency/dp-pd/trm-mrt/rapport-report

Parks Canada. 2017b. "Indigenous Cultures: Guardian and Watchmen Programs." Parks Canada. 11 August. https://www.pc.gc.ca/en/culture/autochtones-indigenous/gardiens-guardians

Parks Canada. 2017c. "Values." Parks Canada. 7 July. https://www.pc.gc.ca/en/docs/pc/guide/vgp-vop/page3

Parks Canada. 2018. "The Parks Canada Mandate and Charter." Parks Canada. 28 December. https://www.pc.gc.ca/en/agence-agency/mandat-mandate

Parks Canada. 2019. *Corporate Book*. Ottawa: Public Works and Procurement. Retrieved from www.pc.gc.ca/en/agence-agency/dp-pd/transition/ministre-minister-dec-2019#stakeholder

Parks Canada. 2020a. "Parks Canada Departmental Plan: 2020–21." Parks Canada. 4 September. Retrieved from Parks Canada Strategies and Plans: https://www.pc.gc.ca/en/agence-agency/bib-lib/plans/dp/dp2020-21/index#section7-3

Parks Canada. 2020b. *Parks Canada Departmental Results Report 2019–2020*. Ottawa: Parks Canada. https://www.pc.gc.ca/en/docs/pc/rpts/rmr-dpr/03312020

Parks Canada History. 2020. "Leaders of Parks Canada." Parks Canada History. 12 March. http://parkscanadahistory.com/centennial/leaders-full.htm

Parliament of Canada. 1976. Hansard. *35(11994)*, 96. Ottawa, ON: Parliament of Canada.

Parliamentary Research Branch. 2000. "Bill C-27: Canada National Parks Act LS-365E." Law and Government Division. http://www.publications.gc.ca/Collection-R/LoPBdP/LS/362/c27-e.html

Reader's Digest Canada. 2012. "Most Trusted Institutions–2012 Trust Poll Results." *Readers Digest Canada*. March 20. https://www.readersdigest.ca/culture/most-trusted-institutions-2012-trust-poll-results/

Sandlos, J. 2011. "Nature's Playgrounds: The Parks Branch and Tourism Promotion in the National Parks, 1911–1929." In *A Century of Parks Canada, 1911–2011*, edited by C. E. Campbell, pp. 53–78. Calgary: University of Calgary Press.

Selznick, P. 1957. *Leadership in Administration*. New York: Harper & Row.

Senate of Canada. 1998. "Proceedings of the Standing Committee on Energy, Environment and Natural Resources." Canadian Senate. 7 October. https://sencanada.ca/en/Content/Sen/committee/361/enrg/11eva-e

Taylor, C. 1991. "Legislating Nature: The National Parks Act of 1930." In *To See Ourselves/To Save Ourselves: Ecology and Culture in Canada*, edited by E. A. Rowland Lorimer, pp. 125–137. Montreal: Association for Canadian Studies.

Taylor, C. 2011. "Banff in the 1960s: Divergent Views of the National Park Ideal." In *A Century of Parks Canada, 1911–2011*, edited by C. E. Campbell, pp. 133–152. Calgary: University of Calgary Press.

TBS. 2020. "2019 Public Service Employee Survey (Parks Canada)." Government of Canada. 25 November. https://www.canada.ca/en/treasury-board-secretariat/services/innovation/public-service-employee-survey/2019.html

Theberge, J. C., J. B. Theberge, and P. Dearden. 2016. "Protecting Park Ecosystems: The Application of Ecological Concepts and Active Management." In *Parks and Protected Areas in Canada: Planning and Management*, edited by P. Dearden, R. Rollins, and M. Needham, pp. 70–103. 4th edn. Don Mills, ON: Oxford University Press.

18

The Great Lakes

Embracing the Complexity of Policy Success

Carolyn M. Johns

Introduction

Almost 55 million people rely on the Great Lakes for drinking water, food, recreation, and their livelihoods (Gold et al., 2018). Some 50 years ago environmental governance of the Great Lakes were viewed by the public, politicians, and the scientific community as a policy failure. The evidence of pollution and ecosystem degradation was visible. The culmination of scientific evidence and stakeholder mobilization resulted in government policy action in the form of the 1972 Great Lakes Water Quality Agreement (GLWQA). This international agreement signed between the Canadian and US federal governments was implemented through domestic policies, led by the environmental agencies in each country with oversight by a transboundary organization—the International Joint Commission (IJC).

Time, space, and scale are important dimensions that must be considered when examining policy success. In keeping with Sabatier's (1993) position, the GLWQA case illustrates that the success or failure of a public policy cannot be properly assessed unless one looks at its evolution and impact across a decade or more from its inception. A temporal dimension or what Compton and 't Hart call 'temporal complexity' (Compton and 't Hart, 2019a) must be included in assessments of policy success. Assessment of policy success thus requires a multi-dimensional, multi-perspective, multi-criteria approach. While there can be indicators of policy success over time and at certain scales, there can also be simultaneous, emergent, and enduring indicators of policy failure. The case of environment and water policy in the Great Lakes illustrates these complexities well.

This chapter assesses policy success using the PPPE framework of this book to tease out the factors that make this 50-year-old case worthy of inclusion in a book on policy success. The chapter unpacks how and why success was achieved, the context in which success arose and evolved, and the setbacks and challenges that continue to endure and cause us to question policy success across time, space,

Carolyn M. Johns, *The Great Lakes.* In: *Policy Success in Canada.*
Edited by Evert A. Lindquist et al., Oxford University Press. © Carolyn M. Johns (2022).
DOI: 10.1093/oso/9780192897046.003.0018

scale, and from counter perspectives. It highlights that even cases that exhibit some evidence of policy success can also include evidence of policy failure. The chapter demonstrates that assessing the success of complex and long-running policies and programs requires us to pay attention to multiple vantage points, intended and unintended consequences, and shifting fortunes over time. This case clearly outlines how policy successes are in the eye of the beholder (Compton and 't Hart 2019b, 3) and are assessed differently by different stakeholders (McConnell et al., 2020).

The first section of this chapter outlines the policy problems and state of the environment before a concerted transboundary policy effort was initiated. This section is followed by an overview of the GLWQA and the decades of policy-making and implementation by the complex transboundary policy regime constituted by two federal countries and high-level policy goals of clean, drinkable, fishable, and swimmable waters. The presentation of evidence and indicators of policy success over the past five decades focuses on the 'context, challenges, and agents' and the assessment dimensions of programmatic, process, political success and endurance that are used in this book. This content is presented chronologically to highlight that, while dimensions of policy success are evident over the past five decades, there can be simultaneous and significant periods of policy failure. Policy success can be followed by periods of inaction, complacency, set-backs, re-emerging issues, enduring challenges, and new threats.

The chapter uses scholarly literature and evidence from the perspective of government actors themselves, who report on policy progress and ecosystem outcomes. In this case there is a well-developed progress reporting and accountability regime that also allows for some analysis of the extent to which key actors have been successful in framing policy as a success. In the final section, the four dimensions of assessment are revisited (program, process, political success, and endurance/temporal dimensions) to examine process inclusivity, degree of innovation, and the pace of change (Compton et al., 2019, 121) to draw lessons from this complex case.

Background: The Policy Problem

The history of pollution in the Great Lakes, and the policy responses by governments in Canada and the United States at all levels, are well documented (Caldwell 1998; Colborn et.al. 1990; Sproule-Jones, 2002; Botts and Muldoon, 2005; Krantzberg and Manno, 2010; Johns, 2009, 2016, Egan 2017; VanNijnatten and Johns 2019). The foundations of the pollution problem, which required policy action, were set by the turn of the century as the region experienced population growth and industrialization (Denning, 2020). As early as 1912, water pollution issues were referred to the IJC—the international body charged with governing the waters of the Great Lakes, which was established in 1909 under the Boundary Waters Treaty (BWT). In 1912, the federal governments in Canada and the United States asked the IJC to investigate the pollution of boundary waters and undertake 'the most expansive bacteriological examination of waters the world has ever known' (IJC, 1918, 10). This joint study involved scientists and public health experts from both countries (Benidickson, 2017).

An IJC report in 1918 drew attention to widespread problems stemming from sewage systems discharging raw sewage into the lakes and ship discharges, highlighting that pollution was indeed transboundary (IJC, 1918, 26). It also outlined that the negative impacts of human and industrial development violated the BWT and the commitment of both federal governments to shared management of the Great Lakes. Over 100 years ago, the report recommended that the IJC be given the necessary jurisdiction and authority to regulate and prohibit the pollution of boundary waters (IJC, 1918).

However, the national governments in both countries, and governments at all levels, were preoccupied from the 1920s to the 1940s with shipping, industrialization, fishing, and other economic activities—not with pollution. This was also a period that saw significant negative impact caused by chemical pollutants and experienced serious environmental injustices that undermined communities, affected the well-being of Indigenous populations, and destroyed valuable ecosystems and fisheries (Benedickson, 2017, 80). Although early pollution problems did result in some legislation, such as the US Federal Pollution Control Act in 1948, scientific studies in the 1940s and 1950s and the transboundary mobilization of scientists began to document ecosystem impacts of pollution in the region (IAGLR, 2020).

Evidence of serious environmental degradation from industrial waste, human sewage, and chemicals began to have grave ecosystem effects. By the mid 1960s Lake Erie was declared 'dead' by *Time Magazine*—described as 'an odorous slime-covered graveyard' (Edmonds, 1965). As fish populations collapsed (Regier et al., 1969), there was considerable research and focus on the implications of pollution for the commercial fishery (Egerton, 1985). Invasive species had also been introduced over the decades, including 34 non-indigenous fish species between 1819 and 1974 (Emery, 1985) and many other invasive species were being introduced through ship ballast water (US EPA, 2020c). The invasion by sea lamprey had a devastating impact on fisheries in the Great Lakes until the scientific discovery of a lampricide in 1958 and the sea lamprey management program, which was implemented by the Great Lakes Fishery Commission (Egerton, 2018).

In 1964, Canada and the United States asked the IJC to broaden its investigative scope and report on whether pollution was a transboundary problem (IJC, 1970). Researchers began to notice the decrease in the loon, eagle, and other bird populations in the late 1960s and early 1970s due to acid rain, mercury, and other toxic contaminants. Shocking events, including large-scale fish kills in Lake Erie and the

Cuyahoga River in Cleveland, Ohio, catching fire in 1969 due to extremely high levels of pollutants in the water, and the contamination of the walleye fishery by mercury, all brought environmental issues to the forefront of government attention. In 1966, a push to create a formal organization of transboundary scientists resulted in the establishment of the International Association of Great Lakes research (IAGLR). By 1968, it had 225 members (IAGLR, 2020) and was important to the evidence-based policy regime that was emerging. At the same time, evidence of severe pollution mobilized the public, newly forming environmental groups, and political leadership at all levels for political action (Botts and Muldoon, 2005). As the 1960s ended, the 1948 US Federal Water Pollution Control Act was replaced by the Clean Water Act (US EPA, 2020a) and the Canada Water Act was under development (Benedickson, 2017, 79).

An IJC report submitted to the Canadian and US federal governments in 1970 provided a comprehensive list of pollution threats to the lakes and concluded that 'there is no doubt that contaminants entering Lake Erie and Lake Ontario from one country move across the boundary and affect the water quality in the other country' (IJC, 1970, 62).

Mounting public concern in the 1970s about the deterioration of water quality and ecosystem degradation (Smith, 1972) led various groups—fishermen, women, scientists, and public health activists—to demand government action (Johns and Sproule-Jones, 2016). Public awareness culminated in the political demand for basin-wide efforts focused on point source pollution controls, effluent limits for industries and municipal sewage treatment systems, and the regulation of toxic substances. Recognizing that environmental problems required transboundary and national action, the IJC recommended that the two federal governments negotiate a binational agreement to address pollution in the Great Lakes.

The federal governments in both countries simultaneously began a period of developing national legislation containing policy goals related to environmental and water protection including the National Environmental Policy Act (1970), the Clean Water Act (1972), and Safe Drinking Water Act (1974) in the United States and the Canada Water Act (1970). Environmental degradation in the Great Lakes region was also an important impetus for the creation of the Environmental Protection Agency (EPA) in the United States in 1970 and the Department of the Environment in Canada in 1971. In 1971 Canada and Ontario signed the first intergovernmental agreement to address environmental pollution in the Great Lakes region (Winfield and Jenish, 1999). A year later, in 1972, President Nixon and Prime Minister Trudeau signed the first GLWQA. This agreement contained important policy goals and officially made the EPA in the United States, and the Environment Department in Canada, the 'Parties' with implementation responsibility, and outlined the role of the IJC as the official transboundary oversight body.

352 THE GREAT LAKES WATER QUALITY AGREEMENT

Policy Success: The First Two Decades

The 1972 GLWQA formalized the water quality and environmental policy goals in the region. The agreement had clearly stated General Objectives and Specific Objectives related to reducing phosphorus, eliminating the use of toxic chemicals, and addressing municipal and industrial point-source pollution. The five General Water Quality Objectives were focused on making the waters 'free from' substances, debris, and nutrients, and focused on municipal, industrial, agricultural, shipping, and hazardous substances. The agreement outlined the role of the IJC as a joint institution to oversee the implementation of the agreement and achievement of water quality objectives. The two federal governments were responsible for implementation of the programs and other measures, including more detailed policy goals outlined in the eight Annexes (IJC, 1972).

The agreement was implemented through federal, provincial, and state government legislation and the newly established and funded environmental bureaucracies. The original agreement focused primarily on reducing algae by limiting phosphorus inputs. However, after decades of pollution, policy progress was initially slow to address the major problems of historical degradation. Scientists continued to inform policy-makers of the need for action. By 1974 IAGLR had its own scholarly journal and many scientists were active in the policy realm, mobilizing evidence to support policy action (Francis, 1987).

Pollution events in the region continued to gain national attention and reinforced the need for more policy effort to address the 'uses and abuses of the Great Lakes' (Kuchenberg, 1978). The Love Canal in Niagara Falls, New York, was the worst toxic pollution tragedy in US history. After several decades of the canal being used as a municipal and industrial chemical dumpsite, a working-class community of 239 families had to be evacuated (US EPA, 1979). In 1978, President Jimmy Carter declared a state of emergency and the US clean-up Superfund was created.

In 1978 the GLWQA was amended to reflect a broadened goal 'to restore and maintain the chemical, physical and biological integrity of the waters of the Great Lakes basin ecosystem'. The two significant shifts of the 1978 GLWQA were the introduction of the 'ecosystem approach'—the notion of taking the whole ecosystem into account (and not just certain parts)—and a call for the 'virtual elimination' of toxic pollution (Binational, 2020). Governments at all levels were committed to the regulation of toxic chemicals, many of which were banned and phased out. Canada and the United States continued to focus on developing policies and programs, and further invested in their bureaucratic capacity to implement the GLWQA.

Phosphorous reductions were one of the first indicators that the GLWQA, through federal leadership and intergovernmental policy efforts, could achieve policy success. According to the US EPA and Environment Canada, 'phosphorus levels in the Great Lakes declined significantly during the 1970s and 1980s.

At the time, this was an unprecedented success in achieving environmental results and demonstrating the value of binational cooperation' (Binational, 2020). In 1983, a supplement to the GLWQA further limited phosphorus discharges, and included firmer commitments by Canada and the United States to implement regulations and programs. In addition to regulations, there was major investment in municipal water, sewage plants, and infrastructure. Scientific evidence began to indicate policy success in reducing phosphorous (Dove and Chapra, 2015); significant reductions in phosphorus levels were reached by the mid-1980s and the lakes, ecosystems, and fisheries showed signs of restoration (IJC, 2018). Populations of several species that were previously considered endangered, including the Canada Goose, trumpeter swan, and the grey wolf began to increase.

However, despite some evidence of policy success, many environmental problems remained. The GLWQA was amended in 1987 to incorporate new commitments to reduce toxic pollutants through Lakewide Management Plans for each lake. This effort was to focus on 43 Areas of Concern (AOCs) that had been identified by the IJC as particularly problematic watersheds with serious pollution challenges (see Figure 18.1). An additional policy goal was to clean up and 'delist' AOCs through the implementation of Remedial Action Plans (RAPs). The latter involved engaging local decision-makers, citizens, and local governments

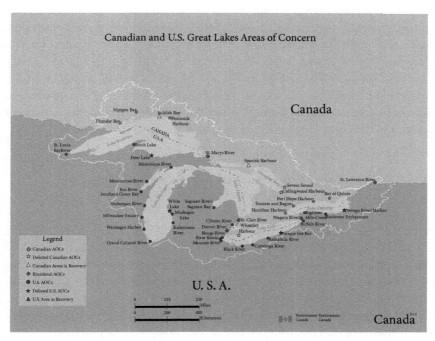

Fig. 18.1 Map of Great Lakes Basin and Areas of Concern
Source: Environment and Climate Change Canada, 2020.

to restore water quality by focusing on 14 'beneficial use impairments' in these highly polluted communities.

By the late 1980s, the policy regime had developed into a complex system with many structures, functions, and actors that made water governance difficult to fully comprehend and analyse (Francis, 1987; Caldwell, 1988). Policy success was evident through ecosystem science and the momentum generated by stakeholder and community engagement as a part of the AOC and RAP process. The 1987 GLWQA and AOC program mobilized local governments and NGOs in a two-staged process: problem-definition and watershed planning in Stage 1 and implementation in Stage 2, both focused on engaging key stakeholders (Hartig and Zarell, 1992; Sproule-Jones, 2002; Greitens et al., 2012). Although unprecedented policy action was taken with regard to AOCs, decades of historical degradation and ongoing pollution meant that programmatic success was elusive. At the end of the 1980s an estimated 57 million tonnes of liquid waste were still being poured into the Great Lakes annually (Colborn et al., 1990, 64). Zebra and quagga mussels had been discovered, and within two years of their discovery, had invaded all five Great Lakes (Egerton, 2018). The degraded state of ecosystems and the magnitude of the policy challenge was well known (Caldwell, 1988).

By the 1990s there was clear evidence of success from the efforts focused on point source pollution regulation. At the local scale, the transboundary water policy regime had some positive impacts. The Great Lakes scientific community and policy community were both well-developed. Stable coalitions of government-led, multi-level, multi-issue, multi-actor policy efforts underpinned some successful outcomes (Sproule-Jones, 2002). The US EPA and Environment Canada, as signatories of the GLWQA, established biennial progress reporting through the State of the Lakes Ecosystem Conference (SOLEC). Biodiversity and fish population recoveries were evident, reductions of harmful algal blooms indicated ecosystem health, and there was progress in reducing acid rain.

Plateauing Policy Success and Emerging Failures: The Next Two Decades

Policy success in addressing end-of-pipe municipal and industrial pollution, chemical pollution, and some clean-up efforts seemed to have peaked by the mid 1990s. Indeed, the narrative of policy success might have contributed to waning public and political attention, resulting in periods where significant policy challenges were not viewed as requiring a concerted policy effort (Botts and Muldoon, 2005). Some major pollution events and the newly developing scientific reporting regime indicated the complexity of several enduring pollution problems.

The 1993 Milwaukee cryptosporidium outbreak became the largest waterborne disease outbreak in US history (Gradus, 2014). The incident, where a water treatment plant became contaminated from run-off, resulted in 403,000 residents becoming ill and thousands being hospitalized. Immediate repairs and upgrades were made to the treatment facilities and the total cost of outbreak-associated illnesses was $96.2 million (Corso et al., 2003). This outbreak highlighted the weaknesses of the policy regime related to non-point source water pollution (Johns, 2000).

The first SOLEC report in 1994 highlighted the importance of scientific evidence related to the fundamental policy goals of fishable, swimmable, drinkable waters (US EPA, 1995, 3). The work on environmental indicators and reporting was just beginning amidst the simultaneous demands from policy-makers for environmental reporting and performance measurement. Three ecosystem indicators were contained in the first SOLEC report: the state of aquatic communities, human health, and aquatic habitat. Overall, the assessment of ecosystem health in the region in 1994 was 'mixed and improving' (US EPA SOLEC, 1995).

Policy success began to slow and change by the late 1990s. Two decades of concerted policy effort and early indications that things were moving in the right direction may have led to waning public attention. As Great Lakes governance was becoming touted as a 'model' of transboundary cooperation and action (Linton and Hall, 2013), changes in the ideological and economic context led to a shift in policy instruments, whereby regulatory instruments and government-led programs started to give way to market-based and voluntary policy instruments (Johns, 2000). Federal governments in both countries turned their attention away from the Great Lakes agenda (Botts and Muldoon, 2005). Despite evidence of subnational actors increasingly engaging in transboundary environmental policy networks related to the GLWQA (Johns, 2009; Norman and Bakker, 2015), the focus on the GLWQA declined, particularly in Canada. The twenty-fifth anniversary of the GLWQA in 1997 celebrated policy success but also marked the creeping decline in political and public interest in the region.

The government of Canada and the provincial government in Ontario reduced their policy efforts and the GLWQA was no longer a priority. The Canada-Ontario intergovernmental agreement related to implementing the GLWQA was essentially suspended during this period (Winfield and Jenish, 1999; Botts and Muldoon, 2005). The policy challenge became how to sustain political will, maintain bureaucratic capacity, and continue to engage key water users, stakeholders, and the private sector in implementation. In order to remediate and restore the AOCs, Phase 2 of the RAPs required significant resources and changes to the status quo to successfully remediate polluted areas (Sproule-Jones, 2002) and the few AOCs that had been de-listed had higher levels of subnational and local government participation, which was noticeably declining (Greitens et al., 2012). Investments required to clean up and de-list AOCs, in line with policy goals of the GLWQA, were viewed by political leaders as too significant and long term. Remaining policy challenges related to non-point source pollution were more

356 THE GREAT LAKES WATER QUALITY AGREEMENT

complex and political (Johns, 2000). Funding for policy implementation was cut by many jurisdictions in the region during this time (Botts and Muldoon, 2005).

By 1998, the scientific community had developed 80 SOLEC indicators to report on the progress and the state of the lakes. Its report that year noted several successes indicating 'adequate and successful control of sea lamprey (p. 12), phosphorous regulations and controls have been successful in reducing nutrient concentrations in the lakes (p. 17), contaminants from PCBs in waterbirds have been significantly and substantially reduced from 25 years ago (p. 18) and mercury and DDT have declined significantly in fish' (US EPA, 1998, 40–41). The use of Ontario Farm Plans and several protection and agricultural incentive programs were noted as indicators of progress (US EPA, 1998, 30–33).

However, the 1998 SOLEC report also noted that some successes were less pronounced and plateauing. The report outlined that 'contaminant trends after a decade or more of decline in concentrations appear to not be decreasing at the same rate as in previous years (p. 39), atmospheric deposition success from control programs in the late 70s and 80s appear to be levelling out (p.79), bird and wildlife biodiversity is mixed, and loss of wetlands remains a problem in several lakes' (US EPA SOLEC, 1998). In the United States and Canada, as the frequency in monitoring and reporting increased, more advisories, postings, and closures were observed. In 2000, both the United States and Canada experienced a doubling of beaches that had advisories or closings for more than 10 per cent of the season (US EPA, 2004).

In May 2000 another water pollution tragedy shocked the policy community. Drinking water contamination from agricultural run-off permeated the local drinking water system in Walkerton, Ontario making over 2,000 residents ill and killing seven people due to high levels of E. coli bacteria in their water supply. The two-year public inquiry found systemic policy and management problems and made numerous recommendations related to drinking water in the province. Despite this crisis generating a concerted water policy focus in Ontario and highlighting some recognition of regulatory failure (Johns, 2008, 2014; Schwartz and McConnell, 2009), connections to Great Lakes water quality and the decline in effort related to the GLWQA were not made until several years after the tragedy (Johns, 2014). The Walkerton Inquiry also highlighted the poor state of water quality and the problem of boil water advisories in Ontario's First Nations. This new dimension of policy—drinking water safety—also highlighted the fact that Indigenous peoples were marginalized from the Great Lakes policy community.

Although the Wisconsin and Ontario drinking water outbreaks did put water policy back on the subnational political agenda in Canada and the United States in the early 2000s, broader connections to the state of the environment and water policy in the Great Lakes were not made (Johns, 2014). Scholarship and public critiques by environmental groups highlighted the lack of political leadership and effort at the federal levels, particularly in Canada, and outlined some of the failures in terms of governance and political will. The Great Lakes were not on the national political agenda in Canada during the Chrétien Liberal government years from 1993 to 2003. In the United States, implementation of the GLWQA proceeded through Congressional funding in several US statutes that mandate regular funding and leadership by the Great Lakes Office in the US EPA. However, several SOLEC reports between 1996 and 2008 indicated that progress had stalled. Phosphorous levels were increasing in Lake Erie; algal blooms began to reappear and had grown rapidly since 2002, with the five worst blooms occurring since 2011 (IJC, 2018). Voluntary policy instruments related to run-off from agriculture were not working (Johns, 2000, 2008). Concerted, government-led action across the region slowed, particularly in Canada (Canada Office of the Auditor General, 2001). For almost two decades a period of policy inaction and ambivalence was evident in the Great Lakes (Botts and Muldoon, 2005).

This is an important period in terms of assessing policy success, as policy inaction also offers us an opportunity to analyse policy success and failure (McConnell and 't Hart, 2019). Policy inaction in this case was partially the result of a changing context and competing policy mandates. However, it was also related to a period of declining political interest after a period of policy success. By the mid-2000s there was mounting evidence that serious policy challenges remained and new ones were emerging (Dempsey, 2004). There were also growing demands for the renewal of the GLWQA, as it had been almost 25 years since the signing of the last agreement in 1987.

The 2012 GLWQA: Setbacks and a Push to Rekindle Early Successes

The signing of the 2012 GLWQA was considered a major policy achievement and indicator of political success in reinstating the goals of environment and water quality on the federal and subnational policy agenda in the region. The new agreement reconfirmed the commitment to the original general and specific objectives, but also added new annexes to articulate policy goals and address new issues, such as climate change and groundwater. There was also a renewed interest in implementation, reporting, and accountability for progress (VanNijnatten and Johns, 2019). Using nine key indicators, the reporting regime was strengthened to better align the policy goals of fishable, swimmable, drinkable waters, with the nine general objectives of the GLWQA. Implementation began with a re-engagement of policy efforts and actors in 2013.

The policy community, directed by both federal governments through leadership of the US EPA and Environment Canada, mobilized financial and human resources to implement the general and specific objectives and the 10 annexes of the agreement. As the lead agencies of the Great Lakes Executive Committee

(GLEC), the federal governments worked in partnership with states and provinces, Indigenous representatives, municipalities, and other key stakeholders. Policy implementation remained government-led, progress was being made, and success was evident, particularly on US AOCs, which had significant investments that had been made by the Obama administration starting in 2010 under the Great Lakes Restoration Initiative (GLRI). Programmatic, process, and political success was evident. However, shortly after the 2012 GLWQA went into force, two major water pollution events and flooding in several cities in the region highlighted enduring environmental challenges.

The drinking water pollution scandal in Flint, Michigan, made headlines in 2014. The economic policy decision to switch the town's water source from Detroit to the Flint River had devastating human health impacts and was a clear case of environmental injustice (NRDC, 2015). The second water pollution event happened in the summer of 2014 in Toledo, when Ohio's fourth most populous city was shut down due to toxic harmful algal blooms (HABs) caused by agricultural run-off which had contaminated the city's drinking water. Some 500,000 residents were under a 'do not drink' advisory for three days. These events and the return of HABs to Lake Erie were a wake-up call to policy-makers and the IJC, resulting in a major study (IJC, 2014) and new efforts by governments at all levels to develop new, more stringent targets for phosphorous and nitrogen loadings. In addition, several cities experienced unprecedented floods and fluctuations levels in 2013, 2015, and 2017, bringing climate change to the attention of political leaders.

At the same time, momentum from renewed commitments and implementation of the 2012 GLWQA, along with US reinvestments under GLRI, began to indicate some success. Several endangered species populations witnessed population increases, including the bald eagle, the great blue heron, and the piping plover (Freedman and Neuzil, 2018). Similarly, the grey wolf populations went from record lows of 300 in 1960 to 5,400 in 2013 (USFWS, 2020). By 2016 the Progress Report of the Parties indicated that four additional AOCs were de-listed (see Figure 18.1). As of 2019, seven AOCs were de-listed, two were designated as 'Areas in Recovery', and 79 out of 137 known use-impairments in Canadian AOCs and 90 out of 255 known use-impairments in US AOCs were eliminated (US EPA and ECCC, 2019).

There is some evidence the new GLWQA and US-GLRI indicated a shift in the policy paradigm, as policy-makers increasingly viewed environmental policy and water policy as sound economic policy, whereby pollution clean-up, prevention, and green technology investments were seen as important economic investments in the region. Between 1985 and 2019, a total of US $22.78 billion was spent on restoring AOCs: investments that helped revitalize communities and were estimated to provide a 3 to 1 return on investment (Hartig et .al., 2020). Although after 35 years, only seven (of 43) AOCs have been cleaned up and de-listed, AOC restoration is now viewed as a slow, long-term item on the policy agenda with realistic implementation horizons. Policy practitioners in the region seem to now view implementation as a complex process, requiring sustained resources and the engagement of key stakeholders who have previously not been at the table nor involved in policy efforts.

At the same time, enduring and new challenges underpin some impatience with the pace of policy success. The third-largest algal bloom occurred in Lake Erie in 2017 (IJC, 2018). Agricultural run-off and oxygen-depleted 'dead zones' appear to regularly cause toxic seasonal algae blooms in Lake Erie and the western basin, resulting in them being classified as 'impaired' and on 'life support' (Great Lakes Now, 2018). Policy-makers are aware that successes and failures in this case are observable, and policy inaction has direct environmental, social, and economic costs.

The well-developed ecosystem indicators and the reporting regime indicates that policy success is complex. Under the new GLWQA there are two reports produced by the federal governments: i) the *Progress Report of the Parties* (PROP) and ii) the *State of the Great Lakes Report* (SOGL). The IJC also issues its own oversight report, the *Triennial Assessment of Progress Report* (TAP), following submissions and public feedback on the reports submitted by the Parties. The PROP and SOGL reports in 2016 and 2019 indicate some clear policy success stories and state that progress has been made. The latest SOGL report indicates the overall state of the Great Lakes is 'fair and unchanging', with invasive species 'deteriorating', and climate change 'undermined' (see Table 18.1).

The overall assessment of 'fair and unchanging' raises questions about how the status quo, slow progress, and external assessments factor into valuations of policy success. The IJC's TAP report likewise acknowledged evidence of success and progress, but also highlighted several new and enduring challenges related to the general and specific objectives in the GLWQA (IJC, 2020). A survey of 35 policy experts from the United States and Canada, related to the fiftieth anniversary of the GLWQA, indicates the main success has been the multi-national, multi-level

Table 18.1 State of the Great Lakes Ecosystem Indicators, 2019

Indicator	Status	Trend
Climate change and watersheds	Fair	Watersheds unchanging; climate change undetermined
Habitat and species	Fair	Unchanging
Invasive species	Poor	Deteriorating
Nutrients and algae	Fair	Unchanging
Groundwater	Fair	Undetermined
Toxic chemicals	Fair	Unchanging to improving
Fish consumption	Fair	Unchanging
Drinking water	Good	Unchanging
Beaches	Good	Unchanging

Source: https://binational.net/wp-content/uploads/2020/05/May-4.2020-2019-SOGL-FINAL.pdf

360   THE GREAT LAKES WATER QUALITY AGREEMENT

cooperation and partnerships. Some 74 per cent felt this was the most notable success of the GLWQA and the cooperative policy regime (IJC, 2020).

Assessing the Great Lakes Policy Saga

The review of the GLWQA over five decades highlights the complexity of policy success. It illustrates how evidence of success can be punctuated by events that indicate policy failure. Indeed, the overall assessment may be characterized as 'mixed', particularly in terms of ecosystem outcomes. However, the framework and dimensions used in this book provide an opportunity to more closely examine the programmatic, process, and political success of the policy, as well as its endurance.

Table 18.2 lists the assessment factors associated with policy success and the PPPE framework used in this book. Using these assessment criteria, the Great Lakes case exhibits key elements of a policy success over the past 50 years. In addition to the factors evident in other chapters, this case offers some additional features that seem to be important determinants of policy success, which are particularly evident over longer periods of time. These additions are highlighted in blue text in Table 18.2.

Programmatic Assessment: Mixed Success

Assessing programmatic success over five decades presents a challenge, especially given the transboundary, intergovernmental, multi-issue policy goals of the GLWQA. This dimension reflects a focus on 'classic' evaluation criteria, such as policy goals, the theory of change underpinning it, and the selection of the policy instruments it deploys—all culminating in judgements about the degree to which a policy achieves valuable social (environmental) impacts (Compton and 't Hart, 2019a). Programmatic performance is essentially about designing smart programs that will have an impact on the issues they are supposed to tackle, while delivering those programs in a manner to produce social (environmental) outcomes that are valuable (Compton et al., 2019, 121).

Over the past five decades, there have been some observable programmatic successes in the Great Lakes region as a result of the GLWQA. These successes include: point source pollution reductions; banning of many toxic chemicals; clean-up and removal of many beneficial use impairments in AOCs; building community awareness; mobilization of environmental and community organizations; return of some fish populations; effective management of sea lamprey; effective regulation of ballast water effluent from shipping; return of some endangered species; protection of some habitat and wetlands; shoreline and nearshore protection; and upgrades of most water and wastewater treatment facilities to secondary treatment.

CAROLYN M. JOHNS 361

Table 18.2 Assessing Policy Success

Assessment Factor	Assessment
Programmatic Assessment: *purposeful and valued action*	
A well-developed and empirically feasible public value proposition	Y
Achievement of (or considerable momentum towards) the policy's intended goals and/or other beneficial social (environmental) outcomes	M
Cost/benefits associated with the policy are distributed fairly and equitably in society across the institutional and community stakeholders	M
Evaluation, progress reporting, and accountability system in place and valuable	Y
Process Assessment: *thoughtful and fair policy-making practices*	
The policy process allows for rigorous deliberation about the relevant values and interests; the hierarchy of goals and objectives contextual constraints; the mix of policy instruments; and the institutional arrangements and capacities necessary for effective policy implementation	Y
Decision-making processes incorporate balanced consideration of a wide range of evidence, expertise, and advice	Y
Offers reasonable opportunities for different stakeholders to exercise influence and engage in policy-making	M
Allows for innovative practices and solutions to be attempted before key policy choices are made	M
Results in adequate levels of funding, realistic timelines, and administrative capacity	M
Delivery process effectively and adaptively deploys mix of policy instruments to achieve policy goals, outcomes with acceptable costs, and with limited unintended negative consequences	Y
Diversity of key stakeholders involved in collective action and policy implementation	M
Political Assessment: *stakeholder and public legitimacy for the policy*	
A relatively broad and deep political coalition supports the policy's value proposition, instruments, and current results	Y
Association with the policy enhances the political capital of the responsible policy-makers and reputations of the actors driving it (both inside and outside government)	Y
Association with the policy enhances the organizational reputation of the relevant public agencies	Y

Continued

362   THE GREAT LAKES WATER QUALITY AGREEMENT

Table 18.2 *Continued*

Assessment Factor	Assessment
A wide array of stakeholders feel they could advance their interests through the process and/or outcomes of the policy	Y
The policy enjoys relatively high levels of social, political, and administrative support	Y
Sustained political leadership and will	M
Sustained public priority and support	M
Endurance/Temporal Assessment	
Endurance of policy's value proposition (high-level ends–means relationships underpinning its rationale and design, combined with the flexible adaptation of its on-the-ground and programmatic features to changing circumstances and in relation to performance feedback)	M
Degree to which the policy's programmatic, process, and political performance and efficacy is maintained over time	Y
Emerging narratives about the policy's success confers legitimacy on the broader political system	Y
Stable or growing strength of social, political, and administrative coalitions favouring continuation of the program over time	Y
Policy implementation efforts are sustained over time	M

Notes
Y = yes, evidence of this factor in the Great Lakes policy case.
N = no, there is no evidence of this factor being present in the case.
M = mixed, inconclusive evidence, the assessment over time does not indicate policy success or failure, or evidence of success and simultaneous evidence of failure.

However, over the same five decades there is some evidence of program failures. These include: the failure to de-list a large number of AOCs designated in 1987 (only seven cleaned-up and de-listed and two in recovery); an increasing number of invasive species; enduring challenges of non-point source pollution, particularly from agricultural run-off; new chemical and toxic pollutants such as microplastics; significant loss of wetlands; enduring reliance on grey infrastructure; new pollution from flooding events; and limited programmatic progress related to climate change. Significant pollution events have also highlighted programmatic failure. Examples include the Cryptosporidium outbreak in Milwaukee, Wisconsin in 1993; the E. coli drinking water tragedy in Walkerton, Ontario in 2000; the drinking water crises in Flint, Michigan and Toldeo, Ohio in 2014; and long-standing boil water advisories in Indigenous communities.

The eutrophication and harmful algal blooms in Lake Erie represent the most pointed evidence of a mixed programmatic assessment. Lake Erie in many ways indicates the overall health of the Great Lakes. It was declared 'dead' in the early 1970s, significantly improved for two decades and deemed a policy success for many years, and then re-emerged as a policy failure in 2011. The re-emergence of significant pollution from run-off has resulted in the policy regime focusing on nutrient management, but Lake Erie remains under stress and a symbol of policy failure, despite the voluntary nutrient management programs.

Using the programmatic criteria in this book, there is evidence of policy success in the form of a well-developed and agreed-upon set of policy goals, some important achievements, some momentum towards the intended goals, and a fair distribution of benefits resulting from the GLWQA agreement. However, the costs are not fairly distributed. The commitment to program evaluation and progress reporting also indicates some degree of programmatic success and a pledge to continuous learning, reflection, and improvement.

Process Assessment: Moderate Success

Much of the narrative of around the success of the GLWQA as a model rests on the criteria highlighted in policy process success. This set of factors focuses on how the processes of policy design, decision-making, and delivery are organized and managed, and whether these processes contribute to 'vigilant public problem-solving' and improved technical problem-solving capacity (effectiveness and efficiency) through the application of rigorous deliberative processes that instil a sense of procedural justice among key stakeholders and a sense of inclusivity among the wider public (Compton et al., 2019, 119).

The Great Lakes case scores well on these indicators. The GLWQA has developed into a mature policy regime with transboundary and federal government leadership, high levels of functional diplomacy (Johns and Thorn, 2015), institutional maturity (Sproule-Jones, 2002), and intergovernmental cooperation (Rabe and Zimmerman, 1995; Johns, 2009). There is a high functioning transboundary machinery led by the IJC and the Parties, and coordinated intergovernmental policy efforts through the binational Great Lakes Executive Committee structure and Annex committees. At all levels (from transboundary, to lake, AOC, and community levels) there is participation from both federal governments, subnational governments, as well as cities, and engagement of some Indigenous communities and key stakeholders.

There are well-developed policy evaluation criteria, ecosystem indicators, coordinated scientific reports, evidence-based decision-making and lesson-drawing, and a mature accountability system (VanNijnatten and Johns, 2019). Application of the OECD's (Organisation for Economic Co-operation and Development)

36 water governance indicators suggests that most of the 12 principles and 36 indicators of a well-operating water governance regime are 'functioning and in place' (Johns and VanNijnatten, 2021). However, the accountability regime has been the target of criticism for some time (McLaughlin and Krantzberg, 2011), notably in Canada where the domestic legal, policy, and accountability regime is weaker, particularly at the federal level.

There are also some notable process challenges. The process has experienced 'considerable setbacks' and 'occasional setbacks' (Compton et al., 2019, 129) as evident in Lake Erie and the drinking water failures. These setbacks and slow progress on many issues highlight weaknesses in the policy process. However, there are still vigilant policy design, decision-making, and implementation practices, as well as an 'institutionally embedded use of quality evidence in the policy process' (Compton et al., 2019, 129), with government and scientists driving process success.

Assessment of process inclusivity, however, is mixed. Environmental groups (Botts and Muldoon, 2005) and Indigenous peoples (Phare, 2013) are important constituencies whose knowledge and involvement would enhance policy success. Engaging the private sector and industry water users (Sproule-Jones, 2002) and the general public through behavioural change policies at all levels (IJC, 2020) is an important frontier for improving the outcomes and process success of the GLWQA. The policy community, IJC, and Parties are aware of these process improvement challenges but have struggled to make the policy process more inclusive.

Political Assessment: Legitimacy Success

The GLWQA enjoys broad legitimacy and relatively high levels of social, political, and administrative support. A deep coalition supports the policy. Association with the policy enhances the reputation and political capital of policy-makers and implementers, as well as the reputation and political legitimacy of both its architects and supporters (Compton et al., 2019, 129). The political success is embedded in a narrative of achievement, with the IJC and GLWQA upheld as a model of transboundary, international, and intergovernmental political cooperation.

The Great Lakes are not, however, generally high on the political agenda. Exceptions are the early 1970s and the critical political leadership and investment by the Obama administration to renegotiate the GLWQA and prioritize both economic and environmental goals under the GLRI. Politics is also arms-length. The IJC Commissioners are political appointees by the president and prime minister (three apiece) whose mandates are to ensure boundary waters are managed cooperatively. The evidence-based, science-based foundations of the GLWQA are often seen as one of the main factors for its political success. Science and evidence are viewed as bases of political agreement and policy work and a wide range of stakeholders feel they can advance their interests through this policy model. However, the case clearly highlights that political leadership and political will matter.

An examination over five decades reveals that sustained political leadership and will, even if low profile and steady, are important to policy success. When political leadership and will wane, programmatic and process dimensions weaken. There is some recognition that the political gains from this case are generally long term, beyond electoral cycles. While investments in clean-up and restoration projects may have some electoral and constituency benefits, and politicians seem to increasingly recognize that environmental investments are economic investments, policy success flows from steady political commitment and buy-in from many key stakeholders.

Endurance Assessment: Slow-Paced Success

The GLWQA has endured for some 50 years. It has been amended, updated, and improved over time by many different governments. The pace of success has been impacted by changes in government. Political ideology has also had some impact. It is notable that the US Great Lakes Legacy Act was passed during Republican President George W. Bush's presidency, and disengagement of the Canadian federal government was evident during both the Chrétien and Harper decades. Thus, it is not necessarily the political party in power that explains the mixed policy success over time.

Ideas and context matter. In the first two decades there was a clear public consensus that policy action was necessary. With some visible successes, and incorporation of new issues like climate change into the GLWQA, a narrative of success developed in the next two decades, to the point that 'fair and unchanging' and the status quo became acceptable to the policy community over time. The maturing of the policy regime and recognition that environment and water policy is a complex arena seems to justify the slow and incremental success.

The renegotiation of the GLWQA in 2012 highlights the limited capacity of an established policy regime to undertake the innovations needed to deal with re-emerging and new challenges such as the pollution of Lake Erie, clean-up of AOCs, and climate change. Institutional arrangements related to the GLWQA have adapted somewhat over time, but earlier decisions, rules, and vested interests have limited policy success (Sproule-Jones et al., 2008). Lake Erie pollution and drinking water outbreaks highlight the insufficiency of efforts to address non-point source pollution. They also indicate deep-rooted challenges and problems with the policy instrument mix. While there was political will and public support for regulations of industrial and municipal point source pollution during the first two decades of the GLWQA, the shift to market-based instruments and reliance on voluntary instruments slowed progress in the next two decades. In the past decade there seems to be more recognition that instruments can have economic and environmental benefits and must result in behavioural change.

366   THE GREAT LAKES WATER QUALITY AGREEMENT

Examination over decades highlights why policy success remains slow. Although policy-makers have been somewhat capable of adapting the goals and instruments to anticipate and to respond to changing circumstances (Compton et al., 2019, 129), the pace of change has been made in gradual steps, rather than occurring in leaps. There are stable coalitions favouring the continuation of the policy over time, and policy efforts have been sustained, but there has been limited policy innovation to address enduring pollution challenges and slow adaptation to new governance realities.

Conclusion

Applying the PPPE framework and assessment dimensions to a historic analysis suggests that the path to policy success can be long and winding. The GLWQA case highlights the complexity of policy success over time, at different scales, and from different perspectives. It highlights the broad array of factors and conditions that must be examined to assess policy success in complex, transboundary, international, multi-level, multi-issue, multi-actor governance systems, especially given the 'temporal dimension' in policy evaluation (Bressers et al., 2013).

The first two decades of institutional innovation and concerted policy action (1970s and 1980s) indicated a period of notable policy success. This was followed by two decades (1990s and 2000s) of slowed success, mixed with indicators of policy failure. During the last decade, since the signing of the 2012 GLWQA, there has been confirmation of commitment to the policy goals, political support, process, and programs to improve policy success. While not much policy innovation was evident, the GLWQA was adapted to some degree, which resulted in renewed dedication to implementation, progress reporting, and improved outcomes. Examining the evolution of policy in this case highlights that there are different paths to policy success.

The 'first route is to ensure the policy design process is inclusive' (Compton et al., 2019, 132). Over time, the regime has enjoyed some success based on the government-led, science-driven model. However, in the past decade critiques have focused on the need to broaden stakeholder engagement and seriously examine the multiple uses and vested interests in the region that continue to undermine policy progress. These are not easy policy fixes and require a serious rebalancing of uses, engagement of critical water users, and more fundamental governance and institutional reform to meet enduring and future challenges (Sproule-Jones et al., 2008).

The exclusion of various publics has limited policy success. Indigenous peoples, who have lived in this region for hundreds of years, would not view this case as a success. In the last decade, Indigenous peoples have gained some representation in the policy process, but not in substantial, meaningful ways (Phare, 2013). Similarly, diverse people of colour and newcomers have also not been incorporated into the policy process. Furthermore, environmental groups who have been working on Great Lakes' issues for decades would also likely not deem this case a success. Policy success according to whom, is an increasingly significant dimension when analysing policy success in this case. There is increasing recognition that the Great Lakes policy process is exclusive and that a more diverse engagement strategy can improve policy outcomes and success.

The second route to programmatic and political success is 'a combination of a slow pace of change and a low degree of innovation' wherein policies 'build on or are in line with previous efforts, and are adopted slowly over a series of steps' (Compton et al., 2019, 132). The Great Lakes' case seems to align better with this path to policy success. The policy does have elements of 'successful process with some unsuccessful programs' (McConnell, 2010, 357); as such, it contains elements of 'resilient success' as well as 'conflicted success' (McConnell, 2010, 354). It contains elements of policy success related to the policy goals in the GLWQA; implementation is in line with objectives, and there is some evidence of program, process, political, and endurance success. However, it also highlights that some policy success is accompanied by unexpected problems and only a partial achievement of goals. Using the PPPE framework, process and political success are most evident. The policy is legitimate, has built a sustainable coalition, and is reinforced by well-developed programs and implementation arrangements. Renegotiations of the GLWQA indicates the policy is adaptable to new challenges but not innovative, and reactive rather than anticipatory. It is successful in the sense that 'government does what it sets out to do, opposition is virtually non-existent, and support nearly universal' (McConnell, 2010, 352).

The Great Lakes case highlights lessons similar to other cases in this book. Clearly stated policy goals and objectives are critical. Political and broad-based public consensus and support for those goals is important. Government-designed policy instruments that are informed by scientific evidence seems to be a key ingredient. Bureaucratic leadership, government-led capacity, and intergovernmental and multi-stakeholder implementation are other key ingredients. Sustained resources, political capital, partnerships, and a cooperative policy community also underpin success in this case. After 50 years there are deeply vested interests in working towards policy success. The costs and benefits are broadly spread. A narrative of policy success and commitment continues momentum and engagement. The program failures that have occurred over the past five decades have not threatened the policy, but they are viewed as setbacks and indicators that more work needs to be done.

References

Benedickson, J. 2017. "The Evolution of Canadian Water Law and Policy: Securing Safe and Sustainable Abundance." *McGill Journal of Sustainable Development Law* 13 (1): pp. 61–104.

Binational. 2020. *The Great Lakes Water Quality Agreement*. Binational.net. https://binational.net/glwqa-aqegl/

Botts, L. and P. Muldoon. 2005. *Evolution of the Great Lakes Water Quality Agreement*. East Lansing: Michigan State University Press.

Bovens, M., P. 't Hart, and B. G. Peters (eds). 2001. *Success and Failure in Public Governance: A Comparative Analysis*. Cheltenham: Edward Elgar.

Bressers, N., M. van Twist, and E. ten Heuvelhof. 2013. "Exploring the Temporal Dimension in Policy Evaluation Studies." *Policy Sciences* 46 (1): pp. 23–37.

Caldwell, L. 1988. *Perspectives on Ecosystem Management for the Great Lakes: A Reader*. Albany, NY: State University of New York Press.

Colborn, T., A. Davidson, S. Green, R. A. Hodge, C. I. Jackson, and R. A. Liroff. 1990. *Great Lakes, Great Legacy?* Washington: Conservation Foundation and Ottawa Institute for Research on Public Policy.

Compton, M., J. Luetjens, and P. 't Hart. 2019. "Designing for Policy Success." *International Review of Public Policy* 1 (2): pp. 119–146.

Compton, M. and P. 't Hart (eds). 2019a. *Great Policy Successes*. Oxford: Oxford University Press.

Compton, M. and P. 't Hart. 2019b. "How to 'See' Great Policy Successes: A Field Guide to Spotting Policy Successes in the Wild." In *Great Policy Successes*, edited by M. Compton and P 't Hart, pp. 1–20. Oxford: Oxford University Press.

Corso, P. S., M. H. Kramer, K. A. Blair, D. G. Addiss, J. P. Davis, and A. C. Haddix. 2003. "Costs of Illness in the 1993 Waterborne Cryptosporidium Outbreak, Milwaukee, Wisconsin." *Emerging Infectious Diseases* 9 (4): pp. 426–431.

Dempsey, D. 2004. *On the Brink: The Great Lakes in the 21st Century*. East Lansing: Michigan State University Press.

Denning, M. 2020. "Construction of a Keystone: How Local Concerns and International Geopolitics Created the First Water Management Mechanisms on the Canada-US Border." In *The First Century of the International Joint Commission*, edited by D. Macfarlane and M. Clamen, pp. 71–112. Calgary: University of Calgary Press.

Dove, A., and S. C. Chapra. 2015. "Long-term Trends of Nutrients and Trophic Response Variables for the Great Lakes Limnology." *Oceanography* 60 (2): pp. 696–721.

Edmonds, A. 1965. "Death of a Great Lakes." *MacLeans Magazine*. 1 November. http://archive.macleans.ca/article/1965/11/1/death-of-a-great-lake

Egan, Dan, 2017. *The Death and Life of the Great Lakes*, New York: W.W. Norton and Company.

Egerton, F. 2018. "History of Ecological Sciences, Part 60: American Great Lakes before 2000." *Ecological Society of America Bulletin* 99 (1): pp. 77–136.

Egerton, F. N. 1985. *Overfishing or Pollution? Case History of a Controversy on the Great Lakes*. Ann Arbour: Great Lakes Fishery Commission.

Emery, L. 1985. *Review of Fish Species Introduced into the Great Lakes, 1819–1974*. Great Lakes Fishery Commission (Report 45), Ann Arbor.

Environment Canada. 2017. *Evaluation of the Great Lakes Program*. Ottawa: Environment Canada. https://www.canada.ca/content/dam/eccc/documents/pdf/evaluation-great-lake-program/Evaluation_of_the_great_Lakes_program.pdf

Francis, G. 1987. "Toward Understanding Great Lakes 'Organizational Ecosystems'." *Journal of Great Lakes Research* 13: pp. 233–45.

Freedman, E. and M. Neuzil (eds). 2018. *Biodiversity, Conservation, and Environmental Management in the Great Lakes Basin*. New York: Routledge.

Geist, E. G. 2018. "Lake Erie Declared Impaired: So What?" *Great Lakes Now*. 3 April. https://www.greatlakesnow.org/2018/04/lake-erie-has-been-declared-impaired-so-what/

Gold, A., R. Pendall, and M. Treskon. 2018. *Demographic Change in the Great Lakes Region: Recent Population Trends and Possible Futures*. Washington: Urban Institute. https://www.urban.org/sites/default/files/publication/98572/demographic_change_in_the_great_lakes_region_1.pdf

Gradus, S. 2014. "Milwaukee 1993: The Largest Documented Waterborne Disease Outbreak in US History." Water Quality Health Council. 10 January. https://waterandhealth.org/safe-drinking-water/drinking-water/milwaukee-1993-largest-documented-waterborne-disease-outbreak-history/

Greitens, T. J., J. C. Strachan, and C. Welton. 2012. "The Importance of Multi-Level Governance Participation in the 'Great Lakes Areas of Concern'." In *Making Multi-Level Public Management Work: Cases from the EU and North America*, edited by I. Roberge, D. Jesuit, and D. Cepiku, pp. 159–182. New York: Taylor and Francis.

Hartig, J. H., G. Krantzberg, and P. Alsip. 2020. "Thirty-five Years of Restoring Great Lakes Areas of Concern: Gradual Progress, Hopeful Future." *Journal of Great Lakes Research* 46 (3): pp. 429–442.

Hartig, J. H., and Z. Zarrell. 1992. *Under RAPs*. Ann Arbor: University of Michigan Press.

International Association of Great Lakes Research. 2020. "History of IAGLR." IAGLR. http://iaglr.org/about/history/

International Joint Commission. 1918. *Final Report of the International Joint Commission on the Pollution of Boundary Waters Reference*. Washington and Ottawa: IJC. https://www.ijc.org/sites/default/files/A62.pdf

International Joint Commission. 1970. *Pollution of Lake Erie, Lake Ontario and the International Section of the St. Lawrence River*. Windsor: IJC.

International Joint Commission. 1972. *Great Lakes Water Quality Agreement*. Windsor: IJC. https://www.ijc.org/sites/default/files/C23.pdf

International Joint Commission. 2014. *A Balanced Diet for Lake Erie: Reducing Phosphorous Loadings and Harmful Algal Blooms, Report of the Lake Erie Ecosystem Priority*. Windsor: IJC. https://legacyfiles.ijc.org/publications/2014%20IJC%20LEEP%20REPORT.pdf

International Joint Commission. 2018. "Understanding and Solving Lake Erie's Nutrient Problems." IJC. 11 January. https://www.ijc.org/en/understanding-and-solving-lake-eries-nutrient-problems

International Joint Commission. 2020. *Second Triennial Assessment of Progress Related to the Great Lakes Water Quality Agreement*. Windsor: IJC. https://www.ijc.org/en/2020-TAP-Report

Johns, C. 2000. "Non-point Source Water Pollution Management in Canada and the US: A Comparative Analysis of Institutional Arrangements and Policy Instruments. PhD dissertation. McMaster University.

Johns, C. 2008. "Non-Point Source Water Pollution Institutions in Ontario before and after Walkerton." In *Canadian Water Politics*, edited by M. Sproule-Jones, C. Johns, and B. Timothy Heinmiller, pp. 203–242. Montreal-Kingston: McGill-Queens University Press.

Johns, C. 2009. "Water Pollution in the Great Lakes Basin: The Global–Local Dynamic." In *Environmental Challenges and Opportunities: Local-Global Perspectives on Canadian Issues*, edited by C. Gore and P. Stoett, pp. 95–129. Toronto: Emond Montgomery.

Johns, C. 2014. "The Walkerton Inquiry and Policy Change." In *Commissions of Inquiry and Policy Change in Canada*, edited by G. J. Inwood and C. M. Johns, pp. 214–243. Toronto: University of Toronto Press.

Johns, C. and M. Sproule-Jones. 2016. "Great Lakes Water Policy: The Cases of Water Levels and Water Pollution in Lake Erie." In *Canadian Environmental Policy and Politics: Prospects for Leadership and Innovation*, edited by D. VanNijnatten, pp. 252–277. 4th edn. Don Mills: Oxford University Press.

Johns, C. and A. Thorn. 2015. "Subnational Diplomacy in the Great Lakes Region: Toward Explaining Variation between Water Quantity and Quality Regimes." *Canadian Foreign Policy Journal* 21 (3): pp. 195–211.

Johns, C. and D. VanNijnatten. 2021. "Comparing the Application of the OECD's Water Governance Indicators in the Great Lakes and Rio Grande/Bravo Regions." *Environmental and Sustainability Indicators* 10: pp. 100, 102.

Krantzberg, G. and J. Manno. 2010. "Renovation and Innovation: It's Time for the Great Lakes Regime to Respond." *Water Resources Management* 24 (15): pp. 4273–4285.

Kuchenberg, T. 1978. *Reflections in a Tarnished Mirror: The Use and Abuse of the Great Lakes*. Sturgeon Bay: Golden Glow Publishing.

Linton, J. and N. Hall. 2013. "The Great Lakes: A Model of Transboundary Cooperation." In *Water without Borders? Canada, the United States and Shared Waters*, edited by E. Norman, A. Cohen, and K. Bakker, pp. 221–246. Toronto: University of Toronto Press.

McConnell, A. 2010. "Policy Success, Policy Failure and Grey Areas In-between." *Journal of Public Policy* 30 (3): pp. 345–362.

McConnell, A., L. Grealy, and T. Lea. 2020. "Policy Analysis for Whom? A Framework for Analysis." *Policy Sciences* 53 (4): pp. 589–608.

McConnell, A. and P. 't Hart. 2019. "Inaction and Public Policy: Understanding Why Policymakers 'Do Nothing'." *Policy Sciences* 52 (4): pp. 645–661.

McLaughlin, C., & Krantzberg, G. 2011. "An appraisal of policy implementation deficits in the Great Lakes." *Journal of Great Lakes Research*, 37(2), 390–396.

Natural Resources Defence Council (NRDC). 2020. "Flint Water Crisis", https://www.nrdc.org/stories/flint-water-crisis-everything-you-need-know

Norman, E. and K. Bakker. 2015. "Do Good Fences Make Good Neighbors? Canada-United States Transboundary Water Governance, the Boundary Waters Treaty, and 21st-century Challenges." *Water International* 40 (1): pp. 199–213.

Office of the Auditor General. 2001. *A Legacy Worth Protecting: Charting a Sustainable Course in the Great Lakes and St. Lawrence River Basin, Report of the Commissioner of the Environment and Sustainable Development*. Ottawa: Government of Canada.

Phare, M.-A. 2013. "Indigenous Peoples and Water: Governing across Borders." In *Water without Borders? The Future of Canada-US Transboundary Water Governance*, edited by E. S. Norman, A. Cohen, and K. Bakker, pp. 27–46. Toronto: University of Toronto Press.

Rabe, B. G. and J. B. Zimmerman. 1995. "Beyond Environmental Regulatory Fragmentation: Signs of Integration in the Case of the Great Lakes Basin." *Governance* 8 (1): pp. 58–77.

Regier, H. A., V. C. Applegate, and R. A. Ryder. 1969. *The Ecology and Management of the Walleye in Western Lake Erie*. Technical report 15. Ann Arbor: Great Lakes Fishery Commission.

Sabatier, P. 1993. "Policy Change over a Decade or More." In *Policy Change and Learning*, edited by P. Sabatier and H. Jenkins-Smith, pp. 143–174. Boulder, CO: Westview Press.

Schwartz, A. M. 2005. "The Canada–US Environmental Relationship: Calm Waters But Slow Sailing." *International Journal* 60 (2): pp. 437–448.

Schwartz, R. and A. McConnell. 2009. "Do Crises Help Remedy Regulatory Failure? A Comparative Study of the Walkerton Water and Jerusalem Banquet Hall Disasters." *Canadian Public Administration* 52 (1): pp. 91–112.

Smith, S. H. 1972. "Destruction of the Ecosystem in the Great Lakes and Possibilities for its Reconstruction." *Progress in Fishery and Food Science* 5: pp. 41–46.

Sproule-Jones, M., C. Johns, and B. Timothy Heinmiller (eds). 2008. *Canadian Water Politics: Conflicts and Institutions*. Montreal-Kingston: McGill-Queens University Press.

Sproule-Jones, M. H. 2002. *Restoration of the Great Lakes: Promises, Practices, Performance*. Vancouver: University of British Columbia Press.

United States Environmental Protection Agency (US EPA). 1979. "The Love Canal Tragedy." EPA. January. https://archive.epa.gov/epa/aboutepa/love-canal-tragedy.html

United States Environmental Protection Agency (US EPA). 1995. *State of the Great Lakes Report*. Washington: EPA. https://archive.epa.gov/solec/web/pdf/state_of_the_great_lakes_1995_highlights_report.pdf

United States Environmental Protection Agency (US EPA). 1998. *State of the Lakes Ecosystem Conference (SOLEC) Report*. https://archive.epa.gov/solec/web/pdf/solec_1998_conference_proceedings.pdf

United States Environmental Protection Agency (US EPA). 2002. *Lake Erie Dead Zone*. https://www.epa.gov

United States Environmental Protection Agency (US EPA). 2003. *State of the Great Lakes Ecosystem Conference Report*. Washington: EPA. https://archive.epa.gov/solec/web/pdf/state_of_the_great_lakes_2003_summary_report.pdf

United States Environmental Protection Agency (US EPA). 2004. *State of the Lakes Ecosystem Conference Report: Highlights*. Washington: EPA. https://archive.epa.gov/solec/web/pdf/2004_highlights.pdf

United States Environmental Protection Agency (EPA). 2020. Invasive Species in the Great Lakes, https://www.epa.gov/greatlakes/invasive-species-great-lakes

United States Environmental Protection Agency. 2020a. "Summary of the Clean Water Act (1972)." EPA. https://www.epa.gov/laws-regulations/summary-clean-water-act

United States Environmental Protection Agency. 2020b. "Invasive Species in the Great Lakes." EPA. https://www.epa.gov/greatlakes/invasive-species-great-lakes

United States Environmental Protection Agency (EPA) and Environment and Climate Change Canada (ECCC). 2019. *Progress Report of the Parties*. https://binational.net/wp-content/uploads/2020/01/2019-ProgressReport_EN.pdf

United Stated Fish and Wildlife Service, (USFWS), 2020c. "Grey Wolves in Western Great Lakes States", https://www.fws.gov/midwest/wolf/

VanNijnatten, D. and C. Johns. 2019. "The International Joint Commission and the Evolution of the Great Lakes Water Quality Agreement: Accountability, Progress Reporting, and Measuring Performance." In *The First Century of the International Joint Commission*, edited by M. Clamen and D. Macfarlane, pp. 395–430. Calgary: University of Calgary Press.

Winfield, M. and G. Jenish. 1999. *Troubled Waters? A Review of the Performance of the Governments of Canada and Ontario under the 1994 Canada–Ontario Agreement Respecting the Great Lakes Basin Ecosystem*. Toronto: Canadian Institute of Environmental Law and Policy.

19

Phasing Out Coal-Fired Electricity in Ontario

Mark S. Winfield and Abdeali Saherwala

Introduction

The phase-out of coal-fired electricity production in the Canadian province of Ontario has been widely described as one of the most significant measures taken by any government in the world to reduce greenhouse gas (GHG) emissions (Petravan, 2017). The phase-out of coal, which in the early 2000s constituted a quarter of the province's electricity supply, was completed in 2014. The phase-out has been associated with dramatic improvements in air quality in the southern part of the province. As such, it is regarded as a core environmental legacy of the 2003–2018 Liberal governments of premiers Dalton McGuinty and Kathleen Wynne.

As shown in Table 19.1, the phase-out was an undeniable success in terms of reducing emissions of GHGs, smog and acid rain precursors, and heavy metals, like mercury. These reductions in emissions translated into direct positive impacts on air quality in Ontario. In 2001, the province issued seven smog advisories covering 23 days, the most on record at that time. 2005 was the worst year, with 15 advisories covering 53 days. The number of advisories dropped to virtually zero from 2013 onwards (Ontario, 2017), coinciding with the closure of the coal plants.

The Ontario coal phase-out had national impacts as well. In 2012 the Conservative federal government adopted a regulation establishing the national phase-out of conventional coal-fired electricity generation, although with an implementation timeline reaching into the early 2060s (Government of Canada, 2012). The phase-out date, principally affecting Alberta, Nova Scotia, and Saskatchewan, was subsequently advanced to 2030 by the Liberal federal government that has been in office since 2015 (ECCC, 2018). Coal phase-outs are central features of the 2016 Pan-Canadian Framework for Clean Growth and Climate Change (PCF), and provincial climate change plans.

Mark S. Winfield and Abdeali Saherwala, *Phasing Out Coal-Fired Electricity in Ontario*. In: *Policy Success in Canada*. Edited by Evert A. Lindquist et al., Oxford University Press. © Mark S. Winfield and Abdeali Saherwala (2022). DOI: 10.1093/oso/9780192897046.003.0019

Table 19.1 Electricity-Sector Emissions Reductions in Ontario

Pollutant	2005 Emissions	Decrease (%)	2015 Emissions (est.)
Greenhouse gases (GHGs)—megatonnes (MT)	32.9	87%	4.25
Nitrogen oxides (NOx)—kilotonnes (Kt)	48.1	86%	6.8
Sulphur oxides (SOx)—kilotonnes (Kt)	114.3	99.6%	0.4
Mercury (Hg)—kilograms (Kg)	326	100%	0.0

Source: (Ontario 2017) https://www.ontario.ca/page/end-coal

At the same time, Ontario's approach to the phase-out did involve a series of significant environmental, economic, and political trade-offs, the benefits of which continue to be debated, and whose consequences have affected the province's politics profoundly. With respect to the environment, although energy conservation and an expansion of renewable energy played significant roles in the phase-out, the process also involved a major recommitment to nuclear energy, and a noteworthy expansion of natural gas-fired generation. Both technologies are associated with very substantial environmental impacts of their own. The economic costs of the phase-out, in terms of the overall reconstruction of the province's electricity system and the impacts on electricity prices, remain a central controversy in Ontario politics. The phase-out was also embedded within a deepening explicit politicization of decision-making regarding the province's electricity system. Using McConnell's (2010) framework for assessing policy outcomes around programmatic results, policy processes, and politics, the coal phase-out itself can be considered a 'resilient' and 'political success'. However, other aspects of the process, like the McGuinty (2003–2013) and Wynne (2013–2018) governments' overall handling of electricity policy, can also be considered what McConnell terms a 'political failure'.

The Ontario case is also a striking illustration of the potential impacts of policy entrepreneurship on the part of non-governmental organizations. It is doubtful whether the Ontario and subsequent national phase-outs would have occurred without the work of the Ontario Clean Air Alliance, and the coalition of health professions, municipal governments, unions, and other NGOs assembled by the alliance.

This case study provides a brief history of the Ontario coal phase-out, beginning with acid rain control efforts in the 1970s and 1980s, through to its completion in 2014. This is followed by a discussion of the landscape, as well as the institutional and policy factors that contributed to the feasibility of a phase-out in the

374 PHASING OUT COAL-FIRED ELECTRICITY IN ONTARIO

province. Finally, the chapter assesses the outcomes of the coal phase-out in terms of its programmatic environmental and economic impacts, policy resiliency and endurance, and wider policy effects. The influence of the phase-out on the policy-making process and broader political dynamics within the province are evaluated as well.

The Coal Phase-Out: A History

The Role of Coal-Fired Electricity in Ontario

As shown in Table 19.2, Ontario constructed six coal-fired electricity plants between the early 1950s and mid-1980s. Up to the 1950s, the province's electricity system had been almost entirely hydro-electric. However, the dramatic post-war growth in electricity demand outstripped the province's supply of readily developable hydro sites. The coal-fired plants were constructed to bridge supply until the province's planned nuclear energy program could be realized. That process would stretch from the 1960s to the mid-1990s (Freeman1996). Even then, the coal-fired plants provided back-up supply for periods of high electricity demand.

The Beginnings: Acid Rain Control

While the Ontario coal phase-out is generally viewed as a response to issues related to climate change and air quality, environmental questions about the role of coal-fired electricity in the province first arose around an earlier issue—acid rain. A complex process of domestic and international agenda-setting and advocacy through the 1970s and early 1980s culminated in the 1986 imposition, by the newly

Table 19.2 Ontario's Coal-Fired Electricity Plants

Name and Location	Commissioned	Capacity	Fate
Hearn (Toronto)	1951	1200MW	Shutdown 1983, abandoned.
Lakeview (Mississauga)	1962	2400MW	Shutdown 2005, demolished.
Thunder Bay	1963	306MW	Converted to biomass 2015, shutdown 2018.
Lambton (Sarnia)	1969	1980MW	Shutdown 2013, demolished.
Nanticoke	1972–1978	3964MW	Shutdown 2013, demolished
Atikokan	1985	211MW	Converted to biomass, 2014.

elected Liberal minority government led by David Peterson, of special regulations on the four largest sources of acid-rain-causing emissions in the province. Under the program—known as Countdown Acid Rain—Inco, Ontario Hydro, Falconbridge Ltd., and the Algoma Steel Co. Ltd. were required to reduce their total sulphur dioxide emissions from the 1980 level of 1,772,000 tonnes per year to 795,000 tonnes by 1995. Ontario Hydro, for its part, planned to meet its 1995 target of 175,000 tonnes per year largely by mothballing its coal-fired generating facilities as new nuclear plants, particularly the Darlington facility east of Toronto, came into service (Winfield, 2012). The coal-fired plants would, however, be held in reserve.

Coal and the 'Common Sense Revolution'

The arrival of a Progressive Conservative government led by Mike Harris in 1995 had major, if initially unexpected, implications for the fate of Ontario Hydro's coal-fired plants. The new government's 'Common Sense Revolution' (CSR) platform had said little about electricity issues, other than to promise a five-year freeze on hydro rates. In practice, the government embarked on what would be the most extensive restructuring of the electricity sector in Ontario since the creation of the Ontario Hydro Electric Commission in 1906. Strongly influenced by developments in the United Kingdom and the United States, the government moved to abandon Ontario Hydro's near monopoly on electricity system planning and abolish its control of major generating assets in order to embrace a 'market' model for the system. Under this model, the role of public utilities in long-term planning for electricity supply would be removed. Rather, investors would make decisions about where and when electricity generating facilities should be built, and these decisions would be based on their assessments of the potential market for the power they would produce (Dewees, 2005).

As part of the process, Ontario Hydro was divided into five separate entities: Ontario Power Generation (OPG), which would own the utility's generating assets (including the coal-fired plants); Ontario Services Corporation (later named Hydro One) to operate the transmission infrastructure; an Independent Market Operator (IMO) to operate and administer a wholesale electricity market; the Ontario Hydro Financial Corporation, which assumed responsibility for the $20 billion of Ontario Hydro's $38 billion debt that was 'stranded' as a result of the utility's break-up; and the Electrical Safety Authority (ESA), which was to assume Ontario Hydro's regulatory functions with respect to electrical safety. All the successor entities, except for the ESA, would continue, like Ontario Hydro, to be owned by the province. One of the major goals of the government was to reduce Ontario Hydro's dominant position in the system, reducing its ownership of generating assets from 85 per cent to 35 per cent by 2010 (Winfield, 2012, 102–103).

376 PHASING OUT COAL-FIRED ELECTRICITY IN ONTARIO

Table 19.3 Ontario Power Generation's Coal Plants: Electricity Generation and Emissions 1995–2001

Parameter	1995	1996	1997	1998	1999	2000	2001
Electricity generation (Gwh)	16,699	18,915	24,523	33,275	34,068	41,446	37,185
GHGs (megatonnes)	15.4	17.9	22.43	29.8	30.5	37.64	35.1
Sulphur dioxide (kilotonnes)	74.1	84.5	123.15	140.81	140.58	163.51	147.19
Nitogen oxides (no.) (kilotonnes)	28.2	35.1	42.77	54.32	49.24	49.45	42.17

Source: Gibbons (2003).

New problems emerged at Ontario Hydro even as the government was moving towards its dissolution. In July 1997 an external review raised major concerns regarding the maintenance and safety of Ontario's nuclear power plants (Ontario Hydro, 1997). In response, Ontario Hydro adopted a Nuclear Asset Optimization Plan (NAOP). Under the plan, seven of the utility's 19 operating power reactors[1] were taken out of service for repair and overhaul. Although not immediately apparent, the NAOP and its consequences would set in motion the chain of events that would lead to the phase-out of coal-fired electricity generation in Ontario.

As part of the NAOP, Ontario Hydro relied on its five operational coal-fired generating facilities (Lakeview, Nanticoke, Lambton, Thunder Bay, and Atikokan) to replace the power supplies lost by taking the seven nuclear units out of service. This, inevitably, led to major increases in emissions of smog and acid rain precursors, heavy metals, and GHGs from these facilities. Therefore (see Table 19.3), as the plants' outputs rose between 1995 and 2001, their GHG emissions increased by a factor of 2.3, and emissions of the smog and acid rain precursors, sulphur dioxide (SO_2) and nitrogen oxide (NOx), doubled and increased by a factor of 1.7, respectively.

The Emergence of the Smog Issue

The large increases in emissions associated with the NAOP occurred as the health impacts of the increasingly regular smog episodes in southern Ontario became a major public concern. The situation triggered a number of high-profile

[1] Pickering A Units 1–4 and Bruce A Units 1, 3, and 4. Bruce A Unit 2 had been shut down in October 1995.

interventions by health professionals. A major report released by the Ontario Medical Association (OMA) in May 1998 characterized the smog situation as posing a 'serious health risk to the people of Ontario' (OMA, 1998, 1). The report, marking the first major intervention by the OMA in an environmental issue since the late 1960s, was critical of the likely impacts of the NAOP on air quality, and more generally, of the province's performance on air quality issues.

Three of OPG's coal-fired plants, Lambton, Nanticoke, and Lakeview, were located directly in the southern Ontario airshed most affected by smog. The province's electricity consumption patterns, which were now moving towards peaking in the summer due to increased air conditioning loads, further reinforced the problem. Summer peaks meant that the coal plants were being run at maximum capacity at a time when the conditions for smog formation were at their worst (Cundiff, 2015).

The emergence of the smog issue, combined with the implementation of the NAOP, led to the establishment of what would become the key policy entrepreneur in the coal phase-out story—the Ontario Clean Air Alliance (hereafter, the Alliance). The Alliance was founded in 1997 as a project of the Canadian Institute for Environmental Law and Policy. (It later moved its institutional home to Pollution Probe, one of the oldest NGOs in the sector). The Alliance rapidly assembled a diverse coalition of supporters including municipalities, private-sector companies, unions, health professions and their associations, and other environmental organizations. Its presence, and the active engagement and advocacy by the health professions through the OMA, Registered Nurses Association of Ontario, and Ontario Public Health Association, were particularly important in overcoming opposition from the major institutional actors in the system (e.g. OPG and OPA/IESO), industrial power consumers represented by the Association of Major Power Consumers of Ontario (AMPCO), and the Power Workers' Union, which represented OPG's workers (Cundiff, 2015; Harris et al., 2015).

The Alliance initially focused on the establishment of emission caps for GHGs, nitrogen oxides, and sulphur dioxide for the electricity sector (Gibbons and Bjorkquist, 1998). It was specifically with the government's direction to Ontario Hydro to sell generating assets in order to reduce its dominant position in the emerging market. The utility was under pressure to sell those assets, including the coal-fired plants, as going concerns, to maximize the revenues their sale would generate. In turn, these revenues would contribute to paying down Ontario Hydro's debt.

The federal government added on to provincial pressures around air quality issues by initiating discussions with the US federal government to develop an Ozone Annex to the 1991 Canada-US Air Quality Agreement, which had been principally focused on combating acid rain. The Annex was eventually signed in October 2000. Its provisions included a cap on nitrogen oxide emissions from coal-fired power stations in central and southern Ontario, opening the possibility of federal

378 PHASING OUT COAL-FIRED ELECTRICITY IN ONTARIO

regulation of these facilities if the province did not take steps to reduce their emissions on its own. In May 2001, that possibility was reinforced with the addition of particulate matter 10 microns in diameter (PM_{10}) and then, in July 2002, sulphur dioxide and nitrogen oxides, volatile organic compounds, nitric oxide, ozone, and gaseous ammonia—all smog components or precursors—to the list of toxic substances under the Canadian Environmental Protection Act (CEPA). The listing of these substances under CEPA would permit the federal government to regulate their emissions directly.

In response to these pressures, in January 2000, the province announced its intention to impose new sulphur dioxide and nitrogen oxide emission caps on OPG's coal- and oil-fired plants by January 2001 as part of its 'strategic attack' on air pollution (Ontario Ministry of the Environment, 2000). Under continuing pressure from the Alliance's campaign, and in anticipation of reports from the OMA (OMA, 2000) and the City of Toronto's medical officer of health (Toronto Public Health, 2000) highlighting the role of the coal-fired plants in southern Ontario's air quality problems, the province announced in May 2000 an 'environmental' moratorium on the sale of OPG's coal-fired plants (Clark and Yacoumidis, 2000).

A phase-out of the Lakeview coal-fired plant by April 2005 was announced by Environment Minister Elizabeth Witmer. Any replacement facility would be required to meet the same emission standards of an 'efficient natural gas technology' (Elwell et al., 2001, 72). That requirement was incorporated into a regulation in October 2001. The government subsequently refused to approve proposed sales of the Thunder Bay and Atikokan plants for 'environmental reasons', and made any future sales conditional on the conversion of the coal-fired plants to natural gas (Smith and Stewart, 2004, 173). These steps, sometimes referred to as the 'Witmer standard', represented the beginning of the end for the province's coal-fired plants.

The 2003 Election: A Coal Phase-Out Moves to Centre Stage

All three major political parties in Ontario entered the October 2003 election with platform commitments to phase out coal-fired electricity. The governing Progressive Conservatives, now led by Ernie Eves, committed to closing all of Ontario's coal-fired power plants by 2015 (PC Ontario 2003, paper 6). The NDP's *Publicpower* platform was more ambitious, proposing a 2007 closure date (NDP, 2003). The Liberals, led by Dalton McGuinty, who would emerge from the election with a strong majority government, also committed to 'shut down' Ontario's coal-burning power plants by 2007 (Ontario Liberal Party, 2003, 3–5).

The new Liberal government began to move away from the market model for the electricity system, towards what it described as a 'hybrid' system of markets and planning, symbolized by the re-badging of the Independent Market Operator as the Independent Electricity System Operator (IESO). The Electricity

Restructuring Act, adopted in 2004, created a new entity, the Ontario Power Authority (OPA). The OPA was mandated to develop a 20-year Integrated Power System Plan (IPSP) for the province's electricity system. The legislation allowed the minister of energy to issue directives to the OPA with respect to the content of the IPSP.

In response to a request for advice from the minister of energy on the appropriate mix of supply options for Ontario's future electricity system over the next 20 years, the OPA recommended that coal be phased out between 2005 and 2015. The coal plants would be replaced by a combination of natural-gas-fired generation and new renewables—principally a combination of refurbished hydro facilities and new wind-power projects (OPA, 2005).

A Supply Mix Directive was issued on 13 June 2006 to the OPA regarding the IPSP that it was to develop. Consistent with the OPA's advice, the directive signalled a backing away from the government's commitment to phase out coal-fired electricity by 2007, simply requiring that the plan provide for the replacement of coal-fired generation 'in the earliest practical time frame that ensures adequate generating capacity and electricity system reliability in Ontario' (Duncan 2006, 2–3). The directive was widely criticized by environmental advocates for its focus on nuclear energy, abandonment of the 2007 coal-phase-out target date, and exemption of the overall planning process from the Environmental Assessment Act (Ontario Clean Air Alliance, 2006).

The IPSP, proposing $60 billion in investments in energy supply and conservation (including $27 billion on nuclear energy), was filed with the Ontario Energy Board on 29 August 2007, just prior to the start of the 2007 election campaign. A regulation (Ontario Regulation 496/07), which required the cessation of the use of coal at the province's four remaining coal-fired power plants by 2014, was also adopted at the same time. From the government's perspective, a renewed commitment to a coal phase-out and modest support for renewable energy and conservation helped divide some of the environmental opposition to the plan, overriding the political risk of some members of the ENGO community actively campaigning against the IPSP (*Toronto Star* 2007).

The move in the direction of a coal phase-out was further reinforced by the emerging issue of climate change. Ontario announced its Go Green climate change plan in June 2007. The plan committed to reducing the province's GHG emissions to 6 per cent below 1990 levels by 2014, 15 per cent by 2020, and 80 per cent by 2050. The commitment to phase out coal-fired electricity generation was the centrepiece of the plan. The plan included major investments in public transit and a cap-and-trade system for other large industrial pollutant sources (ECO, 2009).

The Liberal platform going into the October 2007 election committed to carrying through on the climate change plan, including a coal phase-out by 2014. However, the government's wider plans were profoundly disrupted by the autumn 2008 Global Financial Crisis. Among other things, the financial collapse triggered

380 PHASING OUT COAL-FIRED ELECTRICITY IN ONTARIO

a further crisis in the North American automobile manufacturing industry. As a result, the province's economy lost nearly 250,000 jobs between the autumn of 2008 and the spring of 2009.

Picking up on signals from the incoming Obama administration in the United States, the province made strong moves to link its economic recovery strategy to environmental sustainability, particularly in the form of the 2009 Green Energy and Green Economy Act (GEGEA). The act provided, among other things, the authority for a feed-in tariff (FIT) mechanism, similar to those employed in Germany, Spain, and Denmark, for low-impact renewable energy sources. FIT mechanisms pay the owners and operators of renewable energy projects a guaranteed fixed price for the electricity produced by their facilities (Winfield, 2015).

Along with a number of competitive request-for-proposal processes, the FIT did facilitate a large increase in the renewable energy capacity in the province. From a starting point of virtually zero in 2005, approximately 4500MW of wind and 450MW of solar PV capacity had been installed by the end of 2018 (IESO, 2020a). At the same time, however, the program became the target of growing criticism over rising electricity costs and questions about the need for additional power supplies in the face of declining electricity demands (Winfield and Dolter, 2014). It would be effectively terminated by McGuinty's successor, Kathleen Wynne, for larger projects in 2013, and for smaller ones in 2017 (Winfield, 2016).

Completing the Phase-Out: 2011–2014

The 2011 Liberal platform again committed to completing the phase-out of coal-fired electricity. The Liberals emerged from the election just short of a majority government but secured a historic third term in office. Yet the electricity question marred that third term. In the run-up to the election, serious complications arose around the government's cancellation of proposed gas-fired electricity plants in Oakville and Mississauga, which were designed to be part of the coal-phase-out process. The plants had faced very strong local opposition in both communities. It would emerge in the aftermath of the election that the cost of cancelling the plants, for which contracts had been signed between the OPA and the proponents, approached $600 million (Artuso, 2013).

The legislative opposition's pursuit of the issue, in the context of a minority government produced by the October 2011 election, would be central to McGuinty's October 2012 decision to prorogue the legislature and announce his intention to resign. McGuinty was succeeded as premier by Kathleen Wynne in February 2013. Wynne's leadership platform was silent on electricity issues other than containing a specific commitment to continue the coal phase-out. The phase-out would ultimately be completed at the end of 2014 with the closure of the Nanticoke and Lambton facilities, and the conversion of the Thunder Bay and Atikokan facilities to burn biomass (i.e. wood pellets). The phase-out continued to be referenced as a major component of the government's comprehensive 2016 Climate Change Action Plan (CCAP). At the same time, the fallout from the Liberal government's handling of the electricity file would continue to play a defining role in the province's politics.

The Aftermath: The Fair Hydro Plan and Doug Ford

In June 2016, the government adopted legislation merging the IESO and OPA.[2] Perhaps more significantly, the legislation eliminated the requirement for the development and publication of IPSPs by the merged entity and for their review by the OEB before implementation. Instead, system plans would be developed by the minister of energy and approved by the cabinet. The OEB and IESO would then be required to implement those plans. In effect, the legislation dropped the pretence of rational planning and meaningful independent public review of the province's electricity system. Instead, it formalized a paradigm of political management in electricity system planning (Winfield and MacWhirter, 2019).

A major expression of the politicization of decision-making on electricity policy came at the beginning of March 2017. With high hydro costs being consistently identified as the leading public concern facing the province (Nanos, 2016), the government announced a 'Fair Hydro Plan'. The plan was to reduce electricity rates by 25 per cent for the following five years, beginning 1 July 2017, (Office of the Premier, 2017) with the intention of removing the issue of hydro rates from the political agenda before the provincial election in 2018. The plan relied principally on extending the financing period for debt associated with new electricity infrastructure, typically from 20 to 30 years. The potential additional financing costs of this approach, along with the elimination of the HST, on hydro bills, were estimated at $45 billion, with the costs largely falling on future consumers (Auditor General of Ontario, 2017).

In the end, the plan had no impact on the election outcome in 2018, which resulted in a major defeat for the Liberals and the election of a populist Progressive-Conservative premier, Doug Ford. Relief from energy costs, particularly electricity costs, was a major theme in Ford's electoral platform. Blame for these costs was laid squarely at the feet of the GEGEA FIT program and the GHG emission cap and trade system that was at the heart of the 2016 CCAP (PC Ontario, 2018). Although the Ford government moved quickly to dismantle the cap and trade program and the CCAP programs financed through it, and to repeal the GEGEA, there was no effort to reverse the coal phase-out (Winfield and Kaiser, 2020).

---

[2] Bill 135—The Energy Statute Law Amendment Act, 2016, S.O. 2016, c. 10.

Indeed, it was referenced as an important success in the Ford government's own 'made-in-Ontario' environment plan, released in December 2018 (Ontario, 2018).

Drivers of the Phase-Out: External, Policy, and Institutional Factors

The Ontario Clear Air Alliance's policy entrepreneurship, and the consistent political commitment of the McGuinty and Wynne governments to a phase-out were the central factors in its completion. A number of other external and institutional factors and complementary policy decisions converged to facilitate a coal phase-out in Ontario, as well. These included a decline in electricity demand, the construction of new gas-fired and renewable energy sources, and the return to service of some of the NAOP 'laid-up' nuclear facilities. The fact that OPG was owned by the province, as opposed to being an investor-owned utility, also helped to facilitate the phase-out. The following section discusses each of these elements in detail.

Firstly, the phase-out of coal-fired generation was assisted by a significant decline in electricity demand in the province from the mid-2000s onwards, as shown in Figure 19.1. The decline occurred despite continuing growth in the province's population and economy. The shift has been attributed in large part to economic restructuring away from energy-intensive manufacturing, resource extraction and processing activities, towards less energy-intense service, knowledge, and information-based sectors. The impact of the conservation programs put in place from 2003 onwards was also a factor (Winfield and Gelfant, 2020).

Secondly, between 2004 and 2012 the province added 5500 MW of natural-gas-fired generating capacity, in the form of new combined cycle facilities, single cycle peaking plants, and combined heat and power facilities (Ontario, 2017). The

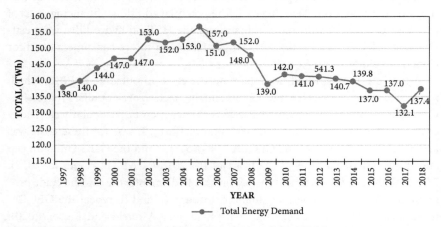

Fig. 19.1 Total Annual Ontario Electricity Demand (in TWh) 1997–2018
Source: Data from IESO n.d.

contracts for these facilities were structured around capacity payments, ensuring that the capital costs of facility construction would be retired at the end of these contracts, regardless of facility utilization rates. The development of new natural gas-fired generating facilities in Ontario coincided with historically low natural gas prices in North America, a product of the increasing availability of 'fracked' natural gas. The situation has prompted a widespread displacement of coal-fired generation by natural gas throughout the United States (Saha, 2019).

Thirdly, four of the seven nuclear reactors 'laid up' through the NAOP were eventually refurbished and returned to service. They included two units each at the Pickering[3] and Bruce[4] facilities. Two un-refurbished units at Bruce were also returned to service.[5] Although making significant contributions to the province's electricity supply, the refurbishment and repair projects ran billions of dollars over budget and years behind schedule (Winfield et al., 2006, Table 6.4). Along with a number of competitive request-for-proposal processes, the GEGEA did facilitate a large increase in renewable energy capacity in the province. As noted earlier, from a starting point of virtually zero in 2005, approximately 5400 MW of wind and 2600 MW of solar PV capacity was installed by the end of 2018 (IESO, 2020a). A number of upgrades and refurbishments were also undertaken on OPG's existing hydro-electric facilities.

A final factor contributing to the feasibility of a coal phase-out in Ontario was that OPG was the owner of the five coal plants and OPG itself remained in provincial ownership throughout the restructuring of the electricity sector. As the ultimate owner of OPG, the province could give directives directly to the utility, and choose to write off whatever residual capital value might have remained in the coal-fired plants at their time of closure. This was a very different approach from that taken by the NDP Notley government in Alberta to its phase-out of coal-fired electricity. Alberta's coal-fired plants were owned by private utilities, and rather than risking legal battles with those utilities, the province used the revenues from its carbon pricing systems to compensate the owners for the lost value of their facilities arising from the phase-out (Vriens, 2018).

A Policy Success? Assessing the Phase-Out

An overall assessment of the Ontario coal phase-out has to recognize that while this policy can be seen as a stand-alone initiative in programmatic, process, political, and endurance terms, it was intimately connected to the province's overall

---

[3] Unit A1 (515MW) returned to service 2003. Unit A4 (515MW) returned to service 2005. Refurbishment of units A2 and A3 was abandoned as uneconomic.
[4] Units A1 and A2 (both 830MW) returned to service 2012.
[5] Unit A3 2004; Unit A4 2003.

384   PHASING OUT COAL-FIRED ELECTRICITY IN ONTARIO

handling of the electricity file. Any final evaluation must account for both of these components, as they were so intimately intertwined.

Programmatic Assessment

When taking into consideration its environmental and economic 'balance sheets', the Ontario coal phase-out itself can be rated as a 'resilient success' in programmatic terms. The phase-out has delivered significant and measurable improvements in environmental quality, although the question of its costs to the overall reconstruction of the province's electricity system remained controversial. As shown in Table 19.1, the phase-out of coal-fired electricity in Ontario resulted in major reductions in emissions of GHGs, smog and acid rain precursors, and hazardous air pollutants—particularly heavy metals—leading to substantial, measurable improvements in air quality in southern Ontario.

At the same time, the phase-out did involve some important environmental trade-offs. The province's approach to the phase-out involved a significant 'comeback' of nuclear generation, which grew from 43 per cent of electricity output in 2003 to more than 60 per cent from 2014 onwards (Ontario, 2017). The growth in nuclear generation resulted in increased production of extremely hazardous and long-lasting waste up stream and down stream. Nuclear energy is also associated with unique and severe accidents and security risks, and is associated with significant losses in system flexibility at the operational and planning levels (Sovacool et al., 2020; Winfield et al., 2006).

A sustainability assessment of the 2007 IPSP concluded that the replacement of coal with refurbished and expanded nuclear power, which underpinned the plan, was unacceptable from a sustainability perspective. Both options presented severe, although different, immediate and long-term negative consequences, while better options were available (Winfield et al., 2010). As noted earlier, the phase-out was also associated with the construction of a large fleet of new natural gas-fired generating facilities, whose operations can have significant air quality impacts, particularly in terms of emissions of GHGs, nitrogen oxides, and particulate matter. Unconventional or 'fracked' natural gas production, which constitutes a growing portion of North American natural gas supplies, is also associated with significant environmental effects, including methane leakage, and groundwater and landscape impacts (Barcelo and Bennett, 2016).

In purely economic terms, coal-fired generation offered a relatively cheap and reliable electricity source. Viewed in wider terms, the cost of coal-fired generation was much higher. A 2005 study completed for the province estimated that the total annual cost of coal-fired electricity, including health, financial, and environmental costs, was $4.4 billion (Ontario Ministry of Energy, 2005). At the same time, the period over which the phase-out occurred was associated with major increases in electricity prices, particularly for residential consumers. Consumers' costs per kWh of electricity more than doubled from the early 2000s to 2018 (IESO, 2020b). The situation with rising electricity costs became a point of major political controversy, leading to the 2017 Fair Hydro Plan. Even then, it was widely seen as a contributing factor in the Wynne government's 2018 electoral defeat (Gurney, 2018).

The Electricity Conservation and Supply Task Force had estimated in 2003 that two-thirds of the system's generating assets (including the coal plants) would need to be refurbished or replaced over the following twenty years (ECSTF, 2004, Figure 1A). The capital costs of these investments were embedded in what is referred to as the 'Global Adjustment' (GA) component of electricity bills. As shown in Figure 19.2, in recent years, the GA has risen to account for approximately 80 per cent of the electricity portion of consumers' bills (IESO, 2020b).

Although the 2009 GEGEA FIT program has been widely blamed for the increases in the GA (McKitrick, 2013), a breakdown of the contributors to the charge tells a more complex story. As of 2020, renewables, principally wind and solar, accounted for approximately 25 per cent of the GA. Nuclear, mainly the costs of the first Pickering and Bruce refurbishments, accounted for over 50 per cent, and was expected to account for an ever-higher portion as the refurbishments of

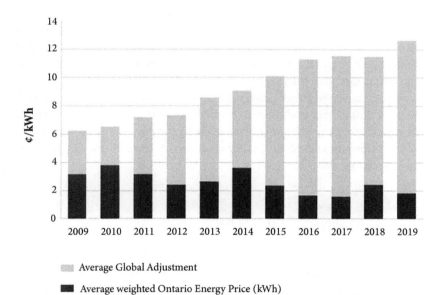

Fig. 19.2 Average Global Adjustment vs. Average Market Electricity Price (2009–2019)

Source: IESO (2020b). Copyright © 2001–2020 Independent Electricity System Operator, all rights reserved. This information is subject to the Terms of Use set out in the IESO's website (www.ieso.ca).

the facilities proceeded. Natural gas-fired generation accounted for 10 per cent, largely driven by capacity payments for the natural gas-fired plants constructed between 2004 and 2012 (IESO, 2020b). The upgrading and refurbishment of transmission and distribution infrastructure, reflected in the 'delivery' portion of bills and usually accounting for about one third of the total bill, added further costs (Environmental Defense, 2017). Industrial consumers were able to avoid the GA part of their electricity bills through a variety of mechanisms (Winfield and Gelfant, 2020), meaning that the bulk of the capital costs of rebuilding the system fell on residential consumers.

Although the Ford government took steps to clarify the costs of the 2017 Fair Hydro Plan (Bill 87), it left its core elements in place. The result has been a situation where hydro rates are being kept artificially low through subsidies out of general revenues of $7 billion per year (FAO, 2020). There are ongoing debates about whether the reconstruction of the system could have been achieved at lower costs. Particularly strong arguments occur over the necessity and costs of new renewable energy sources, new gas-fired generation and nuclear refurbishments, as well as the availability of lower-cost alternatives through conservation and hydro imports from Quebec (Winfield and MacWhirter, 2019).

Given the scale of the overall system reconstruction that took place between 2004 and 2020, the range of elements that contributed to the phase-out (conservation, declining demand, new renewable and natural gas-fired generation and nuclear refurbishments), and the scope of possible scenarios for the retention of coal (such as major pollution control retrofits), it is virtually impossible to define a specific marginal cost for the coal phase-out. Any assessment is further complicated by the reality that, with the possible exceptions of Nanticoke and Atikokan, the province's coal-fired power plants were at, or approaching, technical end-of-life in the early 2000s, and would have required major reconstructions or replacements regardless of any policy decisions made by the province (Cui et al., 2019).[6] At the same time, the coal phase-out per se, is rarely blamed for the electricity cost increases seen over the period.

Process Assessment

One of the central critiques of the province's post-2003 approach to decision-making around the electricity system has been that it has become increasingly and explicitly politicized (Vegh, 2018). That process culminated in the adoption of Bill 135 in 2016. The bill effectively eliminated the requirement for a formal

---

[6] The anticipated life for coal-fired power plants is in the range of 40–50 years. Cui et al. (2019). This would suggest non-policy-driven closure dates as follows: Nanticoke 2012–2028; Atikokan 2025–2035; Thunder Bay 2003–2013; Lambton 2009–2019; and Lakeview 2002–2012.

evidence-based planning process around the electricity system, and instead established a directive-based system which ran from the political level to the province's energy agencies.

The coal phase-out highlighted several trade-offs associated with this politized decision-making model. On the one hand, the phase-out was strongly resisted by key institutional actors in Ontario's electricity system (e.g. OPG/OPA/IESO) and the major industrial consumers represented by the Association of Major Power Consumers of Ontario (AMPCO). In that context, it is highly unlikely that the phase-out would have occurred without the consistent political direction and formal directives provided by the McGuinty and Wynne governments to the OPA and IESO. The same could be said regarding the province's progress on energy conservation, and renewable energy development and programming, designed to assist low-income energy consumers. At the same time, the province has been left with no real electricity system planning process, and there is an apparent acceptance of political direction as opposed to open, evidence-based decision-making around major infrastructure decisions (MacWhirter and Winfield, 2019).

The overall result in policy process terms might be considered a 'conflicted success' (McConnell, 2010). On the one hand, the coal phase-out was successfully implemented. At the same time, the overall process of energy and electricity policy-making remains precarious, indeed controversial, in political terms.

Political Assessment

The conflicting outcomes are also witnessed in political assessments. The coal phase-out itself can be seen as a politically successful policy insofar as by 2003 there was support for it from all of the province's major political parties. At the same time, the overall state of the province's electricity system planning efforts must be seen as a political failure (as defined by McConnell, 2010). This is particularly evident in the role that electricity costs played in the outcome of the province's 2018 election. The election saw the defeat of the Liberal government and its replacement by a populist Progressive Conservative administration, whose promises to 'clean up the Hydro mess', and 'cut hydro rates' (PC Ontario, 2018) were central to the outcome of the campaign.

Endurance Assessment

To what extent have these programmatic benefits now been 'locked in'? The demolition of the southern Ontario coal plants (Lakeview in 2006–07, Nanticoke in 2018–19, and Lambton in 2019–20) make a large-scale return to coal virtually impossible. The Thunder Bay plant was converted to burn biomass (wood pellets)

388 PHASING OUT COAL-FIRED ELECTRICITY IN ONTARIO

but is now retired. Only the Atikokan plant remains in service, running on wood pellet biomass. There seems no serious consideration of restoring the role of coal in the province's electricity system. Indeed, the phase-out is referenced as a major achievement in the Ford government's December 2018 Environment Plan.

In the longer term, however, some of the environmental gains from the coal phase-out may be significantly eroded. The province currently plans to run the fleet of gas-fired plants, commissioned between 2004 and 2012, to make up for potential power shortfalls from the retirement of the Pickering nuclear facility in 2024, and refurbishments at the Bruce (six units) and Darlington (four units) nuclear plants between 2020 and 2033. Thirty to 40 per cent of the reductions in emissions of GHGs and smog precursors obtained through the coal phase-out could be lost through such a strategy (IESO, 2020c).

A national phase-out of conventional coal-fired electricity generation was announced by Stephen Harper's Conservative federal government in 2012, although full implementation would not have occurred until the 2060s. In 2018, the Trudeau government advanced the phase-out date to 2030, principally affecting facilities in Alberta, Saskatchewan, and Nova Scotia (Canada 2018).

In sum, although some of the environmental gains from the phase-out are at risk of partial erosion, there is little or no risk of a full-scale reversal. While there is broad consensus around the positive environmental and health impacts of the coal phase-out, the overall costs and directions for the restructuring of the province's electricity sector remain a point of political conflict, and might be considered a 'conflicted' or even 'precarious' success at best (McConnell, 2010).

Conclusions

The overall assessment of the province's handling of the coal phase-out is summarized in Table 19.4. The conclusions highlight the relative successes around the coal phase-out per se, and also draw attention to failures around the handling of the electricity question more generally.

The phase-out of coal-fired electricity generation in Ontario, completed in 2014, has had significant and measurable positive effects on environmental quality, particularly with respect to acid rain, smog, and GHG emissions. The Ontario phase-out ultimately prompted the federal government to pursue a national phase-out of conventional coal-fired electricity, initially by the 2060s, and later by 2030. At the same time, the Ontario phase-out involved significant trade-offs in terms of the environmental sustainability of the province's electricity system. Assessments of the economic costs of the phase-out are difficult, given its complex relationship with the overall reconstruction of the province's electricity system.

The phase-out was also a product of a wider explicit politicization of decision-making around the system. The phase-out demonstrated both the advantages of

Table 19.4 Assessing the Ontario Coal Phase-Out

	Programmatic Assessment	Process Assessment	Political Assessment	Endurance Assessment
Coal phase-out	Resilient success	Conflicted Success	Political success	Resilient success
Electricity policy overall	Conflicted/ precarious success	Precarious success/ process failure	Political failure	Conflicted/ precarious success

Source: Authors

politicization as well as its drawbacks. On the one hand, significant structural changes were made to a system with deeply embedded institutional interests; on the other hand, the politicized process eroded transparent, evidence-based decision-making regarding major infrastructure projects. The coal phase-out itself was politically successful, gaining support from all major Ontario political parties, and even featuring in the populist Ford government's 2018 environmental plan. However, the arrival of that government was in no small part due to the failures, in political terms, of the McGuinty and Wynne governments' overall handling of the electricity file.

On a final note, the Ontario Clean Air Alliance's role as the key policy entrepreneur in the province's coal phase-out must be recognized. Without the Alliance's work it is unlikely the phase-out would have occurred. The engagement of the province's health professions around air quality issues was also a critical factor in overcoming the objections of key institutional actors and economic interests to a phase-out. The federal interventions in the early 2000s, like the Ozone Annex agreement with the United States, also contributed to the all-party consensus around a phase-out going into the crucial 2003 provincial election.

References

Artuso, A. 2013. "Gas Plant Cancellations Cost $585 Million: Ontario Power Authority." *The Toronto Sun*. 30 April. https://torontosun.com/2013/04/30/gas-plant-cancellations-cost-585-million-ontario-power-authority

Auditor General of Ontario. 2017. *Special Report: The Fair Hydro Plan: Concerns about Fiscal Transparency, Accountability and Value for Money*. Toronto: Queen's Printer.

Barcelo, D. and J. P. Bennett (eds). 2016 "Human Health and Environmental Risks of Unconventional Shale Gas Hydro Fracking." *Science of the Total Environment* 100 (544): pp. 1139–1140.

CBC. 2020. "Ontario to Spend Extra $1.6bn Stabilizing Hydro Rates, Minister Says." CBC News. 30 January. https://www.cbc.ca/news/canada/toronto/ontario-hydro-rates-spending-1.5446353

Clark, K. and J. Yacoumidis. 2000. *Ontario's Environment and the 'Common Sense Revolution': A Fifth Year Report*. Toronto: Canadian Institute for Environmental Law and Policy.

Cui, R. Y., N. Hultman, M. R. Edwards, L. He, A. Sen, K. Surana, H. McJeon, G. Iyer, P. Patel, S. Yu, and T. Nace. 2019. "Quantifying Operational Lifetimes for Coal Power Plants under the Paris Goals." *Nature Communications* 10 (1): pp. 1–9.

Cundiff, B. 2015. *Ontario's Coal Phase-Out: Lessons Learned from a Massive Climate Achievement*. Toronto: Ontario Clear Air Alliance. https://www.cleanairalliance.org/wp-content/uploads/2015/04/CoalPhaseOut-web.pdf

Dewees, D. N. 2005. "Electricity Restructuring in Canada." In *Canadian Energy Policy and the Struggle for Sustainable Development*, edited by G. B. Doern, pp. 128–150. Toronto: University of Toronto Press.

Duncan, D. 2006. *Directive to OPA re: Integrated Power System Plan*. 13 June. Ontario Ministry of Energy.

Electricity Conservation and Supply Task Force (ECSTF). 2004. *Final Report*. Toronto: Ministry of Energy.

Elwell, C., J. Castrilli, and E. Chau. 2001. *Ontario's Environment and the Common Sense Revolution: Sixth Annual Report*. Toronto: Canadian Institute for Environmental Law and Policy.

Environment and Climate Change Canada (ECCC). 2018. "Canada's Coal Power Phase-Out Reaches Another Milestone." ECCC. 12 December. https://www.canada.ca/en/environment-climate-change/news/2018/12/canadas-coal-power-phase-out-reaches-another-milestone.html

Environmental Commissioner of Ontario (ECO). 2009. *Finding a Vision for Change: Annual Greenhouse Gas Progress Report 2008/09*. Toronto: ECO.

Environmental Defence. 2017. *Ontario's Electricity System: Backgrounder*. Toronto: Environmental Defence Canada. https://environmentaldefence.ca/wp-content/uploads/2017/02/17-05_ED_MediaBackgrounder_Electricity-FINAL.pdf

Financial Accountability Office (FAO) (2022). *Ontario's Energy and Electricity Subsidy Programs* Toronto: FAO 2022. https://www.fao-on.org/en/Blog/publications/energy-and-electricity-2022

Freeman, N. B. 1996. *The Politics of Power: Ontario Hydro and its Government 1906–1995*. Toronto: University of Toronto Press.

Gibbons, J. 2003. *Countdown Coal: How Ontario Can Improve Air Quality by Phasing Out Coal-Fired Electricity Generation*. Toronto: Ontario Clean Air Alliance.

Gibbons, J. and S. Bjorkquist. 1998. *Electricity Competition and Clean Air*. Toronto: Ontario Clean Air Alliance.

Government of Canada. 2012. "Reduction of Carbon Dioxide Emissions from Coal-Fired Generation of Electricity Regulations." *Canada Gazette Part II* 146 (19). http://www.gazette.gc.ca/rp-pr/p2/2012/2012-09-12/pdf/g2-14619.pdf

Government of Ontario. 2018. *A Made-in-Ontario Environment Plan*. Toronto: Queen's Printer for Ontario.

Gurney, M. 2018. "Commentary: Ontario Voters Punished Kathleen Wynne's 'Stretch Goal' Approach to Politics." Global News. 8 June. https://globalnews.ca/news/4263200/matt-gurney-kathleen-wynne-stretch-goal-politics/

Harris, M., M. Beck, and I. Gerasimchuk. 2015. *The End of Coal: Ontario's Coal Phase-Out*. Winnipeg: International Institute for Sustainable Development, https://www.iisd.org/library/end-coal-ontarios-coal-phase-out

IESO. 2020a. "Ontario's Supply Mix." IESO. ishttps://www.ieso.ca/en/Power-Data/Supply-Overview/Transmission-Connected-Generation

IESO. 2020b. "Price Overview: Global Adjustment." IESO. http://ieso.ca/power-data/price-overview/global-adjustment

IESO. 2020c. "The IESO's Annual Planning Outlook in Six Graphs." IESO. http://www.ieso.ca/Powering-Tomorrow/Data/The-IESOs-Annual-Planning-Outlook-in-Six-Graphs

Independent Electricity System Operator (IESO). n.d. "Demand Overview. Historical Demand." IESO.

McConnell, A. 2010. "Policy Success, Policy Failure and Grey Areas In-Between." *Journal of Public Policy* 30 (3): pp. 345–362.

McKitrick, R. R. 2013. *Environmental and Economic Consequences of Ontario's Green Energy Act*. Vancouver: The Fraser Institute. https://www.fraserinstitute.org/sites/default/files/environmental-and-economic-consequences-ontarios-green-energy-act.pdf

Nanos Research. 2016. "Hydro Rates Are the Top Issue for Ontarians; PCs Lead and Wynne Takes an Image Hit." Nanos Research. November. http://www.nanosresearch.com/sites/default/files/POLNAT-S15-T711.pdf

Office of the Premier. 2017. "Ontario Cutting Electricity Bills by 25 Per Cent: System Restructuring Delivers Lasting Relief to Households across Province." Government of Ontario. 2 March.

Ontario. 2017. "The End of Coal." The Government of Ontario. 15 December. https://www.ontario.ca/page/end-coal

Ontario Clean Air Alliance. 2006. "Liberals Blackout on Energy." OCAA. 20 July.

Ontario Hydro. 1997. *Report to Management IIPA/SSFI Evaluation Findings and Recommendations*. Toronto: Ontario Hydro.

Ontario Liberal Party. 2002. *Growing Strong Communities*. Toronto: Ontario Liberal Party.

Ontario Medical Association (OMA). 1998. *The Health Effects of Ground Level Ozone, Acid Aerosols and Particulate Matter*. Toronto: Ontario Medical Association.

Ontario Medical Association (OMA). 2000. *Illness Costs of Air Pollution: Summary of Findings*. Toronto: OMA.

Ontario Ministry of Energy. 2005. *Cost Benefit Analysis: Replacing Ontario's Coal-Fired Electricity Generation*. Prepared by DSS Management Consultants Inc. RWDI Air Inc.

Ontario Ministry of Environment, Conservation and Parks. 2018. *A Made-in-Ontario Environment Plan*. Toronto: Queen's Printer. https://www.ontario.ca/page/made-in-ontario-environment-plan

Ontario Ministry of the Environment. 2000. "Enhancing Ontario's Air Quality." Ontario Government. 24 January.

Ontario New Democratic Party. 2003. *Publicpower: Practical Solutions for Ontario*. Toronto: Ontario NDP.

Ontario Power Authority (OPA). 2005. *Supply Mix Advice and Recommendations*. Toronto: Ontario Power Authority. http://www.powerauthority.on.ca/Report_Static/1139.htm

Ontario Liberal Party. 2002. *Growing Strong Communities: The Ontario Liberal Plan for Clean, Safe Communities that Work*. Toronto: Ontario Liberal Party.

Petrevan, S. 2017. "Ontario's Coal Phase-Out in Perspective." Clean Energy Canada. 17 January. http://cleanenergycanada.org/ontarios-coal-phaseout-perspective/

Progressive Conservative Party of Ontario. 2003. *The Road Ahead: Policy Paper 6: Safeguarding the Natural Environment*. Toronto: PC Ontario Party.

Progressive Conservative Party of Ontario. 2018. *Plan for the People*. Toronto: PC Ontario Party.

Saha, D. 2019. "Natural Gas Beat Coal in the US. Will Renewables and Storage Soon Beat Natural Gas?" World Resources Institute. 8 July. https://www.wri.org/blog/2019/07/natural-gas-beat-coal-us-will-renewables-and-storage-soon-beat-natural-gas

Sovacool, B. K., P. Schmid, A. Stirling, G. Walter, and G. MacKerron. 2020. "Differences in Carbon Emissions Reduction between Countries Pursuing Renewable Electricity versus Nuclear Power." *Nature Energy* 5 (11): pp. 928–935.

Swift, J. and K. Stewart. 2004. *Hydro: The Decline and Fall of Ontario's Electric Empire*. Toronto: Between the Lines.

Toronto Public Health. 2000. *Air Pollution Burden of Illness in Toronto: Summary Report*. Toronto: City of Toronto.

Toronto Star. 2007. "New Energy Plan for a New Era." *The Toronto Star*. 30 August.

Vegh, G. 2018. *Energy Policy—-Transition Briefing: Establishing Greater Evidence-Based Analysis of Ontario's Energy Procurement*. Toronto: Ontario360 Project. https://on360.ca/30-30/ontario-360-reforming-ontarios-energy-policy-transition-briefing/

Vriens., L. 2018. *The End of Coal: Alberta's Coal Phase-Out*. Winnipeg: International Institute for Sustainable Development.

Winfield, M. 2012. *Blue-Green Province: The Environment and the Political Economy of Ontario*. Vancouver: University of British Columbia Press.

Winfield, M. 2015. "Ontario's Green Energy and Green Economy Act as an Industrial Development Strategy" In *Work and the Challenge of Climate Change: Canadian and International Perspectives*, edited by S. McBride and C. Carla Lipsig-Mummé. Kingston and Montreal: McGill-Queens University Press.

Winfield, M. 2016. "Environmental Policy: Greening the Province from the Dynasty to Wynne" In *Government and Politics of Ontario*, edited by J. Malloy and C. Collier, pp. 251–273. 6th edn. Toronto: University of Toronto Press.

Winfield, M. and B. Dolter. 2014. "Energy, Economic and Environmental Discourses and their Policy Impact: The Case of Ontario's Green Energy and Green Economy Act." *Energy Policy* 68: pp. 423–435.

Winfield, M. and G. Gelfant. 2020. "Distributed Energy Resource Development in Ontario: A Socio-Technical Transition in Progress?" *Energy Regulation Quarterly* 7 (4): pp. 11–23.

Winfield, M., R. Gibson, T. Markvart, K. Gaudreau, and J. Taylor. 2010. "Implications of Sustainability Assessment for Electricity System Design: The Case of the Ontario Power Authority's Integrated Power System Plan." *Energy Policy* 38 (8): pp. 4115–4126.

Winfield, M., A. Jamison, R. Wong, and P. Czajkowski. 2006. *Nuclear Power in Canada: An Examination of Impacts, Risks and Sustainability*. Drayton Valley: Pembina Institute.

Winfield, M. and C. Kaiser. 2020. "Ontario and Climate Change." In *Ontario since Confederation: A Reader*, edited by J. Onusko and D. Anastakis. Toronto: University of Toronto Press.

Winfield, M. and R. MacWhirter. 2019. "The Search for Sustainability in Ontario Electricity Policy." In *Divided Province: Ontario Politics in the Age of Neoliberalism*, edited by G. Albo and R .MacDermid, pp. 359–393. Kingston/Montreal: Queens-McGill University Press.

PART VI
GOVERNANCE POLICY SUCCESSES

20

How Indigenous Nations Have Been Transforming Public Policy through the Courts

Satsan (Herb George), Kent McNeil, and Frances Abele

Introduction

Through political action and litigation, Indigenous people have transformed the Canadian constitutional landscape—peacefully, and in a fashion largely unremarked by casual observers (Cairns 2011). Of the many aspects of this transformation, our focus here is on legal developments regarding Aboriginal rights and title and concomitant changes to federal policy. After explaining the jurisprudential starting point in British colonial law, we explore the political context of selected Supreme Court of Canada decisions and their impact on public policy. Although the process is far from complete, the transformation of public policy through Indigenous political activism and the courts is well underway. The goal of many—though not all—Indigenous leaders is to achieve acknowledgement and implementation of the status of Indigenous nations as a third order of government alongside the federal and provincial governments, with constitutional jurisdiction as an Aboriginal and treaty rights recognized and affirmed by s.35 of the Constitution Act 1982. In this chapter, we assess their progress towards this goal.

Policy development in this political context presents a particular challenge to the McConnell (2010) and McConnell et al. (2020) frameworks for gauging policy success, which presume that governments initiate and then implement policy, with varying degrees of success. Indigenous peoples have resorted to Canadian courts as a result of dissatisfaction with existing government policies, inaction on treaties and other undertakings, and insufficient recognition of inherent governance authority and land and resource rights. This chapter demonstrates how, through a succession of court cases, Indigenous leaders have challenged established colonial policies, and successfully created a new landscape for policy development and negotiations between Indigenous nations and federal, provincial, and local governments. These court challenges, reaching back to the early 1970s, along with

---

Satsan (Herb George), Kent McNeil, and Frances Abele, *How Indigenous Nations Have Been Transforming Public Policy through the Courts.* In: *Policy Success in Canada.* Edited by Evert A. Lindquist et al., Oxford University Press.
© Satsan (Herb George), Kent McNeil, and Frances Abele (2022). DOI: 10.1093/oso/9780192897046.003.0020

the impact of the Constitution Act, 1982, have been enduring and profound, affecting every policy domain relating to Indigenous peoples. Even so, much has yet to be accomplished for Indigenous nations to achieve recognition as a third order of government and for Indigenous law to be accepted as part of the legal landscape in Canada.

The Beginning

During the age of imperial expansion, European powers competed for global dominance and wealth by trading, pillaging, making war, entering into treaties, and often simply asserting ownership of other nations' land and resources (Seed, 1995; Weaver, 2003). A legacy of British North America has been a legal tradition that assumes unitary Crown sovereignty and obliterates the sovereign rights of the original nations (Nichols, 2020). For well over a century, this stance provided the underpinning of colonial administration under the Indian Act and its predecessor legislation (RCAP Report, 1996, 137–332).

Indigenous nations have never shared this European perspective. All over what are now called the Americas, Indigenous nations met European traders, explorers, and sojourners from within the prevailing Indigenous legal framework (Ray, 1996; Witgen, 2012). They applied the diplomatic protocols in use in their territories at the time of contact. Migrant Europeans tended to comply with these local rules for international relations—until, of course, they did not. Every Indigenous nation experienced a distinctive history of relations with the newcomers, but in general terms these followed a similar pattern. After a period of Indigenous predominance and then reciprocity, the balance of power shifted as Indigenous societies were weakened by new diseases and the arrival of ever-growing numbers of settlers (RCAP Report, 1996).

Through all these changes, Indigenous nations defended their territorial rights by every means available: assertion and explanation, petitions, negotiation of treaties, military alliances, and forceful resistance. They took representatives of the Crown at their word, engaging in diplomatic negotiations and visiting European capitals for diplomatic purposes. In the mid-nineteenth century, Anishinaabe in the area north of the Great Lakes responded to incursions by miners through demanding, with reference to the Royal Proclamation of 1763 (discussed later), that treaties be negotiated. The result was the Robinson Treaties of 1850, followed by 11 numbered treaties negotiated after Confederation to formalize relations between the Crown and Indigenous authorities, and bring order to the society being created by immigration (Henderson, 2007; Miller, 2009). Indigenous nations in British Columbia demanded treaties for similar reasons, beginning in the second half of the nineteenth century as disease and migrants entered their country (Tennant, 1990).

There have been multiple peaceful attempts by Indigenous peoples to have their sovereign rights respected. An attempt to organize a national representative body in the twentieth century prompted a 1927 amendment to the Indian Act that prohibited raising funds or paying lawyers to pursue Indian claims.[1] This prohibition, along with other repressive measures, impeded political organization, but did not entirely halt it (Tennant, 1982).

By the mid-nineteenth century British colonial law and policy, while acknowledging some Indigenous land rights, had hardened into a denial of Indigenous nations' sovereign rights—and indeed their agency—in British North America. In Canada, the most famous legal decision in this tradition is the *St. Catherine's Milling* case (1888), in which the Judicial Committee of the Privy Council adjudicated a dispute between the federal government and Ontario over the right to issue timber licenses on treaty land (McNeil, 2019). Although the Indigenous people concerned were neither parties nor witnesses, the judges ruled that 'the tenure of the Indians was a personal and usufructuary right, dependent upon the good will of the Sovereign' (*St. Catherine's Milling*, 1888, 54). This was the Privy Council's interpretation of the Royal Proclamation of 1763—a prerogative instrument issued by the British Crown at the end of the Seven Years War that was supposed to protect pre-existing Indigenous land rights, but instead was construed as the source of limited rights that could be taken away at any time.

Post-World War II Developments

The *St. Catherine's Milling* reasoning prevailed in Canadian jurisprudence, though not in Indigenous legal or political thought, until the latter half of the twentieth century, when a new social and political basis for dialogue between Indigenous people and the Crown began to form. This change affected both Indigenous people's capacity to achieve their goals and the political context for reaching them.

The global depression of the 1930s, followed by global warfare of the 1940s, transformed popular and elite expectations of both citizenship and the state. The war effort had broken old conventions about the limits to the role of the state in the economy, while the combination of a strengthening labour movement and the prospect of thousands of veterans returning to the labour force stimulated a new conception of citizens' rights that included social and economic security and a larger role for the state (Owram, 1986). The overheated wartime economy and booming US demand for Canadian resources provided the necessary fiscal capacity to act on these principles. At the same time, the horrors of World War II had begun to shift public opinion and elite assumptions away from race-based discrimination and towards universal citizenship rights (Weaver, 1975).

[1] RSC 1927, c.98, s.141.

398　INDIGENOUS NATIONS TRANSFORMING PUBLIC POLICY

This changed climate was the basis for the Canadian version of the welfare state, and it was to have many implications for Indigenous people, not all of them favourable (e.g. Tester and Kulchyski, 1994). But the new times also brought political opportunities. Returning Indigenous veterans were unwilling to accept discriminatory treatment, and discrimination was also beginning to be regarded as unacceptable by non-Indigenous veterans and their families, as well as other members of the public. Discriminatory treatment and the impoverished circumstances of 'Indians' were discussed by a series of Parliamentary committees beginning in 1944, leading to major amendments to the Indian Act in 1951, including the removal of the prohibition that impeded funded legal action. Indian organizations seized the opportunity to address these committees, putting forth a political program and set of demands for increased self-sufficiency, treaty rights, and full Canadian citizenship. In turn, these ideas were reflected in the report of the Hawthorn Task Force, appointed in 1964 to study Indian conditions. The two-volume Hawthorn Report described what many saw as a reasonable—if not perfect—reflection of Indian conditions and perspectives. A major recommendation was that Indians should be 'citizens plus'—that is, entitled to full Canadian citizenship rights as well as special rights flowing from their status as 'charter' citizens of Canada. (Cairns, 2000; Canada, 1966–1967).

However, the basis for negotiated progress in First Nations–Crown relations created by these initiatives was shattered in 1969 when Pierre Trudeau's newly elected government proposed a fresh start in a discussion paper on Indian policy (Canada, 1969). The unfortunately labelled 'White Paper' ignored most of the Hawthorn findings and recommendations, as well as consultations on the Indian Act then underway, proposing instead the termination of special status for Indians, the transfer of responsibilities for them to the provinces, and moth-balling the treaties (Weaver, 1975). These proposals shocked Indian leaders and activists, who immediately organized nationally in an atmosphere of anger and mistrust (Cardinal, 1969). The National Indian Brotherhood was formed, protests were organized, and the Indian Association of Alberta countered with a 'Red Paper', which rejected the government's assimilationist approach and insisted upon treaty rights and federal responsibilities (Indian Association of Alberta, 1970). As a result, the White Paper was withdrawn in March 1971 (Canada, 1971; Weaver, 1975, 187). While these events were unfolding, Lloyd Barber, who had been appointed Indian Claims Commissioner in 1969, and other officials were advocating behind the scenes for the establishment of a process for the negotiation of Indigenous rights (Scholtz, 2006).

Resort to the Courts

Around this time, pressure from three crucial court actions, initiated by First Nations to have their land rights acknowledged, came into play. Two of these responded to development pressure on Indigenous lands in the North that had been accelerating since World War II, fuelled by rising demand for energy and natural resources in southern Canada and the United States. Major energy projects sparked two almost concurrent conflicts over land use.

In late 1968, Dene in the Northwest Territories discovered that preparations were underway to construct a massive pipeline in their territory in the Mackenzie Valley. They united in the Indian Brotherhood of the Northwest Territories and prepared to defend their lands, filing a caveat on the lands to be traversed by the pipeline system. The 1973 decision of the Supreme Court of the Northwest Territories in *Re Paulette* found that the Indian Brotherhood had standing and that their claim of an interest in 400,000 square miles of the NWT was cognizable, regardless of Treaties 8 (1899) and 11 (1921). In its ruling the Supreme Court stated that the land surrender provisions in the written versions of those treaties had never been explained and were probably ineffective (Fumoleau, 1973). This decision was overturned on appeal for different reasons. However, given certain factors like the factual findings at trial regarding the treaty provisions, the importance of the Mackenzie Valley pipeline to Canadian energy exports, the urging of the Indian Claims Commissioner, and sustained Dene opposition, the federal Cabinet moved towards accepting that a process for negotiating land rights should be formulated (Scholtz, 2013).[2]

Additional pressure came from a similar conflict in northern Quebec. In April 1971, Robert Bourassa's new Liberal government announced plans for a massive hydro-electric development in Cree and Inuit territories in northern Quebec. After their objections to the project and demands for negotiated land rights were ignored, the Cree and Inuit commenced court action, pointing out that the province had not fulfilled its obligations to negotiate with Indigenous peoples on this land when it received transfers of territory from the federal government in 1898 and 1912. In November 1973, the Quebec Superior Court found in their favour (*Gros-Louis*). Although this decision was reversed by the Quebec Court of Appeal, the province, federal government, and Hydro Quebec commenced negotiations with the Cree and Inuit, resulting in the first modern land claims agreement, signed in 1975 (Feit, 1983; Nungak, 2017).

A third court case was brought by the Nisga'a Nation in British Columbia. Faced with decades of having their assertions of land rights ignored, they sought a declaration that their Aboriginal title had never been extinguished (Foster et al., 2007). If they could get a favourable court decision, they would be in a strong position to negotiate a settlement with the province, which had consistently refused to acknowledge Indigenous land rights (Tennant, 1990). In *Calder* (1973), the Supreme Court split three/three on whether extinguishment had occurred

---

[2] The pipeline project was put on hold after Justice Thomas Berger recommended that land claims be settled first: Berger (1977). The pipeline has not been built.

legislatively before British Columbia joined Canada in 1871, but four out of seven judges dismissed the action on a technicality.

The decision was nonetheless a victory for the Nisga'a and other Indigenous nations that had not entered into treaties because six of the judges decided that, absent extinguishment, Aboriginal title exists as a legal right enforceable in Canadian courts. After the *Calder* decision, Prime Minister Trudeau reportedly said in reference to First Nations: 'Perhaps you had more legal rights than we thought you had when we did the white paper' (Canada, 1985, 12). Meeting with Frank Calder and other Nisga'a leaders after the decision, Trudeau committed the Canadian government to negotiations (Calder and Berger, 2007, 47).

A broader shift in federal policy soon followed. After substantial internal debate and increasing pressure from Indigenous organizations and the Indian Claims Commissioner, the federal Cabinet decided that negotiation of unresolved land claims was necessary. The 1973 *Statement on the Claims of Indian and Inuit People* announced this reversal and the establishment of the Office of Native Claims to undertake negotiations (Canada, 1985, 12).

Modern Treaties

The Office of Native Claims and its bureaucratic descendants have negotiated 26 comprehensive claim agreements since 1975, resolving land rights over millions of hectares in Labrador, Quebec, the three territories, and British Columbia. Together, the agreements confirm Indigenous ownership of 600,000 square kilometers of land and provide for capital transfers of $3.2 billion to compensate Indigenous parties for land rights they have ceded.

The modern treaties have had enormous consequences for the institutions and practice of Canadian governance. Decision-making about major development projects in vast areas of Canada is now subject to mandatory public hearings by panels appointed jointly by subnational governments and Indigenous authorities. Two new territories, including the majority-Inuit territory of Nunavut, were created by division of the old Northwest Territories, mandated under the 1993 Nunavut Agreement. Indigenous nations own surface and subsurface rights to portions of their original territories and have the capacity to levy land taxes and royalties on development.

Federal negotiating parameters have shifted somewhat in response to policy changes. Much of this has been prompted by judicial decisions, as discussed later. For this reason, and because the circumstances of Indigenous nations vary, modern treaties are not all the same (Abele et al., 2016). For example, treaties negotiated between 1982 and 1995 do not contain self-government provisions because the federal government did not want such provisions to be constitutionally protected, as they would be if included in land claims agreements (s.35(3), Constitution

Act, 1982). In 1995, the federal government changed its policy and decided to acknowledge that constitutional protection would extend to subsequently negotiated self-government rights.[3]

Constitution Act, 1982, Sections 25, 35, and 37

Perhaps the greatest-ever mobilization of a Canada-wide Indigenous lobby occurred during the intense four years leading to the patriation of the Canadian Constitution (Manuel and Derrickson, 2015). While many expressed disappointment with the results, as history has unfolded the clauses in the Constitution Act, 1982 that directly address Indigenous peoples' rights have proven to be remarkably important and consequent on litigation either brought by Indigenous parties or against them when they have exercised their constitutional rights.

As mentioned earlier, s.35 recognized and affirmed existing Aboriginal and treaty rights. In addition, s.25 shielded the rights of the Aboriginal peoples from the Charter, and s.37 mandated a constitutional conference for the purpose of defining Aboriginal and treaty rights. In fact, four such conferences were held in the 1980s, with little progress being made other than additions to s.35 clarifying that the rights in modern land claims agreements are treaty rights for the purposes of the section, and guaranteeing s.35 rights to men and women equally (McNeil, 1994, 122–126). A subsequent round of negotiations and a broad process of public deliberation led to the 1992 Charlottetown Accord, which included affirmation of the inherent right of self-government, recognition of Indigenous governments as a third order, and several other provisions of great consequence to Indigenous peoples' constitutional position. The Accord included other important provisions, such as recognition of Quebec as a distinct society. It was put to a referendum and defeated, damaging Quebec–Canada relations and leaving the task of defining Aboriginal and treaty rights to the courts.

This process was already underway. Litigation initiated by the Musqueam Nation resulted in an important Supreme Court decision in 1984. *Guerin v The Queen* involved a surrender to the Crown of part of the Musqueam Reserve in Vancouver for lease as a golf course. Officials of the federal Department of Indian Affairs negotiated the lease on behalf of the Musqueam but did not reveal the actual terms to them until years later. These terms were so unfavourable that the Court held the Crown had breached the fiduciary obligation it owed the Musqueam Nation and ordered the federal government to pay $10 million in damages. This decision shifted the legal landscape by reining in Crown discretion and forcing

---

[3] For criticism of the contingent rights approach in this policy, see Manuel and Derrickson (2015: 111).

402 INDIGENOUS NATIONS TRANSFORMING PUBLIC POLICY

policy-makers to abide by legally enforceable standards when making decisions that impact Indigenous peoples' cognizable interests (Reynolds, 2020).

R. v Sparrow, which also involved the Musqueam people, was the first Supreme Court decision to interpret and apply s.35 of the Constitution Act, 1982. Ronald Sparrow had been fishing in the Fraser River in the traditional territory of the Musqueam, using a drift net longer than permitted by federal fishery regulations. He admitted the facts but claimed that, as a Musqueam person, he had an Aboriginal right to catch fish for food, societal, and ceremonial purposes. The Supreme Court agreed but held that this constitutional right is not absolute and can be limited by regulations that have a valid legislative purpose, such as conservation, and that respect the Crown's fiduciary obligations. Respect for these obligations requires consultation with the right holders, minimal impairment of the right, and compensation in appropriate circumstances. The case was sent back to the trial court (but never retried) to determine if the regulations infringed the Aboriginal right and could be justified.

Despite allowing for legislative infringement of Aboriginal rights in some instances, *Sparrow* was a win for Indigenous peoples because it limited government discretion even further. The Court ruled that s.35 provides significant constitutional protection for Aboriginal rights (and, by implication, treaty rights), and the ruling gave those rights priority over commercial and sports interests, acknowledged that the rights can have an economic component, and required consultation when infringement of them was contemplated. Consequently, the federal government has had to modify fisheries policy to take account of the Aboriginal fishing rights that many Indigenous nations possess.[4] As discussed later, the Court has since expanded the application of the consultation requirement, ensuring that Indigenous peoples are policy players whenever government action that might impact their claimed rights is contemplated.

The *Sparrow* decision did not provide guidance on how Aboriginal rights are to be identified because the existence of the Musqueam fishing right was not seriously disputed. The Supreme Court faced the definition issue six years later in *R. v Van der Peet* (1996), which, together with *R. v Gladstone* and *R. v N.T.C. Smokehouse* (decided the same day), involved claims of rights to fish commercially. In *Van der Peet*, the Court created what is known as the 'integral to the distinctive culture test' for Aboriginal rights. Dorothy Van der Peet, a member of the Stó:lō Nation whose territory is along the lower Fraser River in British Columbia, had sold ten salmon caught by her spouse and another relative. Her defence to the charge of selling fish caught under an Indian food fish licence was that she had a s.35 Aboriginal right to sell the salmon. The Court decided that s.35 Aboriginal rights are derived from practices, customs, and traditions integral to the distinctive culture of a particular

---

[4] See Allain and Fréchette (1993), Canada (2003). For an unsuccessful court challenge to federal policy giving priority to Aboriginal fishing rights, see *R. v Kapp* (2008).

Indigenous people at the time of first contact with Europeans.[5] As the evidence did not show that exchange of fish for money or other goods had been integral to Stó:lō culture at the time of contact, the Court held that the right had not been established. A similar conclusion was reached regarding the claimed right in the *Smokehouse* case, but in *Gladstone* it was different: the Heiltsuk were able to prove that they had exchanged herring spawn on kelp in commercial quantities prior to contact, and so were able to establish a s.35 right to do so.

Three years later, the Supreme Court was confronted with a claim to a treaty right to catch and trade fish in *R. v Marshall [No. 1]* (1999). After consideration of the historical record, the Court concluded that the Mi'kmaq, who agreed to trade only at English truck houses (trading posts), have a treaty right to obtain the produce of the sea and forest for that purpose, to the extent required for a 'moderate livelihood'. Donald Marshall Jr. was accordingly acquitted of the charge of selling 463 pounds of eels. As the treaty right was not limited to this species, the Mi'kmaq began fishing for other seafood, especially lobster. This set off a reaction by other fishers, leading to confrontations that sometimes turned violent. Unfortunately, the federal Department of Fisheries was unprepared for such conflict and, instead of calming the situation and quelling the disturbance, even contributed to it (Coates, 2000; Wicken, 2004). Disturbingly, the recurrent confrontations and violence in 2020, initiated by non-Indigenous fishers opposed to Mi'kmaw treaty rights, reveal an ongoing failure by the federal government to develop and implement effective public policy to deal with the reality of Indigenous peoples' constitutional fishing rights in Atlantic Canada.

The Supreme Court also appears to have been taken aback by the reaction to its judgement. On an application to rehear the case, which it dismissed in *R v Marshall [No. 2]* (1999), the Court took the unprecedented step of issuing a clarification judgement to clearly explain the ways in which the treaty right is limited (Cameron, 2009; Wildsmith, 2001).

Section 35 Aboriginal and treaty rights are rights of the Métis and Inuit as well as First Nations. Métis tested the implications of this in *R. v Powley* (2003). Steve Powley and his son, Roddy, killed a moose for food near Sault Ste. Marie, Ontario, and were charged under provincial law with unlawful hunting. They proved that hunting was integral to the distinctive culture of the Métis in the area prior to 1850 when effective European control was established. The Court decided that this was an appropriate timeframe for determining the existence of Métis Aboriginal rights. The Métis did not exist prior to European contact, the time used for First Nation Aboriginal rights in *Van der Peet*. The Powleys also proved the existence of a present-day Métis community at Sault Ste. Marie, to which they belong. The *Powley* decision has required governments to change their policies regarding

---

[5] For application of this test to harvesting of wood for domestic purposes, see *R. v Sappier; R. v Gray* (2006).

404   INDIGENOUS NATIONS TRANSFORMING PUBLIC POLICY

the application of fish and game laws to Métis, though the requirement of identifying historical and contemporary Métis communities has become a stumbling
block for some Métis claimants. The issue of membership in contemporary Métis
communities can also be controversial (Chartrand, 2019).[6]

The early Supreme Court decisions in *Guerin* and *Sparrow* likely contributed
to a change of policy in British Columbia. The New Democratic government of
Premier Mike Harcourt, elected in 1991, officially abandoned the province's long-
standing position that Aboriginal title did not exist or had been extinguished.
This decision, which also reflected the NDP's openness to recognizing First Nation rights, led to the creation in 1993 of the British Columbia Treaty Commission
by the province, Canada, and the First Nations Summit, a made-in-BC process for
resolving Aboriginal title claims through negotiations (Mckee, 1996, 30–33).

Unfortunately, the federal and provincial negotiating mandates regarding both
Indigenous territory and the inherent right of self-government proved unaccept-
ably narrow for some of the Indigenous nations who had been part of the process
to establish the Commission. The Gitxsan and Wet'suwet'en Nations, who had already taken their claim to court in the mid-1980s and been handed a dismissive
judgement by the BC Supreme Court in *Delgamuukw* (1991), chose to continue the
litigation and appealed their case to the Supreme Court of Canada. In a landmark
decision in 1997, the Court overturned the trial judgement and ordered a new trial
(the case has not, however, been retried). Nonetheless, in a lengthy judgement,
Chief Justice Lamer ruled that Indigenous oral histories are admissible as evidence
and must be given the same respect and weight as written histories. The Court also
provided guidelines on Aboriginal title's nature, content, proof, and constitutional
status. Very significantly, the Court decided that Aboriginal title is a property right
that enjoys the same legal protection as other property rights, as well as constitutional protection against extinguishment and unjustifiable infringement by, or
pursuant to, legislation.

The 1997 *Delgamuukw* decision does not appear to have had much direct impact
on the positions of the British Columbia and federal governments in land claims
negotiations (Browne, 2009; Manuel and Derrickson, 2017, 102). The Nisga'a Final
Agreement (2000), for example, does not appear to have been modified in the final
months of negotiations to take the *Delgamuukw* decision into account—though
after almost 25 years of negotiations the Nisga'a themselves appear to have been
willing to proceed without significant changes (Rynard, 2000; Molloy and Ward,
2000, 96–97, 106–107). However, the *Delgamuukw* decision, and more recently
the Supreme Court's ruling in *Tsilhqot'in Nation* (2014), have probably fortified
the unwillingness of many First Nations to participate in a treaty process that they
regard as providing less than they are entitled to in Canadian constitutional law,
let alone under their own legal orders (de Costa, 2003). Almost half of the First

---

[6] Métis land rights have been addressed only in relation to the Manitoba Act, 1870: *Manitoba Metis Federation* (2013).

Nations in British Columbia are not participating in the BC treaty process, in part because, unlike the Nisga'a, they are unwilling to give up their title to over 90 per cent of their territories, nor do they regard the self-governance provisions in the Nisga'a and other post-1995 land claims agreements as adequate (Manuel and Derrickson, 2015).

The *Delgamuukw* decision did not rule on a key issue brought by the Gitxsan and Wet'suwet'en: whether Aboriginal title is limited to specific sites of intensive use as the Crown argued, or if it extends over entire Indigenous territories. In *R. v Marshall*; *R. v Bernard* (2005), on appeal from Nova Scotia and New Brunswick where no treaties involving land have been negotiated, the Supreme Court appeared to take a site-specific approach. However, in *Tsilhqot'in Nation* (2014) it rejected that approach in favour of a territorial concept of Aboriginal title. The case is especially significant because the Court, for the first time, issued a declaration of title derived from the Tsilhqot'in Nation's exclusive occupation of land when the Crown asserted sovereignty in British Columbia in 1846. However, a downside of the judgement for Indigenous peoples is the Court's decision that provincial legislatures as well as Parliament have the constitutional authority to infringe Aboriginal and treaty rights if the infringement can be justified using the *Sparrow* test (Wilkins, 2017).

After the 1997 *Delgamuukw* decision, the BC government's position was that Aboriginal title does not exist until proven, and so lands that are neither federal nor privately owned were considered provincial Crown lands. In other words, despite *Delgamuukw* the province acted as though nothing had changed—it could carry on 'business as usual' and continue granting various rights (eg. mining rights, timber rights, etc.) on lands subject to Aboriginal title claims. With *Delgamuukw* in mind, the Haida Nation challenged this position in an important case that went to the Supreme Court. In *Haida Nation* (2004), the Court ruled that the province could not ignore unproven Aboriginal title claims and act as though lands it regarded as Crown lands were at its disposal. In the memorable words of Chief Justice McLachlin, 'The Crown, acting honourably, cannot cavalierly run roughshod over Aboriginal interests where claims affecting these interests are being seriously pursued in the process of treaty negotiation and proof. It must respect these potential, but yet unproven, interests' (para. 27). In this situation, the Crown owed Indigenous claimants a duty to consult, the depth of which depends on the strength of their claim and the potential impact of the government action on their potential rights. The Crown had to take their concerns seriously and accommodate them by modifying its plans in appropriate circumstances (Newman, 2014).

The *Haida Nation* case arose on Haida Gwaii, a non-treaty area where the Haida have a strong Aboriginal title claim. In other parts of Canada, where there are either historical treaties or recent land claims agreements, it was not immediately apparent that the Crown would have an equivalent duty to consult. That changed when the Supreme Court handed down its decisions in *Mikisew Cree First Nation* (2005), involving Treaty 8 (1899), and *Quebec (Attorney General)* (2010) and

406 INDIGENOUS NATIONS TRANSFORMING PUBLIC POLICY

Beckman (2010), involving modern treaties (comprehensive land claims agreements) in Quebec and the Yukon. In those cases, the Court decided that the honour of the Crown requires consultation whenever government action could have a negative impact on the Indigenous parties' treaty rights. In a more recent case, *Mikisew Cree First Nation* (2018), the Supreme Court held that no duty to consult arises when legislation is enacted, but if a statute once passed infringes Aboriginal or treaty rights, the infringement will have to be justified.

The duty to consult cases have been extremely significant because they have forced the federal and provincial governments to seriously consider Indigenous rights that have not yet been acknowledged by Canadian courts or governments, and treat Indigenous peoples as participants in resource development and other major projects, such as pipelines (Gallagher, 2011). If affected Indigenous groups think they have not been adequately consulted, they can take governments to court and, if successful, block projects until adequate consultation takes place.[7] This provides Indigenous nations that have not signed treaties with rights similar to those affirmed in modern treaties, potentially including negotiation of impact benefit agreements that can provide revenue, employment, and business opportunities (Newman, 2014).

Indigenous Law and Governance

An area where Supreme Court decisions have not had much impact on public policy is with regard to Indigenous law and governance, even though it was disagreement over self-government that resulted in lack of progress during the constitutional talks in the 1980s. It was this lack of progress that resulted in the matter of Aboriginal and treaty rights being taken to the courts. However, courts appear to be uncomfortable addressing governance issues because they regard them as more political than legal. There is a long history of the courts dealing with distribution of governance authority between Parliament and the provincial legislatures in division-of-powers cases, where the issue is which order of government has legislative authority under the enumerated powers in the Constitution Act 1867. For the courts, it is a different matter trying to determine what governance authority Indigenous peoples have under s.35 of the Constitution Act 1982, which contains no list of powers.

The Supreme Court has often stated that Indigenous law is part of the Indigenous perspective on s.35 rights and must be taken into account.[8] However, one

---

[7] E.g. see *Clyde River* (2017); *Tsleil-Waututh Nation* (2018).

[8] E.g. see *Delgamuukw* (1997), paras. 114, 126, 145–147, 157; *Mitchell* (2001), para. 10; Tsilhqot'in Nation (2014), para. 35; *R v Desautel* (2021) SCC 17, para. 86 ('It is for Aboriginal peoples ... to define themselves and to choose by what means to make their decisions, according to their own laws, customs and practices').

searches in vain for decisions in which the Court has actually applied Indigenous law. Lower court decisions have acknowledged the application of Indigenous law in relation to marriages and adoptions (Zlotkin, 1984),[9] but judges have been more reluctant to apply it in other contexts. For example, in *Coastal GasLink Pipeline Ltd.* (2019), a case involving protests and blockades over the construction of a gas pipeline through Wet'suwet'en territory in British Columbia, Justice Church stated: 'As a general rule, Indigenous customary laws do not become an effectual part of Canadian common law or Canadian domestic law until there is some means or process by which the Indigenous customary law is recognized as being part of Canadian domestic law, either through incorporation into treaties, court declarations, such as Aboriginal title or rights jurisprudence, or statutory provisions' (para. 127). On the other hand, in *Pastion* (2018) Justice Grammond said that 'Indigenous legal traditions are among Canada's legal traditions. They form part of the law of the land' (para. 8).

While acknowledging Indigenous law's existence,[10] Canadian courts are obviously uncertain about how to deal with it and incorporate it into Canada's common law, civil law, and statute law. It remains for Indigenous peoples to take the initiative by exercising the inherent right of self-government that the Canadian government acknowledged in 1995 (Canada 1995), breathing new life into their traditional laws and legislating in areas where those laws do not address current social and economic realities.

With respect to Indigenous governance authority, counsel in *R. v Sparrow* argued that the Musqueam's Aboriginal right to fish included authority to regulate fishing by Musqueam people. The British Columbia Court of Appeal dismissed that argument, stating that their fishing right 'cannot be defined as if the Musqueam band had continued to be a self-governing entity, or as if its members were not citizens of Canada and residents of British Columbia' (BCCA, para. 74). While not addressing this issue directly, the Supreme Court stated that 'there was from the outset never any doubt that sovereignty and legislative power ... vested in the Crown' (*R. v Sparrow*, SCC, para. 49).[11]

In *Delgamuukw*, the Gitxsan and Wet'suwet'en claimed a right of self-government over their territories, as well as Aboriginal title to their lands. The Supreme Court largely avoided the self-government claim. In two short paragraphs, Chief Justice Lamer explained that this complex matter had not been sufficiently argued by counsel and had been framed in overly broad terms at the trial that had taken place before the Court's decision on *R. v Pamajewon* (1996), a case involving a claim by two First Nations in Ontario of a right to engage in and regulate gaming on their reserves. In *Pamajewon*, the Supreme Court applied the

---

[9] E.g. see *Connolly* (1867); *Re Adoption of Katie* (1961); *Casimel* (1993).

[10] For examples of the growing literature on Indigenous law, see Law Commission of Canada (2007), Borrows (2010), Hanna (2018).

[11] For critical commentary, see Asch and Macklem (1991); Nichols (2020).

408 INDIGENOUS NATIONS TRANSFORMING PUBLIC POLICY

Van der Peet test, which in this context required proof that high-stakes gambling had been integral to the distinctive Anishinaabe culture prior to contact with Europeans. As the accused were unable to meet this burden of proof, their convictions of unlawful gaming under the *Criminal Code* of Canada were upheld.

The *Pamajewon* decision has been subjected to severe academic criticism but has not been overruled.[12] However, in *Campbell* (2000) Justice Williamson of the BC Supreme Court found a way to get around it. That case involved an allegation that the self-government provisions of the Nisga'a Final Agreement (2000) are invalid because there is no room for Indigenous governance in the Canadian Constitution. Justice Williamson dismissed that argument, holding instead that the Nisga'a's right of self-government existed prior to Confederation and had not been extinguished by the division of powers in the Constitution Act, 1867 or at any time since. It was therefore recognized and affirmed by s.35 of the Constitution Act, 1982. What the Nisga'a Final Agreement did was acknowledge and define, not create, this right. Justice Williamson found support for this conclusion in a passage from *Delgamuukw* in which Chief Justice Lamer said that Aboriginal title land 'is held communally ... Decisions with respect to that land are also made by that community' (*Delgamuukw*, para. 115, Lamer C.J.'s emphasis). Justice Williamson observed that, for the Nisga'a Nation to be able to make communal decisions, a government structure would be necessary.

As mentioned previously, the federal government acknowledged Indigenous peoples' inherent right of self-government as being fulfilled through negotiations, circumscribed by certain conditions (Canada, 1997). Recently, Parliament has gone further in An Act Respecting First Nations, Inuit and Métis Children, Youth and Families,[13] s.8 of which states the following: 'The purpose of this Act is to (a) affirm the inherent right of self-government, which includes jurisdiction in relation to child and family services.'[14] This legislation was prompted by the Canadian Human Rights Tribunal's decision in *First Nations Child and Family Caring Society of Canada* (2016), which outlined that the Canadian government had systematically discriminated against First Nation children in the provision of child welfare services (Bezanson, 2018). This revealed the impact quasi-judicial decisions can have on public policy regarding Indigenous peoples. The statute goes

---

[12] For example, Morse (1997) notes that the court did not take Indigenous law into account, rather adopting the view that any rights were 'frozen' at the time of contact.

[13] SC 2019, c.24 (in force as of 1 January 2020).

[14] The constitutionality of the Indigenous governance provisions in this statute was challenged by Quebec in *Renvoi à la Cour d'appel du Québec relatif à la Loi concernant les enfants, les jeunes et les familles des Premières Nations, des Inuits et des Métis* (2022). The Quebec Court of Appeal, in a unanimous decision, upheld the statute's validity with the exception of two provisions and affirmed the inherent right of self-government. An English summary of the lengthy French decision is at https://courdappelduquebec.ca/en/judgments/details/reference-to-the-court-of-appeal-of-quebec-in-relation-with-the-act-respecting-first-nations-inuit/. As this decision was handed down on 10 February 2022 while this chapter was being copyedited, it was too late for us to include discussion of it. The decision is on appeal to the Supreme Court of Canada.

on to state in s.18(1): 'The inherent right of self-government recognized and affirmed by section 35 of the Constitution Act, 1982 includes jurisdiction in relation to child and family services, including legislative authority in relation to those services and authority to administer and enforce laws made under that legislative authority.' While this legislative acknowledgement of the right of self-government should have been unnecessary, given that the right is inherent and constitutionally protected (Metallic, 2018), the fact that Parliament has affirmed that the right exists and has constitutional status under s.35 does provide the courts with statutory authority to enforce the right—something they appear to be hesitant to do on their own initiative (see *R. v Pamajewon* (1996); *Delgamuukw* (1997), paras. 170–171).

Another important development, which is beyond the scope of this chapter, is the Trudeau government's unqualified 2016 endorsement of and promise to implement the *United Nations Declaration on the Rights of Indigenous Peoples*, adopted by the UN General Assembly on 13 September 2007. Statutes enacted by British Columbia and the Parliament of Canada are designed to make BC and Canadian law consistent with the Declaration.[15] Although Canada's acceptance of the Declaration appears not to have been motivated by court decisions, its adoption and legislative endorsement represent major policy shifts, the consequences of which are hard to predict.

Conclusions

Supreme Court of Canada decisions have been instrumental in motivating governments to change public policy to take account of Indigenous rights, as defined by the Court. Prominent examples are *Calder* (1973) in relation to Aboriginal title, *Guerin* (1984) on the Crown's fiduciary obligations, and *Haida Nation* (2004) and *Mikisew Cree* (2005) on the duty to consult. These cases were initiated by Indigenous nations with the goal of forcing governments to respect their rights and enter into negotiations to settle their just claims. Nonetheless, governments do not always react positively to court decisions, often interpreting them narrowly and showing reluctance to modify some government policies, as shown by the land claims negotiations after *Delgamuukw*.

On the whole, however, Indigenous peoples have been remarkably successful in achieving some of their legal and political goals through court action: transforming the discourse, creating new venues for challenging government policies, and establishing their constitutional rights. Supreme Court decisions have forced governments to revise their policies regarding land rights, access to natural resources, treaty rights, involvement of Indigenous peoples in decision-making through

[15] Declaration on the Rights of Indigenous Peoples Act, SBC 2019, c.44; United Nations Declaration on the Rights of Indigenous Peoples Act, SC 2021, c.14.

410 INDIGENOUS NATIONS TRANSFORMING PUBLIC POLICY

consultation, and so on. These court decisions have significantly shaped—and will continue to shape—the development and remaking of polices pertaining to Indigenous peoples.

However, neither the Court nor the Canadian government has questioned Crown assertion of sovereignty. In Eastern Canada, reliance continues to be placed on cession of sovereignty by France to Britain in the Treaty of Utrecht in 1713 and the Treaty of Paris in 1763, which was the Privy Council's understanding in the *St. Catherine's Milling* case in 1888. The rest of Canada is regarded as having been acquired by 'settlement', an original means of acquisition that ignores the existence of Indigenous nations and relies on the discredited doctrine of discovery.[16] In the *Haida Nation* decision in 2004, the Court acknowledged the pre-existing sovereignty of the Indigenous nations,[17] and yet in 2014 in *Tsilhqot'in Nation* it reaffirmed that Crown sovereignty in British Columbia dated from the 1846 Oregon Boundary Treaty between Britain and the United States, a bilateral international treaty that took no account of Indigenous sovereignty. These contradictions continue to plague the jurisprudence and need to be addressed politically for Indigenous and Crown sovereignty to be reconciled—a sentiment echoed by Chief Justice McLachlin in *Haida Nation*.[18] The reality of Indigenous sovereignty can no longer be ignored.

Our assessment of the impact of court decisions on Canadian public policy in relation to Indigenous rights challenges the McConnell (2010, 2020) frameworks which inform this collection. As we noted in our introduction, this is not the typical situation of appraising how well a policy has been implemented by a government. Rather, our discussion has focused on part of a longer-term effort to undo and remake framework policies that damaged Indigenous peoples across Canada, gain standing and affirm rights that political authorities have to deal with, and lay the groundwork for additional assertion of Indigenous rights and policies in negotiations with governments. Using McConnell's typology, the succession of Supreme Court victories by Indigenous peoples should be viewed as a long-overdue 'process success'. On the other hand, the extent to which Indigenous rights have been recognized and self-governance achieved on the 'program' and 'political' dimensions might be categorized as somewhere between a 'conflicted' success and 'resilient' success, given the ongoing foot-dragging and resistance on the part of the federal and provincial governments to fully embrace and factor these rights into policy and legislation. More generally, the analysis in this chapter points to the

---

[16] In *Guerin* (1984), page 378, and *R. v Sparrow* (1990), para. 49, the Supreme Court relied explicitly upon *Johnson v M'Intosh* (1823), in which the US Supreme Court applied the discovery doctrine. See Miller (2010).

[17] See also *Manitoba Metis Federation* (2013), para. 67, and *Mikisew Cree First Nation* (2018), para. 21.

[18] See Hoehn (2012), Nichols (2020).

long-term horizons involved: Indigenous peoples and a succession of leaders have steadily argued for well over a hundred years for recognition of their prior societies and governance traditions, for agreements negotiated with Europeans and settlers to be honoured, and for use and control of their traditional lands and resources. Our assessment shows that, looking forward, realizing the potential of the 'process success' will require similar determination on the part of Indigenous peoples in the decades ahead.

References

Court Cases

Beckman v Little Salmon/Carmacks First Nation [2010] 3 SCR 103.
Calder v Attorney General of British Columbia [1973] SCR 313.
Campbell v British Columbia (Attorney General) [2000] 4 CNLR 1.
Casimel v Insurance Corporation of British Columbia [1993] 106 DLR (4th) 720.
Clyde River (Hamlet) v Petroleum Geo-Services Inc. [2017] 1 SCR 1069.
Coastal GasLink Pipeline Ltd. v Huson, [2019] BCSC 2264.
Connolly v Woolrich [1967] 17 RJRQ 75 (QSC); *Johnstone v Connolly* [1969] 17 RJRQ 266 (QQB).
Delgamuukw v British Columbia [1991] 79 DLR (4th) 185 (BCSC); (1993) 104 DLR (4th) 470 (BCCA); [1997] 3 SCR 1010.
First Nations Child and Family Services Caring Society of Canada v Canada (Attorney General) [2016] CHRT 2, [2016] 2 CNLR 270.
Gros-Louis c. La Société de Développement de la Baie James [1974] Que PR 38 (QSC), reversed *Société de Développement de la Baie James c. Kanatewat* [1975] Que CA 166, leave to appeal dismissed [1975] 1 SCR 48.
Guerin v The Queen [1984] 2 SCR 335.
Haida Nation v British Columbia (Minister of Forests) [2004] 3 SCR 511.
Johnson v M'Intosh, 8 Wheat (21 US) 543 [1823].
Manitoba Metis Federation Inc. v Canada (Attorney General) [2013] 1 SRC 623.
Mikisew Cree First Nation v Canada (Minister of Canadian Heritage) [2005] 3 SCR 388.
Mikisew Cree First Nation v Canada (Governor General in Council) [2018] 2 SCR 765.
Mitchell v M.N.R. [2001] 1 SCR 911.
Pastion v Dene Tha' First Nation [2018] 4 FCR 467.
Quebec (Attorney General) v Moses [2010] 1 SCR 557.
R. v Desautel [2021] SCC 17.
R. v Gladstone [1996] 2 SCR 723.
R. v Kapp [2008] 2 SCR 483.
R. v Marshall [No. 1] [1999] 3 SCR 456.
R v Marshall [No. 2] [1999] 3 SCR 533.
R. v Marshall; R. v Bernard [2005] 2 SCR 220.
R. v N.T.C. Smokehouse [1996] 2 SCR 672.
R. v Pamajewon [1996] 2 SCR 821.
R. v Powley [2003] 2 SCR 207.
R. v Sappier; R. v Gray [2006] 2 SCR 686.

R. v Sparrow [1986] 36 DLR (4th) 246 (BCCA); (1990) 1 SCR 1075.
R. v Van der Peet [1996] 2 SCR 507.
Re Adoption of Katie [1961] 32 DLR (2d) 686 (NWTTC).
Re Paulette et al. and Registrar of Titles (No. 2) [1973] 42 DLR (3d) 8 (NWTSC), reversed (1975) 63 DLR (3d) 1 (NWTCA), reversal affirmed [1977] 2 SCR 628.
Renvoi à la Cour d'appel du Québec relatif à la Loi concernant les enfants, les jeunes et les familles des Premières Nations, des Inuits et des Métis, 2022 QCCA 185 (CanLII)
St. Catherine's Milling and Lumber Company v The Queen [1888] 14 App Cas 46.
Tsilhqot'in Nation v British Columbia [2014] 2 SCR 257.
Tsleil-Waututh Nation v Canada (Attorney General) [2019] 2 FCR 3 (Fed CA), leave to appeal dismissed, 2019 CanLII 37489 (SCC).

Other Sources

Abele, F., S. Irlbacher-Fox, and J. Gladstone (eds). 2016. "Special Issue on Modern Treaty Implementation." *Northern Public Affairs* 6 (2) http://www.northernpublicaffairs.ca/index/volume-6-special-issue-2-special-issue-on-modern-treaty-implementation-research/

Allain, J., and J.-D. Fréchette. 1993. "The Aboriginal Fisheries and the *Sparrow* Decision." Government of Canada. http://www.publications.gc.ca/Collection-R/LoPBdP/BP/bp341-e.htm

Asch, M., and P. Macklem. 1991. "Aboriginal Rights and Canadian Sovereignty: An Essay on *R v Sparrow*." *Alberta Law Review* 29 (2): pp. 498–517.

Berger, T. R. 1977. *Northern Frontier, Northern Homeland: The Report of the Mackenzie Valley Pipeline Inquiry*. Ottawa: Minister of Supply and Services Canada.

Bezanson, K. 2018. "*Caring Society v Canada*: Neoliberalism, Social Reproduction, and Indigenous Child Welfare." *Journal of Law and Social Policy* 28 (1): pp. 152–173.

Borrows, J. 2010. *Canada's Indigenous Constitution*. Toronto: University of Toronto Press.

Browne, M. 2009. "The Promise of *Delgamuukw* and the Reality of Treaty Negotiations in British Columbia." In *Aboriginal Law since Delgamuukw*, edited by M. Morellato, pp. 465–505. Aurora: Canada Law Book.

Cairns, A. C. 2000. *Citizens Plus: Aboriginal Peoples and the Canadian State*. Vancouver: University of British Columbia Press.

Cairns, A. 2011. "Preface." In B. Gallagher *Resource Rulers: Fortune and Folly on Canada's Road to Resources*, pp. vii–xi. Waterloo, ON: Bill Gallagher.

Calder, F., and T. Berger. 2007. "Frank Calder and Thomas Berger: A Conversation." In *Let Right Be Done: Aboriginal Title, the Calder Case, and the Future of Indigenous Rights*, edited by H. Foster, H. Raven, and J. Webber, pp. 37–53. Vancouver: University of British Columbia Press.

Cameron, A. M. 2009. *Power without Law: The Supreme Court of Canada, the Marshall Decisions, and the Failure of Judicial Activism*. Montreal and Kingston: McGill-Queen's University Press.

Canada. 1966–1967. *A Survey of the Contemporary Indians of Canada: Economic, Political, Educational Needs and Policies (Hawthorn Report)*. Ottawa: Queen's Printer.

Canada. 1969. "Statement of the Government of Canada on Indian Policy [White Paper]." Government of Canada. https://www.aadnc-aandc.gc.ca/eng/1100100010189/1100100010191

Canada. 1971. "The Unfinished Tapestry—Indian Policy in Canada." Ottawa: Department of Indian Affairs and Northern Development. 17 March. http://publications.gc.ca/site/eng/9.852496/publication.html

Canada. 1985. *Living Treaties: Lasting Agreements. Report of the Task Force to Review Comprehensive Claims Policy.* Ottawa: Department of Indian Affairs and Northern Development.

Canada. 1997. *Gathering Strength: Canada's Aboriginal Action Plan.* Ottawa: Services Canada.

Canada. 2003. *Strengthening our Relationship—The Aboriginal Fisheries Strategy and Beyond—October 2003.* Ottawa: Fisheries and Oceans Canada. https://www.dfo-mpo.gc.ca/fisheries-peches/aboriginal-autochtones/afs/afsoct03-eng.html

Cardinal, H. 1969. *The Unjust Society.* Vancouver: Douglas & McIntyre.

Chartrand, L. 2019. "The Constitutional Determination of a Métis Rights-Bearing Community: Reorienting the *Powley* Test." In *Renewing Relationships: Indigenous Peoples and Canada*, edited by K. Drake and B. L. Gunn, pp. 169–192. Saskatoon: University of Saskatchewan Native Law Centre.

Coates, K. S. 2000. *The Marshall Decision and Native Rights.* Montreal and Kingston: McGill-Queen's University Press.

de Costa, R. 2003. "Treaties in British Columbia: The Search for a New Relationship." *International Journal of Canadian Studies* (27): pp. 173–196.

Feit, H. A. 1983. "Negotiating Recognition of Aboriginal Rights: History, Strategies and Reactions to the James Bay and Northern Quebec Agreement." In *Aborigines, Land and Land Rights*, edited by N. Petersen and M. Langton, pp. 416–438. Canberra: Institute of Aboriginal Studies.

Foster, H., H. Raven, and J. Webber (eds). 2007. *Let Right Be Done: Aboriginal Title, the Calder Case, and the Future of Indigenous Rights.* Vancouver: University of British Columbia Press.

Fumoleau, R. 1973. *As Long as This Land Shall Last: A History of Treaty 8 and Treaty 11, 1870–1939.* Toronto: McClelland and Stewart.

Gallagher, B. 2011. *Resource Rulers: Fortune and Folly on Canada's Road to Resources.* Waterloo, ON: Bill Gallagher.

Hanna, A. 2018. "Spaces for Sharing: Searching for Indigenous Law on the Canadian Legal Landscape." *UBC Law Review* 51 (1): pp. 105–159.

Henderson. J. (S.) Y. 2007. *Treaty Rights in the Constitution of Canada.* Toronto: Thomson Carswell.

Hoehn, F. 2012. *Reconciling Sovereignties: Aboriginal Nations and Canada.* Saskatoon: University of Saskatchewan Native Law Centre.

Indian Association of Alberta. 1970. "Citizens Plus." Indian Chiefs of Alberta. June. Online: http://caid.ca/RedPaper1970.pdf

Law Commission of Canada (ed). 2007. *Indigenous Legal Traditions.* Vancouver: University of British Columbia Press.

McConnell, A. 2010. Policy Success, "Policy Failure and Grey Areas In-Between," *Journal of Public Policy*, 30(20): pp. 345-362.

McConnell, A., Grealy, L., and Lea, T. 2020. "Policy success for whom? A framework for analysis," *Policy Sciences* 53: pp. 589-608.

Manuel, A., and R. M. Derrickson. 2015. *Unsettling Canada: A National Wake-up Call.* Toronto: Between the Lines.

Manuel, A., and R. M. Derrickson. 2017. *The Reconciliation Manifesto: Recovering the Land, Rebuilding the Economy.* Toronto: Lorimer.

McKee, C. 1996. *Treaty Talks in British Columbia: Negotiating a Mutually Beneficial Future.* Vancouver: University of British Columbia Press.

McNeil, K. 1994. "The Decolonization of Canada: Moving toward Recognition of Aboriginal Governments." *Western Legal History* 7 (1): pp. 113–141.

McNeil, K. 2019. *Flawed Precedent: The* St. Catherine's *Case and Aboriginal Title.* Vancouver: University of British Columbia Press.

Metallic, N. W. 2018. "A Human Right to Self-Government over First Nation Child and Family Services and Beyond: Implications of the *Caring Society* Case." *Journal of Law and Social Policy* 28 (2): pp. 4–41.

Miller, J. R. 2009. *Compact, Contract, Covenant: Aboriginal Treaty-Making in Canada.* Toronto: University of Toronto Press.

Miller, R. J., J. Ruru, L. Behrendt, and T. Lindberg. 2010. *Discovering Indigenous Lands: The Doctrine of Discovery in the English Colonies.* Oxford: Oxford University Press.

Molloy, T., and D. Ward. 2000. *The World Is our Witness: The Historic Journey of the Nisga'a into Canada.* Calgary: Fifth House.

Morse, B. 1997. "Permafrost Rights: Aboriginal Self-Government and the Supreme Court in *R. v Pamajewon.*" *McGill Law Journal* 42 (4): pp. 1011–1042.

Newman, D. G. 2014. *Revisiting the Duty to Consult Aboriginal Peoples.* Saskatoon: Purich Publishing.

Nichols, J. B. D. 2020. *Reconciliation without Recollection? An Investigation of the Foundations of Aboriginal Law in Canada.* Toronto: University of Toronto Press.

Nungak, Z. 2017. *Wrestling with Colonialism on Steroids: Quebec Inuit Fight for their Homeland.* Montréal: Véhicule Press.

Owran, D. 1986. *The Government Generation: Canadian Intellectuals and the State 1900–1945.* Toronto: University of Toronto Press.

Ray, A. J. 1996. *I Have Lived Here since the World Began: An Illustrated History of Canada's Native Peoples.* Toronto: Lester Publishing.

Reynard, P. 2000. "'Welcome in, But Check your Rights at the Door': The James Bay and Nisga'a Agreements in Canada." *Canadian Journal of Political Science* 33 (2): pp. 211–243.

Reynolds, J. 2020. *From Wardship to Rights: The* Guerin *Case and Aboriginal Law.* Vancouver: University of British Columbia Press.

Royal Commission on Aboriginal Peoples. 1996. *Report of the Royal Commission on Aboriginal Peoples*, Vol. 1, *Looking Forward, Looking Back.* Ottawa: Supply and Services Canada.

Scholtz, C. 2006. *Negotiating Claims: The Emergence of Indigenous Land Claim Negotiation Policies in Australia, Canada, New Zealand, and the United States.* New York: Routledge.

Seed, P. 1995. *Ceremonies of Possession in Europe's Conquest of the New World 1492–1640.* Cambridge: Cambridge University Press.

Tennant, P. 1982. "Native Indian Political Organization in British Columbia, 1900–1969: A Response to Internal Colonialism." *BC Studies* 55 (Autumn): pp. 3–47.

Tennant, P. 1990. *Aboriginal Peoples and Politics: The Indian Land Question in British Columbia, 1849–1989.* Vancouver: University of British Columbia Press.

Tester, F., and P. Kulchyski. 1994. *Tammamiit (Mistakes): Inuit Relocation in the Eastern Arctic 1936–1963*. Vancouver: University of British Columbia Press.

UN General Assembly. 2007. *United Nations Declaration on the Rights of Indigenous Peoples United Nations General Assembly*. 2 October. https://undocs.org/A/RES/61/295

Weaver, J. C. 2003. *The Great Land Rush: The Making of the Modern World 1650–1900*. Montreal and Kingston: McGill-Queen's University Press.

Weaver, S. M. 1975. *Making Canadian Indian Policy: The Hidden Agenda 1968–1970*. Toronto: University of Toronto Press.

Wicken, W. C. 2004. *Mi'kmaq Treaties on Trial: History, Land, and Donald Marshall Junior*. Toronto: University of Toronto Press.

Wildsmith, B. H. 2001. "Vindicating Mi'kmaq Rights: The Struggle before, after, and during Marshall." *Windsor Yearbook of Access to Justice* 19: pp. 203–240.

Wilkins, K. 2017. "Life among the Ruins: Section 91(24) after *Tsilhqot'in* and *Grassy Narrows*." *Alberta Law Review* 55 (1): pp. 91–125.

Witgen, M. 2012. *An Infinity of Nations: How the Native New World Shaped Early North America*. Philadelphia: University of Pennsylvania Press.

Zlotkin, N. K. 1984. "Judicial Recognition of Aboriginal Customary Law in Canada: Selected Marriage and Adoption Cases." *Canadian Native Law Reporter* 4: pp. 1–17.

21

The Canadian Federal 1994–1996 Program Review

Appraising a Success 25 Years Later

Geneviève Tellier

Introduction

This is the story of an initiative that has stirred much debate in Canada and attracted a lot of attention from abroad. It is about a battle to bring back balanced budgets and responsible budgeting, which was fought successfully by the Canadian federal government. From the end of the 1990s until the Global Financial Crisis of 2007–09, the federal government managed to deliver a balanced budget every year, cut its debt by a third and lowered its interest payments significantly. Even though Canada was severely impacted by two major economic crises since (the great financial crisis of 2007–08 and the current Covid-19 pandemic), its fiscal position remains enviable: its net debt to gross domestic product (GDP) has remained among the lowest in the industrialized world (International Monetary Fund, 2020).

This success can be largely attributed to one specific initiative, the 1994–1996 Program Review. Its goal was 'to ensure that the government's diminished resources are directed to the highest priority requirements and to those areas where the federal government is best placed to deliver services to' (Department of Finance, 1995, 32). The operating spending of all departments were examined which led to the termination, downsizing, or redesigning of many programs. This exercise was not easy to conduct: many tensions emerged within departments and government agencies, between departments, among Cabinet ministers, and also among those outside the government machinery. The initiative nonetheless produced the expected outcomes. The role of the federal government was redefined, and its fiscal position was, without a doubt, strengthened.

However, not everyone would agree, that the 1994–1996 Program Review was a success. There was a social cost to be paid. The redefinition of the role of the state

Geneviève Tellier, *The Canadian Federal 1994–1996 Program Review.* In: *Policy Success in Canada.*
Edited by Evert A. Lindquist et al., Oxford University Press. © Geneviève Tellier (2022).
DOI: 10.1093/oso/9780192897046.003.0021

meant that fewer Canadians, not-for-profit organizations, and businesses would have access to public services. One important consequence of this redefinition was that cuts were highly uneven across departments and programs. The new responsibilities allocated to the federal government also significantly changed the nature of fiscal federalism in the country, to the dismay of most if not all the provinces. On the other hand, it was clear that the program review attained its primary goal, which was to eliminate the federal deficit. In this sense, it was undeniably a success and it is in these terms that we will assess it and examine how it was brought about.

This chapter begins by offering a description of the political and fiscal context that led to the 1994–1996 Program Review. We then consider how the initiative was designed and implemented. Next, we examine the supports and objections it received outside the government, and what it was able to accomplish. Finally, using the framework of Compton and 't Hart (2019), we conclude by assessing the success of the 1994–1996 Program Review. We will demonstrate that while not all conditions for a 'great policy success' were met, most of them were. Furthermore, our analysis will point to a few lessons that can be learned for this initiative.

The Political, Financial, and Institutional Context

A New Government Wrestling with a Nagging Problem

On 22 February 1994, Finance Minister Paul Martin proudly tabled his first budget (Martin, 2008). The Liberal Party of Canada had just won the October 1993 Canadian general elections, and the new minister was eager to promote the initiatives he and his team had assembled in just two months. The new governing party had obtained a clear mandate from the voters, winning 40.5 per cent of the popular vote and 177 of the 295 seats in the House of Commons. The outgoing Conservative government had almost disappeared from the political landscape (only two of the 295 Conservative candidates were elected), while a new Québec nationalist party, the Bloc Québécois, became the official opposition party (with 54 seats). The finance minister was, therefore, confident that he would be able to implement the commitments made by his party during the electoral campaign. The 1994 Budget was the first step taken towards that end.

The party manifesto presented during the electoral campaign (which would be known as the 'Liberal Red Book') clearly laid out the objectives and policies the Liberal Party intended to carry out if elected. The overall goal was to restore fiscal discipline without dismantling the welfare state. This could be achieved, it was argued, by increasing public revenues through economic growth and by constraining the growth of public expenditures. More precisely, the Liberals were committed to reducing the deficit to 3 per cent of GDP by the end of the third year of

418   THE CANADIAN FEDERAL 1994–1996 PROGRAM REVIEW

their electoral mandate, and promised to adopt new programs only if funding was available (Liberal Party of Canada, 1993).

The 1994 Budget put this vision into action. New initiatives were presented to stimulate the economy, while some cuts were made to operating departmental budgets. Total expenditures would increase by a mere $0.8 billion, while total revenues would grow by $9.7 billion. The growth of revenues was mainly the result of favourable economic circumstances, not tax increases. The 1994 Budget also forecasted a deficit reaching 5.4 per cent of GDP in the first year (1994–95), 4.2 per cent the following year (1995–1996) and 3.0 per cent in the third (1996–97). Overall, the new finance minister was confident his government had delivered on its promises, and believed, therefore, that his budget would be well received by the financial community.

Yet Martin's optimism was short lived. As he recalled years later, convincing the financial sector about the merits of his first budget proved to be particularly difficult. While touring the country and abroad to 'sell' his budget, he was met with deep scepticism, as many questioned the federal government's new-found commitment to fiscal responsibility. For Paul Martin, the message was clear:

> I came back convinced after the '94 tour that not only did we have to attack the deficit with an aggressiveness that had not been seen before, but we had to do it in a very different way if we were going to re-establish our credibility.
>
> Martin (2005)

This assessment would have important consequences, as it directly and rapidly triggered the 1994–1996 Program Review.

A Problem Rooted in History

The skepticism manifested towards the federal government engagement to restore fiscal discipline was understandable. Over the years, all governments had come to rely more and more on borrowed funds to finance their new initiatives, while sustaining existing programs. As Figure 21.1 shows, federal deficits have increased substantially during the 1970s and remained high throughout the 1980s, reaching peaks during the aftermath of the 1982–83 and 1991 recessions. So, to try and restore fiscal stringency would constitute a major break with a well-established practice.

Public expenditures had grown significantly more than revenues, especially during the 1970s (see Figure 21.2). Even though public revenues also increased during that period, they remained insufficient to cover the accelerating aggregate spending. It seemed that the federal government, and probably a majority of Canadians, wanted the benefits of the welfare state but did not want to have

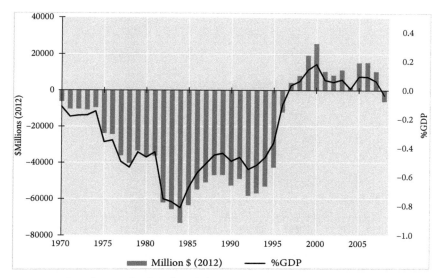

Fig. 21.1 Canadian Federal Budget Balance, 1970–2008

Notes: Figures are in constant Canadian dollars (2012). Computations were made by the author. The federal Canadian government and Statistics Canada have changed the methodology used to compute public budget data and price indexes over the years, and so, year-by-year comparisons should be done with caution. However, the data displayed in this figure provide a good overview of the evolution of the fiscal outlook over this period.
Sources: Department of Finance (2014). *Fiscal Reference Tables*. Ottawa: Government of Canada; Statistic Canada, *CANSIM Database*, 'Gross domestic product price indexes, quarterly', Table 36-10-0106-01. https://www150.statcan.gc.ca/t1/tbl1/en/tv.action?pid=3610010601 (accessed December 18, 2020).

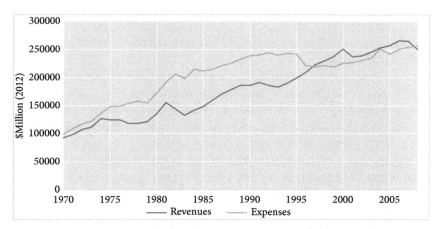

Fig. 21.2 Canadian Federal Revenues and Expenditures, 1970–2008

Source: Department of Finance (2014). *Fiscal Reference Tables*. Ottawa: Government of Canada. Statistic Canada, *CANSIM Database*, 'Gross domestic product price indexes, quarterly', Table 36-10-0106-01. https://www150.statcan.gc.ca/t1/tbl1/en/tv.action?pid=3610010601 (accessed December 18, 2020).

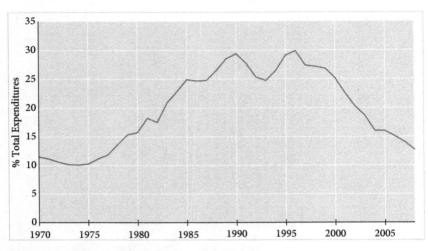

Fig. 21.3 Canadian Federal Interest Payments, 1970–2008
Source: Department of Finance (2014). *Fiscal Reference Tables.* Ottawa: Government of Canada

a tax system that would enable the government to collect the revenue needed to pay for these benefits. As Gillespie has explained: 'the growth in government spending was never more than a minor contributor to increasing deficits [...]. The major cause of the increase in deficit financing from the mid-1970s onwards was the decline in total tax revenues relative to the size of the economy' (1991, 212).

One element that exacerbated the situation was the rising cost of debt. While the charges related to interest payments amounted to 11 per cent of total public expenditures on average during the 1970s, they doubled to 22 per cent during the 1980s (see Figure 21.3). This meant that fewer financial resources were available to fund public programs.

The accumulation of annual deficits over the years directly impacted the size of the public debt. The federal net debt rose from about 15 per cent of GDP in 1980 to almost 50 per cent in 1990 (see Figure 21.4). This sharp increase would continue until 1995, when the federal net debt reached 70 per cent of GDP. Moreover, a sizable portion of the debt was now held by non-residents, constituting an increasingly concerning situation. In 1992, the federal government's net foreign liabilities reached 44 per cent of GDP, which was the highest rate, by far, observed among G-7 countries (Italy came in second, with a ratio of about 15 per cent) (Department of Finance, 1993).

This indebtedness translated into higher interest rates for the federal government. Foreign financial markets usually charge a premium because of the risks associated with foreign investment (caused, among other things, by the volatility of exchange rates). Credit-rating agencies provide risk assessment analyses to help foreign investors. Although Canada has historically enjoyed positive reviews

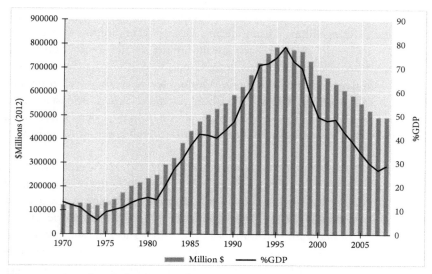

Fig. 21.4 Canadian Federal Net Debt, 1970–2008

Note: Net debt is gross debt less financial and nonfinancial assets.
Source: Department of Finance (2014). *Fiscal Reference Tables.* Ottawa: Government of Canada; Statistic Canada, *CANSIM Database*, 'Gross domestic product price indexes, quarterly', Table 36-10-0106-01. https://www150.statcan.gc.ca/t1/tbl1/en/tv.action?pid=3610010601 (accessed December 18, 2020).

from credit-rating agencies, things were starting to change in the early 1990s. Standard & Poor's downgraded Canada's credit rating in 1992, and Moody's also did so twice, in 1994 and in 1995. When *The Wall Street Journal* (1995) commented bluntly that Canada had become an 'honorary member of the Third World' (1995) this declaration did not go unnoticed in Canada (McMurdy, 1995), especially among members of Cabinet (Savoie, 1999).

Previous Attempts to Restore Fiscal Discipline

The Canadian federal government was well aware of the high level of indebtedness and the financial burden it generated. Several initiatives were launched over the years to address the issue. In 1979, the Conservative Clarke government launched the Expenditure Management System (EMS) to impose strict limits on the overall size of public expenditures. Despite the fall of the government in 1980, the EMS was continued by the Trudeau Liberal government, yet it was relabelled as the Policy and Expenditure Management System (PEMS). To allow some flexibility, all departments were regrouped in to different 'sectors', and each sector was allocated a spending envelope. The budget of all departments assigned to a specific sector could not exceed the value of their respective envelope. If a department wanted additional spending, it had to secure the support of the other departments assigned to its sector, which probably meant finding savings in other programs. The main feature of this reform was to make ministers aware that financial government resources were not unlimited. Within a few years, however, it became obvious that the promises of the PEMS would not materialize. Consensus among ministers proved difficult to attain, and more importantly, the federal government was still not able to maintain a limit on the size of overall spending (Good, 2014; Savoie, 1990).

The newly elected Conservative government under Mulroney decided to tackle the problem differently. The focus would now be placed on the management of programs. The goal was to eliminate waste, find savings, and improve the delivery of each program. To that effect, a Ministerial Task Force on Program Review, better known as the Nielsen Task Force, was set up in 1984. The Task Force was composed of only a handful of senior ministers (four in total). One distinctive feature of this review was that it would seek the expertise and vision of outside stakeholders. Nineteen working groups were set up, composed of various representatives from the private and public (federal and provincial) sectors. The recommendations of each working group were then evaluated by the Task Force, and later, by the Cabinet. The recommendations of the 19 working groups amounted to spending and tax reductions worth between $7 and $8 billion. However, very few were adopted: savings resulting from the Nielsen Task Force was estimated to be about $500 million (Bourgon, 2009). At that time, it became very clear that eliminating or cutting programs would have important negative political costs (Wilson, 1988; Good, 2014; Savoie, 1990).

Following the Nielsen Task Force, the Conservative government tried various case-by-case strategies to limit the growth of public expenditures and bring down the deficit: across-the-board cuts to departments, public-service layouts, de-indexation of public benefits, a public-sector wage freeze, privatizations, legislation that prohibits forecasting deficits, among others. A few months before the 1993 general elections, Prime Minister Kim Campbell, who had replaced Mulroney in a desperate bid by the Conservatives to re-energize their fading popularity, launched another ambitious initiative. This time, the focus would be on reorganizing the machinery of government. Small departments were merged to create large ministries. The Treasury Board Secretariat, one of the government's central agencies, was given new responsibilities with the transfer to it of the Office of the Comptroller General (which manages and supervises internal auditing). The number of Cabinet ministers was reduced from 40 to 24. The objective of this reform was to place tight financial controls on spending. It did not succeed amidst continuing confusion about the role of watchdogs and central agencies within the machinery of government (Good, 2014).

Clearly, something had to be done. That, at least, was what Finance Minister Paul Martin, a key player in the Chrétien Liberal government, believed when he took office.

Designing and Implementing the 1994–1996 Review Program

Redefining the Role of the Federal Government

Committed to restoring Canada's financial credibility, Martin realized that the promises made by his party during the electoral campaign were untenable (Martin, 2005). Just weeks after the presentation of his first budget, he opted for a drastic policy change. Not only would the deficit be reduced to 3 per cent of GDP in one year instead of three, but the government would also commit to presenting a balanced budget before the end of its four-year term. This meant that operational program spending had to be cut by a whopping 20 per cent, consigning the Liberal Red Book's campaign promises to the dustbin. This target was set up by Martin and his closest advisors at the Finance Department, without extensive research, consultations, and negotiations:

> I was accused of using arbitrary numbers, and I agree. I was told I was being unreasonable and I agree. If I wasn't arbitrary and unreasonable, we would be nickeled and dimed and delayed to death. [...] We had no alternative. Or actually we did: that we would fail.
>
> Martin (2008, 138)

The cornerstone of this exercise would be the 1994–1996 Review Program. This initiative was designed to address two specific issues: how to decide which programs should be maintained, and how these programs should be managed financially. The programs to be terminated or transformed (meaning severely cut) were to be identified by senior managers in each department and agency. In addition, each program that would continue to be funded would have to be examined to find savings. All programs would be subject to this review with a few exceptions (such as the Department of Indian Affairs and transfer payments to individuals). Overall, the review program examined about $52 billion worth of spending (Department of Finance, 1995).

This was not the first time the government was launching a program review. This time, however, department managers were directly involved in the exercise. Furthermore, they were provided clear and strict guidelines to execute their task. This technocratic and transparent approach contrasted sharply with past reforms, where across-the-board cuts, and top-down and often secretive modes of political decision-making, had prevailed. The guidelines were presented as a series of 'tests'

424 THE CANADIAN FEDERAL 1994–1996 PROGRAM REVIEW

that each and every program under review had to undergo. Each test was presented in the form of a question. These were:

1. Public Interest Test: Does the program area or activity continue to serve a public interest?
2. Role of Government Test: Is there a legitimate and necessary role for government in this program area or activity?
3. Federalism Test: Is the current role of the federal government appropriate, or is the program a candidate for realignment with the provinces?
4. Partnership Test: What activities or programs should or could be transferred in whole or in part to the private or voluntary sector?
5. Efficiency Test: If the program or activity continues, how could its efficiency be improved?
6. Affordability Test: Is the resultant package of programs and activities affordable within the fiscal restraint? If not, what programs or activities should be abandoned?

These six questions were intended to be answered sequentially. Each question was therefore a 'necessary condition' to be met before addressing the following one. In the end, each and every program had to pass all six tests to have any chance to be maintained.

These tests show clearly that the program review promoted a new vision for the Canadian federal state. It was one where the government would play more of a 'subsidiary' role, only stepping in when other actors (citizens themselves, community organizations, businesses, or other levels of government) were not able to assume responsibility (Paquet and Shepherd, 1996). The program review, therefore, entailed significant devolution of responsibilities to other levels of government and enhanced partnership with various outside stakeholders. In addition to its subsidiary role, the program review also prioritized fiscal restraint and cost-saving measures. No provision was made to explicitly address the issue of budget reallocation or budget increases. None of the six tests provided clear guidelines to examine if the savings that were found within some programs could be reallocated to other programs, or if some programs could receive additional funding. The program review exercise was clearly intended to find savings and bring down public spending by reducing the scope and the size of state interventions.

Managing the Review: The Decision-Making Structure

Once launched, the program review was to be conducted rapidly: most programs were to be reviewed in the coming year. A smaller number of programs would be examined in the following year. Martin had made it clear that he wanted to announce permanent, structural changes in the next budget. This meant that the Cabinet would have to make important decisions within months and that it needed the support of the public machinery.

The process was essentially designed as a top-down decision-making mechanism. Two committees were created at the top of the apparatus to oversee the program review. First, a special committee, called The Program Review Cabinet Committee, was set up in Cabinet to provide political guidance and coherence. The members of this committee were carefully selected by the prime minister to obtain a diversity of regional representation, political views, and institutional perspectives (Bourgon, 2009). Marcel Massé, a former experienced civil servant who had become the minister responsible for public service renewal, was appointed to chair this committee. This choice was welcomed by both public servants (the chair understood the government machinery) and Cabinet members (relieved that the committee was not presided over by the finance minister, who would have gained too much control over the exercise) (Savoie, 1999; Manley, 2005).

Second, a steering Deputy Ministers' Committee was established to review the work of departments and to provide advice to departments and ministers. This committee also played a key role in mobilizing the community of top department managers to support the government initiative, and it built consensus around various propositions (Bourgon, 2009). The clerk of the Privy Council and secretary to the Cabinet (the highest public servant in the apparatus hierarchy), Jocelyn Bourgon, chaired this committee. The committee included experienced deputy ministers from central agencies and line departments.

A Program Review Secretariat was also set up to facilitate coordination among the two committees, the Cabinet, and departments. Each department was asked to appoint a program review coordinator to act as a *liaison* with the Program Review Secretariat. The secretariat was located within the Privy Council Office (which is the department of the prime minister) and reported directly to the deputy secretary to the Cabinet (the second top-ranking public servant).

There was an important bottom-up component to this otherwise top-down process. As it was simply impossible for the Cabinet to review all programs in detail, each department had to set up their own internal program review process to provide proposals for budget cuts. Considerable resources were mobilized for this exercise in each department. At Industry Canada, for instance, the programs were grouped and examined by 14 distinct working teams that involved more than 200 officials (Doern, 1996). Each team was responsible for applying the six tests to each program falling under its responsibility. A departmental Program Review Council was established to coordinate the work of each team and assess the proposals. The final decisions fell upon the minister, and the department's Strategic Action Plan was then submitted to the Program Review Cabinet Committee and the Deputy Minister Committee.

The 1994–1996 Program Review Timetable

The program review started officially in May 1994. All departments were asked to review their respective programs over the next three months. Early in the process, the minister of finance met with each minister to present some notional cuts the government was contemplating. These cuts were severe: 20 per cent on average, up to 60 per cent for some departments (Kroeger, 1996; Martin, 2005). Ministers soon realized, however, that these targets were more than just mere suggestions, and they were non-negotiable (Savoie, 1999).

In September, the Deputy Ministers and the Program Review Cabinet Committee began to review the departmental Strategic Action Plans. Meetings occurred regularly between the chairs of the two committees, while Cabinet members received regular updates. The prime minister was continuously briefed. Cabinet retreats (one-day sessions usually held outside the capital) were also used to build and consolidate political support (Bourgon, 2009). There were indications, however, that debates in Cabinet were acrimonious, as ministers were fighting each other to save their own programs (Kelly, 2000). Some ministers argued their case directly to the prime minister in an effort to circumvent cuts imposed by the minister of finance. Yet Chrétien held the line and was unequivocal in his support for the operation (Greenspoon and Wilson-Smith, 1996; Savoie, 1999; Manley, 2005; Martin, 2005).

The budget plan was almost finalized when the Mexican peso crisis occurred in December: the value of the Mexican currency plummeted, which caused interest rates to increase. This impacted the federal budget directly, as more spending would necessarily be redirected to interest payments. The minister of finance therefore asked for additional cuts to departments. Departments and programs that had been protected from cuts until now (such as defence, which had faced important cuts in the 1993 Budget, and social policy programs, such as the unemployment insurance program) were now asked to generate savings rapidly. The 1995 Budget was tabled on 27 February and the government subsequently enacted several bills to afford legal protection to these changes (Bourgon, 2009). A team was set up to oversee the program review implementation.

The second phase of the program review started immediately after the 1995 Budget was tabled. Its scope was much more modest, as departments were asked to reduce their respective budget by an additional 3.5 per cent, which would take effect in 1998–99. The Treasury Board Secretariat oversaw the review process, thus replacing the Deputy Ministers' Committee and the Program Review Cabinet Committee, which were abolished (Kelly, 2000). The objective of this second round was mainly to 'further clarify the core program responsibilities of the federal government in the economy—through further reductions in business subsidies, privatization, and commercialization and new partnerships with other jurisdictions' (Department of Finance, 1996, 35).

Breaking the Pattern: Outcomes

The 1995 and 1996 Federal Budgets

The changes introduced by the program review were first announced in the 1995 Budget, while the cuts resulting from the second phase of the review were presented in the 1996 Budget. The spending reductions were initially planned to be deployed over a three-year period. This period was extended by one additional year when the second phase was implemented. The budget cuts announced in both the 1995 and 1996 Budgets totalled $18.8 billion. The government also reaffirmed its commitment to the spending reductions that were announced previously in the 1994 Budget (totalling $8.4 billion). Therefore, the cumulative expenditure reduction would amount to $27.2 billion between 1994–95 and 1998–99. Most of the cuts would occur in the second and third years. Total expenditures would be reduced by $4.1 billion in 1995–96, $9.3 in 1996–97, $12.3 in 1997–98, and $1.9 billion in 1998–99.

About 70 per cent of the reductions initiated by the program review directly targeted the operational budget of departments. The remaining savings came from reductions to transfer payments to individuals (mainly to the unemployment insurance benefits) and to other levels of government (basically provinces). Total federal departmental spending would decline by 21.5 per cent over the next four years. As shown in Table 21.1, these cuts were not distributed evenly across programs. Some departments were severely hit. The largest declines occurred in the Departments of Transport and Natural Resources. Many other departments saw their budgets reduced by 30 per cent or more. Only the Department of Indian and Northern Affairs was shielded from these cuts (as promised by the finance minister).

The program review led to the adoption of a wide range of initiatives: subsidies to businesses were eliminated, user fees and cost recovery strategies were implemented, Crown corporations were privatized, public operations were commercialized, departmental management operations were rationalized, and staff was reduced. Programs that supported industrial and economic policies were the most impacted by the reform. This was consistent with the redefinition of the role of government that the Liberals wanted to implement.

The 1994–1996 Program Review also triggered a major restructuring of federal transfers programs. The cost-sharing initiatives that have characterized the funding of several provincial programs for many years were terminated and replaced by one block-funding program the Canada Health and Social Transfer (CHST). In

428   THE CANADIAN FEDERAL 1994–1996 PROGRAM REVIEW

Table 21.1 1994–1996 Program Review Department Spending Reductions

Departments	Spending Levels		Changes	
	1994–95	1997–98	$ million	%
Transport	2,273	704	−1,569	−69.0
Natural resources	1,422	592	−830	−58.4
Human resources development	2,415	1,452	−964	−39.9
International assistance envelope	2,910	1,912	−998	−34.3
Environment	716	480	−236	−32.9
Central agencies	369	248	−122	−32.9
Industry	2,940	2,052	−888	−30.2
Agriculture	2,080	1,455	−625	−30.1
Heritage and cultural programs	2,906	2,051	−855	−29.4
Defence/emergency preparedness	11,801	9,252	−2,549	−21.6
Fisheries and oceans	1,307	1,037	−269	−20.6
Regional agencies	882	708	−174	−19.7
Parliament and general government services	4,635	3,979	−656	−14.1
Foreign affairs and international trade	1,464	1,320	−143	−9.8
Canada mortgage and housing	1,988	1,808	−180	−9.0
Solicitor general	2,623	2,421	−202	−7.7
Health	1,818	1,682	−136	−7.5
Veterans' affairs	1,975	1,840	−136	−6.9
Citizenship and immigration	658	615	−43	−6.5
Justice	752	719	−33	−4.5
Indian and northern affairs	3,786	4,268	481	12.7
Total	**51,720**	**40,593**	**−11,127**	**−21.5**

Source: Department of Finance (1996, 39) *Budget Plan.*

total, federal transfers to the provinces would be reduced by $6.5 billion between 1995–96 and 1998–99.

Finally, the government was on track to reduce its deficit to 3 per cent of GDP, and even beyond. The deficit would reach 4.2 per cent of GDP in 1995–96 (or $32.7 billion), 3.0 per cent in 1996–97 ($21.3 billion), and 2.0 per cent in 1997–1998 ($17 billion).

Divided Reactions

The 1995 Budget tabled by Paul Martin attracted a lot of attention, as the minister of finance had built high expectations about its strategy to restore the credibility of the federal government on financial markets. In addition, he had launched some extensive public pre-budget consultations during the fall, which helped him shape public expectations (Good, 2014). Overall, business financial markets were pleased and found the budget 'credible': 'We gave them an A,' said a Goldman

Sachs representative; 'The government has finally walked the deficit-reduction talk,' added the Bank of Nova Scotia chief economist (Dow Jones, 1995; Blinch, 1995).

The deficit reduction strategy came, however, with a high price tag for many: severe cuts were made to various programs that provided financial support to community groups and the voluntary sector (Cardozo, 1996). Many advocacy and social justice groups strongly denounced the cuts (Monsebraaten, 1995; Dutrisac, 1995). Most premiers were also furious about the reduction of provincial transfers. Ontario stated that 'the fight has just begun,' while Québec denounced a 'greater centralization of powers in the hands of Ottawa' (Séguin, 1995; *Globe and Mail*, 1995).

Opposition parties joined the chorus of critics. Their respective grievances were along traditional party lines. The right-leaning leaders of the Reform Party and the Conservative Party insisted that the cuts were not deep enough, and the deficit should have been eliminated sooner, while the leaders of the left-wing New Democratic Party and the nationalist Bloc Québécois denounced the massive cuts to social programs and to provincial transfers respectively (Ferguson, 1995; Presse canadienne, 1995). Unsurprisingly, all opposition parties voted against the Budget in the House of Commons.

The Canadian public's support for this budget was not as polarized, however, something the Liberal government had learned from previous public consultations (Lindquist, 1994). Opinion polls indicated that the size of the deficit had become a significant concern for many Canadians. As illustrated in Figure 21.5, an increasing number of people were of the opinion that it was important that the federal government brought its budget under control. Just after the 1994 Budget was tabled, almost three-quarters of Canadians thought that it was 'very important' that the federal government tries to reduce the deficit. Opinion polls also showed that Canadians were generally supportive of the Liberal government strategy. An Angus Reid survey conducted only days after the presentation of the 1995 Budget found that 67 per cent of respondents believed the budget 'was on the right track' (with only 23 per cent indicating the contrary), while 57 per cent said the budget was better than what most had seen in the past 10 years (Little and Freeman, 1995). They were some concerns, however, about the pace of the reform: 70 per cent of respondents to an Environics opinion poll conducted a few months after the 1995 Budget was tabled, stated that the government should take a more gradual approach to reduce the deficit (Environics, 1995). They nonetheless approved the government's strategy to cut spending (57.8 per cent supported this strategy) instead of raising taxes (2.3 per cent support) or both (29.8 per cent support) and maintained that reducing the deficit should remain a high priority for the next budget (with 62.1 per cent support for this).

In fact, the Liberal government enjoyed high levels of popularity among voters. In the Ipsos-Reid and Environics polls, the approval rating of the prime minister

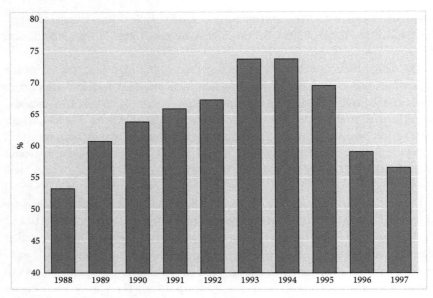

Fig. 21.5 Public Opinion about the Size of the Federal Deficit, 1988–1997

Notes: Percentage of respondents that answered 'yes' to the following question: 'Is it important that the federal government try to reduce the deficit?'. For 1995, the survey was conducted after the presentation of the 1995 Budget (in the fall).
Source: Environics Focus Canada, various quarterly opinion polls. Data are available at the Scholars Portal Canadian Public Opinion Polls Collection (ODESI), https://search1.odesi.ca/#/.

was steadily above 50 per cent, and even at times over 60 per cent. The popularity of Jean Chrétien only started to decline seriously in 2002, when his approval rate fell below 50 per cent for the first time (Ipsos-Reid, 2002). This popularity translated to two subsequent majority victories for the Liberals in 1997 and 2000. One factor that can explain this political success was the absence of a solid opposition party, as existing parties were unable to present themselves as an acceptable alternative to the governing party. The right was divided, with the Reform Party successfully challenging the Progressive Conservative Party, while the Bloc Québécois was solidly established in Québec. The left was also struggling with the New Democratic Party (NDP), which was unable to articulate a serious left-wing opposition. At the 1993 general federal election, only 7.1 per cent of the electorate voted for the NDP. It seemed that the electorate was leaning towards the right of the political spectrum.

The Liberal government's lasting popularity can also be linked to the state of the economy. At the time the 1995 Budget was tabled, the country was slowly recovering from the 1991 economic downturn. Production and employment were on the rise, while interest rates were gradually decreasing and, more importantly, were becoming less volatile. These favourable economic circumstances helped keep public spending under control (especially for social programs such as unemployment benefits) and generated additional public revenues (from individuals and businesses). At the end of the 1990s, the price of oil started to increase substantially, producing unanticipated revenues for the federal government. The deep cuts to public programs would quickly be a thing of the past, as the government started to increase spending. The government projected that it would spend an additional $55.2 billion on new initiatives between 1997–98 and 2002–03 (Department of Finance, 2000, 155). Despite these new commitments, total spending would remain below total revenues (see Figure 21.1).

Beyond the 1996 Budget

Did the Review Program achieve its objectives? From a financial perspective, the answer is an undeniable yes. Table 21.2 shows the federal government's fiscal outcomes for the 1995–1999 period. The deficit was lower than forecasted, near 3 per cent of GDP in 1995, and surpluses appeared in 1997—much sooner than anticipated. Surpluses would occur annually until the Global Financial Crisis of 2007–08 (as shown in Figure 21.1). In addition, the federal government debt was reduced from 74.4 per cent of GDP in 1995 to 28.9 per cent of GDP in 2008 (see Figure 21.3). This achievement was obtained mostly through a tight control on public expenditures. Even though spending would eventually increase, it would always remain below total revenues (see Figure 21.2). The federal government proudly reminded Canadians that the last time a federal budget was balanced for three consecutive years was in 1951 (Department of Finance, 1998, 140).

The answer to the above question is also affirmative from a policy perspective. Structural changes regarding the downsizing and the delivery of programs

Table 21.2 Federal Fiscal Transactions, $ million

	1995–96	1996–97	1997–98	1998–99	1999–2000
Revenues	140,257	149,889	160,864	165,520	176,408
Program expenditures					
Operating expenses	55,659	50,339	55,329	51,031	55,366
Transfers to individuals	39,121	38,826	38,952	39,884	40,157
Transfers to other governments	26,076	22,162	20,504	25,523	23,243
Total	120,856	111,327	114,785	116,438	118,766
Operating surplus	19,401	38,562	46,079	49,082	57,642
Debt servicing	49,407	47,281	43,120	43,303	43,384
Budgetary surplus	−30,006	−8,719	2,959	5,779	14,258
(% of GDP)	(−3.6%)	(−1.0%)	(0.3%)	(0.6%)	(1.4%)

Source: Department of Finance (2014) *Fiscal Reference Tables.*

432   THE CANADIAN FEDERAL 1994–1996 PROGRAM REVIEW

were introduced by the Liberal government. User fees and commercial activities were implemented, while several responsibilities were transferred to the private sector (privatization) or to the provinces (devolution). More generally, the subsidiary role of the Canadian federal state was now clear: its core mission was to create an environment conducive for businesses; to help the most vulnerable citizens in society; and to manage financial resources responsibly. In the end, the program review proved an important vehicle for forging a new, albeit controversial (e.g. Paquet and Shepherd, 1996), vision for the role of the federal government.

Subsequent governments sought to implement a permanent program review process, directly inspired by the 1994–96 exercise. The focus was less on fiscal restraint and more on periodic budget reallocations. One of its key components, the six tests, would still be used regularly, with a few alterations to evaluate existing and new programs (Bourgon, 2009; Good, 2014; Shepherd, 2013). The attempts to incorporate a program review as a permanent exercise failed, however. Subsequent governments were not committed to devoting the requisite amount of time, resources, and commitment from the highest levels of the political and administrative machinery (Lindquist, 2006). In addition, the need to make significant changes no longer existed after 1997, as the deficit was already eliminated, and economic conditions markedly improved. Any additional budget reductions would therefore come at a higher political cost for the government (Kelly, 2003). Finally, budget reductions and budget reallocation are not the same, as reprioritizing spending does not necessarily entail reducing spending (Kelly, 2003). The problem was that subsequent governments continued to use the six tests and the subsidiarity principles used for the 1994–1996 Review Program, even though expenditure cuts were no longer necessary. At the turn of the millennium, the federal government was generating surpluses higher than expected, which created new challenges, such as identifying new spending priorities without compromising the fiscal wealth of the government (for a good example of the new challenges faced by the federal government after the 1994–1996 Program Review, see Chapter 8 by Allan Tupper in this volume).

Assessing the Success and Legacy of the 1994–1996 Program Review

The aim of the 1994–1996 Program Review was to rethink the role of the Canadian federal government in a context of budgetary restraint. The federal government was facing considerable deficits in the early 1990s, and the initiative was implemented to drastically change this course of action. From a financial point of view, the initiative fulfilled its promises. By abolishing, reallocating, consolidating, and streamlining programs, the federal government was able to save almost $30 billion over a three-year period. The federal deficit, which stood at $42 billion in 1994, was gone by 1997. Afterwards, the federal government produced an accumulated surplus of $95.6 billion between 1998 and 2003 (Standing Committee on Finance, 2004). Federal budget surpluses occurred every year until the Global Financial Crisis of 2007–08.

To what extent can the 1994–1996 Program Review be deemed a policy success? Compton and 't Hart (2019) argue that a policy can be considered a 'complete success' if it has a) created widely valued social outcomes (programmatic assessment); b) been implemented through the use of sound design, decision-making, and delivery mechanisms (process assessment); c) achieved the support of a broad political coalition (political assessment); and d) sustained success over time (temporal assessment) (Compton and 't Hart, 2019, 5; see also McConnell, 2010).

From a *programmatic* perspective, the 1994–1996 Program Review can be deemed a success because it has accomplished its objectives. The program review was launched because the federal government wanted to reduce federal public spending by restructuring programs and redefining the role of government in society. This goal was attained. There were no across-the-board reductions, which proved ineffective in the past. Instead, the government elected to employ carefully targeted program cuts, which were designed to have lasting effects. Furthermore, these cuts were guided by a clear vision about what the mission of the Canadian federal government ought to be. Even today, the changes introduced in 1995 and 1996 are still visible. Subsequent governments did not seek to restore programs that were cut and transformed by the Liberals (for instance, Crown Corporations that were privatized were not renationalized, and user fees and block-funding programs remained). Furthermore, total expenditures remained below total revenues, indicating that the government only spent within its limits. In addition, Canada's fiscal position was strengthened. The diminution of interest payments meant that more revenues could be directed to fund public programs. While interest payments almost reached 30 per cent of total expenditures in 1995, they were down to 12 per cent in 2008 (see Figures 21.2 and 21.3).

The 1994–1996 Program Review exercise was also successful from a *process* perspective. The government seemed to have learned lessons from past reforms and tried to avoid making the same mistakes. Experienced and skilled individuals were leading the reform, while various committees were set up to establish communication lines among departments, central agencies and the Cabinet. Outside stakeholders did not participate directly in the program review process, which also illustrated the determination of the prime minister and his close advisors to rely on people who had a good understanding of the government machinery. A key element of the 1994–1996 Program Review were the six tests that would be used to assess each program. These tests provided structure and coherence in the decision-making process. Even though people could disagree with the cuts and the reasons behind those cuts, they knew why these cuts were made. More broadly, the 1994–1996 Program Review constituted the end of an era when departmental spenders had enjoyed a high degree of influence in the decision-making process. The program review gave more power to the Department of Finance, thus strengthening the influence of the guardians of prudent budgeting (Good, 2014). The program review disproved the then widely held view that the size of the public sector simply could not be reduced.

From a *political perspective*, despite its controversial nature, the Review got through the Cabinet and Parliament largely unscathed, and the Liberal government did not see its popularity diminished. Unlike some provinces and organized interests, the Canadian public by and large accepted the 're-set' as inevitable. The 1994–1996 Program Review was also well received by the financial and business community. Canada's fiscal credibility was restored. At the same time, however, not everyone applauded the government initiative. The cuts made to many programs meant that several public services were no longer available for many Canadians.

Some actors questioned the choice of reducing expenditures instead of raising taxes. This was not the view shared by a majority of Canadians, however. Opinions polls regularly showed that most Canadians did not want deficits to be eliminated through tax hikes. The Canadian provinces were also strongly dissatisfied with the 1994–1996 Program Review, as they were directly hit by the cuts. Yet, the misfortune of Canadian provinces is that they do not vote. Therefore, the federal governments tend to incur few political costs when they reduce transfer payments to the provinces.

A precondition for the political efficacy of the Review was the disciplined commitment of the prime minister to this reform. To paraphrase Donald Savoie (1999), 'there was no light' between the minister of finance and the prime minister. Cabinet ministers who tried to appeal directly to the prime minister to shield their program from cuts were rapidly reminded to comply with the program review's directives. In addition to strong leadership from the centre, the political landscape was another factor that led to the success of the initiative. The Liberal Party was able to implement unpopular measures (programs cuts) because it faced no serious threat from opposition parties. The right was deeply divided, the left was struggling to offer some propositions that would appeal to a significant portion of Canadians and, overall, the Liberal Party enjoyed a strong popular support. The government also benefited from favourable economic conditions. The Canadian economy was faring better than expected at the end of the twentieth century, which meant more revenues for the federal government. The fiscal restraint imposed by the Program Review only lasted a few years. It is not certain whether the popularity of the government would have remained as strong if the program cuts had been maintained for a longer period, or if the deficit was not eliminated.

An *endurance assessment* of the 1994–1996 Program Review is mixed. On the one hand, the elimination of the deficit and the reduction of debt considerably strengthened the fiscal position of the Canadian federal government, leaving a legacy that would last many years. On the other hand, many failed to recognize the exceptional features of the 1994–1996 Program Review. This initiative was devised to address a specific problem that occurred at a particular moment in time. Several subsequent governments tried to replicate this success by emulating the 1994–1996 Program Review to implement new budget reforms, yet they seemed unaware that they were pursuing different objectives, which required different tools.

This is not to say that a successful program review will never occur again. A new program review that is as transformative as the 1994–1996 Program Review can be implemented in the future. However, it needs strong leadership, considerable resources, and a bit of luck, in the form of favourable political and economic conditions. With the current pandemic, many will question the role of the state in our society. A program review exercise could be the way for a future government to implement a new vision for the Canadian federal government. The 1994–1996 Program Review has provided some interesting and important lessons on how to conduct a successful program review.

References

Blinch, R. 1995. "Canada Slashes Government in Budget, Markets Cheers." *Reuters.* 28 February.

Bourgon, J. 2009. *Program Review: The Government of Canada's Experience Eliminating the Deficit, 1994–1999—-A Canadian Case Study.* Waterloo: The Centre for International Governance Innovation.

Cardozo, A. 1996. "Lion Taming: Downsizing the Opponents of Downsizing." In *How Ottawa Spends, 1996–1997: Life under the Knife,* edited by G. Swimmer, pp. 303–336. Ottawa: Carleton University Press.

Compton, M. E. and P. 't Hart. 2019. "How to 'See' Great Policy Successes: A Field Guide to Spotting Policy Successes in the Wild." In *Great Policy Successes,* edited by M. E. Compton and P. 't Hart, pp. 1–20. Oxford: Oxford University Press.

Department of Finance. 1993. *The Budget 1993.* Ottawa: Government of Canada.

Department of Finance. 1995. *Budget Plan.* Ottawa: Government of Canada.

Department of Finance. 1996. *Budget Plan.* Ottawa: Government of Canada.

Department of Finance. 1998. *The Budget Plan 1998: Building Canada for the 21st Century.* Ottawa: Government of Canada.

Department of Finance. 2000. *The Budget Plan 2000: Better Finances, Better Lives.* Ottawa: Government of Canada.

Department of Finance. 2014. *Fiscal Reference Tables.* Ottawa: Government of Canada.

Doern, B. G. 1996. "Looking for the Core: Industry Canada and Program Review." In *How Ottawa Spends, 1996–1997: Life under the Knife,* edited by G. Swimmer, pp. 73–97. Ottawa: Carleton University Press.

Dutrisac, R. 1995. "Satisfaction tranquille des milieux d'affaires". *Le Devoir.* 28 February.

436 THE CANADIAN FEDERAL 1994–1996 PROGRAM REVIEW

Environics. 1995. *Environics Focus Canada 1995-4*. Toronto: Environics Research Group.

Ferguson, D. 1995. "Manning Says Cuts Don't Go Far Enough." *Toronto Star*. 28 February.

International Monetary Fund. 2020. *Fiscal Monitor: Policies for the Recovery*. Washington, DC: International Monetary Fund.

Gillespie, W. I. 1991. *Tax, Borrow and Spend Financing Federal Spending in Canada, 1867–1990*. Ottawa: Carleton University Press.

Globe and Mail. 1995. "The Federal Budget: Provinces Cry the Blues in Spite of Feeling Relief." *Globe and Mail*. 28 February.

Good, D. A. 2014. *The Politics of Public Money*. Toronto: University of Toronto Press.

Greenspoon, E. and A. Wilson-Smith. 1996. *Double Vision: The Inside Story of the Liberals in Power*. Toronto: Doubleday Canada.

Ipsos-Reid. 2002. "Lowest Level of Job Approval (46%) for Jean Chretien since Becoming Prime Minister." *IPSOS*. 6 June. https://www.ipsos.com/sites/default/files/publication/2002-06/mr020606-3.pdf

Dow Jones. 1995. "Cdn dlr, bonds strengthen after cdn govt budget release." *Dow Jones News Service*. 27 February.

Wall Street Journal. 1995. "Bankrupt Canada?" *The Wall Street Journal*. 12 January.

Kelly, J. 2000. "Budgeting and Program Review in Canada 1994–2000." *Australian Journal of Public Administration* 59 (3): pp. 72–78.

Kelly, J. 2003. "The Pursuit of an Elusive Ideal: Spending Review and Reallocation under the Chrétien Government." In *How Ottawa Spends, 2003–2004: Regime Change and Policy Shift*, edited by B. G. Doern, pp. 118–133. Don Mills: Oxford University Press.

Kroeger, A. 1996. "Changing Course: The Federal Government's Program Review of 1994–95." In *Hard Choices or No Choices: Assessing Program Review = L'heure des choix difficiles : l'évaluation de l'examen des programmes*, edited by A. Armit and J. Bourgault, pp. 21–28. Toronto: Institute of Public Administration of Canada.

Liberal Party of Canada. 1993. *Creating Opportunity: The Liberal Plan for Canada*. Liberal Party of Canada.

Lindquist, E. 1994. "Citizens, Experts, and Budgets: Evaluating Ottawa's Emerging Budget Process." In *How Ottawa Spends, 1994–1995. Making Change*, edited by S. D. Philipps, pp. 91–128. Ottawa: Carleton University Press.

Lindquist, E. 2006. "How Ottawa Reviews Spending: Moving beyond Adhocracy?" In *How Ottawa Spends, 2006/2007: In from the Cold: The Tory Rise and the Liberal Demise*, edited by B. G. Doern, pp. 185–207. Montreal and Kingston: McGill-Queen's University Press.

Little, B., and A. Freeman. 1995. "Cuts Are Good Politics, Martin Declares as Dollar Sags, Finance Minister Sees 'Overwhelming National Will' to Attack Deficit." *The Globe and Mail*. 3 March.

Manley, J. 2005. "How Canada Slayed the Deficit Dragon and Created the Surplus." *Policy Options/Options politiques*. 1 October. https://polwicyoptions.irpp.org/magazines/fiscal-federalism/how-canada-slayed-the-deficit-dragon-and-created-the-surplus/

Martin, P. 2005. '*Testimony*'. *Commission of Inquiry into the Sponsorship Program and Advertising Program*. Ottawa: Government of Canada. 10 February.

Martin, P. 2008. *Hell or High Water: My Life in and out Politics*. Toronto: McClelland & Stewart.

McConnell, A. 2010. "Policy Success, Policy Failure and Grey Areas In-Between." *Journal of Public Policy* 30 (3): pp. 345–362.

McMurdy, D. 1995. "How Bad Can It Get?" *Maclean's*. 23 January.

Monsebraaten, L. 1995. "'Nothing to Offer Women and Children' Groups Lament Cuts to Funding." *Toronto Star*. 28 February.

Paquet, G. and R. Shepherd. 1996. "The Program Review Process: A Deconstruction." In *How Ottawa Spends, 1996-1997: Life under the Knife*, edited by G. Swimmer, pp. 39–72. Ottawa: Carleton University Press.

Presse canadienne. 1995. "Un budget trop dur juste pour les démunis, dit Bouchard." *La Presse*. 28 February.

Savoie, D. J. 1990. *The Politics of Public Spending in Canada*. Toronto: University of Toronto Press.

Savoie, D. J. 1999. *Governing from the Centre: The Concentration of Power in Canadian Politics*. Toronto: University of Toronto Press.

Séguin, R. 1995. "The Federal Budget: Budget Worse Than Status Quo, PQ Says." *Globe and Mail*. 28 February.

Shepherd, R. P. 2013. "How Ottawa Controls: Harper Era Strategic Reviews in the Context of the 1993–1996 Liberal Program Review." In *How Ottawa Spends, 2013-2014. The Harper Government: Mid-Term Blues and Long-Term Plans*, edited by C. Stoney and B. G. Doern, pp. 101–113. Montreal and Kingston: McGill-Queen's University Press.

Standing Committee on Finance. 2004. *Moving Forward: Balancing Priorities and Making Choices for the Economy of the Twenty-First Century, House of Commons*. Ottawa: Parliament of Canada.

Wilson, S. 1988. "What Legacy? The Nielsen Task Force Program Review." In *How Ottawa Spends, 1988-89. The Conservatives Heading into the Stretch*, edited by K. A. Graham, pp. 23–47. Ottawa: Carleton University Press.

22

Canadian Airport Authorities

A Success Story

David J. Langlois

Introduction

Beginning in the late 1920s the nascent Department of Transport (DOT)[1] began the development of air transport in Canada.[2] Much of this development involved the building and maintenance of airports. However, costs ballooned after World War II, and by 1984 the department was costing the federal government over $750 million a year. In the late 1970s there was interest in privatizing DOT-owned airports in a fashion similar to the Canadian seaports. This was not acceptable politically and the idea faded. However, in 1984, the Mulroney Progressive Conservative government won the election on a platform of economic regulatory reform, and the idea of 'privatizing' government-owned functions gained traction once again. Removing the DOT's involvement in the day-to-day operation of airports, and reducing significant financing costs for maintenance and upgrading, moved from a thought to a priority by 1987.

The first four Canadian airport authorities (AAs) were created in 1992, and by 2003, another 17 AAs had been established to govern airport facilities in the country's major airports (see Figure 22.1). These 21 AAs have achieved far more success than initially expected of them in the late 1980s.[3] They have spent over $32 billion in infrastructure development. They employ almost 100,000 people

---

[1] This was the official name of the department from its inception in 1935 until the 1980s, when it began using 'Transport Canada' as a branding or marketing device. Its official name remains the Department of Transport.

[2] This chapter is based upon research by the author from 2002 to 2019. More detail can be found in Langlois (2019).

[3] Airport authorities and date of transfer: Vancouver (1992), Edmonton (1992), Calgary (1992), Montreal (1992), Toronto (1995), Winnipeg (1996), Moncton (1997), Ottawa (1997), Thunder Bay (1997), Victoria (1997), London (1998), St. John's (1998), Charlottetown (1999), Regina (1999), Saint John (1999), Saskatoon (1999), Halifax (2000), Fredericton (2001), Gander (2001), Quebec City (2001), Prince George (2003).

David J. Langlois, *Canadian Airport Authorities*. In: *Policy Success in Canada*.
Edited by Evert A. Lindquist et al., Oxford University Press. © David J. Langlois (2022).
DOI: 10.1093/oso/9780192897046.003.0022

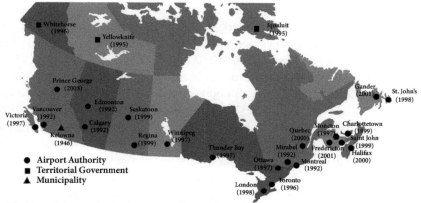

The National Airports System: Locations and Dates of Transfer

Fig. 22.1 The National Airports System—Transfer Dates
Source: Langlois, D. 2019. 386

directly and indirectly in airport operations. They spend almost $7 billion a year in their local economies. Before the Covid-19 pandemic, rather than cost $1.4 billion a year to operate, the AAs contributed $400 million a year to the General Revenue Fund. AAs have been a remarkable success (McConnell 2010), having been in place for 30 years and returning net revenues to the Government of Canada. The governance framework and accompanying management and oversight rules under which the AAs operate have not fundamentally changed since 1992, surviving transitions across successive Liberal and Conservative governments of different political stripes. How this devolution was conceived, planned, and initially implemented is the focus of this chapter.

Creating public policy is usually a long and tedious process, fraught with pitfalls and traps. In this case, policy development was undertaken in an unusual manner, having to contend with impatient political leaders and extremely conservative and suspicious public bureaucrats, who saw the reform as a threat to their domain.

This chapter tells the story of the creation of Canada's AAs and the innovative administration and policy process which allowed this innovation to occur. It is a story about how a small team of officials was established with direct access to ministers and top officials in Transport Canada to research and develop a policy framework. This team consulted with key actors and learned from other jurisdictions, it then proceeded to develop a principle-based, innovative devolution model and secured the necessary approvals for its implementation. The team worked with local communities to develop corporate vehicles for the transfer and management of airports. The planning for, and the implementation of, the devolution succeeded beyond anyone's imagination.

440   CANADIAN AIRPORT AUTHORITIES

After positioning this case as an instance of policy success in terms of this volume's PPPE assessment framework, the chapter provides background on the impetus for rethinking the operation and management of Canada's airports. It then describes how and why a small team—the Airport Transfer Task Force (ATTF)—was created in Transport Canada to design and implement the transfers, and it examines the guiding principles and options the ATTF developed and had approved. This discussion is followed by three sections, which outline the resistance the ATTF encountered from its own Department of Transport and others, the needs of the private sector if non-government financing was to be forthcoming, and the ATTF's approach to dealing with would-be AAs and public-sector unions. Two subsequent sections examine the first four transfers in 1992, the introduction of the National Airports Policy, and the next 17 transfers between 1994 and 2003. The final two sections flag some enduring challenges confronting the AAs, Transport Canada's response to them, and consider why, despite these challenges, the airport transfers can be considered as success using the McConnell (2010) framework.

A Policy Success

The transfer of responsibility for governing and managing Canada's airports from 1992 to 2003 can be considered an enduring policy success. Adroit planning and handling of the transfer process was a critical factor in laying the groundwork, designing the policy framework, and later implementing the devolution of AAs across Canada. At one level 'process' refers to building the requisite design capacity of the ATTF, building a small team, and situating the team in the much larger Transport Canada where it was overseen by ministers and deputy ministers and supported and guided by the Airport Transfer Advisory Board (ATAB). At another level, process refers to how this policy worked: professionally eliciting advice from key internal and external stakeholders in anticipation of all phases of the process (e.g. developing policy principles, negotiating agreements, working with new AAs). The ATTF built momentum by developing principles and complementary frameworks. It then secured political approval for them, finalized project details, and later, piloted transfers with four AAs.

Success occurred in the programmatic dimension. The ATTF developed an innovative institutional design based on clear principles: first, it would give AAs independence and relative freedom from financial regulatory encumbrances, so they could raise capital and financing from financial markets and generate revenues from concessions and travellers; and second, it would devolve authority to AAs as nonprofit entities rather than transferring them to local governments and associated politics. The result was the creation of 21 AAs over several governments and eight ministers. Ultimately, these AAs performed well; they also brought in vast amounts of financing after 1992 that generated a great deal of revenue for the government and promoted local economic activity. Given the number and pace of transfers, as well as the limited capacity of the ATTF group and many other restructuring initiatives during the 1990s, it is not surprising that there were challenges in securing approvals, implementation, and fully developing a complete oversight regime. However, by 2018 the 21 AAs had spent more than $32 billion on infrastructure and were contributing about $3 billion annually to local economies. In 2018, they paid $175 million in municipal taxes, $400 million in rent to the federal government, and employed more than 100,000 persons directly and indirectly, who earned more than $550 million in salaries. Using McConnell's (2010) criteria, the AAs were a 'program success' because they clearly met the intended objectives of shifting the responsibility for financing airport infrastructure away from the federal government through securing sustainable external financing for airports across the country.

The extent of political success is somewhat harder to ascertain. The political goal of shifting responsibility for maintaining and improving airport infrastructure away from the Government of Canada's balance sheet was certainly achieved, and successive governments did not suffer political setbacks based on the creation of local AAs. Indeed, the creation of AAs was part of a much larger transformation of policies and programs as the federal government dealt with significant and unsustainable deficits and debt. The Conservative government's economic and regulatory review of 1984 as well as the Liberal government's Program Review (1994–96), (examined in this volume by Tellier in Chapter 21) were taking place in the background. Although creating local AAs was a significant policy change, it was not a top election issue for voters and hence not critical to the electoral success of any party. However, it did receive the support of successive Conservative and Liberal governments, and no serious attempts were made to roll back the governance model. Creating Canadian AAs, then, was not the object of political contention and proceeded relatively smoothly.

Background and Impetus for Transferring Airports

The DOT model of developing an airport, and then operating and maintaining it using federal tax monies, had worked well during the late 1940s and early-to-mid 1950s. However, by the late 1950s air travel was increasingly more competitive, especially for the lucrative North Atlantic air routes, and the increased number of passengers carried by airlines began to stress airport passenger-handling capacity. The DOT's plans for developing and re-developing airports under its control always lagged behind the curve, and during the 1960s it was becoming increasingly reactive. By the early 1970s, it was apparent that significant financial outlays would be required to support increased aerodrome services and airport infrastructure.

442 CANADIAN AIRPORT AUTHORITIES

At the same time, the Canadian economy faced a challenging period of inflation, low economic growth, increasing federal deficits, and national debt. As such, dramatically increasing funding to Transport Canada was considered politically unacceptable.

In the mid-1970s, under the Liberal government led by Prime Minister Pierre Elliott Trudeau, the minister of transport, Otto Lang, and DOT officials began actively exploring how airport lands might be better used for commercial purposes even while they were also preserved for possible future strategic government uses in case of war, crisis, or other circumstances. They also toyed with the possibility of relying on local AAs to improve operations (Langlois, 2019: 30). These concerns led to the creation of a Task Force on Airport Management in 1979, which prepared a report in July 1979 (The Haglund Report). The report observed that the Revolving Fund that Transport Canada operated to maintain 169 airports across the country was inadequate and recommended the principal airports be governed by autonomous airport commissions and a Canadian Airports Authority. However, there was little interest at the time in outright divestiture by the current minister and his successor, Jean-Luc Pepin.

In 1984, a Conservative government led by Prime Minister Brian Mulroney was elected on a platform of reducing the federal debt and undertaking regulatory reform. The divestiture of airports was consistent with this agenda, particularly since outlays for airports had reached $750 million per year. The new minister of transport, Don Mazankowski, indicated that transportation reform based on reduced regulation and greater reliance on market forces was a top priority, to be complemented by proper oversight and inspection. There were also additional incentives for reform: overload on the minister's office for approvals of leases, contracts, and many other matters from all of the airports; too many opportunities for political interference; and inconsistent administration of airports in different regions across the country. In 1984, the minister created a group to tackle these issues and realize the aforementioned objectives. A year later, this group recommended creating AAs. Meanwhile, the Ministerial Task Force on Program Review (the Nielsen Task Force), a government-wide review exercise, issued a report on real property management which recommended moving 'from ownership and centralized public service operations to managed and owned airports' (Nielsen, 1986, 28–29).

The Mulroney government accepted the recommendation of the Nielsen Task Force and in April 1987, under the new minister of transport, Benoit Bouchard, a new management policy framework was announced, which sought to encourage local management of airports. It emphasized that the government would be interested in receiving proposals from provinces, municipalities, local authorities, or the private sector to own or operate airports, and to place more reliance on business principles for those not transferred. These principles animated the new National Transportation Act of 1987, which applied to rail, road, marine, and air transportation modes, and emphasized furthering regional economic development and securing investments in airport infrastructure.

However, there was a political view that Transport Canada was not doing enough to make progress on the file, and there was perceived resistance from the Airports Group, which did not wish to relinquish control over airports. Government officials were less experienced in the use of contracts and the practices of devolving authority and responsibility to non-government entities. As such, before devolution and contracting could be used as the main tools for the airport transfer initiative, the government needed to experience a paradigm shift. The biggest challenge was that the government and its officials needed to do more than just consult and then decide; success would require negotiating and working with proponents who were no longer 'subjects' but 'partners' of the transfer initiative, and these individuals would have to agree to the proposed transactions. In March 1988, the prime minister appointed a new minister of state for airport transfers, Gerry St. Germain, to drive the initiative forward.

Building the Transfer Team and Negotiating Capacity

In 1987, after discussion between Gerry St. Germain (secretary of state[4] for airport transfers) and Glen Shortliffe (Transport Canada's deputy minister), the latter created the ATTF. Policy development in Transport Canada (with 20,000 staff) was normally handled by its Policy Group, but initiatives would often take months, even years, to develop. In the case of airport transfers, such thoroughness had already been interpreted as bureaucratic resistance and departmental reluctance to give up the management of airports.

Accordingly, a small ATTF team was established in January 1987, with five staff: an executive director, a negotiator, and three project managers assigned to each airport transfer file. The project managers had liaison, coordination, and facilitation roles between the ATTF and the AAs. The ATTF's executive director formally reported directly to the deputy minister (DM) and indirectly to the minister of transport. The ATTF had total independence from the department and could deal directly with the media, but it also had access to the DM, minister, the staff, the Transition Groups, and stakeholders if it needed support.[5] All the executive director had to do was to pick up the telephone and call. His mandate was the day-to-day

---

[4] Secretaries of state are junior members of the ministry and the Queen's Privy Council for Canada. Just as ministers of state, they are assigned to assist Cabinet ministers, but unlike ministers of state are not themselves members of Cabinet.

[5] For example, with respect to communications, the ATTF did newspaper interviews, radio spots, TV interviews, met with city councillors to explain the policy and processes, and with opposition MPs to keep them informed and abreast of what was happening. The outreach undertaken by the ATTF 'just became normal for us as part of our modus operandi. The operational freedom was both rewarding and productive (Farquhar, 2018).

444 CANADIAN AIRPORT AUTHORITIES

conduct of analysis, negotiations, and policy development. ATTF's small size enabled it to be responsive, flexible, and transparent, and it had full authority to take any decision it thought necessary to move the agenda forward. All of these were important ingredients underpinning the success of its work.

Later, the ATTF relied heavily on the Department of Justice's legal counsel in drafting the proposed agreements and instruments for airport transfers, and for securing approval on legal documentation by the governor in Council (the legal arm of Cabinet). There were no off-the-shelf forms of contract or precedents that legal counsel could draw on. Counsel had to construct the legal documentation, informed only by the eight guiding and 36 supplementary principles. Counsel proposed that it should serve as chief negotiator for the ATTF negotiations with AAs, which was accepted. Indeed, ATTF's executive director realized that discussions with the AAs could get heated, so the project managers were not directly involved in the negotiations. The ATTF also ensured that legal counsel was an integral part of the team when consulting the rating agencies and investment bankers. It was important for their legal counsel to have depth, breadth, and scope of awareness regarding the industry, the financing, and other issues as they became germane. In order to draft lease texts that could withstand challenges, the Counsel was involved in the process from the very beginning.

Developing Principles and Options for Devolution

Early on, the ATTF commissioned several studies and soon had several models to consider, particularly the British Airports Authority (BAA) and the United States government approach of either providing capital assistance to airports by means of national funds or allowing bond-financing for municipal-owned airports (Langlois, 2019, 38–45). Other countries had begun to explore the possibility of using public private partnerships (PPPs) to supply services that were formerly the sole domain of the public sector. Great Britain had privatized its major airports in the 1960s by creating the BAA. The United States had a well-developed airport industry that went hand-in-hand with the airlines. So, for many in the Canadian political and airline arena, it was not a great leap to apply these principles to the air transport industry in Canada.

ATTF identified four options for consideration: private-sector-run airports; airports run through local AAs; the Transport Canada airport authority model; and the formation of a Crown corporation. For all options, Transport Canada would retain responsibility for safety, security, navigation, air regulations, and airport certification. However, maintaining the status quo was not an option and the ATTF had no desire to pursue total privatization. This was because the ATTF believed that selling all the airports and their assets was not in the public interest, since the Canadian government had invested billions of dollars into these airports. Essentially, they argued that transferring this investment to the private sector would not be good public policy. The prime motivation for the ATTF was to avoid future government expenditure on airport infrastructure and management by encouraging the commercialization of airport lands and facilities. The BAA model was deemed unattractive, even though it was profitable in aggregate, because it involved cross-subsidization across airports.

If neither privatization nor subsidization were the answer, what, then, was the option? To tackle this, the ATTF began to develop a policy framework for undertaking airport divestiture. It articulated eight guiding principles:

- Safety and security regulation would remain under federal government control and the new operator would have to adhere to aerodrome certificate conditions.
- An equitable benefits package for the transfer of federal government employees would have to be negotiated.
- All federal taxation revenues, including the Air Transportation Tax (which brought in $435 million in 1987/88) would be retained by the federal government.
- No long-term funding for leases would be undertaken by the federal government.
- Reasonable compensation for the airport transfer, whether by sale or by lease, would be required.
- Existing leases, licenses, and commercial contracts would have to be honoured.
- Special federal programs, such as accommodation of official languages and the transportation of the disabled, would have to be maintained.
- The new operator would be subject to the Competition Act and the new National Transportation Act (Langlois 2019, 35–36).

These principles and the accompanying framework were approved by Minister St Germain and Deputy Minister Shortcliffe in April 1988. Then ATTF and Transport Canada went to Cabinet to secure its approval to prevent the possibility of end-runs by opponents within the bureaucracy. Cabinet approval also was given.

Nevertheless, St Germain believed that the department was not moving forward concertedly enough on the issue, so he established the ATAB to support the ATTF. Chaired by Shortcliffe and comprised of eight private-sector members with broad air industry experience from across Canada, the Board reported directly to the minister of transport, and had the mandate of providing the minister with advice on submissions related to the transfer of airports to local AAs.

The ATAB anticipated that, once it recommended a not-for-profit model over the other models on the table, there was a likelihood that AAs would face challenges raising equity capital to fully finance construction, given that bank and bond market practices related to 100 per cent financing for major capital projects. The US model of a passenger facility charge (PFC) was identified as a means for financing airport capital investment. It was anticipated that every airport would eventually have the freedom to levy a PFC, or an equivalent. Unlike the BAA (which is privatized) and the US airports model (with federal and municipal governments having direct political control), the Canadian AA governance structure would have a board of directors with members variously nominated by municipal, regional, provincial, and federal governments. This board would also represent local social and economic stakeholder groups, such as the Board of Trade, the Chamber of Commerce, and labour and professional organizations. All AA boards would have one federal government representative, who would be appointed by the minister of transport.

Another challenge was determining at what rates the government would set rent for different AAs. The airports that the ATTF was initially trying to transfer ranged from larger facilities, like Toronto Pearson Airport (50 million passengers per year) to smaller ones, like Saint John Airport (280,000 passengers per year). As such, the group had to identify various feasible options that would apply equitably to any airport, whether it was Pearson or Saint John.

Since the ATTF was working for the taxpayer, it had a responsibility to act in the public interest. Accordingly, a core objective when choosing the Canadian AAs' governance structure was to ensure that the Canadian taxpayer was receiving the best possible return on its 60-year investment in the national airport system.[6] And, since AAs were to take stewardship of public property and resources, any governance arrangements would have to bear public scrutiny.

Since airport transfers had also come about because Transport Canada, as the operator, had not been proactively or sufficiently responding to the financial or operational demands of airports, it also had to reflect the airports' needs and those of their local community.

Navigating Bureaucratic Politics

ATTF's view that the Government of Canada should make a return on the previous 60 years of investment was not met with universal support. For months during 1990 and 1991, the transfer process was a large focus of ongoing discussions with the Department of Finance. Very few people in Transport Canada or Finance understood what the rent formula would produce. There was a strong view

---

[6] The actual investment is difficult to determine with any precision because the financial records no longer exist. From my research it would seem that the total amount invested over a period of 60 years by Canada into the 22 airports which are managed by 21 AAs, from their creation in the 1920s and 1930s to when they became AAs in the 1990s and 2000s, is anywhere from $8 to $10 billion (actual dollars, not accounting for inflation) (Langlois, 2019).

in Transport Canada that the proposed shift in policy could not happen, would not happen, or should not happen—that it was wrong for the government to make a 'profit' on a public asset.

In the late 1980s, federal Department of Finance officials wanted to sell all the airports since the sale revenues would offset the large national debt. The Department's reasoning was that at the time of divestiture, there would be a large cheque from private interests to the federal government. However, once the ATTF met with Finance officials and informed them that these airports were costing the federal government $750 million a year, it became quite clear that the government was not going to get any such cheque at all, as potential buyers were not going to finance money-losing entities. It was within this context that discussions shifted in favour of exploring lease options. Once this decision was made, the ATTF was given the mandate to say: 'the government is going to rent, it's going to continue to own the land.'[7]

The ATTF considered airports as being engaged in three types of activities: airside, concessions, and land development (there was a lot of land available for businesses which required airport proximity), which made it easier to fully document all functions conducted by an airport. But the ATTF team found that it was particularly difficult to communicate the asset value of airports to both Transport Canada and the Ministry of Finance, as this value could not be defined solely in terms of tangible financial assets, since airport lands also contained inherent strategic, military, and commercial value. Land is important to a nation: for military purposes, for industrial purposes, and for strategic purposes; and the people of Canada owned this vast and incredibly well-situated land. People needed to appreciate the non-monetary value of such land. The government had to ensure it could reclaim these assets, when necessary, primarily for national security reasons.

The ATTF team met with the auditor general of Canada several times to critically examine the policy principles in great detail. The ATTF light-heartedly suggested that 'We're more worried that you're going to find the deal was too good'[8] rather than find it lacking in some measure. Indeed, many in Transport Canada agreed with the auditor general's scepticism about the benefits of the transfer policy. However, because the ATTF had an excellent relationship with St. Germain, it obtained political support directly from him, and consequently, indirectly from Cabinet. Without that support it would have never received government approval of the policy principles, let alone the airport transfer agreements. Even Transport Canada's finance group had difficulty understanding, let alone agreeing, with the lease option.

---

[7] Michael Farquhar and John Cloutier. 23 October 2018. Interview with the author.
[8] Farquhar and Cloutier (2018).

448 CANADIAN AIRPORT AUTHORITIES

Private-Sector Financing in Return for No Financial Regulation

The question posed by ATTF to financial markets was 'How does this thing need to be structured so that the bank will lend the AA money?'[9] The ATTF went to syndicate bankers and rating agencies in New York and Toronto to seek their views on how to structure AAs as corporate entities so they could receive financing from markets. The ATTF soon realized that the AAs would need full freedom in what they could control and charge to secure such financing. Accordingly, the Canadian government imposed no financial regulations on AAs, so that, after the transfer, an AA could immediately seek financing from banks and other financial institutions. The ATTF provided financial markets with the background to the AAs, their structure, and a detailed vision for the future. A key ATTF condition to financial institutions was that AAs had no recourse to suborn any of the debt to the federal government. Once an AA accepted control and management over an airport, they could borrow any amount they wanted to, but financial institutions had to appreciate there would be no federal government intervention or recourse to repay an AA bank debt.

The ATTF sought clarification from financial institutions regarding the assurances they would need in order for AAs to raise capital. It adjusted and fine-tuned the formula and policy based on the answers that it received from financial institutions. With no equity and no shareholders, why would banks lend money to an AA? The short answer was there would be no regulation of user charges set by AAs, who were free to set future site-specific user fees for landing, terminal usage, passenger facility fees, and other charges. Moreover, the AA had the authority to issue airport revenue bonds for financing major capital undertakings (Langlois, 2019, 61). The AA would have a greater scope to develop concessions in the air terminal building and to develop commercial operations on airport lands (Langlois, 2019, 61). The airport authority, not airlines, would make final decisions on capacity expansions (Daniels and Trebilcock, 1993). Finally, the ATTF became convinced that the ability to levy passenger charges would be an invaluable tool for removing pressure on terminal charges and placing more responsibility directly and visibly on passengers. Such charges could be applied in a flexible manner and be directly linked to capital improvement projects undertaken by the AA (Farquhar, 1991).

With this lack of interference in the operations of AAs and their financing tools, and greater awareness raised around the rules of the airport game, private financing began to flow. For example, within a year of transfer, the Vancouver AA arranged financing from the banks for a half-billion-dollar capital expenditure.

---

[9] Farquhar and Cloutier (2018).

Negotiating with Airport Authorities and Unions

During 1988, the negotiating principles for divestiture were developed, takeover feasibility studies were undertaken, and discussions commenced between Transport Canada and the organizing AA's in Vancouver, Edmonton, Calgary, and Montréal. Airport authority organizing committees were also at work in Victoria, Winnipeg, and Halifax; however, for various reasons the early efforts by the committees in these three cities did not progress as expected.

The key underlying principle during transfer negotiations was that the government had to remain financially 'no worse off than it otherwise would have been had it continued to operate the airport' (Langlois, 2019, 256). The ATTF counselled the minister and deputy minister many times that if they caved into a demand from any of the AAs, within days they would have a line-up of AAs wanting to meet the minister for the same consideration. The AA management teams engaged and informed each other. There was a 'jungle telegraph' out there so, if they gave money to an AA, could they afford to give twenty other AAs the same?[10]

The legal counsel drafted all the agreements for the government, and the lawyers of the AAs also commented on these documents. This strategy paid dividends as it ensured consistency among all the AA offerings. It also avoided confusion that would have resulted if each AA had worked in parallel on their own agreements. A key goal of the negotiations was to settle the business contents of the legal documentation that the minister and the Governor in Council had recommended. Legal counsel also supported the ATTF in its negotiations by having several 'legal discussions' with their counterparts from private law firms representing the AAs.

A critical element of the transfer was informing and negotiating with the union representatives of Transport Canada's employees about protections and opportunities of working under the new AA governance framework. Here, too, the strategy of ATTF involved thorough preparation in order to anticipate the questions and needs of employees and union representatives. Prior to engaging or negotiating with an AA, the ATTF undertook a series of analyses and brain-storming exercises to establish its basic position, its fall-back position, and its bottom-line. Each position developed by the ATTF had various degrees of flexibility, which was predetermined. On occasion, the ATTF found itself in the position of being able to assist the AA in identifying a mutually acceptable solution to a specific problem the AA was attempting to address.

Challenges emerged during the negotiations. The first concerned how employees would be treated within the AA transfer provisions, which had major policy implications. The ATTF had hired experts to advise on the human resource issues, pensions, retention, termination, and recruitment, among other relevant issues. The ATTF introduced a policy requiring each AA to accept all Transport Canada

---

[10] Farquhar and Cloutier (2018).

450   CANADIAN AIRPORT AUTHORITIES

employees working at the airport. They would receive a compensation package equal to or better than the public-service compensation package they were receiving prior to the transfer. Another challenge involved informing and persuading Transport Canada employees, who would soon have an AA as their employer—not the government—that the transfer was good for them. The ATTF dealt with the unions and met with many employees one-on-one to assure them they were not going to lose their jobs or take a cut in pay; in fact, they might be better off (Farquhar, 1991).

When each AA developed its proposed compensation package, the ATTF would hire an external HR expert to review and assess the broader hiring policy and compensation structure. The ATTF expert would then contact the AA's expert and the two parties would undertake adjustments, as necessary. By the time of the sixth or seventh transfer, the AAs had essentially shared information on their HR policies, compensation structures, and other employee information with other AAs. This, in turn, ensured that transfers progressed in a uniform manner.

The ATTF had the foresight to ensure that the public interest was protected against private gain, since airports in Canada were located on federally owned Crown land,[11] and were considered strategic assets of Canada. The government thus believed the federal lands should not be sold to a private interest. The ATTF team had intellect, energy, foresight, and an endurance that would support their success. They were tough negotiators, looking to get the best deal for the Canadian public. They wanted devolution to succeed, and to succeed beyond public expectations.

The private-sector perspective of AA creation was different. They found it difficult to understand the public-sector timelines, the governance structure, the logistics, and structural approval and implementation processes (Langlois, 2019, 4). However, private-sector members of the AAs expressed respect for their public-sector counterparts. When the lease agreements were signed, both private and public sector noted that flexibility, risk-taking, and ability to see divergent and conflicting perspectives from an alternate view had enabled both parties to arrive at an equitable solution. As a result, Canada's airports are now owned and governed by the federal government and operationally managed by non-profit AAs. Those involved in creating 'their' organizing committee, which eventually morphed into the local AA, were considered as the movers and shakers of their communities. They put their heart and soul into ensuring that 'their' local airport received what

---

[11] All land in Canada, regardless of whether ceded or not is claimed to be held by the Crown (i.e. Her Majesty). Those who hold land from the Crown such as airports acquire the responsibility to deal with the land as an agent of the Crown and so their lease does not allow them to do whatever they want with the land without consultation. Although Her Majesty has title to all lands in Canada, some of that land may be subject to the Crown's duty to consult arising from its relationship with aboriginal people. This may become an issue if the airport is privatized. See *Haida Nation v British Columbia* [2004] 3 SCR 511.

it deserved. They had a passion for the job that went far beyond just wanting to ensure their airport survived.

Negotiating the First Four Transfers

Authorized by the policy statement on the management of Canadian airports, Transport Canada officials initiated negotiations to transfer the Vancouver, Edmonton, Calgary, and Montreal airports, which accounted for the majority of air traffic in the country (except for Toronto Pearson), as well as with groups on Victoria, Winnipeg, and Halifax. Negotiations for the first four were concluded in 1992 with clauses indicating that the agreements were leases, meaning that ownership was to remain with the government. These leases were to remain in effect for a period of 60 years, with a 20-year extension if requested by the AA and approved by the minister.

Effecting a transfer had two stages: the local organizing committee had to form and incorporate an AA, and then the AA had to sign an Agreement to Transfer with Transport Canada. The AA then had to meet several preconditions by certain dates established during the negotiations, such as its personnel package, insurance arrangements, and purchase of chattels.

The accountability of AA board members provoked lively debate. Some stakeholders argued that the appointment of AA board members should be under municipal control, which would ensure direct accountability to the electorate. Other stakeholders argued that this would make the AAs too responsive to local municipal concerns—for example: should airport runway resurfacing take precedence over a new library, a new swimming pool, a sports complex (Farquhar, 1989)? This discussion was not fully resolved until the issuance of the Public Accountability Principles in 1995. To counter challenges and impediments, the ATTF created airport-site communications committees as a forum for the exchange of information on the status of transfer negotiations. These forums allowed for discussions between Transport Canada employees and the ATTF on many issues like job security, surplus status, salaries and job classifications, pension and health benefits, and collective agreements (Farquhar, 1992).

The ATTF, which would be subjected to scrutiny by Parliament, the auditor general, central agencies, and the general public, had to ensure the transfer of airports to the private sector was in the public interest. Consequently, it had to ensure that: files and records were complete; independent reports were undertaken on the validity and acceptability of the audit and insurance clauses; AAs' employee benefits plans, business plans, and financial proposals were assessed; the financial provisions of the ground leases were acceptable to insurance companies and financial institutions in Canada and the United States; and independent reviews of all legal documentation were conducted. Although the federal government retained

452   CANADIAN AIRPORT AUTHORITIES

responsibility for protective policing, particularly relating to terrorism, the provision of crash, fire, and rescue services was the responsibility of each AA (Farquhar, 1989).

The other three cities who had tried to create AAs (Victoria, Winnipeg, and Halifax) were unsuccessful in negotiating an agreement with Transport Canada by 1992. Victoria had found it difficult to achieve consensus with the thirteen municipalities that would be served by the airport. Winnipeg had had to deal with intense municipal interference in the organization of its AA. And the airport lands at Halifax were of great environmental concern since they contained pyritic slate, which, when exposed to water, produces acid.

From Principles to a National Airport Policy: The Next Seventeen AAs (1994–2003)

After the election of the Liberal Government in 1993, the government decided that the transfer of Toronto Pearson Airport to a private-sector consortium was a flawed decision on the part of the previous Conservative government. Subsequently, when Public Works reviewed the awarded contract, it realized that a group seeking to create an AA had been unfairly excluded from the bidding process despite being the most suited group to take over operations for Toronto Pearson Airport (Langlois, 2019, 361). The examination process also determined that a National Airports Policy was required for subsequent transfers to be accomplished in an efficacious manner.

In 1994, the Liberal government introduced and secured approval of a new National Airport Policy. It was the first formal federal government policy on the transfer of airports. Previously, the Conservative government had simply approved the Guiding Principles and Supplementary Principles as a high-level framework for the negotiation of airport transfers. The responsibility for interpreting and applying these principles for transferring airports had been left to the ATTF, which translated them into business terms and legal documentation. The agreements, of course, were subject to ratification by the Governor in Council.

The National Airport Policy was built on the eight guiding principles and the 36 supplementary principles (although it did not reference them). With very minor adjustments (mostly related to the public accountability principles), the Liberal government relied on the generic legal documentation for AAs developed by the Conservative government for the first four airport transfers when it transferred the remaining 17 airports.

The transfers of the remaining 17 airports took another seven years, with the last one completed in 2003. The size of the ATTF influenced these long timelines: there were only three program managers and each could only handle one airport file at a time, thus, aspiring AAs had to wait in line before going through the application, negotiation, and approval process. This meant, though, that the ATTF staff became expert in handling the transfers and good at managing expectations. Through these acquired skills, they were able to maintain the support of the government, even if each transfer was significant for the communities involved and was associated with idiosyncratic negotiations.[12]

Beyond the Success of Transfers: Some Regrets and Emergent Challenges

This chapter has argued that the creation and transfer of responsibilities to 21 airport transfers along with the development of the National Airports Policy has been a policy success. This initiative substantially reduced growing pressure on the Government of Canada to upgrade and expand airport infrastructure and attracted substantial private-sector investments in airport infrastructure, while maintaining safety standards. This initiative was successful, too, because of how its small team of designers and negotiators were given a mandate for change, scope to act, and protection from the traditional culture of Transport Canada by the minister and deputy minister. However, this does not mean that there were no issues, criticisms, and regrets about AA negotiations, the implementation of AAs or the oversight provided by Transport Canada. There were also two attempts to introduce a revised Act to audit and govern the AAs.

In a 2000 audit of the airport transfers, the Office of the Auditor General of Canada raised criticisms of the negotiation and approval process (Auditor General of Canada, 2000). It found that Transport Canada had not assessed the fair market value of the airports to be transferred before entering into the second round of negotiations and any renegotiations, had provided some incomplete and inaccurate information to decision-makers, and had failed to adhere to some key government directions. The auditor general suggested that contributing factors might have been the absence of a codified application framework in support of the transfers and renegotiations, and the lack of independent review to determine whether the proposed final deals were consistent with government directions. The auditor general also noted that Transport Canada did not yet have a framework for evaluating and reporting on the overall financial impact of the entire transfer initiative. It had been slow to complete a five-year policy review of airport transfers and had not adequately reported on the concerns surrounding the initiative. The auditor general, not surprisingly, called for more diligence in Transport Canada's handling of future transfers and renegotiation of agreements, and better reporting to Parliament. It also recommended that Transport Canada be more proactive and rigorous in articulating its role as overseer of the National Airports System

---

[12] This is more fully explained in Langlois (2019), with a full chapter on each airport.

454   CANADIAN AIRPORT AUTHORITIES

and guarantor of its integrity and viability. Finally, the auditor general suggested that Transport Canada protect the public interest better by clarifying its role as a landlord of the transferred facilities and properly monitoring the growing use of airport improvement fees, sole-source contracting, and the use and activities of subsidiaries by AAs.

The ATTF regretted that it had neither asked for nor received specific instructions about governance of the authorities during its deliberations and negotiations of the AAs. The first AAs formed in 1992 were guided only by a set of accountability principles, which did not directly address governance. When the Mulroney and Chrétien governments undertook the transfers, they had less interest in controlling AAs as entities. The ATTF was focused on enabling the AAs to operate independently, effectively, and efficiently, and more generally, Transport Canada was largely concerned with oversight and regulation to further the safe operation of airports. The Liberal government made two attempts in the 2000s to articulate a new governance framework with a new Canada Airports Act. A bill introduced in 2003 would have allowed Transport Canada to conduct fiscal audits of the AAs, while a bill introduced in 2006 bill included accountability principles for the AAs (Canada, 2003, 2006). However, both bills died on the order paper and were not reintroduced. That there was no subsequent push on the part of Transport Canada suggests continued disinterest in controlling AAs as corporate entities.

By 2005, in the follow-up audit, the auditor general of Canada observed that Transport Canada had made good progress in addressing the issues identified in the earlier audit (Auditor General of Canada, 2005). The auditor general acknowledged that Transport Canada had: clarified and taken up its oversight role of the airports and their authorities; established good relations with the AAs; instituted a lease monitoring program, which had led to a high level of compliance by AAs; ensured that airport facilities were in as good or better condition than before the transfers; monitored whether AAs were adhering to environmental protection and other lease provisions regarding the public interest and governance; and started to monitor the financial situation of the AAs annually and oversee the long-term viability of the National Airports System. However, the auditor general noted that Transport Canada had fallen behind with its National Airports Rent Policy Review and was measuring only the airports' financial performance. It did not yet have a performance framework. However, a regime of five-year performance reviews for all the AAs had long been in place.[13]

Several other issues surfaced over the intervening years. First, prior to 1992, the main Canadian air carriers (Air Canada, WestJet, and Canadian Pacific) had been able to lobby Transport Canada about needed infrastructure enhancements.

---

[13] The first Five-Year Performance Review was done in 1997. Since then 88 Five-Year Performance Reviews have been conducted on all of the AAs; the author conducted 45 of them. They examined safety, security, financial probity, and governance.

Once taken over by AAs, such lobbying had little or no effect, and the AAs made infrastructure decisions based on their own best economic interests. Second, the AAs had to incur many costs such as advertising and promotion, insurance, debt-servicing, security, rent, depreciation, professional fees, travel, training of airport managers,[14] and directors' fees and expenses. Finally, the need for safety management and airport security programs did not become top a priority until the 9/11 attacks in 2001, when Transport Canada was in the midst of reducing its inspections due to public-service downsizing. More substantial safety management and airport security systems were gradually introduced during the 2000s and 2010s.

Finally, Canadian AAs have been profoundly negatively affected by the Covid-19 pandemic and, like the entire transportation and service sectors, are under considerable stress, with passenger volumes at 10–15 per cent of pre-Covid-19 levels. This has greatly affected their capital investment activities but not their safety and security. It will be interesting to see how quickly, and to what extent, the Canadian AAs rebound in the post-Covid-19 era. Post 9/11, passenger volumes fell by 60–80 per cent but had rebounded and were exceeding 2000 levels by 2005. The question is not whether air travel returns to pre-Covid-19 levels, but when?

References

Auditor General for Canada. 2000. *Chapter 10: Transport Canada–Airport Transfers: National Airports System*. Ottawa: Government of Canada.

Auditor General for Canada. 2005. *Chapter 2: Transport Canada–Overseeing the National Airports System*. Ottawa: Government of Canada.

Bennett, M. J. 2019. "Privatization Would Allow Toronto's Airport to Reach New Heights." The Portage Citizen. 27 September. https://theportagecitizen.ca/business/toronto-airport-privatization-necessary/

Canada. 2003. "Transport Minister Introduces Canada Airports Act." Government of Canada. 20 March. https://www.canada.ca/en/news/archive/2003/03/transport-minister-introduces-canada-airports-act.html

Canada. 2006. "Transport Minister Introduces Canada Airports Act." Government of Canada. 15 June. https://www.canada.ca/en/news/archive/2006/06/transport-minister-introduces-canada-airports-act.html

Collenette, D. 2019. Interview with the author. 5 February.

Daniels, R. and M. Trebilcock. 1993. *Policy Instruments: Financing and Delivery of Infrastructure in the Public and Private Sector*. Toronto: University of Toronto Press.

Farquhar, M. 1989. "Privatization of Airports and Airport Operators, Airport Transfers, the Canadian Approach." Speech to the American Transportation Research Board. Washington, DC. 23 January.

Farquhar, M. 1992. *An Executive Briefing on Partnership, Devolution and Power Sharing: Implications for Management*. Ottawa: Transport Canada.

---

[14] Transport Canada had an excellent training program for airport managers, which disappeared with the airport transfers. The AAs had to organize their own training programs.

456 CANADIAN AIRPORT AUTHORITIES

Farquhar, M. and J. Cloutier. 2018. Interview with the author. 23 October.

Farquhar, Michael. 1991. "The Future of Airports in the U.S. and Canada." Speech to the American Association of Airport Executives. Ottawa. 29 July.

Langlois, D. 2019. *Courage and Innovation: The Story of the Men and Women Who Created Canada's Airport Authorities*. Hudson, QC: Sans Souci Publishing.

McConnell, A. 2010. "Policy Success, Policy Failure and Grey Areas In-Between." *Journal of Public Policy* 30 (3): pp. 345–362.

Milne, G. 2000. *Making Policy: A Guide to the Federal Government's Policy Process*. Ottawa: Glen Milne.

Nielsen, E. 1986. *Regulatory Programs: A Study Team Report to the Task Force on Program Review*. Supply and Services Canada, Ottawa.

Rovinescu, C. 2016. "Letters." *Globe and Mail*. 19 December.

Tretheway, Dr. M. 2018. Interview with the author. 22 November.

Young, D. 2014. "Letters." *Globe and Mail*. 15 January.

23
Canada's Response to the Global Financial Crisis
Pivoting to the Economic Action Plan

Evert A. Lindquist

Introduction

When comparing policy responses to the 2007–09 Global Financial Crisis, Canada was a top-performing jurisdiction for three reasons (Wanna et al., 2015). First, among OECD nations, it entered into the tumult with a relatively prudently regulated banking and financial sector (see Williams, Chapter 13 this volume). Second, before the crisis, Canada had a relatively strong balance sheet, a well-managed budget process, a capable Department of Finance, and independent central bank (Good and Lindquist, 2015). Third, the government's policy response and focus of this chapter—the Economic Action Plan (EAP)—provided significant infrastructure funding to all levels of government, underpinned by many creative policy and administrative features. The EAP was quickly designed and announced in early 2009 by a newly formed Conservative minority government led by Prime Minister Stephen Harper. Due in large measure to the concerted implementation of this policy intervention, the prime minister was rewarded with a majority government in the subsequent May 2011 federal election. Relying on the 'policy success' literature (McConnell, 2010), this chapter argues that the EAP can be viewed as a process, programmatic, and political success, especially when it is understood that it was designed as a time-limited intervention.

However, this apparent success masks considerable controversy and a near-death experience for that newly elected minority government, revealing significant blind spots and hubris. The prime minister and his then-minister of finance, oblivious to the gravity of the emerging crisis and shifting public mood, engaged in petty manoeuvres in the party's first economic statement and misread the extent to which opposition parties were willing to collaborate and bring down the Conservative government. The Harper government almost fell as three opposition parties joined forces for an imminent vote of non-confidence. This led to the remarkable

Evert A. Lindquist, *Canada's Response to the Global Financial Crisis*. In: *Policy Success in Canada*.
Edited by Evert A. Lindquist et al., Oxford University Press. © Evert A. Lindquist (2022).
DOI: 10.1093/oso/9780192897046.003.0023

458   CANADA'S RESPONSE TO THE GLOBAL FINANCIAL CRISIS

request of Prime Minister Harper, just two months after the 14 October 2008 federal election, to meet the Governor General and request the prorogation of Parliament. Indeed, the government's initial ham-fisted approach during the early stage of the crisis stands in considerable contrast to how it later regained its bearings and developed a strategy and disciplined policy response, leading to what arguably was a political and administrative success. Accordingly, this case adds another success trajectory to the mix: how a government can move from an 'own goal' situation, rapidly reassess its prospects, and pivot to concertedly design and adroitly steer the implementation of a major policy intervention, which helped stabilize the Canadian economy and ultimately led to political success.

This chapter has four sections. The first provides an overview of the Harper government's initial reaction to the Global Financial Crisis, which led to a political crisis, and how it controversially 're-set' matters by requesting the prorogation of Parliament, promising to introduce a new budget and plan for dealing with the economic crisis. The second section reviews the consultations and general design animating the sprawling EAP, while the third section outlines key features of the implementation strategy. The fourth section appraises the EAP as a policy success, using criteria from McConnell (2010), Compton and 't Hart (2019), and McConnell et al. (2020). The conclusion steps back and considers EAP's relevance for contemporary challenges.

The GFC and the Harper Government: From Economic to Political Crisis

The 14 October 2008 federal election produced mixed results for every one of the major federal parties. Among other reasons, Prime Minister Harper had called the election in order to move from a minority to a majority government, as well as to head off support for the Kyoto Protocol and take on the Liberal Party for its support of a carbon tax as part of a broader climate change strategy. While the election did not deliver a majority for the Conservative Party, it delivered a greater number of seats for Prime Minister Harper, largely at the expense of the Liberal Party in Quebec. Moreover, the net loss of 24 seats meant that Stephane Dion's leadership of the Liberal Party seemed fatally wounded. On the other hand, the NDP had modest gains, building on its totals in the previous two elections. The Bloc Québécois (BQ), benefitting from the collapse of the Liberal vote in Quebec, prevented the Conservatives from securing a majority government. The election campaign and outcome, though, had come amidst gathering storms in the international economy.

In late 2006, the first signs of serious difficulties in the US housing market had emerged, leading to its collapse and increasing pressure on mortgage firms and banks holding mortgage-backed securities. This led to liquidity problems for many well-known banks, brokerage houses, and insurance firms in late 2007 and early 2008, causing some collapses. In response, the US Bush administration introduced a major stimulus package in February 2008 and later took significant steps to bail out its major lending institutions and stabilize the subprime mortgage market, such as the Troubled Asset Relief Program (TARP) in October 2008 (Posner and Fantone, 2015; Lindquist et al., 2015). Similar responses in other countries, rising demands for coordinated responses by central banks, and interventions from the European Union (EU), International Monetary Fund (IMF) and World Bank fuelled concerns about international financial markets and spill-over effects in Canada.

First Response: An Economic Statement

It was against this backdrop that the minister of finance, Jim Flaherty, delivered the new minority government's first economic statement, which set off an intriguing chain of events. Canadian federal governments typically present their budgets in February and March, with dates sometimes shifted to April and May. They are preceded by the autumn economic statements and fiscal updates, usually delivered each November, which help to inform and frame consultations in advance of the main Budget. These dates vary depending on election cycles and broader developments in the economy and government finances. Following the recent election, and the rapidly evolving fiscal and economic climate, along with worries expressed by the newly established Parliamentary Budget Office about the government's budget staying in balance in the current fiscal year, the November 2008 economic statement and fiscal update took on added importance.

Flaherty noted that the budget was in balance and lauded the country's strong financial system. While not ruling out an economic stimulus in the months ahead, he projected that the budget would remain in surplus until 2013–14 (Good and Lindquist, 2015). It offered a 'stand pat' approach despite aggressive actions occurring south of the border, in other countries, and by international agencies in response to rapidly deteriorating financial markets. But it also proposed to remove per-voter subsidies for national political parties, have pay equity for public servants handled through collective bargaining and not the courts, and suspend public servants' right to strike until 2011. The non-fiscal measures looked petty and manipulative, which did not seem warranted or advisable when financial, fiscal, and monetary turbulence was well in motion. These announcements played to the caricatures of the prime minister's critics of his leadership: controlling, anti-democratic, and strongly biased towards small government. It misread the public mood, misinterpreted the economy, and was seen as a miscalculation by a seemingly smug government that had just been returned to power.

Opposition Parties Concert

Despite not securing a majority in the House of Commons, the Conservative strategists must have presumed that the opposition parties would not have the energy or gumption to challenge the measures in the economic statement. Indeed, the Liberals had suffered significant losses in the October election and its leader was now a lame-duck; the NDP had failed to secure as many seats as it had hoped; the BQ, though having had a credible showing in Quebec, would have little interest in collaborating with the other opposition parties; and there was considerable antipathy among these parties. However, the audacity and incongruity of the statement with emerging news, the direct assault on public financing of political parties, and the prospect of more such initiatives by the Conservatives, galvanized the opposition parties and caused a media storm.

Within days (see Valpy, 2009, for details) the backlash from political commentators and opposition parties led the government to withdraw its political-party-financing proposal and move forward the date for introducing the Budget to late January. Another 48 hours later, on Monday 1 December, the government withdrew its economic statement and reversed its statement on banning public-service strikes, and a day later they withdrew the motion to approve the Economic and Fiscal Statement, which would have been a vote of confidence.

While the government was performing these U-turns, the opposition parties laid the groundwork for bringing the government down. They announced a coalition agreement between the Liberals and NDP that, with the support of the BQ, created an existential threat to the Harper government.

On Tuesday 2 December, the government mounted a campaign-style media blitz, casting the coalition agreement as a coup supported by a separatist party (the BQ) and inherently undemocratic given that an election had just taken place, and presenting novel and misleading interpretations of constitutional conventions, principles, and practices (Leduc, 2009; Smith, 2009; Weinrib, 2009; Malloy, 2010). Prime Minister Harper delivered a prime-time television address to the nation the next day, later followed by a maladroit televised response by the leader of the Liberal Party. On Thursday, to avoid certain defeat and re-set his government's agenda, Harper requested a meeting with the Governor General to discuss his proposal to prorogue Parliament.

The Proroguing of Parliament

Requesting a prorogation of Parliament just two weeks after its first sitting following a national election was an extraordinary move that generated considerable public debate (see Russell and Sossin, 2009; Brodie, 2018). The choices confronting the Governor General were difficult (prorogue Parliament, call an election, or allow the government to fall and allow the Liberal-NDP coalition to test the waters as a government), but she decided to grant Harper's request and allow the prorogation of Parliament for six weeks until 26 January 2009. When Parliament was back in session, the minister of finance would present the government's Budget to the House of Commons, several weeks earlier than it normally would in the budget cycle. Despite the Harper government's strained public arguments and rationale, the decision was on balance reasonable (Franks, 2009; Cameron, 2009) given the strange proposed coalition alternative. Moreover, if the returning government did fall, it would not preclude the possibility of the Governor General giving the new coalition a chance to succeed.

Successfully arguing for prorogation meant that the Harper government had a very short window to rethink its approach and tone, develop a credible economic strategy, and secure the support of at least one of the opposition parties, whom it had deeply offended with the economic statement and its subsequent media blitz. The Harper government 'pivot' involved acknowledging the rapidly deepening economic slump, recognizing the political crisis it had sparked, and, with its back to the wall, devising a breathtaking and controversial 'crisis management' strategy to turn around the situation.

The Governor General's decision and tactical whirlwinds of the previous week accelerated the end of Stephane Dion's leadership of the Liberal Party, with star recruit and former Harvard professor Michael Ignatieff appointed as his successor just after the prorogation of Parliament was announced. The critical question quickly moved beyond whether the Harper government would survive, to how it would use its grace period to navigate this new political and economic landscape amidst acute time pressures.

Designing and Approving the Economic Action Plan

Preparing a national budget in six weeks is a challenge in the best of times, but for an ordinarily conservative government to rethink its fiscal stance and prepare a credible stimulus package that would stabilize all sectors of the economy, was quite another. The near-death experience of the government focused not only the minds of ministers, but also central agencies and top executives across the Canadian public service. Developing the new assumptions and fiscal framework fell to the Department of Finance and its minister, but an aggressive stimulus package would involve all ministers and their departments, requiring considerable coordination from the Privy Council Office, its intergovernmental affairs secretariat, and the Treasury Board Secretariat. To re-build trust meant that, at the very least, the government had to be seen as consulting with other levels of government and key stakeholders to forge a credible and effective policy response.

Consultations with a New Fiscal Framework

The government adopted a multi-pronged approach. First, officials in the Department of Finance had to revisit the 27 November Economic Statement. By

462 CANADA'S RESPONSE TO THE GLOBAL FINANCIAL CRISIS

taking advantage of new data, they needed to prepare a new economic outlook and operating assumptions for engaging stakeholders and provide the assumptions that would underpin the budget. The revised economic outlook—informed by consultations and forecasts elicited from private-sector economic forecasters—was made public on 17 December, less than two weeks after the prorogation. It included dramatically different baseline forecasts of deficits for the next two fiscal years that took into account the rapidly deteriorating US economic outlook and global economy, and anticipating different scenarios given the rapidly unravelling financial carnage and uncertainties it was generating.

Second, the *Budget Plan* noted that the government had undertaken 'an unprecedented consultative effort. It has consulted the provinces and territories. It has considered the views of private sector economists, academics, business leaders and thousands of Canadians who participated in on-line consultations. The Minister of Finance also sought advice from his Economic Advisory Council and Members of Parliament from all parties' (p. 10). Whether the consultations were, in fact, the most extensive is an open question, but they were certainly the most extensively showcased pre-budget consultations since the early 1990s when then-minister of finance, Paul Martin, consulted with numerous groups to grapple with a burgeoning deficit for a newly elected Chrétien Liberal government (Lindquist, 1994). The minister of finance met first with provincial and territorial counterparts on 17 December and the next day with his newly established Economic Advisory Council of business and financial leaders, asking them to provide their advice before Christmas. Meetings held with economic forecasters and the Standing Committee on Finance in the House of Commons were part of the normal cycle of budget consultations, but seemed of more importance than in recent years.

Citizens and groups were invited to submit suggestions on budget priorities as part of a National Consultation on Budget Actions to Protect Canada's Economy via an online portal. Thousands took up the government's offer. The minister and Department of Finance were in regular touch with colleagues in other countries and international entities to compare notes and coordinate interventions, including commitments made with other G20 countries. Finally, a few short weeks later, the prime minister met with provincial and territorial premiers on 16 January.

Introducing the Budget and Economic Action Plan

As agreed, Parliament reopened on 26 January 2009, with a curt five-minute Throne Speech delivered by the Governor General, followed the next day with the Budget. Much of what was in the 27 January Budget had been shared through several pre-budget announcements and leaks on training, housing, tax cuts for individuals and businesses, and a variety of initiatives for Aboriginal communities. The budget itself used five main categories to describe the EAP (Canada, 2009):

- Improving Access to Financing and Strengthening Canada's Financial System ($200 billion);
- Action to Help Canadians and Stimulate Spending ($8.3 billion for skills development and $20 billion in income tax relief over five years);
- Action to Stimulate Housing Construction ($7.8 billion for a variety of housing programs);
- Immediate Action to Build Infrastructure ($12 billion in infrastructure investments);
- Action to Support Businesses and Communities.

Much of the $200 billion associated with the Extraordinary Financing Framework focused on providing backstops and higher limits for loans and insurance for financial institutions and recipients, but would not involve direct costs (as long as the economy recovered and risks were not realized). Otherwise, the initial plan was for a $40 billion infusion of support (2.5 per cent of GDP) over a two-year period, targeted towards creating jobs, helping those most in need, and meeting international obligations. But such measures were also temporary, so that the programs and outlays would not become part of the structural deficit (but with leveraged funds the estimates were $50 billion or 3.25 per cent of GDP). These funds supported a bewildering array of programs and initiatives and became the focus of attention within the EAP. The $40 billion fund was later increased to $47 billion. The predicted deficits of over $15 billion in 2009–10 and at least $84 billion in 2012–13 signalled the dramatic shift in the government's fiscal policy since 27 November.

The many different interventions in the 2009 Budget paper defied easy categorization. It contained a mixture of high-level and specific announcements designed to show that the government had listened to and had supports and initiatives for a diverse range of stakeholders. The goal was to show that the plan was comprehensive and that it would reach different sectors and different categories of citizens and businesses, with many receiving indirect forms of support. The government also sought to communicate that the infrastructure program was to be quickly launched and delivered by the 31 March 2011 deadline to make good on its promise that it would be a temporary initiative.

Securing Support in Parliament

Budget 2009 reflected an extraordinary change in the mindset of a frugally inclined Conservative government. Earlier confidence in Canada's financial system and balanced-budget rectitude were cast aside in recognition of the rapidly evolving economic landscape, and growing domestic and international clamouring for decisive action in the midst of a crumbling global economy. In preparing the budget,

464 CANADA'S RESPONSE TO THE GLOBAL FINANCIAL CRISIS

the government had a critical hurdle to overcome: to secure the support of one party in order to pass the budget in the House of Commons and ensure the government did not fall. If it failed that test, there would be a return to the Governor General, and the possibility of either an election or a new coalition government. The government's dominant strategy since the prorogation of Parliament was to be seen as taking criticism seriously and listening to stakeholders, identifying and generating public support for the measures it was proposing. Its aim was to propose an ambitious package of stabilization and support measures that opposition parties could not readily dismiss.

Since the prorogation of Parliament, the balance among the opposition parties had shifted. The Liberals' new leader, Michael Ignatieff, along with many of his caucus colleagues, had been uneasy about his predecessor forming a coalition with the NDP. Yet the Harper government had acknowledged that the country was grappling with a serious international economic crisis, and had since pivoted to produce a budget that might have looked like a Liberal budget. This meant that the Liberal party had cause to support the budget on its merits and give the Harper government its due.

Seeking a concession in return for supporting the budget, though, Ignatieff's demand was for reporting, transparency, and accountability on progress with the EAP. Accountability and oversight were in the air. While in opposition, the Conservative Party had feasted on the Human Resources Development Canada (HRDC) grants and contributions 'billion-dollar boondoggle' (Good, 2003) and capitalized on the subsequent federal sponsorship and advertising scandal (Gomery, 2006). Back in June 2006, with a new minority government, Prime Minister Harper had secured passage of the Federal Accountability Act (Good, 2014). Now, he was reminded of its potential as a check on the minority government's budget strategy. Harper responded by outlining an 'Accountability Stimulus Framework' that would 'provide an initial report on progress this summer, and responsible ministers will provide an update to Parliament the first week following the summer recess' (Budget 2009, Ch. 3). This was not a sufficient commitment for the Liberals, who introduced an amendment requiring quarterly reporting to Parliament on the EAP. The amendment was accepted by the Conservatives, and the budget was approved with support from the Liberals on 3 February 2009. The NDP and BQ members voted against the budget.

Implementing the Economic Action Plan

With prorogation, departments and agencies reviewed all their programs to identify those that could be topped up, limits and levels that could be changed, and given their client groups or sectors, what new programs could be put in place to preserve or stabilize jobs and business, providing stimulus or support in the shorter term. The selection of instruments, initiatives, and programs was guided by three 'design' principles: *timeliness* (interventions and programs had to be able to start within four months of the budget); *clear targeting* (to families, sectors, and entities most in need); and *time-limited* (needed to be wound down after two years). Infrastructure programs in particular had two-year horizons with a strong emphasis on so-called 'shovel-ready' projects. The goal was to identify programs that could be scaled up or accelerated directly by the federal government, or whose revenues indirectly flowed to Aboriginal communities or provinces and territories, and in turn, to municipalities.

As further consultations, negotiations, and planning progressed, the EAP began to take shape as a more coherent package of infrastructure programs. The federal outlay was just over $47 billion over two years, levering over $14 billion from the provinces, with the following breakdown:

- Social housing ($1 billion for the Canada Housing and Mortgage Corporation and to the provinces)
- Building Canada Fund (Infrastructure Canada with regional agencies, $500 million)
- Community Adjustment Fund (regional agencies, $1 billion)
- First Nations On-Reserve Housing, Schools, and Water and Wastewater Projects (Indian and Northern Affairs Canada, $515 million, which did not include CMHC funding)
- Infrastructure Stimulus Program (Infrastructure Canada, $4 billion)
- Marquee Tourism Events Program (Industry Canada, $100 million)
- Knowledge Infrastructure Program (Industry Canada, $2 billion)
- Recreational Infrastructure Canada Program (five regional agencies, $500 million)
- Investing in Federal Buildings (Public Works and Government Services Canada, $264 million)
- Modernizing Federal Laboratories (Treasury Board of Canada Secretariat and Public Works and Government Services Canada, $250 million).

Other support was directed to industries and communities ($14 billion), support for enhancing Employment Insurance payments ($7 billion), and tax cuts ($6.2 billion).

The sheer number of funded programs (90) and the aggressive timelines meant the government had to rely on partners and existing delivery networks to implement them, especially where events and infrastructure programs were concerned (otherwise the government relied on tax, financing, and employment insurance instruments, which it directly controlled). To reach municipal and regional governments, the government collaborated with provincial and territorial governments to receive approved proposals, and from these it selected and approved

466 CANADA'S RESPONSE TO THE GLOBAL FINANCIAL CRISIS

projects using repertoires developed in the 1990s, essential because the Infrastructure Stimulus Program required matching funding from these governments. The federal government received permission from the provinces to deal directly with universities and colleges across Canada to elicit proposals and provide infrastructure in support of research infrastructure. For First Nations communities' projects, the government relied on established links through Indian and Northern Affairs Canada. To move funding to the country's diverse regions for infrastructure and recreation projects, the government relied on its regional development agencies to identify projects and deliver others. The federal government turned to Public Works and Government Services (PWGS) to accelerate approvals and move forward the backlog of upgrades to buildings, laboratories, and other infrastructure projects.

This distributed approach—relying on multiple networks to deliver diverse EAP programs under tight timelines—presented a massive coordination challenge inside the federal government. The prime minister and top advisors made it abundantly clear to ministers, deputy ministers, and the public service as a whole that the EAP was the signal priority of the government—the reputation of the government hinged on successful implementation. The prime minister, though perhaps not having anticipated launching such a comprehensive intervention, had appointed his strongest and most trusted ministers to key portfolios (Finance, Treasury Board, Industry, Infrastructure, etc.) when he formed his new cabinet after the October 2008 election. Keeping on top of 90 programs that would involve 35 departments and agencies across the government meant that there had to be a combination of strong and modestly distributed coordination across key central agencies: the Privy Council Office (Canada's cabinet office), the Department of Finance, the Treasury Board of Canada Secretariat, the Department of Industry, and Infrastructure Canada (an agency). They not only had to coordinate with each other, but they also had to smooth the way for various combinations of departments and agencies to take up particular responsibilities. This required securing early approval of eligibility criteria for eliciting project proposals, and finding creative ways to coordinate and streamline approval processes for tens of thousands of projects,

The aftershocks of the HRDC and sponsorship scandals meant that all political parties, officials, media, and the public had their antennae up about possible improprieties in financial management arising from the outlays associated with the EAP, especially since its scale significantly dwarfed those programs. An intriguing development occurred early on when the auditor general of Canada publicly communicated to the secretary of the Treasury Board the criteria her office would use to undertake audits. This information enabled departments and agencies to design projects and oversight regimes with them in mind, and to develop internal capacity and repertoires when designing program implementation frameworks (Auditor General of Canada, 2009). This task presaged a concerted effort to engage the risk-management and audit community. The Office of the Comptroller General—which is the internal accounting entity attached to TBSC that sets standards for financial, risk, and audit management across the federal government—brought representatives of departments and agencies together to compare notes on challenges and share innovative practices, and to encourage executive teams to work closely with departmental audit committees (DAAs), which included advisors external to government. Indeed, in its first performance audit of the EAP programs, the auditor general assessed the extent to which risk-management strategies were in place and whether DAAs were engaged (Auditor General of Canada, 2010).

Reporting and communications were important features of the EAP. The government, of course, had committed to quarterly reporting to Parliament in order to secure passage of its budget, and it wanted to avoid the scandals that had plagued the Liberal government. Moreover, the goal of the EAP was to build confidence in the Canadian economy despite economic uncertainties. Finally, the government wanted to demonstrate to funding partners, opposition parties, and the public that promised programs and specific initiatives were on track. The government astutely converted a modest reporting requirement into a sustained government-wide communications strategy. The EAP soon had its own brand and logo, a central website for progress reporting ($2 million was spent on this alone), advertising on every media platform (over $136 million over 2009–10 alone), and 5,000 signs at construction sites across the country (Marland, 2016; Curry, 2014). In addition to the signage, there was a constant stream of public announcements on television, radio, and social media. The government submitted seven quarterly reports on the EAP to Parliament, which were reviewed by the Standing Committee on Government Operations and Estimates. In short, the government moved well beyond the simple task of reporting on projects and providing transparency, to a comprehensive effort to build confidence in the EAP and restore its own credibility.

The final report of the government—*The Stimulus Phase of Canada's Economic Action Plan*—was released on 29 March 2012, a 70-page annex to the Budget. Here, the government reported that the EAP had led to over $63 billion in overall stimulus spending, supporting 30,200 projects, and contributing an estimated 610,000 jobs since July 2009. Spending items included: a whopping 7,500 provincial, territorial, and municipal infrastructure projects; 500 college and university and college infrastructure projects; upgrading small craft harbours (258); community adjustment projects administered by regional agencies across the country (1,850); cultural infrastructure projects (147); national parks and national historic sites facilities (200+); modernizing federal laboratories (249); renovating and repairing federal buildings (1,800); improving accessibility of Crown-owned buildings for persons with disabilities (300); First Nations infrastructure projects (97); and creating 16,500 social housing and First Nations housing units. The report noted that the government had granted a seven-month extension for partners to complete over 2,270 projects (with them due on 31 October 2011), and framed the extension as a response to provincial, territorial, and municipal requests for another construction season. It also reviewed the other EAP initiatives, such as tax and employment insurance relief, extension of employment insurance and other benefits (e.g. Working Income Tax Benefit, National Child Benefit, Age Credit, and first-time homebuyers), tax relief and incentives for small businesses, several job training and retraining programs, and targeted assistance to particular communities and sectors. The report emphasized the timeliness, sound stewardship, and regular reporting of the government, and indicated that Canada had the strongest growth in employment amongst the G7 countries since July 2009.

Having declared victory, the government recast the 'old' EAP as the 'stimulus phase' in the 2012 Budget. It was a launching pad for the EAP 2012, which was designed to help the economy move into full recovery. The EAP branding and advertising continued well beyond the two-year time horizon originally envisioned in January 2009, helping the government position itself for the next election.

A Mistake Made Good? Assessing the Economic Action Plan

Many Canadians will readily recall the controversy over the prorogation of Parliament at the request of Prime Minister Harper in early December 2009 and the extensive advertising associated with the EAP from 2009 through to 2015, when Harper's Conservatives lost power. They may also recall that Canada did not suffer the economic and social carnage wrought by the subprime mortgage crisis in the United States and the subsequent turmoil in international financial markets. This benign trajectory was partly attributable to Canada's prudent regulation of its financial sector, but it was also due to the Harper government's astute EAP. Memory fades about the extent to which the second Harper minority government's future was in doubt at the time, as were its motivations and competence. Introducing and then delivering on the EAP was a crucial step in restoring credibility and public trust after the government's political miscalculation with the November 2008 statement. What follows uses McConnell (2010) to appraise the EAP as a policy success, first considering the process, program, and political dimensions—and stepping back to consider its temporal, design, and distributional dimensions, as suggested by Compton et al. (2019) and McConnell et al. (2020).

Process Assessment: Pivoting from Failure

The November 2008 Economic Statement was a failure, the product of political miscalculation and over-confidence after an election by a new minority government. It presumed a weakened opposition and was predicated on the notion that Canada had little to worry about when it came to the emerging global financial crisis. After this misfire, the prime minister took calculated risks and steps to remedy the political situation: he and his advisors took stock of the situation, made political calculations, swallowed their pride and sought a reprieve via a prorogation request to the Governor General, creating an opportunity to prepare a new economic statement and budget to match. In the process, Harper and various cabinet ministers did make misleading claims to the public, party members, and the Governor General about the supposed illegitimacy of an alternative coalition government, which misrepresented constitutional and governance practice in Canada and elsewhere (Leduc, 2009). They revealed the lines of argument that would be made were an election called or a Liberal-NDP coalition invited to form a new minority government. This tactic increased the perceived risks and costs of pursuing these options with a financial crisis at hand.

With its reprieve obtained, the Harper government then proceeded to consult widely, asserting that they were the most substantial consultations ever, even if these were not nearly as substantial as the budget and other consultations that had occurred in the late 1980s and early 1990s (Longo, 2017; Lindquist, 1994, 2015). Still, the government's consultative events were showcased prominently, and the high political stakes meant there was considerably more media and public interest in them. Given the prorogation agreement, the consultation period was time-limited, yet sufficiently inclusive and public to show that the government was listening. It helped build credibility for the budget. The government openly canvassed for ideas, but the ultimate test of how well the process worked would be determined by the public reception to the budget. It would indicate whether the government had listened and developed a credible response. Later, the government would rely on consultative repertoires developed in the early 1990s for working with provincial and territorial governments to identify projects for municipal governments while respecting jurisdictional responsibilities.

Process-wise the development of the EAP was a *resilient success* (McConnell, 2010). While many actors would continue to be in fundamental opposition to, or sceptical of, the Harper government's motivations, and would still see prorogation and the arguments advanced in support of it as offensive, most could not disagree with the pressing need for a timely budget and a consultative approach to preparing one. The BQ and NDP voted against the budget because they knew the Liberals were not in a position to bring the government down, and given the chance, would propose a similar program of action. More fundamentally, there was considerable public support for a government to focus on dealing with the economic crisis, muting opposition demands.

Program Assessment: Clear Criteria, Distributing Benefits, and Smoothing Approvals

There were clear criteria (targeted, timely, transparent) informing the EAP portfolio of policy instruments and programs, and, in the case of the Infrastructure

Stimulus Program, the selection of projects. The decision not to focus on more transformative programs—such as multi-year programs that would prepare the country for climate change and increase sustainability (Stoney and Krawchenko, 2012)—was pragmatic and political. It was pragmatic in seeking a short-term stimulus into the economy, and not increasing the cost of government over the longer term, reflecting its own principles. It was political because the government could not have felt comfortable making transformative investments, particularly with respect to climate change programs (which could be seen as indirectly embracing the Liberals' Green Shift strategy, which it had ridiculed during the election campaign) and because of its support for the energy and natural resource sectors. Nevertheless, it did create a modest green infrastructure fund as part of the stimulus package. The strict timelines for eliciting, approving, and completing projects (before 31 March 2011) were largely met, although, as noted, deadlines were eventually extended by seven months for some projects. The time horizon and pace of change was clear: two years, and certainly less than a government's typical term.

The 'targeting' of programs is interesting to probe from a distributional perspective (Compton and 't Hart, 2019; McConnell et al., 2020). Because there was great potential for 'pork-barrel' politics in the awarding of infrastructure funding for projects, there were predictions that the government would approve more projects in crucial swing ridings. Indeed, some journalists and opposition members suggested that the government did favour certain ridings over others (Chase et al., 2009). However, most careful analyses concluded there was surprisingly little such behaviour (Bennett, 2012; Dutil and Park, 2012). Moreover, provincial, territorial, municipal, First Nations, universities and colleges, community partners, as well as assorted federal regional public works agencies proposed projects for consideration by the federal government. There was little outcry about the overall mix of projects approved by the government (perhaps because observers were overwhelmed by the sheer volume of projects). Many more eyebrows were raised about the huge advertising budget and unrelenting exposure in all forms of media, and whether those activities transgressed guidelines on political advertising. Indeed, the government seemed less determined to win over marginal electoral ridings and more interested in demonstrating to the entire country that it could concertedly deliver projects for every imaginable sector, region, and community.

Different actors within the government found ways to accelerate approvals, transparency, and audit processes. First, the Treasury Board Secretariat worked with the Privy Council Office and departments and agencies to coordinate what hitherto had been sequential appropriations approval processes, enabling them to proceed in parallel, short-circuiting what would have been a longer pathway relying on Supplementary Estimates (Kennedy, 2009). While the Auditor General of Canada (2010) approvingly observed that the time required for central-agency approvals was reduced from six to two months, many projects benefited from streamlined environmental reviews or exemptions. Second, the auditor general shared 'pre-audit' criteria in early 2009 so that deputy ministers and heads of agencies, along with their executive teams and departmental audit committees, could build tracking and paperwork repertoires into their project-management systems, which later led to a clean audit (Auditor General of Canada, 2009, 2010). Third, it is not widely known that, through Infrastructure Canada, the government relied on consultative repertoires developed in the early 1990s to move funding to priority projects for municipal governments. Fourth, along with quarterly reporting, the government developed a gateway website platform for tracking infrastructure projects rolling out across the country. While acknowledging the government was delivering on what it had promised, an important criticism was that such reporting focused more on 'outputs' as opposed to touted 'outcomes' (Chase, 2009).

In short, the EAP and its infrastructure stimulus were programmatic successes in that the government accomplished what it set out to do, the benefits were distributed across the country to a variety of stakeholders, and there was little serious opposition from the other political parties. Even though the programs were not the only reason why Canada performed well, they were delivered on time and received international recognition (IMF 2010, 2011). The public servants responsible for designing and implementing the program also received an Innovation Award from the Association of Public Service Executives (APEX).

Political Assessment: The Art of the U-Turn

During the first stage of the crisis hubris almost led to the fall of the minority Harper government. With its back against the wall, the government was forced to focus on what was important. Having launched a high-stakes effort to suspend Parliament, the Conservative government needed to play its cards well, since it had put all of its reputational eggs in one policy basket. The government's approach was pragmatic, ideologically conditioned, and unabashedly political. The EAP's time-limited design allowed the government to claim it was adhering to conservative principles (i.e. not permanently growing the size of government), and it demonstrated that the government was capable of managing programs that could look out for all Canadians.

Indeed, the Harper government was single-minded in delivering infrastructure outputs within clear timelines, working with delivery partners to smooth the path for projects, dealing with blockages, and regularly reporting on projects via a centralized website platform. This, along with the prime minister having already appointed strong ministers in key portfolios (Finance, Treasury Board, Industry, Transportation), meant that the feet of officials were put to the fire. As one public-service executive observed, the EAP was the 'only priority' of the government. This, in turn, motivated senior officials in departments and central agencies to

472 CANADA'S RESPONSE TO THE GLOBAL FINANCIAL CRISIS

find innovative ways to move various EAP programs forward. All of this mirrored the United Kingdom's 'deliverology' initiative (Barber, 2008), well before a diluted version came to Ottawa years later (Lindquist, 2015).

The government's political astuteness was on display in its shrewd levering of the quarterly reporting demanded by the Liberal opposition in return for its support of the Budget. The quarterly reports became just one part of an integrated, continuous, and national EAP advertising campaign. While such advertising eventually wore thin, and the opposition parties and many commentators complained it was a political, as opposed to legitimate, public advertising of programs (Curry, 2014)—this strategy made use of what had long been a grey area. It focused on an initiative of national importance, involving many projects with provincial, territorial, municipal, and First Nations governments, as well as higher education institutions and communities across all regions. Moreover, we forget that for years, a succession of Canadian governments had emphasized advertising of the 'federal presence' across the country. Most importantly, this communications and branding strategy worked as a political strategy because the government was not only promising but also acting and delivering the promised programs.

Many citizens did not particularly care for Prime Minister Harper or his controlling instincts, but it became apparent to them that his government delivered on its promises to meet this challenge, and many probably believed that governments with other political stripes would not have done much differently. Quickly moving funding to all regions, sectors, and cities across the country proved to be an effective and good political strategy. Charges of pork-barrel politics did not stick. No scandals emerged remotely of the order associated with the HRDC grants and contributions or political advertising mishaps. None of the opposition parties seriously challenged the need for a stimulus program. Moreover, Canada was considered a relatively strong performer by international standards (Canada, 2012; Wanna et al., 2015). This put the government in a stronger position, despite it losing a vote of confidence in the House of Commons over its 2011 budget and subsequently being held in contempt of Parliament for refusing to share financial information with Parliament as matters of Cabinet confidence (House of Commons 2011).

On 26 March, Prime Minister Harper called an election for 2 May 2011, buttressed by themes outlined in the 22 March budget labelled *The Next Phase of Canada's Economic Action Plan* (Minister of Finance, 2011). The Conservative Party won a majority in the House of Commons, while support for the Liberal Party and BQ plummeted, with the NDP making surprising gains in Quebec and Ontario. The Conservative government had campaigned on its EAP record and secured enough voter support to win an additional 23 seats. Once elected, it continued to rely on the EAP brand, modifying its content for the post-recession context (Minister of Finance, 2012), which would carry it through until the October 2015 election.

Conclusion: Learning in a Crisis

This case shows that, despite the early inability of a government to recognize and address an emerging crisis, it could retreat and make politically shrewd decisions to buy time in the face of political and fiscal realities, and move on to design and implement a successful policy package. However, this case also shows that a *mea culpa* is not sufficient to produce good outcomes: a full and successful pivot requires good political strategy, delineation and adherence to critical policy and administrative design principles, and fusion of political and administrative leadership to engage a capable public service to get the job done. This is a case where political survival instinct triggered a steep learning curve and produced a good policy result.

It is important to locate this case against the range of other successful public policy interventions. This was not a fundamental structural shift in a Canadian policy domain, but rather, a sustained but time-limited response to a daunting challenge, which the country came through quite well. We need to acknowledge the solid foundation of a prudently regulated financial services sector, which meant the Harper government did not have to bail out failing financial institutions and could focus its attention and money squarely on making the fiscal stimulus work (cf. Wanna et al., 2015). That said, this was more than a conventional crisis-management situation: the government had to design and implement an effective stimulus package that would achieve its effects over a two- or three-year horizon, requiring a fusion of pragmatic and focused political leadership, supported by concerted and often creative administrative implementation.

This chapter has argued that the EAP stimulus package constituted a success according to McConnell's (2010) criteria, rating highly along the process, program, and political dimensions. The key ingredients of this success were that it was conceived and implemented as a time-limited intervention (Compton et al., 2019) and intended benefits were widely distributed and focused on the greater public good (McConnell et al., 2020). Such success may seem surprising given that the government did not see, nor initially respond well to the crisis and had styled itself as a party that was, in principle, against big government. Yet in this case, early failure propelled the leaders of the government to introduce policies they had never imagined supporting. Like other policy-makers around the world, they evolved from fiscal conservatives into overnight Keynesians, quickly pivoting to a comprehensive policy intervention. This rapid learning served the country well amidst an economic crisis and favourably positioned the governing party for the next federal election, despite some of its own flaws.

Looking back from the early 2020s, one would likely cast an even more critical eye on the almost exclusive reliance on so-called 'shovel-ready' infrastructure programs. There would be more insistence by governments and the public for more transformative programs in the context of climate change, reconciliation,

474 CANADA'S RESPONSE TO THE GLOBAL FINANCIAL CRISIS

and preparing for a post-Covid-19 mix of economic and social policies. Indeed, when grappling with the Covid-19 pandemic, the Trudeau government took a serious look at the EAP, contacting ministers, officials, and auditors familiar with that era (Curry, 2020). Its reaching back to the EAP experience showed recognition that there is much to learn there concerning design and implementation strategies, even if future governments might be more interested in supporting more transformative projects and less inclined to rely on brazen branding and advertising regimes.

References

Auditor General of Canada. 2009. *Letter to Secretary of the Treasury Board*. Ottawa: Government of Canada. 5 March.

Auditor General of Canada. 2010. "Canada's Economic Action Plan." In *2010 Fall Report of the Auditor General of Canada*. pp. 1–39 Ottawa: Public Works and Government Services Canada. https://www1.oag-bvg.gc.ca/internet/English/parl_oag_201010_01_e_34284.html

Auditor General of Canada. 2011. "Canada's Economic Action Plan." In *2011 Fall Report of the Auditor General of Canada*. p.1–32 Ottawa: Public Works and Government Services Canada. https://www1.oagbvg.gc.ca/internet/English/parl_oag_201111_01_e_35933.html#hd3a

Barber, M. 2008. *Instruction to Deliver: Fighting to Transform Britain's Public Services*, Revised Paperback Edition. York: Methuen.

Bennett, S. E. 2012. "Federal Infrastructure Program Benefits: Perceptions at the Community Level." In *How Ottawa Spends, 2012–2013: The Harper Majority, Budget Cuts, and the New Opposition*, edited by G. B. Doern, and C. Stone, pp. 190–206. Montreal: McGill-Queen's University Press.

Brodie, I. 2018. "Democratizing or Bureaucratizing the Constitution?" In *At the Centre of Government: The Prime Minister and the Limits on Political Power*, pp. 156–159. McGill-Queen's University Press.

Cameron. D. R. 2009. "Ultimately, the System Worked." In *Parliamentary Democracy in Crisis*, edited by P. H. Russell, and L. Sossin, pp. 189–194. Toronto: University of Toronto Press.

Canada. 2009. *Canada's Economic Action Plan: A Fourth Report to Canadians*. Ottawa: Public Works and Government Services Canada.

Canada. 2010. "News Release: PM Highlights the Success of Canada's Economic Action Plan." Government of Canada. 2 December. https://www.canada.ca/en/news/archive/2010/12/highlights-success-canada-economic-action-plan-578259.html

Canada, House of Commons, Standing Committee on Procedure and House Affairs. 2011. "Question of Privilege Relating to the Failure of Government to Fully Provide the Documents as Ordered by the House." In *Report of the Standing Committee on Procedure and House Affairs*.pp. 1–18 Ottawa: Public Works and Government Services Canada.

Canada, House of Commons, Standing Committee on Public Accounts. 2012. "Chapter 1, Canada's Economic Action Plan, of the Fall 2011 Report of the Auditor General of Canada." In *Report of the Standing Committee on Public Accounts*.

pp1–17 Ottawa: Public Works and Government Services Canada. https://www.ourcommons.ca/Content/Committee/411/PACP/Reports/RP5846025/411_PACP_Rpt10/411_PACP_Rpt10-e.pdf

Chase, S. 2009. "Ottawa's Stimulus Reporting Gets Poor Grade from Watchdog." *Globe and Mail*. 10 October. https://www.theglobeandmail.com/news/politics/ottawas-stimulus-reporting-gets-poor-grade-from-watchdog/article1204078/

Chase, S., E. Anderssen, and B. Curry. 2009. "Stimulus program favours Tory ridings." *Globe and Mail*. 21 October. https://www.theglobeandmail.com/news/politics/stimulus-program-favours-tory-ridings/article4295068/

Compton, M. E., J. Luetjens, and P. 't Hart. 2019. "Designing for Policy Success." *International Review of Public Policy* 1 (1–2): pp. 119–146.

Curry, B. 2011. "Harper Government Opens Wallet to Hype its Stimulus Package." *Globe and Mail*. 24 February. https://www.theglobeandmail.com/news/politics/harper-government-opens-wallet-to-hype-its-stimulus-package/article568169/

Curry, B. 2014. "Government Spends Millions on Ads for 'Economic Action Plan' That Ended Two Years Ago." *Globe and Mail*. 25 January. https://www.theglobeandmail.com/news/politics/federal-ad-spending-exceeds-projections/article16503725/

Curry, B. 2020. "Ottawa Seeks 'Shovel-Ready' Projects for Post Shutdown Stimulus Plan." *Globe and Mail*. 15 April. https://www.theglobeandmail.com/politics/article-mckenna-seeking-shovel-ready-projects-for-post-shutdown-stimulus/

Department of Finance. 2009. "Canada's Economic Action Plan." In *Budget Plan 2009*. Ottawa: Department of Finance Canada. https://www.budget.gc.ca/2009/plan/bpc3a-eng.html

Doern, G. B., A. M. Maslove, and M. J. Prince. 2013. *Canadian Budgeting in the Age of Crises: Shifting Budget Domains and Temporal Budgeting*. Montreal and Kingston: McGill-Queen's University Press.

Dutil, P. and B. Park. 2012. "How Ontario Was Won: The Harper Economic Action Plan." In *How Ottawa Spends, 2012–2013: The Harper Majority, Budget Cuts, and the New Opposition*, edited by G. B. Doern and C. Stoney, pp. 207–226. Montreal: McGill-Queen's University Press.

Fenna, A. and P. 't Hart. 2019. "The 53-Billion-Dollar Question: Was Australia's 2009–2010 Fiscal Stimulus a Good Thing?" In *Successful Public Policy: Lessons from Australia and New Zealand*, edited by J. Luetjens, M. Mintrom, and P. 't Hart, pp. 87–112. Acton: ANU Press.

Franks, C. E. S. 2009. "To Prorogue or Not to Prorogue: Did the Governor General Make the Right Decision?" In *Parliamentary Democracy in Crisis*, edited by P. H. Russell, and L. Sossin, pp. 33–46. Toronto: University of Toronto Press.

International Monetary Fund. 2010. *Canada: Staff Report for the 2010 Article IV Consultation—-Supplementary Information*. Washington: IMF. 10 December.

International Monetary Fund. 2011. *Canada: Staff Report for the 2010 Article IV Consultation—-Supplementary Information*. Washington: IMF. 23 November.

Gomery, J. H. 2006. *Restoring Accountability: Recommendations, Commission of Inquiry into the Sponsorship Program and Advertising Activities*. Ottawa: Public Works and Government Services Canada.

Good, D. A. 2003. *The Politics of Public Management: The HRDC Audit of Grants and Contributions*. Toronto: University of Toronto Press.

Good, D. A. 2014. *The Politics of Public Money*. 2nd edn. Toronto: University of Toronto Press.

Good, D. A., and E. A. Lindquist. 2015. "Canada's Reactive Budget Response to the Global Financial Crisis: From Robust Stimulus and Brinksmanship to Agility and Innovation." In *The Global Financial Crisis and its Budget Impacts on OECD Nations*, edited by J. Wanna, E. A. Lindquist, and J. de Vries, pp. 59–91. Cheltenham: Edward Elgar.

Ireland, D. and K. Webb. 2010. "The Canadian Escape from the Subprime Crisis? Comparing the US and Canadian Approaches." In *How Ottawa Spends, 2010–2011: Recession, Realignment, and the New Deficit Era*, edited by G. B. Doern, and C. Stoney, pp. 87–108. Montreal: McGill-Queen's University Press.

Kennedy, S. 2009. "Testimony to the Standing Committee on Government Operations and Estimates." Parliament of Canada. 12 March. https://www.ourcommons.ca/DocumentViewer/en/40-2/OGGO/meeting-10/evidence

Leduc, L. 2009. "Coalition Government: When It Happens, How It Works." In *Parliamentary Democracy in Crisis*, edited by P. H. Russell, and L. Sossin, pp. 123–135. Toronto: University of Toronto Press.

Lindquist, E. A. 1994. "Citizens, Experts and Budgets: Evaluating Ottawa's Emerging Budget Process." In *How Ottawa Spends 1994–95: Making Change*, edited by S. D. Phillips, pp. 91–128. Ottawa: Carleton University Press.

Lindquist, E., J. de Vries, and J. Wanna. 2015. "Meeting the Challenge of the Global Financial Crisis in OECD Nations: Fiscal Responses and Future Challenges." In *The Global Financial Crisis and its Budget Impacts on OECD Nations*, edited by J. Wanna, E. A. Lindquist, and J. de Vries, pp. 1–30. Cheltenham: Edward Elgar.

Longo, J. 2017. "The Evolution of Citizen and Stakeholder Engagement in Canada, from Spicer to #Hashtags." *Canadian Public Administration* 60 (4): pp. 517–537.

Macklem, T. 2010. "Fiscal Policy during and after the Crisis." Notes for presentation to CMFE Conference. 13–14 May. https://carleton.ca/economics/wp-content/uploads/2p-Macklem.pdf

Malloy, J. 2010. "The Drama of Parliament under Minority Government." In *How Ottawa Spends, 2010–2011: Recession, Realignment, and the New Deficit Era*, edited by G. B. Doern, and C. Stoney, pp. 31–47. Montreal: McGill-Queen's University Press.

Marland, A. 2016. "Short Case Study: The Economic Action Plan." In *Brand Command: Canadian Politics and Democracy in the Age of Message Control*, pp. 335–349. Vancouver: University of British Columbia Press.

McConnell, A. 2010. "Policy Success, Policy Failure and Grey Areas In-Between." *Journal of Public Policy* 30 (20): 345–362.

McConnell, A., L. Grealy, and T. Lea. 2020. "Policy Success for Whom? A Framework for Analysis." *Policy Sciences* 53 (4): pp. 589–608.

Minister of Finance. 2011. *The Next Phases of Canada's Economic Action Plan: A Low-Tax Plan for Jobs and Growth*. Ottawa: Public Works and Government Services Canada.

Minister of Finance. 2012. "Annex 2—The Stimulus Phase of Canada's Economic Action Plan: A Final Report to Canadians." In *Economic Action Plan: Jobs, Growth and Economic Prosperity*, pp. 285–356. Ottawa: Public Works and Government Services Canada.

Modhora, R. and D. Rowlands. 2014. *Crisis and Reform: Canada and the International Financial System*. Waterloo: Centre for International Governance Innovation in partnership with the Norman Paterson School of International Affairs.

CBC News. 2008. "Harper Shuffles Cabinet to Create 'Right Team for These Times."
Canadian Broadcasting Corporation. 30 October. https://www.cbc.ca/news/canada/
harper-shuffles-cabinet-to-create-right-team-for-these-times-1.706956

CBC News. 2010. "How the Economic Action Plan Works: Criteria for Qualifying
Projects." Canadian Broadcasting Corporation. 26 October. https://www.cbc.ca/
news/canada/how-the-economic-action-plan-works-1.923188

Pal, L. A. 2011. "Into the Wild: The Politics of Economic Stimulus." In *How Ottawa
Spends, 2011–2012: Trimming Fat or Slicing Pork?* edited by C. Stoney, and G. B.
Doern, pp. 39–59. Montreal: McGill-Queen's University Press .

Posner, P. L., and D. M. Fantone. 2015. "The United States' Response to the Global
Financial Crisis: From Robust Stimulus to Fiscal Gridlock." In *The Global Financial
Crisis and its Budget Impacts on OECD Nations,* edited by J. Wanna, E. A. Lindquist,
and J. de Vries, pp. 31–58. Cheltenham: Edward Elgar.

Russell, P. H., and L. Sossin (eds). 2009. *Parliamentary Democracy in Crisis.* Toronto:
University of Toronto Press.

Smith, J. 2009. "Parliamentary Democracy versus Faux Populist Democracy." In *Parliamentary Democracy in Crisis,* edited by P. H. Russell, and L. Sossin, pp. 175–188.
Toronto: University of Toronto Press.

Stoney, C. and G. B. Doern. 2011. "Harper Budgeting in a New Majority Government:
Trimming Fat or Slicing Pork?" In *How Ottawa Spends, 2011–2012: Trimming Fat
or Slicing Pork?* edited by C. Stoney, and G. B. Doern, pp. 3–37. Montreal: McGill-
Queen's University Press.

Stoney, C. and Krawchenko, T. 2012, Transparency and accountability in infrastructure
stimulus spending. *Canadian Public Administration* 55: 481-503.

't Hart, P. and J. Wanna. 2011. *The Treasury and the Financial Crisis.* Canberra:
Australian National University. https://www.anzsog.edu.au/preview-documents/
case-study-level-1/682-treasury-and-the-global-financial-crisis-the-b-2010-119-2/
file?aid=2682&return=aHR0cHM6Ly93d3cuYW56c29nLmVkdS5hdS9yZXNvdXJ
jZS1saWJyYXJ5L2Nhc2UtdbGlicmFyeS90cmVhc3VyeS1hbmQtdGhlLWdsb2JhbC1
maW5hbmNpYWwtY3Jpc2lzLXRoZS1iLTIwMTAtMTE5LTlv

Valpy, M. 2009. "The 'Crisis': A Narrative." In *Parliamentary Democracy in Crisis,* edited
by P. H. Russell, and L. Sossin, pp. 3–18. Toronto: University of Toronto Press.

Wanna, J., E. A. Lindquist, and J. de Vries (eds). 2015. *The Global Financial Crisis
and its Budget Impacts on OECD Nations: Fiscal Responses and Future Challenges.*
Cheltenham: Edward Elgar.

Weinrib, L. E. 2009. "Prime Minister Harper's Parliamentary 'Time Out': A Constitutional Revolution in the Making?" In *Parliamentary Democracy in Crisis,* edited by
P. H. Russell, and L. Sossin, pp. 63–75. Toronto: University of Toronto Press.

24

Conclusion

Public Policy Success: Lessons from the Canadian Experience

Grace Skogstad, Geneviève Tellier, Paul 't Hart, Michael Howlett, and Evert A. Lindquist

This volume, like its predecessors dealing with New Zealand and Australia (Luetjens et al., 2019) and more globally (Compton and 't Hart, 2019), has aimed to correct a perceived bias of the public policy literature to focus on policy failures to the neglect of policy success. Following in the wake of McConnell's (2010) pioneering multi-dimensional conceptualization of policy success, each of these volumes has addressed the question of the elements of policy success using a methodology of detailed case studies that track policy histories and assess policy processes and outcomes over time. This volume's 22 case studies, comprising a wide span of carefully pre-selected instances of successful policies across Canada, thereby shed light not only on how best to conceptualize policy success, but also on the contextually specific conditions that contribute to policy success. Each chapter in this collection has added to this body of knowledge by describing the historical context and pathways to programmatic, process, political, and enduring success in a particular policy or public management domain. In this concluding chapter, our objective is to collate their findings to generate broader lessons and themes for conceptualizing and explaining policy success.

To accomplish these knowledge-building goals, we begin with a summary of the success ratings of the case studies. This scorecard, supplemented by authors' elaborations of any caveats to their ratings, allows us to demonstrate the considerable extent to which our authors have found useful the multidimensional PPPE (programmatic, process, political, endurance) assessment framework that has been presented in the introductory chapter of this volume in ascertaining the nature and degree of policy success in discrete cases of public policy in Canada. Second, drawing on the findings of the individual case studies, we identify the factors across policy domains—some common, some particular, some contingent—that contribute to the different dimensions of policy success. Third, and relatedly, we

---

Grace Skogstad et al., *Conclusion*. In: *Policy Success in Canada.*
Edited by Evert A. Lindquist et al., Oxford University Press. © Grace Skogstad et al., (2022).
DOI: 10.1093/oso/9780192897046.003.0024

extract from our case studies the complex role of macro-institutions—federalism, executive-dominated parliamentary government, and the judiciary in the case of Canada—in accounting for programmatic, process, political, and enduring policy success. Finally, we offer suggestions on lines of future research to strengthen our understanding of policy success.

Applying the PPPE Framework to Canadian Cases

The authors of the 22 Canadian case studies provide further, confirmatory, evidence of the usefulness of the PPPE conceptualization and indicators of policy success advanced by McConnell (2010), Compton and 't Hart (2019), and Luetjens et al. (2019). As described in the Introduction to this collection, their framework identifies clear criteria for judging policy success even while it recognizes that success is a matter of degree and rarely complete. Accordingly, it places policy success on a continuum, with intermediate categories from success to failure. It also recognizes that a policy's placement on the continuum can vary over time, as can judgements of the success of a policy by different stakeholders. Moreover, success on one dimension may entail trade-offs on another dimension: a successful program traded off for unsuccessful politics, successful politics traded off for an unsuccessful program, or a successful process traded off for unsuccessful programs.

A summary of authors' assessments of their individual case studies is presented in Table 24.1. By way of reminder in reviewing their assessments, programmatic success reflects the extent to which outcomes are consistent with the objectives of government and stakeholders. Process success refers to the extent to which government policy goals and favoured instruments are preserved throughout the policy process, the policy process is consistent with norms of legitimacy, the policy is sustained by a durable coalition of supporting actors, and the policy process encourages innovation. Political success represents the extent to which the policy's political benefits outweigh its political costs, maintain the broad values of government, and marginalize critics (McConnell, 2010, 352–356). The fourth criterion, endurance, is the sustainability of programmatic, process, and political benefits of a policy over time.

As Table 24.1 shows, authors generally were able to use McConnell's (2010) success–failure continuum to provide a more granular assessment of their cases. In most instances, and not surprisingly given the deliberate case selection's focus on policy success, numerous cases were rated highly across all four criteria of programmatic, process, political, and enduring success. Yet intermediate categories on the spectrum proved helpful for assessing some of the cases when contributors sought to make more qualified assessments. Even while judging a policy as a success, authors also acknowledge that some stakeholders, depending on their own policy goals, ability to shape policy developments, and/or accrue political benefits

480 CONCLUSION: LESSONS FROM THE CANADIAN EXPERIENCE

Table 24.1 Summary of Case Assessments on the Success Spectrum

Chapter	Topic	Programmatic Assessment	Process Assessment	Political Assessment	Endurance Assessment
2	Medicare	Success	Success	Success	Success
3	Tobacco use regulation	Success	Success	Success	Success
4	Safe injection of drugs	Success	Success	Success	Success
5	Elementary to secondary education	Success	Success	Success	Success
6	Quebec universal childcare	Success	Success	Success	Success
7	Early years policies	Success	Success	Success	Success
8	University research policy	Success	Success	Success	Success
9	Immigration	Success	Success	Success	Success
10	Multiculturalism	Success	Resilient to conflicted success	Resilient to conflicted success	Success
11	Pensions (OAS & GIC)	Success	Success	Success	Resilient success
12	Equalization	Success	Conflicted success	Conflicted success	Success
13	Bank regulation	Success	Success	Success	Success
14	Dairy and Poultry supply management	Success	Precarious to resilient success	Success	Resilient success
15	Canola development	Resilient success	Success	Success	Success
16	Developing Canada's wine industry	Success	Success	Success	Contested success
17	Managing national parks	Success	Success	Success	Success
18	Great Lakes Water Quality Agreement	Mixed success	Moderate success	Success	Success
19	Ontario coal phase-out	Resilient success	Conflicted success	Success	Resilient success

Continued

Table 24.1 *Continued*

Chapter	Topic	Programmatic Assessment	Process Assessment	Political Assessment	Endurance Assessment
20	First Nations and the courts	Conflicted-resilient	Success	Conflicted-resilient	Conflicted/ Precarious Success
21	Federal 1995–1996 Program Review	Success	Success	Success	Mixed
22	Creation of Canadian Airport Authorities	Success	Success	Success	Success
23	2009 Economic Action Plan	Success	Resilient Success	Success	Not applicable (policy was a one-off crisis response)

from the policy, would render harsher judgements of the policy (cf. McConnell et al., 2020).

Medicare is widely viewed by Canadians as a policy success, yet Marchildon (Chapter 2) records some deterioration in its ability to achieve its programmatic goal of universal access to essential health care services. He further acknowledges that while public support for Medicare remains high, its political success is marred by intergovernmental conflict over federal health transfers to provinces and court challenges on the part of doctors seeking to run for-profit clinics inside Medicare. Callard (Chapter 3) judges Canada's regulation of tobacco use a success in reducing smoking but also observes that other countries have higher levels of tobacco control than Canada. Wallner (Chapter 5) rates Canada's public education system from elementary to secondary school as highly successful—except for Indigenous children. Burlone (Chapter 6) describes the province of Quebec's provision of affordable and high quality childcare spaces as a 'huge success' but still reports that available spaces fall short of demand for them. Davidson and White (Chapter 7) rate early years policies of the federal government and some provinces an overall success, even while noting that Canada lags behind other OECD countries when it comes to investments in children. Banting (Chapter 10) describes multiculturalism as a strong success as judged against its explicit goals but also notes its success has not ended racial economic inequality and discrimination in the Canadian labour market. Lecours, Béland, and Tombe (Chapter 12) describe equalization, by virtue of achieving its goals of reducing provincial inequality and preserving provincial autonomy, as a programmatic success. Still, they note equalization is also subject to criticisms in the name of both fairness and efficiency. This

482   CONCLUSION: LESSONS FROM THE CANADIAN EXPERIENCE

criticism is one that Skogstad (Chapter 14) also observes with respect to supply management plans in the Canadian dairy and poultry sectors. Wilder (Chapter 15) describes Canada's development of the popular and healthy oilseed, canola, to be an example of successful innovation, even while environmental groups and organic farmers see themselves as losers of the policy. Johns (Chapter 18) judges the Great Lakes Water Quality Agreement between Canada and the United States to be a 'mixed' success of program successes and failures, and a 'moderate' success of a well-designed process but also one subject to some 'notable challenges'. 'Mixed success' is also the verdict of Satsan, McNeil, and Abele when it comes to the efforts of Canada's first nations to transform public policy through the courts (Chapter 20). Although they describe Indigenous peoples as 'remarkably successful' in achieving some of their legal and political goals through court action, they also believe that 'much has yet to be accomplished' when it comes to Indigenous nations being recognized as a third order of government and Indigenous law being accepted as part of Canada's legal architecture. To cite one final example, Tellier (Chapter 21) rates the Canadian Government's 1995–1996 Program Review an 'undeniable' programmatic success, but also acknowledges that those who bore the social cost of the federal government eliminating its deficit would disagree. In short, judgements of success are rarely unanimous or without caveats.

As mentioned earlier, the continuum of intermediate categories from full success to complete failure also proved helpful, as has the proposition that the success of a policy can vary over time. Banting describes public policies with respect to multiculturalism (Chapter 10) as transitioning over time from a resilient success (that is, as subject to but also overcoming non-life threatening challenges via policy adjustments) to a conflicted success (subject to substantial controversy) as the policy process became undermined by politicization and ideological conflicts. Lecours, Béland, and Tombe (Chapter 12) document the same politicization occurring with equalization; a policy that was uncontroversial at its origins is now a highly charged area of intergovernmental dispute, beset by conflict on both process and political grounds. Winfield and Saherwala (Chapter 19) rate Ontario's phase out of coal in electricity generating facilities by 2014 a conflicted success on process grounds, and, further, describe the McGuinty (2003–2013) and Wynne (2013–2018) governments' overall handling of electricity policy as a political failure. Skogstad (Chapter 14) tracks the transition of supply management plans in the dairy and poultry sectors from their precarious early days, when their very existence hung in the balance, to their current resilient success. And Johns observes that over its five-decade history, the 1972 Great Lakes Water Quality Agreement has undergone 'simultaneous and significant periods of policy failure'.

The Canadian case studies also lend some support to the proposition in the policy success literature that success on one policy dimension can come at the expense of success on another dimension. Although he judges Canada's immigration policy a success across the board, Triadafilopoulos (Chapter 9) argues that in response to public pressure the Canadian government has made it very difficult for asylum seekers to enter Canada, trading off process success for normative standards of justice for refugees. Supply management, notes Skogstad (Chapter 14), is seen by its critics as a case of 'good politics but bad policy', with the political benefits politicians accrue from supporting the policy undermining their incentives to reform it. Winfield and Saherwala (Chapter 19) also see clear trade-offs between programmatic, process, and political success. They argue that the coal phase-out—a programmatic success in improving the quality of air in Ontario by reducing emissions of GHGs, smog and acid rain precursors, and heavy metals, like mercury—would not have occurred without political direction from the Wynne government. Yet, this politicization of the policy process 'eroded transparent, evidence-based decision-making regarding major infrastructure projects'. Notwithstanding these examples of trade-offs across policy dimensions, and as we discuss further later, our case studies also reveal a different pattern whereby success on one policy dimension can have positive feedback effects for success on another policy dimension.

Even while Canadian case studies thus collectively affirm the merits of Chapter 1's PPPE framework for evaluating policy success, individually they also suggest some ways to further enhance its utility. In its focus on the success of what governments do, the framework overlooks developments that, by delimiting the parameters within which governments operate, also establish new criteria for policy success. Indigenous peoples' use of the courts to secure recognition of their traditional rights and self-government is a case in point (Chapter 20). Satsan, McNeil, and Abele observe that through a succession of court cases, Indigenous peoples have achieved some of their legal and political goals, forced governments to revise their policies, and thereby 'significantly shaped' the development of future policies pertaining to Indigenous peoples. In other words, what counts as success in terms of governments' relations with Indigenous peoples on both programmatic and process grounds has itself been re-defined. In other cases, a government-centric approach can ignore public policies co-produced by governments and private firms, examples of which are Wilder's case study of the Canadian development of canola (Chapter 15) and Migone's of the development of the Canadian wine industry (Chapter 16). As Wilder observes, an important measure of the programmatic success of such public–private partnerships must be the extent to which the beneficiary (private firm) bears the risk so that the public is spared excessive costs.

Other case studies also point to the efficiency of public policies—that is, the extent to which policy objectives are met at a reasonable cost—as a criterion of programmatic success but not one explicitly identified in the PPPE framework.[1]

---

[1] We are grateful to an external reviewer for suggesting this criterion of policy success.

484 CONCLUSION: LESSONS FROM THE CANADIAN EXPERIENCE

Healthcare and pensions are examples of cost-efficient policies. Canada's single-payer healthcare system delivers high health outcomes at lower administrative costs (Chapter 2), while Canada's pension policy mix of Old Age Security and a Guaranteed Income Supplement is effective at fighting poverty among older people at public costs significantly below the OECD average (Chapter 11). The transfer of responsibility for governing and managing Canada's airports to private airport authorities is another example of policy efficiency (Chapter 22). The federal government achieved its intended objective of off-loading its responsibility for financing airport infrastructure, even while the airport authorities generated considerable revenue for the government prior to the Covid-19 pandemic.

Finally, several case studies reference the diffusion of a policy to other provinces or to the national level as a criterion to judge policy success. Examples include Saskatchewan's universal healthcare insurance being taken up by the federal government to become Canada-wide Medicare (Chapter 2), other Canadian cities' adoption of Vancouver's innovative supervised safe injection of drugs site (Chapter 4), the interprovincial spread of and convergence on quality public education programs and practices (Chapter 5), and other provinces' emulation of Ontario's full-day kindergarten (Chapter 7). They also include the diffusion of provincial agricultural marketing boards and their coordination in national supply management plans (Chapter 14) and Ontario's phase-out of conventional coal-fired electricity to the national level (Chapter 19). However, Quebec's universal and low-cost childcare centres (Chapter 6) have failed to be adopted by other provinces. Its counter-example suggests limits to treating diffusion as a measure of success in federal systems. An important federal principle is respect for the distinct preferences and values of citizens within constituent units. That divergent societal preferences can result in policies unique to one province should not therefore necessarily be a minus on that policy's success scorecard.

Policy Success Factors in the Canadian Context

The PPPE framework is intended to be a cross-jurisdictional template for *assessing* policy success by identifying outcomes associated with success/failure. In order to advance the policy success literature further, we now ask whether there are any commonalities across the cases in terms of structures, actors, styles, and processes of policy-making that are associated with these outcomes. Here, our discussion is necessarily specific to the Canadian policy-making context: one constituted by executive-dominated parliamentary government, a professional public service, a federal system in which governments at both federal and provincial orders are legally powerful, and a liberal market economy. Are there some broad conclusions that can be drawn about the overall effects of this policy-making context on policy success in general? For example, are there some types of political actors and policy processes that are generally associated with successful outcomes? If factors like careful policy design, administrative capacity, and fiscal resources are important to programmatic and overall policy success, how does the Canadian political-institutional context affect their supply? At the same time, variation in policy success across policy domains (see Table 24.1) suggests the importance of sectoral-level contextual factors. And hence, another important question is what are the sectoral-level dynamics associated with different dimensions of policy success, and particularly with the durability of public policies, over time? We begin by providing an overview of factors associated with policy success across our cases before turning to sectoral-level dynamics.

Taken as a whole, the Canadian experience highlights, first, the importance of *leadership* in many Canadian policy successes. The concentration of political authority in the political executive (the prime minister/premier and Cabinet) in Canada's parliamentary system means that political leadership at the highest levels of government is critical for policy success. Provincial leadership on universal healthcare insurance from Saskatchewan Premier Tommy Douglas produced the template for Canadian Medicare (Chapter 2). The success of the federal university research program (Chapter 8) and the 1995–1996 Program Review exercise (Chapter 21) owed a great deal to the strong leadership and commitment of Prime Minister Jean Chrétien. Having narrowly escaped a political crisis following his initial failed reaction to the 2008 Global Financial Crisis, Prime Minister Stephen Harper was subsequently motivated to act quickly to design and implement a politically saleable economic action plan (Chapter 23). At the cost of his own political career, Vancouver Mayor Phillip Owen's leadership proved pivotal to legitimizing the harm reduction strategy advanced by the coalition supporting safe injection sites for drug users in the city (Chapter 4).

Leadership need not come from the very top of government; ideologically committed cabinet ministers can provide the crucial political support for policy innovations, as illustrated by the creation of Canadian supply management in the agriculture sector (Chapter 14). Nor is leadership necessarily associated with a single individual. Liberal premiers Dalton McGuinty and Kathleen Wynne provided the requisite political leadership to phase out coal-fired electricity production in Ontario (Chapter 19). Political leadership can also be observed across party lines. Although Canada's multiculturalism policy was initiated by Prime Minister Pierre Elliott Trudeau in the 1970s, it was embedded in legislation by Prime Minister Mulroney in 1988 (Chapter 10).

Leadership outside government in the form of 'policy entrepreneurs' who seize opportunities to put issues on the government's agenda (Kingdon, 1984) and stay the course over time has also been an ingredient in policy success. A good illustration has been the regulation of tobacco products where civil society organizations

486 CONCLUSION: LESSONS FROM THE CANADIAN EXPERIENCE

repeatedly faced severe opposition from the industry (Chapter 3). In other instances, activists had to convince governments and the population about the merits of their proposal. For instance, the idea of setting up safe injection sites for drug users seemed counterintuitive at first. Yet by gradually building a coalition for their initiative, proponents of safe-site injection centres were able to convince governments to adopt this policy (Chapter 4).

Second, resources of *independent legal authority* and *fiscal capacity* are associated with policy success at both the federal and provincial levels. Several areas of programmatic, process and political success in this volume occurred where the federal government had the legal authority to exercise its regulatory and the fiscal powers to act independently of the provinces. They are tobacco and banking regulation (Chapters 3 and 13, respectively); university research funding (Chapter 8); multiculturalism (Chapter 10); seniors' pensions (Chapter 11); equalization (Chapter 12); national parks (Chapter 17); Great Lakes water quality (Chapter 18); the government of Canada's 1995–1996 Program Review (Chapter 21) and response to the 2008–09 great financial crisis (Chapter 23); and the devolution of responsibility for managing airports (Chapter 22).

At the provincial level, the programmatic, process, and political success of policies is also facilitated by provinces having exclusive legal authority over a problem or policy. Examples are supervised injection sites in Vancouver, British Columbia (Chapter 4) and the phase-out of coal-fired electricity in Ontario (Chapter 19). At other times, provinces can only redress problems by accessing federal fiscal resources. Illustrative cases in this volume of the latter are provinces' early years (pre-school) and childcare policies, as well as their elementary and secondary education policies (Chapters 5–7). In have-not provinces, the federal equalization program (Chapter 12) has been crucial to the fiscal capacity of provinces to carry out these social programs.

The nation-wide diffusion of provincial social and economic/regulatory policies—such that they can be described as national policy successes—has usually required a role for the Government of Canada. The federal role is normally fiscal, as in the support of social policies, like Medicare. However, the intergovernmental negotiations required to finance them are usually not only opaque (Béland et al., 2017) but also subject to the shifting fiscal fortunes and priorities of governments at the two federal orders (Bakvis and Skogstad, 2020). Accordingly, the policy success of these shared-cost programs, from a durability perspective, can be subject to the priorities of an incumbent federal government. The case study examples cited earlier of policies diffusing cross-provincially are consistent with findings of other studies (Poel, 1976; Lutz, 1989; Boyd and Olive, 2021).

Public resources—in the form of the fiscal and regulatory support from both federal and provincial governments—are also usually needed for successful innovation and economic development policies. The examples here are the development of one of Canada's top agricultural products, canola (Chapter 15), and the domestic wine industry (Chapter 16).

Third, skilful *administrative professionalism* and *government capacity* are also important, especially with respect to programme success and successful implementation (Wu et al., 2015). In some instances, success comes after several trials and errors. For example, the 1995–1996 Program Review sought to avoid replicating the mistakes of several previous administrative reforms (Chapter 21). In the same vein, the government's response to the 2008–09 Global Financial Crisis benefited from concerted consultations with diverse stakeholders, a mechanism previously used by the Department of Finance (Chapter 23). Expertise within a single or several departments has also been a key element of success for the establishment of a radically new governance model. Johns identifies bureaucratic leadership, policy instruments informed by scientific evidence, and sustained resources as important ingredients in the successful implementation of the Canada-United States Great Lakes Water Quality Agreement (Chapter 18), while Langlois credits the success of the creation of Canadian airport authorities to manage Canadian airports to a small team of government officials working in concert with key internal and external stakeholders (Chapter 22).

Fourth, although not sufficient to guarantee success, *popular support* has often been critical in forcing an issue onto the agenda, giving rise to a public policy to address it and maintaining the policy in the face of pockets of determined opponents. Examples include the implementation of the Canadian Medicare program, which was forcefully opposed by the medical profession and the insurance industry (Chapter 2), and the Canadian Pension Plan, which most provinces initially viewed as too expensive (Chapter 11). However, in both cases the opposition dissipated once it became clear that most Canadians supported the initiatives. Sometimes it takes a considerable amount of time and energy to convince the population of the social desirability of a policy: examples here include regulating the tobacco industry (Chapter 3) and implementing supervised injection sites (Chapter 4). However, governments usually initiate policies that already enjoy considerable popular support, such as early childhood policies (Chapters 6 and 7), immigration (Chapter 9), national parks (Chapter 17), and banking regulation (Chapter 13).

Fifth, *contingencies and chance* have played a role in the success of public policies. Triadafilopoulos attributes some of the success of Canadian immigration policy to 'place luck': Canada's isolated geography limits flows of asylum seekers and other unwanted immigrants to Canada (Chapter 9). Besides strong leadership and administrative capacity, Tellier attributes 'a bit of luck', in the form of favourable political and economic conditions, to the success of the Liberal Party's implementation of unpopular program cuts in its 1995–1996 Program Review.

Sixth, notwithstanding some common patterns of success, there are also discernible *sectoral-level dynamics* associated with different dimensions of policy

488 CONCLUSION: LESSONS FROM THE CANADIAN EXPERIENCE

success. One dynamic is the political actors who dominate the policy process. Elite political and bureaucratic actors have dominated, and often monopolized, successful innovations in Canadian public management. Examples are university research funding (Chapter 8), equalization payments (Chapter 12), the 1994–1996 Program Review (Chapter 21), the devolution of responsibility for managing airports (Chapter 22), and the Economic Action Plan in response to the 2007–09 Global Financial Crisis (Chapter 23). In all these cases, although parliament's approval was eventually required to turn elite actors' decisions into law, the policy process was relatively closed to civil-society actors. At the same time, the relative lack of contestation around these policies demonstrates, as Tupper says of university research, that 'good processes need not engage large groups of people, interest groups or even parliamentarians to be successful' (Chapter 8).

By contrast, a plurality of non-state actors—interest groups and civil-society actors—has been involved in the agenda-setting, policy formulation and/or policy implementation phases of policy-making in many other policy domains. Examples are tobacco and banking regulation (Chapters 3 and 13, respectively), multiculturalism (Chapter 10), seniors' pensions (Chapter 11), supervised injection sites in the city of Vancouver (Chapter 4), elementary through secondary education (Chapter 5), the phase-out of coal-fired electricity in Ontario (Chapter 19), and early years (pre-school) and childcare policies (Chapters 6 and 7). In some cases, such as with respect to multiculturalism and the Ontario coal phase-out, opening the policy process to a broader array of political actors has been associated with greater politicization and contestation. In other cases, such as the deregulation of banking, the approval of transgenic canola (Chapter 15), and the management of Canada's national parks (Chapter 17), a more open and pluralist policy process has enhanced the legitimacy and effectiveness of a policy.

Our case studies also provide insights regarding the conditions for the durability or maintenance of a policy's performance over time. In addition to the capacity for political actors to adjust policy processes (as earlier) or policy instruments (as with supply management boards, Chapter 14) as altered circumstances require, other self-reinforcing material and interpretive feedback effects are also evident (Pierson, 1993, 2000). As demonstrated by the examples of pensions (Chapter 11), equalization (Chapter 12), and agricultural supply management (Chapter 14), policies endure because their beneficiaries have strong incentives to sustain them. Policies also persist over time by self-generating a narrative of achievement and/or by becoming part of the identity of Canadians. National parks (Chapter 17) and the Great Lakes Water Quality Agreement (Chapter 18) are examples of the former, while Medicare (Chapter 2) and, to a lesser extent, multiculturalism (Chapter 10) are examples of the latter.

As illustrated by the instances of conflicted success in this volume, policy endurance should not be equated with the absence of negative or self-undermining feedback effects (Jacobs and Weaver, 2015). The constitutional entrenchment that fortifies the principle of equalization has not eliminated intergovernmental con-testation over the government of Canada's determination of the formula used to distribute equalization payments. Nor has the joint decision trap (Scharpf 1997), which requires agreement across multiple federal and provincial governments for changes to supply management in the Canadian dairy and poultry industries (Chapter 14). Institutional and constitutional bulwarks can thus make policies resilient even when they fall short on some programmatic or process grounds.

Looking Ahead: Learning through Comparative Research

Policy dynamics—understood as motors of innovation, continuity, and change—are complex phenomena and the role played in these dynamics by policy-makers and publics learning from previous policy experience has rightly drawn much attention in attempts to explain not only how policy change occurs but also en-dures (Dunlop and Radaelli, 2018b; Capano, 2012). This endeavour extends to the derivation of different types, triggers, and modes of learning including 'positive', 'negative', and 'non-learning' among others (Dunlop and Radaelli, 2018a).

In exploring these types of policy learning, it is necessary to build upon a clear understanding and analysis of policy success and failure. In particular, un-derstanding the processes through which policies evolve and endure over time requires learning from policy successes—a reorientation away from focusing only or mostly on policy failure and non-learning or 'negative' learning.

In this way, the book aims to improve the understanding of policy learning and especially the possibility of 'positive' learning and lesson-drawing (Rose, 1993). Such an effort, we argue, is needed not only to improve policy scholarship but also to enhance policy practice in many countries, including Canada. The impor-tance of policy learning is arguably greatest during crises, such as the Covid-19 pandemic which began in 2020. If the experience of the Canadian Harper govern-ment's response to the 2008–9 Global Financial Crisis (Chapter 23) is any guide, governments need to learn quickly, and the expertise of seasoned public servants who have dealt with political crises in the past is a key ingredient in their ability to do so. In addition, the Covid-19 crisis has also demonstrated that programmatic success depends upon governments' political leadership and their ability to draw on the expertise of medical professional experts.

The suite of Canadian cases presented in this collection also suggests further lines of inquiry for learning about policy success processes and patterns. One avenue of research is the cross-national generalizability of the Canadian pattern of province-led innovation, as well as the requisite of joint federal and provincial action for policy innovation and success. Whether these patterns are distinct to Canada, or found in other federal countries such as Australia, is an example of the kind of future inquiry the book may help engender. Comparative research can

490 CONCLUSION: LESSONS FROM THE CANADIAN EXPERIENCE

also profit from examining the extent to which specific sectoral dynamics of policy successes—in particular, their distinctive policy processes—are generalizable to other countries. That is, are the elite-dominated and comparatively closed policy processes of public management successes associated with policy success in other jurisdictions and countries? Do the more open, pluralist, and contested processes of policy successes in social policy fields prevail in the same social policy domains elsewhere? Finally, as demonstrated by the Canadian cases, future research can also profit from broadening analyses beyond cases of unqualified policy success to those of precarious and/or conflicted success on one or more of programmatic, process, or political grounds.

References

Bakvis, Herman and Grace Skogstad (eds). 2020. *Canadian Federalism: Performance, Effectiveness and Legitimacy*. Toronto: University of Toronto Press.

Béland, Daniel, André Lecours, Gregory P. Marchildon, Haizhen Mou, and M. Rose Olfert. 2017. *Fiscal Federalism and Equalization Policy in Canada: Political and Economic Dimensions*. Toronto: University of Toronto Press.

Boyd, Brendan and Andrea Olive. 2021. *Provincial Policy Laboratories: Policy Diffusion and Transfer in Canada's Federal System*. Toronto: University of Toronto Press.

Capano, G. 2012. "Policy Dynamics and Change: The Never-Ending Puzzle". In *Routledge Handbook of Public Policy*, edited by E. Araral, S. Fritzen, M. Howlett, M. Ramesh, and X. Wu, pp. 451–472. New York: Routledge.

Compton, M. and 't Hart, P. (eds). 2019. *Great Policy Successes*. Oxford: Oxford University Press.

Dunlop, C. A. and C. M. Radaelli. 2018a. "The Lessons of Policy Learning: Types, Triggers, Hindrances and Pathologies." *Policy and Politics* 46 (2): 255–272.

Dunlop, C. A., and C. M. Radaelli (eds). 2018b. *Learning in Public Policy: Analysis, Modes and Outcomes*. London: Palgrave Macmillan.

Jacobs, A. M. and R. K. Weaver. 2015. "When Policies Undo Themselves: Self-Undermining Feedback as a Source of Policy Change." *Governance* 28 (4): 441–457. https://doi.org/10.1111/gove.12101

Kingdon, J. W. 1984. *Agendas, Alternatives, and Public Policies*. Boston: Little, Brown.

Luetjens, J., M. Mintrom, and P. 't Hart (eds). 2019. *Successful Public Policy: Lessons from Australia and New Zealand*.Canberra, Australia: ANU Press and Australian and New Zealand School of Government (ANZSOG).

Lutz, J. M. 1989. "Emulation and Policy Adoptions in the Canadian Provinces." *Canadian Journal of Political Science* 22 (2): 147–154.

McConnell, A. 2010. "Policy Success, Policy Failure and Grey Areas In-Between." *Journal of Public Policy* 30 (20): 345–362.

McConnell, A. 2017. "Policy Success and Failure." In *Oxford Research Encyclopedia of Politics*, edited by William R. Thompson, Oxford: Oxford University Press.

McConnell, A., L. Grealy, and T. Lea. 2020. "Policy Success for Whom? A Framework for Analysis." *Policy Sciences* 53 (4): 589–608.

Pierson, P. 1993. "When Effect Becomes Cause: Policy Feedback and Political Change." *World Politics* 45 (4): 595–628. https://doi.org/10.2307/2950710

Pierson, P. 2000. "Increasing Returns, Path Dependence, and the Study of Politics," *American Political Science Review* 94 (2): 251–267.

Poel, D. H. 1976. "The Diffusion of Legislation among the Canadian Provinces: A Statistical Analysis." *Canadian Journal of Political Science* 9 (4): 605–626.

Rose, R. 1993. *Lesson-Drawing in Public Policy: A Guide to Learning across Time and Space.* Chatham: Chatham House Publishing.

Scharpf, F. W. 1997. "Introduction: The Problem-Solving Capacity of Multi-Level Governance." *Journal of European Public Policy* 4 (4): 520–538.

Wu, X., M. Ramesh, and M. Howlett. 2015. "Policy Capacity: A Conceptual Framework for Understanding Policy Competences and Capabilities." *Policy and Society* 34 (3–4).

Index

Aberhart, William 88

Aboriginal *see* First Nations; Indigenous; Inuit; Metis

Actors 6–7, 10, 56–7, 59–60, 63, 65, 78, 86, 88–9, 110, 117, 119, 121, 125, 131, 140, 148–9, 171, 211, 219, 232, 240, 247–8, 250–1, 264, 287, 289, 297, 303–4, 308, 310–1, 313–5, 317, 319–21, 349, 354–5, 361, 377, 387, 424, 434, 439, 469–70, 479, 484, 488

  academics 4, 58, 68, 88–9, 150, 161, 177, 194, 429, 462

  activists 39, 56–7, 59–62, 64–5, 71, 103, 189, 194, 298, 338, 351, 398

  adults 207, 209, 211, 216

  advisors 56, 155

  Chief Executive Officers (CEOs) 256, 302, 333, 336–7

  consultants 188, 340

  consumers 166, 247, 252, 254, 267, 273–4, 277–9, 311, 318, 320, 377, 381, 385–7

  doctors, nurses, or other medical profession-als 19, 22–4, 28–31, 43, 58–61, 65, 67, 69–70, 481, 487, 489

  educators *see* Actors, teachers

  elites 142, 148, 152, 155, 397, 488, 490

  employees 25, 192, 307, 332, 335–6, 340, 343–4, 445, 449–51 *see also* Actors, workers

  employers 44, 129–30, 166, 170, 214–5, 441, 450

  entrepreneurs 10, 64, 88, 165, 303–4, 341, 373, 377, 382, 389, 485

  experts 6, 8, 50–1, 103, 127–8, 149, 167, 240, 255, 257–8, 339, 350, 360, 422, 450, 487, 489

  farmers 41–3, 163, 267–8, 272–5, 278–82, 300, 304, 307–11, 482

  investors 165, 254, 258, 262, 375, 420

  journalists 161, 470

  judges 171, 397, 400, 404–8

  lawyers 397, 444, 449

  lobbyists 18, 20, 22, 39–40, 255, 264

  managers 26, 300, 312, 423, 425, 443–4, 452, 455,

  merchants 40, 62

  officials 8, 43–4, 45, 56, 60–1, 63, 65, 67, 85–6, 93, 141–2, 145, 149–51, 156, 171, 188, 214,

333, 338, 341, 398, 401, 425, 439, 442–3447, 451, 461, 466, 471, 474, 487

  practitioners 19, 77, 221, 242, 359

  politicians 24, 67–8, 71, 86, 232, 278, 483

  public servants 24, 44–5, 58, 141, 148, 166, 189, 233, 341, 425, 471, 489

  researchers 40–1, 58, 141, 145–6, 153, 288, 291–3, 350

  residents 20, 23, 26, 29, 57, 61, 68–9, 90, 93, 130, 165, 170, 173, 216, 331–2, 338, 341, 355–6, 358, 407, 420

  retirees 206–7, 209

  scholars 1, 143–4, 151, 153, 192, 194, 206, 221, 225, 242, 278, 338

  scientists 37, 42, 145, 290–1, 296, 299, 302, 351–2, 356, 363

  seniors 206–21, 486, 488

  soldiers 40, 197

  staff 65, 145, 153–4, 293, 330, 333, 335–6, 341, 344, 427, 443, 453

  stakeholders 5–7, 43, 48, 110, 142, 161–3, 166, 176–7, 211, 276–7, 283, 300, 328, 333, 339–43, 348–9, 354–5, 358–60, 363–4, 366–7, 402, 422, 424, 433, 440, 446, 451, 461–4, 471, 479, 487

  students 77, 80, 83, 90, 93, 130, 142, 151, 153, 155, 169–70

  teachers 78, 81–2, 85–90, 92, 126–7, 140, 149

  veterans 397–8

  winemakers 307

  workers 41, 45–6, 104, 109, 117, 122, 128–30, 143, 148, 169–70, 214–5, 219, 307, 377

  youth 49, 81, 103, 214, 342, 408

Acts 44, 64–5, 121, 161–7, 188, 318, 335–7, 350, 378

  Balanced Refugee Reform Act 171

  Bank Act 249, 251, 253, 261–2

  BC Wine Act 312

  Broadcasting Act 185

  Canada Child Care Act 121

  Canada Health Act 24–5, 30–1

  Canada National Parks Act 332, 339

  Canada Water Act 351

  Canadian Citizenship Act 191

  Canadian Dairy Commission Act 270, 277

Canadian Environmental Protection Act
(CEPA) 378
Canadian Multiculturalism Act 188
Competition Act 262, 445
Constitution Act 93, 230–1, 234, 242, 318,
395–6, 401–2, 406, 408–9
Controlled Drugs and Substances Act
(CDSA) 64–8
Dominion Forest Reserves and Parks
Act 330–1
Dominion Lands Act 329
Electricity Restructuring Act 378–9
Environmental Assessment Act 379
Farm Products Marketing Agencies Act 272,
277
Federal Accountability Act 464
Food and Drugs Act 48–9
Great Lakes Legacy Act 365
Green Energy and Green Economy Act
(GEGEA) 380, 383
Gwaii Haanas National Park Act 337
Hospital Insurance and Diagnostic Services
Act (HIDSA) 21, 24
Immigration Act 161–2, 164–8, 175, 188
Immigration and Refugee Protection Act
(IRPA) 161–2, 168, 172, 175
Indian Act 78, 396–8
Intoxicating Liquor Act (ILA) 318
Medical Care Act 23–4
National Day-Care Act 121
National Marine Conservation Act 339
National Parks Act 331–2, 337, 339
National Transportation Act 442, 445
Non-Smoker's Health Act 46
Old Age Assistance Act 213
Old Age Security Act 213, 216–7
Old Ages Pensions Act 212
Ontario Vintners Quality Alliance Act 314
Ontario Wine Content Act 312
Parks Canada Agency Act 332, 336, 339
Preventing Human Smugglers from Abusing
Canada's Immigration System Act 172
Protecting Canada's Immigration System
Act 172
Respecting First Nations, Inuit and Metis
Children, Youth and Families 408
Rocky Mountain Park Act 330
Tobacco Act 46
Tobacco and Vaping Products Act 49
Tobacco Product Control Act 46
Tobacco Restraint Act 40
Wine Content and Labelling Act 313
Zero Tolerance for Barbaric Cultural Practices
Act 190–1

see also Bills
Administration 9, 70, 81, 88–9, 113, 127, 141–3,
153, 165, 176, 209–13, 216, 242, 248, 268,
271–2, 276, 295, 319, 330, 358, 361, 364,
380, 387, 396, 432, 439, 442, 458, 473, 483–7
capacity 210, 241, 321, 361, 485, 487–8
costs 25–6, 216, 479, 483–4
success 458, 487
Advertising 36–47, 103, 378, 470, 472–4
Advocacy Coalition Framework (ACF) 57 fn
Africa 184, 188
Agencies 29, 242, 272, 276–7, 292, 314–5, 328–9,
331–5, 341–3, 348, 351, 361, 387, 422–3,
425, 433, 444, 451, 459, 466–7
Atlantic Opportunities Agency 155
British Columbia Wine Authority 315
Canadian Agency for Drugs and Technologies
in Health 29
Canadian Blood Agency 29
Canadian Egg Marketing Agency
(CEMA) 273
Canadian Food Inspection Agency 299
Credit-rating agencies 420–1, 444
Environmental Protection Agency (EPA) 351,
354, 357
Foreign Investment Review Agency
(FIRA) 292
Parks Canada Agency 327–9, 331–44
Statistics Canada 77, 168, 419
see also Marketing
Agriculture 9, 41–2, 163, 267–70, 273–5,
279–80, 286–305, 307–16, 352, 356, 358–9,
482, 484–6
Agricultural Policy Framework 295
Canadian Agricultural Partnership 316
Canadian Federation of Agriculture
(CFA) 270, 272
canola 286–305, 482–3, 486, 488
International Centre for Agricultural Science
and Technology (ICAST) 295–6
United Grain Growers 291–4, 298, 302
viticulture 307–8, 311–3, 315–6
Alberta 20, 22–3, 32, 80, 88–90, 133, 141, 153,
226–8, 230–3, 235–6, 238–9, 241, 274,
288–9, 291, 295–6, 298, 309, 318, 329,
331–2, 372, 383, 388, 398
Banff Management Plan 332
Conservative (party) 230–1
Fair Deal Panel 230
New Democratic Party (party - NDP) 383
Social Credit (party) 20
Ambrose, Rona 49
America *see* United States
see also North America

494 INDEX

Analysis, analysts 2–3, 8, 10, 17, 58, 119, 148, 193, 198, 206, 208–9, 211, 233, 239, 255, 259, 308, 317, 321, 349, 417–8, 420, 444, 470, 490
  cost-benefit 1, 58, 361
  empirical 119, 195, 201, 228, 418
  evidence 10, 50–1, 58–9, 64, 66, 68, 71, 161, 192–5, 199, 267, 337, 349, 351–5, 357, 361–4, 367, 387, 389, 404, 483, 487
  meta-analysis 207, 210
  see also Knowledge; Policy, analysis; Reports; Studies; Think tanks
Arctic 399
Argentina 314, 319
Asia 47, 169, 188, 230, 279, 288, 301, 316
Associations 19, 22, 24, 28–9, 42, 45, 48, 62, 65, 85–6, 88, 104, 121, 141, 148, 186, 253–5, 287, 289–90, 295, 300, 307, 310–1, 316, 338, 377, 398
  Alberta Teachers' Association (ATA) 88, 90
  Association of Major Power Consumers of Ontario (AMPCO) 377, 387
  Association of Universities and Colleges of Canada (AUCC) 141, 149–52, 154, 156
  Banff Citizens Association 338
  Canadian Association of University Teachers (CAUT) 140, 149, 151–2, 156
  Canadian Automobile Dealers Association 260
  Canadian Bankers Association (CBA) 253, 255–7, 259
  Canadian Day Care Advocacy Association 121
  Canadian Education Association (CEA) 85–6
  Canadian Medical Association 22, 42
  Canadian Police Association 65
  Chinatown Merchants Association 62
  Dairy Farmers of Canada 270
  Dominion Education Association (DEA) 85, 88
  International Association of Great Lakes Research (IAGLR) 351–2
  Investment Dealers Association (IIDA) 254
  Non-Partisan Association (NPA) 62, 65
  Ontario Public Health Association 377
  Ontario Public School Boards' Association 126
  Rapeseed Association of Canada 289–90
  Registered Nurses Association of Ontario 377
  Regroupement interorganismes pour une politique familiale au Quebec (RIOPFQ) 104
  Trust Companies Association of Canada (TCAC) 254

Women's Christian Temperance Union (WCTU) 39–40
Australasia 30
Australia 8, 83, 90, 176, 186, 211, 241, 281, 290, 307, 314, 317, 478, 489
Austria 186
Banks, banking 2, 9, 45, 47, 247–9, 251, 253–9, 262–4, 295, 302, 416, 428–9, 444–5, 448, 457, 459, 480, 486–8
  Bank of Montreal (BMO) 254–6
  Canadian Imperial Bank of Commerce (CIBC) 256, 295
  Goldman Sachs 428–9
  International Monetary Fund (IMF) 416, 459
  oversight 249, 263, 457, 464
  pillarization 251, 253–4, 262
  Royal Bank of Canada (RBC) 254–6, 295–6
  Scotiabank 259, 263, 428
  Toronto Dominion 256
  World Bank 47, 459

Barber, Lloyd 398
Begin, Monique 24
Behaviour 2, 365
Belgium 186, 296
Bennett, W. A. C. 23, 227, 233, 236
Bernier, Maxime 174
Bills 44–6, 121, 167–8, 171–2, 240, 260, 286, 327, 426, 454
  Bill-85 327
  Bill-135 286
  C-8 260
  C-11 171
  C-24 240
  C-31 172
  C-49 172
  C-86 167
  C-144 121
  C-248 44
  see also Acts; Canada, Parliament
Borders 69, 88, 112, 131, 133, 167, 172, 198, 280, 318, 360, 459
  see also International Relations; Treaties
Bouchard, Benoit 442
Bouchard, Lucien 98, 102, 105, 109–12, 129
Bourassa, Robert 399
Bloc Quebecois (BQ) 280, 417, 429–30, 458, 460, 464, 469, 472
Britain *see* United Kingdom
British Columbia (BC) 20–1, 23, 28–9, 32, 44, 48, 56, 64–70, 79–80, 88–9, 91, 125, 132–3, 141, 150, 154, 171, 175, 227, 232–3, 235–6, 274, 307, 309–14, 317–20, 331, 396, 399–400, 402–5, 407, 409, 450 fn, 486

BC Liquor Distribution Board (BCLDB) 310
BC Teachers' Federation 91
Liberal (party) 20, 64
Liquor and Cannabis Regulation Branch 310
New Democratic Party (party - NDP) 404
Social Credit (party) 236
Supreme Court 28, 66, 399, 401–5, 408
see also Universities
Budgets, budgeting 10, 17, 92, 98–9, 102, 109,
    111–3, 122–4, 139, 143, 146, 150, 152,
    172, 219–20, 231, 241, 290, 295, 332, 334,
    339–41, 383, 416–9, 421, 423–9, 432, 434–5,
    447, 457, 459–60, 462–3, 468–9, 472
    debt, deficits 99, 121, 123, 153, 218, 377, 381,
        416, 418, 420–1, 423, 428–30, 433–5, 441–2,
        447–8, 463, 482
    revenue 30–1, 41, 82–3, 93, 109, 209, 216,
        218–9, 225, 227–8, 231, 234–40, 269–70,
        278, 308–9, 315, 331, 339, 341, 377, 383,
        386, 406, 417–20, 431–4, 439–41, 445,
        447–8, 465, 484
    spending, expenditures 77, 118, 121, 124,
        141–3, 156, 208–9, 211–2, 225, 239, 273,
        327, 417–8, 420–2, 424, 426–35, 483
    surplus 139–41, 143, 146, 150, 219, 269, 273,
        275, 341, 431–3, 451, 459
    see also Business; Economy; Finance, funding
Bureaucracy, bureaucrats 52, 63, 65, 85, 88, 92,
    171, 188–9, 199, 233, 300–1, 327–8, 352,
    355, 367, 400, 439, 443, 445, 487
Bush, George W. 68, 365, 459
Business 20, 22, 25, 28, 39–47, 49, 51–2, 65,
    147–8, 152–3, 165, 172, 235, 247–9, 252–5,
    257–9, 261–2, 271, 276–7, 286–90, 292–8,
    300–2, 307–21, 329, 331–2, 375, 406, 417,
    424, 426, 432, 443–7, 449, 451–2, 462–4,
    468
    Canadian Federation of Independent Business
        (CFIB) 258, 260
    Chamber of Commerce 446
    conglomeration, mergers 249, 251–63, 278,
        297–8, 302
    monopolies 41, 47, 299, 309, 375
    monopsony 318
    multinational 47, 254–5, 287, 292, 295, 298,
        304, 307
    retail sector 38, 41, 46–7, 50–1, 308–12,
        317–21
    see also Privatization, private sector

Cabinet 20–1, 40, 42, 44–5, 49, 52, 85, 92, 102,
    109, 229, 233, 253–4, 333, 341, 381, 399,
    416, 421–2, 425–6, 433–4, 444–5, 447, 459,
    466, 469, 472, 485

    see also Departments; Ministers
Calgary 438 fn, 449, 451
California 292, 307, 313
Campbell, Gordon 64–6, 71
Campbell, Kim 422
Campbell, Larry 61–4, 71
Canada, Canadians 3–4, 7, 9–10, 17–22, 24–6,
    29–30, 32, 36–8, 41–3, 45–8, 56, 60, 64–70,
    77–9, 84–9, 93–4, 103, 106–8, 118–20,
    131–2, 139–45, 149, 161–2, 172–7, 183–9,
    192–4, 198–9, 207, 211, 213–7, 225, 227–8,
    230, 238–43, 248–9, 253–8, 262–5, 269,
    276, 287–8, 294–7, 300–5, 307–9, 312–5,
    319, 329, 331–4, 336–7, 341, 348–50, 356,
    360, 363–5, 377, 396–405, 416–8, 435, 441,
    444–6, 451, 463–7, 478, 482, 486, 489
Atlantic 4, 38, 87, 155, 217, 227, 235, 239, 307,
    334, 403–5
Atlantic Accord 240
Auditor General 143, 341, 344, 447, 451,
    453–4, 466–7, 470–1
Canada National Parks Branch 330, 334
Canada-Quebec Accord 170
Canada Wheat Board 282
Canadian Development Corporation 292–3
Canadian Experience Class (CEC) 169–70
Canadian Government Specification
    Board 289
Canadian Pacific Railway (CPR) 329–31
Canadian Parks and Wilderness Society 338
Canadian Teachers' Federation (CTF) 86, 89
Canola Council of Canada 290, 297
Central 87
Charter of Rights and Freedoms 28–9, 66–7,
    70–1, 185, 189, 192, 233, 401
Competition Bureau 252–3, 256, 258, 261–3,
    298
Comptroller General 422, 467
Confederation 77, 83, 85, 147, 396, 408
Council of Ministers of Education, Canada
    (CMEC) 80, 83, 86, 93
Council on Smoking and Health 45
Crown 92, 121, 396–7, 401, 405–7, 427, 444,
    450 fn
Crown Investment Corporation (CIC) 295–6,
    302
Eastern 21–4, 28, 38, 42, 46, 48, 77, 85, 89,
    98–112, 230, 259, 351, 355–6, 362, 393,
    399–401, 403–6, 407–8, 410, 458, 472
Economic Council of Canada 258, 273, 462
Farm Products Council of Canada 272, 276,
    278
Governor General 458, 460–2, 464, 469
Governor in Council 444

496 INDEX

Canada, Canadians (*Continued*)
  Historic Sites and Monuments Board of
    Canada 331
  Human Resources Development Canada
    (HRDC) 149, 464, 466, 472
  Human Rights Tribunal 408
  Immigration and Refugee Review Board 167
  Macdonald-Laurier National Policy 147, 163
  Maritime 87, 334
  Medical Research Council of Canada 144
  National Airports Policy 440, 452–3
  National Biotechnology Strategy 295
  National Farmers Union 270, 303–4
  Northern 336
  Office Superintendent of Financial Institutions
    (OSFI) 249, 251, 253, 256, 261–2
  Pacific 236
  Parliament 18, 21, 40, 42–6, 48–9, 63, 155,
    164–5, 168, 171, 174, 188, 201, 231, 239,
    251–3, 256–64, 267–8, 280, 327, 330, 333,
    339, 398, 405–6, 409, 417, 428–9, 434, 451,
    453, 458–62, 464, 467–8, 472, 484, 488
  Parliamentary Budget Office (PBO) 459
  Privy Council Office 111, 149–50, 397, 410,
    425, 443, 461, 466, 470
  Senate 79, 164, 171, 209, 259–60
  Solicitor General 428
  Supreme Court 28, 38, 46, 66–7, 91, 167,
    190–1, 272, 298–9, 304, 318, 395, 405–7,
    409
  Victoria Charter 230 fn
  Western 20–1, 22–3, 28–9, 32, 44, 48, 77,
    84–5, 87–8, 163, 228, 230, 233, 289, 295,
    329, 332, 396, 398–400, 402–5, 407, 409
  see also Associations; Government; Institutes;
    Policy; Programs; Provinces; Research
Capital (money) 121, 127, 142, 302, 383–5, 400,
  403, 418, 421, 440, 444, 446, 448
  see also Finance, funding
Caplan, Elinor 168
Caribbean 188
Carter, Jimmy 352
Charest, Jean 106, 111, 191
Children, childcare 40, 43–4, 46, 63, 79, 89–91,
  98–9, 103–13, 117–25, 128–9, 131–4, 169,
  231, 408–9, 468, 481, 486–8
  Centres de la petite enfance (CPE) 98–100,
    104–9, 111, 113
  Child Tax Benefit (CTB) 118, 122–3
  daycare 9, 100, 103, 108
  Early Learning Advisor 126
  Home Child Care 128
  Multilateral Early Learning and Child Care
    Framework 124

  National Child Benefit (NCB)
    supplement 122–3, 129
  Unified Child Allowance (UCA) 104
  universalization 103–4, 119–21, 123, 131
  see also Families, households; Programs
Chile 314, 342
China 47, 167, 169, 197, 293, 308, 342
Chretien, Jean 4, 48, 123, 139–43, 145–8, 150–6,
  166, 219, 336, 340–1, 357, 365, 422, 426,
  430, 454, 462
  family of 146
Cigarettes *see* Tobacco
Cities *see* Government, municipal
Citizens, citizenship 1, 3, 26–7, 31, 58, 87, 90, 93,
  117, 162–3, 165, 173, 175, 184–6, 189–94,
  197, 201, 212, 216, 226, 229, 231, 332, 344,
  353, 397–8, 424, 462, 484
Civil rights 71, 184
Clarke, Charles Joseph 421
Class 39, 56–7, 62, 84, 99, 117, 120, 211, 229
  low income or poor 57, 120–2, 127–8, 131,
    190, 209–10, 229
  middle income or class 57, 62, 120, 122–3,
    210, 219, 221
  high income or wealthy 124, 129, 131, 218,
    229, 277
  see also Actors, elites; Actors, workers; Poverty
Climate change 9, 329, 339, 341, 358–9, 365,
  372, 379, 458, 470, 473, 482–3
  acid rain 372–6, 384, 388, 483
  Climate Change Action Plan (CCAP) 381
  flooding 358, 362
  greenhouse gas (GHG) 372–3, 375–9, 384,
    388, 483
  Kyoto Protocol 458
  ozone depletion 377, 389
  Pan-Canadian Framework for Clean Growth
    and Climate Change (PCF) 372
  see also Environment, stewardship
Coal *see* Energy, hydrocarbons; Resources,
  natural, coal
Coalitions *see* Politics, coalitions
Cold War 47, 167
Colombia 342
Colonialism, decolonization 77, 84, 164, 184,
  395–7, 411
Commerce, companies *see* Business; Economy;
  Markets
Commercialization 289–92, 297, 301, 427, 432,
  445
  see also Privatization, private sector
Commissions, commissioners 19, 23, 27, 89,
  105, 118, 120–1, 125, 127, 129, 187, 192,

229, 234, 239–41, 259, 262, 270, 291, 330, 339, 398, 442
Airport Transfer Task Force (ATTF) 440–1, 443–50, 452, 454
Barber Commission 398
BC Treaty Commission 404–5
Canadian Dairy Commission 270, 277
Commissioner of National Parks 338
Controller of the National Parks Bureau 334
Expert Panel on the Ecological Integrity of Canada 339
Electricity Conservation and Supply Task Force 385
Federal Task Force on Agriculture 272
Gomery Commission 4
Great Lakes Fishery Commission 350
Hall Commission 23
Hawthorn Task Force 398
Ianno Report 259–61
Indian Claims Commissioner 398–400
International Joint Commission (IJC) 348–51, 358–9, 363–4
MacKay Task Force 253–7, 259–61, 263
Massey Commission 334
Nielsen Task Force 422, 442
on Price Spread 41
Ontario Hydro Electric Commission 375
Parliamentary Task Force on Federal-Provincial Fiscal Arrangements 239–41
Romanow Commission 27
Rowell-Sirois Commission 234, 239
Royal Commission on Education 105 fn
Royal Commission on the Status of Women 120–1
Sigerist Commission 19
Task Force on Airport Management, Haglund Report 442
Task Force on Childcare 121
Truth and Reconciliation Commission (TRC) 78–9
see also Reports; Studies
Committees 18, 37, 44–5, 48–9, 52, 86, 103, 109–10, 121, 164, 209, 258–62, 264, 270, 337, 398, 425, 449–51
Aboriginal Consultative Committee 337
Canadian Dairy Advisory Committee 270
Canadian Milk Supply Management Committee (CMSMC) 271
Commons Finance Committee 260–1, 462
Commons Health Committee 49
Departmental Audit Committees (DAAs) 467, 471
Deputy Ministers' Committee 425–6

Great Lakes Executive Committee (GLEC) 357–8, 363
Judicial Committee of the Privy Council 397
National Strategy To Reduce Tobacco Use (NSTRTU) 45–6, 48
on Cigarette Evils 40
on Government Operations and Estimates 467
on Health Insurance 18
on Health, Welfare and Social Affairs 43–4
Program Review Cabinet Committee 425–6
Senate Banking Committee 259–61
Senate Special Committee on Aging 214
Special Joint Committee 164
Special Parliamentary Committee on Childcare 121
Taxation Review Committee 104
Communication 47, 84, 291, 336, 443, 447, 451, 467, 472
Communities 39, 46–7, 49–50, 57, 59–61, 64, 68, 70, 79, 90, 122, 126, 143, 185, 187, 191, 193, 277–8, 295, 328, 330, 332, 336–7, 339, 342–3, 350, 354–8, 361–3, 379–80, 404, 418, 424, 439, 446, 450, 453, 463, 465, 470
see also Government, municipal; Indigenous; Policy, community
Competition 139, 147, 214, 226, 251–7, 261–4, 269, 275, 280, 298, 303, 310, 314, 316, 319–20
see also Business, monopolies; Economy; Regulation and deregulation
Computers, computing 148
Conferences 18–19, 21, 42, 61–2, 86, 88, 129, 338, 341, 355, 401
Conference on Teacher Education 88
State of Lakes Ecosystem Conference (SOLEC) 355–7
Summit on the Economy and Employment 129
UN World Summit on Sustainable Development 341
Conservation see Environment, stewardship
Conservative (party) 41, 45, 65–7, 117, 122–5, 127, 169–72, 188–90, 198, 219, 240, 263, 272, 280, 282, 340–1, 372, 388, 417, 421–2, 429, 439, 441–2, 444–5, 452, 457–60, 463–4, 468, 471–2
see also Progressive Conservative (party)
Contracts, contracting 10, 130, 380, 383, 442–3, 445, 452, 454
Cooperatives (farming) 268, 281, 293, 298
Co-operative Commonwealth Federation (CCF) 18–9, 214
Copps, Sheila 332, 339

498 INDEX

Corporations *see* Business
Corruption 4, 249
Cory, W. W. 331
Couillard, Philippe 106, 111
Courts, court cases 28–9, 31, 42, 46, 48, 51, 66,
  70, 171, 190–1, 272, 287, 298–9, 303, 318,
  320, 395, 397–407, 409, 481–2
  appeals 171–2, 298, 399, 404, 407
Covid-19 (coronavirus) 2, 9, 69, 77, 109, 134,
  143, 168, 198, 222, 416, 439, 455, 474, 484,
  489
Crime 56, 58–60, 63, 67, 69, 71, 79, 168, 317
  see also Policing; RCMP
Crises 7, 56, 57 fn, 59, 61–2, 64–5, 67–8, 71, 98,
  190, 233, 249, 380, 267, 272, 416, 426, 433,
  442, 457–8, 461, 464, 469, 471, 473, 485, 489
  see also Great or Global Financial Crisis of
  2007-2009 (GFC)
Culture 39, 50, 79, 81, 84, 87, 90, 165, 169,
  183–4, 186–8, 190–3, 195–9, 232, 329, 339,
  402–3, 408, 467
  minorities 83, 87, 169, 184–6, 190–1, 193–7,
  200–1
  see also Multiculturalism

Davis, William 89
Decision-making, decision-makers 2, 46, 50, 60,
  69, 71, 80, 90, 109, 161, 169, 225, 233, 282,
  302, 309, 334, 337, 343–4, 353, 363, 373,
  381–2, 386–9, 400, 410, 423, 425, 433–4,
  453, 483
Democracy *see* Government, social democratic
Demographics 81, 84, 98–9, 101, 161, 165, 168,
  170, 175, 184–5, 194, 199, 207, 218–9, 315,
  340, 349
  see also Culture; Ethnicity; Gender; Language;
  Multiculturalism; Race, racism; Society,
  social
Denmark 186, 207, 380
Departments 45–6, 49, 52, 66, 82–3, 87–8, 103,
  106, 109–10, 190, 229, 232–3, 295–6, 316,
  327, 331, 334, 336, 343–4, 357, 401, 416–8,
  422, 425–8, 434, 445–7, 466, 471, 487
  Agriculture and Agri-Food 270–4, 288,
  290–2, 299, 301–2, 307, 316, 428
  Canadian Heritage 189, 191, 332
  Central Agencies 428
  Children and Youth Services 125
  Citizenship and Immigration 171, 190, 428
  Defence 426, 428
  Education 82–3, 85–8, 103, 109, 127
  Environment and Climate Change 332, 341,
  351–2, 354, 357, 428
  Family 106, 109

Finance 103, 109, 111, 149–50, 218–9, 229,
  232–3, 252, 254, 260, 276, 416–9, 434, 441,
  446–7, 457, 459, 461–2, 466, 487
Fisheries and Oceans 402–3, 428
Foreign Affairs and International Trade 428
Forest Branch, Department of Interior 330
Health and Welfare 290, 428
Health Canada 45–6, 49, 68–9
Heritage and Cultural Programs 428
Human Resources 428
Immigration 168, 171, 189–90
Indian and Northern Affairs 334, 336, 401,
  427–8, 465–6
Industry 149, 425, 428, 465
Infrastructure Canada 465–6, 471, 473
Intergovernmental Affairs 109, 461
Interior 327, 329–31, 338
International Assistance 428
Justice 428, 444
Mortgage and Housing 428
Multiculturalism 189–90
Natural Resources 427–8
Pensions 103
Public Works and Government Services
  (PWGS) 452, 465–6
Regional Agencies 428
Revenue 109
Social Solidarity 103
Transport 427–8, 438–47, 449–54
Treasury Board (Secretariat) 109, 151, 422,
  426, 461, 465–7, 470–1
Veterans' Affairs 428
Western Economic Diversification 295–6
  see also Cabinet; Ministers; Provinces
Detroit 358
Development 4, 70, 90, 127, 174, 212, 214, 231,
  233, 241, 286–7, 289–91, 294, 296, 300, 304,
  308, 313, 315, 317, 328, 332, 338, 400, 416,
  421, 438, 441, 447, 482, 486
  see also Policy, development
Devine, Grant 301
Diefenbaker, John G. 21, 164, 235
Dion, Stephane 340, 458, 461
Diplomacy 363, 365, 396, 482
Disease 39, 41, 297, 354–6, 362
  see also Health, healthcare
Discourse, discussion 2–3, 5, 61–2, 68, 78, 91,
  123, 195, 198, 228, 231, 409, 447, 484
  see also Policy, deliberation; Politics, debate
Diversity 56, 61, 71, 99, 118, 142, 153, 168, 174,
  183–5, 187–9, 191–3, 195–9, 310, 327, 340,
  361, 377, 425, 487
  see also Demographics; Inclusivity;
  Multiculturalism

Douglas, Thomas "Tommy" 18–21, 485
Duplessis, Maurice 232
Drug use 56–71
North American Opiate Medication Initiative (NAOMI) 65
Overdose Prevention Sites (OPS) 68–9
War on Drugs 59
see also Health, healthcare

East Asia 286
Economy 1, 4–5, 8–9, 47, 51–2, 57–8, 63, 79–80, 83, 90, 99, 113, 125–6, 128, 144, 147–8, 150, 153, 155, 162–3, 165–8, 170, 174, 185, 189, 194, 198, 214, 221, 225–6, 228, 232, 236, 238, 241–2, 254–5, 257–8, 267–9, 272–3, 276, 281, 290, 295, 307, 314–5, 318, 327, 329, 343, 355, 358–9, 364, 373, 380, 384, 388, 397, 402, 416–8, 420, 427–30, 434, 438–9, 441–2, 446, 457, 459–61, 463, 467–9, 481, 484, 486–8
Economic Action Plan (EAP) 457, 461–9, 471–2, 474, 481, 488
gross domestic product (GDP) 237, 281, 307, 314, 416–21, 423, 428, 431, 463
prices 39, 41, 47, 101, 127, 221, 230, 233, 238–9, 241, 267–71, 274–5, 277–8, 281, 309–10, 312, 315, 373, 375, 380–3, 385–7, 416, 419, 421, 429, 431, 453
production 39, 238, 240, 267–81, 287–90, 293, 295, 297–8, 302–4, 307–13, 315, 320–1, 372, 384, 430, 485
see also Budgets, budgeting; Business; Policy
Edmonton 88, 438 fn, 449, 451
Education 3, 9, 43–6, 62, 77–94, 100–5, 107, 109, 118, 124–6, 128, 131, 133, 140–1, 146, 150–6, 161, 164, 169, 190, 195, 197, 201, 226, 229, 331, 470, 472, 480–1, 486, 488
Anishnabek Nation Education Agreement 79
Council of Public Instruction 84–5, 87
Early Childhood Education and Care (ECEC) 118–122, 124–34
Elementary Teachers Federation 126
kindergarten 124–9, 132–3, 484
literacy 84
post-secondary 9, 81, 83, 140–1, 150–1, 153–4
secondary 77, 83, 86–7, 90–1, 93, 480–1, 486, 488
universality, universalizing 81, 86, 89–91, 93
see also Children, childcare; First Nations; Schools; Universities
Elections *see* Politics
Employment, unemployment 77, 93, 101, 104, 117, 119, 164–5, 167, 169–70, 186, 194–5,

198, 211, 213, 216, 260, 338, 406, 423, 426, 430, 463, 468
see also Actors, employees; Actors, employers; Business
Energy, electricity 230, 232, 238, 241, 291–2, 372–84, 399, 470, 482, 485–6
biomass 381, 388
Fair Hydro Plan 385–6
heating 382
hydrocarbons 230, 232–3, 235, 238–41, 372–86, 482, 485–6, 488
hydroelectricity 399, 374–5, 379, 381, 383
National Energy Program 228, 239
nuclear 373–6, 379, 382–5, 388
Nuclear Asset Optimization Plan (NAOP) 376–7, 382–3
pipelines 228, 230–1, 233, 399, 407
renewable 373, 379–80, 382–3, 385, 387
Engineering 145, 154, 286
see also Genetic engineering, genomics
Environment, stewardship 9, 47, 142, 228, 304, 309, 327–30, 332–44, 348, 350–5, 358–62, 364–5, 372–4, 377–84, 388, 402, 452, 482
air quality 372, 374, 378
ecosystems 328–9, 332, 335, 338–40, 342, 358–60, 362
Environment Impact Assessments 341
see also Agencies; Departments; Pollution; Wildlife
Environmentalism 287, 298, 300, 304, 332, 335, 343, 358, 363, 366, 379, 482
Epp, Jake 45
Equality, inequality 7, 78, 80–1, 83–4, 93, 102, 119, 121, 188, 194–5, 198–9, 225, 229–31, 236, 238, 481
Ethics 153
Ethnicity 39, 163, 184–6, 188, 194, 196, 199, 201
see also Culture; Language; Multiculturalism; Race, racism
Europe 27, 30, 47, 61, 74, 79, 81, 87, 162 fn, 169, 176, 184–5, 187, 199, 212, 220, 230, 279, 286, 288, 297, 301, 311, 396, 403, 411
European Union (EU) 281, 316, 319, 459
Eves, Ernie 378

Families, households 4, 57–8, 79, 81, 91, 98–104, 107, 109–12, 117–20, 122–4, 128–33, 161, 163–6, 169, 175–6, 190, 206–7, 216–7, 398, 407, 409, 465
income 57, 190, 219
marriages 98, 217–8, 407
maternity 118–9, 121, 126, 128–30
see also Children, childcare

500 INDEX

Federalism 9, 30, 32, 66–7, 70, 78, 82–3, 85, 92,
  119, 140, 156, 226, 228–9, 232, 234–5, 242,
  309, 318, 416–7, 424, 479, 481
Feminism 119, 121, 129, 131, 219
  see also Gender; Women
Finance, funding 17–20, 22–5, 27, 30, 41, 43–5,
  60–1, 63–5, 81–4, 86, 91–3, 107, 119, 121–3,
  127–9, 139–46, 149–55, 172–3, 186, 189–91,
  201, 209, 211, 218–9, 225–7, 229, 231–9,
  241, 247, 250, 257–8, 271–2, 294–5, 302,
  308, 316–7, 320, 332–4, 339–40, 344, 356–7,
  361, 379, 381, 384, 397, 416, 418, 420–4,
  427–8, 431–4, 438, 440–2, 444–8, 451, 459,
  461, 463, 465–8, 470–3, 484, 486, 488
  Canadian Millennium Scholarship Fund 146
  capacity 225–6, 236–41, 487–8
  equalization 225–43, 480–2, 486, 488–9
  Established Programs Financing (EPF) 23–4
  Expenditure Management System (EMS) 421
  financial services and instruments 247–50,
    252–4, 257–9, 263–4, 270, 300, 463, 473
  interest, interest rates 258, 416, 420, 426, 430,
    433–5
  investments, investing 51, 77, 93, 118–9, 123,
    125, 131, 133, 228, 294, 302–3, 311, 340,
    358, 364, 379, 443–6, 453, 455
  mortgages 251, 458
  mutual funds 254
  public 19–23, 31
  see also Budgets, budgeting; Business
Finland 80–1, 186
First Nations 4, 9, 39, 78–9, 337, 350, 356,
  395–8, 400–11, 462, 465–7, 470, 472, 480–2
  Aboriginal Affairs Secretariat 337
  Anishinaabe 79, 396, 408
  Charlottetown Accord 401
  Cree 399, 405–6, 409–10
  Dene 399
  Gitxsan 404–5, 407
  Haida 337, 405, 409–10, 450 fn
  Heiltsuk 403
  land claims 336–7, 395, 399–401, 407–10
  Mi'kmaq 403
  Musqueam 401–2, 407
  National Indian Brotherhood 398–9
  Nisga'a 399–400, 404–5, 408
  Office of Native Claims 400
  reconciliation 473
  residential schools 4, 78–9, 84
  Statement on the Claims of Indian and Inuit
    People 400
  Sto:lo 402
  Tsilqot'in 404–5, 410
  Wet'suwet'en 404–5, 407

  see also Indigenous; Law
First World War 40–1
Flaherty, Jim 459
Flint, Michigan 358, 362
Ford, Doug 67, 127–8, 381–2, 386, 388–9
France 26, 79–80, 84, 87, 106, 164, 183, 186–7,
  191, 194, 296, 410

Gender 4, 117, 119, 131, 189
Genetic engineering, genomics 286–97
  Allelix 292–4, 296–7, 300, 302
  Monsanto 292, 296–9, 304
  Proctor and Gamble 297
  see also Agriculture; Technology
Geography 162–3, 174, 307, 310, 316, 425, 487
Georgia 314
Germany 26, 80, 83, 176, 186, 194, 292, 380
Giroux, Robert 151
Globalization 47, 153, 164, 166, 168, 247,
  249–50, 253–4, 257, 259, 264, 273, 307–8,
  311, 313–4, 316–7, 320, 478
  see also Internationalization
Globe and Mail 235–6, 340, 429
  see also Media
Goldenberg, Eddie 145, 149–50
Government 1–4, 18, 21, 23–5, 27, 29–31, 36,
  40, 42–6, 49, 63–6, 77, 79, 81–3, 85–6, 98,
  109–111, 148–56, 161, 167, 171–2, 175–7,
  189–91, 225–7, 230–2, 238, 254–5, 257–9,
  272, 287, 291, 307–9, 314–7, 339–40, 343,
  350–1, 355–7, 363, 388, 395–6, 401, 406,
  408, 416–7, 422, 427–9, 432–4, 439, 446,
  459–61, 467, 472, 479, 481, 486
  accountability 143, 333, 340, 361, 363
  authority 84, 268, 272, 313, 409
  capacity 4, 131, 187, 241, 264, 267, 363, 365
  coalitions *see* Politics, coalitions
  constitutions 9, 32, 46, 66–8, 83, 118, 140,
    142, 187, 189, 201, 226, 230, 233, 242, 318,
    395, 400–3, 406, 408, 469, 488–9
  devolution 432
  double majority rule 21
  executive branch 70, 92, 109, 111, 162–4, 168,
    175–6, 188, 242, 479, 484–5
  expenses *see* Finance, funding; Budgets,
    budgeting
  failures 2–4, 328, 357, 373, 403, 468, 482, 484,
    489
  federal 18, 21–4, 26, 30–2, 37, 41–2, 44–6,
    49, 51–2, 60, 63–6, 69, 77, 83, 86, 100, 104,
    117–9, 121–4, 129, 133, 139–41, 146–7,
    149–51, 154, 162–3, 165, 185, 189, 192, 198,
    209, 212–4, 219, 225–8, 230–2, 234, 238–9,
    241–2, 249–51, 253, 264, 267–9, 274, 280,

288, 290–1, 301, 304, 308, 316, 319–20, 329–31, 336, 338, 340–1, 348, 351–2, 355, 358–9, 363–5, 372, 378, 388, 395, 397, 400–1, 403, 406, 410, 416–7, 420, 423, 431–4, 438, 441, 445–8, 451, 458, 464–6, 470, 486, 489

goals 1, 5, 10, 45, 48, 50, 58, 68, 89, 102, 156, 165, 177,195–6, 199, 237, 248–50, 264, 276, 316–7, 320, 328, 341, 357, 362, 364, 397, 416–7, 463, 479, 481

green books 18

institutions 2, 4, 10, 23, 57, 70–1, 78, 82, 84–7, 92, 117, 132–3, 139, 142–4, 150, 152, 185, 190, 193, 208, 232, 247, 253, 267, 270, 273, 277, 282, 286, 300, 302–5, 327–8, 343, 361, 366, 373, 382, 400, 440, 448, 485, 489

interprovincial 85–6, 225, 231, 272, 276, 282, 307, 317–20, 484

jurisdictions 3–4, 63, 67, 78, 82–3, 85, 88, 90, 92, 118–22, 131–2, 176, 192, 225, 248, 251–2, 265, 270, 282, 307, 310–1, 318, 331, 338, 342, 356, 409, 427, 457, 484

legislature 19, 21, 40, 44, 85, 331, 380, 399, 402, 405, 407, 409

local 50, 56, 60–7, 82, 92, 142, 228, 258, 314, 332–6, 338, 343, 353–5, 380, 395, 439–40, 442, 446, 450–1

machinery 142, 363, 416, 422, 425, 432–3

minority 183, 199, 212, 230, 380, 457, 459, 464, 468–9

multi-level 5, 36, 56, 313, 337, 352, 354, 366, 387, 424, 482, 489

municipal 8, 20, 42, 45, 47, 51, 56, 59–60, 62–3, 67, 152, 201, 235, 330, 332, 338, 352, 358, 363, 377, 439, 441, 444, 446, 449, 451–2, 465, 467–8, 470–2, 485

national dairy authority 270

one-party 41, 302

parliamentary 18, 37, 45, 81, 85, 92, 484–5

powers of 85, 118, 230, 268–72, 275, 338, 406, 408, 429, 486

programs *see* Programs

provincial 3, 17–9, 23–4, 26–8, 30–1, 42, 44–6, 48, 51–2, 60, 63–7, 69, 77–8, 80, 85–6, 92–3, 99, 117–9, 121–5, 128–9, 132, 140, 142, 144, 146, 148–9, 155–6, 211–2, 228, 230–4, 237–8, 241–2, 251, 257, 267–73, 288, 291, 301, 304, 308–9, 312, 316–20, 331, 333–4, 337, 352, 377, 381–3, 395, 410, 446, 467–8, 470, 484–6, 489

referendum 22, 128, 188, 230–1, 233

scandals 4, 358

self-governance 405–10

Single Member Plurality (SMP) 162, 175

social democratic 2, 161, 163–4, 175–6, 185–6, 194, 198, 200, 207

technocracy, technocratic 92, 242, 423

traditions 4, 70, 166, 190, 402, 407, 410

white papers 98, 104, 109, 111, 129, 398, 400

Great or Global Financial Crisis of 2007-2009 (GFC) 9, 127, 168, 241, 247, 252, 258, 262–4, 379, 416, 433, 457–9, 468–9, 471, 485–9

Great Depression 18, 233, 397

Great Lakes 9, 348–67, 396, 482, 486–7

   Areas of Concern (AOC) 353, 358, 360, 362, 365

   Great Lakes Restoration Initiative (GLRI) 358, 364

   Great Lakes Water Quality Agreement (GLWQA) 348–9, 351–5, 357–60, 362–7, 482, 487–8

   Lake Erie 350–1, 357–9, 362–3, 365

   Lake Ontario 351

   Remedial Action Plans (RAP) 353–4

Greece 186

Green (party) 67

Greenpeace 298, 303

Groups *see* Interest groups

Growth 40, 93, 106, 113, 131, 175, 198, 221, 238, 278–9, 308, 311, 313, 315–7, 338, 349, 372, 374, 382, 384, 417–8, 420, 422, 442, 468

Halifax 438 fn, 449, 451–2

Harcourt, Mike 404

Harkin, James Bernard 330–1, 334–5, 344

Harper, Stephen 48, 66, 68, 70, 79, 123, 142, 169–71, 190, 219, 226, 233, 280, 282, 365, 388, 457–8, 460–1, 464, 468–9, 471–3, 485, 489

Harris, Mike 125, 375

Harris, Walter 232

Hays, Harry 280

Health, healthcare 2, 8, 17–26, 28–31, 37, 39–43, 45–9, 51, 56–64, 66–7, 69–70, 77, 83, 133, 139, 143–5, 154, 198, 211, 217, 226–7, 229, 290, 299, 330, 350–1, 354–5, 358, 362, 373, 376–8, 384, 388, 427, 451, 481, 483–5

   addiction 56–8, 60, 62–3, 66, 71

   disabilities 91, 122, 153, 211

   dual practice 27, 30

   Health Services Survey 19

   HIV/AIDS 58–9, 69

   Hospitals, clinics 17, 19–26, 28, 31, 37, 355, 481

   mental health 56–9, 63, 68

   multi-payer 21, 23, 25, 28, 31

502 INDEX

Health, healthcare (*Continued*)
 nationalization 19, 21
 Pharmacare 30
 prescription drugs 19, 30, 217
 safe injection sites (SIS - Insite) 8, 56–71, 480,
  484–6, 488
 single-payer 19–23, 25, 28–31
 universal 18–23, 27, 30–2, 481
 see also Insurance; Medicare
History 10, 17, 24, 31, 39, 57–8, 71, 77–8, 81,
  83–5, 88, 102–3, 119, 122, 140, 162–4, 166,
  183–4, 186, 190, 212, 215, 219, 228, 230,
  233, 237, 269, 307, 309, 328–9, 334–6,
  343–4, 350–2, 354, 373, 396, 401, 403–4,
  416, 418, 420, 478, 482
House of Commons *see* Canada, Parliament
Housing 57, 61, 68, 458, 463, 465, 467
Hudak, Tim 127
human trafficking 168
Human Resources (HR), or capital 93, 119, 149,
  164, 332, 344, 357, 449–50
Human Rights 51, 164, 170–4, 184, 397
 universal 397

Ideology 62, 65, 70–1, 106, 162–4, 175–7, 187,
  199, 207, 221, 227, 280, 282, 355, 365, 471,
  482
 conservatism 62, 65, 67–8, 71, 117, 184,
  188–92, 199, 219, 439
 liberalism 65, 163–4, 175, 184, 198, 207, 211,
  221, 281, 286, 301, 303–4
 national socialism 164
 neoliberalism 68, 106, 166
Ignatieff, Michael 461, 464
Immigration, immigrants 9, 22, 81, 161–77,
  183–200, 207, 217, 340, 396, 480, 482, 487
 Temporary Foreign Workers (TFWs) 169–70
Imperialism 396
Inclusivity 57, 86, 183, 192, 199, 336, 363
India 169
Indigenous 4, 39, 78–80, 84, 147, 153, 169, 189,
  210, 328, 330, 333–9, 342–4, 350, 356, 358,
  362–3, 366, 395–411, 450 fn, 481–3
 see also First Nations; Inuit; Metis; Recreation
Indochina 167
Industry, industries 9, 20, 37–8, 41, 43–5, 48,
  52, 147–8, 163–4, 212, 247–9, 252–5, 257,
  259–60, 263, 269–70, 278, 281, 283, 286–9,
  291–2, 294, 296–8, 300–4, 307–17, 319–20,
  349–51, 354, 365, 377, 379–80, 386–7, 416,
  427, 444–5, 447, 465, 485–6
Inflation 29, 221, 230, 233, 239, 258, 276, 442
 see also Economy, prices

Information 47, 83, 91, 110, 172, 288, 317–8,
  337, 450–1, 453, 461, 466, 472
Infrastructure 2, 29, 93, 141, 143–5, 151, 208,
  331, 340, 353, 362, 374, 386–7, 438, 441,
  443, 445, 453, 455, 457, 463, 465–7, 470,
  483–4
Innovation 9, 32, 51, 65, 78, 84–5, 87–8, 112,
  139, 141–3, 147, 149, 152, 155, 254, 276–9,
  286, 294–6, 299–302, 311–2, 316, 332–3,
  365, 471, 479, 482, 486
 see also Policy, innovation
Inquiries, investigations 77, 79, 254, 256, 262,
  356, 489
 Walkerton 358, 362
 see also Commissions, commissioners;
  Reports
Institutes 141–4, 174, 280, 289, 296, 311, 317
 Canada Foundation for Innovation (CFI) 139,
  141–5, 149, 152, 155
 Canadian Institutes for Health Research
  (CIHR) 139, 142–4
 Canadian Institute for Environmental Law
  and Policy 377
 BC Wine Institute 312, 317
 Edible Oils Institute 289
 Environics Institute for Survey Research 174,
  429
 Plant Biotechnology Institute 296
 see also Government, institutions; Think tanks
Institutions *see* Government, institutions
Insurance 18, 20–1, 28, 104, 129–30, 249, 251,
  259–60, 426, 430, 451, 459, 465, 484–5
 Employment Insurance (EI) 129–30
 health insurance 18, 20–1, 25–6, 28, 30, 484–5
 see also Health, healthcare
Interest groups 28, 40, 62, 65, 71, 86, 112, 121,
  140, 148–50, 189, 218, 221, 226, 267, 274,
  287, 300, 304, 335, 338, 343, 350, 363, 366,
  429, 446, 450, 482, 488
International Relations 86, 161, 167, 172,
  217, 267–8, 274–6, 278, 312, 317–9,
  339, 351–5, 364–6, 396, 416, 420, 482,
  487
 see also Diplomacy; First Nations; Treaties
Internationalization 154, 317
 see also Globalization
Internet 140
Inuit 79, 337, 399–400, 403, 408
Iranian Revolution 238
Ireland 186, 207
Italy 186–7, 420

Japan 186, 297
Judiciary *see* Actors

INDEX   503

see also Courts, court cases

Kenney, Jason 190, 228, 233
Keynesianism 147, 418, 473
  see also Economy
King, William Lyon Mackenzie 41, 212
Klein, Ralph 233
Knowledge 59, 69, 84, 140, 143, 150, 153, 164,
  166, 317, 321, 333, 478
  see also Information; Actors, workers

Labour 21, 79, 99, 102, 108–9, 112, 117, 126,
  128–9, 161, 163, 166, 170, 174, 194–5, 214,
  218, 277, 307, 397, 481
  see also Actors, workers; Employment,
  unemployment; Unions
Labrador 400
Lacroix, Robert 145, 150
LaMarsh, Judy 42
Land claims *see* First Nations
Landry, Bernard 109
Lang, Otto 442
Language 79–81, 83–4, 87, 164, 183, 186–7,
  190–1, 197, 201, 445
Lapalme, Georges-Emile 85
Law 21, 24, 29, 32, 39–40, 44, 46, 49, 56, 62–7,
  153, 164, 167, 176, 185, 242, 271–2, 294,
  302, 363, 396–7, 402–3, 406–7, 409, 426,
  444, 451, 482, 484, 488
  bylaws 45, 47
  colonial 395, 397
  firms 30
  indigenous 396, 482
Leaders, leadership 4, 50, 56, 59, 62, 65, 70–1,
  83–4, 87, 91–2, 112, 140, 148, 151, 154–5,
  174, 188, 216, 232, 255, 270, 333, 335–6,
  343–4, 350, 355–8, 361, 363–4, 367, 387,
  411, 417–8, 429, 433–4, 439, 460, 464, 473,
  485, 487, 489
Lee, Thomas 332, 336, 339–40
Legault, Francois 107, 111
Legislation, legislative 19, 24, 37, 39, 43–6,
  49–50, 77, 91, 121, 128, 168, 175,
  187, 191–2, 212–3, 262–3, 270, 272,
  277, 309, 312, 316, 318–9, 327, 330,
  334, 340, 344, 352, 379–81, 396, 410,
  485
  see also Acts; Bills; Government
Legislature *see* Government
Liberal (party) 4, 18, 20–1, 23, 41, 48, 63, 67,
  100, 121, 123–4, 139, 142, 147–8, 150, 164,
  166, 170, 187, 190–1, 198, 212, 214, 219,
  236, 238, 257–60, 272, 280, 336, 340, 357,
  372, 399, 417, 421, 423, 427, 429–30, 432,

  434, 439, 441–2, 452, 458, 460–2, 464, 467,
  469–70, 472, 487
  Red Book 417, 423
Liberalism (economic) 51, 212
Libraries 145
Literature 7, 119, 207–8, 220, 457, 478, 482,
  484
  see also Scholarship; Research
Litigation *see* Courts, court cases
Lobbying 18, 20–2, 29, 39–40, 45–6, 91, 152,
  255, 257, 264, 270, 275, 289, 311, 316, 338,
  401, 454–5
  see also Actors, lobbyists; Interest groups
Logistics 450
Louisbourg 334

MacEachen, Allan 43
Management 26, 57, 82, 92, 143, 149, 153, 165,
  176, 184, 241–2, 252, 267, 269–70, 274,
  276–7, 299, 309, 312, 318, 320–1, 327,
  329–30, 332–7, 341–2, 344, 350, 353, 356–7,
  362, 381, 422–3, 425, 427, 432, 440, 442–3,
  449, 451–2, 455, 466, 470–1, 473, 482–4,
  486, 488
  see also Administration
Manitoba 21, 80, 89, 170, 227, 231, 237, 288–91,
  295–6, 298, 318, 331, 410 fn
Manning, Ernest 20, 23
Marketing 9, 36–9, 44, 49, 268–78, 281–2,
  287–8, 292–4, 297, 302–3, 309–10, 316, 428
  fn, 484
  see also Advertising; Agencies; Business
Markets 27–8, 30, 39–40, 46–8, 69, 99, 101–2,
  112, 117, 129–30, 161, 163, 166, 170, 194–5,
  230, 247–9, 251, 253–4, 258, 263, 268–71,
  274–5, 278–81, 283, 289, 297, 300–3, 307–9,
  311–20, 340, 355, 375, 378, 385, 420, 428,
  440, 442, 446, 448, 453, 459, 468, 481, 484
Marois, Pauline 101, 109, 112
Martin, Paul (jr.) 123–4, 142, 166, 219, 254–6,
  260–3, 417–8, 423–4, 428, 462
Martin, Paul (sr.) 20–1
Massie, Marcel 425
Mazankowski, Don 442
McGuinty, Dalton 125–7, 372–3, 378, 380, 382,
  387, 389, 485
Media 2, 4, 23, 28, 41–2, 44–5, 81, 152, 174, 185,
  188, 197, 201, 216, 219, 227–8, 235–6, 248,
  253, 255–6, 273, 287, 298, 303, 340, 350,
  355, 421, 460, 466–7, 469–70
Medicare 8, 17, 19, 22–31, 481, 484, 486–7
  see also Health, healthcare
Meighen, Arthur 331

504 INDEX

Members of Legislative Assemblies
(MLAs) 63–4
Members of Parliament (MPs) 18, 39–40, 43, 45,
63–4, 140, 150, 212, 253, 255, 258–61, 270,
272, 327, 417, 462, 470–1, 488
Men 37–9, 41–2, 51, 117, 119, 130, 133, 219, 401
Metis 79, 403–4, 408, 410 fn
Mexico 147, 275, 342, 426
Military 190, 197, 212, 447
Ministers 18, 20–1, 24, 42–3, 60, 64–8, 70, 82,
85–8, 92, 101, 103, 110–1, 168, 188–90, 218,
232–3, 254–6, 276, 330–3, 336, 339–41, 343,
378, 416–8, 422–3, 425–7, 434, 439–42, 445,
449, 451, 453, 461–2, 466, 469, 471, 485
deputies 43, 86, 88, 149, 330–2, 425, 440, 443,
445, 449, 453, 466, 471
of Agriculture 270, 272–6, 282
of Canadian Heritage 332–3
of Citizenship, Immigration, and
Multiculturalism 190–1
of Education 80, 82–3, 85–7, 92, 109, 127
of Energy 379, 381
of Environment 340–1, 378
of Finance 109, 150, 218–9, 232–3, 254–5,
260–3, 417–8, 423, 425–8, 457, 459–60, 462,
466, 471
of Health 49, 52, 66, 68, 149
of Immigration and Citizenship 168
of Indian Affairs and Northern
Development 336, 423
of Industry 466
of Infrastructure 466
of Interior 330–1, 338
of National Health and Welfare 20–1, 24,
42–4, 45
of Transport 442–3, 445–6, 451, 453, 471
see also Cabinet, Departments, Prime
Ministers
Ministries see Departments
Mississauga 374, 380
Moe, Scott 233
Money see Capital
Montreal 4, 41, 85, 129, 145–7, 150, 175, 254–6,
288, 438 fn, 449, 451
see also Banks, banking; Universities
Mowat, Oliver 85
Mulroney, Brian 121–2, 165–7, 188, 218, 422,
438, 442, 454, 485
Multiculturalism 9, 162, 174, 183–201, 480–2,
485, 488
pluralism 194, 490
Municipalities see Government, municipal
Munro, John 43–4
Muskrat Falls 4

National Adjustment Grants 234
National Health Service (NHS) 19, 22
Nationalism 147–8, 184, 187–8, 191, 352, 357
Negativity-bias 3
Netherlands 26, 186
Networks see Policy, networks
New Brunswick 23, 80, 84 fn, 87, 125, 132, 217,
229 fn, 231, 237–8, 336, 405
Liberal (party) 23
New Democratic Party (party - NDP) 45, 63, 67,
198, 214, 219, 280, 404, 429–30, 458, 460,
464, 469, 472
Newfoundland and Labrador 4, 84, 132–3,
231–2, 238, 240, 271, 446
New York 352, 448
New Zealand 8, 80, 211, 281, 314–5, 317, 319,
478
Niagara, ON 311, 316, 352–3
Nixon, Richard 351
Non-Governmental Organizations (NGOs) see
Organizations
Norms 41, 134, 164, 177
North America 56–7, 65, 77, 83, 87, 106, 199,
238, 253–4, 256, 275, 286, 293, 296–7, 302,
309, 311–2, 380, 383–4, 396–7
North American Free Trade Agreement
(NAFTA) see Treaties
Northwest Territories 133, 399
Supreme Court 399
Norway 186
Notley, Rachel 383
Nova Scotia 4, 80, 84 fn, 87, 89, 91, 125, 132–3,
167, 217, 229 fn, 231, 238, 318–9, 372, 388,
405, 429
Nova Scotia Teachers' Union 91
Nunavut 400

Oakville, ON 380
Obama, Barack H. 358, 364, 380
Ohio 351, 358, 362
Okanagan, BC 311–2, 316
Oligopoly 249
Olson, Bud 272
Ontario 21–4, 28, 46, 48, 67, 79–80, 84–5, 87–9,
91, 118–20, 124–7, 129, 132–3, 141, 148,
154, 175, 229, 232, 234–6, 239–40, 242,
259, 268, 270–2, 274, 281–2, 289, 291–2,
296, 307, 309–12, 314–5, 317–20, 331, 351,
355–6, 362, 372–9, 382–9, 396, 403, 407,
429, 446, 472, 483–6, 488
Best Start Plan 126
Clean Air Alliance 373, 377, 382, 389
Conservative (party) 127–8
Electrical Safety Authority (ESA) 375

Full-day kindergarten (FDK) 118–20, 125–8, 132–3, 484
Grape Growers of Ontario (GGO) 309
Liberal (party) 85, 125, 128, 372, 375, 378–81, 441, 485
Liquor Control Board of Ontario (LCBO) 309–10, 318 fn, 319
New Democratic Party (party - NDP) 378
Ontario Energy Board 379
Ontario Hydro 375–7
Ontario Institute for Studies in Education Survey of Educational Issues 91
Ontario Medical Association (OMA) 22, 24, 28, 377
Ontario Milk Marketing Board 270
Ontario Power Authority (OPA) 378–9, 381, 387
Ontario Power Generation (OPG) 375, 383, 387
Ontario Services Corporation 375
Progressive Conservative (party) 127, 375, 378, 381, 387, 430
Opinion, polling 67, 174–5, 189, 241, 429
Organisation for Economic Co-operation and Development (OECD) 80–1, 86, 118, 132, 161, 192, 209, 211–2, 220, 363, 457, 481, 484
Organization of the Petroleum Exporting Countries (OPEC) 238
Organizations 30–1, 42, 45, 47, 50, 60, 62, 85–6, 151, 156, 161, 164, 168, 173–4, 186, 188, 201, 215, 218, 238, 251, 257–8, 269–70, 275, 282, 289, 310–1, 328, 333, 335, 342–3, 348, 351, 373, 377, 398, 417
culture 328–30, 336, 342
Non-Governmental Organizations (NGOs) 45, 61, 129, 295, 343, 354, 373, 377, 379, 443
not-for-profit organizations 131, 295, 416, 445
Private Sponsorship Agreement Holders (SAHs) 173
see also Canada; Politics; World Health Organization (WHO); World Trade Organization (WTO)
Ottawa 23, 31, 45, 60, 64, 66–7, 83, 139–43, 145, 147–52, 154–6, 198, 212–3, 227, 234, 251, 255–6, 273, 281–2, 291–2, 301, 310, 313, 316–8, 321, 421, 426, 429, 472
Owen, Philip 61–2, 71, 485

Pandemics see Covid-19
Paris 410
Parliament see Canada, Parliament; Members of Parliament (MPs)

Parties see Government, parliamentary; Politics, coalitions; Politics, partisan; Provinces
Pascal, Charles 126–7
Patents, copyright 292–4, 303
Peacekeeping 4
Pearson, Lester B. 23, 164, 214, 236
Pensions see Departments, Pensions; Welfare, pensions
People's Party of Canada (PPC) 174, 198
Pepin, Jean-Luc 442
Peterson, David 375
Philippines 169
Phoenix (payroll system) 4
Piper, Martha 150
Policing, law enforcement 59–63, 65, 71, 172, 176, 197, 452
Prisons, incarceration 59, 217
see also Drug use; Royal Canadian Mounted Police (RCMP)
Policy 1–9, 19–20, 40–2, 44, 46–7, 49, 51, 56–8, 60–3, 65–6, 68, 71, 80–3, 86–7, 92–3, 98–9, 101, 117, 121, 142, 147, 152–4, 161–8, 172–6, 183–7, 191, 196, 222, 225–6, 229, 237–9, 241–2, 249, 257–9, 270, 286, 294, 307–9, 312–3, 315, 317, 329, 333, 335, 339, 341–2, 349, 354–7, 363, 396, 398, 401–2, 425, 433, 443–7, 449, 457, 461, 478, 481–3
action, inaction 357, 359, 361
activity 2, 31, 77, 83–4, 86, 90, 110, 424
adaptation, adaptability 241, 333
advice 154, 271, 333, 337, 339, 361, 379, 425, 440, 445, 462
agenda 85–6, 93, 121, 127, 129, 149, 151, 357–8, 364, 444, 485, 487
alternatives 20, 29, 31, 47, 51, 56, 63, 85, 131, 214, 221, 232–4, 258, 386, 423, 430, 461, 469
analysis 3, 177, 193, 233, 239, 420
approach 8, 18–9, 21, 30–1, 40, 42–4, 46–52, 59–63, 67–8, 70–1, 78, 81, 88, 92, 100, 109, 118, 120, 122, 124, 126, 128–9, 148, 162, 166–7, 177, 183–94, 234, 237, 240, 242, 253, 299, 303, 307, 309–10, 312–4, 317, 319–21, 340, 348, 352, 373, 380–1, 383–4, 386, 398, 401 fn, 405, 423, 429, 440, 444, 458–9, 461, 466, 469, 471, 483
architecture 25, 82, 93, 129, 215, 219–20, 482
areas 63, 70, 83, 93, 140, 142, 152, 177, 211, 311, 321, 327
arrangements 119
assessments 7, 25, 80–1, 139–40, 148–9, 198–9, 208, 278, 328, 348, 360–1, 363, 386–8, 433, 439, 479, 484
autonomy 321, 329
calibration 220

506   INDEX

Policy (*Continued*)
  capacity 122, 139, 148, 151, 241, 440
  capture 343
  challenges 59, 163, 240, 273, 310, 357, 359, 482
  change 28, 31, 36, 45, 50–1, 57 fn, 62, 64–5, 69, 98, 188, 220, 248, 268, 282, 287, 298, 304, 336, 400, 441, 489
  choices 6, 82, 87, 92–3, 247, 320, 361
  community 60, 85–6, 88, 93, 126, 150, 299–300, 357, 364–5, 425
  consultations 86, 110, 150, 165, 225, 242, 319, 332, 334, 336–8, 342–4, 406, 423, 428, 443, 458, 462, 465, 469, 471
  content 149, 190
  control 149
  criticism 67–8, 148, 166, 193, 225–6, 228, 429, 479, 481, 483
  decisions *see* Decision-making
  deliberation 163, 177, 264
  delivery 10, 81, 238, 240–1, 361, 465
  design 10, 21, 31–2, 78, 81, 87, 118–9, 122, 126–7, 130, 150, 156, 162–3, 168, 176, 210, 215–7, 221–2, 226, 233–4, 237, 241–2, 335, 363, 440, 465, 485
  development 52, 61, 63, 70–1, 98, 111–2, 118–9, 129, 174, 187, 233, 250, 289, 308–9, 335, 410, 439, 443–4, 479, 483
  diffusion 88
  dimensions 483
  direction 44, 189, 332–3
  dividends 51, 296, 320, 449
  domains 7, 59, 63, 80, 188–9, 396, 439, 444, 473, 478, 485, 488, 490
  dominance 1, 70, 101, 117, 140, 156, 162, 212
  dynamics 2, 70, 89, 119, 123, 167, 242, 267–8, 282, 302, 315, 317, 374, 485, 487, 489–90
  economic *see* Economy
  education *see* Education
  effectiveness, efficiency 3, 71, 90, 132, 142, 161–2, 210, 225, 229, 276, 333, 361, 422–4, 434, 452, 481, 484
  efforts 365
  emulation 119, 131–3
  endurance 17, 25, 57, 70, 78, 91, 100, 111–2, 128, 130–1, 139, 161, 237, 241, 286, 299, 320, 349, 374, 383, 389, 440, 478–9, 488
  energy *see* Energy, electricity
  enforcement 40, 409
  environment *see* Environment, stewardship
  evaluation 8, 65, 91, 134, 234, 248, 268, 276, 286, 299, 328, 360–3, 432, 453
  evolution 118, 120, 163, 188, 276, 366

experience 1–2, 4, 7, 30, 109–10, 132, 141, 338, 425, 433, 443, 445, 478, 485, 489
facilitation 32, 92–3, 112, 155, 185, 215, 234, 331, 380, 382–3, 425
failure 1–5, 7, 57, 177, 248, 348–9, 357, 359–60, 362, 366, 468, 482
family 98–101, 103, 106–9, 112–3, 118, 121–9
  see also Families, households
feedback 150, 210–1, 215
fields 83, 313
fiscal *see* Budgets, budgeting; Finance, funding
fish and game *see* Recreation
formulation 488
framework 57, 67, 82, 87, 110, 124, 128, 131–2, 162, 166, 168, 187, 227, 308, 310, 313, 317–9, 328–9, 339, 341, 439–40, 445, 452–3, 479, 483–4
goals 1, 7, 10, 58, 68, 84, 89, 132, 147–8, 177, 183, 187, 195–6, 199, 210, 220, 264–5, 277–8, 299, 313, 316–8, 328, 341, 351–3, 355, 360–2, 365–7, 417, 422, 433, 441, 463, 478
ideas 10, 59–61, 78, 83–4, 87, 89–90, 103, 120, 126, 132, 146, 150, 166, 258, 260, 283, 304, 365, 469
immigration 161- 77, 183–96
impact 1, 3, 8, 10, 18, 24, 42, 62, 65, 82, 102, 107, 140, 142, 148–9, 152–3, 184, 192–3, 195, 211, 226, 261, 309, 328, 348, 350, 354, 372, 377, 381–2, 395–6, 402, 405–6, 410, 427, 453
implementation 4–5, 10, 19, 22, 50, 52, 63, 65, 98–9, 106, 109–10, 112, 118, 121, 126, 129, 132, 168, 189, 192, 213, 233–4, 308, 338, 343, 349, 354–9, 362–6, 417, 426–7, 432–5, 439, 441, 450, 453, 464, 466, 471, 473–4, 485, 487–8
Indian *see* First Nations; Indigenous
influence 6, 18, 20, 25, 51–2, 80, 84, 92, 98, 129, 149, 150–1, 166, 196, 228, 282, 321, 328, 338, 341, 374–5, 434, 452
initiatives 65, 68, 83, 86, 147, 150, 152, 154, 156, 186, 191, 199, 212, 296, 312, 331–2, 338, 416–7, 421, 427, 431–2, 434, 441, 453, 486–7
innovation 6, 50–1, 61, 65, 78, 85, 107, 112, 117–9, 125, 132, 139, 162–3, 276, 282, 286, 299–300, 328, 332–3, 336–8, 342, 365–6, 439–40, 484–6, 488–9
instruments 6, 10, 44, 90, 99, 110–1, 113, 119, 126, 153, 207, 209, 220, 239, 249, 267–8, 275–6, 280–1, 299, 355, 357, 360–1, 365, 367, 397, 444, 465, 469, 479, 487–8

intergovernmental 29, 63, 70, 83, 85–6, 119, 123, 132, 233, 241–2, 268, 282, 335, 360, 363, 367, 486, 489
intervention 44, 51, 67, 77, 117, 124–6, 176, 199, 252, 269, 274, 308, 377, 389, 424, 448, 457–9, 462–3, 465–6, 473
language 151
learning 131–3, 307, 339, 489
legitimacy 57, 67, 70, 163–4, 227, 229, 276, 300, 328, 335, 341–2, 344, 364, 367, 424, 479
lessons 17, 71, 86, 242, 435
levels 148
measures 18, 40, 44–52, 99–104, 107, 109–12, 118, 164, 168, 170, 175–6, 190, 193, 250, 294, 307, 317, 320, 339, 352, 372, 397, 434, 459–60, 463–4
measurements 208, 308, 355, 454
mechanisms 220, 235, 252, 333, 340, 343, 433
mix 132, 206, 212, 220, 222
narrative 121–8
networks 144, 211, 302, 316, 341, 355
objectives 25, 31, 43, 50, 56, 111, 155, 164, 207, 220, 230, 237, 241–2, 267, 289, 304, 352, 357, 361, 367, 417, 422, 431, 433–5, 441, 446, 483–4
observers 149
options 52
outcomes 2, 6–7, 51, 57, 80, 82, 174, 208, 225, 247, 250, 277, 366, 373, 416, 427, 433, 473, 483–4
paradigms 32, 56, 59–60, 62, 90, 119, 358, 381
participants 150, 193
path-dependency 17, 22, 251
perspective 431
planning 354, 381
practitioners see Actors, practitioners
priorities 86, 89, 109, 149, 188, 291, 317, 333, 338–9, 462, 486
principles 164, 230, 234, 440, 447
problems 56, 63, 65, 121–2, 132, 141
process 25, 30, 50–1, 57 fn, 109, 113, 119, 139–42, 148–9, 151, 156, 161–3, 176, 184, 186, 188–9, 199, 225, 229, 233, 253, 261, 264, 274, 299–300, 308, 317, 319–20, 329, 334, 337–9, 358, 361, 363–4, 366–7, 373, 375, 383–7, 404, 411, 426, 433–4, 439, 450, 458, 468–9, 473, 478–9, 483, 486, 488–90
progress 366
public 1–5, 8, 45, 62, 67, 78, 82, 90–1, 99, 139–40, 147, 155, 164, 210, 222, 242, 248, 262, 267, 300–2, 395, 403, 406, 410, 439, 445, 473, 482
questions 147, 257
recommendations 31, 48, 239

reform 32, 119, 129, 167, 169, 230, 233, 235–9, 241–2, 276, 317, 366, 422, 427, 429–30, 433–5, 438–9, 442, 483, 487
refugees and asylum seekers see Refugees
regime 131, 312, 318–9, 349, 354–5, 362–3, 365
research see Research; Universities
resources 140, 147–8, 206, 229, 235, 332, 359, 416, 420, 425, 432, 446, 486
response 149
review 233, 236–7, 239, 241, 253, 256, 381, 416–7, 422–7, 432–3, 441, 453–4, 479–82
roles 143
sectors 77, 83, 251, 290, 320
social 3, 6, 9, 18, 65, 83, 107, 208–19, 226–7, 426, 474, 486
solutions 65
space 87
stability 210, 240
statement 451
style 70, 263, 484
subfield 308
subsystem 57 fn, 248, 268, 282
success 1–10, 18, 25–6, 28–30, 36, 50–1, 56, 67, 71, 80–2, 85, 87, 89, 91, 98, 100, 107, 113, 117–9, 132, 139–41, 161–3, 168, 173, 176–7, 183, 186, 192–3, 199–200, 206–7, 209, 211, 215, 225, 227–8, 238, 241–3, 247–50, 264, 267–8, 273–4, 277–8, 281, 286, 299–301, 307–8, 315, 319–20, 327–9, 335, 337–8, 342–3, 348–9, 352–4, 356–66, 373, 383, 388, 395, 410, 416, 432–5, 438, 440, 453, 457, 468–9, 471–3, 478–90
survival 66
sustainment 31, 51, 106, 211, 250, 355, 362
team 62
template 187
theories 208
thinking 147, 151
tools 1, 69, 166, 195, 209–10, 221, 242, 311, 314, 320, 435, 443, 448
trajectory 315
window 43–4, 64
Policy-making, policy-makers 1–2, 6–7, 10, 26, 39, 56–7, 59, 61, 70, 81, 85, 89, 111, 117, 119, 122, 132, 142, 147, 149–52, 162, 165–8, 177, 221, 229, 233, 247, 250–1, 253, 257, 264, 267–8, 282, 287, 310, 338, 343, 349, 352, 355, 358–9, 361, 363–5, 374, 387, 402, 473, 484, 488–9
Politics 2–3, 5–6, 10, 17, 21–2, 24–5, 29–30, 51–2, 56–7, 62, 65, 67, 86, 88, 100, 111–2, 119–21, 123, 131, 142, 146, 148–9, 152, 156,

508 INDEX

Politics (*Continued*)
    161–2, 174–7, 184–5, 187, 189, 193, 199, 212, 214, 225–9, 234–6, 240, 247, 250–2, 255–7, 259–60, 262–5, 267, 270, 299, 301, 327–8, 343, 351, 356, 361, 364, 366, 372, 381, 385, 395, 398, 406, 417, 422, 426, 434, 439, 457–8, 460–1, 464, 466–73, 478, 481–2, 485
    action 349, 352, 354, 395
    bureaucratic 52, 328, 487
    campaigning 22, 63, 71, 86, 126–7, 164, 190, 198, 212, 218, 235–6, 378–9, 387, 417, 423
    capital 364
    caucus 146, 150, 261 fn, 464
    coalitions 10, 20, 30–1, 46, 56, 64, 131, 148, 219, 248, 267, 277, 300, 302, 364, 373, 377, 433, 460–1, 464, 469, 479, 485–6
    compromise 19, 40, 155, 240, 282, 302,
    consensus 90, 161–3, 166, 184, 187–8, 199, 247, 388, 422
    constituencies 151, 164, 216, 221
    cooperation and coordination 43, 47, 69, 268–71, 282, 310, 317, 353, 355, 360, 363–4, 425
    debate 44, 59–62, 70, 120–1, 146–8, 152, 162–4, 188, 191, 195, 198, 200, 209, 225, 251, 299, 327, 361, 373, 386, 416, 451, 460
    see also Discourse, discussion
    elections 21, 45, 65, 88, 121, 123, 125–7, 131, 142, 146, 162, 168, 172, 174–6, 187–92, 198, 218–9, 235, 240, 257, 282, 302, 364, 378–81, 384, 389, 417, 422–3, 430, 441, 452, 457–60, 468, 470, 472–3
    engagement 193, 320
    financing 257
    legacy 78–9, 84, 86, 92, 146, 190, 249, 262, 344, 372, 396, 432, 435
    mobilization 198, 218
    nativism 161, 176
    negotiations 56, 70, 230, 233, 274–5, 279–81, 318–9, 321, 331, 337, 365, 398, 400–2, 404, 406, 408–9, 423, 426, 440, 443–5, 449–54, 465
    opposition 18–9, 22–3, 59, 62, 127, 140, 198, 213, 218–9, 228, 229 fn, 231, 233, 248, 257, 260–1, 263, 272, 286–7, 301–4, 329, 367, 377, 379–80, 399, 417, 429–30, 434, 443 fn, 457, 459–61, 464, 470–2, 487
    organization 397
    participation 149, 193
    partisan 1–2, 18, 45, 71, 98, 124, 144, 155, 187, 248, 255, 257, 281, 301, 328, 343, 417, 429, 460
    petitions 396

    philosophy 50, 60–1, 64, 68
    platforms, manifestos 121, 189, 214, 235, 375, 378, 380, 417, 423, 442
    populism 3, 175–6, 188–9, 198–200
    pressure 211, 215
    representation 287
    see also Government; Policy
Pollution 133, 348–56, 358–60, 362, 365, 378–9, 384, 483
    air pollution 372, 374–9, 384, 483
    water pollution 348–56, 358–60, 362, 365, 486
    see also Climate change; Environment, stewardship
Portugal 186–7
Poverty 56, 59–60, 68, 99, 102, 104, 108, 118–22, 126, 129, 194, 206–8, 210, 212–5, 219–20, 484
    alleviation 121, 208, 220–1
    homelessness, 56, 59, 68
Praxis 57, 78, 91–3, 119, 311, 342, 361
Premiers 20–1, 23, 64, 66–7, 85, 88–9, 98, 102, 105–7, 109–13, 125–6, 128–9, 191, 227–8, 232–3, 236, 301, 372–5, 378, 381–3, 387, 399, 404, 429, 484
Prichard, Robert 150
Prime Ministers 4, 18, 21, 23, 41, 48, 65–6, 68, 70, 79, 111, 121–4, 139–43, 145–8, 150–6, 164–72, 187–8, 190, 212, 214, 218–9, 226, 230, 232–3, 235–6, 254–6, 260–1, 280, 282, 292, 333, 336, 340–1, 344, 351, 365, 388, 397, 400, 417, 421–3, 425–6, 428, 433–4, 438, 442–3, 454, 457–60, 464, 466, 468–9, 471–4, 484, 489
Prime Minister's Office 142, 149–50
    Senior Policy Advisor 145, 149
Prince Edward Island (PEI) 38, 84 fn, 87, 89, 132, 229 fn, 231–2, 237, 318, 334
Privatization, private sector 9, 20, 26, 47, 61, 64, 81–2, 90, 106, 109, 131, 144, 152, 221, 282, 291, 294–5, 298, 304, 310, 335, 364, 377, 383, 422, 427, 432, 438, 440, 444–7, 450–3, 483
    see also Business, Commercialization
Production *see* Business; Economy, production; Industry, industries
Professors *see* Actors, scholars
Programs 3, 5–6, 8–10, 18, 21, 25–7, 31–2, 42, 44, 50, 56, 58, 63, 68, 78, 80–3, 87–8, 90, 92–3, 99, 101–2, 105, 107, 109, 112–3, 117–9, 121–2, 127–33, 139, 141–6, 149, 151–5, 161–3, 165, 167–73, 176, 186–7, 189–92, 198–9, 206–11, 214–21, 225–7, 229, 233, 235–9, 248, 250, 263, 286, 290,

300, 312–3, 319, 329, 334–5, 338, 340, 342, 344, 349, 352, 356, 360–2, 374, 380, 384, 387, 410, 416–8, 420, 422–9, 440–1, 445, 459, 463, 466–71, 478–9, 481, 486–9
1995-1996 Program Review 416–7, 423–6, 431–5, 481, 485–7
Allowance Program 217
assessment 80, 199, 433
Blended Visa Office-Referred (BVOR) Program 173
Canada Assistance Plan (CAP) 122
Canada Child Benefit (CCB) 118, 120, 123–4, 132
Canada Child Tax Benefit (CCTB) 122–3, 132
Canada Health and Social Transfer (CHST) 122, 226, 242, 427
Canada Pension Plan (CPP) 206–10, 214–5
Canada Research Chairs (CRCs) 141, 144–6, 149, 152–3, 155
Canadian Smoking and Health Program 42
Countdown Acid Rain 375
delivery 81, 149, 236, 240–2
design 81, 150, 168, 416, 433
equalization *see* Finance, funding
evaluation 362
experimental 32
failure 6, 57, 64, 167, 273–4, 286, 300–1, 362, 388, 484, 489
federal government annuities program 212
Federal Skilled Workers Program (FSWP) 169–70
Grape and Wine Adjustment Assistance Program (GWAAP) 312
Guaranteed Income Supplement (GIS) 206–12, 214–8, 220–1, 484
Historic Sites Program 334
In-Canada Asylum Program
Indigenous Guardians and Watchmen initiative 338
Integrated Power System Plan (IPSP) 379
legitimacy 5, 90, 163, 227, 362, 424, 479
means-testing 122–3, 206, 209–11, 213, 215, 217
Old Age Security (OAS) program 206–14, 216–21
Ontario Wine Assistance Programme (OWAP) 312
Pan Canadian Assessment Program (PCAP) 78, 80
Program Review Council 425
Program Review Secretariat 425
Programme for International Student Assessment (PISA) 78, 80–1, 86
Provincial Nominee Program (PNP) 169–70

Rapeseed Utilization Assistance Program 290
Red Chair program 336
Refugee and Humanitarian Resettlement Program 170, 172
Registered Pension Plans (RPPs) 215
Registered Retirement Savings Plans (RRSPs) 214–5
Resettlement Assistance Program 172–3
Seniors Benefit 219
social *see* Welfare
structure 216, 484
success 6, 9–10, 25–6, 56, 58, 67, 78, 80, 82, 85, 112, 162, 168, 176–7, 192, 206, 221, 225, 233, 238, 267, 276, 279, 299–301, 313, 316, 327–8, 354, 358, 373, 410, 432–3, 441, 481, 484–7
Troubled Asset Relief Program (TARP) 459
Universal Child Care Benefit (UCCB) 123
see also Canada; Government; Welfare
Progressive Conservative (party) 21, 28, 164–6, 188, 218, 230, 235, 438
see also Conservative (party)
Projects 3–5, 8, 153, 440
mega-projects 4
see also Programs
Property 65, 237, 303, 404, 442, 446
intellectual 153, 294
Protests, protestors 60, 103
Provinces 3–4, 8–9, 17–25, 27, 30–2, 38, 42, 44–6, 48–9, 56, 67, 77–8, 80, 82–5, 88–90, 92–3, 98–9, 102, 106–7, 110, 112–3, 121–5, 130, 133, 141, 148, 156, 162, 165, 169–70, 175, 184, 191–2, 209, 211, 213–4, 216–7, 225–8, 231–2, 234–8, 241–2, 251, 257, 269–72, 276, 281, 307, 310, 312, 315–8, 320–1, 331, 334, 337, 343, 356, 358, 372–4, 378–82, 398–9, 404–6, 410, 417, 424–5, 428, 434, 462, 465, 470, 472, 481, 484
see also Government, provincial
Public 2–5, 10, 17, 21, 23–4, 27, 31, 56, 59, 62–3, 65–7, 71, 77–8, 80, 84, 86, 90–1, 110, 125, 161, 163, 171, 176, 192, 196–7, 206, 216, 219, 222, 226, 228, 230–1, 237–8, 241–2, 254, 256, 267, 280, 287, 298, 327–8, 333, 336, 338, 351, 354–5, 359, 363–4, 398, 418, 420, 422, 424, 427, 440, 450, 460, 466–7, 469, 478, 481–2, 484–5
assets 447
attitudes 52, 196–7
consensus 90, 365
earnings 207, 214
education 62
finance *see* Finance, funding
good(s) 247, 287, 344

510 INDEX

Public (*Continued*)
  hearings 400
  interest 66, 141, 156, 236, 257, 260, 265, 274,
    328, 354–5, 389, 424, 444, 446, 454, 469
  operations 427
  opinion 27–8, 67, 174, 176–7, 189, 259, 280,
    343, 397, 429–30, 434
  perceptions 5
  Public Service Employee Survey 336
  relations 42, 256
  scrutiny 328
  sector 90, 192, 291, 434, 440, 444, 450
  services 4–5, 23–4, 26, 31, 59–61, 63, 77,
    92–3, 127, 148, 192, 199, 212, 216, 226,
    228–32, 234, 237–8, 241–2, 335, 416–7, 422,
    425, 455, 461, 484
  support 5, 17, 28, 31, 41, 50, 56–7, 61, 65, 67,
    77, 91, 111, 161, 163, 176, 197–8, 211, 241,
    282, 327, 342, 361, 366, 422, 425, 429, 434,
    464, 469, 481, 487
  transport 379, 438–51
  value proposition 6, 361
  see also Actors, public servants; Policy, public;
    Programs
Public-Private Partnerships (PPPs) 148, 291–2,
  300, 302, 444, 483

Quebec 23, 28, 38, 42, 46, 80, 83–5, 87, 90,
  98–112, 118–21, 125, 128–34, 141, 148, 162
  fn, 170, 175, 184, 187–9, 191–4, 196–7, 200,
  206–8, 213–7, 227–8, 231–4, 236, 238, 268,
  271–2, 274, 276, 280–2, 307, 310–1, 317,
  319–20, 336–7, 386, 399–401, 405–6, 408
  fn, 417, 429, 458, 472, 481
  Caisse de depot et placement du Quebec
    (CDPQ) 214
  Charter of Values 192, 194, 196
  Coalition Avenir Quebec (CAQ) 112, 131, 192
  Cullen-Couture Agreement 170
  interculturalism 191
  Liberal (party) 85, 106, 112, 131, 191, 399
  Parti Quebecois (PQ) 102, 107, 111–3, 128–9,
    192
  Policy Statement on Integration and
    Immigration 191
  Quebec Milk Marketing Board 277
  Quebec Parental Insurance Plan
    (QPIP) 129–30, 133
  Quebec Pension Plan (QPP) 206–10, 214–5
  Saguenay-St. Lawrence Marine Park 337
  Societe des Alcools (SAQ) 317
  sovereignty 128, 188, 227, 232, 417
  Superior Court 399
  Union Nationale (UN) 232

Race, racism 117, 153, 162–4, 169, 184–8, 191,
  193–5, 197, 199, 366, 397, 481
Reagan, Ronald 2
Refugees 161, 163, 165–74, 190, 482–3, 487
  Designated Foreign Nationals (DFNs) 172
  Government Assisted Refugees (GARs) 172
  Privately Sponsored Refugees (PSRs) 173
Regulation and deregulation 2, 29, 36, 42–4,
  46, 63–4, 67–8, 83–4, 117–8, 122, 124, 128,
  163–4, 168, 185–6, 195, 228, 247–9, 251–3,
  257–61, 263–5, 268–72, 274–5, 279, 287–8,
  294, 297, 301–3, 309–14, 317–21, 338, 350,
  353–6, 378–9, 402, 438, 440–2, 444–5,
  447–8, 454, 457, 473, 481, 485–8
Religion 18, 40, 79, 84, 87, 103, 173, 184–5, 187,
  190–4, 197
  Anglicanism 79
  Catholicism 79, 84, 87, 103
  Christianity 185, 187
  churches 18, 40, 79, 84, 126
  Islam 190–1, 194, 197–8
  Judaism 187
  Methodism 79
  Presbyterianism 79
  Protestantism 84, 87
  Sikhism 191
Reports 2, 8, 19, 42–3, 121, 127, 165–6, 208, 211,
  234, 270, 281, 307, 332, 339, 354–9, 361–2,
  366, 381, 398, 442, 451, 453, 467–8
Republican (party) 2, 365
Research 1–3, 8, 36, 40, 43, 50, 58, 64, 86, 91,
  139–46, 148–56, 189, 241, 243, 248, 252,
  287–93, 295–8, 300, 311–3, 340, 343, 350,
  423, 479, 485, 488–90
  National Research Council 288, 291, 294
  see also Scholarship; Studies; Universities
Residency 169–72, 209, 212–3, 217
Resources, natural 147–8, 228, 232–3, 235–6,
  238–9, 267–8, 329–31, 339–40, 352–3,
  378–9, 397, 399, 405, 409, 411, 470, 480,
  485–6
  coal 372–6, 378–9, 387, 480, 482, 485–6, 488
  dairy 267–281, 289, 480–2, 489
  fisheries 339, 353–4, 402–3
  forestry 291–2, 327, 331, 405
  fracking 383–4
  livestock 267–8
  mining 327, 405
  poultry 267–8, 271–81, 482, 489
  renewable 148
  water 9, 329, 340–1, 348–59, 362–6, 384, 486
  see also Agriculture; Departments; Energy,
    electricity; Environment, stewardship;
    Policy

Retirement *see* Welfare, retirement income system; Actors, retirees
Robart, John 23
Ross, George 87
Royal Canadian Mounted Police (RCMP) 4, 65
Recreation 145–7, 327, 330–2, 336–9, 342, 348–9, 355, 403–4, 407, 451, 467
  Auyuittuq National Park 336
  Banff National Park 332, 334
  Dominion Parks Branch 327, 330, 343
  expos 147
  fishing 337, 349–50, 354–5, 407
  gambling 408
  hunting 331, 337, 403, 407
  International Union for Conservation of Nature (IUCN) 342
  Kluane National Park Reserve 336
  L'Anse aux Meadows 342
  Nahanni National Park Reserve 336, 342
  National Historic Parks 334
  parks 60, 69, 327–36, 467, 486–8
  Parks Canada Corporate Plan 341
  Rocky Mountain Forest Park 330, 340–1
  sports 145–6, 451
  tourism 314, 333, 335, 340, 465
  see also Environment, stewardship; Departments; Indigenous
Reform (party) 166, 188–9, 260–1, 429
  Blue Book 189
Risk 43, 51, 57, 61–2, 64, 69–71, 109, 127, 150, 171, 226, 248, 252–3, 255, 258, 261–4, 281, 286–7, 302–4, 312, 377, 379, 383–4, 388, 420, 450, 463, 467–9, 483,
Ryerson, Egerton 84–5, 87–8

Saint John's 438 fn, 446
Saskatchewan 18–23, 31–2, 79, 83, 89, 133, 217–8, 232–3, 241, 288–9, 291, 294–8, 301, 304, 318, 331, 372, 388, 484–5
  Co-operative Commonwealth Federation (CCF) 18–9
  Court of Appeal 298
  Saskatchewan Economic Development Corporation (SEDCO) 294–6, 302
  Saskatchewan Organic Directorate 298, 303–4
  Seniors Income Plan (SIP) 217–8
  Wheat Pool 296–8
  see also Government; Provinces
Saskatoon 288, 290–2, 294, 296, 301, 438 fn
Scandinavia 208, 221
Scholarship 1, 3, 119, 150, 153–5, 192, 206–7, 220–1, 343, 356, 489
  social sciences and humanities 153–4, 334

  see also Actors, scholars; Knowledge; Research; Universities
Schools 9, 77–80, 82–94, 99, 105, 108, 119, 126–7, 133, 197, 201, 465, 470
  normal schools 87–9
  school boards 82, 85–6, 92
  see also Education; First Nations; Universities
Science 42, 47, 50, 57, 64–5, 68, 80, 122, 125, 139, 144, 154, 164, 287–8, 290, 295, 299, 309, 316, 321, 334–5, 337, 348, 350–1, 354, 356, 364, 366, 487
  see also Actors; Research; Technology
Second World War 1, 18, 32, 41, 100, 147, 164, 184, 213, 231, 234–5, 281, 288, 334, 397, 399, 438
Security 66, 168, 384, 447, 455
  see also Military; Policing
Seven Years War 397
Shawinigan 146
Shipping *see* Transport, shipping
Shortliffe, Glen 443, 445
Sinclair, Murray 79
Social Credit (party) 20
  see also Alberta; British Columbia
Social security *see* Welfare, social security
Society, social 10, 31, 36, 39, 41–2, 45, 48, 50, 57–8, 60, 65, 69, 79–80, 90, 98–9, 101, 112, 117, 124, 128, 131, 164, 174, 185, 187–9, 193, 198–9, 208–11, 214, 218, 221, 226, 231, 242, 278, 286, 302, 328, 335, 343, 359–61, 402, 407, 416, 426, 433, 446, 468, 474, 486
  social economy 58, 80, 90, 112, 131, 163, 165, 209, 214, 221, 242
  see also Culture; Demographics; Economy; Multiculturalism; Policy, social; Welfare
Somalia 4
South Africa 42, 314
South Korea (Republic of Korea – ROK) 308
Sovereignty 337, 396–7
  see also First Nations, land claims; Quebec, sovereignty
Soviet Union 19, 47
Spain 186, 380
Sponsorship Affair 4
Sport *see* Recreation
St. Germain, Gerry 443, 445, 447
St-Laurent, Louis 21, 232
Stakeholders *see* Actors
Studies 58, 64, 192, 195, 208, 210, 289, 332, 339, 358, 444, 478, 480–3, 486
  see also Analysis, analysts; Knowledge; Reports; Research
Strategy, strategic 45, 47–8, 56, 62–5, 71, 80, 119, 125–6, 151, 172, 186, 190, 192, 199,

512 INDEX

Strategy, strategic (*Continued*)
  216, 236, 248–9, 252, 260, 291–2, 295–6,
  302, 308–9, 315–7, 320, 340, 366, 380, 388,
  422, 425–6, 429, 442, 447, 449–50, 458, 464,
  467, 470, 472–4
Strikes 22, 24, 460
Subsidies, subsidization 9, 20–1, 23, 27, 98, 100,
  105–11, 112, 118–20, 122, 125, 128, 131,
  133, 214, 217, 231, 236, 269, 271, 273, 275,
  294–5, 303, 312, 316–7, 386, 427, 445
Supply management 65, 70–1, 111, 267–83, 288,
  309, 318 fn, 356, 372, 374–5, 379, 383, 385,
  480–5, 488–9
  see also Administration; Management;
  Resources; Transport
Surveillance 68, 117
Sweden 26, 80, 106, 186, 206–7, 288, 293
Switzerland 186
Syria 169, 190

Task Forces *see* Commissions, commissioners
Taxation 18, 23, 27, 38–40, 45–7, 68, 93, 100–1,
  104, 109, 111, 119–20, 122–3, 129, 132, 155,
  209, 214–6, 220, 225, 228–32, 234–5, 237,
  241, 309, 315–6, 319, 338, 418, 420, 422,
  429, 441, 445–6, 458, 463, 465, 468
  Air Transportation Tax 445
  see also Welfare, TFSAs
Technology 29, 39, 86, 147–8, 153, 257, 276,
  286–7, 291–8, 301–5, 311, 316, 358, 373,
  378–9
  Ag-West Biotech 295–6
  biotechnology 286–305
  North American Biotechnology Initiative
  (NABI) 296
  see also Engineering; Genetic engineering
Territories 17, 25, 29–30, 32, 77–8, 80, 82–3, 86,
  90, 92–3, 121, 124, 133, 170, 226, 318, 331,
  333–4, 337, 343, 398, 400, 405, 462, 465,
  468, 470, 472
Terrorism 168, 452
Theory of change 6, 360
Think tanks 67, 241, 258
  Centre for Policy Alternatives 258
  see also Institutes; Research
Thompson, Lisa 127
Time 67–8, 70, 110, 149–50, 174, 226, 239, 241,
  248, 250, 264, 307, 320, 328, 348–9, 361,
  365, 372, 383, 420, 432, 435, 450, 461, 465,
  468–71, 473, 479, 486–8
Tobacco 36–48, 50–2, 291, 481, 485–8
  British American 47
  Federal Tobacco Control Strategy 48

Framework Convention on Tobacco
  Control 47–8, 51
  Imperial 42
  Philip Morris 47
  prohibition of 40, 43
  Rothmans 42
Toronto 67, 86–8, 150, 153–4, 175, 256, 288,
  374–5, 378, 438 fn, 446, 448, 451–2
  Greater Toronto Hamilton Area (GTHA) 175
  Toronto Normal School 87–8
Trade 36, 40, 43, 47, 49, 51–2, 69, 147–8, 238,
  249, 253, 267–72, 274–82, 289, 297–8,
  307–9, 311–4, 316–21, 379–81, 396, 403,
  428, 446
  Board of Trade 446
  exports 270–1, 275, 278–9, 307–9, 313–6, 319
  imports 267, 270–1, 275, 297, 308, 313, 318,
  320
  Most Favoured Nation 316
  securities 249, 251, 257
  tariffs 271, 275, 279, 297, 311–2, 317, 320, 380
  see also Treaties
Transport 9, 45, 170, 318, 329, 331, 334, 379,
  438–55, 471, 481, 484, 487
  aerospace 148
  Air Canada 45, 318 fn
  Airport Authorities (AAs) 438–46, 448–55,
  481, 487
  airports 4, 9, 170, 190, 438–55, 481, 484,
  486–8
  Airport Transfer Advisory Board (ATAB) 445
  automobiles 260, 331, 380
  harbours, ports 9, 438, 467
  railways 329–30
  roads and highways 331, 334
  shipping 297, 319, 350, 352, 360
  see also Public, transport
Treaties 47, 172, 217, 276, 278, 312, 350–2, 357,
  395–6, 398, 400, 404–6, 310
  Agreement on Internal Trade (AIT) 317
  Boundary Waters Treaty (BWT) 350
  Canada-US Air Quality Agreement 377
  Canada-US Safe Third Country
  Agreement 172
  Canadian Free Trade Agreement (CFTA) 275,
  317–8
  General Agreement on Tariffs and Trade
  (GATT) 271, 275, 311, 320
  North American Free Trade Agreement
  (NAFTA) 253, 274–6, 279–80, 312
  Numbered treaties 396, 399
  Ozone Annex agreement 389
  Robinson treaties 396
  social security agreements 217

Trans-Pacific Partnership 280
Treaty of Paris 1763 410
Treaty of Utrecht 1713 410
Trudeau, Justin 120, 123, 168–9, 172, 219, 388, 474
Trudeau, Pierre 121, 187, 230, 233, 292, 336, 351, 398, 400, 421, 442, 485
Trump, Donald J. 2, 176
Turkey 190

Ukraine 187
Unions, unionization 21, 25, 86, 90–1, 103, 109, 127, 129, 152, 214, 270, 303, 377, 440, 449
United Kingdom 3, 19, 22, 26–7, 41, 77, 79–80, 83–4, 87, 164, 176, 183, 186–7, 190–1, 194, 206, 210–2, 221, 375, 395–7, 403, 410, 444, 472
British Airports Authority (BAA) 444–6
Royal Proclamation of 1763 396
United Nations 118, 161, 165–6, 171–2, 341–2, 409
United Nations Convention on Torture 171
United Nations Educational, Scientific and Cultural Organization (UNESCO) 342
United Nations High Commissioner for Refugees (UNHCR) 161, 172–3, 176
United Nations International Children's Fund (UNICEF) 118
United States 2, 4, 9, 25–7, 41, 48, 68, 83, 88–9, 92–3, 106, 144–5, 147, 152, 162 fn, 169, 172–3, 176, 184, 186, 194, 206–7, 211–2, 216, 220–1, 225–6, 229, 249, 254, 271, 275–6, 278–9, 291, 296, 299, 308, 312, 314, 316, 319, 348–53, 356–8, 360, 365, 375, 377, 380, 383, 389, 397–8, 410 fn, 444, 446, 451, 458–9, 462, 468, 482, 487
Congress 357
Universities 1, 9, 19, 81–2, 88–9, 92, 139–51, 153–4, 287–90, 294, 313, 343, 470, 485, 488
Brock University 313
Dalhousie University 343
faculties 89, 145, 152–4
G-10 group 151
McGill University 153–4
McMaster University 153
Universite de Montreal 145, 150, 153
University of Alberta 88–9, 153
University of British Columbia 145, 150, 153–4, 313
University of Calgary 296–7
University of Guelph 293, 302
University of Manitoba 288, 290, 293
University of Saskatchewan 294
University of Toronto 150, 153–4

see also Education; Research; Scholarship
Urban 152, 164, 175, 333, 340, 342
Uruguay 314
Utilities 382–3

Vancouver 28, 56–8, 60–6, 68–71, 150, 175, 401, 438 fn, 448, 451, 484–6, 488
Downtown Eastside (DTES) 57–61, 63, 66, 68–71
Portland Hotel Society (PHS) 61, 64, 66
Vancouver Agreement 63–4, 70
Vancouver Area Network of Drug Users (VANDU) 61, 66
Victoria 60, 64, 438 fn, 449, 451–2
Vietnam 47
Volunteering 127, 129, 289, 314, 333, 355, 357, 362, 424
Voting, voters 45, 62, 67, 93, 162, 164, 175, 189–90, 193, 199, 211, 226, 302, 417, 429, 434, 441
electorate 162, 175, 189, 199, 235, 451

Wall Street Journal 421
War 1, 18, 32, 40–1, 167, 213, 231, 234–5, 286, 288, 334, 396–7, 442
post-war 147, 184, 213, 231, 234, 281, 374
see also Cold War; First World War; Military; Second World War
Washington, DC 289
Welfare 18, 63, 99, 102, 104, 107 fn, 108, 117, 122, 129, 131, 147, 166, 172, 195, 206–8, 210, 213, 216–20, 226, 228, 231, 398, 408, 417–8, 426, 429–31
benefits 215–7
home care 217
indexation mechanism 219–21
pensions 9, 109, 206–21, 449, 451, 480, 483–4, 486–8
regimes 221
retirement income system 208
social security 206–7
Social Security Supplemental 208
state 207–8, 211, 213, 226, 231, 417
Supplemental Security Income (SSI) 211
Targeted Minimum Benefit Plan 208
Tax Free Savings Accounts (TFSAs) 216
universality 83, 207, 209–10, 213, 218–9
Working Income Supplement 122
see also Children, childcare; Education; Health, healthcare; Programs; Provinces; Quebec; Refugees
Weather see Climate change
Westminster 85
Westray 4

514   INDEX

Whelan, Eugene 273–4
White Papers *see* Government
Wildlife 334–6, 339, 351–4, 356, 359, 362
  endangered species 334, 340–2, 358, 360
  see also Environment, stewardship; Recreation
Williamson, Frank H. H. 334
Wilson, Michael 218
Wine 9, 307–21, 480, 483, 486
  Cellared in Canada (CIC) 315–6
  ice wine 308–10, 316, 320
  Organisation Internationale de la Vigne et du Vin (OIV) 308, 315
  Vintners Quality Alliance (VQA) 311–2, 314–6, 320
  wineries 307, 310–6, 320
  World Wine Trade Group (WWTG) 314, 317

see also Business; Industry
Winnipeg 288, 327, 438 fn, 449, 451–2
Wisconsin 356
Witmer, Elizabeth 378
Women 21, 26, 37–42, 51, 98–9, 101–4, 108–10, 112–3, 117–9, 121, 126, 134, 146, 190, 207, 210, 216, 219, 351, 401–2
World Health Organization (WHO) 47, 299
World Trade Organization (WTO) 253, 271, 275, 280, 311, 316, 319–20
  Agreement on Agriculture 275
Wynne, Kathleen 128, 372–3, 380, 382, 385, 387, 389, 483, 485

Yukon 406

Zeitgeist 7